W9-CMB-706

Options

3rd Edition

AS A
STRATEGIC
INVESTMENT

Options
3rd Edition

AS A
STRATEGIC
INVESTMENT

LAWRENCE G. McMILLAN

NEW YORK INSTITUTE OF FINANCE
NEW YORK • TORONTO • SYDNEY • TOKYO • SINGAPORE

Library of Congress Cataloging-in-Publication Data

McMillan, L. G.
    Options as a strategic investment : a comprehensive analysis of
listed option strategies / Lawrence G. McMillan.—3rd ed.
      p. cm.
    Includes index.
    ISBN 0-13-636002-5
    1. Options (Finance)   I. Title.
HG6042.M35   1993   92-26130
332.63′228—dc20   CIP

Printed in the United States of America

10

This publication is designed to provide accurate and authoritative information in regard
to the subject matter covered. It is sold with the understanding that the publisher is not
engaged in rendering legal, accounting, or other professional service. If legal advice or
other expert assistance is required, the services of a competent professional person
should be sought.
—*From the Declaration of Principles jointly adopted by a Committee of the American
Bar Association and a Committee of Publishers and Associations*

ISBN 0-13-636002-5   0-13-099661-0

 NEW YORK INSTITUTE OF FINANCE
Paramus, NJ 07652

Contents

CHAPTER **18**
Buying Puts in Conjunction with Call Purchases   261

Straddle Buying 262, Selecting a Straddle Buy 265, Follow-Up Action 266, Buying a Combination 269

CHAPTER **19**
The Sale of a Put   273

The Uncovered Put Sale 273, Follow-Up Action 276, Evaluating a Naked Put Write 277, Buying Stock Below Its Market Price 280, The Covered Put Sale 281, Ratio Put Writing 281

CHAPTER **20**
The Sale of a Straddle   282

The Covered Straddle Write 282, The Uncovered Straddle Write 285, Selecting a Straddle Write 287, Follow-Up Action 288, Equivalent Stock Position Follow-Up 292, Starting Out with the Protection in Place 293, Combination Writing 295, Further Comments on Uncovered Straddle and Combination Writing 298

CHAPTER **21**
Synthetic Stock Positions Created by Puts and Calls   301

Synthetic Long Stock 301, Synthetic Short Stock 303, Splitting the Strikes 304, Summary 307

CHAPTER **22**
Basic Put Spreads   309

Bear Spread 309, Bull Spread 312, Calendar Spreads 313

CHAPTER **23**
Spreads Combining Calls and Puts   316

The Butterfly Spread 316, Three Useful, But Complex Strategies 319, Selecting the Spreads 327, Summary 330

CHAPTER **24**
Ratio Spreads Using Puts   332

The Ratio Put Spread 332, Using Deltas 335, The Ratio Put Calendar Spread 335, A Logical Extension (The Ratio Calendar Combination) 338, Put Option Summary 340

Preface

When the listed option market originated in April, 1973, a new world of investment strategies was opened to the investing public. The standardization of option terms and the formation of a liquid secondary market created new investment vehicles that, adapted properly, can enhance almost every investment philosophy, from the conservative to the speculative. This book is about those option strategies—which ones work in which situations and why they work.

Some of these strategies are traditionally considered to be "complex," but, with the proper knowledge of their underlying principles, most investors can understand them. While this book contains all the basic definitions concerning options, little time or space is spent on the most elementary definitions. For example, the reader should be familiar with what a call option is, what the CBOE is, and how to find and read option quotes in a newspaper. In essence, everything is contained here for the novice to build on, but the bulk of the discussion is above the beginner level. The reader should also be somewhat familiar with technical analysis—understanding at least the terms "support" and "resistance."

Certain strategies can be, and have been, the topic of whole books—call buying, for example. While some of the strategies discussed in this book receive a more thorough treatment than others, this is by no means a book about only one or two strategies. Current literature on stock options generally does not treat covered call writing in a great deal of detail, even though it is one of the most widely used option strategies by the investing public. Therefore, call writing is the subject of one of the most in-depth discussions presented here. Another writing strategy—straddle writing--receives a great deal of attention. The material presented herein on call and put buying is not particularly lengthy, although much of it is of an advanced nature and should be useful even to sophisticated traders.

In discussing each strategy, particular emphasis is given to showing why one would want to implement the strategy in the first place and to demonstrating under which market scenarios the strategy works and under which ones it does not. The full details of each strategy are presented, including many graphical and tabular layouts of the profit and loss potentials, margin requirements, and criteria for the selection of a position. A great deal of attention is also given to follow-up action. It is often easier to decide to establish a position than it is to take action to limit loss or take profits. Therefore, in the cases where follow-up action applies, many of the reasonable alternatives are spelled out in detail, with examples. Comparisons among similar strategies are also made. An investor who is bullish, for example, may want to implement a variety of strategies. A comparison of the benefits and deficiencies of similar strategies helps the investor decide which one is right for his or her particular case. Pitfalls that should be avoided are also pointed out.

I have used the fictional stock XYZ to illustrate the examples, rather than naming actual stocks. Many of the examples are drawn from actual prices that existed. It is, however, rather pointless to give an example starting Bally at 60 when it might easily be 20 or 200 by the time the reader peruses the example. The purpose of examples is to illustrate concepts, not record history. XYZ fits this purpose best since it is very versatile: It can, as the need arises, be low-priced or high-priced, volatile or nonvolatile; and it changes price at will in order to illustrate follow-up strategies.

Call option strategies are presented in the first part of the book, and put option strategies are in the latter portion. While this order of presentation may interrupt the purely strategic flow a bit—for example, bear spreads are discussed using call options in the first part of the book and then are discussed again later using put options—this format is designed to aid the novice and intermediate option investor in that they are more familiar with calls than puts. For the majority of option investors, the development of the strategies in the more familiar environment of calls should make them more understandable. Then the application of the concepts to put options is easier. Put option strategies are not slighted, however. Their applications are necessary for strategists to have a full range of possibilities at their command, and such strategies therefore occupy a sizable amount of text. Certain special subjects are treated as well, such as computer models and their applications, how to use options in arbitraging, and how the actions of market-makers and arbitrageurs affect the public option investor.

Second Edition

The bulk of the material added to the second edition concerned index options and futures. The same concepts used to describe equity option strategies are used to describe strategies for these vehicles as well. The approach is necessarily slightly different in some cases. The general concepts surrounding these options are introduced and then many examples are given. In these examples, the details of many of the more popular futures and options contracts are presented.

Many of the same strategies available to the equity option trader are applicable to index options. These strategies are explained in the first 30 chapters of the book, using equity options. In most cases, one only need substitute terms. For example, where "underlying stock" is referred to, merely substitute "underlying security." Such a security could be a future, a bond, a currency, or an index.

A great deal of attention is given to hedging portfolios of stocks with index futures and options. The techniques presented herein are applicable for any investor owning stocks, from the individual to the large institution. Variations on the basic hedging strategies are presented as well. These variations are strategies unto themselves, allowing strategists to profit from pricing discrepancies in futures or options. In addition, strategies wherein one attempts to take advantage of the movement of a certain group of stocks in the marketplace are described. Spreads between various stock indices are also discussed in detail.

The chapter on taxes was revised to reflect the changes in the tax laws. These changes have made tax preparation more difficult, especially for the covered call writer. Several tax strategies are no longer applicable, especially those in which gains could be rolled from one year to the next. In addition, the shrinking of the holding periods to qualify for long-term gains has changed some of the tax aspects of options. Non-equity options are subject to a different tax rate than equity options. This difference in rates is discussed as well.

Certain additions and modifications were made to the original 28 chapters also. One of the largest expansions was in the discussion of risk arbitrage. This subject has been the object of much attention in recent years, due to the well-advertised profits made by risk arbitrageurs. The new material emphasizes the use of options to reduce the risk in risk arbitrage situations. Another section that was expanded is the one discussing equivalence arbitrage—reversals, conversions, and boxes. More of the concepts involving these popular forms of arbitrage were described. In addition, the risks of these strategies were delineated more fully.

Modifications were made to other chapters. Position limits changed, for example. There is also a greater emphasis on using the method of equivalent stock position (ESP) to analyze a neutral position for follow-up action. This method is applicable to most ratio writing strategies, straddle writes, and combinations. Both chapters on calendar spreads—puts and calls—were expanded to discuss more fully the ratio calendar spread, a neutral strategy that has limited risk if established with in-the-money options. A detailed example of a Black-Scholes model calculation was added to the chapter on mathematics. This is in response to the many questions that were received over the years regarding computations involving the model. Finally, more suggestions have been made for using the computer as a tool in follow-up action, including an example printout of an advanced follow-up analysis.

Third Edition

There are six entirely new chapters in the third edition. In addition, substantial revisions have been made to three others. There are new chapters covering LEAPS, CAPS, and PERCS. Each of these are option or option-related products that have been recently introduced.

LEAPS are merely long-term options. However, as such they require a little different viewpoint that regular short-term options. For example, short-term interest rates have a much more profound influence on a longer-term option than on a short-term one. Strategies are presented for using LEAPS as a substitute for stock ownership, as well as for using LEAPS in standard strategies.

PERCS are actually a type of preferred stock, which has a redemption feature built in. They also pay a significantly larger dividend than the ordinary common stock. This redemption feature makes a PERCS exactly like a covered call option write. As such, several strategies apply to PERCS that would also apply to covered writers. Moreover, suggestions are given for hedging PERCS.

CAPS are index options that resemble vertical spreads. They contain an upper limit on their price appreciation (the cap price), and this limit is automatically invoked if the underlying index should close above the cap price on a given day. Strategies that utilize vertical spreads can be considered with CAPS, although the automatic exercise feature introduces some new wrinkles. Finally, suggestions for pricing CAPS are given, using boundary conditions.

The chapters on futures and other non-equity options that were written for the second edition have been deleted and replaced by two entirely new chapters on futures options. The strategist should familiarize himself with futures options, for many profit opportunities exist in this area. Thus, even though futures trading may be unfamiliar to many customers and brokers who are equity traders, it behooves the serious strategist to acquire a knowledge of futures options. The first new chapter on futures concentrates on definitions, pricing, and on strategies that are unique to futures options. The second new chapter centers on the use of futures options in spreading strategies. These spreading strategies are different from the ones described in the first part of the book, although the "calendar spread" looks similar, but is really not. Futures traders and strategists spend a great deal of time looking at futures spreads, and the option strategies presented in this new chapter are designed to help make that type of trading more profitable.

Chapter 38 is a new chapter dealing with advanced mathematical concepts. As option trading has matured and the computer has become more of an integral way of life in monitoring and evaluating positions, more advanced techniques are used to monitor risk. This chapter describes the six major measures of risk of an option position or portfolio. The application of these measures to initialize positions which are doubly or triply neutral are discussed. Moreover, the use of the computer to predict the results and "shape" of a position at points in the future is described.

There have been substantial revisions to the chapters on index options as well. Part of the revisions are due to the fact that these were relatively new products at the time of the writing of the second edition; as a result, many changes have been made to the products—delisting of some index options and introduction of others. Also, after the crash of 1987, the use of index products has been changed somewhat (the introduction of circuit breakers, for example).

I am certain that many readers of this book expect to learn what the "best" option strategy is. While there is a section discussing this subject, there is no definitively "best" strategy. The optimum strategy for one investor may not be best for another. Option professionals who have the time to closely monitor positions may be able to utilize an array of strategies that could not possibly be operated diligently by a public customer employed in another full-time occupation. Moreover, one's particular investment philosophy must play an important part in determining which strategy is best for him. Those willing to accept little or no risk other than that of owning stock may prefer covered call writing. More speculative strategists may feel that low-cost, high-profit potential situations suit them best.

Every investor must read the Options Clearing Corporation Prospectus before trading in listed options. Options may not be suitable for every investor. There are risks involved in any investment, and certain option strategies may involve large risks. The reader must determine whether his or her financial situation and investment objectives are compatible with the strategies described. The only way in which an investor can reasonably make a decision on his or her own suitably to trade options is to attempt to acquire a knowledge of the subject.

Several years ago, I wrote that "the option market shows every sign of becoming a stronger force in the investment world. Those who understand it will be able to benefit the most." Nothing has happened in the interim to change the truth of that statement, and, in fact, it could probably be even more forcefully stated today. The universal purpose of this book is to provide the reader with that understanding of options.

I would like to express my appreciation to several people who helped make this book possible: to Ron Dilks and Howard Whitman, who brought me into the brokerage business; to Art Kaufman, whose broad experience in options helped to crystalize many of these strategies; to Peter Kopple for his help in reviewing the chapter on arbitrage; to Shelly Kaufman for his help in designing the graphs for the third edition and to Ben Russell and Fred Dahl for their suggestions on format and layout. Special thanks to go Bruce Nemirow for his invaluable assistance, especially for comprehensively reading and critiquing the entire manuscript. Most of all, I am grateful to my wife, Janet, who typed the original manuscript, and to Karen and Glenn, our children, all of whom graciously withstood the countless hours of interrupted family life that were necessary in order to complete this work.

Lawrence G. McMillan

Options

3rd Edition

AS A
STRATEGIC
INVESTMENT

BASIC PROPERTIES OF STOCK OPTIONS

PROLOG

Each chapter in this book presents information in a logically sequential fashion. Many chapters build on the information presented in preceding chapters. One should therefore be able to proceed from beginning to end without constantly referring to the glossary or index. However, the reader who is using the text as a reference—perhaps scanning one of the later chapters—many find that terms are being encountered that have been defined in an earlier chapter. In this case, the extensive glossary at the back of the book should prove useful. The index may provide aid as well, since some subjects are described, in varying levels of complexity, in more than one place in the book. For example, call buying is discussed initially in Chapter 3; and mathematical applications, as they apply to call purchases, are described in Chapter 30. The latter chapters address more complex topics than do the early chapters.

Chapter *1* _____

Definitions

The successful implementation of various investment strategies necessitates a sound working knowledge of the fundamentals of options and option trading. The option strategist must be familiar with a wide range of the basic aspects of stock options—how the price of an option behaves under certain conditions or how the markets function. A thorough understanding of the rudiments and of the strategies helps the investor who is not familiar with options to decide not only whether a strategy seems desirable, but also—and more important—*whether it is suitable*. Determining suitability is nothing new to stock market investors, for stocks themselves are not suitable for every investor. For example, if the investor's primary objectives are income and safety of principal, then bonds, rather than stocks, would be more suitable. The need to assess the suitability of options is especially important: Option buyers can lose their entire investment in a short time, and uncovered option writers may be subjected to large financial risks. Despite follow-up methods designed to limit risk, the individual investor must decide whether option trading is suitable for his or her financial situation and investment objective.

ELEMENTARY DEFINITIONS

A *stock option* is the right to buy or sell a particular stock at a certain price for a limited period of time. The stock in question is called the *underlying security*. A *call option* gives the owner (or holder) the right to buy the underlying security, while a *put option* gives the holder the right to sell the underlying security. The price at which the stock may be bought or sold is the *exercise price*, also called the *striking price*. (In the listed options market, "exercise price" and "striking price" are synonymous; in the older, over-the-counter options market, they have different meanings.) A stock option affords this right to buy or sell for only a limited period of time; thus, each option has an *expiration date*. Throughout the book, the term "options" is always understood to mean *listed options*, that is, options traded on national option exchanges where a secondary market exists. Unless specifically mentioned, the older type of option, the over-the-counter (OTC) option, is not included in any discussion.

Describing Options

Four specifications uniquely describe any option contract:

1. the type (put or call),
2. the underlying stock name,
3. the expiration date, and
4. the striking price.

As an example, an option referred to as an "XYZ July 50 call" is an option to buy (a call) 100 shares (normally) of the underlying XYZ stock for $50 per share. The option expires in July. The price of a listed option is quoted on a per-share basis, regardless of how many shares of stock can be bought with the option. Thus, if the price of the XYZ July 50 call is quoted at $5, buying the option would ordinarily cost $500 ($5 × 100 shares), plus commissions.

The Value of Options

An option is a "wasting" asset; that is, it has only an initial value that declines (or "wastes" away) as time passes. It may even expire worthless, or the holder may have to exercise it in order to recover some value before expiration. Of course, the holder may sell the option in the listed option market *before* expiration.

An option is also a security by itself, but it is a derivative security. The option is irrevocably linked to the underlying stock; its price fluctuates as the price of the underlying stock rises or falls. Splits and stock dividends in the underlying stock affect the terms of listed options, although cash dividends do not. The holder of a call does not receive any cash dividends paid by the underlying stock.

Standardization

The listed option exchanges have standardized the terms of option contracts. The *terms* of an option constitutes the collective name that includes all of the four descriptive specifications. While the type (put or call) and the underlying stock are self-evident and essentially standardized, the striking price and expiration date require more explanation.

Striking Price. Striking prices are *generally* spaced 5 points apart for stocks selling at or under $100 per share, 10 points apart for stocks up to $200 per share, and 20 points apart for stocks over $200 per share. A $35 stock might, for example, have options with striking prices, or "strikes," of 30, 35, and 40, while a $155 stock might have one at 150 and one at 160. Moreover, stocks selling at less than $25 per share may have strikes that are 2½ points apart. That is, a $17 stock might have strikes at 15, 17½, and 20.

These striking price guidelines are not iron-clad, however. Exchange officials may alter the intervals to improve depth and liquidity, perhaps spacing the strikes 5 points apart on a nonvolatile stock even if it is selling for more than $100. For example, if a 155 dollar stock were very active, and possibly not volatile, then there might well be a strike at 155, in addition to those at 150 and 160.

Expiration Dates. Options have expiration dates in one of three fixed cycles:

1. the January/April/July/October cycle,
2. the February/May/August/November cycle, or
3. the March/June/September/December cycle.

In addition the two nearest months have listed options as well. However, at any given time, the longest-term expiration dates are normally no farther away than 9 months. Longer-term options, called LEAPS, are available on some stocks (see Chapter 25). Hence in any cycle, options may expire in 3 of the 4 major months (series) plus the near-term months. For example, on February 1 of any year, XYZ options may expire in February, March, April, July, and October—not in January. The February option (the closest series) is the *short-* or *near-term* option; and the October, the *far-* or *long-term* option.

The exact date of expiration is fixed within each month. The last trading day for an option is the third Friday in the expiration month. Although the option actually does not expire until the following day (the Saturday following), a public customer must invoke the right to buy or sell stock by 5:30 P.M., New York time, on the last day of trading.

The Option Itself: Other Definitions

Classes and Series. A *class* of options refers to all put and call contracts on the same underlying security. For instance, all IBM options—all the puts and calls at various strikes and expiration months—form one class. A *series*, a subset of a class, consists of all contracts of the same class (IBM, for example) having the same expiration date and striking price.

Opening and Closing Transactions. An *opening transaction* is the initial transaction, either a buy or a sell. For example, an opening buy transaction creates or increases a long position in the customer's account. A *closing transaction* reduces the customer's position. Opening buys are often followed by closing sales; correspondingly, opening sells often precede closing buy trades.

Open Interest. The option exchanges keep track of the amount of opening and closing transactions in each option series. This is called the *open interest.* Each opening transaction adds to the open interest and each closing transaction decreases the open interest. The open interest is expressed in number of option contracts, so that one order to buy 5 calls opening would increase the open interest by 5. Note that the open interest does not differentiate between buyers and sellers—there is no way to tell if there is a preponderance of either one. While the magnitude of the open interest is not an extremely important piece of data for the investor, it is useful in determining the liquidity of the option in question. If there is a large open interest, then there should be little problem in making fairly large trades. However, if the open interest is small—only a few hundred contracts outstanding—then there might not be a reasonable secondary market in that option series.

The Holder and Writer. Anyone who buys an option as the initial transaction—that is, *buys opening*—is called the *holder.* On the other hand, the investor who sells an option as the initial transaction—an *opening sale*—is called the *writer* of the option. Commonly, the writer (or seller) of an option is referred to as being *short* the option contract. The term "writer" dates back to the over-the-counter days, when a direct link existed between buyers and sellers of options; at that time, the seller was the *writer* of a new contract to buy stock. In the listed option market, however, the issuer of all options is the Options Clearing Corporation, and contracts are standardized. This important difference makes it possible to break the direct link between the buyer and seller, paving the way for the formation of the secondary markets that now exist.

Exercise and Assignment. An option owner (or *holder*) who invokes the right to buy or sell is said to *exercise* the option. Call option holders exercise to buy stock; put holders exercise to sell. The holder may exercise the option any time after taking possession of it up until 8:00 P.M. on the last trading day; the holder does not have to wait until the expiration date itself before exercising. Whenever a holder exercises an option, somewhere a writer is *assigned the obligation* to fulfill the terms of the option contract: Thus, if a call holder exercises the right to buy, a call writer is assigned the obligation to sell; conversely, if a put holder exercises the right to sell, a put writer is assigned the obligation to buy. A more detailed description of the exercise and assignment of call options follows later in this chapter; put option exercise and assignment are discussed in the second half of the book.

Relationship of the Option Price and Stock Price

In- and Out-of-the-Money. Certain terms describe the relationship between the stock price and the option's striking price. A call option is said to be *out-of-the-money* if the stock is selling below the striking price of the option. A call option is *in-the-money* if the stock price is above the striking price of the option. (Put options work in a converse manner, which is described later.)

Example: XYZ stock is trading at $47 per share. The XYZ July 50 call option is out-of-the-money, just like the XYZ October 50 call and the XYZ July 60 call. However, the XYZ July 45 call, XYZ October 40, or XYZ January 35 are in-the-money.

The *intrinsic value* of an in-the-money call is the amount by which the stock price exceeds the striking price. If the call is out-of-the-money, its intrinsic value is zero. The price that an option sells for is commonly referred to as the *premium*. The premium is distinctly different from the *time value premium* (called *time premium*, for short), which is the amount by which the option premium itself exceeds its *intrinsic value*. The time value premium is quickly computed by the following formula for an in-the-money call option:

Call time value premium = call option price + striking price − stock price

Example: XYZ is trading at 48, and XYZ July 45 call is at 4. The premium—the total price—of the option is 4. With XYZ at 48 and the striking price of the option at 45, the in-the-money amount (or *intrinsic value*) is 3 points (48 − 45), and the time value is 1 (4 − 3).

If the call is out-of-the-money, then the premium and the time value premium are the same.

Example: With XYZ at 48 and an XYZ July 50 call selling at 2, both the premium and the time value premium of the call are 2 points. The call has no intrinsic value by itself with the stock price below the striking price.

An option normally has the largest amount of time value premium when the stock price is equal to the striking price. As an option becomes deeply in- or out-of-the-money, the time value premium shrinks substantially. Table 1-1 illustrates this effect. Note how the time value premium increases as the stock nears the striking price (50) and then decreases as it draws away from 50.

Parity. An option is said to be trading *at parity* with the underlying security if it is trading for its intrinsic value. Thus, if XYZ is 48 and the XYZ July 45 call is selling for 3, the call is *at parity*. A common practice of particular interest to option writers (as shall be seen later) is to refer to the price of an option by relating how close it is to parity with the common stock. Thus, the XYZ July 45 call is said to be a half-point over parity in any of the cases shown in Table 1-2.

TABLE 1-1.
Changes in time value premium.

XYZ Stock Price	XYZ July 50 Call Price	Intrinsic Value	Time Value Premium
40	½	0	½
43	1	0	1
45	2	0	2
47	3	0	3
⟶ *50*	*5*	*0*	*5*
53	7	3	4
55	8	5	3
57	9	7	2
60	10½	10	½
70	19½	20	−½[a]

[a]Simplistically, a deeply in-the-money call may actually trade at a discount from intrinsic value, because call buyers are more interested in less expensive calls that might return better percentage profits on an upward move in the stock. This phenomenon is discussed in more detail when arbitrage techniques are examined.

TABLE 1-2.
Comparison of XYZ stock and call prices.

Striking Price	+	XYZ July 45 Call Price	−	XYZ Stock Price	=	Over Parity
(45	+	1	−	45½)	=	½
(45	+	2½	−	47)	=	½
(45	+	5½	−	50)	=	½
(45	+	15½	−	60)	=	½

FACTORS INFLUENCING THE PRICE OF AN OPTION

An option's price is the result of properties of both the underlying stock and terms of the option. The major quantifiable factors influencing the price of an option are the:

1. price of the underlying stock,
2. striking price of the option itself,
3. time remaining until expiration of the option,
4. volatility of the underlying stock,
5. the current risk-free interest rate (such as for 90-day Treasury bills), and
6. dividend rate of the underlying stock.

The first four items are the major determinants of an option's price, while the latter two are generally less important, although the dividend rate can be influential in the case of high-yield stock.

The Four Major Determinants

Probably the most important influence on the option's price is the stock price, because if the stock price is far above or far below the striking price, the other factors have little influence. Its dominance is obvious on the day that an option expires. On that day, only the stock price and the striking price of the option determine the option's value; the other four factors have no bearing at all. At this time, an option is worth only its intrinsic value.

   Example: On the expiration day in July, with no time remaining, an XYZ July 50 call has the value shown in Table 1-3; each value depends on the stock price at the time.

   The Call Option Price Curve. The *call option price curve* is a curve that plots the prices of an option against various stock prices. Figure 1-1

TABLE 1-3.
XYZ option's values on the expiration day.

XYZ Stock Price	XYZ July 50 Call (Intrinsic) Value at Expiration
40	0
45	0
48	0
50	0
52	2
55	5
60	10

FIGURE 1-1.
The value of an option at expiration, its intrinsic value.

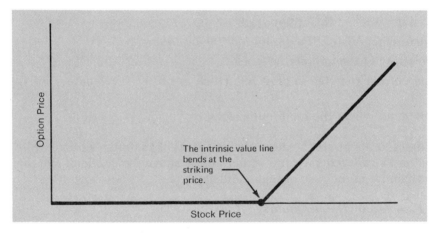

shows the axes needed to graph such a curve. The vertical axis is called Option Price. The horizontal axis is for Stock Prices. This figure is a graph of the intrinsic value. When the option is either out-of-the-money or equal to the stock price, the intrinsic value is zero. Once the stock price passes the striking price, it reflects the increase of intrinsic value as the stock price goes up. Since a call is usually worth at least its intrinsic value at any time, the graph thus represents the minimum price that a call may be worth.

When a call has time remaining to its expiration date, its total price consists of its intrinsic value plus its time value premium. The resultant call option price curve takes the form of an inverted arch that stretches along the stock price axis. If one plots the data from Table 1-4 on the grid supplied in Figure 1-2, the curve assumes two characteristics:

TABLE 1-4.
The prices of a hypothetical July 50 call with 6 months of time remaining, plotted in Figure 1-2.

XYZ Stock Price (Horizontal Axis)	XYZ July 50 Call Price (Vertical Axis)	Intrinsic Value	Time Value Premium (Shading)
40	1	0	1
45	2	0	2
48	3	0	3
→50	4	0	4
52	5	2	3
55	6½	5	1½
60	11	10	1

FIGURE 1-2.
Six-month July call option (see Table 1-4).

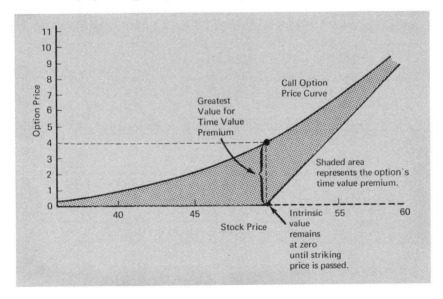

1. The time value premium (the shaded area) is greatest when the stock price and the striking price are the same.

2. When the stock price is far above or far below the striking price (near the ends of the curve), the option sells for nearly its intrinsic value. As a result, the curve nearly touches the intrinsic value line at either end. [Figure 1-2 thus shows both the intrinsic value and the option price curve.]

This curve, however, shows only how one might expect the XYZ July 50 call prices to behave with 6 months remaining until expiration. As the time to expiration grows shorter, the arched line drops lower and lower, until, on the final day in the life of the option, it merges completely with the intrinsic value line. In other words, the call is worth only its intrinsic value at expiration. Examine Figure 1-3, which depicts three separate XYZ calls. At any given stock price (a fixed point on the stock price scale), the longest-term call sells for the highest price and the nearest-term call sells for the lowest price. At the striking price, the actual differences in the three option prices are the greatest. Near either end of the scale, the three curves are much closer together, indicating that the actual price differences from one option to another are small. For a given stock price, therefore, option prices decrease as the expiration date approaches.

Example: On January 1, XYZ is selling at 48. An XYZ July 50 call will sell for more than an April 50 call, which in turn will sell for more than a January 50 call.

This statement is true no matter what the stock price is. The only reservation is that with the stock deeply in- or out-of-the-money, the actual difference between the January, April, and July calls will be smaller than with XYZ stock selling at the striking price of 50.

Time Value Premium Decay. In Figure 1-3, notice that the price of the 9-month call is not three times that of the 3-month call. Note next that the curve in Figure 1-4 for the decay of time value premium is not straight;

FIGURE 1-3.
Price curves for the 3-, 6-, and 9-month call options.

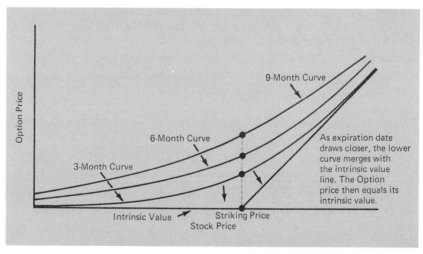

FIGURE 1-4.
Time value premium decay, assuming the stock price remains constant.

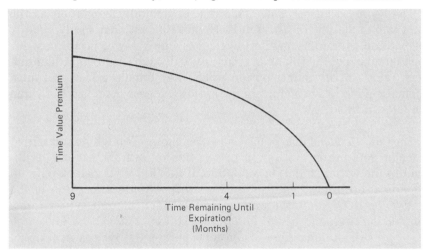

that is, *the rate of decay of an option is not linear*. An option's time value premium decays much more rapidly in the last few weeks of its life (that is, in the weeks immediately preceding expiration) than it does in the first few weeks of its existence. The rate of decay is actually related to the square root of the time remaining. Thus a 3-month option decays (loses time value premium) at twice the rate of a 9-month option, since the square root of 9 is 3. Similarly, a 2-month option decays at twice the rate of a 4-month option ($\sqrt{4} = 2$).

This graphic simplification should not lead one to believe that a 9-month option necessarily sells for twice the price of a 3-month option, because the other factors also influence the actual price relationship between the two calls. Of those other factors, the *volatility* of the underlying stock is particularly influential. *More volatile underlying stocks have higher option prices*. This relationship is logical, because if a stock has the ability to move a relatively large distance upward, buyers of the calls are willing to pay higher prices for the calls—and sellers demand them as well. For example, if AT&T and Xerox sell for the same price (as they have been known to do), the Xerox calls would be more highly priced than the AT&T calls because Xerox is a more volatile stock than AT&T.

The interplay of the four major variables—stock price, striking price, time, and volatility—can be quite complex. While a rising stock price (for example) is directing the price of a call upward, decreasing time may be simultaneously driving the price in the opposite direction. Thus the purchaser of an out-of-the-money call may wind up with a loss even after a rise in price by the underlying stock, because time has eroded the call value.

The Two Minor Determinants

The Risk-Free Interest Rate. This rate is generally construed as the current rate of 90-day Treasury bills. Higher interest rates imply slightly higher option premiums, while lower rates imply lower premiums. Although members of the financial community disagree as to the extent that interest rates actually affect option price, they remain a factor in most mathematical models used for pricing options. (These models are covered much later in this book.)

The Cash Dividend Rate of the Underlying Stock. Though not classified as a major determinant in option prices, this rate can be especially important to the writer (seller) of an option. If the underlying stock pays no dividends at all, then a call option's worth is strictly a function of the other five items. *Dividends, however, tend to lower call option premiums: the larger the dividend of the underlying common stock, the lower the price of its call options.* One of the most influential factors in keeping option premiums low on high-yielding stock is the yield itself.

Example: XYX is a relatively low-priced stock with low volatility selling for $25 per share. It pays a large annual dividend of $2 per share in four quarterly payments of $.50 each. What is a fair price of an XYZ call with striking price 25?

A prospective buyer of XYZ options is determined to figure out a fair price. In six months XYZ will pay $1 per share in dividends, and the stock price will thus be reduced by $1 per share when it goes ex-dividend over that time period. In that case, if XYZ's price remains unchanged except for the ex-dividend reductions, it will then be $24. Moreover, since XYZ is a nonvolatile stock, it may not readily climb back to 25 after the ex-dividend reductions. Therefore, the call buyer makes a low bid—even for a 6-month call—because the underlying stock's price will be reduced by the ex-dividend reduction, and the call holder does not receive the cash dividends.

This particular call buyer calculates the worth of the XYZ July 25 call in terms of what it is worth with the stock discounted to 24—not at 25. He knew for certain that the stock was going to lose 1 point of value over the next 6 months, providing the dividend rate of XYZ stock did not change. In actual practice, option buyers tend to discount the upcoming dividends of the stock when they bid for the calls. However, not all dividends are discounted fully; usually the nearest dividend is discounted more heavily than are dividends to be paid at a later date. The less-volatile stocks with the higher dividend payout rates have lower call prices than volatile stocks with low payouts. In fact, in certain cases, an impending large dividend payment can substantially increase the probability of an exercise of the call in advance of expiration. (This phenomenon is discussed more fully in the following section.) In any case, to one degree or another, dividends are an important influence on the price of some calls.

Other Influences

These six factors, major and minor, are only the quantifiable influences on the price of an option. In practice, nonquantitative market dynamics—investor sentiment—can play various roles as well. In a bullish market, call premiums often expand because of increased demand. In bearish markets, call premiums may shrink due to increased supply or diminished demand. These influences, however, are normally short-lived and generally come into play only in dynamic market periods when emotions are running high.

EXERCISE AND ASSIGNMENT: THE MECHANICS

The holder of an option can exercise his right at any time during the life of an option: Call option holders exercise to buy stock, while put option holders exercise to sell stock. In the event that an option is exercised, the writer of an option with the same terms is assigned an obligation to fulfill the terms of the option contract.

Exercising the Option

The actual mechanics of exercise and assignment are fairly simple, due to the role of the Options Clearing Corporation (OCC). As the issuer of all listed option contracts, it controls all listed option exercises and assignments. Its activities are best explained by an example.

Example: The holder of an XYZ January 45 call option wishes to exercise his right to buy XYZ stock at $45 per share. He instructs his broker to do so. The broker then notifies the administrative section of the brokerage firm that handles such matters. The firm then notifies the OCC that they wish to exercise one contract of the XYZ January 45 call series.

Now the OCC takes over the handling. OCC records indicate which member (brokerage) firms are short or which have written and not yet covered XYZ Jan 45 calls. The OCC selects, at random, a member firm who is short at least one XYZ Jan 45 call, and it notifies the short firm that is has been assigned. That firm must then deliver 100 shares of XYZ at $45 per share to the firm who exercised the option. The assigned firm, in turn, selects one of its customers who is short the XYZ January 45 call. This selection for the assignment may be either:

1. at random,

2. on a first-in/first-out basis, or

3. on any other basis that is fair, equitable, and approved by the appropriate exchange.

The selection of the customer who is short the XYZ January 45 completes the exercise/assignment process. (If one is an option writer, he should obviously determine exactly how his brokerage firm assigns its option contracts.)

Honoring the Assignment

The assigned customer *must* deliver the stock—he has no other choice. It is too late to try buying the option back in the option market. He must, without fail, deliver 100 shares of XYZ stock at $45 per share. The assigned writer does, however, have a choice as to how to fulfill the assignment. If he happens to be already long 100 shares of XYZ in his account, he merely delivers that 100 shares as fulfillment of the assignment notice. Alternatively, he can go into the stock market and buy XYZ at the current market price—presumably something higher than $45—and then deliver the newly purchased stock as fulfillment. A third alternative is merely to notify his brokerage firm that he wishes to go short XYZ stock and to ask them to deliver the 100 shares of XYZ at 45 out of his short account. At times, borrowing stock to go short may not be possible; so this third alternative is not always available on every stock.

Margin Requirements. If the assigned writer purchases stock to fulfill a contract, reduced margin requirements generally apply to the transaction, so that he would not have to fully margin the purchased stock merely for the purpose of delivery. Generally, the customer only has to pay a day-trade margin of the difference between the current price of XYZ and the delivery price of $45 per share. If he goes short to honor the assignment, then he has to fully margin the short sale at the current rate for stock sold short on a margin basis.

After Exercising the Option

The OCC and the customer exercising the option are not concerned with the actual method in which the delivery is handled by the assigned customer. They want only to ensure that the 100 shares of XYZ at 45 are, in fact, delivered. The holder who exercised the call can keep the stock in his account if he wants to, but he has to margin it fully or pay cash in a cash account. On the other hand, he may want to sell the stock immediately in the open market, presumably at a higher price than 45. If he has an established margin account, he may sell right away without putting out any money. If he exercises in a cash account, however, the stock must be paid for in full—even if it is subsequently sold on the same day. Alternatively, he may use the delivered stock to cover a short sale in his own account if he happens to be short XYZ stock.

Commissions

Both the buyer of the stock via the exercise and the seller of the stock via the assignment are charged a full stock commission on 100 shares, unless a special agreement exists between the customer and the brokerage firm. Generally, option holders incur higher commission costs through assignment than they do selling the option in the secondary market. So *the public customer who holds an option is better off selling the option in the secondary market than exercising the call.*

Example: XYZ is $55 per share. A public customer owns the XYZ January 45 call option. He realizes that exercising the call, buying XYZ at 45, and then immediately selling it at 55 in the stock market would net a profit of 10 points—or $1,000. However, the combined stock commissions on both the purchase at 45 and the sale at 55 might easily exceed $150. The net gain would actually be only $850.

On the other hand, the XYZ January 45 call is worth (and it would normally sell for) at least 10 points in the listed options market. The commission for selling one call at a price of 10 is roughly $30. The customer therefore decides to sell his XYZ January 45 call in the option market. He receives $1,000 (10 points) for the call and pays only $30 in commissions—for a net of $970. The benefit of his decision is obvious.

Of course, sometimes a customer *wants* to own XYZ stock at $45 per share, despite the stock commissions. Perhaps the stock is an atractive addition that will bring greater potential to a portfolio. Or if the customer is already short the XYZ stock, he is going to have to buy 100 shares and pay the commissions sooner or later in any case; so exercising the call at the lower stock price of 45 may be more desirable than buying at the current price of 55.

Anticipating Assignment

The writer of a call often prefers to buy the option back in the secondary market, rather than fulfill the obligation via a stock transaction. It should be stressed again that once the writer receives an assignment notice, it is too late to attempt to buy back (cover) the call. The writer must buy *before* assignment, or live up to the terms upon assignment. The writer who is aware of the circumstances that generally cause the holders to exercise can anticipate assignment with a fair amount of certainty. In anticipation of the assignment, the writer can then close the contract in the secondary market. As long as the writer covers the position any time during a trading day, he cannot be assigned on that option. Assignment notices are determined on open positions as of the *close* of the trading each day. The crucial question then becomes, "How can the writer anticipate assignment?" Several circumstances signal assignments:

1. a call that is in-the-money at expiration,
2. an option trading at a discount prior to expiration, or
3. the underlying stock paying a large dividend and about to go ex-dividend.

Automatic Exercise. Assignment is all but certain if the option is in-the-money at expiration. Should the stock close even a half-point above the striking price on the last day of trading, the holder will exercise to take advantage of the half-point rather than let the option expire. Assignment is nearly inevitable even if a call is only one-eighth of a point in-the-money at expiration. In fact, even if the call trades in-the-money *at any time* during the last trading day, assignment may be forthcoming. Even if a holder forgets that he owns an option and fails to exercise, the OCC automatically exercises any call that is ¾-point in-the-money at expiration, unless the individual brokerage firm whose customer is long the call gives specific instructions *not* to exercise. This *automatic exercise* mechanism ensures that no investor throws away money through carelessness.

Example: XYZ closes at 51 on the third Friday of January (the last day of trading for the January option series). Since options don't expire until Saturday, the next day, the OCC and all brokerage firms have the opportunity to review their records to issue assignments and exercises and to see if any options could have been profitably exercised but were not. If XYZ closed at 51 and a customer who owned a January 45 call option failed to either sell or exercise it, it is automatically exercised. Since it is worth $600, this customer stands to receive a substantial amount of money back, even after stock commissions.

In the case of an XYZ January 50 call option, the automatic exercise procedure is not as clearcut with the stock at 51. Though the OCC wants to exercise the call automatically, they cannot identify a specific owner. They know only that one or more XYZ January calls are still open on the long side. When the OCC checks with the brokerage firm, it may find that the firm does not wish to have the XYZ January 50 call exercised automatically, because the customer would lose money on the exercise after incurring stock commissions. Yet the OCC must attempt to exercise automatically any in-the-money calls because the holder may have overlooked a long position.

When the public customer sells a call in the secondary market on the last day of trading, the buyer on the other side of the trade is very likely a market-maker. Thus, when trading stops, much of the open interest in in-the-money calls held long belongs to market-makers. Since they can profitably exercise even for an eighth of a point, they do so. Hence the writer may receive an assignment notice even if the stock has been only slightly above the strike price on the last trading day before expiration.

Any writer who wishes to avoid an assignment notice should always buy back (or cover) the option if it appears the stock will be above the strike at expiration. The probabilities of assignment are extremely high if the option expires in-the-money.

Early Exercise Due to Discount. When options are exercised *prior to expiration*, this is called *early, or premature, exercise*. The writer can usually expect an early exercise when the call is trading at or below parity. A parity or discount situation in advance of expiration may mean that an early exercise is forthcoming, even if the discount is slight. A writer who does not want to deliver stock should buy back the option prior to expiration if the option is apparently going to trade at a discount to parity. The reason is that arbitrageurs (floor traders or member firm traders who pay only minimal commissions) can take advantage of discount situations. (Arbitrage is discussed in more detail later in the text, but here it shows why early exercise often occurs in a discount situation.)

Example: XYZ is bid at $50 per share, and an XYZ January 40 call option is offered at a discount price of $9\frac{3}{4}$. The call is actually "worth" 10 points. The arbitrageur can take advantage of this situation through the following actions, all on the same day:

1. Buy the January 40 call at $9\frac{3}{4}$.
2. Sell short XYZ common stock at 50.
3. Exercise the call to buy XYZ at 40.

The arbitrageur makes 10 points from the short sale of XYZ (steps 2 and 3), from which he deducts the $9\frac{3}{4}$ points he paid for the call. Thus his total gain is a quarter-point—the amount of the discount. Since he pays only a minimal commission, this transaction results in a net profit.

Also, if the writer can expect assignment when the option has no time value premium left in it, then conversely the option will usually not be called if time premium is left in it.

Example: Prior to the expiration date, XYZ is trading at 50½, and the January 50 call is trading at 1. The call is not necessarily in imminent danger of being called, since it still has half a point of time premium left.

$$\frac{\text{Time value}}{\text{premium}} = \frac{\text{Call}}{\text{price}} + \frac{\text{Striking}}{\text{price}} - \frac{\text{Stock}}{\text{price}}$$

$$= \quad 1 \quad + \quad 50 \quad - \quad 50\tfrac{1}{2}$$

$$= \quad \tfrac{1}{2}$$

Early Exercise Due to Dividends on the Underlying Stock. Sometimes the market conditions create a discount situation, and sometimes a large dividend gives rise to a discount. Since the stock price is almost invariably reduced by the amount of the dividend, the option price is also most likely reduced after the ex-dividend. Since the holder of a listed option does not receive the dividend, he may decide to sell the option in the secondary market before the ex-date in anticipation of the drop in price. If enough calls are sold because of the impending ex-dividend reduction the option may come to parity or even to a discount. Once again the arbitrageurs may move in to take advantage of the situation by buying these calls and exercising them.

If assigned prior to the ex-date, the writer does not receive the dividend for he no longer owns the stock on the ex-date. Furthermore, if he receives an assignment notice on the ex-date, he must deliver the stock with the dividend. It is therefore very important for the writer to watch for discount situations on the day prior to the ex-date.

A word of caution: Do not conclude from this discussion that a call will be exercised for the dividend if the dividend is larger than the remaining time premium. It won't. An example will show why.

Example: XYZ stock, at 50, is going to pay a $1 dividend with the ex-date set for the next day. An XYZ January 40 call is selling at 10¼; it has a quarter-point of time premium. (TVP = 10¼ + 40 − 50 = ¼). The same type of arbitrage will not work. Suppose that the arbitrageur buys the call at 10¼ and exercises it: He now owns the stock for the ex-date, and he plans to sell the stock immediately at the opening on the ex-date, the next day. On the ex-date, XYZ opens at 49, because it goes ex-dividend by $1. The arbitrageur's transactions thus consist of:

1. Buy the XYZ January 40 call at 10¼.

2. Exercise the call the same day to buy XYZ at 40.

3. On the ex-date, sell XYZ at 49 and collect the $1 dividend.

He makes 9 points on the stock (steps 2 and 3), and he receives a 1-point dividend for a total cash inflow of 10 points. However, he loses $10\frac{1}{4}$ points paying for the call. *The overall transaction is a loser* and the arbitrageur would thus not attempt it.

A dividend payment that exceeds the time premium in the call, therefore, does not imply that the writer will be assigned.

More of a possibility, but a much less certain one, is that the arbitrageur may attempt a "risk arbitrage" in such a situation. *Risk arbitrage* is arbitrage in which the arbitrageur runs the risk of a loss in order to try for a profit. The arbitrageur may suspect that the stock will not be discounted the full ex-dividend amount or that the call's time premium will increase after the ex-date. In either case (or both), he might make a profit: If the stock opens down only five-eighths or if the option premium expands by three-eighths, the arbitrageur could profit on the opening. In general, however, arbitrageurs do not like to take risks and therefore avoid this type of situation. So the probability of assignment as the result of a dividend payment on the underlying stock is small, *unless* the call trades at parity or at a discount.

Of course, the anticipation of an early exercise assumes rational behavior on the part of the call holder. If time premium is left in the call, the holder is always better off financially to sell that call in the secondary market rather than to exercise it. However, the terms of the call contract give a call holder the right to go ahead and exercise it anyway—even if exercise is not the profitable thing to do. In such a case, a writer would receive an assignment notice quite unexpectedly. Though not often, financially unsound early exercises *do* happen, and an option writer must realize that, in a very small percentage of cases, he could be assigned under very illogical circumstances.

THE OPTION MARKETS

The trader of stocks does not have to become very familiar with the details of the way the stock market works in order to make money. Stocks don't expire, nor can an investor be pulled out of his investment unexpectedly. However, the option trader is required to do more homework regarding the operation of the option markets. In fact, the option strategist who does not know the details of the working of the option markets will likely find that he or she eventually loses some money due to ignorance.

Market-Makers

In at least one respect, stock and listed option markets are similar. Stock markets use specialists to do two things: First, they are required to make a market in a stock by buying and selling from their own inventory, when public orders to buy or sell the stock are absent. Second, they keep the public book of orders, consisting of limit orders to buy and sell, as well as stop orders placed by the public. When listed option trading began, the Chicago Board Options Exchange (CBOE) introduced a similar method of trading, the market-maker and the board broker system. The CBOE assigns several *market-makers* to each optionable stock to provide bids and offers to buy and sell options in the absence of public orders. Market-makers cannot handle public orders; they buy and sell for their own accounts only. A separate person, the board broker, keeps the book of limit orders. The board broker, who cannot do any trading, opens the book for traders to see how many orders to buy and sell are placed nearest to the current market (consisting of the highest bid and lowest offer). (The specialist on the stock exchange keeps a more closed book; he is not required to formally disclose the size and price of the public orders.)

In theory, the CBOE system is more efficient. With several market-makers competing to create the market in a particular security, the market should be a more efficient one than a single specialist can provide. Also, the somewhat open book of public orders should provide a more orderly market. In practice, whether the CBOE has a more efficient market is usually a subject for heated discussion. The strategist need not be concerned with the question.

The American Stock Exchange uses specialists for its option trading, but it also has floor traders who function similarly to market-makers. The regional option exchanges use combinations of the two systems; some use market-makers, while others use specialists.

DETAILS OF OPTION TRADING

The facts that the strategist should be concerned with are included in this section. They are not presented in any particular order of importance, and this list is not necessarily complete. Many more details are given in the discussion of specific strategies throughout this text.

1. *Options expire on the Saturday following the third Friday of the expiration month, although the third Friday is the last day of trading.* In general, however, waiting past 3:30 P.M. on the last day to place orders to buy or sell the expiring options is not advisable. In the "crush" of orders during the final minutes of trading, even a market order may not have enough time to be executed.

2. *Option trades have a one-day settlement.* The trade settles on the next business day after the trade. Purchases must be paid for in full, and the credits from sales "hit" the account on the settlement day. Some brokerage firms require settlement on the same day as the trade, when the trade occurs on the last trading day of an expiration series.

3. *Options are opened for trading in rotation.* When the underlying stock opens for trading on any exchange, regional or national, the options on that stock then go into opening rotation on the corresponding option exchange. The rotation system also applies if the underlying stock halts trading and then reopens during a trading day; options on that stock reopen via a rotation.

In the rotation itself, interested parties make bids and offers for each particular option series—the XYZ January 45 call, the XYZ January 50 call, and so on—until all the puts and calls at various expiration dates and striking prices have been opened. Trades do not necessarily have to take place in each series, just bids and offers. Orders, such as spreads, that involve more than one option are not executed during a rotation.

4. *When the underlying stock splits or pays a stock dividend, the terms of its options are adjusted.* Such an adjustment may result in fractional striking prices and in options for other than 100 shares per contract. No adjustments in terms are made for cash dividends. The actual details of splits, stock dividends, and rights offerings, along with their effects on the option terms, are always published by the option exchange that trades those options. Notices are sent to all member firms, who then make that information available to their brokers for distribution to clients. In actual practice, the option strategist should ascertain from the broker the specific terms of the new option series, in case the broker has overlooked the information sent.

Example 1: XYZ is a $50 stock with option striking prices of 45, 50, and 60 for the January, April, and July series. It declares a 2-for-1 stock split. Usually, in a 2-for-1 split situation, the number of outstanding option contracts are doubled and the striking prices halved. The owner of 5 XYZ January 60 calls becomes the owner of 10 XYZ January 30 calls. Each call is still for 100 shares of the underlying stock.

If *fractional striking prices* arise, the exchange also publishes the quote symbol that is to be used to find the price of the new option. The XYZ July 45 call has a symbol of XYZGI: G stands for July and I is for 45. After the 2-for-1 split, one July 45 call becomes 2 July 22½ calls. The strike of 22½ is assigned one of the letters between U and Z for this stock only. Assuming that the letter U has been designated to be the symbol for the 22½ strike, the XYZ July 22½ call is quoted with the symbol of XYZGU.

After the split, XYZ has options with strikes of 22½, 25, and 30. In some cases, the option exchange officials may introduce another strike if they feel such a strike is necessary; in this example, they might introduce a striking price of 20.

Example 2: UVW Corp. is now trading at 40 with strikes of 35, 40, and 45 for the January, April, and July series. UVW declares a 2½ percent stock dividend. The contractually standardized 100 shares is adjusted up to 102, and the striking prices are reduced by 2 percent (rounded to the nearest eighth). Thus, the "old" 35 strike becomes a "new" strike of 34⅜: 1.02 divided into 35 equals 34.314, which is 34⅜ when rounded to the nearest eighth. The "old" 40 strike becomes a "new" strike of 39¼, and the "old" 45 strike becomes 44⅛. Since these new strikes are all fractional, they are given special symbols—probably U, V, and W. Thus the "old" symbol UVWDH (UVW April 40) becomes the "new" symbol UVWDV (UVW April 39¼).

After the split, the exchange usually opens for trading new strikes of 35, 40, and 45—each for 100 shares of the underlying stock. For a while, there are 6 striking prices for UVW options. As time passes, the fractional strikes are eliminated as they expire. Since they are not reintroduced, they eventually disappear as long as UVW does not issue further stock dividends.

5. *All options are quoted on a per-share basis*, regardless of how many shares of stock the option involves. Normally the quote assumes 100 shares of the underlying stock. However, in such a case as that of UVW options just described, a quote of 3 for the UVW April 39¼ means a dollar price of $306 ($3 × 102).

6. *Changes in the price of the underlying stock can also* bring about *new striking prices*. XYZ is a $47 stock with striking prices of 45 and 50. If the price of XYZ stock falls to $40, the striking prices of 45 and 50 do not give option traders enough opportunities in XYZ. So the exchange might introduce a new striking price of 40. In practice, a new series is generally opened when the stock trades at the lowest (or highest) existing strike in any series. For example, if XYZ is falling, as soon as it traded at or below 45—the striking price of 40 may be introduced. The officials of the option exchange that trades XYZ options make the exact decision as to the day when the strike begins trading.

Position Limit and Exercise Limit

7. *An investor or a group of investors cannot be long or short more than a set limit of contracts in one stock on the same side of the market.* The actual limit varies according to the trading activity in the underlying stock.

Heavily traded stocks with a large number of shares outstanding have position limits of 8,000 contracts. Smaller stocks have position limits of either 5,500 or 3,000 contracts. The exchange on which the option is listed makes available a list of the position limits on each of its optionable stocks. So, if one were long the limit of XYZ call options, he cannot at the same time be short *any* XYZ put options. Long calls and short puts are on the same side of the market; that is, both are bullish positions. Similarly, long puts and short calls are both on the same side of the market. While these *position limits* generally exceed by far any position that an individual investor normally attains, the limits apply to "related" accounts. For instance, a money manager or investment advisor, who is managing many accounts, cannot exceed the limit when all the accounts' positions are combined.

8. *The number of contracts that can be exercised in a particular period of time is also limited to the same amount as the position limit.* This *exercise limit* prevents an investor or group from "cornering" a stock by repeatedly buying calls one day and exercising them day after day. *Option exchanges set exact limits, which are subject to change.*

ORDER ENTRY

Order Information

Of the various types of orders, each specifies:

1. whether the transaction is a buy or sell,
2. the option to be bought or sold,
3. whether the trade is opening or closing a position,
4. whether the transaction is a spread (discussed later), and
5. the desired price.

Types of Orders

Many types of orders are acceptable for trading options, but not all are acceptable on all exchanges that trade options. Since regulations change, information regarding which order is valid for a given exchange is best supplied by the broker to the customer. The following orders are acceptable on all option exchanges:

Market Orders. These are simple orders to buy or sell the option at the best possible price as soon as the order gets to the exchange floor.

Market Not Held Order. The customer who uses this type of order is giving the floor broker discretion in executing the order. The floor broker is not held responsible for the final outcome. For example, if a floor broker has a "market not held" order to buy, and he feels that the stock will "downtick" (decline in price) or that there is a surplus of sellers in the crowd, he may often hold off on the execution of the buy order, figuring that the price will decline shortly and that the order can then be executed at a more favorable price. In essence, the customer is giving the floor broker the right to use some judgment regarding the execution of the order. If the floor broker has an opinion and that opinion is correct, the customer will probably receive a better price than if he had used a regular market order. If the opinion used is wrong, however, the price of the execution may be worse than a regular market order.

Limit Orders. The limit order is an order to buy or to sell at a specified price—the limit. It may be executed at a better price than the limit—a lower one for buyers and a higher one for sellers. However, if the limit is never reached, the order may never be executed.

Sometimes a limit order may specify a discretionary margin for the floor broker. In other words, the order may read "buy at 5 with ⅛ discretion." This instruction enables the floor broker to execute the order at 5⅛, if he feels that the market will never reach 5. Under no circumstances, however, can the order be executed at a price higher than 5⅛.

Other orders may or may not be accepted on some option exchanges.

Stop Order. This order is not always valid on all option exchanges. A stop order becomes a market order when the security trades at or through the price specified on the order. Buy stop orders are placed above the current market price, and sell stop orders are entered below the current market price. Such orders are used to either limit loss or protect a profit. For example, if a holder's option is selling for 3, a sell stop order for 2 is activated if the market dropped down below the 2 level, whereupon the floor broker would execute the order as soon as possible. The customer, however, is not guaranteed that the trade will be exactly at 2.

Stop-Limit Order. This order becomes a limit order when the specified price is reached. Whereas the stop order has to be executed as soon as the stop price is reached, the stop-limit may or may not be filled, depending on market behavior. For instance, if the option is trading at 3 while a stop-limit order is put in for 2, the floor broker may not be able to get a trade exactly at 2. If the option continues to decline through 2–1⅞, 1¾, 1½, and so on—without ever regaining the 2 level, then the broker's hands are tied. He may not execute what is now a limit order unless the call trades at 2.

Good-until-Canceled Order. A limit, stop, or stop-limit order may be designated "good until canceled." If the conditions for the order execution do not occur, the order remains valid for 6 months without renewal by the customer.

PROFITS AND PROFIT GRAPHS

A visual presentation of the profit potential of any position is important to the overall understanding and evaluation of it. In option trading, the many multi-security positions especially warrant strict analysis: stock versus options (as in covered or ratio writing) or options versus options (as in spreads). Some strategists prefer a table listing the outcomes of a particular strategy for the stock at various prices; others feel the strategy is more clearly demonstrated by a graph. In the rest of the text, both a table and a graph will be presented for each new strategy discussed.

Example: A customer wishes to evaluate the purchase of a call option. The potential profits or losses of a purchase of an XYZ July 50 call at 4 can be arrayed in either a table or a graph of outcomes at expiration. Both Table 1-5 and Figure 1-5 depict the same information; the graph is merely the line representing the column marked "Profit or Loss" in the table. The vertical axis represents dollars of profit or loss, and the horizontal axis shows the stock price at expiration. In this case, the dollars of profit and the stock price are *at the expiration date*. Often the strategist wants to determine what the potential profits and losses will be before expiration, rather than at the expiration date itself. Tables and graphs lend themselves well to the necessary analysis, as will be seen in detail in various places later on.

TABLE 1-5.
Potential profits and losses for an XYZ call purchase.

XYZ Price at Expiration	Call Price at Expiration	Profit or Loss
40	$ 0	−$ 400
45	0	− 400
50	0	− 400
55	5	+ 100
60	10	+ 600
70	20	+ 1,600

FIGURE 1-5.
Graph of potential profits for an XYZ call purchase.

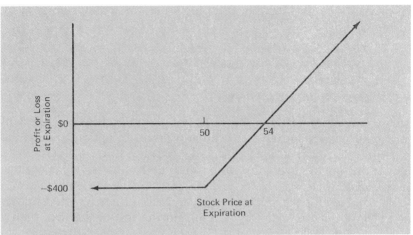

In practice, such an example is too simple to require a table or a graph—certainly not both—to evaluate the potential profits and losses of a simple call purchase held to expiration. However, as more complex strategies are discussed, these tools become ever more useful for quickly determining such things as where a position makes money and where it loses, or how fast one's risk increases at certain stock prices.

CALL OPTION STRATEGIES

The average person dealing in option trading utilizes primarily one of two option strategies—call buying or covered call writing. These strategies are, at face value, simple, and they are therefore the ones most often tried. There are many more strategies involving the use of call options, many of which will be described later in this Part. However, Chapters 2 and 3 deal with the fundamental call option strategies.

Both covered call writing and call buying are relatively simple strategies, but, like any investment, they can be employed with differing levels of skill and complexity. The discussions to follow will begin by describing the basics of each strategy and will then discuss each in depth.

Chapter 2

Covered Call Writing

Covered call writing is the name given to the strategy by which one sells a call option while simultaneously owning the obligated number of shares of underlying stock. The writer should be mildly bullish, or at least neutral, toward the underlying stock. By writing a call option against stock, one always decreases the risk of owning the stock. It may even be possible to profit from a covered write if the stock declines somewhat. However, the covered call writer does limit his profit potential and therefore may not fully participate in a strong upward move in the price of the underlying stock. Use of this strategy is becoming so common that the strategist must understand it thoroughly. It will therefore be discussed at length.

THE IMPORTANCE OF COVERED CALL WRITING

Covered Call Writing for Downside Protection

Example: An investor owns 100 shares of XYZ common stock, which is currently selling at $48 per share. If this investor sells an XYZ July 50 call option while still holding his stock, he establishes a covered write.

Suppose the investor receives $300 from the sale of the July 50 call. If XYZ is below 50 at July expiration, the call option that was sold expires worthless and the investor earns the $300 that he originally received for writing the call. Thus he receives $300, or 3 points, of *downside protection*. That is, he can afford to have the XYZ stock drop by 3 points and still break even on the total transaction. At that time he can write another call option if he so desires.

Note that if the underlying stock should fall by more than 3 points, there will be a loss on the overall position. *Thus, the risk in the covered writing strategy materializes if the stock falls by a distance greater than the call option premium that was originally taken in.*

The Benefits of an Increase in Stock Price

If XYZ increases in price moderately, he may be able to have the best of both worlds.

Example: If XYZ is at or just below 50 at July expiration, the call still expires worthless, and the investor makes the $300 from the option in addition to having a small profit from his stock purchase. Again, he still owns the stock.

Should XYZ increase in price by expiration to levels above 50, the covered writer has a choice of alternatives. As one alternative, he could do nothing, in which case the option would be assigned and his stock would be called away at the striking price of 50. In that case, his profits would be equal to the $300 received from selling the call plus the profit on the increase of his stock from the purchase price of 48 to the sale price of 50. In this case, however, he would no longer own the stock. If as another alternative he desires to retain his stock ownership, he can elect to buy back (or cover) the written call in the open market. This decision might involve taking a loss on the option part of the covered writing transaction, but he would have a correspondingly larger profit, albeit unrealized, from his stock purchase. Using some specific numbers, one can see how this second alternative works out.

Example: XYZ rises to a price of 60 by July expiration. The call option then sells near its intrinsic value of 10. If the investor covers the call at 10, he loses $700 on the option portion of his covered write. (Recall that he originally received $300 from the sale of the option, and now he is buying it back for $1,000.) However, he relieves the obligation to sell his stock at 50 (the striking price) by buying back the call, so he has an unrealized gain of 12 points in the stock, which was purchased at 48. His total profit, including both realized and unrealized gains, is $500.

This profit is exactly the same as he would have made if he had let his stock be called from him. If called, he would keep the $300 from the sale of the call, and he would have made 2 points ($200) from buying the stock at 48 and selling it, via exercise, at 50. This profit, again, is a total of $500. The major difference between the two cases is that the investor no longer owns his stock after letting it be called away, whereas he retains stock ownership if he buys back the written call. Which of the two alternatives is the better one in a given situation is not always clear.

No matter how high the stock climbs in price, the profit from a covered write is limited because the writer has obligated himself to sell stock at the striking price. The covered writer still profits when the stock climbs, but possibly not by as much as he might have had he not written the call. On the other hand, he is receiving $300 of immediate cash inflow, because the writer may take the premium immediately and do with it as he pleases. That income can represent a substantial increase in the income currently provided by the dividends on the underlying stock, or it can act to offset part of the loss in case the stock declines.

For readers who prefer formulae, the profit potential and break-even point of a covered write can be summarized as follows:

$$\text{Maximum profit potential} = \text{strike price} - \text{stock price} + \text{call price}$$

$$\text{Downside break-even point} = \text{stock price} - \text{call price}$$

Quantification of the Covered Write

Table 2-1 and Figure 2-1 depict the *profit graph* for the example involving the XYZ covered write of the July 50 call. The table makes the assumption that the call is bought back at parity. If the stock is called away, the same total profit of $500 results; but the price involved on the stock sale is always 50, and the option profit is always $300.

Several conclusions can be drawn. The break-even point is 45 (zero total profit) with risk below 45; the maximum profit attainable is $500 if

TABLE 2-1.
The XYZ July 50 call.

XYZ Price at Expiration	Stock Profit	July 50 Call at Expiration	Call Profit	Total Profit
40	−$ 800	0	+$300	− $500
45	− 300	0	+ 300	0
48	− 0	0	+ 300	+ 300
50	+ 200	0	+ 300	+ 500
55	+ 700	5	− 200	+ 500
60	+ 1,200	10	− 700	+ 500

FIGURE 2-1.
XYZ covered write.

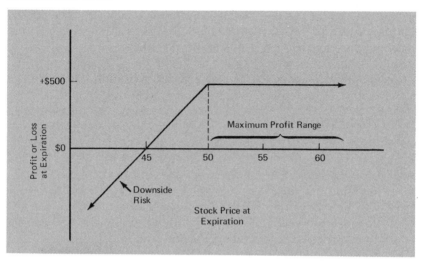

the position is held until expiration; and the *profit if the stock price is unchanged* is $300, that is, the covered writer makes $300 even if his stock goes absolutely nowhere.

The profit graph for a covered write always has the shape shown in Figure 2-1. Note that the maximum profit always occurs at all stock prices equal to or greater than the striking price, if the position is held until expiration. However, there is downside risk. If the stock declines in price by too great an amount, the option premium cannot possibly compensate for the entire loss. Downside protective strategies, which will be discussed later, attempt to deal with the limitation of this downside risk.

COVERED WRITING PHILOSOPHY

The primary objective of covered writing, for most investors, is increased income through stock ownership. An ever-increasing number of private and institutional investors are writing call options against the stocks that they own. The fact that the option premium acts as a partial compensation for a decline in price by the underlying stock, and that the premium represents an increase in income to the stockholder, are evident. *The strategy of owning the stock and writing the call will outperform outright stock ownership if the stock falls, remains the same, or even rises slightly.* In fact, the only time that the outright owner of the stock will outperform a covered writer is if the stock increases in price by a relatively substantial amount during the life of the call. Moreover, if one consistently writes call options against his stock, *his portfolio will show less variability of results from quarter to quarter.* The total position—long stock and short option—has less volatility than the stock alone, so on a quarter-by-quarter basis, results will be closer to average than they would be with normal stock ownership. This is an attractive feature, especially for portfolio managers.

Physical Location of the Stock

Before getting more involved in the details of covered writing strategy, it may be useful to review exactly what stock holdings may be written against. Recall that this discussion applies to listed options. If one has deposited stock with his broker in either a cash or a margin account, he may write an option for each 100 shares that he owns without any additional requirement. However, it is possible to write covered options without actually depositing stock with a brokerage firm. There are several ways in which to do this, all involving the deposit of stock with a bank.

Once the stock is deposited with the bank, the investor may have the bank issue an *escrow receipt* or letter of guarantee to the brokerage firm at which the investor does his option business. The bank must be an "approved" bank in order for the brokerage firm to accept a *letter of guarantee*, and not all firms accept letters of guarantee. These items cost money, and as a new receipt or letter is required for each new option written, the costs may become prohibitive to the customer if only 100 or 200 shares of stock are involved. The cost of an escrow receipt can range from as low as $15 to upwards of $40, depending on the bank involved.

There is another alternative open to the customer who wishes to write options without depositing his stock at the brokerage firm. He may deposit his stock with a bank that is a member of the *Depository Trust Corporation* (DTC). The DTC guarantees the Options Clearing Corporation that it will, in fact, deliver stock should an assignment notice be given to the call writer. This is the most convenient method for the investor to use, and is the one used by most of the institutional covered writing investors. There is usually no additional charge for this service by the bank to institutional accounts. However, since there are only a limited number of banks who are members of DTC, and these banks are generally the larger banks located in metropolitan centers, it may be somewhat difficult for many individual investors to take advantage of the DTC opportunity.

Types of Covered Writes

While all covered writes involve selling a call against stock that is owned, there are different terms used to describe various categories of covered writing. The two broadest terms, under which all covered writes can be classified, are the *out-of-money covered write* and the *in-the-money cov-*

ered write. These refer, obviously, to whether the option itself was in-the-money or out-of-the-money when the write was first established. Sometimes one may see covered writes classified by the nature of the stock involved (low-priced covered write, high-yield covered write, etc.), but these are only subcases of the two broad categories.

In general, out-of-the-money covered writes offer higher potential rewards but have less risk protection than do in-the-money covered writes. One can establish an aggressive or defensive covered writing position, depending on how far the call option is in- or out-of-the-money when the write is established. In-the-money writes are more defensive covered writing positions.

Some examples may help to illustrate how one covered write can be considerably more conservative, from a strategy viewpoint, than another.

Example: XYZ common stock is selling at 45 and two options are being considered for writing: an XYZ July 40 selling for 8, and an XYZ July 50 selling for 1. Table 2-2 depicts the profitability of utilizing the July 40 or the July 50 for the covered writing. The in-the-money covered write of the July 40 afford 8 points, or nearly 18% protection down to a price of 37 (the break-even point) at expiration. The out-of-the-money covered write of the July 50 offers only 1 point of downside protection at expiration. Hence, *the in-the-money covered write offers greater downside protection than does the out-of-the-money covered write.* This statement is true in general—not merely for this example.

In the balance of the financial world, it is normally true that investment positions offering less risk also have lower reward potential. The covered writing example just given is no exception. The in-the-money covered write of the July 40 has a maximum potential profit of $300 at any point above 40 at the time of expiration. However, the out-of-the-

TABLE 2-2.
Profit or loss of the July 40 and July 50 calls.

In-the-Money Write of July 40		Out-of-the-Money Write of July 50	
Stock at Expiration	Total Profit	Stock at Expiration	Total Profit
35	− $200	35	− $900
37	0	40	− 400
40	+ 300	44	0
45	+ 300	45	+ 100
50	+ 300	50	+ 600
60	+ 300	60	+ 600

money covered write of the July 50 has a maximum potential of $600 at any point above 50 at expiration. *The maximum potential profit of an out-of-the-money covered write is generally greater than that of an in-the-money write.*

To make a true comparison between the two covered writes, one must look at what happens with the stock between 40 and 50 at expiration. The in-the-money write attains its maximum profit anywhere within that range. Even a 5-point *decline* by the underlying stock at expiration would still leave the in-the-money writer with his maximum profit. However, *for the maximum profit potential to be realized with an out-of-the-money covered write always requires a rise in price by the underlying stock.* This further illustrates the more conservative nature of the in-the-money write. It should be noted that in-the-money writes, although having a smaller profit potential, can still be attractive on a percentage return basis, especially if the write is done in a margin account.

One can construct a more aggressive position by writing an out-of-the-money call. One's outlook for the underlying stock should be bullish in that case. If one is neutral or moderately bearish on the stock, an in-the-money covered write is more appropriate. If one is truly bearish on a stock he owns, he should sell the stock instead of establishing a covered write.

THE TOTAL RETURN CONCEPT OF COVERED WRITING

When one writes an out-of-the-money option, the overall position tends to reflect more of the result of the stock price movement and less of the benefits of writing the call. Since the premium on an out-of-the-money call is relatively small, the total position will be quite susceptible to loss if the stock declines. If the stock rises, the position will make money regardless of the result in the option at expiration. On the other hand, an in-the-money write is more of a "total" position—taking advantage of the benefit of the relatively large option premium. If the stock declines, the position can still make a profit—in fact, it can even make the maximum profit. Of course an in-the-money write will also make money if the stock rises in price, but the profit is not generally as great in percentage terms as is that of an out-of-the-money write.

Those who believe in the *total return concept of covered writing* consider both downside protection and maximum potential return as important factors and are willing to have the stock called away, if necessary, to meet their objectives. When premiums are moderate or small, only in-the-money writes satisfy the total return philosophy.

Some covered writers prefer never to lose their stock through exercise, and as a result will often write options quite far out-of-the-money to minimize the chances of being called by expiration. These writers receive little downside protection and, to make money, must depend almost entirely on the results of the stock itself. Such a philosophy is more like being a stockholder and *trading options* against one's stock position than actually operating a covered writing *strategy*. In fact, some covered writers will attempt to buy back written options for quick profits if such profits materialize during the life of the covered write. This, too, is a stock ownership philosophy, not a covered writing strategy. The total return concept represents the true strategy in covered writing, whereby one views the entire position as a single entity and is not predominantly concerned with the results of his stock ownership.

The Conservative Covered Write

Covered writing is generally accepted to be a conservative strategy. This is because the covered writer always has less risk than a stockholder, provided that he holds the covered write until expiration of the written call. For, if the underlying stock declines, the covered writer will always offset part of his loss by the amount of the option premium received, no matter how small.

As was demonstrated in previous sections, however, some covered writes are clearly more conservative than others. Not all option writers agree on what is meant by a conservative covered write. Some feel that it involves writing an option (probably out-of-the-money) on a conservative stock, generally one with high yield and low volatility. It *is* true that the stock itself in such a position is conservative, but the position is more aptly termed a *covered write on a conservative stock*. This is distinctly different from a conservative covered write.

A true *conservative covered write* is one in which the *total* position is conservative—offering reduced risk and a good probability of making a profit. An in-the-money write, even on a stock that itself is not conservative, can become a conservative total position when the option itself is properly chosen. Clearly, one cannot write calls that are too deeply in-the-money. If he did, he would get large amounts of downside protection, but his returns would be severely limited. If all that one desired was maximum protection of his money at a nominal rate of profit, he could leave the money in a bank. Instead, the conservative covered writer strives to make a potentially acceptable return while still receiving an above-average amount of protection.

Example: Again assume XYZ common stock is selling at 45 and an XYZ July 40 call is selling at 8. A covered write of the XYZ July 40 would require, in a cash account, an investment of $3,700—$4,500 to purchase 100 shares of XYZ, less the $800 received in option premiums. The write has a maximum profit potential of $300. The potential return from this position is therefore $300/$3,700, just over 8 % for the period during which the write must be held. Since this period can be at most 9 months (listed options have a maximum life of 9 months), this return would be well in excess of 10% on a per annum basis. If the write were done in a margin account, the return would be considerably higher.

Note that we have ignored dividends paid by the underlying stock and commission charges, factors that will be discussed in detail in the next section. Also, one should be aware that if he is looking at an *annualized return* from a covered write, there is no guarantee that such a return could actually be obtained. All that is certain is that the writer could make 8% in 9 months. There is no guarantee that 9 months from now, when the call expires, there will be an equivalent position to establish that will extend the same return for the remainder of the annualization period. Annual returns should only be used for comparative purposes between covered writes.

The writer has a position that has an annualized return (for comparative purposes) of over 10% and the position has 8 points of downside protection. Thus the *total position* is an investment that will not lose money unless XYZ common stock falls by more than 8 points, or about 18%, and is an investment that could return the equivalent of 10% annually should XYZ common stock rise, remain the same, or fall by 5 points (to 40). This is a conservative position. Even if XYZ itself is not a conservative stock, the action of writing this option has made the *total position* a conservative one. The only factor that might detract from the conservative nature of the total position would be if XYZ were so volatile that it could easily fall more than 8 points in 9 months.

In a strategic sense, the total position described above is better and more conservative than one in which a writer buys a conservative stock—yielding perhaps 6 or 7%—and writes an out-of-the-money call for a minimal premium. If this conservative stock were to fall in price, the writer would be in danger of being in a loss situation, because here the option is not providing anything more than the most minimal downside protection. As was described earlier, a high-yielding, low-volatility stock will not have much time premium in its in-the-money options, so that one cannot effectively establish an in-the-money write on such a "conservative" stock.

COMPUTING RETURN ON INVESTMENT

Now that the reader has some general feeling for covered call writing, it is time to discuss the specifics of computing return on investment. One should always know exactly what his potential returns are, including all costs, when he establishes a covered writing position. Once the procedure for computing returns is clear, one can more logically decide which covered writes are the most attractive.

There are three basic elements of a covered write that should be computed before entering into the position. The first is the *return if exercised*. This is the return on investment that one would achieve if the stock were called away. For an out-of-the-money covered write, it is necessary for the stock to rise in price in order for the return if exercised to be achieved. However, for an in-the-money covered write, the return if exercised would be attained even if the stock were unchanged in price at option expiration. Thus it is often advantageous to compute the *return if unchanged*—that is, the return that would be realized if the underlying stock were unchanged when the option expired. One can more fairly compare out-of-the-money and in-the-money covered writes by using the return if unchanged, since no assumption is made concerning stock price movement. The third important statistic that the covered writer should consider is the exact *downside break-even point* after all costs are included. Once this downside break-even point is known, one can readily compute the percentage of *downside protection* that he would receive from selling the call.

Example 1: An investor is considering the following covered write of a 6-month call: buy 500 XYZ common at 43, sell 5 XYZ July 45 calls at 3. One must first compute the net investment required (Table 2-3). In a cash account, this investment consists of paying for the stock in full, less the net proceeds from the sale of the options. Note that this net investment figure includes all commissions necessary to establish the position. (The commissions used here are approximations, as they vary from firm to firm.) Of course, if the investor withdraws the option premium, as he is free to do, his net investment will consist of the stock cost plus commissions. Once the necessary investment is known, the writer can compute the return if exercised. Table 2-4 illustrates the computation. One first computes the profit if exercised and then divides that quantity by the net investment to obtain the return if exercised. Note that dividends

TABLE 2-3.
Net investment required—cash account.

Stock cost (500 shares at 43)	$21,500
Plus stock purchase commissions	+ 320
Less option premiums received	− 1,500
Plus option sale commissions	+ 60
Net cash investment	$20,380

TABLE 2-4.
Return if exercised—cash account.

Stock sale proceeds (500 shares at 45)	$22,500
Less stock sale commissions	− 330
Plus dividends earned until expiration	+ 500
Less net investment	− 20,380
Net profit if exercised	$ 2,290

$$\text{Return if exercised} = \frac{\$2,290}{\$20,389} = 11.2\%$$

TABLE 2-5.
Return if unchanged—cash account.

Unchanged stock value (500 shares at 43)	$21,500
Plus dividends	+ 500
Less net investment	− 20,380
Profit if unchanged	$ 1,620

$$\text{Return if unchanged} = \frac{\$1,620}{\$20,380} = 7.9\%$$

are included in this computation; it is assumed that XYZ stock will pay $500 in dividends on the 500 shares during the life of the call. Moreover, all commissions are included as well—the net investment includes the original stock purchase and option sale commissions, and the stock sale commission is explicitly listed.

For the return computed above to be realized, XYZ stock would have to rise in price from its current price of 43 to any price above 45 by expiration. As noted earlier, it may be more useful to know what return could be made by the writer if the stock did not move anywhere at all. Table 2-5 illustrates the method of computing the *return if unchanged*— also called the *static return* and sometimes *incorrectly* referred to as the "expected return." Again, one first calculates the profit and then calculates the return by dividing the profit by the net investment. An important point should be made here. There is no stock sale commission included in Table 2-5. This is the most common way of calculating the return if unchanged, and is done this way because in a majority of cases, one would continue to hold the stock if it were unchanged and would write another call option against the same stock. Recall again, though, that *if the written call is in-the-money, the return if unchanged is the same as the return if exercised*—stock sale commissions must therefore be included in that case.

Once the necessary returns have been computed and the writer has a feeling for how much money he could make in the covered write, he next computes the exact *downside break-even point* to determine what kind of *downside protection* the written call provides (Table 2-6). The total return concept of covered writing necessitates viewing both potential income *and* downside protection as important criteria for selecting a writing position. If the stock were held to expiration and the $500 in dividends received, the writer would break even at a price of 39¾ when rounded to the nearest eighth. Most computer printouts will express the break-even price in tenths. Again, a stock sale commission is not generally included in the break-even point computation, because the written call would expire totally worthless and the writer might then write another call on the same stock. Later, we will discuss the subject of continuing to write against stocks already owned. It will be seen that in many cases it is advantageous to continue to hold a stock and write against it again rather than to sell it and establish a covered write in a new stock.

Next, we translate the break-even price into *percent downside protection* (Table 2-7), which is a convenient way of comparing the levels of downside protection among variously priced stocks. We will see later that it is actually better to compare the downside protection with the *volatility* of the underlying stock. However, since percent downside protection is a common and widely accepted method that is more readily calculated, it is necessary to be familiar with it as well.

Before moving on to discuss what kinds of returns one should attempt to strive for in which situations, the same example will be worked through again for a covered write in a margin account. The use of margin

TABLE 2-6.
Downside break-even point—cash account.

Net investment	$20,380
Less dividends	− 500
Total stock cost to expiration	$19,880
Divide by shares held	÷ 500
Break-even price	39.8

TABLE 2-7.
Percent downside protection—cash account.

Initial stock price	43
Less break-even price	− 39.8
Points of protection	3.2
Divide by original stock price	÷ 43
Equals percent downside protection	7.4%

will provide higher potential returns since the net investment will be smaller. However, the margin interest charge incurred on the debit balance (the amount of money borrowed from the brokerage firm) will cause the break-even point to be higher, thus slightly reducing the amount of down-side protection available from writing the call. Again, all commissions to establish the position are included in the net investment computation.

Example 2: Recall that the net investment for the cash write was $20,380. A margin covered write requires less than half of the investment of a cash write when the margin rate (set by the Federal Reserve) is 50%. In a margin account, if one desires to remove the premium from the account, he may do so immediately provided that he has enough reserve equity in the account to cover the purchase of the stock. If he does so, his net investment would be equal to the debit balance calculation shown on the right in Table 2-8.

Tables 2-9 to 2-12 illustrate the computation of returns from writing on margin. If one has already computed the cash returns, he can use method 2 most easily. Method 1 involves no prior profit calculations.

TABLE 2-8.
Net investment required—margin account.

Stock cost	$21,500			
Plus stock commissions	+ 320	Debit balance calculation:		
Net stock cost	$21,820	Net stock cost		$21,820
Times margin rate	× 50%	Less equity	−	10,910
Equity required	$10,910	Debit balance		$10,910
Less premiums received	− 1,500	(at 50% margin)		
Plus option commissions	+ 60			
Net margin investment	$ 9,470			

TABLE 2-9.
Return if exercised—margin account.

Method 1		Method 2	
Stock sale proceeds	$22,500	Net profit if exercised—cash	$2,290
Less stock commissions	− 330	Less margin interest charges	− 545
Plus dividends	+ 550	Net profit if exercised—	$1,745
Less margin interest charges		margin	
(10% on $10,910 for 6 months)	− 545		
Less debit balance	− 10,910		
Less net margin investment	− 9,470		
Net profit—margin	$ 1,745		

$$\text{Return if exercised} = \frac{\$1,745}{\$9,470} = 18.4\%$$

TABLE 2-10.
Return if unchanged—margin account.

Method 1		Method 2	
Unchanged stock value (500 shares at 43)	$21,500	Profit if unchanged—cash	$1,620
		Less margin interest charges	− 545
Plus dividends	+ 500	Net profit if unchanged— margin	$1,075
Less margin interest charges (10% on $10,910 debit for 6 months)	− 545		
Less debit balance	− 10,910		
Less net investment (margin)	− 9,470		
Net profit unchanged— margin	$ 1,075		

$$\text{Return if unchanged} = \frac{\$1,075}{\$9,470} = 11.4\%$$

TABLE 2-11.
Break-even point—margin write.

Net margin investment	$ 9,470
Plus debit balance	+ 10,910
Less dividends	− 500
Plus margin interest charges	+ 545
Total stock cost to expiration	$20,425
Divide by shares held	÷ 500
Break-even point—margin	40.9

TABLE 2-12.
Percent downside protection—margin write.

Initial stock price	43
Less break-even price—margin	− 40.9
Points of protection	2.1
Divide by original stock price	÷ 43
Equals percent downside protection—margin	4.9%

The return if exercised is 18.4% for the covered write using margin. In Example 1 the return if exercised for a cash write was computed as 11.2%. Thus the return if exercised from a margin write is considerably higher. In fact, unless a fairly deep in-the-money write is being considered, the return on margin will always be higher than the return from cash. The farther out-of-the-money that the written call is, the bigger the discrepancy between cash and margin returns will be when the return if exercised is computed.

As with the computation for return if exercised for a write on margin, the return if unchanged calculation is similar for cash and margin also. The only difference is the subtraction of the margin interest charges from the profit. The return if unchanged is also higher for a margin write, provided that there is enough option premium to compensate for the margin interest charges. The return if unchanged in the cash example was 7.9% versus 11.4% for the margin write. In general, the farther from the strike in either direction—out-of-the-money or in-the-money—the less return if unchanged on margin will exceed the cash return if unchanged. In fact, for deeply out-of-the-money or deeply in-the-money calls, the return if unchanged will be higher on cash than on margin. Table 2-11 shows that the break-even point on margin, 40⅞, is higher than the break-even point from a cash write, 39¾, because of the margin interest charges. Again, the percent downside protection can be computed as shown in Table 2-12. Obviously, since the break-even point on margin is higher than that on cash, there is less percent downside protection in a margin covered write.

Compound Interest

The astute reader will have noticed that our computations of margin interest have been overly simplistic; the compounding effect of interest rates has been ignored. That is, since interest charges are normally applied to an account monthly, the investor will be paying interest in the later stages of a covered writing position on not only the original debit, but on all previous monthly interest charges. This effect is described in detail in a later chapter on arbitrage techniques. Briefly stated, rather than computing the interest charge as the debit times the interest rate multiplied by the time to expiration, one should technically use:

$$\text{Margin interest charges} = \text{debit} \, [(1 + r)^t - 1]$$

where r is the interest rate per month and t the number of months to expiration (it would be incorrect to use days to expiration since brokerage firms compute interest monthly, not daily).

In Example 2 of the preceding section, the debit was $10,910, the time was 6 months, and the annual interest rate was 10%. Using this more complex formula, the margin interest charges would be $557, as opposed to the $545 charge computed with the simpler formula. Thus the difference is usually small, in terms of percentage, and *it is therefore common practice to use the simpler method.*

Size of the Position

So far it has been assumed that the writer was purchasing 500 shares of XYZ and selling 5 calls. This requires a relatively considerable investment for one position for the individual investor. However, one should be aware that buying too few shares for covered writing purposes can lower his returns considerably.

Example: If an investor were to buy 100 shares of XYZ at 43 and sell 1 July 45 call for 3, his return if exercised would drop from the 11.2% return (cash) that was computed earlier to a return of 9.9% in a cash account. Table 2-13 verifies this statement.

Since commissions are less, on a per-share basis, when one buys more stock and sells more calls, the returns will naturally be higher with a 500- or 1,000-share position than with a 100- or 200-share position. This difference can be rather dramatic, as Tables 2-14 and 2-15 point out. Several interesting and worthwhile conclusions can be drawn from these tables. The first and most obvious conclusion is that *the more shares one writes against, the higher his returns and the lower his break-even point will be.* This is true for both cash and margin and is a direct result of the

TABLE 2-13.
Cash investment vs. return.

Net Investment—Cash (100 shares)		Return if Exercised—Cash (100 shares)	
Stock cost	$4,300	Stock sale price	$4,500
Plus commissions	+ 85	Stock commissions	− 85
Less option premium	− 300	Plus dividend	+ 100
Plus option commissions	+ 25	Less net investment	− 4,110
Net investment	$4,110	Net profit if exercised	$ 405

$$\text{Return if exercised} = \frac{\$405}{\$4,110} = 9.9\%$$

TABLE 2-14.
Cash covered writes (costs included).

	Shares Written Against						
	100	200	300	400	500	1,000	2,000
Return if exercised (%)	9.9	10.0	10.4	10.8	11.2	12.1	12.7
Return if unchanged (%)	7.1	7.2	7.5	7.7	7.9	8.4	8.7
Break-even point	40.1	40.0	39.9	39.9	39.8	39.6	39.5

TABLE 2-15.
Margin covered write (costs included).

	Shares Written Against						
	100	200	300	400	500	1,000	2,000
Return if exercised (%)	10.4	15.8	16.6	17.4	18.4	20.4	21.6
Return if unchanged (%)	4.4	9.8	10.3	10.8	11.4	12.3	13.0
Break-even point	41.2	41.1	41.0	41.0	40.9	40.7	40.6

way commissions are figured—larger trades involve smaller *percentage* commission charges. While the percentage returns increase as the number of shares increases for both cash or margin covered writing, the increase is much more dramatic in the case of margin. Note that in the first table, which depicts cash transactions, the return from writing against 100 shares is 9.9% and increases to 12.7% if 2,000 shares are written against. This is an increase, but not a particularly dramatic one. However, in the margin table, the return if exercised more than doubles (21.6 vs. 10.4) and the return if unchanged nearly triples (13.0 vs. 4.4) when the 100-share write is compared to the 2,000-share write. This effect is more dramatic for margin writes due to two factors—the lower investment required and the more burdensome effect of margin interest charges on the profits of smaller positions. This effect is so dramatic that a 100-share write in a cash account in our example actually offers a higher return if unchanged than does the margin write—7.1% vs. 4.4%. This implies that *one should carefully compute his potential returns if he is writing against a small number of shares on margin.*

What a Difference an Eighth Makes

Another aspect of covered writing that can be important as far as potential returns are concerned is, of course, the prices of the stock and option involved in the write. It may seem insignificant that one has to pay an extra eighth for the stock or possibly receives an eighth or quarter less for the call, but even a relatively small fraction can alter the potential returns by a surprising amount. This is especially true for in-the-money writes, although any write will be affected. Let us use the previous 500-share covered writing example, again including all costs.

As before, the results are more dramatic for the margin write than for the cash write. In neither case does the break-even point change by much. However, the potential returns are altered significantly. Notice that if one pays an extra eighth for the stock and receives an eighth less for the call—the far right-hand column in Table 2-16—he may greatly negate the effect of writing against a larger number of shares. From Tables 2-14 and 2-15, one can see that writing against *300 shares* at those prices (43

TABLE 2-16.
Effect of stock and option prices on writing returns.

	Buy stock at 43 Sell Call at 3	Buy Stock at 43⅛ Sell Call at 3	Buy Stock at 43⅛ Sell Call at 2⅞
Return if exercised	11.2% cash	10.9% cash	10.6% cash
	18.4% margin	17.7% margin	16.9% margin
Return if unchanged	7.9% cash	7.6% cash	7.3% cash
	11.4% margin	10.7% margin	9.9% margin
Break-even point	39.8 cash	39.9 cash	40.0 cash
	40.9 margin	41.0 margin	41.1 margin

for the stock and 3 for the call) is approximately the same return as writing against 500 shares where the stock costs 43⅛ and the option brings in 2⅞.

Table 2-16 should clearly demonstrate that entering a covered writing order *at the market* may not be a prudent thing to do, especially if one's calculations for the potential returns are based on last sales or on closing prices in the newspaper. The next section discusses, in depth, the proper procedure for entering a covered writing order.

EXECUTION OF THE COVERED WRITE ORDER

When establishing a covered writing position, the question often arises: Which should be done first—buy the stock or sell the option? The correct answer is that neither should be done first! In fact, a *simultaneous transaction of buying the stock and selling the option is the only way of assuring that both sides of the covered write are established at desired price levels.*

If one "legs" into the position—that is, buys the stock first and then attempts to sell the option, or vice versa—he is subjecting himself to a risk.

Example: An investor wants to buy XYZ at 43 and sell the July 45 call at 3. If he first sells the option at 3 and *then* tries to buy the stock, he may find that he has to pay more than 43 for the stock. On the other hand, if he tries to buy the stock first and *then* sell the option, he may find that the option price has moved down. In either case the writer will be accepting a lower return on his covered write. Table 2-16 demonstrated how one's returns might be affected if he has to give up an eighth by "legging" into the position.

Establishing a Net Position

What the covered writer really wants to do is ensure that his net price is obtained. If he wants to buy stock at 43 and sell an option at 3, he is attempting to establish the position at 40 net. He normally would not mind paying $43\frac{1}{8}$ for the stock if he can sell the call at $3\frac{1}{8}$, thereby still obtaining 40 net.

A *"net" covered writing order* must be placed with a brokerage firm because it is essential for the person actually executing the order to have full access to both the stock exchange and the option exchange. This is also referred to as a *contingent* order. Most major brokerage firms offer this service to their clients, although some place a minimum number of shares on the order. That is, one must write against at least 500 or 1,000 shares in order to avail himself of the service. There are, however, brokerage firms that will take net orders even for 100-share covered writes. Since the chances of giving away an eighth of a point are relatively great if one attempts to execute his own order by placing separate orders on two exchanges—stock and option—he should avail himself of the broker's service. Moreover, if his orders are for a small number of shares, he should deal with a broker who will take net orders for small positions.

The reader must understand that *there is no guarantee that a net order will be filled.* The net order is always a "not held"order—meaning that the customer is not guaranteed an execution even if it appears that the order could be filled at prevailing market bids and offers. Of course, the broker will attempt to fill the order if it can reasonably be accomplished since that is his livelihood. However, if the net order is slightly away from current market prices, the broker may have to "leg" into the position to fill the order. The risk in this is the broker's responsibility, not the customer's. Therefore, the broker may elect not to take risk and to report "nothing done"—the order is not filled.

If one buys stock at 43 and sells the call at 3, is the return really the same as buying the stock at $43\frac{1}{8}$ and selling the call at $3\frac{1}{8}$? The answer is, yes, the returns are very similar when the prices differ by small amounts. This can be seen without the use of a table. If one pays an eighth more for the stock, his investment increases by $12.50 per 100 shares, or $62.50 total. However, the fact that he has received an eighth extra for the call means that the investment is reduced by $62.50. Thus there is no effect on the net investment except for commissions. The commission on 500 shares at $43\frac{1}{8}$ is slightly higher than the commission for 500 shares at 43. Similarly, the commission on 5 calls at $3\frac{1}{8}$ are slightly higher than those on 5 calls at 3. Even so, these increased commissions would be so small that they would not affect the return by more than one-tenth of 1%. Of course, should the covered write at 40 net be executed with stock at $42\frac{7}{8}$ and the call at $2\frac{7}{8}$, the net investment will still remain essentially the same, but the commissions will go *down* slightly. Again, the effect is miniscule.

To carry this concept to extremes may prove somewhat misleading. If one were to buy stock at $40\frac{1}{2}$ and sell the call at $\frac{1}{2}$, he would still be receiving 40 net, but several aspects would have changed considerably. The return, if exercised, remains amazingly constant, but the return, if unchanged, and the percentage downside protection are reduced dramatically. If one were to buy stock at 48 and sell the call at 8—again for 40 net—he would improve the return if unchanged and the percentage downside protection. In reality, when one places a "net" order with a brokerage firm, he normally gets an execution with prices quite close to the ones at the time the order was first entered. It would be a rare case, indeed, when either upside or downside extremes such as those mentioned here would result in the same trading day.

"Side-by-side" trading of stock and options has been proposed by the option exchanges: that is, both the options and their underlying stocks would trade in close physical proximity. If this were approved, the covered call writer would benefit. In a side-by-side market, a single net order could be given to one exchange and the floor broker on that exchange could then buy stock and sell the call at the stated net price.

SELECTING A COVERED WRITING POSITION

The preceding sections, in describing types of covered writes and how to compute returns and break-even points, have laid the groundwork for the ultimate decision that every covered writer must make—choosing which stock to buy and which option to write. This is not necessarily an easy task, because there are large numbers of stocks, striking prices, and expiration dates to choose from.

Since the primary objective of covered writing for most investors is increased income through stock ownership, the return on investment is an important consideration in determining which write to choose. However, the decision must not be made on the basis of return alone. More volatile stocks will offer higher returns, but they may also involve more risk because of their ability to fall in price quickly. Thus the amount of downside protection is the other important objective of covered writing. Finally, the quality and technical or fundamental outlook of the underlying stock itself are of importance as well. The following section will help to quantify how these factors should be viewed by the covered writer.

Projected Returns

The return that one strives for is somewhat a matter of personal preference. In general, the annualized return if unchanged should be used as the comparative measure between various covered writes. In using this return as the measuring criterion, one does not make any assumptions about the stock moving up in price in order to attain the potential return. A general rule used in deciding what is a minimally acceptable return is to consider a covered writing position only if the return unchanged is at least 1% per month. That is, a 3-month write would have to offer a return of at least 3% and a 6-month write would have to have a return if unchanged of at least 6%. During periods of expanded option premiums, there may be so many writes that satisfy this criterion that one would want to raise his sights somewhat—say to 1½% and 2% per month. Also, one must feel personally comfortable that his minimum return criterion—whether it be 1% per month or 2% per month—is large enough to compensate for the risks he is taking. That is, the downside risk of owning stock, should it fall far enough to outdistance the premium received, should be adequately compensated for by the potential return. It should be pointed out that 1% per month is not a return to be taken lightly, especially if there is a reasonable assurance that it can be attained. However, if less risky investments, such as bonds, were yielding 12% annually, the covered writer must set his sights higher.

Normally, the returns from various covered writing situations are compared by annualizing the returns. One should not, however, be deluded into believing that he can always attain the projected annual return. A 6-month write that offers a 6% return annualizes to 12%. But if one establishes such a position, all that he can achieve is 6% in 6 months. One does not really know for sure that 6 months from now there will be another position available that will provide 6% over the next 6 months.

The deeper that the written option is in-the-money, the higher the probability that the return if unchanged will actually be attained. In an in-the-money situation, recall that the return if unchanged is the same as the return if exercised. Both would be attained unless the stock fell below the striking price by expiration. Thus, for an in-the-money write, the projected return is attained if the stock rises, remains unchanged, or even falls slightly by the time the option expires. Higher potential returns are available for out-of-the-money writes if the stock rises. However, should the stock remain the same or decline in price, the out-of-the-money write will generally underperform the in-the-money write. This is why the return if unchanged is a good comparison.

Downside Protection

Downside protection is more difficult to quantify than projected returns are. As mentioned earlier, the percentage of downside protection is often used as a measure. This is somewhat misleading, however, since the more volatile stocks will always offer a large percentage of downside protection (their premiums are higher). The difficulty arises in trying to decide if 10% protection on a volatile stock is better than or worse than, say, 6%

protection on a less volatile stock. There are mathematical ways to quantify this, but because of the relatively advanced nature of the computations involved, they will not be discussed until later in the text.

Rather than go into involved mathematical calculations, many covered writers use the percentage of downside protection and will only consider writes that offer a certain minimum level of protection—say 10%. Although this is not exact, it does strive to ensure that one has minimal downside protection in a covered write as well as an acceptable return. A standard figure that is often used is the 10% level of protection. Alternatively, one may also require that the write be a certain percent in-the-money, say 5%. This is just another way of arriving at the same concept.

The Importance of Strategy

In a conservative option writing strategy, one should be looking for minimum returns if unchanged of 1% per month, with downside protection of at least 10% as general guidelines. Employing such criteria automatically forces one to write in-the-money options, in line with the total return concept. The overall position constructed by using such guidelines as these will be a relatively conservative position—regardless of the volatility of the underlying stock—since the levels of protection will be large but a reasonable return can still be attained. There is a danger, however, in using fixed guidelines because market conditions change. In the early days of listed options, premiums were so large that virtually every at- or in-the-money covered write satisfied the foregoing criteria. However, now one should work with a ranked list of covered writing positions, or perhaps two lists. A daily computer ranking of either or both of the following categories would help establish the most attractive types of conservative covered writes. One list would rank, by annualized return, the writes that afford, as a minimum, the desired downside protection level, say 10%. The other list would rank, by percentage downside protection, all the writes that meet at least the minimum acceptable return if unchanged, say 12%. If premium levels shrink and the lists become quite small on a daily basis, one might consider expanding the criteria to view more potential situations. On the other hand, if premiums expand dramatically, one might consider using more restrictive criteria, to reduce the number of potential writing candidates.

A different group of covered writers may favor a more aggressive strategy of out-of-the-money writes. *There is some mathematical basis to believe, in the long run, that moderately out-of-the-money covered writes will perform better than in-the-money writes.* In falling or static markets, any covered writer—even the more aggressive one—will outperform the stockowner who does not write calls. The out-of-the-money covered writer does not write calls. The out-of-the-money covered writer has more risk in such a market than the in-the-money writer does. But in a rising market, the out-of-the-money covered writer will not limit his returns as much as the in-the-money writer will. As stated earlier, the out-of-the-money writer's performance will more closely follow the performance of the underlying stock—that is, it will be more volatile on a quarter-by-quarter basis.

There is merit in either philosophy. The in-the-money writes appeal to those investors looking to earn a relatively consistent, moderate rate of return. This is the *total return concept*. These investors are generally concerned with preservation of capital, thus striving for the greater levels of downside protection available from in-the-money writes. On the other hand, some investors prefer to strive for higher potential returns through writing out-of-the-money calls. These more aggressive investors are willing to accept more downside risk in their covered writing positions in exchange for the possibility of higher returns should the underlying stock rise in price. These investors will often rely on a bullish research opinion on a stock in order to select out-of-the-money writes.

Although the type of covered writing strategy pursued is a matter of personal philosophy, it would seem that the benefits of in-the-money strategy—more consistent returns and lessened risk than stock ownership will normally provide—would lead the portfolio manager or less aggressive investor toward this strategy. If the investor is interested in achieving higher returns, some of the strategies to be presented later in the book may be able to provide higher returns with less risk than can out-of-the-money covered writing.

The final important consideration in selecting a covered write is the underlying stock itself. One does not necessarily have to be bullish on the underlying stock to take a covered writing position. As long as one does not foresee a potential decline in the underlying stock, he can feel free to establish the covered writing position. It is generally best if one is neutral or slightly bullish on the underlying stock. *If one is bearish, he should not take a covered writing position on that stock*, regardless of the levels of protection that can be obtained. An even broader statement would be that one should not establish a covered write on a stock that he does not want to own. Some individual investors may have qualms about buying stock they feel is too volatile for them. Impartially, if the return and protection are adequate, the characteristics of the total position are different from those of the underlying stock. However, it is still true that one should not invest in positions that he considers too risky for his portfolio—nor should one establish a covered write just because he likes a particular stock. If the potential return if unchanged or levels of downside protection do not meet one's criteria, the write should not be established.

The covered writing *strategist* strives for a balance between acceptable returns and downside protection. He rejects situations that do not meet his criteria in either category and rejects stocks on which he is bearish. The resulting situations will probably fulfill the objectives of a conservative covered writing program—increased income, protection, and less variability of results on a less volatile investment portfolio.

WRITING AGAINST STOCK ALREADY OWNED

Establishing covered writing positions involves other factors. It is often the case that an investor owns stock that has listed options trading, but feels that the returns from writing are too low in comparison to other covered writes that simultaneously exist in the marketplace. This opinion may be valid, but often arises from the fact that the investor has seen a computer-generated list showing returns on his stock as being low in comparison to similarly priced stocks. One should note that such lists generally assume that stock is bought in order to establish the covered write; the returns are usually not computed and published for writing against stock already held. It may be the case that the commission costs for selling one stock and investing in another may alter the returns so substantially that one would be better off to write against the shares of stock initially held.

Example: An investor owns XYZ stock and is comparing it against AAA stock for writing purposes. If AAA is more volatile than XYZ, the current prices might appear as follows:

	Stock	*Oct 50 Call*
XYZ: 50		4
AAA: 50		6

Table 2-17 summarizes the computation of the return if exercised as one might see it listed on a daily or weekly summary of available covered writing returns. Assume that 500 shares are being written against, that XYZ will pay 50 cents per share in dividends while AAA pays none during the life of the call, and that the October 50 is a 6-month call.

Without going into as much detail, the other significant aspects of these two writes are:

	XYZ	*AAA*
Return if exercised—margin	7.9%	16.2%
Downside break-even point—cash	46.3	44.9
Downside break-even point—margin	47.6	46.1

TABLE 2-17.
Summary of covered writing returns, XYZ and AAA.

	XYZ	AAA
Buy 500 shares at 50	$25,000	$25,000
Plus stock commissions	+ 345	+ 345
Less option premiums received	− 2,000	− 3,000
Plus option sale commissions	+ 77	+ 91
Net investment—cash	$23,422	$22,436
Sell 500 shares at 50	$25,000	$25,000
Less stock sale commissions	− 345	− 345
Dividend received	+ 250	0
Less net investment	− 23,422	− 22,436
Net profit	$ 1,483	$ 2,219
Return if exercised—cash	6.3%	9.9%

Seeing these calculations, the XYZ stockholder may feel that it is not advisable to write against his stock, or he may even be tempted to sell XYZ and buy AAA in order to establish a covered write. Either of these actions could be a mistake.

First, he should compute what his returns would be, at current prices, from writing against the XYZ *he already owns*. Since the stock is already held, no stock buy commissions would be involved. This would reduce the net investment shown above by the stock purchase commissions, or $345, giving a total net investment (cash) of $23,077. In theory, the stockholder does not really make an investment per se—after all, he already owns the stock. However, for the purposes of computing returns, an investment figure is necessary. This reduction in the net investment will then increase his profit by the same amount—$345—thus bringing the profit up to $1,828. Consequently, the return if exercised (cash) would be 7.9% on XYZ stock already held. On margin, the return would increase to 11.3% after eliminating purchase commissions. This return, assumed to be for a 6-month period, is well in excess of 1% per month—the level nominally used for acceptable covered writes. Thus the investor who already owns stock may inadvertently be overlooking a potentially attractive covered write because he has not computed the returns excluding the stock purchase commission on his current stock holding.

It could conceivably be an even more extreme oversight for the investor to switch from XYZ to AAA for writing purposes. The investor may consider making this switch because he thinks that he could substantially increase his return from 6.3% to 9.9% for the 6-month period, as shown in Table 2-17 comparing the two writes.

However, returns are not truly comparable because the investor already owns XYZ. To make the switch, he would first have to spend $345 in stock commissions to sell his XYZ—thereby reducing his profits on AAA by $345. Referring again to the preceding detailed breakdown of the return if exercised, the profit on AAA would then decline to $1,874 on the investment of $22,436, a return if exercised (cash) of 8.4%. On margin, the comparable return from switching stocks would drop to 14.8%.

The real comparison in returns from writing against these two stocks should be made in the following manner. The return from writing against XYZ *that is already held* should be compared with the return from writing AAA *after switching from XYZ:*

	XYZ Already Held	Switch from XYZ to AAA
Return if exercised—cash	7.9%	8.4%
Return if exercised—margin	11.3%	14.8%

Each investor must decide for himself whether it is worth this much *smaller increase* in return to switch to a more volatile stock that pays a smaller dividend. He can, of course, only make this decision by making the true comparison shown immediately above as opposed to the first comparison, which assumed that both stocks had to be purchased in order to establish the covered write.

The same logic applies in situations where an investor has been doing covered writing. If he owns stock on which an option has expired, he will have to decide whether to write against the same stock again or to sell the stock and buy a new stock for covered writing purposes. Generally, the investor should write against the stock already held. This justifies the method of computation of return if unchanged for out-of-the-money writes and also the computation of downside break-even points in which a stock sale commission was not charged. That is, the writer would not normally sell his stock after an option has expired worthless, but would instead write another option against the same stock. It is thus acceptable to make these computations without including a stock sales commission.

A Word of Caution

The stockholder who owns stock from a previous purchase and later contemplates writing calls against that stock must be aware of his situation. He must realize and accept the fact that he might lose his stock via assignment. If he is determined to retain ownership of the stock, he may have to buy back the written option at a loss should the underlying stock increase in price. In essence, he is limiting the stock's upside potential.

If a stockholder is going to be frustrated and disappointed when he is not fully participating during a rally in his stock, he should not write a call in the first place. Perhaps he could utilize the incremental return concept of covered writing—a topic to be covered later in this chapter.

As stressed earlier, a covered writing strategy involves viewing the stock and option as a *total* position—*it is not a strategy wherein the investor is a stockholder who also trades options against his stock position.* If the stockholder is selling the calls because he thinks the stock is going to decline in price and the call trade itself will be profitable, he may be putting himself in a tenuous position. Thinking this way, he will probably only be satisfied if he makes a profit on the call trade, regardless of the unrealized result in the underlying stock. This sort of philosophy is contrary to a covered writing strategy philosophy. Such an investor—he is really becoming a trader—should carefully review his motives for writing the call and anticipate his reaction if the stock rises substantially in price after the call has been written.

DIVERSIFYING RETURN AND PROTECTION IN A COVERED WRITE

Fundamental Diversification Techniques

Quite clearly, the covered writing strategist would like to have as much of a combination of high potential returns and adequate downside protection as he can obtain. Writing an out-of-the-money call will offer higher returns if exercised, but it usually affords only a modest amount of downside protection. On the other hand, writing an in-the-money call will provide more downside cushion but offers a lower return if exercised. For some strategists, this diversification is realized in practice by writing out-of-the-money calls on some stocks and in-the-moneys on other stocks. There is no guarantee that writing in this manner on a list of diversified stocks will produce superior results—one is still forced to pick the stocks that he expects will perform better (for out-of-the-money writing) and that is difficult to do. Moreover, the individual investor may not have enough funds available to diversify into many such situations. There is, however, another alternative to obtaining diversification of both returns and downside protection in a covered writing situation.

The writer may often do best by writing half of his position against in-the-moneys and half against out-of-the-moneys on the same stock. This is especially attractive for a stock whose out-of-the-money calls do not appear to provide enough downside protection, and at the same time, the in-the-money calls do not provide quite enough return. By writing both options, the writer may be able to acquire the return and protection diversification that he is seeking.

Example: The following prices exist for 6-month calls:

XYZ common stock, 42;

XYZ April 40 call, 4; and

XYZ April 45 call, 2.

The writer wishing to establish a covered write against XYZ common stock may like the protection afforded by the April 40 call, but may not find the return particularly attractive. He may be able to improve his return by writing April 45's against part of his position. Assume the writer is considering buying 1,000 shares of XYZ. Table 2-18 compares the attributes of writing the out-of-the-money (April 40) only, or of writing only the in-the-money (April 45), or of writing 5 of each. The table is based on a cash covered write, but returns and protection would be similar for a margin write. Commissions are included in the figures.

It is easily seen that the *"combined" write*—half of the position against the April 40's and the other half against the April 45's—offers the best balance of return and protection. The in-the-money call, by itself, provides over 10% downside protection, but the 5% return if exercised is less than 1% per month. Thus one might not want to write April 40's against his entire position because the potential return is small. At the same time, the April 45's, if written against the entire stock position, would provide for an attractive return if exercised (over 2% per month) but offer only 5% downside protection. The combined write, which has the better features of both options, offers over 8% return if exercised (1⅓% per month) and affords over 8% downside protection. By writing both calls, the writer has potentially solved the problems inherent in writing entirely out-of-the-moneys or entirely in-the-moneys. The "combined" write frees the covered writer from having to initially take a bearish (in-the-money write) or bullish (out-of-the-money write) posture on the stock if he does not want to. This is often necessary on a low-volatility stock trading between striking prices.

TABLE 2-18.
Attributes of various writes.

	In-the-Money Write	Out-of-the Money Write	Write Both Calls
Buy 1,000 XYZ and sell	10 April 40's	10 April 45's	5 April 40's and 5 April 45's
Return if exercised	5.1%	12.2%	8.4%
Return if unchanged	5.1%	6.0%	5.4%
Percent protection	10.5%	5.7%	8.1%

For those who prefer a graphic representation, the profit graph shown in Figure 2-2 compares the combined write of both calls with either the in-the-money write or the out-of-the-money write (dashed lines). It can be observed that all three choices are equal if XYZ is near 42 at expiration—all three lines intersect there.

Since this technique can be useful in providing diversification between protection and return, not only for an individual position but for a large part of a portfolio, it may be useful to see how to exactly compute the potential returns and break-even points. Tables 2-19 and 2-20 calculate the return if exercised and the return if unchanged using the prices from the previous example. Assume XYZ will pay $1 per share in dividends before April expiration.

Note that the profit calculations are similar to those described in earlier sections, except that now there are two prices for stock sales since there are two options involved. In the "return if exercised" section, half

FIGURE 2-2.
Comparison: combined write vs. in-the-money write and out-of-the-money write.

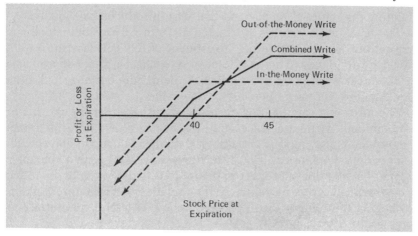

TABLE 2-19.
Net investment—cash account.

Buy 1,000 XYZ at 42	$42,000
Plus stock commissions	+ 460
Less options premiums:	
Sell 5 April 40's at 4	− 2,000
Sell 5 April 45's at 2	− 1,000
Plus total option commissions	+ 140
Net investment	$39,600

TABLE 2-20.
Net return—cash account.

Return if Exercised		Return if Unchanged	
Sell 500 XYZ at 45	$22,500	Unchanged stock value (500 shares at 42)	$21,000
Sell 500 XYZ at 40	20,000	Sell 500 at 40	+ 20,000
Less total stock sale commissions	− 560	Commissions on sale at 40	− 280
Plus dividends ($1/share)	+ 1,000	Plus dividends ($1/share)	+ 1,000
Less net investment	− 39,600	Less net investment	− 39,600
Net profit if exercised	$ 3,340	Net profit if unchanged	$ 2,120

$$\frac{\text{Return if exercised}}{\text{(cash)}} = \frac{3,340}{39,600} = 8.4\% \qquad \frac{\text{Return if unchanged}}{\text{(cash)}} = \frac{2,120}{39,600} = 5.4\%$$

of the stock is sold at 45 and half is sold at 40. The "return if unchanged" calculation is somewhat more complicated now because half of the stock will be called away if it remains unchanged (the in-the-money portion) whereas the other half will not. This is consistent with the method of calculating the return if unchanged that was introduced previously.

The break-even point is calculated as before. The "total stock cost to expiration" would be the net investment of $39,600 less the $1,000 received in dividends. This is a total of $38,600. On a per-share basis, then, the break-even point of 38.6 is 8.1% below the current stock price of 42. Thus the amount of percentage downside protection is 8.1%.

The foregoing calculations clearly demonstrate that the returns on the "combined" write are *not* exactly the averages of the in-the-money and out-of-the-money returns, because of the different commission calculations at various stock prices. However, if one is working with a computer-generated list and does not want to bother to calculate exactly the return on the combined write, he can arrive at a relatively close approximation by averaging the returns for the in-the-money write and the out-of-the-money write.

Other Diversification Techniques

Holders of large positions in a particular stock may want even more diversification than can be provided by writing against two different striking prices. Institutions, pension funds, and large individual stockholders may fall into this category. It is often advisable for such large stockholders to *diversify* their writing *over time* as well as over at least two striking prices. By diversifying over time—for example, writing one-third of the position against near-term calls, writing one-third against the middle-term calls, and the remaining third against long-term calls—one can gain several benefits. First, all of one's positions need not be adjusted at the same time. This includes either having the stock called away, or buying back one written call and selling another. Moreover, one is not subject to the level of option premiums that exist only at the time one series of calls expire. For example, if one only writes 9-month calls and then rolls them over when they expire, he may unnecessarily be subjecting himself to the potential of lower returns. If option premium levels happen to be low when it is time for this 9-month call writer to sell more calls, he will be establishing a less-than-optimum write for up to 9 months. By spreading his writing out over time, he would, at worst, be subjecting only one-third of his holding to the low-premium write. Hopefully, premiums would expand before the next expiration 3 months later, and he would then be getting a relatively better premium on the next third of his portfolio. There is an important aside here. The individual or relatively small investor who only owns enough stock to write one series of options should generally not write the longest-term calls for this very reason. He may not be obtaining a particularly attractive level of premiums but may feel he is forced to retain the position until expiration. Thus he could be in a relatively poor write for as long as 9 months. Finally, this type of diversification may also lead to having calls at various striking prices as the market fluctuates cyclically. All of one's stock is not necessarily committed at one price if this diversification technique is employed.

This concludes the discussion of how to establish a covered writing position against stock. Covered writes against other types of securities will be described later.

FOLLOW-UP ACTION

Establishing a covered write—or any option position for that matter—is only part of the strategist's job. Once the position has been taken, it must be monitored closely so that adjustments may be made should the stock drop too far in price. Moreover, even if the stock remains relatively unchanged, adjustments will need to be made as the written call approaches expiration.

Some writers take no follow-up action at all, preferring to let a stock be called away if it rises above the striking price at the expiration of the option, or preferring to let the original expire worthless if the stock is below the strike. These are not always optimum actions; there may be much more decision making involved.

Follow-up action can be divided into three general categories:

1. protective action to take if the stock drops,
2. aggressive action to take when the stock rises, or

3. action to avoid assignment if the time premium disappears from an in-the-money call.

There may be times when one decides to close the entire position before expiration or to let the stock be called away. These cases will be discussed as well.

Protective Action If the Underlying Stock Declines in Price

The covered writer who does not take protective action in the face of a relatively substantial drop in price by the underlying stock may be risking the possibility of large losses. Since covered writing is a strategy with limited profit potential, one should also take care to limit losses. Otherwise, one losing position can negate several winning positions. The simplest form of follow-up action in a decline is to merely close out the position. This might be done if the stock declines by a certain percentage, or if the stock falls below a technical support level. Unfortunately, this method of defensive action may prove to be an inferior one. The investor will often do better to continue to sell more time value in the form of additional option premiums.

Follow-up action is generally taken by buying back the call that was originally written and then writing another call—with a different striking price and/or expiration date—in its place. Any adjustment of this sort is referred to as a *"rolling" action*. When the underlying stock drops in price, one generally buys back the original call—presumably at a profit since the underlying stock has declined—and then sells a call with a *lower* striking price. This is known as *rolling down*, since the new option has a lower striking price.

Example: The covered writing position described as "buy XYZ at 51, sell the XYZ January 50 call at 6" would have a maximum profit potential at expiration of 5 points. Downside protection is 6 points down to a stock price of 45 at expiration. These figures do not include commissions, but for the purposes of an elementary example the commissions will be ignored.

If the stock begins to decline in price, taking perhaps two months to fall to 45, the following option prices might exist:

XYZ common, 45;

XYZ January 50 call, 1; and

XYZ January 45 call, 4.

The covered writer of the January 50 would, at this time, have a small unrealized loss of one point in his overall position—his loss on the common stock is 6 points, but he has a 5-point gain in the January 50 call (this demonstrates that *prior to expiration*, a loss occurs at the "break-even" point). If the stock should continue to fall from these levels, he could have a larger loss at expiration. The call, selling for one point, only affords one more point of downside protection. If a further stock price drop is anticipated, *additional downside protection can be obtained by rolling down*. In this example, if one were to buy back the January 50 call at 1 and sell the January 45 at 4, he would be rolling down. This would increase his protection by another three points—the credit generated by buying the 50 call at 1 and selling the 45 call at 4. Hence, his downside break-even point would be 42 after rolling down.

Moreover, if the stock were to remain unchanged—that is, if XYZ were exactly 45 at January expiration—the writer would make an *additional* $300. If he had not rolled down, the most *additional* income that he could make, if XYZ remained unchanged, would be the remaining $100 from the January 50 call. So *rolling down gives more downside protection against a further drop in stock price and may also produce additional income if the stock price stabilizes*.

In order to more exactly evaluate the overall effect that was obtained by rolling down in this example, one can either compute a profit table (Table 2-21) or draw a net profit graph (Figure 2-3) that compares the original covered write with the rolled-down position.

Note that the rolled-down position has a smaller maximum profit potential than the original position did. This is because, by rolling down to a January 45 call, the writer limits his profits anywhere above 45 at expiration. He has committed himself to sell stock 5 points lower than the original position, which utilized a January 50 call and thus had limited profits above 50. *Rolling down generally reduces the maximum profit potential of the covered write*. Limiting the maximum profit may be a secondary consideration, however, when a stock is breaking downward.

TABLE 2-21.
Profit table.

XYZ Price at Expiration	Profit from January 50 Write	Profit from Rolled Position
40	− $500	− $200
42	− 300	0
45	0	+ 300
48	+ 300	+ 300
50	+ 500	+ 300
60	+ 500	+ 300

FIGURE 2-3.
Comparison: original covered write vs. rolled-down write.

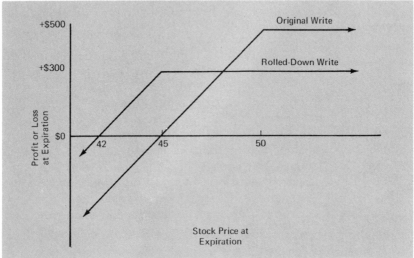

Additional downside protection is often a more pressing criterion in that case.

Anywhere below 45 at expiration, the rolled-down position does $300 better than the original position, because of the $300 credit generated from rolling down. In fact, the rolled-down position will outperform the original position even if the stock rallies back to, but not above, a price of 48. At 48 at expiration, the two positions are equal, both producing a $300 profit. If the stock should reverse direction and rally back above 48 by expiration, the writer would have been better off not to have rolled down. All these facts are clear from Table 2-21 and Figure 2-3.

Consequently, the only case in which it does *not* pay to roll down is the one in which the stock experiences a reversal—a rise in price after the initial drop. The selection of where to roll down is important because rolling down too early or at an inappropriate price could limit the returns. Technical support levels of the stock are often useful in selecting prices at which to roll down. If one rolls down after technical support has been broken, the chances of being caught in a stock-price-reversal situation would normally be reduced.

The above example is rather simplistic; in actual practice, more complicated situations may arise, such as a sudden and fairly steep decline in price by the underlying stock. This may present the writer with what is called a *"locked-in loss."* This means, simply, that there is no option to which the writer can roll down that will provide him with enough premium to realize any profit if the stock were then called away at expiration. These situations arise more commonly on lower-priced stocks, where the striking prices are relatively far apart in percentage terms. Out-of-the-money writes are more susceptible to this problem than are in-the-money writes. Although it is not emotionally satisfying to be in an investment position that cannot produce a profit—at least for a limited period of time—it may still be beneficial to roll down to protect as much of the stock price decline as possible.

Example: For the covered write described as "buy XYZ at 20, sell the January 20 call at 2," the stock unexpectedly drops very quickly to 16, and the following prices exist:

XYZ common, 16;

XYZ January 20 call, ½; and

XYZ January 15 call, 2½.

The covered writer is faced with a difficult choice. He currently has an unrealized loss of 2½ points—a 4-point loss on the stock which is partially offset by a 1½-point gain on the January 20 call. This represents a fairly substantial percentage loss on his investment in a short period of time. He could do nothing, hoping for the stock to recover its loss. Unfortunately, this may prove to be wishful thinking.

If he considers rolling down, he will not be excited by what he sees. Suppose that the writer wants to roll down from the January 20 to the January 15. He would thus buy the January 20 at ½ and sell the January 15 at 2½, for a net credit of 2 points. By rolling down, he is obligating himself to sell his stock at 15—the striking price of the January 15 call. Suppose XYZ were above 15 in January and were called away. How would the writer do? He would lose 5 points on his stock, since he originally bought it at 20 and is selling it at 15. This 5-point loss is substantially offset by his option profits, which amount to 4 points: 1½ points of profit on the January 20—sold at 2 and bought back at ½—plus the 2½ points received from the sale of the January 15. However, his net result is a 1-point loss, since he lost 5 points on the stock and only made 4 points on the options. Moreover, this 1-point loss is the best that he can hope for! This is true because, as has been demonstrated several times, a covered writing position makes its maximum profit anywhere above the striking price. Thus, by rolling down to the 15 strike, he has limited the position severely, to the extent of "locking in a loss."

Even considering what has been shown about this loss, *it is still correct for this writer to roll down to the January 15.* Once the stock has fallen to 16, there is nothing anybody can do about the unrealized losses. However, if the writer rolls down, he *can* prevent the losses from accumulating at a faster rate. In fact, he will do better by rolling down if the stock drops further, remains unchanged, or even rises slightly. Table 2-22 and Figure 2-4 compare the original write with the rolled-down position. It is clear from the figure that the rolled-down position is locked into a loss. However, the rolled-down position still outperforms the original position unless the stock rallies back above 17 by expiration. Thus, if the stock continues to fall, if it remains unchanged, or even if it rallies less than 1 point, the rolled-down position actually outperforms the original write. It is for this reason that the writer is taking the most logical action by rolling down, even though to do so locks in a loss.

Technical analysis may be able to provide a little help for the writer faced with the dilemma of rolling down to lock in a loss or else holding onto a position that has no further downside protection. If XYZ has broken

TABLE 2-22.
Profits of original write and rolled position.

Stock Price at Expiration	Profit from January 20 Write	Profit from Rolled Position
10	− $800	− $600
15	− 300	− 100
18	0	− 100
20	+ 200	− 100
25	+ 200	− 100

FIGURE 2-4.
Comparison: original write vs. "locked-in loss."

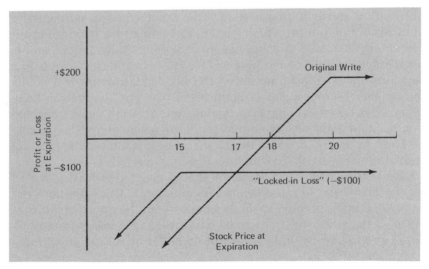

a support level or important trend line, it is added evidence for rolling down. In our example, it is difficult to imagine the case where a $20 stock suddenly drops to become a $16 stock without substantial harm to its technical picture. Nevertheless, if the charts should show that there is support at 15½ or 16, it may be worth the writer's while to wait and see if that support level can hold before rolling down.

Perhaps the best way to avoid having to lock in losses would be to establish positions that are less likely to become such a problem. In-the-money covered writes on higher-priced stocks that have a moderate amount of volatility will rarely force the writer to lock in a loss by rolling down. Of course, any stock, should it fall far enough and fast enough, could force the writer to lock in a loss if he has to roll down two or three times in a fairly short time span. However, the higher-priced stock has striking prices that are much closer together (in percentages) and thus presents the writer with the opportunity to utilize a new option with a lower striking price much sooner in the decline of the stock. Also, higher volatility should help in generating large enough premiums that substantial portions of the stock's decline can be hedged by rolling down. Conversely, low-priced stocks, especially nonvolatile ones, often present the most severe problems for the covered writer when they decline in price.

A related point concerning order entry can be inserted here. When one simultaneously buys one call and sells another, he is executing a *spread*. Spreads, in general, will be discussed at length later. However, the covered writer should be aware that whenever he rolls his position, the order can be placed as a spread order. This will normally help the writer to obtain a better price execution.

An Alternative Method of Rolling Down

There is another alternative that the covered writer can use to attempt to gain some additional downside protection without necessarily having to lock in a loss. Basically, the writer only rolls down part of his covered writing position.

Example: One thousand shares of XYZ were bought at 20 and 10 January 20 calls were sold at 2 points each. As before, the stock falls to 16, with the following prices: XYZ January 20 call, ½; and XYZ January 15 call, 2½. As was demonstrated in the last section, if the writer were to roll all 10 calls down from the January 20 to the January 15, he would be locking in a loss. Although there may be some justification for this action, the writer would naturally rather not have to place himself in such a position.

One can attempt to achieve some balance between added downside protection and upward profit potential by rolling down only part of the calls. In this example, the writer would buy back only 5 of the January 20's and sell 5 January 15 calls. He would then have this position:

long 1,000 XYZ at 20;

short 5 XYZ January 20's at 2;

short 5 XYZ January 15's at 2½; and

realized gain, $750 from 5 January 20's.

This strategy is generally referred to a a *partial roll-down*, in which only a portion of the original calls are rolled, as opposed to the more conventional complete roll-down. By analyzing the partially rolled position, it will be clear that the writer no longer locks in a loss.

If XYZ rallies back above 20, the writer would, at expiration, sell 500 XYZ at 20 (breaking even) and 500 at 15 losing $2,500 on this portion). He would make $1,000 from the five January 20's held until expiration, plus $1,250 from the five January 15's, plus the $750 of realized gain from the January 20's that were rolled down. This amounts to $3,000 worth of option profits and $2,500 worth of stock losses, or an overall net gain of $500, less commissions. Thus, the partial roll-down offers the writer a chance to make *some* profit if the stock rebounds. Obviously, the partial roll-down will not provide as much downside protection as the complete roll-down does, but it does give more protection than not rolling down at all. To see this, compare the results given in Table 2-23 if XYZ is at 15 at expiration.

In summary, the covered writer who would like to roll down, but who does not want to lock in a loss or who feels the stock may rebound somewhat before expiration, should consider rolling down only part of his position. If the stock should continue to drop—making it evident that there is little hope of a strong rebound back to the original strike—the rest of the position can then be rolled down as well.

TABLE 2-23.
Stock at 15 at expiration.

Strategy	Stock loss	Option Profit	Total Loss
Original position	− $5,000	+ $2,000	− $3,000
Partial roll-down	− 5,000	+ 3,000	− 2,000
Complete roll-down	− 5,000	+ 4,000	− 1,000

Utilizing Different Expiration Series When Rolling Down

In the examples thus far, the same expiration month has been used whenever rolling-down action was taken. In actual practice, the writer may often want to use a more distant expiration month when rolling down and, in some cases, he may even want to use a nearer expiraton month.

The advantage of rolling down into a more distant expiration series is that more actual points of protection are received. This is a common action to take when the underlying stock has become somewhat worrisome on a technical or fundamental basis. However, since rolling down reduces the maximum profit potential—a fact that has been demonstrated several times—every roll-down should not be made to a more distant expiration series. By utilizing a longer-term call when rolling down, one is reducing his maximum profit potential for a longer period of time. Thus the longer-term call should be used only if the writer has grown concerned over the stock's capability to hold current price levels. The partial-roll-down strategy is particularly amenable to rolling down to a longer-term call since, by rolling down only part of the position, one has already left the door open for profits if the stock should rebound. Therefore, he can feel free to avail himself of the maximum protection possible in the part of his position that is rolled down.

The writer who must roll down to lock in a loss, possibly because of circumstances beyond his control, such as a sudden fall in the price of the underlying stock, may actually want to roll down to a *near-term* option. This allows him to make back the available time premium in the short-term call in the least time possible.

Example: A writer buys XYZ at 19 and sells a 6-month call for 2 points. Shortly thereafter, however, bad news appears concerning the common stock and XYZ falls quickly to 14. At that time, the following prices exist for the calls with the striking price 15:

XYZ common, 14:

near-term call, 1;

middle-term call, 1½; and

far-term call, 2.

If the writer rolls down into any of these three calls, he will be locking in a loss. Therefore, the best strategy may be to roll down into the near-term call, planning to capture one point of time premium in 3 months. In this way, he will be beginning to work himself out of the loss situation by availing himself of the most potential time premium decay in the shortest period of time. When the near-term call expires—3 months from now—he can reassess the situation to see if he wants to write another near-term call to continue taking in short-term premiums or perhaps write a long-term call at that time.

When rolling down into the near-term call, one is attempting to return to a potentially profitable situation in the shortest period of time. By writing short-term calls one or two times, the writer will eventually be able to reduce his stock cost nearer to 15 in the shortest time period. Once his stock cost approaches 15, he can then write a long-term call with striking price 15 and return again to a potentially profitable situation—he will no longer be locked into a loss.

Action to Take If the Stock Rises

A more pleasant situation for the covered writer to encounter is the one in which the underlying stock rises in price after the covered writing position has been established. There are generally several choices available if this happens. The writer may decide to do nothing and to let his stock be called away, thereby making the return that he had hoped for when he established the position. On the other hand, if the underlying stock rises fairly quickly and the written call comes to parity, the writer may either close the position early or roll the call up. Each case will be discussed.

Example: Someone establishes a covered writing position by buying a stock at 50 and selling a 6-month call for 6 points. His maximum profit potential is 6 points anywhere above 50 at expiration, and his downside break-even point is 44. Furthermore, suppose that the stock experiences a substantial rally and that it climbs to a price of 60 in a short period of time. With the stock at 60, the July 50 might be selling for 11 points and a July 60 might sell for as much as 7 points. Thus, the writer may consider buying back the call that was originally written and rolling up to the call with a higher striking price. Table 2-24 summarizes the situation.

If the writer were to roll-up—that is, buy back the July 50 and sell the July 60—he would be increasing his profit potential. For, if XYZ were above 60 in July and were called away, he would make his option credits— 6 points from the July 50 plus 7 points from the July 60—less the 11 points he paid to buy back the July 50. Thus his option profits would

TABLE 2-24.
Comparison of original and current prices.

Original Position	Current Prices	
Buy XYZ at 50	XYZ common	60
Sell XYZ July 50 call at 6	XYZ July 50	11
	XYZ July 60	7

amount to 2 points, which, added to the stock profit of 10 points, increases his maximum profit potential to 12 points anywhere above 60 at July expiration.

To increase his profit potential by such a large amount, the covered writer has given up some of his downside protection. *The downside break-even point is always raised by the amount of the debit required to roll up.* The debit required to roll up in this example is 4 points—buy the July 50 at 11 and sell the July 60 at 7. Thus the break-even point is increased from the original 44 level to 48 after rolling up. There is another method of calculating the new profit potential and break-even point. In essence, the writer has raised his net stock cost to 55 by taking the realized 5-point loss on the July 50 call. Hence he is essentially in a covered write where he has bought stock at 55 and has sold a July 60 call for 7. When expressed in this manner, it may be easier to see that the break-even point is 48 and the maximum profit potential, above 60, is 12 points.

Note that *when one rolls up, there is a debit incurred.* That is, the investor must deposit additional cash into the covered writing position. This was not the case in rolling down, where credits were generated. Debits are considered by many investors to be a seriously negative aspect of rolling up, and they therefore prefer never to roll up for debits. Although the debit required to roll up may not be a negative aspect to every investor, it does translate directly into the fact that the break-even point is raised and the writer is subjecting himself to a potential loss if the stock should pull back. It is often advantageous to roll to a more distant expiration when rolling up. This will reduce the debit required.

The rolled-up position has a break-even point of 48. Thus, if XYZ falls back to 48, the writer who rolled up will be left with no profit. However, if he had not rolled up, he would have made 4 points with XYZ at 48 at expiration in the original position. A further comparison can be made between the original position and the rolled-up position. The two are equal at July expiration at a stock price of 54—both have a profit of 6 points with XYZ at 54 at July expiration. Thus, although it may appear attractive to roll up, one should determine the point where the rolled-up position and the original position will be equal at expiration. If the writer believes XYZ could be subject to a 10% correction by expiration from 60 to 54—certainly not out of the question for any stock—he should stay with his original position.

Figure 2-5 compares the original position with the rolled-up position. Note that the break-even point has moved up from 44 to 48, that the maximum profit potential has increased from 6 points to 12 points, and that at expiration the two writes are equal, at 54.

In summary, it can be said that rolling up increases one's profit potential but also exposes one to risk of loss if a stock price reversal should occur. Therefore, an element of risk is introduced as well as the possibility

FIGURE 2-5.
Comparison: original write vs. rolled-up position.

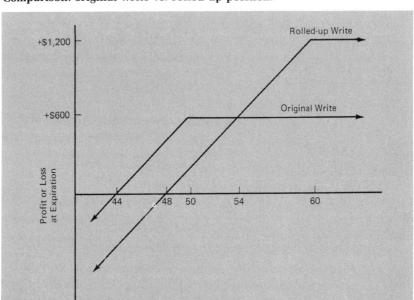

of increased rewards. Generally, it is not advisable to roll up if at least a 10% correction in the stock price cannot be withstood. One's initial goals for the covered write were set when the position was established. If the stock advances and these goals are being met, the writer should be very cautious about risking that profit.

The discussion to this point has been directed at rolling up *before* expiration. At or near expiration, when the time value premium has disappeared from the written call, one may have no choice but to write the next-higher striking price if he wants to retain his stock. This will be discussed soon, when we analyze action to take at or near expiration.

If the underlying stock rises, one's choices are not necessarily limited to rolling up or doing nothing. As the stock increases in price, the written call will lose its time premium and may begin to trade near parity. The writer may decide to close the position himself—perhaps well in advance of expiration—by buying back the written call and selling the stock out, hopefully near parity.

Example: A customer originally bought XYZ at 25 and sold the 6-month July 25 for 3 points—a net of 22. Now, three months later, XYZ has risen to 33 and the call is trading at 8 (parity) because it is so deeply in-the-money. At this point, the writer may want to sell the stock at 33 and buy back the call at 8, thereby realizing an effective net of 25 for the covered write which is his maximum profit potential. This is certainly preferable to remaining in the position for 3 more months with no more profit potential available. The advantage of closing a parity covered write early is that one is realizing the maximum return in a shorter period than anticipated. He is thereby increasing his annualized return on the position. Although it is generally to the cash writer's advantage (margin writers read on) to take such action, there are a few additional costs involved that he would not experience if he held the position until the call expired. First, the commission for the option purchase (buy-back) is an additional expense. Second, he will be selling his stock at a higher price than the striking price, so he will pay a slightly higher commission on that trade as well. If there is a dividend left until expiration, he will not be receiving that dividend if he closes the write early. Of course, if the trade was done in a margin account, the writer will be reducing the margin interest that he had planned to pay in the position because the debit will be erased earlier. In most cases, the increased commissions are very small and the lost dividend is not significant compared to the increase in annualized return that one can achieve by closing the position early. However, this is not always true and one should be aware of exactly what his costs are for closing the position early.

Obviously, getting out of a covered writing position can be as difficult as establishing it. Therefore, one should place the order to close the position with his brokerage firm's option desk, to be executed as a "net" order. The same traders who facilitate establishing covered writing positions at net prices will also facilitate getting out of the position. One would normally place the order by saying that he wanted to sell his stock and buy the option "at parity" or, in the example, at "25 net." Just as it is often necessary to be in contact with both the option and stock exchanges to *establish* a position, so is it necessary to maintain the same contacts to *remove* a position at parity.

Action to Take at or Near Expiration

As expiration nears and the time value premium disappears from a written call, the covered writer may often want to *roll forward*, that is, buy back the currently written call and sell a longer-term call with the same striking price. For an in-the-money call, the optimum time to roll forward is generally when the time value premium has completely disappeared from the call. For an out-of-the-money call, the correct time to move into the more distant option series is when the return offered by the near-term option is less than the return offered by the longer-term call.

The in-the-money case is quite simple to analyze. As long as there is time premium left in the call, there is little risk of assignment, and therefore the writer is earning time premium by remaining with the original call. However, when the option begins to trade at parity or a discount, there becomes a significant probability of exercise by arbitrageurs. It is at this time that the writer should roll the in-the-money call forward. For example, if XYZ were offered at 51 and the July 50 call were bid at 1, the writer should be rolling forward into the October 50 or January 50 call.

The out-of-the-money case is a little more difficult to handle, but there is a relatively straightforward analysis that can be applied to facilitate the writer's decision. One can compute the return per day remaining in the written call and compare it to the net return per day from the longer-term call. If the longer-term call has a higher return, one should roll forward.

Example: An investor previously entered a covered writing situation in which he wrote five January 30 calls against 500 XYZ common. The following prices exist currently, 1 month before expiration:

XYZ common, 29½;

January 30 call, ½; and

April 30 call, 2½.

The writer can only make ½ of a point more of time premium on this covered write for the time remaining until expiration. It is possible that his money could be put to better use by rolling forward to the April 30 call. Commissions for rolling forward must be subtracted from the April 30's premium to present a true comparison.

By remaining in the January 30, the writer could make, at most, $250 for the 30 days remaining until January expiration. This is a return of $8.33 per day. The commissions for rolling forward would be approximately $100—including both the buy-back and the new sale. Since the current time premium in the April 30 call is $250 per option, this would mean that the writer would stand to make 5 times $250 less the $100 in commissions during the 120-day period until April expiration. $1,150 divided by 120 days is $9.58 per day. Thus the per-day return is higher from the April 30 than from the January 30, after commissions are included. The writer should roll forward to the April 30 at this time.

Rolling forward, since it involves a positive cash flow (that is, it is a credit transaction) simultaneously increases the writer's maximum profit potential and lowers the break-even point. In the example above, the credit for rolling forward is 2 points, so the break-even point will be lowered by 2 points and the maximum profit potential is also increased by the 2-point credit.

A simple calculator can provide one with the return-per-day calculation necessary to make the decision concerning rolling forward. The preceding analysis is only directly applicable to rolling forward at the *same striking price*. Rolling-up or rolling-down decisions at expiration, since they involve different striking prices, cannot be based solely on the differential returns in time premium values offered by the options in question.

In the earlier discussion concerning rolling up, it was mentioned that at or near expiration, one may have no choice but to write the next higher striking price if he wants to retain his stock. This does not necessarily involve a debit transaction, however. If the stock is volatile enough, one might even be able to *roll up* for even money or a slight credit at expiration. Should this occur, it would be a desirable situation and should always be taken advantage of.

Example: The following prices exist at January expiration:

XYZ, 50;

XYZ January 45 call, 5; and

XYZ July 50 call, 7.

In this case, if one had originally written the January 45 call, he could now roll up to the July 50 at expiration for a *credit* of 2 points. This action is quite prudent, since the break-even point and the maximum profit potential are enhanced. The break-even point is lowered by the 2 points of credit received from rolling up. The maximum profit potential is increased substantially—by 7 points—since the striking price is raised by 5 points and an additional 2 points of credit are taken in from the roll up. Consequently, whenever one can roll up for a credit, a situation that would normally arise only on more volatile stocks, he should do so.

Another choice that may occur at or near expiration is that of *rolling down*. The case may arise where one has allowed a written call to expire worthless with the stock more than a small distance below the striking price. The writer is then faced with the decision of either writing a small premium out-of-the-money call or a larger premium in-the-money call. Again an example may prove to be useful.

Example: Just after the January 25 call has expired worthless,

XYZ is at 22,

XYZ July 25 call at ¾, and

XYZ July 20 call at 3½.

If the investor were now to write the July 25 call, he would be receiving only ¾ of a point of downside protection. However, his maximum profit potential would be quite large if XYZ could rally to 25 by expiration. On the other hand, the October 20 at 3½ is an attractive write that affords substantial downside protection and its 1½ points of time value premium are twice that offered by the July 25 call. In a purely analytic sense, one should not base his decision on what his performance has been to date, but that is a difficult axiom to apply in practice. If this investor owns XYZ at a higher price, he will almost surely opt for the July 25 call. If, however, he owns XYZ at approximately the same price, he will have no qualms about writing the July 20 call. There is no absolute rule that can be applied to all such situations, but one is usually better off writing the call that provides the best balance between return and downside protection at all times. Only if one is bullish on the underlying stock should he write the July 25 call.

Avoiding the Uncovered Position

There is a margin rule that the covered writer must be aware of if he is considering taking any sort of follow-up action on the day that the written call ceases trading. If another call is sold on that day—even though the written call is obviously going to expire worthless—the writer will be considered uncovered, for margin purposes, over the weekend and will be obligated to put forth the collateral for an uncovered option. This is usually not what the writer intends to do, and being aware of this rule will eliminate unwanted margin calls. Furthermore, uncovered options may be considered unsuitable for many covered writers.

   Example: A customer owns XYZ and has January 20 calls outstanding on the last day of trading of the January series (the third Friday of January; the calls actually do not expire until the following day, Saturday). If XYZ is at 15 on the last day of trading, the January 20 call will almost certainly expire worthless. However, should the writer decide to sell a longer-term call on that day without buying back the January 20, he will be considered uncovered over the weekend. Thus *if one plans to wait for an option to expire totally worthless before writing another call, he must wait until the Monday after expiration before writing again, assuming that he wants to remain covered.* The writer should also realize that it is possible for some sort of news item to be announced between the end of trading in an option series and the actual expiration of the series. Thus call holders might exercise because they believe the stock will jump sufficiently in price to make the exercise profitable. This has happened in the past, two of the most notable cases being IBM in January 1975 and Carrier Corp. in September 1978.

When to Let Stock Be Called Away

Another alternative that is open to the writer, as the written call approaches expiration, is to let the stock be called away if it is above the striking price. In most cases, it is to the advantage of the writer to keep rolling options forward before he is called, thereby retaining his stock ownership. However, in certain cases, it may be advisable to allow the stock to be called away. It should be emphasized that the writer often has a definite choice in this matter, since he can generally tell when the call is about to be exercised—when the time value premium disappears.

The reason that it is *normally* desirable to roll forward is that, over time, the covered writer will realize a higher return by rolling instead of being called. The option commissions for rolling forward every three or six months are smaller than the commissions for buying and selling the underlying stock every 3 or 6 months, and therefore the eventual return will be higher. However, if by rolling forward, an inferior return has to be accepted or the break-even point raised significantly, one must consider the alternative of letting the stock be called away.

Example: A covered write is established by buying XYZ at 49 and selling an April 50 call for 3 points. The original break-even point was thus 46. Near expiration, suppose XYZ has risen to 56 and the April 50 is trading at 6. If the investor wants to roll forward, now is the time to do so, because the call is at parity. However, he notes that the choices are somewhat limited. Suppose the following prices exist with XYZ at 56: XYZ October 50 call, 7; and XYZ October 60 call, 2. It seems apparent that the premium levels have declined since the original writing position was established, but that is an occurrence beyond the control of the writer, who must work in the current market environment.

If the writer attempts to roll forward to the October 50, he could make at most 1 additional point of profit until October (the time premium in the call). This represents an extremely low rate of return and the writer should reject this alternative since there are surely better returns available in covered writes on other securities.

On the other hand, if the writer tries to roll up and forward, it will cost 4 points to do so—6 points to buy back the April 50 less 2 points received for the October 60. This debit transaction means that his break-even point would move up from the original level of 46 to a new level of 50. If the common declines below 54, he would be eating into profits already at hand, since the October 60 provides only 2 points of protection from the current stock price of 56. If the writer is not confidently bullish on the outlook for XYZ, he should not roll up and forward.

At this point, the writer has exhausted his alternatives for rolling. His remaining choice is to let the stock be called away and to to use the proceeds to establish a covered write in a new stock—one that offers a more attractive rate of return with reasonable downside protection. This choice of allowing the stock to be called away is generally the wisest strategy if both of the following *criteria* are met:

1. Rolling forward offers only a minimal return.
2. Rolling up and forward significantly raises the break-even point and leaves the position relatively unprotected should the stock drop in price.

SPECIAL WRITING SITUATIONS

Our discussions have pertained directly to writing against common stock. However, one may also write covered call options against convertible securities or warrants. In addition, a different type of covered writing strategy will be described that has a large amount of appeal to large stockholders, both individuals and institutions.

Covered Writing Against a Convertible Security

It may be more advantageous to buy a security that is convertible into common stock than to buy the stock itself, for covered call writing purposes. Convertible bonds and convertible preferred stocks are securities commonly used for this purpose. One advantage of using the convertible security is that it often has a higher yield than does the common stock itself.

Before describing the covered write, it may be beneficial to review the basics of convertible securities. Suppose XYZ common stock has an XYZ convertible Preferred A stock that is convertible into 1.5 shares of common. The number of shares of common that the convertible security converts into is an important piece of information that the writer *must* know. It can be found in a *Standard & Poor's Stock Guide* (or *Bond Guide,* in the case of convertible bonds).

The writer also needs to determine how many shares of the convertible security must be owned in order to equal 100 shares of the common stock. This is quickly determined by dividing 100 by the *conversion ratio*—1.5 in our XYZ example. Since 100 divided by 1.5 equals 66.666, one must own 67 shares of XYZ cv Pfd A to cover the sale of one XYZ option for 100 shares of common. Note that the market prices of neither XYZ common nor the convertible security are necessary for this computation.

When using a convertible bond, the conversion information is usually stated in a form such as "converts into 50 shares at a price of 20."

The price is irrelevant. What *is* important is the number of shares that the bond converts into—50 in this case. Thus if one were using these bonds for covered writing of 1 call, he would need two (2,000) bonds to own the equivalent of 100 shares of stock.

Once one knows how much of the convertible security must be purchased, he can use the actual prices of the securities, and their yields, to determine whether a covered write against the common or the convertible is more attractive.

Example: The following information is known:

XYZ common, 50;

XYZ cv Pfd A, 80;

XYZ July 50 call, 5;

XYZ dividend, 1.00 per share annually; and

XYZ cv Pfd A dividend, 5.00 per share annually.

Note that, in either case, the same call—the July 50—would be written. *The use of the convertible as the underlying security does not alter the choice of which option to use.* To make the comparison of returns easier, commissions will be ignored in the calculations given in Table 2-25. In reality, the commissions for the stock purchase—either common or preferred—would be very similar. Thus, from a numerical point of view, it appears to be more advantageous to write against the convertible than against the common.

When writing against a convertible security, there are additional considerations that should be looked at. The first is the *premium of the*

TABLE 2-25.
Comparison of common and convertible writes.

	Write against Common	Write against Convertible
Buy underlying security	$5,000 (100 XYZ)	$5,360 (67 XYZ cv Pfd A)
Sell one July 50 call	− 500	− 500
Net cash investment	$4,500	$4,860
Premium collected	$ 500	$ 500
Dividends until July	50	250
Maximum profit potential	$ 550	$ 750
Return (profit divided by investment)	12.2%	15.4%

convertible security. In the example, with XYZ selling at 50, the XYZ cv Pfd A has a true value of 1.5 times 50, or $75 per share. However, it is selling at 80, which represents a premium of 5 points above its computed value of 75. *Normally, one would not want to buy a convertible security if the premium is too large.* In this example, the premium appears quite reasonable. Any convertible premium greater than 15% above computed value might be considered to be too large.

Another consideration when writing against convertible securities is the *handling of assignment.* If the writer is assigned, he may either (1) convert his preferred stock into common and deliver that, or (2) sell the *preferred* in the market and use the proceeds to buy 100 shares of common stock in the market for delivery against the assignment notice. The second choice is usually preferable if the convertible security has any premium at all, since converting the preferred into common causes the *loss* of any premium in the convertible, as well as the loss of accrued interest in the case of a convertible bond.

The writer should also be aware of whether or not the convertible is *callable,* and, if so, what the exact terms are. Once the convertible has been called by the company, it will no longer trade in relation to the underlying stock, but will instead trade at the call price. Thus, if the stock should climb sharply, the writer could be incurring losses on his written option without any corresponding benefit from his convertible security. Consequently, if the convertible is called, the entire position should normally be closed immediately by selling the convertible and buying the option back.

Other aspects of covered writing, such as rolling down or forward, do not change even if the option is written against a convertible security — one would take action based on the relationship of the option price and the common stock price, as usual.

Writing Against Warrants

It is also possible to write covered call options against warrants. Again, one must own enough warrants to convert into 100 shares of the underlying stock—generally, this would be 100 warrants. The transaction must be a cash transaction—the warrants must be paid for in full, and they have no loan value. Technically, listed warrants may be marginable but many brokerage houses still require payment in full. There may also be an *additional investment requirement.* Warrants also have an exercise price. If the exercise price of the warrant is *higher* than the striking price of the call, the covered writer must also deposit the difference between the two as part of his investment.

The advantage of using warrants is that, if they are deeply in-the-money they may provide the cash covered writer with a higher return since less of an investment is involved.

Example: XYZ is at 50 and there are XYZ warrants to buy the common at 25. Since the warrant is so deeply in-the-money, it will be selling for approximately $25 per warrant. XYZ pays no dividend. Thus if the writer were considering a covered write of the XYZ July 50, he might choose to use the warrant instead of the common, since his investment, per 100 shares of common, would only be $2,500 instead of the $5,000 required to buy 100 XYZ. The potential profit would be the same in either case because no dividend is involved.

Even if the stock does pay a dividend (warrants themselves have no dividend), the writer may still be able to earn a higher return by writing against the warrant than the common because of the smaller investment involved. This would depend, of course, on the exact size of the dividend and on how deeply the warrant is in-the-money.

Covered writing against warrants is not a frequent practice because of the small number of warrants on optionable stocks and the problems inherent in checking available returns. However, in certain circumstances, the writer may actually have a decided advantage by writing against a deep in-the-money warrant. It is often not advisable to write against a warrant that is at- or out-of-the-money, since it can decline by a large percentage if the underlying stock drops in price—producing a high-risk position. Also, the writer's investment may increase in this case if he rolls down to an option with a striking price lower than the warrant's exercise price.

PERCS

The PERCS (Preferred Equity Redemption Cumulative Stock) is a form of covered writing. It is discussed in Chapter 26.

The Incremental Return Concept of Covered Writing

The incremental return concept of covered call writing is a way in which *the covered writer can earn the full value of stock appreciation between today's stock price and a target sale price, which may be substantially higher.* At the same time, the writer can earn an incremental, positive return from writing options.

Many institutional investors are somewhat apprehensive about covered call writing because of the upside limit that is place on profit potential. If a call is written against a stock that subsequently declines in price, most institutional managers would *not* view this as an unfavorable situation, since they would be outperforming all managers who owned the stock and who did not write a call. However, if the stock rises substantially after the call is written, many institutional managers do not like having their profits limited by the written call. This strategy is not only for institutional money managers, although one should have a relatively substantial holding in an underlying stock to attempt the strategy—at least 500 shares, and preferably, 1,000 shares or more. *The incremental return concept can be used by anyone who is planning to hold his stock, even if it should temporarily decline in price, until it reaches a predetermined, higher price at which he is willing to sell the stock.*

The basic strategy involves, as an initial step, selecting the target price at which the writer is willing to sell his stock.

Example: A customer owns 1,000 shares of XYZ, which is currently at 60, and is willing to sell the stock at 80. In the meantime, he would like to realize a *positive cash flow* from writing options against his stock. This positive cash flow does not necessarily result in a realized option gain until the stock is called away. Most likely, with the stock at 60, there would not be options available with a striking price of 80, so one could not write 10 July 80's, for example. This would not be an optimum strategy even if the July 80's existed, for the investor would be receiving so little in option premiums—perhaps ⅛ of a point per call—that writing might not be worthwhile. The incremental return strategy allows this investor to achieve his objectives regardless of the existence of options with a higher striking price.

The foundation of the incremental return strategy is to write against only a *part* of the entire stock holding initially, and to write these calls at the striking price nearest the current stock price. Then, should the stock move up to the next higher striking price, one rolls up for a *credit* by adding to the number of calls written. Rolling for a credit is mandatory and is the key to the strategy. Eventually, the stock reaches the target price and the stock is called away, the investor sells all his stock at the target price and, in addition, earns the total *credits* from all the option transactions.

Example: XYZ is 60, the investor owns 1,000 shares, and his target price is 80. One might begin by selling three of the longest-term calls at 60 for 7 points apiece. Table 2-26 shows how a poor case—one in which the stock climbs directly to the target price—might work. As Table 2-26 shows, if XYZ rose to 70 in one month, the three original calls would be bought back and enough calls at 70 would be sold to produce a credit— five XYZ October 70's. If the stock continued upward to 80 in another month, the 5 calls would be bought back and the entire position—10 calls—would be written against the target price.

If XYZ remains above 80, the stock will be called away and *all 1,000 shares will be sold at the target price of 80*. In addition, the investor will earn all the option credits generated along the way. These amount to $2,800. Thus the writer obtained the full appreciation of his stock to the target price plus an *incremental*, positive return from option writing.

TABLE 2-26.
Two months of incremental return strategy.

Day 1: XYZ = 60	
Sell 3 XYZ October 60's at 7	+ $2,100 credit
One month later: XYZ = 70	
Buy back the 3 XYZ Oct 60's at 11 and	− $3,300 debit
sell 5 XYZ Oct 70's at 7	+ $3,500 credit
Two months later: XYZ = 80	
Buy back the 5 Oct 70's at 11 and	− $5,500 debit
sell 10 XYZ Oct 80's at 6	+ $6,000 credit
	+ $2,800 credit

In a flat market, the strategy is relatively easy to monitor. If a written call loses its time value premium, and therefore might be subject to assignment, the writer can roll forward to a more distant expiration series, keeping the quantity of written calls constant. This transaction would generate additional credits as well.

COVERED CALL WRITING SUMMARY

This concludes the chapter on covered call writing. The strategy will be referred to later, when compared to other strategies. The following items are a brief summary of the more important points that were discussed.

Covered call writing is a viable strategy because it reduces the risk of stock ownership and will make one's portfolio less volatile to short-term market movements. The choice of which call to write can make for a more aggressive or more conservative write—writing in-the- money calls is strategically more conservative than writing out-of-the-money calls, because of the larger amount of downside protection received. The total return concept of covered call writing attempts to achieve the maximum balance between income from all sources—option premiums, stock ownership, and dividend income—and downside protection. This balance is usually realized by writing calls when the stock is near the striking price— either slightly in- or out-of-the-money.

The writer should compute various returns before entering into the position—the return if exercised, the return if the stock is unchanged at expiration, and the break-even point. To truly compare various writes, returns should be annualized, and all commissions and dividends should be included in these calculations. Returns will be increased by taking larger positions in the underlying stock—500 or 1,000 shares. Also, by utilizing a brokerage firm's capability to produce "net" executions, buying the stock and selling the call at a specified net price differential, one will receive better executions and realize higher returns in the long run.

The selection of which call to write should be made on a comparison of available returns and downside protection. One can sometimes write part of his position out-of-the-money and the other part in-the-money to force a balance between return and protection that might not otherwise exist. Finally, one should not write against an underlying stock if he is bearish on the stock. The writer should be slightly bullish, or at least neutral, on the underlying stock.

Follow-up action can be as important as the selection of the initial position itself. By rolling down if the underlying stock drops, the investor can add downside protection and current income. If one is unwilling to limit his upside potential too severely, he may consider rolling down only part of his call writing position. As the written call expires, the writer should roll forward into a more distant expiration month if the stock is relatively close to the original striking price. Higher consistent returns are achieved in this manner, because one is not spending additional stock commissions by letting the stock be called away. An aggressive follow-up action can also be taken when the underlying stock rises in price— the writer can roll up to a higher striking price. This action increases the maximum profit potential but also exposes the position to loss if the stock should subsequently decline. One would want to take no follow-up action and let his stock be called if it is above the striking price and if there are better returns available elsewhere in other securities.

Covered call writing can also be done against convertible securities— bonds or preferred stocks. These convertibles sometimes offer higher dividend yields and therefore increase the overall return from covered writing. Also, the use of warrants in place of the underlying stock may be advantageous in certain circumstances because the net investment is lowered while the profit potential remains the same. Therefore, the overall return could be higher.

Finally, the larger individual stockholder or institutional investor who wants to achieve a certain price for his stock holdings should operate his covered writing strategy under the incremental return concept. This will allow him to realize the full profit potential of his underlying stock, up to the target sale price, and to earn additional positive income from option writing.

Chapter *3*

Call Buying

The success of a call buying strategy depends primarily on one's ability to select stocks that will go up and to time the selection reasonably well. Thus call buying is not a strategy in the same sense of the word as most of the other strategies discussed in this text. Most other strategies are designed to remove some of the exactness of stock picking—allowing one to be neutral or at least to have some room for error and still make a profit. Techniques of call buying are important, though, because it is necessary to understand the long side of calls in order to understand more complex strategies correctly.

Call buying is the simplest form of option investment, and therefore is the most frequently used option "strategy" by the public investor. The following section will outline the basic facts that one needs to know to implement an intelligent call buying program.

WHY BUY?

The main attraction in buying calls is that they provide the speculator with a great deal of leverage. One could potentially realize large percentage profits from only a modest rise in price by the underlying stock. Moreover, even though they may be large percentagewise, the risks cannot exceed a fixed dollar amount—the price originally paid for the call. Calls must be paid for in full—they have no margin value and do not constitute equity for margin purposes. The following simple example illustrates how a call purchase might work.

Example: Assume that XYZ is at 48 and the 6-month call, the July 50, is selling for 3. Thus, with an investment of $300, the call buyer may participate, for 6 months, in a move upward in the price of XYZ common. If XYZ should rise in price by 10 points (just over 20%), the July 50 call will be worth at least $800 and the call buyer would have a 167% profit on a move in the stock of just over 20%. This is the leverage that attracts speculators to call buying. At expiration, if XYZ is below 50, the buyer's loss is total, but is limited to his initial $300 investment, even if XYZ declines in price substantially. Although this risk is equal to 100% of his initial investment, it is still small dollarwise. *One should normally not invest more than 15% of his risk capital in call buying*, because of the relatively large percentage risks involved.

Some investors participate in call buying on a limited basis to add some upside potential to their portfolios while keeping the risk to a fixed amount. For example, if an investor normally only purchased low-volatility, conservative stocks because he wanted to limit his downside risk, he might consider putting a small percentage of his cash into calls on more volatile stocks. In this manner, he could "trade" higher risk stocks than he might normally do. If these volatile stocks increase in price, the investor will profit handsomely. However, if they decline substantially— as well they might, being volatile—the investor has limited his dollar risk by owning the calls rather than the stock.

Another reason some investors buy calls is to be able to buy stock at a reasonable price without missing a market.

Example: With XYZ at 75, this investor might buy a call on XYZ at 80. He would like to own XYZ at 80 if it can prove itself capable of rallying and be in-the-money at expiration. He would exercise the call in that case. On the other hand, if XYZ declines in price instead, he has not tied up money in the stock and can lose only an amount equal to the call premium that he paid, an amount that is generally much less than the price of the stock itself.

Another approach to call buying is sometimes utilized, also by an investor who does not want to "miss the market." Suppose an investor knows that, in the near future, he will have an amount of money large enough to purchase a particular stock—perhaps he is closing the sale of his house or a Certificate of Deposit is maturing. However, he would like to buy the stock now, for he feels a rally is imminent. He might buy calls at the present time if he had a small amount of cash available. The call purchases would require an investment much smaller than the stock purchase. Then, when he receives the cash that he knew was forthcoming, he could exercise the calls and buy the stock. In this way, he might have participated in a rally by the stock before he actually had the money available to pay for the stock in full.

RISK/REWARD FOR THE CALL BUYER

The most important fact for the call buyer to realize is that he will normally only win if the stock rises in price. All the worthwhile analysis in the world spent in selecting which call to buy will not produce profits if the underlying stock declines. However, this fact should not dissuade one from making reasonable analyses in his call buying selections. Too often, the call buyer feels that a stock will move up—and is correct in that part of his projection—but still loses money on his call purchase because he failed to analyze the risk and rewards involved with the various calls available for purchase at the time. He bought the wrong call on the right stock.

Since the best ally that the call buyer has is upward movement in the underlying stock, the selection of the underlying stock is the most important choice the call buyer has to make. Since timing is so important when buying calls, the technical factors of stock selection probably outweigh the fundamentals, because even if positive fundamentals do exist, one does not know how long it will take in order for them to be reflected in the price of the stock. One must be bullish on the underlying stock in order to consider buying calls on that stock. Once the stock selection has been made, only then can the call buyer begin to consider other factors, such as which striking price to use and which expiration to buy. The call buyer may have another ally, but not one that he can normally predict: if the stock on which he owns a call becomes more volatile, the call's price will rise to reflect that change.

The purchase of an out-of-the-money call generally offers both larger potential risk and larger potential reward than does the purchase of an in-the-money call. Many call buyers tend to select the out-of-the-money call merely because it is cheaper in price. *Absolute dollar price should in no way be a deciding factor for the call buyer.* If one's funds are so limited that he can only afford to buy the cheapest calls, he should not be speculating in this strategy. If the underlying stock increases in price substantially, the out-of-the-money call will naturally provide the largest rewards. However, if the stock only advances moderately in price, the in-the-money call may actually perform better.

Example: XYZ is at 65 and the July 60 sells for 7 while the July 70 sells for 3. If the stock moves up to 68 relatively slowly, the buyer of the July 70—the out-of-the-money call—may actually experience a loss, even if the call has not yet expired. However, the holder of the in-the-money July 60 will definitely have a profit because the call will sell for at least 8 points—its intrinsic value. The point is that, percentagewise, *an in-the-money call will offer better rewards for a modest stock gain and the out-of-the-money call is better for larger stock gains.*

When risk is considered, the in-the-money call clearly has less probability of risk. In the prior example, the in-the-money call buyer would not lose his entire investment unless XYZ fell by at least 5 points. However, the buyer of the out-of-the-money July 70 would lose all of his investment unless the stock *advanced* by more than 5 points by expiration. Obviously, the probability that the in-the-money call will expire worthless is much smaller than that for the out-of-the-money call.

The time remaining to expiration is also relevant to the call buyer. If the stock is fairly close to the striking price, the near-term call will most closely follow the price movement of the underlying stock, so it has the greatest rewards and also the greatest risks. The far-term call, because it has a large amount of time remaining, offers the least risk and least percentage reward. *The intermediate-term call offers a moderate amount of each, and is therefore often the most attractive one to buy.* Many times an investor will buy the longer-term call because it only costs a point or a point and a half more than the intermediate-term call. He feels that the extra price is a bargain to pay for three extra months of time. This line of thought may prove somewhat misleading, however, because most call buyers don't hold calls for more than 60 or 90 days. Thus, even though it looks attractive to pay the extra point for the long-term call, it may prove to be an unnecessary expense if, as is usually the case, one will be selling the call in two or three months.

Certainty of Timing

The certainty with which one expects the underlying stock to advance may also help to play a part in his selection of which call to buy. If one is fairly sure that the underlying stock is about to rise immediately, he should strive for more reward and not be as concerned about risk. This would mean buying short-term, slightly out-of-the-money calls. Of course, this is only a general rule—one would not normally buy an out-of-the-money call that only has one week remaining until expiration in any case. At the opposite end of the spectrum, if one is very uncertain about his timing, he should buy the longest-term call, to moderate his risk in case his timing is wrong by a wide margin. This situation could easily result, for example, if one feels that a positive fundamental aspect concerning the company will assert itself and cause the stock to increase in price at an unknown time in the future. Since the buyer does not know whether this positive fundamental will come to light in the next month or 6 months from now, he should buy the longer-term call to allow room for error in timing.

In many cases, one is not intending to hold the purchased call for any significant period of time—he is just looking to capitalize on a quick, short-term movement by the underlying stock. In this case, he would want to buy a relatively short-term in-the-money call. Although such a call may be more expensive than an out-of-the-money call on the same underlying stock, it will most surely move up on any increase in price by the under-lying stock. Thus the short-term trader would profit.

The Delta

The reader should by now be familiar with basic facts concerning call options: The time premium is highest when the stock is at the striking price of the call; it is lowest deep in- or out-of-the-money; option prices do not decay at a linear rate—the time premium disappears more rapidly as the option approaches expiration. As a further means of review, the *option pricing curve* introduced in Chapter 1 is reprinted here. Notice that all the facts listed above can be observed from Figure 3-1. The curves are much nearer the "intrinsic value" line at the ends than they are in the middle, implying that the time value premium is greatest when the stock is at the strike and is least when the stock moves away from the

FIGURE 3-1.
Option pricing curve; 3-, 6-, and 9-month calls.

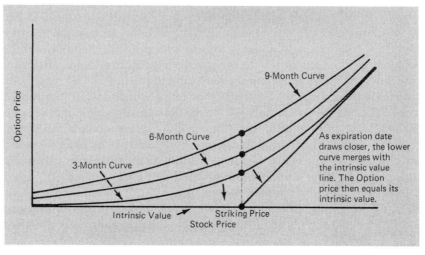

strike—either into- or out-of-the-money. Furthermore, the fact that the curve for the 3-month option lies only about halfway between the intrinsic value line and the curve of the 9-month option implies that the rate of decay of an at- or near-the-money option is not linear. The reader may also want to refer back to the graph of time value premium decay in Chapter 1.

There is another property of call options that the buyer should be familiar with, the *delta* of the option (also called the *hedge ratio*). Simply stated, *the delta of an option is the amount by which the call will increase or decrease in price if the underlying stock moves by 1 point.*

Example: The delta of a call option is close to 1 when the underlying stock is well above the striking price of the call. If XYZ were 60 and XYZ July 50 call were $10\frac{1}{8}$, the call would change in price by nearly 1 point if XYZ moved by 1 point, either up or down. A deeply out-of-the-money call has a delta of nearly zero. If XYZ were 40, the July 50 call might be selling at $\frac{1}{4}$ of a point. The call would change very little in price if XYZ moved by one point—either to 41 or 39. When the stock is *at* the striking price, the delta is usually between one-half of a point and five-eighths of a point. Very long-term calls may have even larger at-the-money deltas. Thus, if XYZ were 50 and the XYZ July 50 call were 5, the call might increase to $5\frac{1}{2}$ if XYZ rose to 51 or would decrease to $4\frac{1}{2}$ if XYZ dropped to 49.

Actually, the delta changes each time the underlying stock changes even fractionally in price—it is an exact mathematical derivation that will be presented in a later chapter. This is most easily seen by the fact that a deep in-the-money option has a delta of 1. However, if the stock should undergo a series of 1-point drops down to the striking price, the delta will be more like $\frac{1}{2}$—certainly not 1 any longer. In reality, the delta changed instantaneously all during the price decline by the stock. For those who are geometrically inclined, the preceding option price curve is useful in determining a graphic representation of the delta. The delta is the *slope* of the tangent line to the price curve. Notice that a deeply in-the-money option lies to the upper right side of the curve, very nearly on the intrinsic value line, which has a slope of 1 above the strike. Similarly, a deeply out-of-the-money call lies to the left on the price curve, again near the intrinsic value line, which has a slope of zero below the strike.

Since it is more common to relate the option's price change to a full point change in the underlying stock (rather than to deal in "instantaneous" price changes), the concepts of "*up delta*" and "*down delta*" arise. That is, if the underlying stock moves up by 1 full point, a call with a delta of .50 might increase by $\frac{5}{8}$. However, should the stock fall by one full point, the call might only decrease by $\frac{3}{8}$. There is a different net price change in the call when the stock moves up by 1 full point as opposed to when it falls by a point—the up delta is observed to be ⅝ while the down delta is ⅜. In the true mathematical sense, there is only one delta and it measures "instantaneous" price change. The concepts of up delta and down delta are practical, rather than theoretical, concepts which merely illustrate the fact that the true delta changes whenever the stock price changes, even by as little as 1 point. In the following examples and in later chapters, only one delta will be referred to.

The delta is an important piece of information for the call buyer because it can tell him how much of an increase or decrease he can expect for short-term moves by the underlying stock. This piece of information may help the buyer decide which call to buy.

Example: If XYZ is 47½ and the call buyer expects a quick, but possibly limited, rise in price in the underlying stock, should he buy the 45 call or the 50 call? The delta may help him decide. He has the following information:

XYZ: 47½   XYZ July 45 call: price = 3½,   delta = ⅝
                  XYZ July 50 call: price = 1,   delta = ¼

It will make matters easier to make a slightly incorrect, but simplifying, assumption that the deltas remain constant over the short term. Which call is the better buy if the buyer expects the stock to quickly rise to 49? This would represent a 1½-point increase in XYZ, which would translate into a 15/16 increase in the July 45 (1½ times ⅝) or a ⅜ increase in the July 50 (1½ times ¼). Consequently, the July 45—if it increased in price by 15/16—would appreciate by 27%. The July 50—if it increased by ⅜—would appreciate by over 37%. Thus the July 50 appears to be the better buy in this simple example. Commissions should, of course, be included when making an analysis for actual investment.

The investor does not have to bother with computing deltas for himself. Any good call-buying data service will supply the information, and some brokerage houses provide this information free of charge.

More advanced applications of deltas will be described in many of the succeeding chapters, as they apply to a variety of strategies.

ADVANCED SELECTION CRITERIA

The criteria presented above are elementary techniques for selecting which call to buy. In actual practice, one is not usually bullish on just one stock at a time. In fact, he would like to have a list of the "best" calls to buy at any given time. Then, using some method of stock selection, either technical or fundamental, he can select three or four calls that appear to offer the best rewards. This list should be ranked in order of the best potential rewards available, but the construction of the list itself is important.

Call option rankings for buying purposes must be based on the volatilities of the underlying stocks. This is not easy to do, mathematically, and as a result many published rankings of calls are based strictly on percentage change in the underlying stock. Such a list is quite misleading and can lead one to the wrong conclusions.

Example: There are two stocks with listed calls—NVS, which is not volatile, and VVS, which is quite volatile. Since a call on the volatile stock will be higher-priced than a call on the nonvolatile stock, the following prices might exist:

NVS:	40	VVS:	40
NVS July 40 call:	2	VVS July 40 call:	4

If these two calls are ranked, for buying purposes, based strictly on a percentage change in the underlying stock, the NVS call will appear to be the better buy. For example, one might see a list such as "best call buys if the underlying stock advances by 10%." In this example, if each stock advanced 10% by expiration, both NVS and VVS would be at 44. Thus the NVS July 40 would be worth 4, having doubled in price, for a 100% potential profit. Meanwhile, the VVS July 40 would be worth 4 also, for a 0% profit to the call buyer. This analysis would lead one to believe that the NVS July 40 is the better buy. Such a conclusion may be wrong, because an incorrect assumption was made in the ranking of the potentials of the two stocks—it is not right to assume that both stocks have the same probability of moving 10% by expiration. Certainly, the volatile stock has a much better chance of advancing by 10% (or more) than the nonvolatile stock does. *Any ranking based on equal percentage changes in the underlying stock, regardless of their volatilities, is useless and should be avoided.*

The correct method of comparing these two July 40 calls is to utilize the actual volatilities of the underlying stocks. Suppose that it is known that the volatile stock, VVS, could expect to move 15% in the time to July expiration. The nonvolatile stock, NVS, however, could only expect a move of 5% in the same period. Using this information, the call buyer can arrive at the conclusion that VVS July 40 is the best call to buy:

Stock Price in July	Call Price
VVS: 46 (up 15%)	VVS July 40: 6 (up 50%)
NVS: 42 (up 5%)	NVS July 40: 2 (unchanged)

By assuming that each stock can rise in accordance with its volatility, the VVS July 40 has the better reward potential, despite the fact that it was twice as expensive to begin with. This method of analysis is much more realistic.

One more refinement needs to be made in this ranking process. Since most call purchases are made for holding periods of from 30 to 90 days, it is not correct to assume that the calls are held to expiration. That is, even if one buys a 6-month call, he will normally liquidate it—to take profits or cut losses—in 1 to 3 months. *The call buyer's list should thus be based on how the call will perform if held for a realistic time period, such as 90 days.*

Suppose the volatile stock in our example, VVS, has the potential to rise by 12% in 90 days while the less-volatile stock, NVS, only has the potential of rising 4% in 90 days. In 90 days, the July 40 calls will not be at parity because there would be some time remaining until July expiration. Thus it is necessary to attempt to predict what their prices would be at the end of the 90-day holding period. Assume that the following prices are accurate estimates of what the July 40 calls would be selling for in 90 days, if the underlying stocks advanced in relation to their volatilities:

Stock Price in 90 Days	Call Price
VVS: 44.8 (up 12%)	VVS July 40: 6 (up 50%)
NVS: 41.6 (up 4%)	NVS July 40: 2½ (up 25%)

With some time remaining in the calls, they would both have time value premium at the end of 90 days. The bigger time premium would be in the VVS call, since the underlying stock is more volatile. Under this method of analysis, the VVS call is still the best one to buy.

The correct method of ranking potential reward situations for call buyers is as follows:

1. Assume each underlying stock can advance in accordance with its volatility over a fixed period (30, 60, or 90 days).
2. Estimate the call prices after the advance.
3. Rank all potential call purchases by highest percentage reward opportunity for aggressive purchases.
4. Assume each stock can *decline* in accordance with its volatility.
5. Estimate the call prices after the decline.
6. Rank all purchases by reward/risk ratio (percentage gain from item 2 divided by percentage loss from item 2).

The list from item 3 will generate more aggressive purchases because it incorporates potential rewards only. The list from item 6 would be a less speculative one. This method of analysis automatically incorporates the criteria set forth earlier, such as buying short-term out-of-the-money calls for aggressive purchases and buying longer-term in-the-money calls for a more conservative purchase. The delta is also a function of the volatility and is essentially incorporated by steps 1 and 4.

It is virtually impossible to perform this sort of analysis without a computer. The call buyer can generally obtain such a list from a brokerage firm or from a data service. For those individuals who have access to a computer and would like to generate such an analysis for themselves, the details of computing a stock's volatility and for predicting the call prices will be provided later in a section on mathematical techniques.

Overpriced or Underpriced Calls

There are formulae available that are capable of predicting what a call should be selling for, based on the relationship of the stock price and the striking price, the time remaining to expiration, and the volatility of the underlying stock. These are useful, for example, in performing the second step in the foregoing analysis—estimating the call price after an advance in the underlying stock. In reality, a call's actual price may deviate somewhat from the price computed by the formula. If the call is actually selling for more than the "fair" (computed) price, the call is said to be *overvalued*. An *undervalued* call would be one that is actually trading at a price that is less than the "fair" price.

Generally, the amount by which a call is overvalued or undervalued may be only a small fraction of a point—such as an eighth or a quarter. In theory, the call buyer who purchases an undervalued call has gained a slight advantage in that the call should return to its *"fair" value*. However, in practice, this information is most useful only to market-makers or firm traders who pay little or no commissions for trading options. The general public cannot benefit directly from the knowledge that such a small discrepancy exists, because of commission costs.

One should not base his call buying decisions merely on the fact that a call is underpriced. It is small solace to the call buyer to find that he bought a "cheap" call which subsequently declined in price. The method of ranking calls for purchase that have been described does, in fact, give some slight benefit to underpriced calls. However, under the recommended method of analysis, a call will not automatically appear as an attractive purchase just because it is slightly undervalued.

FOLLOW-UP ACTION

The simplest follow-up action that the call buyer can implement when the underlying stock drops is to sell his call and cut his losses. There is often a natural tendency to hold out hope that the stock can rally back to or above the striking price. Most of the time, the buyer does best by cutting his losses in situations where the stock is performing poorly. He might use a "mental" stop price, or could actually place a sell stop order, depending on the rules of the exchange where the call is traded.

If the stock should rise, the buyer should be willing to take profits as well. Most buyers will quite readily take a profit if, for example, a call that was bought for 5 points had advanced to be worth 10 points. However, the same investor is often reluctant to sell a call at 2 that he had previously bought for 1 point, because "I've only made a point." The similarity is clear—both cases resulted in approximately a 100% profit—and the investor should be as willing to accept the one as he is the other. This is not to imply that all calls that are bought at 1 should be sold when and if they get to 2, but the same factors that induce one to sell the 10-point call after doubling his money should apply to the 2-point call as well.

It is rarely to the call buyer's benefit to exercise the call if he has to pay commissions. When one exercises a call, he pays a stock commission to buy the stock at the striking price. Then when the stock is sold, a stock sale commission must also be paid. Since option commissions are much smaller, dollarwise, than stock commissions are, the call holder will usually realize more net dollars by selling the call in the option market than by exercising it.

Locking in Profits

When the call buyer is fortunate enough to see the underlying stock advance relatively quickly, there are a number of strategies that he can implement to enhance his position. These strategies are often useful to the call buyer who has an unrealized profit but is torn between taking the profit or holding on in an attempt to generate more profits if the underlying stock should continue to rise.

Example: A call buyer bought an XYZ October 50 call for 3 points when the stock was at 48. Then the stock rises to 58. The buyer might consider selling his October 50 (which would probably be worth about 9 points) and possibly taking one of several actions—some of which might involve the October 60 call, which may be selling for 3 points. Table 3-1

TABLE 3-1.
Present situation on XYZ October calls.

Original Trade		Current Prices	
XYZ common:	47	XYZ Common:	58
Bought XYZ October 50 at 3		XYZ October 50:	9
		XYZ October 60:	3

summarizes the situation. At this point, the call buyer might take one of four basic actions:

1. Liquidate the position by selling the long call for a profit.
2. Sell the October 50 that he is currently long and use part of the proceeds to purchase October 60's.
3. Create a spread by selling the October 60 call against his long October 50.
4. Do nothing and continue to remain long the October 50 call.

Each of these actions would produce different levels of risk and reward from this point forward in time. If the holder sells the October 50 call, he makes a 6-point profit, less commissions, and terminates the position. He can realize no further appreciation from the call, nor can he lose any of his current profits—he has realized a 6-point gain. *This is the least aggressive tactic of the four.* If the underlying stock continues to advance and rises above 63, any of the other three strategies will outperform the complete liquidation of the call. However, if the underlying stock should instead decline below 50 by expiration, this action would have provided the most profit of the four strategies.

The other simple tactic—the fourth one listed above—would be to do nothing. If the call is then held to expiration, *this tactic would be the riskiest of the four.* It is the only one that could produce a loss at expiration if XYZ fell back below 50. However, if the underlying stock continues to rise in price, more profits would accrue on the call. Every call buyer realizes the ramifications of these two tactics—liquidating or doing nothing—and is generally looking for an alternative that might allow him to reduce some of his risk without cutting off his profit potential completely. The remaining two tactics are geared to this purpose—limiting the total risk while providing the opportunity for further profits of an amount greater than those that could be realized by liquidating.

The strategy in which the holder sells the call that he is currently holding—the October 50—and uses part of the proceeds to buy the call at the next higher strike will be called *rolling up.* In this example, he could sell the October 50 at 9, pocket his initial 3-point investment, and use the remaining proceeds to buy two October 60 calls at 3 points each. Thus it is sometimes possible for the speculator to recoup his entire original investment and still increase the number of calls outstanding by rolling up. Once this has been done, the October 60 calls will represent pure profits, whatever their price. *The buyer who "rolls up" in this manner is essentially speculating with someone else's money*—he has put his own money back in his pocket and is using accrued profits to attempt to realize further gains. At expiration, this tactic would perform best if XYZ substantial amount. This tactic turns out to be the worst of the four at expiration if XYZ remains near its current price—staying above 53 but not rising above 63 in this example.

The final alternative of the four is to continue to hold the October 50 call but to sell the October 60 call against it. This would create what is known as a bull spread, and the tactic can be used *only* by traders who have a margin account and can meet their firm's minimum equity requirement for spreading (generally $2,000). This spread position has no risk, for the long side of the spread—the October 50—cost 3 points and the short side of the spread—the October 60—brought in 3 points via its sale. Even if the underlying stock drops below 50 by expiration and all the calls expire worthless, the trader cannot lose anything except commissions. On the other hand, the maximum potential of this spread is 10 points, the difference between the striking prices of 50 and 60. This maximum potential would be realized if XYZ were anywhere above 60 at expiration, for at that time the October 50 call would be worth 10 points more than the October 60 call, regardless of how far above 60 the underlying stock had risen. *This strategy will be the best performer of the four if XYZ remains relatively unchanged*, above the lower strike but not much above the higher strike by expiration. It is interesting to note that this tactic is *never the worst performer of the four tactics*, no matter where the stock is at expiration. For example, if XYZ drops below 50, this strategy has no risk and is therefore better than the "do nothing" strategy. If XYZ rises substantially, this spread produces a profit of 10 points, which is better than the 6 points of profit offered by the "liquidate" strategy.

There is no definite answer as to which of the four tactics is the best one to apply in a given situation. However, if a call can be sold against the currently long call to produce a bull spread which has little or no risk, it may often be an attractive thing to do. It can never turn out to be the worst decision, and it would produce the largest profits if XYZ does not rise substantially or fall substantially from its current levels. Tables 3-2 and 3-3 summarize the four alternative tactics, when a call holder has an unrealized profit. The four tactics, again, are:

1. "Do nothing"—continue to hold the currently long call.

2. "Liquidate"—sell the long call to take profits and do not reinvest.

3. "Roll up"—sell the long call, pocket the original investment, and use the remaining proceeds to purchase as many out-of-the-money calls as possible.

4. "Spread"—create a bull spread by selling the out-of-the-money call against the currently profitable long call, preferably taking in at least the original cost of the long call.

TABLE 3-2.
Comparison of the four alternative strategies.

If the underlying stock then...	The best tactic was...	And the worst tactic was...
continues to rise dramati- cally...	"roll up"	liquidate
rises moderately above the next strike...	do nothing	liquidate or "roll up"
remains relatively unchanged	spread	"roll up"
falls back below the original strike...	liquidate	do nothing

TABLE 3-3.
Results at expiration.

XYZ Price at Expiration	"Roll-up" Profit	"Do Nothing" Profit	"Spread" Profit	Liquidating Profit
50 or below	$ 0	− $ 300(W)	$ 0	+ $600(B)
53	0(W)	0(W)	+ 300	+ 600(B)
56	0(W)	+ 300	+ 600(B)	+ 600(B)
60	0(W)	+ 700	+ 1,000(B)	+ 600
63	+ 600(W)	+ 1,000(B)	+ 1,000(B)	+ 600(W)
67	+ 1,400(B)	+ 1,400(B)	+ 1,000	+ 600(W)
70	+ 2,000(B)	+ 1,700	+ 1,000	+ 600(W)

Note that each of the four tactics proves to be the best tactic in one case or another, but that the spread tactic is never the worst one. Tables 3-2 and 3-3 represent the results from holding until expiration. For those who prefer to see the actual numbers involved in making these comparisons between the four tactics, Table 3-3 summarizes the potential profits and losses of each of the four tactics using the prices from the example above. "W" indicates that the tactic is the worst one at that price, and "B" indicates that it is the best one.

There are, of course, modifications that one might make to any of these tactics. For example, he might decide to sell out half of his long call position—recovering a major part of his original cost—and continue to hold the remainder of the long calls. This still leaves room for further appreciation.

Defensive Action

There are two follow-up strategies that are sometimes employed by the call buyer when the underlying stock declines in price. Both involve spread strategies—that is being long and short two different calls on the same underlying stock simultaneously. Spreads are discussed in detail in a later chapter. This discussion of spreads applies only to their use by the call buyer.

"*Rolling Down.*" If an option holder owns an option at a currently unrealized loss, it may be possible to greatly increase the chances of making a limited profit on a relatively small rebound in the stock price. In certain cases, the investor may be able to implement such a strategy at little or no increase in risk.

Many call buyers have encountered a situation such as this: an XYZ October 35 call was originally bought for 3 points in hopes of a quick rise in the stock price. However, because of downward movements in the stock—to 32, say—the call is now at $1\frac{1}{2}$ with October expiration nearer. If the call buyer still expects a mild rally in the stock before expiration, he might either hold the call or possibly "average down" (buy more calls at $1\frac{1}{2}$). In either case he will need a rally to nearly 38 by expiration in order to break even. Since this would necessitate at least a 15% upward move by the stock before expiration, it cannot be considered too likely. Instead, the buyer should consider implementing the following strategy, which will be explained through the use of an example.

Example: The investor is long the October 35 call at this time:

XYZ, 32;

XYZ October 35 call, $1\frac{1}{2}$; and

XYZ October 30 call, 3.

One could sell two October 35's and, at the same time, buy one October 30 for no additional investment before commissions. That is, the sale of 2 October 35's at $150 each would bring in $300, exactly the cost, before commissions, of buying the October 30 call. *This is the key to implementing the roll-down strategy—that one be able to buy the lower strike call and sell two of the higher strike calls for nearly even money.*

Note that the investor is now *short* the call that he previously owned— the October 35. Where he previously owned one October 35, he has now sold two of them. He is also now long one October 30 call. Thus his position is:

long 1 XYZ October 30 call,

short 1 XYZ October 35 call.

This is technically known as a *bull spread*, but the terminology is not important. Table 3-4 summarizes the transactions that the buyer has made to acquire this spread. The trader now "owns" the spread at a cost of $300, plus commissions. By making this trade, he has lowered his break-

TABLE 3-4.
Transactions in bull spread.

	Trade	Cost before Commissions
Original trade	Buy 1 October 35 call at 3	$300 debit
Later trade	Sell 2 October 35 calls at 1½	$300 credit
	Buy 1 October 30 call at 3	$300 debit
Net position	Long 1 October 30 call	$300 debit
	Short 1 October 35 call	

even point significantly without increasing his risk. However, the maximum profit potential has also been limited—he can no longer capitalize on a strong rebound by the underlying stock.

In order to see that the break-even point has been lowered, consider what the results are if XYZ is at 33 at October expiration. The October 30 call would be worth 3 points and the October 35 would expire worthless with XYZ at 33. Thus the October 30 call could be sold to bring in $300 at that time and there would not be any expense to buy back the October 35. Consequently, the spread could be liquidated for $300—exactly the amount for which it was "bought." The spread then breaks even at 33 at expiration. If the call buyer had not rolled down, his break-even point would be 38 at expiration, for he paid 3 points for the original October 35 call and he would thus need XYZ to be at 38 in order to be able to liquidate the call for 3 points. Clearly, the stock has a better chance of recovering to 33 than to 38. *Thus the call buyer significantly lowers his break-even point by utilizing this strategy.*

Lowering the break-even point is not the investor's only concern. He must also be aware of what has happened to his profit and loss opportunities. The risk remains essentially the same—the $300 in debits, plus commissions that have been paid out. The risk has actually increased slightly, by the amount of the commissions spent in "rolling down." However, the stock price at which this maximum loss would be realized has been lowered. With the original long call, the October 35, the buyer would lose the entire $300 investment anywhere below 35 at October expiration. The spread strategy, however, would result in a total loss of $300 only if XYZ were below *30* at October expiration. With XYZ above 30 in October, the long side of the spread could be liquidated for some value, thereby avoiding a total loss. *The investor has reduced the chance of realizing the maximum loss,* since the stock price at which that loss would occur has been lowered by 5 points.

As with most investments, the improvement of risk exposure—lowering the break-even point and lowering the maximum loss price—necessitates that some potential reward be sacrificed. In the original long call position (the October 35), the maximum profit potential was unlimited. In the new position, the potential profit is limited to 2 points if XYZ should rally back to, *or anywhere above*, 35 by October expiration. To see this, assume XYZ is 35 at expiration. Then the long October 30 call would be worth 5 points, while the October 35 would expire worthless. Thus the spread could be liquidated for 5 points, a 2-point profit over the 3 points paid for the spread. This is the limit of profit for the spread, however, since if XYZ is above 35 at expiration, any further profits in the long October 30 call would be offset by a corresponding loss on the short October 35 call. *Thus, if XYZ were to rally heavily by expiration, the "rolled down" position would not realize as large a profit as the original long call position would have realized.*

Table 3-5 and Figure 3-2 summarize the original and new positions. Note that the new position is better for stock prices between 30 and 40. Below 30, the two positions are equal, except for the additional commissions spent. If the stock should rally back above 40, the original position would have worked out better. *The new position is an improvement, provided that XYZ does not rally back above 40 by expiration.* The chances that XYZ could rally 8 points, or 25%, from 32 to 40 would have to be considered relatively remote. Rolling the long call down into the spread would thus appear to be the correct thing to do in this case.

This example is particularly attractive, because no additional money was required to establish the spread. In many cases, however, one may find that the long call cannot be rolled into the spread at even money. Some debit may be required. This fact should not necessarily preclude making the change, since a small additional investment may still significantly increase the chance of breaking even or making a profit on a rebound.

TABLE 3-5.
Original and spread positions compared.

Stock Price at Expiration	Long Call Result	Spread Result
25	− $300	− $300
30	− 300	− 300
33	− 300	0
35	− 300	+ 200
38	0	+ 200
40	+ 200	+ 200
45	+ 700	+ 200

FIGURE 3-2.
Comparison: original call purchase vs. spread.

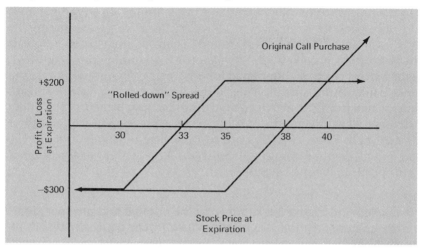

Example: The following prices now exist, rather than the ones used earlier. Only the October 30 call price has been altered:

XYZ, 32;

XYZ October 35 call, 1½; and

XYZ October 30 call, 4.

With these prices, a 1-point debit would be required to roll down. That is, selling 2 October 35 calls would bring in $300 ($150 each), but the cost of buying the October 30 call is $400. Thus the transaction would have to be done at a cost of $100, plus commissions. With these prices, the break-even point after rolling down would be 34—still well below the original break-even price of 38. The risk has now been increased by the additional 1 point spent to roll down. If XYZ should drop below 30 at October expiration, the investor would have a total loss of 4 points plus commissions. The maximum loss with the original long October 35 call was limited to 3 points plus a smaller amount of commissions. Finally, the maximum amount of money that the spread could make is now $100, less commissions. The alternative in this example is not nearly as attractive as the previous one, but it might still be worthwhile for the call buyer to invoke such a spread if he feels that XYZ has limited rally potential up to October expiration.

One should not automatically discard the use of this strategy merely because a debit is required to convert the long call to a spread. Note that to "*average down*" by buying an additional October 35 call at 1½ would require an additional investment of $150. This is more than the $100 required to convert into the spread position in the immediately preceding example. The break-even point on the position that was "averaged down" would be over 37 at expiration, whereas the break-even point on the spread is 34. Admittedly, the averaged-down position has much more profit potential than the spread does, but the conversion to the spread is less expensive than "averaging down" and also provides a lower break-even price.

In summary, then, if the call buyer finds himself with an unrealized loss because the stock has declined, and yet is unwilling to sell, he may be able to improve his chances of breaking even by "rolling down" into a spread. That is, he would sell 2 of the calls that he is currently long—the one that he owns plus another one—and simultaneously buy one call at the next lower striking price. If this transaction of selling 2 calls and buying 1 call can be done for approximately even money, it could definitely be to the buyer's benefit to implement this strategy because the break-even point would be lowered considerably and the buyer would have a much better chance of getting out even or making a small profit should the underlying stock have a small rebound.

Creating a Calendar Spread. A different type of defensive spread strategy is sometimes used by the call buyer who finds that the underlying stock has declined. In this strategy, the holder of an intermediate- or long-term call sells a near-term call, with the same striking price as the call he already owns. This creates what is known as a *calendar spread*. The idea behind doing this is that if the short-term call expires worthless, the overall cost of the long call will be reduced to the buyer. Then, if the stock should rally, the call buyer has a better chance of making a profit.

Example: Suppose that an investor bought an XYZ October 35 call for 3 points sometime in April. By June the stock has fallen to 32, and it appears that the stock might remain depressed for a while longer. The holder of the October 35 call might consider selling a July 35 call—perhaps for a price of 1 point. Should XYZ remain below 35 until July expiration, the short call would expire worthless, earning a small, "1"-point profit. The investor would still own the October 35 call and would then hope for a rally by XYZ before October in order to make profits on that call. Even if XYZ does not rally by October, he has decreased his overall loss by the amount received for the sale of the July 35 call.

This strategy is not as attractive to use as the previous one. If XYZ should rally before July expiration, the investor might find himself with two losing positions. For example, suppose that XYZ rallied back to 36 in the next week. His short call that he sold for 1 point would be selling for something more than that, so he would have an unrealized loss on the short July 35. In addition, the October 35 would probably not have appreciated back to its original price of 3 and he would therefore have an unrealized loss on that side of the spread as well.

Consequehtly, this strategy should be used with great caution, for if the underlying stock rallies quickly before the near-term expiration, the spread could be at a loss on both sides. Note that in the former spread strategy, this could not happen. Even if XYZ rallied quickly, some profit would be made on the rebound.

A FURTHER COMMENT ON SPREADS

Anyone not familiar with the margin requirements for spreads—both under the federal margin rules and the rules of the brokerage firm he is dealing with—should not attempt to utilize a spread transaction. Later chapters on spreads outline the more common requirements for spread transactions. In general, one must have a margin account to establish a spread and he must have a minimum amount of equity in the account. Thus the call buyer who operates in a cash account cannot necessarily use these spread strategies. To do so might incur a margin call and possible restriction of one's trading account. Therefore, check on specific requirements necessary before utilizing a spread strategy. Do not assume that a long call can automatically be "rolled" into any sort of spread.

Chapter *4*

Other Call Buying Strategies

In this chapter, two additional strategies that utilize the purchase of call options will be described. Both of these strategies involve buying calls against the short sale of the underlying stock. Where listed puts are traded on the underlying stock, these strategies become passé—they are better implemented with the use of put options. However, since some stocks have listed calls without listed puts, these strategies are applicable in those cases. Another well-known call buying strategy—the simultaneous purchase of options and fixed-income securities—will be described in Chapter 27.

THE PROTECTED SHORT SALE (OR SYNTHETIC PUT)

Purchasing a call at the same time that one is short the underlying stock is a means of limiting the risk of the short sale to a fixed amount. Since the risk is theoretically unlimited in a short sale, many investors are reluctant to use the strategy. Even for those investors who do sell stock short, it can be rather upsetting if the stock rises in price. One may be forced into an emotional—and perhaps incorrect—decision to cover the short sale in order to relieve the psychological pressure. By owning a call at the same time one is short, the risk is limited to a fixed and generally small amount.

Example: An investor sells XYZ short at 40 and simultaneously purchases an XYZ July 40 call for 3 points. If XYZ falls in price, the short seller will make his profit on the short sale, less the 3 points paid for the call, which will expire worthless. *Thus, by buying the call for protection, a small amount of profit potential is sacrificed.* However, the advantage of owning the call is demonstrated when the results are examined for a stock rise. If XYZ should rise to any price above 40 by July expiration, the short seller can cover his short by exercising the long call and buying stock at 40. Thus the maximum risk that the short seller can incur in this example is the 3 points paid for the call. Table 4-1 and Figure 4-1 depict the results at expiration from utilizing this strategy. Commissions are not included. Note that the break-even point is 37 in this example. That is, if the stock drops 3 points, the protected short sale position will break even because of the 3-point loss on the stock. The short seller who did not spend the extra money for the long call would, of course, have a 3-point profit at 37. To the upside, however, the protected short sale outperforms a regular short sale if the stock climbs anywhere above 43. At 43, both types of short sales have $300 losses. But above that level, the loss would continue to grow for a regular short sale, while it is fixed for the short seller who also bought a call. In either case, the short seller's risk is increased slightly by the fact that he is obligated to pay out the dividends on the underlying stock, if any are declared.

A simple formula is available for determining the maximum amount of risk when one protects a short sale by buying a call option:

Risk = Striking price of purchased call + Call price − Stock price

Depending on how much risk the short seller is willing to absorb, he might want to buy an out-of-the-money call as protection rather than an at-the-money call as was shown in the example above. A smaller dollar amount is spent for the protection when one buys an out-of-the-money call, so

TABLE 4-1.
Results at expiration—protected short sale.

XYZ Price at Expiration	Profit on XYZ	Call Price at Expiration	Profit on Call	Total Profit
20	+$2,000	0	−$ 300	+$1,700
30	+ 1,000	0	− 300	+ 700
37	+ 300	0	− 300	0
40	0	0	− 300	− 300
50	− 1,000	10	+ 700	− 300
60	− 2,000	20	+ 1,700	− 300

FIGURE 4-1.
Protected short sale.

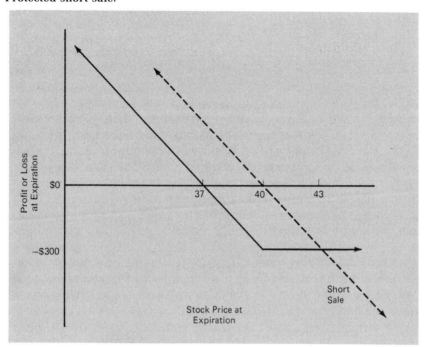

that the short seller does not give away as much of his profit potential. However, his risk is larger because the call does not start its protective qualities until the stock goes above the striking price.

Example: With XYZ at 40, the short seller of XYZ buys the July 45 call at ½ for protection. His maximum possible loss, if XYZ is above 45 at July expiration, would be 5½ points—the five points between the current stock price of 40 and the striking price of 45, plus the amount paid for the call. On the other hand, if XYZ declines, the protected short seller will make nearly as much as the short seller who did not protect, since he only spent ½ point for the long call.

If one buys an *in-the-money* call as protection for the short sale, his risk will be quite minimal. However, his profit potential will be severely limited. As an example, with XYZ at 40, if one had purchased a July 35 call at 5½, his risk would be limited to ½ point anywhere above 35 at July expiration. Unfortunately, he would not realize any profit on the position until the stock went below 34½, a drop of 5½ points. This is too much protection, for it limits the profit so severely that there is only a small hope of making a profit.

   Generally, it is best to buy a call that is at-the-money or only slightly
out-of-the-money as the protection for the short sale. It is not of much
use to buy a deeply out-of-the-money call as protection, since it does very
little to moderate risk unless the stock climbs quite dramatically. Normally, one would cover a short sale before it went heavily against him.
Thus the money spent for such a deeply out-of-the-money call is wasted.

Margin Requirements

Even though one has limited risk in this position, there is no benefit as
far as margin requirements are concerned. A short seller has his position
marked to the market daily—that is, the amount of profit or loss is added
to, or subtracted from, his excess collateral (called SMA) on a daily basis.
Consequently, if a stock that one has sold short should rise dramatically,
one could receive a margin call because of the buildup of unrealized losses.
Even if one has purchased a call as protection for the short sale, this same
margin procedure is followed. It is illogical to mark the short seller to
market even when his risk is limited. However, the federal margin rules
have not been altered to cover this strategy. Should one receive such a
margin call while he owns the long call for protection, he can easily satisfy
the margin requirement by exercising the call option and closing out the
position. This action would return a positive collateral balance to his
margin account.

Follow-Up Action

There is little that the protected short seller needs to perform in the way
of follow-up action in this strategy, other than closing out the position.
If the underlying stock moves down quickly and it appears that it might
rebound, the short sale could be covered without selling the long call. In
this manner, one could potentially profit on the call side as well if the
stock came back above the original striking price. If the underlying stock
rises in price, a similar strategy of taking off only the profitable side of
the transaction is *not* recommended. That is, if XYZ climbed from 40 to
50 and the July 40 call also rose from 3 to 10, it is *not* advisable to take
the 7-point profit in the call, hoping for a drop in the stock price. The
reason for this is that one is entering into a highly risk-oriented situation
by removing his protection when the call is in-the-money. Thus when the
stock *drops*, it is all right—perhaps even desirable—to take the profit
because there is little or no additional risk if the stock continues to drop.
However, when the stock *rises*, it is *not* an equivalent situation. In that
case, if the short seller sells his call for a profit and the stock subsequently
rises even further, large losses could result.

   It may often be advisable to close the position if the call is at or near
parity, in-the-money, by exercising the call. In most strategies, the option

holder has no advantage in exercising the call because of the large dollar difference between stock commissions and option commissions. However, in the protected short sale strategy, the short seller is eventually going to have to cover the short stock in any case and incur the stock commission by so doing. It may be to his advantage to exercise the call and buy his stock at the striking price, thereby buying stock at a lower price and thus paying a slightly lower commission amount.

Example: XYZ rises to 50 from the original short sale price of 40 and the XYZ July 40 call is selling at 10 somewhere close to expiration. The position could be liquidated by either (1) buying the stock back at 50 and selling the call at 10, or (2) exercising the call to buy stock at 40. In the first case, one would pay a stock commission at a price of $50 per share plus an option commission on a $10 option. In the second case, the only commission would be a stock commission at the price of $40 per share. Since both actions accomplish the same end result—closing the position entirely for 40 points plus commissions—clearly the second choice is less costly and therefore more desirable. Of course, if the call has time value premium in it of an amount greater than the commission savings, the first alternative should be used.

THE REVERSE HEDGE (SIMULATED STRADDLE)

There is another strategy involving the purchase of long calls against the short sale of stock. In this strategy, one purchases calls on more shares than he has sold short. The strategist can profit if the underlying stock rises far enough or falls far enough during the life of the calls. This strategy is generally referred to as *reverse hedge* or *simulated straddle*. On stocks where listed puts are traded, this strategy is outmoded—the same results can be better achieved by buying a straddle (a call and a put). Hence the name "simulated straddle" is also applied to the reverse hedge strategy.

This strategy has limited loss potential, usually amounting to a moderate percentage of the initial investment, *and theoretically unlimited profit potential*. The frequency of loss can be high (that is, a large percentage of the trades may result in losses), but the unlimited profit potential feature means that one or two large profits can overcome the losses incurred. These features make this an attractive strategy, especially when call premiums are low in comparison to the underlying stock.

Example: XYZ is at 40 and an investor feels that the stock has the potential of moving by a relatively large distance, but he is not sure of the direction the stock will take. This investor could short XYZ at 40 and buy 2 XYZ July 40 calls at 3 each to set up a reverse hedge. If XYZ moves up by a large distance, he will incur a loss on his short stock, but the fact that he owns *two* calls means that the call profits will outdistance the stock loss. If, on the other hand, XYZ drops far enough, the short sale profit will be larger than the loss on the calls, which is limited to 6 points. Table 4-2 and Figure 4-2 show the possible outcomes for various stock prices at July expiration. If XYZ falls, the stock profits on the short sale will accumulate, but the loss on the two calls is limited to $600 (3 points each) so that, below 34, the reverse hedge can make ever-increasing profits. To the upside, even though the short sale is incurring losses, the call

TABLE 4-2.
Reverse hedge at July expiration.

XYZ Price at Expiration	Stock Profit	Profit on 2 Calls	Total Profit
20	+ $2,000	− $ 600	+ $1,400
25	+ 1,500	− 600	+ 900
30	+ 1,000	− 600	+ 400
34	+ 600	− 600	0
40	0	− 600	− 600
46	− 600	+ 600	0
50	− 1,000	+ 1,400	+ 400
55	− 1,500	+ 2,400	+ 900
60	− 2,000	+ 3,400	+ 1,400

FIGURE 4-2.
Reverse hedge (simulated straddle).

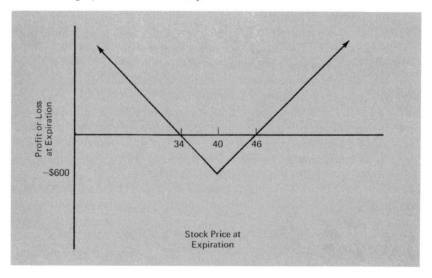

profits grow faster because there are two long calls. For example, at 60 at expiration, there will be a 20-point ($2,000) loss on the short stock, but each XYZ July 40 call will be worth 20 points with the stock at 60. Thus the two calls are worth $4,000, representing a profit of $3,400 over the initial cost of $600 for the calls.

Table 4-2 and Figure 4-2 illustrate another important point—*the maximum loss would occur if the stock were exactly at the striking price at expiration of the calls*. This maximum loss would occur if XYZ were at 40 at expiration and would amount to $600. In actual practice, since the short seller must pay out any dividends paid by the underlying stock, the risk in this strategy is increased by the amount of such dividends.

The net margin required for this strategy is 50% of the underlying stock plus the full purchase price of the calls. In the example above, this would be an initial investment of $2,000 (50% of the stock price) plus $600 for the calls, or $2,600 total plus commissions. The short sale is marked to market so the collateral requirement would grow if the stock rose. Since the maximum risk, before commissions, is $600, this means that the net percentage risk in this transaction is $600/$2,600, about 23%. This is a relatively small percentage risk in a position that could have profits which are potentially very large. There is also very little chance that the entire maximum loss would ever be realized since it occurs only at one specific stock price. One should not be deluded into thinking that this strategy is a sure money maker. In general, stocks do not move very far in a 3- or 6-month period. Thus the probability of loss is high in this strategy. This is balanced out by the fact that significant gains can be realized.

It is obvious from the information above that profits are made if the stock moves far enough in either direction. In fact, one can exactly determine the prices beyond which the stock would have to move by expiration in order for profits to result. These prices are 34 and 46 in the foregoing example. The downside break-even point is 34 and the upside break-even point is 46. These break-even points can be easily computed. First the maximum risk is computed. Then the break-even points are determined.

Maximum risk = Striking price + 2 × Call price − Stock price

Upside break-even point = Striking price + Maximum risk

Downside break-even point = Striking price − Maximum risk

In the preceding example, the striking price was 40, the stock price was also 40, and the call price was 3. Thus the maximum risk = 40 + 2 × 3 − 40 = 6. This confirms that the maximum risk in the position is

6 points, or $600. The upside break-even point is then 40 + 6, or 46, and the downside break-even point is 40 − 6, or 34. These also agree with Table 4-2 and Figure 4-2.

Before expiration, profits can be made even closer to the striking price, because there will be some time value premium left in the purchased calls.

Example: If XYZ moved to 45 in one month, each call might be worth 6. If this happened, the investor would have a 5-point loss on the stock, but would also have a 3-point gain on each of the two options, for a net overall gain of 1 point, or $100. Before expiration, the break-even point is clearly somewhere below 46, because the position is at a profit at 45.

Ideally, one would like to find relatively underpriced calls on a fairly volatile stock in order to implement this strategy most effectively. Unfortunately, this combination occurs mostly in books and not very often in the actual marketplace. Normally, call premiums quite accurately reflect the volatility of the underlying stock. Still, this strategy can be quite viable, because nearly every stock, regardless of its volatility, occasionally experiences a straight-line, fairly large, move. It is during these times that the investor can profit from this strategy.

Generally, the underlying stock selected for the reverse hedge should be volatile. Even though option premiums are larger on these stocks, they can still be outdistanced by a straight-line move in a volatile situation. Another advantage of utilizing volatile stocks is that they generally pay little or no dividends. This is desirable for the reverse hedge, because the short seller will not be required to pay out as much.

The technical pattern of the underlying stock can also be useful when selecting the position. One generally would like to have little or no technical support and resistance within the loss area. This pattern would facilitate the stock's ability to make a fairly quick move either up or down. It is sometimes possible to find a stock that is in a wide trading range, frequently swinging from one side of the range to the other. If a reverse hedge can be set up that has its loss area well within this trading range, the position may also be attractive.

Example: The XYZ stock in the previous example is trading in the range 30 to 50, perhaps swinging to one end and then the other rather frequently. Now the reverse hedge example position, which would make profits above 46 or below 34, would appear more attractive.

Follow-Up Action

Since the reverse hedge has a built-in limited loss feature, it is not necessary to take any follow-up action to avoid losses. The investor could
quite easily put the position on and take no action at all until expiration.
This is often the best method of follow-up action in this strategy.

There is a follow-up strategy that can be applied, although it has
some disadvantages associated with it. This follow-up strategy is sometimes known as *"trading against the straddle."* When the stock moves far
enough in either direction, the profit on that side can be taken. Then if
the stock swings back in the opposite direction, a profit can also be made
on the other side. Two examples will show how this type of follow-up
strategy works.

Example 1: The XYZ stock in the previous example quickly moves
down to 32. At that time, an 8-point profit could be taken on the short
sale. This would leave two long calls. Even if they expired worthless, a
6-point loss would be all that would be incurred on the calls. Thus the
entire strategy would still have produced a profit of 2 points. However,
if the stock should rally above 40, profits could be made on the calls as
well. A slight variation would be to sell one of the calls at the same time
the stock profit is taken. This would result in a slightly larger realized
profit, but, if the stock rallied back above 40, the resulting profits there
would be smaller because the investor would only be long one call instead
of two.

Example 2: XYZ has moved up to a price where the calls are each
worth 8 points. One of the calls could then be sold, realizing a 5-point
profit. The resulting position would be short 100 shares of stock and long
one call, a protected short sale. The protected short sale has a limited risk,
above 40, of 3 points (the stock was sold short at 40 and the call was
purchased for 3 points). Even if XYZ remains above 40 and the maximum
3-point loss has to be taken, the overall reverse hedge would still have
made a profit of 2 points because of the 5-point profit taken on the one
call. Conversely, if XYZ drops below 40, the protected short sale position
could add to the profits already taken on the call.

There is a variation of this upside protective action.

Example 3: Instead of selling the one call, one could instead short
an additional 100 shares of stock at 48. If this was done, the overall position
would be short 200 shares of stock (100 at 40 and the other 100 at 48)
and long two calls—again a protected short sale. If XYZ remained above
40, there would again be an overall gain of 2 points. To see this, suppose

that XYZ was above 40 at expiration and the two calls were exercised to buy 200 shares of stock at 40. This would result in an 8-point profit on the 100 shares sold short at 48 and no gain or loss on the 100 shares sold short at 40. The initial call cost of 6 points would be lost. Thus the overall position would profit by 2 points. This means of follow-up action to the upside is more costly in commissions, but would provide bigger profits if XYZ fell back below 40, because there are 200 shares of XYZ short.

In theory, if any of the foregoing types of follow-up action were taken and the underlying stock did indeed reverse direction and cross back through the striking price, the original position could again be established. Suppose that, after covering the short stock at 32, XYZ rallied back to 40. Then XYZ could be sold short again, reestablishing the original position. If the stock moved outside the break-even points again, further follow-up action could be taken. This process could theoretically be repeated a number of times. If the stock continued to whipsaw back and forth in a trading range, the repeated follow-up actions could produce potentially large profits on a small net change in the stock price. In actual practice, it is unlikely that one would be fortunate to find a stock that moved that far that quickly.

The disadvantage of applying these follow-up strategies is obvious—*one can never make a large profit if he continually cuts his profits off at a small, limited amount.* When XYZ falls to 32, the stock can be covered to ensure an overall profit of 2 points on the transaction. However, if XYZ continued to fall to 20, the investor who took no follow-up action would make 14 points while the one who did take follow-up action would only make 2 points. Recall that it was stated earlier that there is a high probability of realizing limited losses in the reverse hedge strategy, but that this was balanced by the potentially large profits available in the remaining cases. If one takes follow-up action and cuts off these potentially large profits, he is operating at a distinct disadvantage unless he is an extremely adept trader.

Proponents of using the follow-up strategy often counter with the argument that it is frustrating to see the stock fall to 32 and then return back nearly 40 again. If no follow-up action were taken, the unrealized profit would have dissolved into a loss when the stock rallied. This is true as far as it goes, but it is not an effective enough argument to counterbalance the negative effects of cutting off one's profits.

ALTERING THE RATIO OF LONG CALLS TO SHORT STOCK

There is another aspect of this strategy that should be discussed. One does not have to buy exactly two calls against 100 shares of short stock. More bullish positions could be constructed by buying three or four calls against 100 shares short. More bearish positions could be constructed by buying three calls and shorting 200 shares of stock. One might adopt a ratio other than 2:1 because he is more bullish or bearish. He also might use a different ratio if the stock is between two striking prices, but he still wants to create a position that has break-even points spaced equidistant from the current stock price. A few examples will illustrate these points.

Example: XYZ is at 40 and the investor is slightly bullish on the stock but still wants to employ the reverse hedge strategy because he feels there is a chance the stock could drop sharply. He might then short 100 shares of XYZ at 40 and buy 3 July 40 calls for 3 point apiece. Since he paid 9 points for the calls, his maximum risk is that 9 points if XYZ were to be at 40 at expiration. This means his downside break-even price is 31, for at 31 he would have a 9-point profit on the short sale to offset the 9-point loss on the calls. To the upside, his break-even is now $44\frac{1}{2}$. If XYZ were at $44\frac{1}{2}$ and the calls at $4\frac{1}{2}$ each at expiration, he would lose $4\frac{1}{2}$ points on the short sale, but would make $1\frac{1}{2}$ on each of the three calls, for a total call profit of $4\frac{1}{2}$.

A more bearish investor might short 200 XYZ at 40 and buy 3 July 40 calls at 3. His break-even points would be $35\frac{1}{2}$ on the downside and 49 on the upside, and his maximum risk would be 9 points. There is a general formula that one can always apply to calculate the maximum risk and the break-even points, regardless of the ratios involved.

$$\text{Maximum risk} = (\text{striking price} - \text{stock price}) \times \text{round lots shorted} + \text{number of calls bought} \times \text{call price}$$

$$\text{Upside break-even} = \text{striking price} + \frac{\text{maximum risk}}{(\text{number of calls bought} - \text{number of round lots short})}$$

$$\text{Downside break-even} = \text{striking price} - \frac{\text{maximum risk}}{\text{number of round lots short}}$$

To verify this, use the numbers from the example where 100 XYZ was shorted at 40 and three July 40 calls were purchased for 3 each.

$$\text{Maximum risk} = (40 - 40) \times 1 + 3 \times 3 = 9$$

$$\text{Upside break-even} = 40 + 9/(3 - 1) = 40 + 4\frac{1}{2} = 44\frac{1}{2}$$

$$\text{Downside break-even} = 40 - 9/1 = 31$$

It was stated earlier that *one might use an adjusted ratio in order to space the break-even points evenly around the current stock price.*

Example: Suppose XYZ is at 38 and the XYZ July 40 call is at 2. If one wanted to set up a reverse hedge that would profit if XYZ moved either up or down by the same distance, he could not use the 2:1 ratio. The 2:1 ratio would have break-even points of 34 and 46. Thus the stock would start out much closer to the downside break-even point—only 4 points away—than to the upside break-even point, which is 8 points away. By altering the ratio, the investor can set up a reverse hedge that is more neutral on the underlying stock. Suppose that the investor shorted 100 shares of XYZ at 38 and bought *three* July 40 calls at 2 each. Then his break-even points would be 32 on the downside and 44 on the upside. This is a more neutral situation, with the downside break-even point being 6 points below the current stock price and the upside break-even point being 6 points away. The formulae above can be used to verify that, in fact, the break-evens are 32 and 44. Note that the 3:1 ratio has a maximum risk of 8 points, while the 2:1 ratio only had 6 points maximum risk.

A final adjustment that can be applied to this strategy is to short the stock and buy two calls, but with the calls having *different striking prices.* If XYZ were at 37½ to start with, one would have to use a ratio other than 2:1 to set up a position with break-even points spaced equidistant from the current stock price. When these higher ratios are used, the maximum risk is increased and the investor has to adopt a bullish or bearish stance. One may be able to create a position with equidistant break-even points and a smaller maximum risk by utilizing two different striking prices.

Example: The following prices exist:

XYZ, 37½;

XYZ July 40 call, 2; and

XYZ July 35 call, 4.

If one were to short 100 XYZ at 37½ and to buy one July 40 call for 2 and one July 35 call for 4, he would have a position that is similar to a reverse hedge except that *the maximum risk would be realized anywhere between 35 and 40 at expiration.* Although this risk is over a much wider range than in the normal reverse hedge, it is now much smaller in dimension. Table 4-3 and Figure 4-3 show the results from this type of position at expiration. The maximum loss is 3½ points ($350), which is a smaller amount than could be realized using any ratio with strictly the July 35 or the July 40 call. However, this maximum loss is realizable over the entire

TABLE 4-3.
Reverse hedge using two strikes.

XYZ Price at Expiration	Stock Profit	July 50 Call Profit	July 35 Call Profit	Total Profit
25	+ $1,250	− $200	− $ 400	+ $650
30	+ 750	− 200	− 400	+ 150
31½	+ 600	− 200	− 400	0
35	+ 250	− 200	− 400	− 350
37½	0	− 200	− 150	− 350
40	− 250	− 200	+ 100	− 350
43½	− 600	+ 150	+ 450	0
45	− 750	+ 300	+ 600	+ 150
50	− 1,250	+ 800	+ 1,100	+ 650

FIGURE 4-3.
Reverse hedge using two strikes (simulated combination purchase).

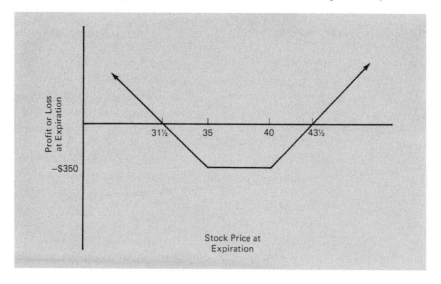

range 35 to 40. Again, large potential profits are available if the stock moves far enough either to the upside or to the downside.

This form of the strategy should only be used when the stock is nearly centered between two strikes and the strategist wants a neutral positioning of the break-even points. Similar types of follow-up action to those described earlier can be applied to this form of the reverse hedge strategy as well.

SUMMARY

The strategies described in this chapter would not normally be used if the underlying stock has listed put options. However, if no puts exist, and the strategist feels that a volatile stock could move a relatively large distance in either direction during the life of a call option, he should consider using one of the forms of the reverse hedge strategy—shorting a quantity of stock and buying calls on more shares than he is short. If the desired movement does develop, potentially large profits could result. In any case, the loss is limited to a fixed amount, generally around 20 to 30% of the initial investment. Although it is possible to take follow-up action to lock in small profits and attempt to gain on a reversal by the stock, it is wiser to let the position run its course to capitalize on those occasions when the profits become large. Normally a 2:1 ratio (long 2 calls, short 100 shares of stock) is used in this strategy, but this ratio can be adjusted if the investor wants to be more bullish or more bearish. If the stock is initially between two striking prices, a neutral profit range can be set up by shorting the stock and buying calls at both the next higher strike and the next lower strike.

Chapter 5

Naked Call Writing

The next two chapters will concentrate various aspects of writing uncovered call options. These strategies have risk of loss if the underlying stock should rise in price, but they offer profits if the underlying stock declines in price. This chapter—on naked, or uncovered, call writing—demonstrates some of the risks and rewards inherent in this aggressive strategy.

THE UNCOVERED (NAKED) CALL OPTION

When one sells a call option without owning the underlying stock or any equivalent security (convertible stock or bond or another call option), he is considered to have written an *uncovered call option*. This strategy has limited profit potential and theoretically unlimited loss. For this reason, this strategy is unsuitable for some investors. This fact is not particularly attractive, but since there is no actual cash investment required to write a naked call—the position can be financed with collateral loan value of marginable securities—the strategy can be operated as an adjunct to many other investment strategies.

A simple example will outline the basic profit and loss potential from naked writing.

Example: XYZ is selling at 50 and a July 50 call is selling for 5. If one were to sell the July 50 call naked—that is, without owning XYZ stock, or any security convertible into XYZ, or another call option on XYZ—he could make, at most, 5 points of profit. This profit would accrue if XYZ were at, or anywhere below, 50 at July expiration as the call would then expire worthless. If XYZ were to rise, however, the naked writer could lose potentially large sums of money. Should the stock climb to 100, say, the call would be at a price of 50. If the writer then covered (bought back) the call for a price of 50, he would have a loss of 45 points on the transaction. In theory, this loss is unlimited, although *in practice the loss is limited by time.* The stock cannot rise an infinite amount during the life of the call. Clearly, defensive strategies are important in this strategy, as one would never want to let a loss run as far as the one here. Table 5-1 and Figure 5-1 (solid line) depict the results of this position at July expiration. Note that the break-even point in this example is 55. That is, if XYZ rose 10%, or 5 points, at expiration, the naked writer would break even. He could buy the call back at parity, 5 points, which is exactly what he sold it for. There is some room for error to the upside. *A naked write will not necessarily lose money if the stock moves up.* It will only lose if the stock advances by more than the amount of the time value premium that was in the call when it was originally written.

Naked writing is not the same as a short sale of the underlying stock. While both strategies have large potential risk, the short sale has much higher reward potential, but the naked write will do better if the underlying stock remains relatively unchanged. It is possible for the naked writer to make money in situations where the short seller would have lost money. For example, in the example above, suppose one investor had written the July 50 call naked for 5 points while another investor sold the stock short at 50. If XYZ were at 52 at expiration, the naked writer could buy the call back at parity, 2 points, for a 3-point profit. The short seller would have

TABLE 5-1.
Position at July expiration.

XYZ Price at Expiration	Call Price at Expiration	Profit on Naked Write
30	0	+$ 500
40	0	+ 500
50	0	+ 500
55	5	0
60	10	− 500
70	20	− 1,500
80	30	− 2,500

FIGURE 5-1.
Uncovered (naked) call write.

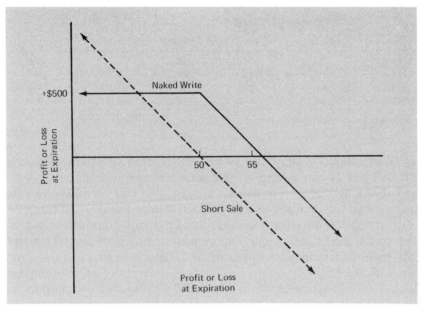

a 2-point *loss*. Moreover, the short seller pays out the dividends on the underlying stock, whereas the naked call writer does not. The naked call will expire, of course, but the short sale does not. This is a situation in which the naked write outperforms the short sale. However, if XYZ were to fall sharply—to 20, say—the naked writer could only make 5 points while the short seller would make 30 points. The dashed line in Figure 5-1 shows how the short sale of XYZ at 50 would compare with the naked write of the July 50 call. Notice that the two strategies are equal at 45 at expiration—they both make a 5-point profit there. Above 45, the naked write does better; it has larger profits and smaller losses. Below 45, the short sale does better, and the farther the stock falls, the better the short sale becomes in comparison. As will be seen later, one can more closely simulate a short sale by writing an in-the-money naked call.

INVESTMENT REQUIRED

The *margin requirements* for writing a naked call are 20% of the stock price plus the call premium less the amount by which the stock is below the striking price. If the stock is below the striking price, the differential is subtracted from the requirement. However, a minimum of 15% of the stock price is required for each call, even if the computation results in a smaller number. Table 5-2 gives four examples of how the initial margin

TABLE 5-2.
Initial collateral requirements for four stock prices.

Call Written	Stock Price When Call Written	Call Price	20% of Stock Price	Out-of-the money Differential	Total Margin Requirement
XYZ July 50	55	$700	$1,100	$ 0	$1,800
XYZ July 50	50	400	1,000	0	1,400
XYZ July 50	46	200	920	− 400	720
XYZ July 50	40	100	800	− 1,000	600*

*Requirement cannot be less than 15%.

requirement would be computed for four different stock prices. The 20% collateral figure is the minimum exchange requirement and may vary somewhat among different brokerage houses. *The call premium may be applied against the requirement.* In the first line of Table 5-2, if the XYZ July 50 call was selling for 7 points, the $700 call premium could be applied against the $1,800 margin requirement, reducing the actual amount that the investor would have to put up as collateral to $1,110.

In addition to the basic requirements, a brokerage firm may require that for a customer to participate in uncovered writing, he have a minimum equity in his account. This equity requirement may range from as low as $2,000 to as high as $10,000. In addition, some brokers require that a *maintenance* requirement be applied against each option written naked. This requirement, sometimes called a "kicker," is usually less than $250 per call and is generally used by the broker to ensure that, should the customer fail to respond to an assignment notice against his naked call, the commissions costs for buying and selling the underlying stock would be defrayed.

Naked Option Positions are Marked to the Market Daily. This means that the collateral requirement for the position is recomputed daily, just as in the short sale of stock. The same margin formula that was described above is applied and, if the stock has risen far enough, the customer will be required to deposit additional collateral or close the position. The need for such a mark to market is obvious. If the underlying stock should rise, the brokerage firm must ensure that the customer has enough collateral to cover the eventuality of buying the stock in the open market and selling it at the striking price if an assignment notice should be received against the naked call. The mark to market works to the customer's favor if the stock falls in price. Excess collateral is then released back into the customer's margin account, and may then be used for other purposes.

It is important to realize that, *in order to write a naked call, collateral is all that is required.* No cash need be "invested" if one owns securities with sufficient collateral loan value.

Example: An investor owns 100 shares of a stock selling at $60 per share. This stock is worth $6,000. If the loan rate on stock is 50% of $6,000, this investor has a collateral loan value equal to 50% of $6,000, or $3,000. This investor could write any of the naked calls in Table 5-2 without adding cash or securities to his account. Moreover, he would have satisfied a minimum equity requirement of at least $6,000, since his stock is equity.

This aspect of naked call writing—using collateral value to finance the writing—is attractive to many investors, since one is able to write calls and bring in premiums without disturbing his existing portfolio. Of course, if the stock underlying the naked call should rise too far in price, additional collateral may be called for by the broker because of the mark to market. Moreover, there is risk whether cash or collateral is used. If one buys in a naked call at a loss, he will then be spending cash, creating a debit in his account.

RISK AND REWARD

One can adjust the apparent risks and rewards from naked call writing by his selection of an in-the-money or out-of-the-money call. Writing an out-of-the-money call naked, especially one quite deeply out-of-the-money, offers a high probability of achieving a small profit. Writing an in-the-money call naked has the most profit potential, but it also has higher risks.

Example: XYZ is selling at 40 and the July 50 is selling for ½. This call could be sold naked. The probability that XYZ could rise to 50 by expiration has to be considered small, especially if there is not a large amount of time remaining in the life of the call. In fact, the stock could rise 25%, or 10 points, by expiration to a price of 50 and the call would still expire worthless. Thus this naked writer has a good chance of realizing a $50 profit, less commissions. There could, of course, be substantial risk in terms of potential profit versus potential loss if the stock rises substantially in price by expiration. Still, this apparent possibility of achieving additional limited income with a high probability of success has led many investors to use the collateral value of their portfolios to sell deeply out-of-the-money naked calls.

For those employing this technique, a favored position is to have a stock at or just about 15 and then sell the near-term option with striking price 20 naked. This option would sell for one-eighth or one-quarter, perhaps, although at times there might not be any bid at all. At this price, the stock would have to rally nearly one-third, or 33%, for the writer to lose money. Although there are not usually many optionable stocks selling at or just above $10 per share, these same out-of-the-money writers would also be attracted to selling a call with striking price 15 when the stock is at 10, because a 50% upward move by the stock would be required for a loss to be realized.

This strategy of selling deeply out-of-the-money calls has its apparent attraction in that the writer is assured of a profit unless the underlying stock can rally rather substantially before the call expires. The danger in this strategy is that one or two losses—perhaps only amounting to a couple of points each—could wipe out many periods of profits. The stock market does occasionally rally heavily in a short period, as witnessed by the January 1976, April 1978, and August 1982 markets. Thus the writer who is adopting this strategy cannot regard it as a "sure thing" and certainly cannot afford to establish the writes and forget them. Close monitoring is required if the market begins to rally and by no means should losses be allowed to accumulate. Even with monitoring, *this is not an attractive strategy and should generally be avoided.*

The opposite end of the spectrum in naked call writing is the writing of fairly deeply in-the-money calls. Since an in-the-money call would not have much time value premium in it, this writer does not have much leeway to the upside. If the stock rallies at all, the writer of the deeply in-the-money naked call will normally experience a loss. However, should the stock drop in price, this writer will make larger dollar profits than will the writer of the out-of-the-money call. The sale of the deeply in-the-money call simulates the profits that a short seller could make, at least until the stock drops close to the striking price, since the delta of a deeply in-the-money call is close to 1.

Example: XYZ is selling at 60 and the July 50 call is selling for 10½. If XYZ rises, the naked writer will lose money, because there is only ½ of a point of time value premium in the call. If XYZ falls, the writer will make profits on a point-for-point basis until the stock falls much closer to 50. That is, if XYZ dropped from 60 to 57, the call price would fall by almost 3 points as well. Thus for quick declines by the stock, the deeply in-the-money write can provide profits nearly equal to those that the short seller could accumulate. Notice that if XYZ falls all the way to 50, the profits on the written call will be large, but will be accumulating at a slower rate as the time value premium builds up with the stock near the striking price.

If one is looking to trade a stock on the short side for just a few points of movement, he might use a deeply in-the-money naked write instead of shorting the stock. His investment will be smaller—20% of the stock price for the write as compared to 50% of the stock price for the short sale—and his return will thus be larger (the requirement for the in-the-money amount is offset by applying the call's premium). The writer should take great caution in ascertaining that the call does have some time premium in it. He does not want to receive an assignment notice on the written call. It is easiest to find time premium in the more distant expiration series, so the writer would normally be safest from assignment by writing the longest-term deep in-the-money call if he wants to make a bearish trade in the stock.

Example: An investor thinks that XYZ could fall 3 or 4 points from its current price of 60 in a quick downward move and wants to capitalize on that move by writing a naked call. If the April 40 was the near-term call, he might have the choice of selling the April 40 at 20, the July 40 at $20\frac{1}{4}$, or the October 40 at $20\frac{1}{2}$. Since all three calls will drop nearly point for point with the stock in a move to 56 or 57, he should write the October 40, as it has the least risk of being assigned. A trader utilizing this strategy should limit his losses in much the same way a short seller would, by covering if the stock rallies, perhaps breaking through overhead technical resistance.

Rolling for Credits

Most writers of naked calls prefer to use one of the two strategies described above. The strategy of writing at-the-money calls, where the stock price is initially close to the striking price of the written call, is not widely utilized. This is because the writer who wants to limit risk will write an out-of-the-money call, whereas the writer who wants to make larger, quick trading profits will write an in-the-money call. There is, however, a strategy that is designed to utilize the at-the-money call. This strategy offers a high degree of eventual success, although there may be an accumulation of losses before the success point is reached. It is a strategy that requires large collateral backing, and is therefore only for the largest investors. We will call this strategy "rolling for credits."

In essence, the writer sells the most time premium that he can at any point in time. This would generally be the longest-term, at-the-money call. If the stock declines, the writer makes the time premium that he sold. However, if the stock rises in price, the writer rolls up for a credit. That is, when the stock reaches the next higher striking price, the writer buys back the calls that were originally sold and sells enough long-term calls at the higher strike to generate a credit. In this way, no debits are incurred, although a realized loss is taken on the rolling up. If the stock persists and rises to the next striking price, the process is repeated. Eventually, the stock will stop rising—they always do—and the last set of written options will expire worthless. At that time, the writer would make an overall profit consisting of an amount equal to all the credits that he had taken in so far.

There are really only two requirements for success in this strategy. The first is that the underlying stock eventually fall back—that it does not rise indefinitely. This is hardly a requirement; it is axiomatic that all stocks will eventually undergo a correction, so this is a simple requirement to satisfy. The second requirement is that the investor have enough collateral backing to stay with the strategy even if the stock runs up heavily against him. This is the harder requirement to satisfy and definitely makes the strategy only applicable to the largest investors. For those investors who do have the collateral available to participate in such a strategy, this is an excellent way of adding additional income to an overall portfolio. Recall that the collateral required for naked call writing may be in the form of cash or securities. Thus a large stock portfolio may be used to finance such a strategy through its loan value. There would be no margin interest charges incurred, because all transactions are credit transactions (no debits are created) and the securities portfolio would remain untouched unless the strategy was terminated before being allowed to reach completion.

Example: The basic strategy in the case of rising stock is shown in Table 5-3. Note that each transaction is a credit and that all (except the last) involve taking a realized loss.

This example assumes that the stock rose so quickly that a longer-term call was never available to roll into. That is, the October calls were always utilized. If there were a longer-term call available (the January series, for example), the writer should roll up and out as well. In this way, larger credits could be generated. The number of calls written increased from 5 to 15 and the collateral required as backing for the writing of the naked calls also increased heavily. Recall that the collateral requirement is equal to 15% of the stock price plus the call premium, less the amount by which the call is out-of-the-money. The premium may be used against

---

TABLE 5-3.
Rolling for credits when stock is rising.

Initially: XYZ = 50	
Sell 5 XYZ October 50's at 7	+ $3,500 credit
Later: XYZ rises to 60	
Buy 5 XYZ October 50's at 11 and	− 5,500 debit
sell 8 XYZ October 60's at 7	+ 5,600 credit
Later: XYZ rises further to 70	
Buy 8 XYZ October 60's at 11 and	− 8,800 debit
sell 15 XYZ October 70's at 6	+ 9,000 credit
Finally: XYZ falls and the October 70's expire worthless	
	Net gain = + $3,800

the collateral requirements. Using the stock and call prices of the example above, the investment is computed in Table 5-4. While the number of written calls has tripled from 5 to 15, the collateral requirement has quadrupled from $5,000 to $21,000. This is why the investor must have ample collateral backing to utilize this strategy. The general philosophy of the large investors who do apply this strategy is that they hope to eventually make a profit and, since they are using the collateral value of large security positions already held, they are not really investing any more money. The strategy does not really "cost" these investors anything. *All profits represent additional income and do not in any way disturb the underlying security portfolio.* Unfortunately, losses taken due to aborting the strategy could seriously affect the portfolio. This is why the investor *must* have sufficient collateral to carry through to completion.

The sophisticated strategist who implements this strategy will generally do more rolling than that discussed in the simple example above. First, if the stock drops, the calls will be rolled down to the next strike—for a credit—in order to constantly be selling the most time premium, which is always found in the longest-term at-the-money call. Furthermore, the strategist may want to roll out to a more distant expiration series whenever the opportunity presents itself. This rolling out, or forward, action is only taken when the stock is relatively unchanged from the initial price and there is no need to roll up or down.

This strategy is very attractive as long as one has enough collateral backing. Should one use up all of his available collateral, the strategy could collapse, causing substantial losses. It may not necessarily generate large rates of return in rising markets, but in stable or declining markets the generation of additional income can be quite substantial. Since the investor is not putting up any additional cash but is utilizing the collateral power of his present securities, his "investment" is actually zero. Any

---

TABLE 5-4.
Increase in collateral requirement.

Initially: XYZ = 50	
Sell 5 XYZ October 50's at 7	$ 5,000 collateral required
($3,500 net credit)	
Later: XYZ = 60	
Sell 8 XYZ October 60's at 7	
Buy 5 October 50's at 11	
($3,600 net credit to date)	$ 9,600 collateral required
Later: XYZ = 70	
Sell 15 XYZ October 70's at 6	
Buy 8 XYZ October 60's at 11	
($3,800 net credit to date)	$21,000 collateral required

profits represent additional income. The investor must be aware of one other factor that can upset the strategy. If a stock should rise so far as to require the number of calls to exceed the position limits set by the OCC, the strategy is ruined. In the example above, XYZ would probably have to rise to about a price of over 200, without a correction, before the sale of 1,000 calls would be required. If the strategist originally started with too many naked calls, he could potentially exceed the limit in a short time period. Rather than attempting to sell too many calls initially in any one security, the strategist should diversity several moderately sized positions throughout a variety of underlying stocks. In this way, he will probably never have to exceed the position limit of contracts short in any one security.

SUMMARY

In a majority of cases, naked call writing is applied as a deeply out-of-the-money strategy in which the investor uses the collateral value of his security holdings to participate in a strategy that offers a large probability of making a very limited profit. It is a poor strategy because one loss may wipe out many profits. The trader who desires an alternative to a short sale may use the sale of an in-the-money naked call in order to attempt to make a quick profit on a smaller investment than the short seller would have to make. Both of these strategies could have large risk if one does not have sufficient capital backing.

A better strategy, but one that is only available to very large investors, is to sell at-the-money calls naked, rolling up and forward for credits if the underlying stock rises in price. This strategy will eventually generate a profit if the underlying stock declines and is therefore a probable way of adding additional income to a large portfolio. However, it is essential that the investor have sufficient collateral backing.

Chapter 6

Ratio Call Writing

Two basic types of call writing have been described in the previous chapters: covered call writing, in which one owns the underlying stock and sells a call, and naked call writing. Ratio writing is a combination of these two types of positions.

THE RATIO WRITE

Simply stated, *ratio call writing* is the strategy in which one owns a certain number of shares of the underlying stock and sells calls against more shares than he owns. Thus there is a ratio of calls written to stock owned. The most common ratio is the 2:1 ratio, where one owns 100 shares of the underlying stock and sells 2 calls. Note that this type of position involves writing a number of naked call options as well as a number of covered options. This resulting position has both downside risk, as does a covered write, and unlimited upside risk, as does a naked write. The ratio write generally will provide much larger profits than either covered writing or naked writing if the underlying stock remains relatively unchanged during the life of the calls. However, the ratio write has two-sided risk, a quality absent from either covered or naked writing.

Generally, when an investor establishes a ratio write, he attempts to be neutral in outlook regarding the underlying stock. This means that he writes the calls with striking price closest to the current stock price.

Example: A ratio write is established by buying 100 shares of XYZ at 49 and selling two XYZ October 50 calls at 6 points each. If XYZ should decline in price and be anywhere below 50 at October expiration, the calls will expire worthless and the writer will make 12 points from the sale of the calls. Thus, even if XYZ drops 12 points to a price of 37, the ratio writer will break even. The stock loss of 12 points would be offset by a 12-point gain on the calls. As with any strategy in which calls are sold, the maximum profit occurs at the striking price of the written calls at expiration. In this example, if XYZ were at 50 at expiration, the calls would still expire worthless for a 12-point gain and the writer would have a 1-point profit on his stock, which has moved up from 49 to 50, for a total gain of 13 points. This position therefore has ample downside protection and a relatively large potential profit. Should XYZ rise above 50 by expiration, the profit will decrease and eventually become a loss if the stock rises too far. To see this, suppose XYZ is at 63 at October expiration. The calls will be at 13 points each, representing a 7-point loss on each call, because they were originally sold for 6 points apiece. However, there would be a 14-point gain on the stock, which has risen from 49 to 63. The overall net is a break-even situation at 63—a 14-point gain on the stock offset by 14 points of loss on the options (7 points each). Table 6-1 and Figure 6-1 summarize the profit and loss potential of this example at October expiration. The shape of the graph resembles a roof with its peak located at the striking price of the written calls—50. It is obvious that the position has both large upside risk above 63 and large downside risk below 37. Therefore, it is imperative that the ratio writer plan to take follow-up action if the stock should move outside these prices. Follow-up action will be discussed later. If the stock remains within the range 37 to 63,

TABLE 6-1.
Profit and loss at October expiration.

XYZ Price at Expiration	Stock Profit	Call Price	Profit on Calls	Total Profit
30	− $1,900	0	+ $1,200	− $ 700
37	− 1,200	0	+ 1,200	0
45	− 400	0	+ 1,200	+ 800
50	+ 100	0	+ 1,200	+ 1,300
55	+ 600	5	+ 200	+ 800
63	+ 1,400	13	− 1,400	0
70	+ 2,100	20	− 2,800	− 700

FIGURE 6-1.
Ratio write (2:1).

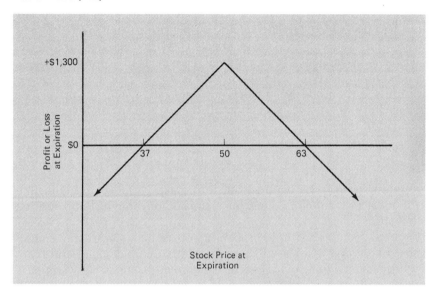

some profit will result before commission charges. This range between the downside break-even point and the upside break-even point is called the *profit range*.

This example represents essentially a neutral position, because the ratio writer will make some profit unless the stock falls by more than 12 points or rises by more than 14 points before the expiration of the calls in October. This is frequently an attractive type of strategy to adopt because, normally, stocks do not move very far in a 3- or 6-month time period. Consequently, this strategy has a rather high probability of making a limited profit. The profit in this example would, of course, be reduced by commission costs and margin interest charges if the stock is bought on margin.

Before discussing the specifics of ratio writing, such as investment required, selection criteria, and follow-up action, it may be beneficial to counter two fairly common objections to this strategy. The first objection, although not heard as frequently today as when listed options first began trading, is "why bother to buy 100 shares of stock and sell 2 calls? You will be naked one call. Why not just sell one naked call?" The ratio writing strategy and the naked writing strategy have very little in common except that both have upside risk. The profit graph for naked writing (Figure 5-1) bears no resemblance to the roof-shaped profit graph for a ratio write (Figure 6-1). Clearly, the two strategies are quite different in profile potential and in many other respects as well.

The second objection to ratio writing for the conservative investor is slightly more valid. The conservative investor may not feel comfortable with a position that has risk if the underlying stock moves up in price. This can be a psychological detriment to ratio writing—when stock prices are rising and everyone who owns stocks is happy making profits, the ratio writer is in danger of losing money. However, in a purely strategic sense, one should be willing to assume some upside risk in exchange for larger profits if the underlying stock does not rise heavily in price. The covered writer has upside protection all the way to infinity; that is, he has no upside risk at all. This cannot be the mathematically optimum situation, because stocks never rise to infinity. Rather, the ratio writer is engaged in a strategy that makes its profits in a price range more in line with the way stocks actually behave. In fact, if one were to try to set up the optimum strategy, he would want it to make its most profits in line with the most probable outcomes for a stock's movement. Ratio writing is such a strategy.

Figure 6-2 shows a simple probability curve for a stock's movement. It is most likely that a stock will remain relatively unchanged and there is very little chance that it will rise or fall a great distance. Now compare the results of the ratio writing strategy with the graph of probable stock outcomes. Notice that the ratio write and the probability curve have their "peaks" in the same area—that is, the ratio write makes its profits in the range of most likely stock prices, because there is only a small chance

FIGURE 6-2.
Stock price probability curve overlaid on profit graph of ratio write.

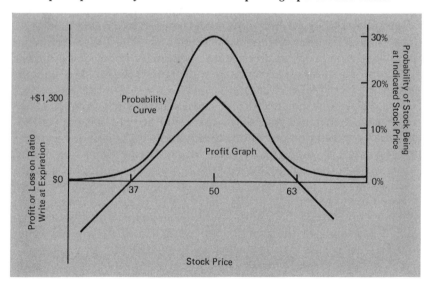

that any stock will increase or decrease by a large amount in a fixed period of time. The large losses are at the edges of the graph, where the probability curve gets very low, approaching zero probability.

INVESTMENT REQUIRED

The ratio writer has a combination of covered writes and naked writes. The margin requirements for each of these strategies have been described previously and the ratio writing strategy is just the sum of the requirements for a naked write and a covered write. Ratio writing is normally done in a margin account, although one could technically keep the stock in a cash account.

Example: Ignoring commissions, the investment required can be computed as follows: Buy 100 XYZ at 49 on 50% margin and sell 2 XYZ October 50 calls at 6 points each (Table 6-2). The commissions for buying the stock and selling the calls would be added to these requirements. A shorter formula (Table 6-3) is actually more desirable to use. It is merely a combination of the investment requirements listed in Table 6-2.

In addition to the basic requirement, there may be minimum equity requirements and maintenance requirements since there are naked calls involved. As these vary from one brokerage firm to another, it is best for the ratio writer to check with his broker to determine the equity and maintenance requirements. Again, since there are naked calls involved in ratio writing, there will be a mark to market of the position. If the stock should rise in price, the investor will have to put up more collateral.

TABLE 6-2.
Investment required.

Covered writing portion (buy 100 XYZ and sell 1 call)	
50% of stock price	$2,450
Less premium received	− 600
Requirement for covered portion	$1,850
Naked writing portion (sell 1 XYZ call)	
20% of stock price	$ 980
Less out-of-money amount	− 100
Plus call premium	+ 600
Less premium received	− 600
Requirement for naked portion	$ 880
Total requirement for ratio write	$2,730

TABLE 6-3.
Initial investment required for a ratio write.

70% of stock cost (XYZ = 49)	$3,430
Plus naked call premiums	+ 600
Less total premiums received	− 1,200
Plus or minus striking price differential on naked calls	− 100
Total requirement	$2,730 (plus commissions)

TABLE 6-4.
Collateral required with stock at upside break-even point of 63.

Covered writing requirement	$1,850 (see above)
20% of stock price (XYZ = 63)	1,260
Plus call premium	1,400
Less initial call premium received	− 600
Total requirement with XYZ at 63	$3,910

Generally, since one would normally take follow-up action at the upside break-even point, he should allow enough collateral for the position in case the stock rises to the upside break-even point. In the example that is being used, the upside break-even point is 63. Thus the requirement for the position with XYZ at 63 should be computed (Table 6-4). In this case, it is necessary to separate the covered writing requirement from the naked call requirement—the covered writing requirement does not change as the stock moves up, but the naked call requirement does.

It is conceivable that the ratio writer would want to stay with his original position as long as the stock did not penetrate the upside break-even point of 63. Therefore, he should allow for enough collateral to cover the eventuality of a move to 63. Assuming the October 50 call is at 14 in this case, he would need $3,910. This is the requirement that the ratio writer should be concerned with—not the initial collateral requirement—and he should therefore plan to invest $3,910 in this position, not $2,730 (the initial requirement). Obviously, he only has to put up $2,730, but from a strategic point of view, he should allow $3,910 for the position. If the ratio writer does this with all his positions, he would not receive a margin call even if all the stocks in his portfolio climbed to their upside break-even points.

SELECTION CRITERIA

To decide whether a ratio write is a desirable position, the writer must first determine the break-even points of the position. Once the break-even points are known, the writer can then decide if the position has a wide-enough profit range to allow for defensive action if it should become necessary. One simple way of determining if the profit range is wide enough is to require that the next higher and lower striking prices be within the profit range.

Example: The writer is buying 100 XYZ at 49 and selling 2 October 50 calls at 6 points apiece. It was seen, by inspection, that the break-even points in the position are 37 on the downside and 63 on the upside. There is a mathematical formula that allows one to quickly compute the break-even points for a 2:1 ratio write.

$$\text{Points of maximum profit} = \text{strike price} - \text{stock price} + 2 \times \text{call price}$$

$$\begin{aligned}\text{Downside break-even point} &= \text{strike price} - \text{points of maximum point} \\ &= \text{stock price} - 2 \times \text{call price}\end{aligned}$$

$$\text{Upside break-even point} = \text{strike price} + \text{points of maximum profit}$$

In this example, the points of maximum profit are $50 - 49 + 2 \times 6$, or 13. Thus the downside break-even point would be 37 $(50 - 13)$ and the upside break-even point would be 63 $(50 + 13)$. These numbers agree with the figures determined earlier by analyzing the position.

This profit range is quite clearly wide enough to allow for defensive action should the underlying stock risk to the next strike of 60 or fall to the next two lower strikes, at 45 and 40. In practice, a ratio write is not automatically a good position only because the profit range extends far enough. Theoretically, one would want the profit range to be wide in relation to the volatility to the underlying stock. If the range is wide in relation to the volatility and the break-even points encompass the next higher and lower striking prices, a desirable position is available. Volatile stocks are the best candidates for ratio writing since their premiums will more easily satisfy both these conditions. A nonvolatile stock may, at times, have relatively large premiums in its calls, but the resulting profit range may still not be wide enough numerically to ensure that follow-up action could be taken. Specific measures for determining volatility may be obtained from many data services and brokerage firms. Moreover, methods of computing volatility will be presented later in a chapter on mathematical applications.

Technical support and resistance levels are also important in establishing the position. If both support and resistance lie within the profit range, there is a better chance that the stock will remain within the range. A position should not necessarily be rejected if there is not support and resistance within the profit range, but the writer is then subjecting himself to a possible undeterred move by the stock in one direction or the other.

The ratio writer is generally a neutral strategist. He tries to take in the most time premium that he can to earn the premium erosion while the stock remains relatively unchanged. If one is more bullish on a particular stock, he can set up a 2:1 ratio write with out-of-the-money calls. This will allow more room to the upside than to the downside, and therefore makes the position slightly more bullish. Conversely, if one is more bearish on the underlying stock, he can write in-the-money calls in a 2:1 ratio.

There is another way to produce a slightly more bullish or bearish ratio write. This is to *change the ratio of calls written* to stock purchased. This method is also used to construct a neutral profit range when the stock is not close to a striking price.

Example: An investor is slightly bearishly inclined in his outlook for the underlying stock, so he might write more than than two calls for each 100 shares of stock purchased. His position might be buy 100 XYZ at 49 and sell 3 XYZ October 50 calls at 6 points each. This position breaks even at 31 on the downside because if the stock dropped by 18 points at expiration, the call profits would amount to 18 points and would produce a break-even situation. To the upside, the break-even point lies at 59½ for the stock at expiration. Each call would be at 9½ at expiration there and would thus be at a loss of 3½ points, for a total loss of 10½ points on the three calls. However, XYZ would have risen from 49 to 59½—a 10½-point gain—therefore producing a break-even situation. Again, a formula is available to aid in determining the break-even point for any ratio.

Maximum profit = (striking price − stock price) × round lots purchased + number of calls written × call price

Downside break-even = $\frac{\text{striking}}{\text{price}} - \frac{\text{maximum profit}}{\text{number of round lots purchased}}$

Upside break-even = $\frac{\text{striking}}{\text{price}} + \frac{\text{maximum profit}}{(\text{calls written} - \text{round lots purchased})}$

Note that in the case of a 2:1 ratio write, where the number of round lots purchased equals 1 and the number of calls written equals 2, these formulae reduce to the ones given earlier for the more common 2:1 ratio write. To verify that the formulae above are correct, insert the numbers from the most recent example.

Example: Three XYZ October 50 calls at a price of 6 were sold against the purchase of 100 XYZ at 49. The number of round lots purchased is 1.

Maximum profit = (50 − 49) × 1 + 3 × 6 = 19

Downside break-even = 50 − 19/1 = 31

Upside break-even = 50 + 19/(3 − 1) = 59½

In the 2:1 ratio writing example given earlier, the break-even points were 37 and 63. The 3:1 write has lower break-even points of 31 and 59½, reflecting the more bearish posture on the underlying stock.

A more bullish write is constructed by buying 200 shares of the underlying stock and writing three calls. To quickly verify that this ratio (3:2) is more bullish, again use 49 for the stock price, 6 for the call price, and now assume that two round lots were purchased.

Maximum profit = (50 − 49) × 2 + 3 × 6 = 20

Downside break-even = 50 − 20/2 = 40

Upside break-even = 50 + 20/(3 − 2) = 70

Thus this ratio of 3 calls against 200 shares of stock has break-even points of 40 and 70, reflecting a more bullish posture on the underlying stock.

A 2:1 ratio may not necessarily be neutral. There is, in fact, a mathematically correct way of determining exactly what a neutral ratio should be. *The neutral ratio is determined by dividing the delta of the written call into 1.* Assume that the delta of the XYZ October 50 call in the previous example is .60. Then the neutral ratio is 1.0/.60, or 5-to-3. This means that one might buy 300 shares and sell 5 calls. Using the formulae above, the details of this position can be observed:

Maximum profit = (50 − 49) × 3 + 5 × 6 = 33

Downside break-even = 50 − 33/3 = 39

Upside break-even = 50 + 33/(5 − 3) = 66½

According to the mathematics of the situation, then, this would be a neutral position initially. It is often the case that a 5:3 ratio is approximately neutral for an at-the-money call.

By now, the reader should have recognized a similarity between the ratio writing strategy and the reverse hedge (or simulated straddle) strategy presented in Chapter 4. The two strategies are the reverse of each other—in fact, this is where the reverse hedge strategy acquires its name. The ratio write has a profit graph that looks like a roof, while the reverse hedge has a profit graph that looks like a trough—the roof upside down. In one strategy the investor buys stock and sells calls while the other strategy is just the opposite—the investor shorts stock and buys calls. Which one is better? The answer depends on whether the calls are "cheap" or "expensive." Even though ratio writing has limited profits and potentially large losses, the strategy will result in a profit in a large majority of cases. The reverse hedge strategy, with its limited losses and potentially large profits, only provides profits on large stock moves—a less frequent event. Thus in stable markets, the ratio writing strategy is generally superior. However, in times of depressed option premiums, the reverse hedge strategy gains a distinct advantage. If calls are underpriced, the advantage lies with the buyer of calls, and that is inherent in the reverse hedge strategy.

THE VARIABLE RATIO WRITE

In ratio writing, one generally likes to establish the position when the stock is trading relatively close to the striking price of the written calls. However, it is sometimes the case that the stock is nearly exactly between two striking prices and neither the in-the-money nor the out-of-the-money call offers a neutral profit range. If this is the case, and one still wants to be in a 2:1 ratio of calls written to stock owned, he can sometimes write one in-the-money call *and* one out-of-the-money call against each 100 shares of common. This strategy, often termed a variable ratio write or trapezoidal hedge, serves to establish a more neutral profit range.

   Example: Given the following prices: XYZ common, 65; XYZ October 60 call, 8; and XYZ October 70 call, 3.
   If one were to establish a 2:1 ratio write with only the October 60's, he would have a somewhat bearish position. His profit range would be 49 to 71 at expiration. Since the stock is already at 65, this means that he would be allowing room for 16 points of downside movement and only 6 points on the upside. This is certainly not neutral. On the other hand, if he were to attempt to utilize only the October 70 calls in his ratio write, he would have a bullish position. This profit range for the October 70 ratio write would be 59 to 81 at expiration. In this case, the stock at 65 is too close to the downside break-even point in comparison to its distance from the upside break-even point.
   A more neutral position can be established by buying 100 XYZ and selling one October 60 and one October 70. This position has a profit range that is centered about the current stock price. Moreover, the new position has both an upside and a downside risk as does a more normal ratio write. However, now *the maximum profit can be obtained anywhere between the two strikes at expiration.* To see this, note that if XYZ is anywhere between 60 and 70 at expiration, the stock will be called away

at 60 against the sale of the October 60 call and the October 70 call will
expire worthless. It makes no difference whether the stock is at 61 or at
69—the same result will occur. Table 6-5 and Figure 6-3 depict the results
from this variable hedge at expiration. In the table, it is assumed that the
option is bought back at parity to close the position, but if the stock were
called away, the results would be the same.

Note that the shape of Figure 6-3 is something like a trapezoid. This
is the source of the name "trapezoidal hedge," although the strategy is
more commonly known as a variable hedge or variable ratio write. The
reader should observe that the maximum profit is indeed obtained if the
stock is anywhere between the two strikes at expiration. The maximum

TABLE 6-5.
Results at expiration of variable hedge.

XYZ Price at Expiration	XYZ Profit	October 60 Profit	October 70 Profit	Total Profit
45	− $2,000	+ $ 800	+ $ 300	− $900
50	− 1,500	+ 800	+ 300	− 400
54	− 1,100	+ 800	+ 300	0
60	− 500	+ 800	+ 300	+ 600
65	0	+ 300	+ 300	+ 600
70	+ 500	− 200	+ 300	+ 600
76	+ 1,100	− 800	− 300	0
80	+ 1,500	− $1,200	− 700	− 400
85	+ 2,000	− 1,700	− 1,200	− 900

FIGURE 6-3.
Variable ratio write (trapezoidal hedge).

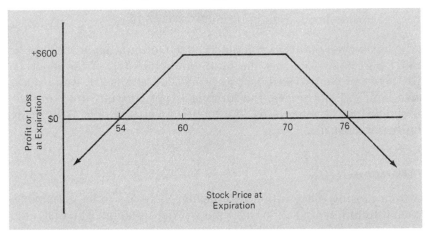

profit potential in this position, $600, is smaller than the maximum profit potential available from writing only the October 60's or only the October 70's. However, there is a vastly greater probability of realizing the maximum profit in a variable ratio write than there is of realizing the maximum profit in a normal ratio write.

The break-even points for a variable ratio write can be computed most quickly by first computing the maximum profit potential, which is equal to the time value that the writer takes in. The break-even points are then computed directly by subtracting the points of maximum profit from the lower striking price to get the downside break-even point and adding the points of maximum profit to the upper striking price to arrive at the upside break-even point. This is a similar procedure to that followed for a normal ratio write:

Points of maximum profit = total option premiums + lower striking price − stock price

Downside break-even point = lower striking price − points of maximum profit

Upside break-even point = higher striking price + points of maximum profit

Substituting the numbers from the example above will help to verify the formula. The total points of option premium brought in were 11 (8 for the October 60 and 3 for the October 70). The stock price was 65, and the striking prices involved were 60 and 70.

Points of maximum profit = 11 + 60 − 65 = 6

Downside break-even point = 60 − 6 = 54

Upside break-even point = 70 + 6 = 76

Thus the break-even points as computed by the formula agree with Table 6-5 and Figure 6-3. Note that the formula applies only if the stock is initially between the two striking prices and the ratio is 2:1. If the stock is above both striking prices, the formula is not correct. However, the writer should not be attempting to establish a variable ratio write with two in-the-money calls.

FOLLOW-UP ACTION

Aside from closing the position completely, there are three reasonable approaches to follow-up action in a ratio writing situation. The first, and most popular, is to roll the written calls up if the stock rises too far or to roll down if the stock drops too far. The second method uses the delta of the written calls. The third follow-up method is to utilize stops on the underlying stock to alter the ratio of the position as the stock moves either up or down. In addition to these types of defensive follow-up action, the investor must also have a plan in mind for taking profits as the written calls approach expiration. These types of follow-up action will be discussed separately.

Rolling Up or Down as a Defensive Action

The reader should already be familiar with the definition of a rolling action—the currently written calls are bought back and calls at a different striking price are written. The ratio writer can use rolling actions to his advantage to readjust his position if the underlying stock moves to the edges of his profit range.

The reason one of the selection criteria for a ratio write was to encompass both the next higher and lower striking prices was to facilitate the rolling actions that might become necessary as a follow-up measure. Since an option has its greatest time premium when the stock price and the striking price are the same, one would normally want to roll exactly at a striking price.

Example: A ratio writer bought 100 XYZ at 49 and sold two October 50 calls at 6 points each. Subsequently, the stock drops in price and the following prices exist: XYZ, 40; XYZ October 50, 1; and XYZ October 40, 4.

One would roll down to the October 40 calls by buying back the 2 October 50's that he is short and selling 2 October 40's. In so doing, he would reestablish a somewhat neutral position. His profit on the buy-back of the October 50 calls would be 5 points each—they were originally sold for 6—and he would realize a 10-point gain on the two calls. This 10-point gain effectively reduces his stock cost from 49 to 39, so that he now has the equivalent of the following position: long 100 XYZ at 39 and short 2 XYZ October 40 calls at 4. This adjusted ratio write has a profit range of 31 to 49 and is thus a new, neutral position with the stock currently at 40. He is now in a position where he can make profits if XYZ remains near this level or he could take further defensive action if the stock experiences a relatively large change in price again.

Defensive action to the upside—rolling up—works in much the same manner.

Example: The initial position again consists of buying 100 XYZ at 49 and selling two October 50 calls at 6. If XYZ then rose to 60, the following prices might exist: XYZ, 60; XYZ October 50, 11; and XYZ October 60, 6.

The ratio writer could thus roll this position up to reestablish a neutral profit range. If he bought back the two October 50 calls, he would take a 5-point loss on each one for a net loss on the calls of 10 points. This would effectively raise his stock cost by 10 points to a price of 59. The rolled-up position would then be long 100 XYZ at 59 and short 2 October 60 calls at 6. This new, neutral position has a profit range of 47 to 73 at October expiration.

In both of the examples above, the writer could have closed out the ratio write at a very small profit of about 1 point before commissions. This would not be advisable, because of the relatively large stock commissions, unless he expects the stock to continue to move dramatically. Either rolling up or rolling down gives the writer a fairly wide new profit range to work with and he could easily expect to make more than 1 point of profit if the underlying stock stabilizes at all.

Having to take rolling defensive action immediately after the position is established is the most detrimental case. If the stock moves very quickly after having set up the position, there will not be much time for time value premium erosion in the written calls, and this will make for smaller profit ranges after the roll is done. It may be useful to use technical support and resistance levels as keys for when to take rolling action if these levels are near the break-even points and/or striking prices.

It should be noted that this method of defensive action—rolling at or near striking prices—automatically means that one is buying back little or no time premium and is selling the greatest amount of time premium currently available. That is, if the stock rises, the call's premium will consist mostly of intrinsic value and very little of time premium value since it is substantially in-the-money. Thus the writer who rolls up by buying back this in-the-money call is buying back mostly intrinsic value and is selling a call at the next strike. This newly sold call consists mostly of time value. By continually buying back "real" or intrinsic value and by selling "thin air" or time value, the writer is taking the optimum neutral action at any given time.

If a stock undergoes a dramatic move in one direction or the other, the ratio writer will not be able to keep pace with the dramatic movement by remaining in the same ratio.

Example: If XYZ was originally at 49, but then undergoes a fairly straight-line move to 80 or 90, the ratio writer who maintains a 2:1 ratio will find himself in a deplorable situation. He will have accumulated rather substantial losses on the calls and will not be able to compensate for these losses by the gain in the underlying stock. A similar situation could arise to the downside. If XYZ were to plunge from 49 to 20, the ratio writer would make a good deal of profit from the calls by rolling down, but may still have a larger loss in the stock itself than the call profits can compensate for.

Many ratio writers who are large enough to diversify their positions into a number of stocks will continue to maintain 2:1 ratios on all their positions and will just close out a position which has gotten out of hand by running dramatically to the upside or to the downside. They feel that the chances of such a dramatic move occurring are small, and that they will take the infrequent losses in such cases in order to be basically neutral on the other stocks in their portfolio.

There is, however, a way to combat this sort of dramatic move. This is done by *altering the ratio* of the covered write as the stock moves either up or down. For example, as the underlying stock moves up dramatically in price, the ratio writer can decrease the number of calls outstanding against his long stock each time that he rolls. Eventually, the ratio might decrease as far as 1:1—which is nothing more than a covered writing situation. As long as the stock continues to move in the same upward direction, the ratio writer who is decreasing his ratio of calls outstanding will be giving more and more weight to the stock gains in the ratio write and less and less weight to the call losses. It is interesting to note that this decreasing ratio effect can also be produced by buying extra shares of stock at each new striking price as the stock moves up and simultaneously keeping the number of outstanding calls written constant. In either case, the ratio of calls outstanding to stock owned is reduced.

When the stock moves down dramatically, a similar action can be taken to increase the number of calls written to stock owned. Normally, as the stock falls, one would sell out some of his long stock and roll the calls down. Eventually, after the stock falls far enough, he would be in a naked writing position. The idea is the same here—as the stock falls, more weight is given to the call profits and less weight is given to the stock losses that are accumulating.

This sort of strategy is more oriented to extremely large investors or to firm traders, market-makers, and the like. Commissions will be exorbitant if frequent rolls are to be made and only those investors who pay very small commissions or who have such a large holding that their commissions are quite small on a percentage basis will be able to profit substantially from such a strategy.

Adjusting with the Delta

The delta of the written calls can be used to determine the correct ratio to be used in this ratio-adjusting defensive strategy. The basic idea is to use the call's delta to remain as neutral as possible at all times.

Example: An investor initially sets up a neutral 5:3 ratio of XYZ October 50 calls to XYZ stock, as was determined previously. The stock is at 49 and the delta is .60. Furthermore, suppose the stock rises to 57 and the call now has a delta of .80. The neutral ratio would currently be 1/.80 (= 1.20) or 5:4. The ratio writer could thus buy another 100 shares of the underlying stock. Alternatively, he might buy in one of the short calls.

In this particular example, buying in one call would produce a 4:3 ratio, which is not absolutely correct. If he had had a larger position initially, it would be easier to adjust to fractional ratios. When the stock declines, it is necessary to increase the ratio. This can be accomplished by either selling more calls or selling out some of the long stock. In theory, these adjustments could be made constantly to keep the position neutral. In practice, one would allow for a few points of movements by the underlying stock before adjusting. If the underlying stock rises too far, it may be logical for the neutral strategist to adjust by rolling up. Similarly, he would also roll down if the stock fell to or below the next lower strike. The neutral ratio in that case is determined by using the delta of the option into which he is rolling.

Example: With XYZ at 57, an investor is contemplating rolling up to the October 60's from his present position of long 300 shares and short 5 XYZ October 50's. If the October 60 has a delta of .40, the neutral ratio for the October 60's is 2.5:1 (1 ÷ .40). Since he is already long 300 shares of stock, he should now be short 7.5 calls (3 × 2.5). Obviously, he would sell 7 or 8, probably depending on his short-term outlook for the stock.

If one prefers to adopt an even more sophisticated approach, he can make adjustments between striking prices by altering his stock position, and can make adjustments if the stock reaches a new striking price by rolling up or down. For those who prefer formulae, the following ones summarize this information:

1. When establishing a new position or when rolling up or down, at the next strike:

$$\text{Number of calls to sell} = \frac{\text{round lots held long}}{\text{delta of call to be sold}}$$

   Note: When establishing a new position, one must first decide how many shares of the underlying stock he can buy before utilizing the formula; 1,000 shares would be a workable amount.

2. When adjusting between strikes by buying or selling stock:

Number of round lots to buy

$$= \text{current delta} \times \text{number of short calls} - \text{round lots held long}$$

Note: If a negative number results, stock should be sold, not bought.

These formulae can be verified by using the numbers from the examples above. For example, when the delta of the October 50 was .80 with the stock at 57, it was seen that buying 100 shares of stock would reestablish a neutral ratio.

$$\text{Number of round lots to buy} = .80 \times 5 - 3 = 4 - 3 = 1$$

Also, if the position was to be rolled up to the October 60 (delta = .40), it was seen that 7.5 October 60's would theoretically be sold:

$$\text{Number of calls to sell} = \frac{3}{.40} = 7.5$$

There is a more general approach to this problem, one that can be applied to any strategy no matter how complicated. It involves computing whether the position is net short or net long. The net position is reduced to an equivalent number of shares of common stock and is commonly called the "equivalent stock position" (ESP). There is a simple formula for the equivalent stock position of any option position:

$$\text{ESP} = \text{option quantity} \times \text{delta} \times \text{shares per option}$$

Example: Suppose that one is long 10 XYZ July 50 calls, which currently have a delta of .45. The option is an option on 100 shares of XYZ. Thus, the ESP can be computed:

$$\text{ESP} = 10 \times .45 \times 100 = 450 \text{ shares}$$

This is merely saying that owning 10 of these options is *equivalent* to owning 450 shares of the underlying common stock, XYZ. The reader should already understand this, in that an option with a delta of .45 would appreciate by .45 points if the common stock moved up 1 dollar. Thus, 10 options would appreciate by 4.5 points, $450. Obviously, 450 shares of common stock would also appreciate by $450 if they moved up by one point.

Note that there are some options—those that result from a stock split—that are for more than 100 shares. The inclusion of the term "shares per option" in the formula accounts for the fact that such options are equivalent to a different amount of stock than most options.

The ESP of an entire option and stock position can be computed, even if there are several different options included in the position. The advantage of this simple calculation is that an entire, possibly complex, option position can be reduced to one number. The ESP shows how the position will behave for short-term market movements.

Look again at the previous example of a ratio write. The position was long 300 shares and short 5 options with a current delta of .80 after the stock had risen to 57. The ESP of the 5 October 50's is short 400 shares (5 × .80 × 100 shares per option). The position is also long 300 shares of stock, so the total ESP of this ratio write is short 100 shares.

This figure gives the strategist a measure of perspective on his position. He now knows that he has a position that is the equivalent of being short 100 shares of XYZ. Perhaps he is bearish on XYZ and therefore decides to do nothing. That would be fine—at least he knows that his position is short.

Normally, however, the strategist would want to adjust his position. Again returning to the previous example, there are several choices that he has in reducing the ESP back to neutral. An ESP of 0 is considered to be a perfectly neutral position. Obviously, one could buy 100 shares of XYZ to reduce the 100-share delta short. Or, given that the delta of the October 50 call is .80, he could buy in 1.25 of these short calls (obviously he could only buy 1; fractional options cannot be purchased).

In later chapters, there will be more discussions and examples using the ESP. It is a vital concept that no strategist who is operating positions involving multiple options should be without. The only requirement for calculating it is to know the delta of the options in one's position. Those are easily obtainable from one's broker or a number of computer services.

For investors who do not have the funds or are not in a position to utilize such a ratio adjusting strategy, there is a less time-consuming method of taking defensive action in a ratio write.

Using Stop Orders as a Defensive Strategy

A ratio writer can use buy or sell stops on his stock position in order to automatically and unemotionally adjust the ratio of his position. This type of defensive strategy is not an aggressive one and will provide some profits unless a whipsaw occurs in the underlying stock.

As an example of how the use of stop orders can aid the ratio writer, let us again assume that the same basic position was established by buying XYZ at 49 and selling two October 50 calls at 6 points each. This produces a profit range of 37 to 63 at expiration. If the stock begins to move up too far or to fall too far, the ratio writer can adjust the ratio of calls short to stock long automatically through the use of stop orders on his stock.

Example: An investor places a stop order to buy 100 shares of XYZ at 57 at the same time that he establishes the original position. If XYZ should get to 57, the stop would be set off and he would then own 200 shares of XYZ and be short 2 calls. That is, he would have a 200-share covered write of XYZ October 50 calls.

To see how such an action affects his overall profit picture, note that his average stock cost is now 53—he paid 49 for the first 100 shares and then paid 57 for the second 100 shares bought via the stop order. Since he sold the calls at 6 each, he essentially has a covered write in which he bought stock at 53 and sold calls for 6 points. This does not represent a lot of profit potential, but it will ensure some profit unless the stock falls back below the new break-even point. This new break-even point is 47—the stock cost, 53, less the 6 points received for the call. He will realize the maximum profit potential from the covered write as long as the stock remains above 50 until expiration. Since the stock is already at 57, the probabilities are relatively strong that it will remain above 50 and even stronger that it will remain above 47 until the expiration date. If the buy stop order was placed just above a technical resistance area, this probability is even better.

Hence *the use of a buy stop order on the upside allows the ratio writer to automatically convert the ratio write into a covered write* if the stock moves up too far. Once the stop goes off, he has a position that will make some profit as long as the stock does not experience a fairly substantial price reversal.

Downside protective action using a sell stop order works in a similar manner.

Example: The investor placed a sell stop for 100 shares of stock after establishing the original position. If this sell stop were placed at 41, for example, the position would become a naked cell writer's position if the stock fell to 41. At that time, the 100 shares of stock that he owned would be sold, at an 8-point loss, but he would have the capability of making 12 points from the sale of his two calls as long as the stock remained below 50 until expiration. In fact, his break-even point after converting into the naked write would actually be 52 at expiration, since at that price, the calls could be bought back for 2 points each, or 8 points total profit, to offset the 8-point loss on the stock. This action limits his profit potential but will allow him to make some profit as long as the stock does not experience a strong price reversal and climb back above 52 by expiration.

There are several advantages to using this method of protection for inexperienced ratio writers. First, the implementation of the protective strategies—buying an extra 100 shares of stock if the stock moves up, or selling out the 100 shares that are long if the stock moves down—is unemotional *if the stop orders are placed at the same time that the original position is established.* This prevents the writer from attempting to impose his own market judgment "in the heat of battle." That is, if XYZ has moved up to 57, the writer who has not placed a buy stop order may be tempted to wait just a little longer, hoping for the stock to fall in price. If the stop orders are placed as soon as the position is established, a great deal of emotion is removed. Second, *this strategy will produce some profit*—assuming that the stops are properly placed—*as long as the stock does not whipsaw*, or experience a price reversal and go back through the striking price in the other direction. Most follow-up actions in *any* writing strategy, whether they involve rolling actions or the use of stops, are subject to losses if the stock whipsaws back and forth.

The disadvantage to using this type of protective action is that the writer may be tying up relatively large amounts of capital in order to make only a small profit after the stop order is set off. However, in a diversified portfolio, only a small percentage of the stocks may go through their stop points, thereby still allowing the ratio writer plenty of profit potential on his other positions.

Once either the buy stop or the sell stop is set off, the writer still needs to watch the position. His first action *after one stop is touched should be to cancel the other stop order*, because the stops are good orders until they are canceled. From that time on, the writer need do nothing if the stock does not experience a price reversal. In fact, he would just as soon have the stock experience a greater move in the same direction to minimize the chances of a price reversal.

If a price reversal does occur, the most conservative action is to close out the position just after the stock crosses back through the striking price. This will normally result in a small loss, but, again, it should happen in only a relatively small number of his positions. Recall that in a limited profit strategy such as ratio writing, it is important to limit losses as well. If the stock does indeed whipsaw and the position is closed, the writer will still have most of his original equity and can then reestablish a new position in another underlying stock.

Placement of Stops. The writer would ideally like to place his stops at prices that allow a reasonable rate of return to be made, while also having the stops far enough away from the original striking price to reduce the chances of a whipsaw occurring. It is a fairly simple matter to calculate the returns that could be made, after commissions are included, if one or the other of the stops goes off. Dividends should be included as well, since they will accrue to the writer. If the writer is willing to accept returns as low as 5% annually for those positions that go through their stop points, he will be able to place his stops farther from the original striking price. If he feels that he needs a higher return when the stops go off, the stops must be placed closer in. As with any stock or option investment, the writer who operates in large size will experience less of a commission charge, percentagewise. That is, the writer who is buying 500 shares of stock and selling 10 calls to start with, will be able to place his stop points farther out than the writer who is buying 100 shares of stock and selling 2 calls.

Technical analysis can be helpful in selecting the stop points as well. If there is resistance overhead, the buy stop should be placed above that resistance. Similarly, if there is support, the sell stop should be placed beneath the support point. Later, when straddles are discussed, it will be seen that this type of strategy can be operated at less of a net commission charge since the purchase and sale of stock will not be involved.

Closing Out the Write

The methods of follow-up action discussed above deal with the eventuality of preventing losses. However, if all goes well, the ratio write will begin to accrue profits as the stock remains relatively close to the original striking price. *To retain these paper profits that have accrued, it is necessary to move the protective action points closer together.*

Example: XYZ is at 51 after some time has passed and the calls are at 3 points each. The writer would, at this time, have an unrealized profit of $800—$200 from the stock purchase at 49 and $300 each on the two calls, which were originally sold at 6 points each. Recall that the maximum potential profit from the position—if XYZ were exactly at 50 at expiration—is $1,300. The writer would like to adjust the protective points so that nearly all of the $800 paper profit might be retained while still allowing for the profit to grow to the $1,300 maximum.

At expiration, $800 profit would be realized if XYZ were at 45 or at 55. This can be verified by referring again to Table 6-1 and Figure 6-1. The 45 to 55 range is now the area that the writer must be concerned with. The original profit range of 39 to 61 has become meaningless, since the position has performed well to this point in time. If the writer is using the rolling method of protection, he would roll forward to the next expiration series if the stock were to reach 45 or 55. If he is using the stop-out method of protection, he could either merely close the position at 45 or 55 or he could also roll to the next expiration series and readjust his stop points. The neutral strategist using deltas would determine the number of calls to roll forward to by using the delta of the longer-term call.

By moving the protective action points closer together, the ratio writer can then adjust his position while he still has a profit; he is attempting to "lock in" his profit. As even more time passes and expiration draws nearer, it may be possible to move the protective points even closer together. Thus, as the position continues to improve over time, the writer should be constantly "telescoping" his action points and finally roll out to the next expiration series. This is generally the more prudent move, because the commissions to sell stock to close the position and then buy another stock to establish yet another position may prove to be prohibitive. In summary, then, as a ratio write nears expiration, the writer should be concerned with an ever-narrowing range within which his profits can grow but outside of which his profits could dissipate if he does not take action.

SUMMARY

Ratio writing is a viable, neutral strategy that can be employed with differing levels of sophistication. The initial ratio of short calls to long stock can be selected simplistically by comparing one's opinion for the underlying stock with projected break-even points from the position. In a more sophisticated manner, the delta of the written calls can be used to determine the ratio.

Since the strategy has potential large losses either to the upside or the downside, follow-up action is mandatory. This action can be taken by simple methods such as rolling up or down in a constant ratio, or by placing stop orders on the underlying stock. A more sophisticated technique involves using the delta of the option to either adjust the stock position or to roll to another call. By using the delta, a theoretically neutral position can be maintained at all times.

Ratio writing is a relatively sophisticated strategy that involves selling naked calls. It is therefore not suitable for all investors. Its attractiveness lies in the fact that vast quantities of time value premium are sold and the strategy is profitable for the most probable price outcomes of the underlying stock. It has a relatively large probability of making a limited profit.

AN INTRODUCTION TO CALL SPREAD STRATEGIES

A *spread* is a transaction in which one simultaneously buys one option and sells another option, with different terms, on the same underlying security. In a call spread, the options are all calls. The basic idea behind spreading is that the strategist is using the sale of one call to reduce the risk of buying another call. The short call in a spread is considered covered, for margin purposes, only if the long call has an expiration date equal to or longer than the short call. Before delving into the individual types of spreads, it may be beneficial to cover some general facts that pertain to most spread situations.

All spreads fall into three broad categories: *vertical, horizontal,* or *diagonal. A vertical spread* is one in which the calls involved have the same expiration date but different striking prices. An example might be to buy the XYZ October 30 and sell the October 35 simultaneously. A *horizontal spread* is one in which the calls have the same striking price but different expiration dates. This would be a horizontal spread: Sell the XYZ January 35 and buy the XYZ April 35. A *diagonal spread* is any combination of vertical and horizontal and may involve calls that have different expiration dates as well as different striking prices. These three names that classify the spreads can be related to the way option prices are listed in any newspaper summary of closing option prices. A vertical spread would involve two options from the same column in a newspaper listing. Newspaper columns run vertically. A horizontal spread would involve two calls whose prices are listed in the same row in a newspaper listing—rows are horizontal. This relationship to the listing format in newspapers is not important, but it is an easy way to remember what vertical spreads and horizontal spreads are. There are several types of vertical and horizontal spreads, and many of them will be discussed in detail in the following chapters.

Spread Order

The term "spread" designates not only a type of strategy, but a type of order as well. *All spread transactions in which both sides of the spread are opening (initial) transactions must be done in a margin account.* This means that the customer must generally maintain a minimum equity in the account—normally $2,000. Some brokerage houses may also have a maintenance requirement, or "kicker."

It *is* possible to transact a spread in a cash account, but one of the sides must be a closing transaction. In fact, many of the follow-up actions taken in the covered writing strategy are actually spread transactions. Suppose that a covered writer is currently short one XYZ April call against 100 shares of the underlying stock. If he wants to roll forward to the July 35 call, he will be buying back the April 35 and selling the July 35 simultaneously. This is a spread transaction, technically, since one call is being bought and the other is being sold. However, in this transaction the buy side is a closing transaction and the sell side is an opening transaction. This type of spread could be done in a cash account. Whenever a covered writer is rolling—up, down, or forward—he should place the order as a spread order to facilitate a better price execution.

The spreads to be discussed in the following chapters are predominantly spread strategies, ones in which both sides of the spread are opening transactions. These are designed to have their own profit and risk potentials, and are not merely follow-up actions to some previously discussed strategy.

When a spread order is entered, the options being bought and sold must be specified. Two other items must be specified as well—the price at which the spread is to be executed and whether that price is a credit or a debit. If the total price of the spread results in a cash inflow to the spread strategist, the spread is a *credit spread*. This merely means that the sell side of the spread brings in a higher price than is paid for the buy side of the spread. If the reverse is true—that is, there is a cash outflow from the spread transaction—the spread is said to be a *debit spread*. This means that the buy side of the spread costs more than is received from the sell side. It is also common to refer to the purchased side of the spread as the *long side* and to refer to the written side of the spread as the *short side*.

The price at which a certain spread can be executed is generally *not* the difference between the last sale prices of the two options involved in the spread.

Example: An investor wants to buy an XYZ October 30 and simultaneously sell an XYZ October 35 call. If the last sale price of the October 30 was 4 points and the last sale price of the October 35 was 2 points, it does not necessarily mean that the spread could be done for a 2-point debit (the difference in the last sale prices). In fact, *the only way to determine the market price for a spread transaction is to know what the bid and asked prices of the options involved are.* Suppose the following quotes are available on these two calls:

	Bid	Asked	Last Sale
October 30 call	$3\frac{7}{8}$	$4\frac{1}{8}$	4
October 35 call	$1\frac{7}{8}$	2	2

Since the spread in question involves buying the October 30 call and selling the October 35, the spreader will, at market, have to pay $4\frac{1}{8}$ for the October 30 (the asked or offering quote) and will receive only 1⅞ (the bid quote) for the October 35. This results in a debit of 2¼ points, significantly more than the 2-point difference in the last sale prices. Of course, one is free to specify any price he wants for any type of transaction. One might enter this spread order at a 2⅛-point debit and could have a reasonable chance of having the order filled if the floor broker can do better than the bid side on the October 35 or better than the offering side on the October 30.

   The point to be learned here is that *one cannot assume that last sale prices are indicative of the price at which a spread transaction can be executed.* This makes computer analysis of spread transactions via closing price data somewhat difficult. Some computer data services offer—generally at a higher cost—closing bid and asked prices as well as closing sale prices. If a strategist is forced to operate with closing prices only, however, he should attempt to build some screens into his output to allow for the fact that last sale prices might not be indicative of the price at which the spread can be executed. One simple method for screening is to look only at relatively liquid options—that is, those that have traded a substantial number of contracts during the previous trading day. If an option is experiencing a great deal of trading activity, there is a much better chance that the current quote is "tight"—that is, the bid and offering prices are quite close to the last sale price.
   In the early days of listed options, it was somewhat common practice to *"leg"* into a spread. That is, the strategist would place separate buy and sell orders for the two transactions comprising his spread. As the listed markets have developed—adding depth and liquidity—*it is generally a poor idea to leg into a spread.* If the floor broker handling the transaction knows the entire transaction, he has a much better chance of "splitting a quote," buying on the bid, or selling on the offering. "*Splitting a quote*" merely means executing at a price that is between the current bid and asked prices. For example, if the bid is 3⅞ and the offering is 4⅛, a transaction at a price of 4 would be "splitting the quote."
   The public customer must be aware that spread transactions may involve substantially higher commission costs, because there are twice as many calls involved in any one transaction. Some brokers offer slightly lower rates for spread transactions, but these are not nearly as low as spreads in commodity trading, for example.

Chapter 7

Bull Spreads

The *bull spread* is one of the most popular forms of spreading. In this type of spread one buys a call at a certain striking price and sells a call at a higher striking price. Generally, both options have the same expiration date. This is a vertical spread. *A bull spread tends to be profitable if the underlying stock moves up in price—hence it is a bullish position.* The spread has both limited profit potential and limited risk. Although both can be substantial percentagewise, the risk can never exceed the net investment. In fact, a bull spread requires a smaller dollar investment and therefore has a smaller maximum dollar loss potential than does an outright call purchase of a similar call.

Example: The following prices exist:

XYZ common, 32;

XYZ October 30 call, 3; and

XYZ October 35 call, 1.

A bull spread would be established by buying the October 30 call and simultaneously selling the October 35 call. Assume that this could be done at the indicated 2-point debit. *A call bull spread is always a debit transaction*, since the call with the lower striking price must always trade for more than a call with a higher price, if both have the same expiration date. Table 7-1 and Figure 7-1 depict the results of this transaction at expiration. The indicated call profits or losses would be realized if the calls were liquidated at parity at expiration. Note that *the spread has a maximum profit and that this profit is realized if the stock is anywhere above the higher striking price at expiration.* The maximum loss is realized if the stock is anywhere below the lower strike at expiration and is equal to the net investment, 2 points in this example. Moreover, there is a break-

TABLE 7-1.
Results at expiration of bull spread.

XYZ Price at Expiration	October 30 Profit	October 35 Profit	Total Profit
25	− $ 300	+ $100	− $200
30	− 300	+ 100	− 200
32	− 100	+ 100	0
35	+ 200	+ 100	+ 300
40	+ 700	− 400	+ 300
45	+ 1,200	− 900	+ 300

FIGURE 7-1.
Bull spread.

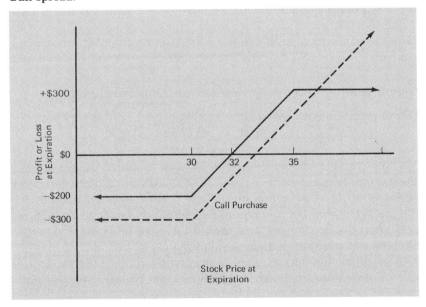

even point which always lies between the two striking prices at expiration. In this example, the break-even point is 32. All bull spreads have profit graphs with the same shape as the one shown above when the expiration dates are the same for both calls.

The investor who establishes this position is bullish on the underlying stock, but is generally looking for a way to hedge himself. If he were rampantly bullish, he would merely buy the October 30 call outright. However, the sale of the October 35 call against the purchase of the October 30 allows him to have a position that will outperform the outright purchase of the October 30—dollarwise—as long as the stock does not rise above 36 by expiration. This fact is demonstrated by the dashed line on Figure 7-1. Therefore, *the strategist establishing the bull spread is bullish, but not overly so.* To verify that this comparison is correct, note that if one bought the October 30 call outright for 3 points, he would have a 3-point profit at expiration if XYZ were at 36. Both strategies have a 3-point profit at 36 at expiration. Below 36, the bull spread does better because the sale of the October 35 call brings in the extra point of premium. Above 36 at expiration, the outright purchase outperforms the bull spread, because there is no limit on the profits that can occur in an outright purchase situation.

The net investment required for a bull spread is the net debit plus commissions. Since the spread must be transacted in a margin account, there will generally be a minimum equity requirement imposed by the brokerage firm. In addition, there may be a maintenance requirement by some brokers. Suppose that one was establishing 10 spreads at the prices given in the example above. His investment, before commissions, would be $2,000 ($200 per spread), plus commissions. It is a simple matter to compute the break-even point and the maximum profit potential of a call bull spread:

Break-even point = lower striking price + net debit of spread

Maximum profit potential = higher striking price − lower striking
price − net debit of spread

In the example above, the net debit was 2 points. Therefore, the break-even point would be 30 + 2, or 32. The maximum profit potential would be 35 − 30 − 2, or 3 points. These figures agree with Table 7-1 and Figure 7-1. *Commissions may represent a significant percentage of the profit and net investment*, and should therefore be calculated *before* establishing the position. If these commissions are included in the net debit to establish the spread, they conveniently fit into the preceding formulae. Commission charges can be reduced, percentagewise, by spreading a larger quantity of calls. For this reason, it is generally advisable to spread at least 5 options at a time.

DEGREES OF AGGRESSIVENESS

Aggressive Bull Spread

Depending on how the bull spread is constructed, it may be an extremely aggressive or more conservative position. The most commonly used bull spread is of the *aggressive* type—the stock is generally well below the higher striking price when the spread is established. This aggressive bull spread generally has the ability to generate substantial percentage returns if the underlying stock should rise in price far enough by expiration. *Aggressive bull spreads are most attractive when the underlying common stock is relatively close to the lower striking price at the time the spread is established.* A bull spread established under these conditions will generally be a low-cost spread with substantial profit potential, even after commissions are included.

Extremely Aggressive Bull Spread

An extremely aggressive type of bull spread is the "out-of-the-money" spread. In such a spread, *both* calls are out-of-the-money when the spread is established. These spreads are extremely inexpensive to establish and have large potential profits if the stock should climb to the higher striking price by expiration. However, they are usually quite deceptive in nature— the underlying stock has only a relatively remote chance of advancing such a great deal by expiration and the spreader could realize a 100% loss of his investment even if the underlying stock advances moderately, since both calls are out-of-the-money. This spread is akin to buying a deeply out-of-the-money call as an outright speculation. It is not recommended that such a strategy be pursued with more than a very small percentage of one's speculative funds.

Least Aggressive Bull Spread

Another type of bull spread can be found occasionally—the "in-the-money" spread. In this situation, both calls are in-the-money. This is a much less aggressive position, since it offers a large probability of realizing the maximum profit potential, although that profit potential will be substantially smaller than the profit potentials offered by the more aggressive bull spread.

Example: XYZ is at 37 some time before expiration, and the October 30 call is at 7 while the October 35 call is at 4. Both calls are in-the-money and the spread would cost 3 points (debit) to establish. The maximum profit potential is 2 points, but it would be realized as long as XYZ were above 35 at expiration. That is, XYZ could *fall* by 2 points and the spreader would still make his maximum profit. This is certainly a more conservative position than the aggressive spread described above. The commission cost in this spread would be substantially larger than those in the spreads above, which involve less expensive options initially, and they should therefore be figured into one's profit calculations before entering into the spread transaction. Since this stock would have to decline 7 points to fall below 30 and cause a loss of the entire investment, it would have to be considered a rather low probability event. This facts adds to the less aggressive nature of this type of spread.

RANKING BULL SPREADS

To accurately compare the risk/reward potentials of the many bull spreads that are available in a given day, one has to use a computer to perform the mass calculations. It is possible to use a strictly arithmetic method of ranking bull spreads, but such a list will not be as accurate as the correct method of analysis. In reality, it is necessary to incorporate the volatility of the underlying stock, and possibly the expected return from the spread as well, into one's calculations. The concept of expected return is described in detail in Chapter 30, where a bull spread is used as an example.

The exact method for using volatility and predicting an option's price after an upward movement are presented later. Many data services offer such information. However, if the reader wants to attempt a simpler method of analysis, the following one may suffice. In any ranking of bull spreads, *it is important not to rank the spreads by their maximum potential profits at expiration.* Such a ranking will always give the most weight to deeply out-of-the-money spreads which can rarely achieve their maximum profit potential. It would be better to screen out any spreads whose maximum profit prices are too far away from the current stock price. A simple method of allowing for a stock's movement might be to assume that the stock could, at expiration, advance by an amount equal to twice the time value premium in an at-the-money call. Since more volatile stocks have options with greater time value premium, this is a simple attempt to incorporate volatility into the analysis. Also, since longer-term options have more time value premium than do short-term options, this will allow for larger movements during a longer time period. Percentage returns should include commission costs. This simple analysis is not completely correct, but it may prove useful to those traders looking for a simple, arithmetic method of analysis that can be quickly computed.

The bull spreads described in previous examples utilize the same expiration date for both the short call and the long call. It is sometimes useful to buy a call with a longer time to maturity than the short call has. Such a position is known as a diagonal bull spread and will be discussed in a later chapter.

With most types of spreads, it is necessary for some time to pass for the spread to become significantly profitable, even if the underlying stock moves in favor of the spreader. For this reason, *bull spreads are not for traders* unless the options involved are very short-term in nature. If a speculator is bullishly oriented for a short-term upward move in an underlying stock, it is generally better for him to buy a call outright than to establish a bull spread. Since the spread differential changes mainly as a function of time, small movements in price by the underlying stock will not cause much of a short-term change in the price of the spread. However, the bull spread has a distinct advantage over the purchase of a call if the underlying stock advances moderately by *expiration*.

In the previous example, a bull spread was established by buying the XYZ October 30 call for 3 points and simultaneously selling the October 35 call for 1 point. This spread can be compared to the outright purchase of the XYZ October 30 alone. There is a short-term advantage in using the outright purchase.

Example: The underlying stock jumps from 32 to 35 in one day's time. The October 30 would be selling for approximately 5½ points if that happened, and the outright purchaser would be ahead by 2½ points, less one option commission. The long side of the bull spread would do as well, of course, since it utilizes the same option, but the short side— the October 35—would probably be selling for about 2½ points. Thus the bull spread would be worth 3 points in total (5½ points on the long side, less 2½ points loss on the short side). This represents a 1-point profit to the spreader, less two option commissions, since the spread was initially established at a debit of 2 points. Clearly, then, for the shortest time period—one day—the outright purchase outperforms the bull spread on a quick rise.

For a slightly longer time period, such as 30 days, the outright purchase still has the advantage if the underlying stock moves up quickly. Even if the stock should advance above 35 in 30 days, the bull spread will still have time premium in it and thus will not have yet reached its maximum spread potential of 5 points. Recall that the maximum potential of a bull spread is always equal to the difference between the striking prices. Clearly, the outright purchaser will do very well if the underlying stock should advance that far in 30 days' time. When risk is considered, however, it must be pointed out that the bull spread has fewer dollars at risk and, if the underlying stock should drop rather than rise, the bull spread will often have a smaller loss than the outright call purchase would.

The longer it takes for the underlying stock to advance, the more the advantage swings to the spread. Suppose XYZ does not get to 35 until expiration. In this case, the October 30 call would be worth 5 points and the October 35 call would be worthless. The outright purchase of the October 30 call would make a 2-point profit less one commission, but the spread would now have a 3-point profit, less two commissions. Even with the increased commissions, the spreader will make more of a profit—both dollarwise and percentagewise.

The conclusion that can be drawn from these examples is that, in general, the outright purchase is a better strategy if one is looking for a quick rise by the underlying stock. Overall, the bull spread is a less aggressive strategy than the outright purchase of a call. The spread will not produce as much of a profit on a short-term move, or on a sustained large upward move. It will, however, outperform the outright purchase of a call if the stock advances slowly and moderately by expiration. Also, the spread always involves fewer actual dollars of risk, because it requires a smaller debit to establish initially. Table 7-2 summarizes which strategy has the upper hand for various stock movements over differing time periods.

FOLLOW-UP ACTION

Since the strategy has both limited profit and limited risk, it is not mandatory for the spreader to take any follow-up action prior to expiration. If the underlying stock advances substantially, the spreader should watch the time value premium in the short call closely in order to close the spread if it appears that there is a possibility of assignment. This possibility would increase substantially if the time value premium disappeared

TABLE 7-2.
Bull spread and outright purchase compared.

	If the underlying stock . . .			
	Declines	Remains Relatively Unchanged	Advances Moderately	Advances Substantially
in. . .				
1 week	Bull spread	Bull spread	Outright purchase	Outright purchase
1 month	Bull spread	Bull spread	Outright purchase	Outright purchase
At expiration	Bull spread	Bull spread	Bull spread	Outright purchase

from the short call. If the stock falls, the trader may want to close the spread in order to limit his losses even further.

When the spread is closed, the order should also be entered as a spread transaction. If the underlying stock has moved up in price, the order to liquidate would be a *credit* spread involving two closing transactions. *The maximum credit that can be recovered from a bull spread is an amount equal to the difference between the striking prices.* In the previous example, if XYZ were above 35 at expiration, one might enter an order to liquidate the spread as follows. Buy the October 35 (it is common practice to specify the buy side of a spread first when placing an order); sell the October 30 at a 5-point credit. In reality, because of the difference between bids and offers, it is quite difficult to obtain the entire 5-point credit even if expiration is quite near. Generally, one might ask for a $4\frac{3}{4}$ or $4\frac{7}{8}$ credit. It *is* possible to close the spread via exercise, although this method is normally advisable only to traders who pay little or no commissions. If the short side of a spread is assigned, the spreader may satisfy the assignment notice by exercising the long side of his spread. There is no margin required to do so, but there are stock commissions involved. Since these stock commissions—to a public customer—would be substantially larger than the option commissions involved in closing the spread by liquidating the options, *it is recommended that the public customer attempt to liquidate rather than exercise.*

A minor point should be made here. Since the amount of commissions paid to liquidate the spread would be larger if higher call prices are involved, the actual net maximum profit point for a bull spread is for the stock to be exactly at the higher striking price at expiration. If the stock exceeds the higher striking price by a great deal, the gross profit will be the same (it was demonstrated earlier that this gross profit is the same anywhere above the higher strike at expiration), but the net profit will be slightly smaller since the investor will pay more in commissions to liquidate the spread.

Some spreaders prefer to buy back the short call if the underlying stock drops in price in order to lock in the profit on the short side. They will then hold the long call in hopes of a rise in price by the underlying stock in order to make the long side of the spread profitable as well. This amounts to "legging" out of the spread, although the overall increase in risk is small—the amount paid to repurchase the short call. If he attempts to "leg" out of the spread in such a manner, the spreader should not attempt to buy back the short call at too high a price. If it can be repurchased at $\frac{1}{8}$ or $\frac{1}{16}$, the spreader will be giving away virtually nothing by buying back the short call. However, he should not be quick to repurchase it if it still has much more value than that unless he is closing out the entire spread. At no time should one attempt to "leg" out after a stock price increase—taking the profit on the long side and hoping for a stock price decline to make the short side profitable as well. The risk is too great.

OTHER USES OF BULL SPREADS

Superficially, the bull spread is one of the simplest forms of spreading. However, it can be an extremely useful tool in a wide variety of situations. Two such situations were described in Chapter 3. If the outright purchaser of a call finds himself with an unrealized loss, he may be able to substantially improve his chances of getting out even by "rolling down" into a bull spread. If, however, he has an unrealized profit, he may be able to sell a call at the next higher strike—creating a bull spread—in an attempt to lock in some of his profit.

In a somewhat similar manner, a common stockholder who is faced with an unrealized loss may be able to utilize a bull spread to lower the price at which he can break even. He may often have a significantly better chance of breaking even or making a profit by using options. The following example illustrates the stockholder's strategy.

Example: An investor buys 100 shares of XYZ at 48, and later finds himself with an unrealized loss with the stock at 42. A 6-point rally in the stock would be necessary in order to break even. However, if XYZ has listed options trading, he may be able to significantly reduce his break-even price. The prices are:

XYZ common, 42:

XYZ October 40, 4; and

XYZ October 45, 2.

The stock owner could enhance his overall position by buying one October 40 call and selling two October 45 calls. Note that no extra money, except commissions, is required for this transaction, because the credit received from selling two October 45's is $400 and is equal to the cost of buying the October 40 call. However, maintenance and equity requirements still apply because a spread has been established.

The resulting position does not have an uncovered, or naked, option in it. One of the October 45 calls that was sold is covered by the underlying stock itself. The other is part of a bull spread with the October 40 call. It is not particularly important that the resulting position is a combination of both a bull spread and a covered write. What is important is the profit characteristic of this new total position.

If XYZ should continue to decline in price and be below 40 at October expiration, all the calls will expire worthless, and the resulting loss to the stock owner will be the same (except for the option commissions spent) as if he had merely held onto his stock without having done any option trading.

Since both a covered write and a bull spread are strategies with a limited profit potential, *this new position obviously must have a limited profit*. If XYZ is anywhere above 45 at October expiration, the maximum profit will be realized. To determine the size of the maximum profit, assume that XYZ is at exactly 45 at expiration. In that case, the two short October 45's would expire worthless and the long October 40 call would be worth 5 points. The option trades would have resulted in a $400 profit on the short side ($200 from each October 45 call) plus a $100 profit on the long side, for a total profit of $500 from the option trades. Since the stock was originally bought at 48 in this example, the stock portion of the position is a $300 loss with XYZ at 45 at expiration. The overall profit of the position is thus $500 less $300, or $200.

For stock prices between 40 and 45 at expiration, the results are shown in Table 7-3 and Figure 7-2. Figure 7-2 depicts the two columns from the table labeled "Profit on Stock" and "Total Profit" so that one can visualize how the new total position compares with the original stockholder's profit. There are several points that should be noted from either the graph or the table. First, the break-even point is lowered from 48 to 44. The new total position breaks even at 44, so that only a 2-point rally by the stock by expiration is necessary in order to break even. The two strategies are equal at 50 at expiration. That is, the stock would have to rally more than 8 points from 42 to 50 by expiration for the original stockholder's position to outperform the new position. Below 40, the two strategies produce the same result. Finally, between 40 and 50, the new position outperforms the original stockholder's position.

TABLE 7-3.
Lowering the break-even price on common stock.

XYZ Price at Expiration	Profit on Stock	Profit on Short October 45's	Profit on Long October 40	Total Profit
35	− $1,300	+ $400	− $400	− $1,300
38	− 1,000	+ 400	− 400	− 1,000
40	− 800	+ 400	− 400	− 800
42	− 600	+ 400	− 200	− 400
43	− 500	+ 400	− 100	200
44	− 400	+ 400	0	0
45	− 300	+ 400	+ 100	+ 200
48	0	− 200	+ 400	+ 200
50	+ 200	− 600	+ 600	+ 200

FIGURE 7-2.
Lowering the break-even price on common stock.

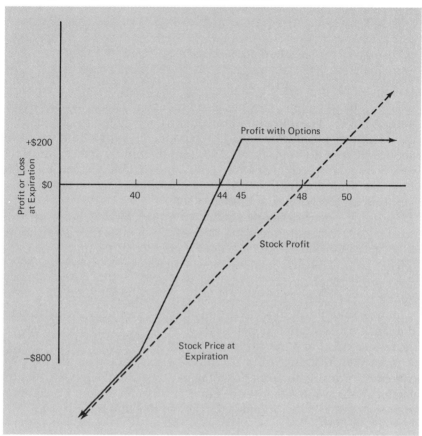

In summary, then, the stockholder stands to gain much and gives away very little by adding the indicated options to his stock position. If the stock stabilizes at all—anywhere between 40 and 50 in the example above—the new position would be an improvement. Moreover, the investor can break even or make profits on a small rally. If the stock continues to drop heavily, nothing additional will be lost except for option commissions. Only if the stock rallies very sharply will the stock position outperform the total position.

This strategy—combining a covered write and a bull spread—is sometimes used as an initial (opening) trade as well. That is, an investor who is considering buying XYZ at 42 might decide to buy the October 40 and sell two October 45's (for even money) at the outset. The resulting position would not be inferior to the outright purchase of XYZ stock, in terms of profit potential, unless XYZ rose above 46 by October expiration.

Bull spreads may also be used as a "substitute" for covered writing. Recall from Chapter 2 that writing against *warrants* can be useful because of the smaller investment required, especially if the warrant was in-the-money and was not selling at much of a premium. The same thinking applies to call options. *If there is an in-the-money call with little or no time premium remaining in it, its purchase may be used as a substitute for buying the stock itself.* Of course the call will expire, whereas the stock will not, but the profit potential of owning a deeply in-the-money call can be very similar to owning the stock. Since such a call costs less to purchase than the stock itself would, the buyer is getting essentially the same profit or loss potential with a smaller investment. It is natural, then, to think that one might write another call—one closer to the money— against the deeply in-the-money purchased call. This position would have profit characteristics much like a covered write since the long call "simulates" the purchase of stock. This position really is, of course, a *bull spread*, where the purchased call is well in-the-money and the written call is closer to the money. Clearly, one would not want to put all of his money into such a strategy and forsake covered writing, since, with bull spreads, he could be entirely wiped out in a moderate market decline. In a covered writing strategy, one still owns the stocks even after a severe market decline. However, one may achieve something of a compromise by investing a much smaller amount of money in bull spreads than he might have invested in covered writes. He can still retain the same profit potential. The balance of the investor's funds could then be placed in interest-bearing securities.

Example: The following prices exist:

XYZ common, 49;

XYZ April 50 call, 3; and

XYZ April 35 call, 14.

Since the deeply in-the-money call has no time premium, its purchase will perform much like the purchase of the stock until April expiration. Table 7-4 summarizes the profit potential from the covered write or the bull spread. The profit potentials are the same from a cash covered write or the bull spread. Both would yield a $400 profit before commissions if XYZ were above 50 at April expiration. However, since the bull spread requires a much smaller investment, the spreader could put $3,500 into interest-bearing securities. This interest could be considered as the equivalent of receiving the dividends on the stock. In any case, the spreader can lose only $1,100 even if the stock declines substantially. The covered writer could have a larger unrealized loss than that if XYZ were below

TABLE 7-4.
Results for covered write and bull spread compared.

	Covered Write: Buy XYZ and Sell April 50 Call	Bull Spread: Buy XYZ April 35 Call and Sell April 50 Call
Maximum profit potential (stock over 50 in April)	$ 400	$ 400
Break-even point	46	46
Investment	$4,600	$1,100

35 at expiration. Also, in the bull spread situation, the writer can "roll down" the April 50 call if the stock declines in price, just as he might do in a covered writing situation.

Thus the bull spread offers the same dollar rewards, the same break-even point, smaller commission costs, less potential risk, and interest income from the fixed income portion of the investment. While it is not always possible to find a deeply in-the-money call to use as "substitute" for buying the stock, when one does exist, the strategist should consider using the bull spread instead of the covered write.

SUMMARY

The bull spread is one of the simplest and most popular forms of spreading. It will generally perform best in a moderately bullish environment. The bull spread can also be applied for more sophisticated purposes in a far wider range of situations than merely wanting to attempt to capitalize on a moderate advance by the underlying stock. Both call buyers and the stock buyers may be able to use bull spreads to "roll down" and produce lower break-even points for their positions. The covered writer may also be able to use bull spreads as a substitute for covered writes in certain situations where a deeply in-the-money call exists.

Bear Spreads Using
Call Options

Options are a versatile investment vehicle. For every type of bullish position that can be established, there is normally a corresponding bearish type of strategy. For every neutral strategy there is an aggressive strategy for the investor with an opposite opinion. One such case has already been explored in some detail—the ratio write is a neutral strategy with a relatively large probability of making a limited profit. The reverse hedge strategy was the opposite side of the spectrum. Many of the strategies to be described from this point on will have a correspondingly similar strategy, designed for the strategist with the opposite point of view. In this vein, the bear spread is the opposite of a bull spread.

THE BEAR SPREAD

In a call bear spread, one buys a call at a certain striking price and sells a call at a lower striking price. This is a vertical spread, as was the bull spread. The bear spread tends to be profitable if the underlying stock declines in price. Like the bull spread, it has limited profit and loss potential. However, unlike the bull spread, the bear spread is a *credit* spread when the spread is set up with call options. Since one is selling the call with the lower strike, and a call at a lower strike always trades at a higher price than a call at a higher strike with the same expiration, the bear spread must be a credit position. It should be pointed out that most bearish strategies that can be established with call options may be more advantageously constructed using put options. Many of these same strategies will therefore be discussed again in Part III.

Example: An investor is bearish on XYZ. Using the same prices that were used for the examples in Chapter 7, an example of a bear spread can be constructed for:

XYZ common, 32;

XYZ October 30 call, 3; and

XYZ October 35 call, 1.

A bear spread would be established by buying the October 35 call and selling the October 30 call. This would be done for a 2-point credit, before commissions. *In a bear spread situation, the strategist is hoping that the stock will drop in price and that both options will expire worthless.* If this happens, he will not have to pay anything to close his spread—he will profit by the entire amount of the original credit taken in. In this example, then, the maximum profit potential is 2 points, since that is the amount of the initial credit. This profit would be realized if XYZ were anywhere below 30 at expiration, because both options would expire worthless in that case.

If the spread expands in price, rather than contracts, the bear spreader will be losing money. This expansion would occur in a rising market. The maximum amount that this spread could expand to is 5 points—the difference between the striking prices. Hence the most that the bear spreader would have to pay to buy back this spread would be 5 points, resulting in a maximum potential loss of 3 points. This loss would be realized if XYZ were anywhere above 35 at October expiration. Table 8-1 and Figure 8-1 depict the actual profit and loss potential of this example at expiration (commissions are not included). The astute reader will note that the figures in the table are exactly the reverse of those shown for the bull spread example in Chapter 7. Also, the profit graph of the bear spread looks like a bull spread profit graph that has been turned upside down. All bear spreads have a profit graph with the same shape as the graph shown in Figure 8-1, at expiration.

The break-even point, maximum profit potential, and investment required are all quite simple computations for a bear spread.

TABLE 8-1.
Bear spread.

XYZ Price at Expiration	October 30 Profit	October 35 Profit	Total Profit
25	+ $300	− $100	+ $200
30	+ 300	− 100	+ 200
32	+ 100	− 100	0
35	− 200	− 100	− 300
40	− 700	+ 400	− 300

FIGURE 8-1.
Bear spread.

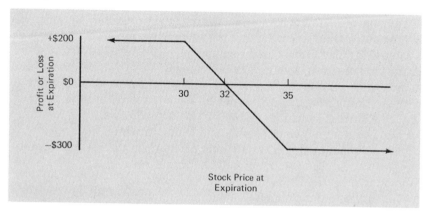

Maximum profit potential = net credit received

Break-even point = lower striking price + amount of credit

Maximum risk = collateral investment required = difference in
              striking prices − credit received + commissions

In the example above, the net credit received from the sale of the
October 30 call at 3 and the purchase of the October 35 call at 1 was two
points. This is the maximum profit potential. The break-even point is then
easily computed as the lower striking price, 30, plus the amount of the
credit, 2, or 32. The risk is equal to the investment. It is the difference
between the striking prices—5 points—less the net credit received—2
points—for a total investment of 3 points plus commissions. Since this
spread involves a call that is not "covered" by a long call with a striking
price equal to or lower than that of the short call, some brokerage firms
may require a higher maintenance requirement per spread than would be
required for a bull spread. Again, since a spread must be done in a margin

account, most brokerage firms will require that a minimum amount of equity be in the account as well.

Since this is a credit spread, the investor does not really "spend" any dollars to establish the spread. The investment is really a reduction in the buying power of the customer's margin account, but it does not actually require dollars to be spent when the transaction is initiated.

SELECTING A BEAR SPREAD

Depending on where the underlying stock is trading with respect to the two striking prices, the bear spread may be very aggressive, with a high profit potential, or it may be less aggressive, with a low profit potential. If a large credit is initially taken in, there is obviously the potential for a good deal of profit. However, for the spread to take in a large credit, the underlying stock must be well above the lower striking price. This means that a relatively substantial downward move would be necessary in order for the maximum profit potential to be realized. Thus *a large credit bear spread is usually an aggressive position*—the spreader needs a substantial move by the underlying stock in order to make his maximum profit. The probabilities of this occurring cannot be considered large.

A less aggressive type of bear spread is one in which the underlying stock is actually *below* the lower striking price when the spread is established. The credit received from establishing a bear spread in such a situation would be small, but the spreader would realize his maximum profit even if the underlying stock remained unchanged or actually rose slightly in price by expiration.

Example: XYZ is at a price of 29. The October 30 call might be sold for 1½ points and the October 35 call bought for ½ point with the stock at 29. While the net credit, and hence the maximum profit potential, is a small dollar amount—1 point—it will be realized even if XYZ rises slightly by expiration, as long as it does not rise above 30.

It is not always clear which type of spread is better—the large credit bear spread or the small credit bear spread. One has a small probability of making a large profit and the other has a much larger probability of making a much smaller profit. In general, *bear spreads established when the underlying stock is closer to the lower striking price will be the best ones.* To see this, note that if a bear spread is initiated when the stock is at the higher striking price, the spreader is selling a call that has mostly intrinsic value and little time value premium (since it is in-the-money) and is buying a call that is nearly all time value. This is just the opposite of what the option strategist should be attempting to do. *The basic phi-*

losophy of option strategy is to sell time value and buy intrinsic value. For this reason, the larger credit bear spread is not an optimum strategy. It will be interesting to observe later that bear spreads with puts are more attractive when the underlying stock is at the *higher* striking price!

FOLLOW-UP ACTION

Follow-up strategies are not difficult, in general, for bear spreads. The major thing that the strategist must be aware of is impending assignment of the short call. If the short side of the spread is in-the-money and has no time premium remaining, the spread should be closed regardless of how much time remains until expiration. This disappearance of time value premium could be caused either by the stock being significantly above the striking price of the stock call, or by an impending dividend payment. In either case, the spread should be closed to avoid assignment and the resultant large commission costs on stock transactions. Note that the large credit bear spread—one established with the stock well above the lower striking price—is dangerous from the viewpoint of early assignment, since the time value premium in the call will be small to begin with.

SUMMARY

The call bear spread is a bearishly oriented strategy. Since the spread is a credit spread—requiring only a reduction in buying power, but no actual layout of cash to establish—it is a moderately popular strategy. The bear spread using calls may not be the optimum type of bearish spread that is available—a bear spread using put options may be.

Chapter 9

Calendar Spreads

A *calendar spread*, also frequently called a *time spread*, involves the sale of one option and the simultaneous purchase of a more distant option, both with the same striking price. In the broad definition, the calendar spread is a horizontal spread. The neutral philosophy for using calendar spreads is that time will erode the value of the near-term option at a faster rate than it will the far-term option. If this happens, the spread will widen and a profit may result at near-term expiration. With call options, one may construct a more aggressive, bullish calendar spread. Both types of spreads will be discussed.

Example: The following prices exist sometime in late January:

	April 50 Call (3-month call)	July 50 Call (6-month call)	October 50 Call (9-month call)
XYZ: 50	5	8	10

If one sells the April 50 call and buys the July 50 at the same time, he will pay a debit of 3 points—the difference in the call prices—plus commissions. That is, *his investment is the net debit of the spread plus commissions.* Furthermore, suppose that in 3 months, at April expiration, XYZ is unchanged at 50. Then the 3-month call should be worth 5 points, and the 6-month call should be worth 8 points, as they were previously, all other factors being equal.

	April 50 Call (Expiring)	July 50 Call (3-month call)	October 50 Call (6-month call)
XYZ: 50	0	5	8

The spread between the April 50 and the July 50 has now widened to 5 points. Since the spread cost 3 points originally, this widening effect has produced a 2-point profit. The spread could be closed at this time in order to realize the profit, or the spreader may decide to continue to hold the July 50 call which he is long. By continuing to hold the July 50 call, he is risking the profits that have accrued to date, but he could profit handsomely if the underlying stock rises in price over the next 3 months before July expiration.

It is not necessary for the underlying stock to be exactly at the striking price of the options at near-term expiration for a profit to result. In fact, some profit can be made in a range that extends both below and above the striking price. The risk in this type of position is that the stock will drop a great deal or rise a great deal, in which case the spread between the two options will shrink and the spreader will lose money. Since the spread between two calls at the same strike cannot shrink to less than zero, however, *the risk is limited to the amount of the original debit spent to establish the spread, plus commissions.*

THE NEUTRAL CALENDAR SPREAD

As mentioned earlier, the calendar spreader can either have a neutral outlook on the stock or he can construct the spread for an aggressively bullish outlook. The neutral outlook will be described first. The calendar spread that is established when the underlying stock is at or near the striking price of the options used is a neutral spread. The strategist is interested in selling time and not in predicting the direction of the underlying stock. If the stock is relatively unchanged when the near-term option expires, the neutral spread will make a profit. *In a neutral spread, one should initially have the intent of closing the spread by the time the near-term option expires.*

Let us again turn to our example calendar spread described earlier in order to more accurately demonstrate the potential risks and rewards from that spread when the near-term, April, call expires. To do this, it is necessary to estimate the price of the July 50 call at that time. Notice that, with XYZ at 50 at expiration, the results agree with the less detailed example presented earlier. The graph shown in Figure 9-1 is the "total profit" from Table 9-1. The graph is a curved, rather than straight, line since the July 50 call still has time premium. There is a slightly bullish bias to this graph: the profit range extends slightly farther above the striking price than it does below the striking price. This is due to the fact that the spread is a call spread. If puts had been used, the profit range would have a bearish bias. The total width of the profit range is a function of

FIGURE 9-1.
Calendar spread at near-term expiration.

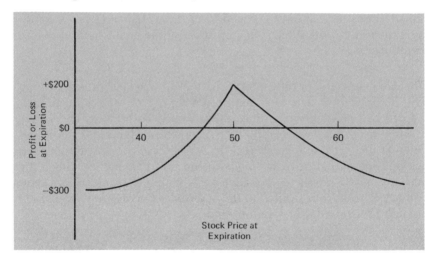

TABLE 9-1.
Estimated profit or losses at April expiration.

XYZ Stock Price	April 50 Price	April 50 Profit	July 50 Price	July 50 Profit	Total Profit
40	0	+ $500	½	− $750	− $250
45	0	+ 500	2½	− 550	− 50
48	0	+ 500	4	− 400	+ 100
50	0	+ 500	5	− 300	+ 200
52	2	+ 300	6	− 200	+ 100
55	5	0	8	0	0
60	10	− 500	10½	+ 250	− 250

the volatility of the underlying stock—since that will determine the price of the remaining long call at expiration—as well as a function of the time remaining to near-term expiration.

Table 9-1 and Figure 9-1 clearly depict several of the more significant aspects of the calendar spread. *There is a range within which the spread is profitable at near-term expiration.* That range would appear to be about 46 to 55 in the example. Outside that range, losses can occur, but they are limited to the amount of the initial debit. Notice in the example that the stock would have to be well below 40 or well above 60 for the maximum loss to occur. Even if the stock is at 40 or 60, there is some time premium left in the longer-term option and the loss is not quite as large as the maximum possible loss of $300.

This type of calendar spread has limited profits and relatively large commission costs. It is generally best to establish such a spread 8 to 12 weeks before the near-term option expires. If this is done, one is capitalizing on the maximum rate of decay of the near-term option with respect to the longer-term option. That is, when a call has less than 8 weeks of life, the rate of decay of its time value premium increases substantially with respect to the longer-term options on the same stock.

FOLLOW-UP ACTION

Ideally, the spreader would like to have the stock be just below the striking price when the near-term call expires. If this happens, he can close the spread with only one commission cost—that of selling out the long call. If the calls are in-the-money at the expiration date, he will, of course, have to pay two commissions to close the spread. As with all spread positions, the order to close the spread should be placed as a single order. "Legging" out of a spread is highly risky and is not recommended.

Prior to expiration, the spreader should close the spread if the near-term, short call is trading at parity. He does this to avoid assignment. Being called out of spread position is devastating from the viewpoint of the stock commissions involved for the public customer. The near-term call would not normally be trading at parity until quite close to the last day of trading, unless the stock has undergone a substantial rise in price.

In the case of an early *downside* breakout by the underlying stock, the spreader has several choices. He could immediately close the spread and take a small loss on the position. Another choice he has is to leave the spread alone until the near-term call expires and then to hope for a partial recovery from the stock in order to be able to recover some value from the long side of the spread. Such a holding action is often better than the immediate close-out, because the expense of buying back the short call can be quite large percentagewise. A riskier downside defensive action is to sell out the long call if the stock begins to break down heavily. In this way, the spreader recovers something from the long side of his spread immediately, and then looks for the stock to remain depressed so that the short side of the spread will expire worthless. This action requires that one have enough collateral available to margin the naked call—often an amount substantially in excess of the original debit paid for the spread. Moreover, if the underlying stock should reverse direction and rally back to or above the striking price, the short side of the spread is naked and could produce substantial losses. The risk assumed by such a follow-up violates the initial neutral premise of the spread, and should therefore be avoided. Of these three types of downside defensive action, *the easiest and most conservative one is to do nothing at all*—letting the short call expire worthless and then hoping for a recovery by the underlying stock. If this tack is taken, the risk still remains fixed at the original debit paid for the spread, and occasionally a rally may produce large profits on the long call. Although this rally is a nonfrequent event, it generally costs the spreader very little to allow himself the opportunity to take advantage of such a rally if it should occur.

In fact, the strategist can employ a slight modification of this sort of action, even if the spread is not at a large loss. If the underlying stock is moderately below the striking price at near-term expiration, the short option will expire worthless and the spreader will be left holding the long option. He could sell the long side immediately and perhaps take a small gain or loss. However, it is often a reasonable strategy to sell out a portion of the long side—recovering all, or a substantial portion, of the initial investment—and hold the remainder. If the stock rises, the remaining long position may appreciate substantially. Although this sort of action deviates from the true nature of the time spread, it is not overly risky.

An early breakout to the upside by the underlying stock is generally handled in much the same way as downside breakout. Doing nothing is often the best course of action. If the underlying stock rallies shortly after the spread is established, the spread will shrink by a small amount, but not substantially, because both options will hold premium in a rally. If the spreader were to rush in to close the position, he would be paying commissions on two rather expensive options. He will usually do better by waiting and giving himself as much of a chance for a reversal as possible. In fact, even at near-term expiration, there will normally be some time premium left in the long option so that the maximum loss would not have to be realized. A highly risk-oriented upside defensive action is to cover the short call on a technical breakout and continue to hold the long call. This can become disastrous if the breakout fails and the stock drops, possibly resulting in losses far in excess of the original debit. Therefore this action cannot be considered anything but extremely aggressive and illogical for the neutral strategist.

If a breakout does not occur, the spreader will normally be making unrealized profits as time passes. Should this be the case, he may want to set some mental stop-out points for himself. For example, if the underlying stock is quite close to the striking price with only 2 weeks to go, there will be some more profit potential left in the spread, but the spreader should be ready to close the position quickly if the stock begins to get too far away from the striking price. In this manner, he can leave room for more profits to accrue, but he is also attempting to protect the profits that have already built up. This is somewhat similar to the action that the ratio writer takes when he narrows the range of his action points as more and more time passes.

THE BULLISH CALENDAR SPREAD

A less neutral and more bullish type of calendar spread is preferred by the more aggressive investor. In a bullish calendar spread, one sells the near-term call and buys a longer-term call, but *he does this when the underlying stock is some distance below the striking price of the calls.* This type of position has the attractive features of low dollar investment and large potential profits. Of course, there is risk involved as well.

Example: One might set up a bullish calendar spread in the following manner:

XYZ common, 45;

sell the XYZ April 50 for 1; and

buy the XYZ July 50 for 1½.

This investor ideally wants two things to happen. *First, he would like the near-term call to expire worthless.* That is why the bullish calendar spread is established with out-of-the-money calls—to increase the chances of the short call expiring worthless. If this happens, the investor will then own the longer-term call at a net cost of his original debit. In this example, his original debit was only ½ of a point to create the spread. If the April 50 call expires worthless, the investor will own the July 50 call at a net cost of ½ point, plus commissions.

The investor now needs a second criterion to be fulfilled—the stock must rise in price by the time the July 50 call expires. In this example, even if XYZ were to rally to only 52 between April and July, the July 50 call could be sold for at least 2 points. This represents a substantial percentage gain because the cost of the call has been reduced to ½ point. Thus there is the potential for large profits in bullish calendar spreads if the underlying stock rallies above the striking price before the longer-term call expires, provided that the short-term call has already expired worthless.

What chance does the investor have that both ideal conditions will occur? There is a reasonably good chance that the written call will expire worthless since it is a short-term call and the stock is below the striking price to start with. If the stock falls, or even rises a little—up to, but not above, the striking price—the first condition will have been met. It is the second condition—a rally above the striking price by the underlying stock before the longer-term expiration date—that normally presents the biggest problem. The chances of this happening are usually small, but the rewards can be large when it does happen. Thus *this strategy offers a small probability of making a large profit.* In fact, one large profit can easily offset several losses, because the losses are small, dollarwise. Even if the stock remains depressed and the July 50 call in the example expires worthless, the loss is limited to the initial debit of ½ a point. Of course, this loss represents 100% of the initial investment, so one cannot put all his money into bullish calendar spreads.

This strategy is a reasonable way to speculate, provided that the spreader adheres to the following criteria when establishing the spread:

1. *Select underlying stocks that are volatile enough to move above the striking price within the allotted time.* Bullish calendar spreads may appear to be very "cheap" on nonvolatile stocks that are well below the striking price. But if a large stock move—say 20%—is required in only a few months, the spread is not worthwhile for a nonvolatile stock.

2. *Do not use options more than one striking price above the current market.* For example, if XYZ were 26, use the 30 strike, not the 35 strike, since the chances of a rally to 30 are many times greater than the chances of a rally to 35.

3. *Do not invest a large percentage of available trading capital in bullish calendar spreads.* Since these are such low-cost spreads, one should be able to follow this rule easily and still diversify into several positions.

FOLLOW-UP ACTION

If the underlying stock should rally before the near-term call expires, the bullish calendar spreader must *never* consider "legging" out of the spread, or consider covering the short call at a loss and attempting to ride the long call. Either action could turn the initial small limited loss into a disastrous loss. Since the strategy hinges on the fact that all the losses will be small and the infrequent large profits will be able to overcome these small losses, one should do nothing to jeopardize the strategy and possibly generate a large loss.

The only reasonable sort of follow-up action that the bullish calendar spreader can take in advance of expiration is to close the spread if the underlying stock has moved up in price and the spread has widened to become profitable. This might occur if the stock moves up to the striking price after some time has passed. In the example above, if XYZ moved up to 50 with a month or so of life left in the April 50 call, the call might be selling for $1\frac{1}{2}$ while the July 50 call might be selling for 3 points. Thus the spread could be closed at $1\frac{1}{2}$ points, representing a 1-point gain over the initial debit of $\frac{1}{2}$ point. Two commissions would have to be paid to close the spread, of course, but there would still be a net profit in the spread.

USING ALL THREE EXPIRATION SERIES

In either the neutral calendar spread or the bullish calendar spread, the investor has three choices of which months to use. He could sell the nearest-term call and buy the intermediate-term call. This is usually the most common way to set up these spreads. However, there is no rule that prevents him from selling the intermediate-term and buying the longest-term, or possibly selling the near-term and buying the long-term. Any of these situations would still be a calendar spread.

Some proponents of calendar spreads prefer initially to sell the near-term and buy the long-term call. Then, if the near-term call expires worthless, they have an opportunity to sell the intermediate-term call if they so desire.

Example: An investor establishes a calendar spread by selling the April 50 call and buying the October 50 call. The April call would have less than 3 months remaining and the October call would be the long-term call. At April expiration, if XYZ is below 50, the April call will expire worthless. At that time, the July 50 call could be sold against the October 50 which is held long, thereby creating another calendar spread with no additional commission cost on the long side.

The advantage of this type of strategy is that it is possible for the two sales (April 50 and July 50 in this example) to actually bring in more credits than were spent for the one purchase (October 50). Thus the spreader might be able to create a position where he has a guaranteed profit. That is, if the sum of his transactions is actually a credit, he cannot lose money in the spread (provided that he does not attempt to "leg" out of the spread). The disadvantage of using the long-term call in the calendar spread is that the initial debit is larger, and therefore more dollars are initially at risk. If the underlying stock moves substantially up or down in the first 3 months, the spreader could realize a larger dollar loss with the April/October spread because his loss will approach the initial debit.

The remaining combination of the expiration series is to initially buy the longest-term call and sell the intermediate-term call against it. This combination will generally require the smallest initial debit, but there is not much profit potential in the spread until the intermediate-term expiration date draws near. Thus there is a lot of time for the underlying stock to move some distance away from the initial striking price. For this reason, this is generally an inferior approach to calendar spreading.

SUMMARY

Calendar spreading is a low-dollar-cost strategy that is a nonaggressive approach, provided that the spreader does not invest a large percentage of his trading capital in the strategy, and provided that he does not attempt to "leg" into or out of the spreads. The neutral calendar spread is one in which the strategist is mainly selling time—he is attempting to capitalize on the known fact that the near-term call will lose time premium more rapidly than will a longer-term call. A more aggressive approach is the bullish calendar spread, in which the speculator is essentially trying to reduce the net cost of a longer-term call by the amount of credits taken in from the sale of a nearer-term call. This bullish strategy requires that the near-term call expire worthless and then that the underlying stock rise in price. In either strategy, the most common approach is to sell the nearest-term call and buy the intermediate-term call. However, it may sometimes prove advantageous to sell the near-term and buy the longest-term initially, with the intention of letting the near-term expire and then possibly writing against the longer-term call a second time.

Chapter *10*

The Butterfly Spread

The recipient of one of the more exotic names given to spread positions, *the butterfly spread is a neutral position that is a combination of both a bull spread and a bear spread*. This spread is for the neutral strategist—one who thinks the underlying stock will not experience much of a net rise or decline by expiration. It generally requires only a small investment and has limited risk. Although profits are limited as well, they are larger than the potential risk. For this reason, the butterfly spread is a viable strategy. However, it is costly in terms of commissions. In this chapter, the strategy will be explained using only calls. The strategy can also be implemented using a combination of puts and calls, or with puts only, as will be demonstrated later. Also see Chapter 34 on CAPS.

There are three striking prices involved in a butterfly spread. Using only calls, the butterfly spread consists of buying one call at the lowest striking price, selling two calls at the middle striking price and buying one call at the highest striking price. The following example will demonstrate how the butterfly spread works.

Example: A butterfly spread is established by buying a July 50 call for 12, selling 2 July 60 calls for 6 each, and buying a July 70 call for 3.

The spread requires a relatively low debit of $300 (Table 10-1), although there are four option commissions involved and these may represent a substantial percentage of the net investment. As usual, *the maximum amount of profit is realized at the striking price of the written calls.* With most types of spreads, this is a useful fact to remember, for it can aid in quick computation of the potential of the spread. In this example, if the stock were at the striking price of the written options at expiration—60— the two July 60's which are short would expire worthless for a $1,200 gain. The long July 70 call would expire worthless—a $300 loss—and the long July 50 call would be worth 10 points, for a $200 loss on that call. The sum of the gains and losses would thus be a $700 gain, less commissions. This is the maximum profit potential of the spread.

The risk is limited in a butterfly spread—both to the upside and to the downside—and is equal to the amount of the net debit required to establish the spread. In the example above, the risk is limited to $300 plus commissions.

Table 10-2 and Figure 10-1 depict the results of this butterfly spread at various prices at expiration. The profit graph resembles that of a ratio write except that the loss is limited on both the upside and the downside. There is a profit range within which the butterfly spread makes money— 53 to 67 in the example, before commissions are included. Outside this profit range, losses will occur at expiration, but these losses are limited to the amount of the original debit plus commissions.

The *collateral investment* required for the butterfly spread is not equal to the net debit expended. Since the spread consists of both a bull spread and a bear spread, the collateral requirement for the butterfly spread is the sum of the requirements for the bull spread and the bear spread. The bull spread—buying the July 50 and selling the July 60 in the example

TABLE 10-1.
Butterfly spread example.

Current prices:	
XYZ common:	60
XYZ July 50 call:	12
XYZ July 60 call:	6
XYZ July 70 call:	3
Butterfly spread:	
Buy 1 July 50 call	$1,200 debit
Sell 2 July 60 calls	$1,200 credit
Buy 1 July 70 call	$300 debit
Net debit	$300 (plus commissions)

TABLE 10-2.
Results of butterfly spread at expiration.

XYZ Price at Expiration	July 50 Profit	July 60 Profit	July 70 Profit	Total Profit
40	− $1,200	+ $1,200	− $300	− $300
50	− 1,200	+ 1,200	− 300	− 300
53	− 900	+ 1,200	− 300	0
56	− 600	+ 1,200	− 300	+ 300
60	− 200	+ 1,200	− 300	+ 700
64	+ 200	+ 400	− 300	+ 300
67	+ 500	− 200	− 300	0
70	+ 800	− 800	− 300	− 300
80	+ 1,800	− 2,800	+ 700	− 300

FIGURE 10-1.
Butterfly spread.

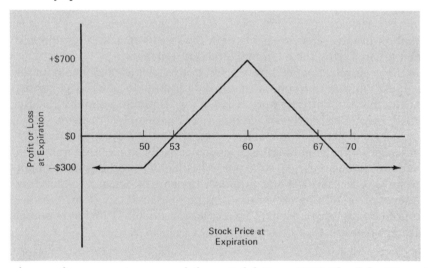

above—has a requirement of the net debit, or $600 (the July 50 cost 12 and the July 60 was sold for 6). The bear spread—buying the July 70 and selling the July 60—has a margin requirement of $700 (the 10-point difference between the strikes plus the 3 points paid for the July 70 less the 6 points received from the sale of the July 60). The butterfly spread, then, has a requirement of $1,300, even though the strategist only directly pays out the $300 debit plus commissions required to establish the spread. The rest of the requirement represents a reduction in the excess buying power in the spreader's margin account. When the striking prices are evenly spaced—the spacing is 10 points in this example—the following formulae can be used to quickly compute the important details of this spread.

Net collateral investment = distance between strikes + net debit

Maximum profit = distance between strikes − net debit

Downside break-even = lowest strike + net debit

Upside break-even = highest strike − net debit

In the example, the distance between strikes is 10 points, the net debit is 3 points (before commissions), the lowest strike used is 50, and the highest strike is 70. These formulae would then yield the following results for this example spread.

Net investment = 10 + 3 = $1,300

Maximum profit = 10 − 3 = $700

Downside break-even = 50 + 3 = 53

Upside break-even = 70 − 3 = 67

Note that all of these answers agree with the results that were previously obtained by analyzing the example spread in detail.

In this example, the maximum profit potential is $700, the maximum risk is $300, and the investment required is $1,300. In percentage terms, this means that the butterfly spread has a loss limited to about 22% and could make profits of nearly 54% in this case. These represent an attractive risk/reward relationship. This is, however, just an example, and two factors that exist in the actual marketplace may greatly affect these numbers. First, commissions are large—it is possible that eight commissions might have to be paid to establish and liquidate the spread. Second, depending on the level of premiums to be found in the market at any point in time, it may not be possible to establish a spread for a debit as low as 3 points when the strikes are 10 points apart.

SELECTING THE SPREAD

Ideally, one would want to establish a butterfly spread at as small of a debit as possible in order to limit his risk to a small amount, both dollarwise and percentagewise. One would also like to have the stock be near the middle striking price to begin with, because he will then be in his maximum profit area if the stock remains relatively unchanged. Unfortunately, it is difficult to satisfy both conditions simultaneously.

The smallest-debit butterfly spreads are those where the stock is some distance away from the middle striking price. To see this, note that if the stock were well above the middle strike and all the options were at parity, the net debit would be zero. Although no one would attempt to establish a butterfly spread with parity options because of the risk of early assignment, it may be somewhat useful to try to obtain a small debit by taking an opinion on the underlying stock. For example, if the stock is close to the higher striking price, the debit would be small normally, but the investor would have to be somewhat bearish on the underlying stock in order to maximize his profit—that is, the stock would have to decline in price from the upper striking price to the middle striking price for the maximum profit to be realized. An analogous situation exists when the underlying stock is originally close to the lower striking price. The investor could establish the spread for a small debit in this case also, but he would now have to be somewhat bullish on the underlying stock in order to attempt to realize his maximum profit.

Example: XYZ is at 70. One may be able to establish a low-debit butterfly spread with the 50's, 60's, and 70's if the following prices exist:

XYZ common, 70;

XYZ July 50, 20;

XYZ July 60, 12; and

XYZ July 70, 5.

The butterfly spread would require a debit of only $100 plus commissions to establish because the cost of the calls at the higher and lower strike is 25 points, and a 24-point credit would be obtained by selling two calls at the middle strike. This is indeed a low-cost butterfly spread, but the stock will have to move down in price for much of a profit to be realized. The maximum profit of $900 less commissions would be realized at 60 at expiration. The strategist would have to be bearish on XYZ for him to want to establish such a spread.

Without the aid of an example, the reader should be able to determine that if XYZ were originally at 50, a low-cost butterfly spread could be established by buying the 50, selling two 60's, and buying a 70. In this case, however, the investor would have to be bullish on the stock because he would want it to move up to 60 by expiration in order for the maximum profit to be realized.

In general, then, if the butterfly spread is to be established at an extremely low debit, the spreader will have to make a decision as to whether he wants to be bullish or bearish on the underlying stock. Many strategists prefer to remain as neutral as possible on the underlying stock at all times in any strategy. This philosophy would lead to slightly higher debits, such as the $300 debit in the example at the beginning of this chapter, but would theoretically have a better chance of making money because there would be a profit if the stock remained relatively un-changed—the most probable occurrence.

In either philosophy, there are other considerations for the butterfly spread. *The best butterfly spreads are generally found on the more ex-pensive and/or more volatile stocks which have striking prices spaced 10 or 20 points apart.* In these situations, the maximum profit is large enough to overcome the weight of the commission costs involved in the butterfly spread. When one establishes butterfly spreads on lower-priced stocks where the striking prices are only 5 points apart, he is normally putting himself at a disadvantage unless the debit is extremely small. One excep-tion to this rule is that attractive situations are often found on higher-priced stocks with striking prices 5 points apart (50, 55, and 60, for ex-ample). They do exist from time to time.

In analyzing butterfly spreads, one commonly works with closing prices. It was mentioned earlier that using closing prices for analysis can prove somewhat misleading since the actual execution will have to be done at bid and asked prices, and these may differ somewhat from closing prices. Normally, this difference is small, but since there are three different calls involved in a butterfly spread, the difference could be substantial. Therefore, it is usually necessary to check the appropriate bid and asked price for each call before entering the spread in order to be able to place a reasonable debit on the order. As with other types of spreads, the but-terfly spread order can be placed as one order.

Before moving on to discuss follow-up action, it may be worthwhile to describe a tactic for stocks with five points between striking prices. For example, the butterfly spreader might work with strikes of 45, 50, and 60. If he sets up the usual type of butterfly spread, he would end up with a position that has too much risk near 60 and very little or none at all near 45. If this is what he wants, fine, but if he wants to remain neutral, the standard type of butterfly spread will have to be modified slightly.

Example: The following prices exist:

XYZ common, 50;

July 45 call, 7;

July 50 call, 5; and

July 60 call, 2.

The normal type of butterfly spread—buying one 45, selling two 50's, and buying one 60—can actually be done for a credit of 1 point. However, the profitability is no longer symmetric about the middle striking price. In this example, the investor cannot lose to the downside, because, even if the stock collapses and all the calls expire worthless, he will still make his 1-point credit. However, to the upside, there is risk: if XYZ is anywhere above 60 at expiration, the risk is 4 points. This is no longer a neutral position—the fact that the lower strike is only 5 points from the middle strike while the higher strike is 10 points away has made this a somewhat bearish position. If the spreader wants to be neutral and still use these striking prices, he will have to put on *two* bull spreads and only one bear spread. That is, he should:

Buy 2 July 45's:	$1,400 debit
Sell 3 July 50's:	$1,500 credit
Buy 1 July 60:	$200 debit

This position now has a net debit of $100 but has a better balance of risk at either end. If XYZ drops and is below 45 at expiration, the spreader will lose his $100 initial debit. But now, if XYZ is at or above 60 at expiration, he will lose $100 in that range also. Thus by establishing two bull spreads with a 5-point difference between the strikes versus one bear spread with a 10-point difference between strikes, the risk has been balanced at both ends.

The same analysis obviously applies anywhere that 5-point striking price intervals exist. There are numerous combinations that could be worked out for lower-priced stocks by merely skipping over a striking price (using the 25's, 30's, and 40's, for example). Although there are not normally many stocks trading over $100 per share, the same analysis is applicable by using 130's, 140's, and 160's for example.

FOLLOW-UP ACTION

Since the butterfly spread has limited risk by its construction, there is usually little that the spreader has to do in the way of follow-up action other than avoiding early exercise or possibly closing out the position early to take profits or limit losses even further. The only part of the spread that is subject to assignment is the call at the middle strike. If this call trades at or near parity, in-the-money, the spread should be closed. This may happen before expiration if the underlying stock is about to go ex-dividend.

If the stock is near the middle strike after a reasonable amount of time has passed, an unrealized profit will begin to accrue to the spreader. If one feels that the underlying stock is about to move away from the middle striking price and thereby jeopardize these profits, it may be advantageous to close the spread to take the available profit. Be certain to include commission costs when determining if an unrealized profit exists. As a general rule of thumb, if one is doing 10 spreads at a time, he can estimate that the commission cost for each option is about ⅛ point. That is, if one has 10 butterfly spreads and the spread is currently at 6 points, he could figure that he would net about 5½ points after commissions to close the spread. This ⅛ estimate is only valid if the spreader has at least 10 options at each strike involved in a spread.

Normally, one would not close the spread early to limit losses since these losses are limited to the original net debit in any case. However, if that original debit was large and the stock is beginning to break out above the higher strike or to break down below the lower strike, the spreader may want to close the spread to limit losses even further.

It has been repeatedly stated that one should not attempt to "leg" out of a spread because of the risk that is incurred if one is wrong. However, there is a method of legging out of a butterfly spread that is acceptable and may even be prudent. Since the spread consists of both a bull spread and a bear spread, it may often be the case that the stock experiences a relatively substantial move in one direction or the other during the life of the butterfly spread and that the bull spread portion or the bear spread portion could be closed out near their maximum profit potentials. If this situation arises, the spreader may want to take advantage of it in order to be able to profit more if the underlying stock reverses direction and comes back into the profit range.

Example: This strategy can be explained by using the initial example from this chapter and then assuming that the stock falls from 60 to 45. Recall that this spread was initially established with a 3-point debit and a maximum profit potential of 7 points. The profit range was 53 to 67 at July expiration. However, a rather unpleasant situation has occurred: The stock has fallen quickly and is below the profit range. If the spreader does nothing and keeps the spread on, he will lose at most 3 points if the stock remains below 50 until July expiration. However, by increasing his risk slightly, he may be able to improve his position. Notice in Table 10-3 that the bear spread portion of the overall spread—short July 60, long July

TABLE 10-3.
Initial spread and current prices.

	Initial Spread		Current Prices
XYZ common:	60	XYZ common:	45
July 50 call:	12	July 50 call:	2
July 60 call:	6	July 60 call:	1
July 70 call:	3	July 70 call:	½

70—has very nearly reached its maximum potential. The bear spread could be bought back for ½ of a point total (pay 1 point to buy back the July 60 and receive ½ point from selling out the July 70). Thus the spreader could convert the butterfly spread to a bull spread by spending ½ of a point. What would such an action do to his overall position? First, his risk would be increased by the ½ point spent to close the bear spread. That is, if XYZ continues to remain below 50 until July expiration, he would now lose 3½ rather than 3 points, plus commissions in either case. He has, however, potentially helped his chances of realizing something close to the maximum profit available from the original butterfly spread.

After buying back the bear spread, he is left with the following bull spread:

$$\left.\begin{array}{l}\text{Long July 50 call} \\ \text{Short July 60 call}\end{array}\right\} - \text{net debit } 3\frac{1}{2} \text{ points}$$

He has a bull spread at the total cost paid to date—3½ points. From the earlier discussion of bull spreads, the reader should know that the break-even point for this position is 53½ at expiration, and it could make a 6½-point profit if XYZ is anywhere over 60 at July expiration. Hence the break-even point for the position was raised from 53 to 53½ by the expense of the ½ point to buy back the bear spread. However, if the stock should rally back above 60, the strategist will be making a profit nearly equal to the original maximum profit that he was aiming for (7 points). Moreover, this profit is now available anywhere over 60, not just exactly at 60 as it was in the original position. Although the chances of such a rally cannot be considered great, it does not cost the spreader much to restructure himself into a position with a much broader maximum profit area.

A similar situation is available if the underlying stock moves up in price. In that case, the bull spread may be able to be removed at nearly its maximum profit potential, thereby leaving a bear spread. Again, suppose that the same initial spread was established but that XYZ has risen to 75. When the underlying stock advances substantially, the bull spread portion of the butterfly spread may expand to near its maximum potential. Since the strikes are 10 points apart in this bull spread, the widest that it can grow to is 10 points. At the prices shown in Table 10-4, the bull spread—long July 50 and short July 60—has grown to 9½ points. Thus the bull spread position could be removed within ½ point of its maximum profit potential and the original butterfly spread would become a bear spread. Note that the closing of the bull spread portion generates a 9½-point *credit*—the July 50 is sold at 25½ and the July 60 is bought back at 16. The original butterfly spread was established at a 3-point debit, so the net position is the remaining position:

TABLE 10-4.
Initial spread and new current prices.

Initial Spread		Current Prices	
XYZ common:	60	XYZ common:	75
XYZ July 50 call:	12	July 50 call:	25½
July 60 call:	6	July 60 call:	16
July 70 call:	3	July 70 call:	7

$$\left. \begin{array}{l} \text{Long July 70 call} \\ \text{Short July 60 call} \end{array} \right\} - \text{net credit } 6\frac{1}{2} \text{ points}$$

This bear spread has a maximum profit potential of 6½ points anywhere below 60 at July expiration. The maximum risk is 3½ points anywhere above 70 at expiration. Thus the original butterfly spread was again converted into a position where a stock price reversal to any price below 60 could produce something close to the maximum profit. Moreover, the risk was only increased by an additional ½ point.

SUMMARY

The butterfly spread is a viable, low-cost strategy with both limited profit potential and limited risk. It is actually a combination of a bull spread and a bear spread, and involves using three striking prices. The risk is limited should the underlying stock fall below the lowest strike or rise above the highest strike. The maximum profit is obtained at the middle strike. One can keep his initial debits to a minimum by initially assuming a bullish or bearish posture on the underlying stock. If he would rather remain neutral, he will normally have to pay a slightly larger debit to establish the spread, but may have a better chance of making money. If the underlying stock experiences a large move in one direction or the other prior to expiration, the spreader may want to close the profitable side of his butterfly spread near its maximum profit potential in order to be able to capitalize on a stock price reversal, should one occur.

Chapter 11

Ratio Call Spreads

A *ratio call spread* is a neutral strategy in which one buys a number of calls at a lower strike and sells more calls at a higher strike. It is somewhat similar to a ratio write in concept, although the spread has less downside risk and normally requires a smaller investment than does a ratio write. The ratio spread and ratio write are similar in that both involve uncovered calls, and both have profit ranges within which a profit can be made at expiration. Other comparisons will be demonstrated throughout the chapter.

    Example: The following prices exist:

XYZ common, 44;

XYZ April 40 call, 5; and

XYZ April 45 call, 3.

A 2:1 ratio call spread could be established by buying one April 40 call and simultaneously selling two April 45's. This spread would be done for a credit of 1 point—the sale of the two April 45's bringing in 6 points and the purchase of the April 40 costing 5 points. This spread can be entered as one spread order, specifying the net credit or debit for the position. In this case, the spread would be entered at a net credit of 1 point.

Ratio spreads, unlike ratio writes, have a relatively small, limited downside risk. In fact, if the spread is established at an initial credit, there is no downside risk at all. In a ratio spread, *the profit or loss at expiration is constant below the lower striking price*, because both options would be worthless in that area. In the example above, if XYZ is below 40 at April expiration, all the options would expire worthless and the spreader would have made a profit of his initial 1-point credit, less commissions. This 1-point gain would occur anywhere below 40 at expiration—it is a constant.

The maximum profit at expiration for a ratio spread occurs if the stock is exactly at the striking price of the written options. This is true for nearly all types of strategies involving written options. In the example, if XYZ were at 45 at April expiration, the April 45 calls would expire worthless for a gain of $600 on the two of them, and the April 40 call would be worth 5 points, resulting in no gain or loss on that call. Thus the total profit would be $600 less commissions.

The greatest risk in a ratio call spread lies to the upside, where the loss may theoretically be unlimited. The upside break-even point in this example is 51, as shown in Table 11-1. The table and Figure 11-1 illustrate the statements made in the preceding paragraphs.

In a 2:1 ratio spread two calls are sold for each one purchased. The maximum profit amount and the upside break-even point can be easily computed by using the following formulae:

Points of maximum profit = initial credit + difference between strikes or

= difference between strikes − initial debit

Upside break-even point = higher strike price + points of maximum profit

TABLE 11-1.
Ratio call spread.

XYZ Price at Expiration	April 40 Call Profits	April 45 Call Profits	Total Profits
35	− $ 500	+ $ 600	+ $100
40	− 500	+ 600	+ 100
42	− 300	+ 600	+ 300
45	0	+ 600	+ 600
48	+ 300	0	+ 300
51	+ 600	− 600	0
55	+ 1,000	− 1,400	− 400
60	+ 1,500	− 2,400	− 900

FIGURE 11-1.
Ratio call spread (2:1).

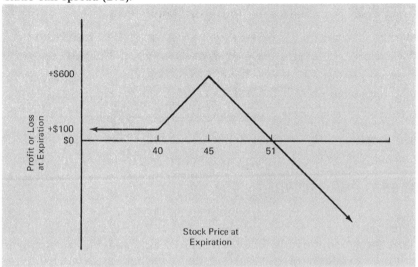

In the preceding example, the initial credit was 1 point, so the points of maximum profit = 1 + 5 = 6, or $600. The upside break-even point is then 45 + 6, or 51. This agrees with the results determined earlier. Note that if the spread is established at a debit rather than a credit, the debit is subtracted from the striking price differential to determine the points of maximum profit.

Many neutral investors prefer ratio spreads over ratio writes for two reasons:

1. The downside risk or gain is predetermined in the ratio spread at expiration, and therefore the position does not require much monitoring on the downside.
2. The margin investment required for a ratio spread is normally smaller than that required for a ratio write, since on the long side one is buying a call rather than buying the common stock itself.

For margin purposes, a ratio spread is really the combination of a bull spread and a naked call write. There is no margin requirement for a bull spread other than the net debit to establish the bull spread. The net investment for the ratio spread is thus equal to the collateral required for the naked calls in the spread plus or minus the net debit or credit of the spread. In the example above, there is one naked call. The requirement for the naked call is 20% of the stock price plus the call premium, less the out-of-the-money amount. So the requirement in the example would be 20% of 44, or $880, plus the call premium of $300, less the one point that the stock is below the striking price—a $1,060 requirement for the naked call. Since the spread was established at a credit of one point, this credit can also be applied against the initial requirement, thereby reducing that requirement to $960. Since there is a naked call in this spread, there will be a *mark to market* if the stock moves up. Just as was recommended for the ratio write, *it is recommended that the ratio spreader allow at least enough collateral to reach the upside break-even point.* Since the upside break-even point is 51 in this example, the spreader should allow 20% of 51, or $1,020, plus the 6 points that the call would be worth less the 1-point initial net credit—a total of $1,520 for this spread ($1,020 + $600 − $100).

DIFFERING PHILOSOPHIES

As in many strategies, there is more than one philosophy of how to implement the strategy. Ratio spreads are no exception, with three philosophies being predominant. One philosophy holds that ratio spreading is quite similar to ratio writing—that one should be looking for opportunities to purchase an in-the-money call with little or no time premium in it so that the ratio spread simulates the profit opportunities from the ratio write as closely as possible with a smaller investment. The ratio spreads established under this philosophy may have rather large debits if the purchased call is substantially in-the-money. Another philosophy of ratio spreading is that spreads should be established for credits so that there is no chance of losing money on the downside. Both philosophies have merit and both will be described. A third philosophy, called the "delta spread," is more concerned with neutrality, regardless of the initial debit or credit.

Ratio Spread as Ratio Write

There are several spread strategies similar to strategies that involve common stock. In this case, the ratio spread is similar to the ratio write. Whenever such a similarity exists, it may be possible for the strategist to buy an in-the-money call with little or no time premium as a substitute for buying the common stock. This was seen earlier in the covered call writing strategy, where it was shown that the purchase of in-the-money calls or warrants might be a viable substitute for the purchase of stock. *If one is able to buy an in-the-money call as a substitute for the stock, he will not affect his profit potential substantially.* When comparing a ratio spread to a ratio write, the maximum profit potential and the profit range are reduced by the time value premium paid for the long call. If this call is at parity (the time value premium is thus zero), the ratio spread and the ratio write have exactly the same profit potential. Moreover, the net investment is reduced and there is less downside risk should the stock fall in price below the striking price of the purchased call. The spread also involves smaller commission costs than does the ratio write, which involves a stock purchase. The ratio writer does receive stock dividends, if any are paid, whereas the spreader does not.

Example: XYZ is at 50, and an XYZ July 40 call is selling for 11 while an XYZ July 50 call is selling for 5. Table 11-2 compares the important points between the ratio write and the ratio spread.

In Chapter 6, it was pointed out that ratio writing was one of the better strategies from a probability of profit viewpoint. That is, the profit potential conforms well to the expected movement of the underlying stock. The same statement holds true for ratio spreads as substitutes for ratio writes. In fact, the ratio spread may often be a better position than the ratio write itself when the long call can be purchased with little or no time value premium in it.

Ratio Spread for Credits

The second philosophy of ratio spreads is to establish them only for credits. Strategists who follow this philosophy generally want a second criterion fulfilled also—that the underlying stock be below the striking price of the written calls when the spread is established. In fact, the farther the stock is below the strike, the more attractive the spread would be. This type of ratio spread has no downside risk, because, even if the stock collapses, the spreader will still make a profit equal to the initial credit received. This application of the ratio spread strategy is actually a subcase of the application discussed above. That is, it may be possible both to buy a long call for little or no time premium, thereby simulating a ratio write, and also to be able to set up the position for a credit as well.

Since the underlying stock is generally below the maximum profit point when one establishes a ratio spread for a credit, *this is actually a*

TABLE 11-2.
Ratio write and ratio spread compared.

	Ratio Write: Buy XYZ at 50 and Sell 2 July 50's at 5	Ratio Spread: Buy 1 July 40 at 11 and Sell 2 July 50's at 5
Profit range	40 to 60	41 to 59
Maximum profit	10 points	9 points
Downside risk	Unlimited	1 point
Upside risk	Unlimited	Unlimited
Initial investment	$3,000	$1,600

mildly bullish position. The investor would want the stock to move up slightly in order for his maximum profit potential to be realized. Of course, the position does have unlimited upside risk, so it is not an overly bullish strategy.

These two philosophies are not mutually exclusive. The strategist who uses ratio spreads without regard to whether they are debit or credit spreads will generally have a broader array of spreads to choose from and will also be able to assume a more neutral posture on the stock. The spreader who insists on generating credits only will be forced to establish spreads where his return will be slightly smaller if the underlying stock remains relatively unchanged. However, he will not have to worry about downside defensive action since he has no risk to the downside. The third philosphy—the "delta spread"—will be described after the next section, in which the uses of ratios other than 2:1 are described.

Altering the Ratio

Under either of the two philosophies discussed above, the strategist may find that a 3:1 ratio or a 3:2 ratio better suits his purposes than the 2:1 ratio. It is not common to write in a ratio of greater than 4:1 because of the large increase in upside risk at such high ratios. The higher the ratio that is used, the higher will be the credits of the spread. This means that the profits to the downside will be greater if the stock collapses. The lower the ratio that is used, the higher the upside break-even point will be, thereby reducing upside risk.

Example: If the same prices are used as in the initial example in this chapter, it will be possible to demonstrate these facts using three different ratios (Table 11-3):

XYZ common, 44;

XYZ April 40 call, 5; and

XYZ April 45 call, 3.

TABLE 11-3.
Comparison of three ratios.

	3:2 Ratio: Buy 2 April 40's Sell 3 April 45's	2:1 Ratio: Buy 1 April 40 Sell 2 April 45's	3:1 Ratio: Buy 1 April 40 Sell 3 April 45's
Price of spread (downside risk)	1 debit	1 credit	4 credit
Upside break-even	54	51	49½
Downside break-even	40½	None	None
Maximum profit	9	6	9

In Chapter 6, on ratio writing, it was seen that it was possible to alter the ratio to adjust the position to one's outlook for the underlying stock. The altering of the ratio in a ratio spread accomplishes the same objective. In fact, as will be pointed out later in the chapter, the ratio may be adjusted continuously to achieve what is considered to be a "neutral spread." A similar tactic, using the option's delta, was described for ratio writes.

The following formulae allow one to determine the maximum profit potential and upside break-even point for any ratio:

$$\text{Points of maximum profit} = \text{net credit} + \text{number of long calls} \times \text{difference in striking prices } or$$

$$= \text{number of long calls} \times \text{difference in striking prices} - \text{net debit}$$

$$\text{Upside break-even point} = \frac{\text{points of maximum profit}}{\text{number of naked calls}} + \text{higher striking price}$$

These formulae can easily be verified by checking the numbers in Table 11-3.

The "Delta Spread"

The third philosophy of ratio spreading is a more sophisticated approach that is often referred to as the "*delta spread*," because the deltas of the options are used to establish and monitor the spread. Recall that the delta of a call option is the amount by which the option is expected to increase in price if the underlying stock should rise by one point. *Delta spreads are neutral spreads* in that one uses the deltas of the two calls to set up a position that is initially neutral.

Example: The deltas of the two calls that appeared in the previous examples were .80 and .50 for the April 40 and April 45, respectively. If one were to buy 5 of the April 40's and simultaneously sell 8 of the April 45's, he would have a delta neutral spread. That is, if XYZ moved up by one point, the 5 April 40 calls would appreciate by .80 point each, for a net gain of 4 points. Similarly, his 8 April 45 calls that he is short would each appreciate by .50 point for a net loss of 4 points on the short side. Thus the spread is initially neutral—the long side and the short side will offset each other. *The idea of setting up this type of neutral spread is to be able to capture the time value premium decay in the preponderance of short calls without subjecting the spread to an inordinate amount of market risk.* The actual credit or debit of the spread is not a determining factor.

It is a fairly simple matter to determine the correct ratio to use in the delta spread—merely *divide the delta of the purchased call by the delta of the written call.* In the example, this implies that the neutral ratio is .80 divided by .50, or 1.6:1. Obviously, one cannot sell 1.6 calls, so it is common practice to express that ratio as 16:10. Thus the neutral spread would consist of buying 10 April 40's and selling 16 April 45's. This is the same as an 8:5 ratio. Notice that this calculation does not include anything about debits or credits involved in the spread. In this example, an 8:5 ratio would involve a small debit of one point (5 April 40's cost 25 points and 8 April 45's bring in 24 points). Generally, reasonably selected delta spreads involve small debits.

Certain selection criteria can be offered to help the spreader eliminate some of the myriad possibilities of delta spreads on a day-to-day basis. First, one does not want the ratio of the spread to be too large. An absolute limit, such as 4:1, can be placed on all spread candidates. Also, if one eliminates any options selling for less than ½ point as candidates for the short side of the spread, the higher ratios will be eliminated. Second, one does not want the ratio to be too *small.* If the delta neutral ratio is less than 1.2:1 (6:5), the spread should probably be rejected. Finally, if one is concerned with downside risk, he might want to limit the total debit outlay. This might be done with a simple parameter, such as not paying a debit of more than 1 point per long option. Thus in a spread involving 10 long calls, the total debit must be 10 points or less. These screens are quickly applied, especially with the aid of a computer analysis. One merely uses the deltas to determine the neutral ratio. Then if it is too small or too large, or if it requires the outlay of too large of a debit, the spread is rejected from consideration. If not, it is a potential candidate for investment.

FOLLOW-UP ACTION

Depending on the initial credit or debit of the spread, it may not be necessary to take any downside defensive action at all. *If the initial debit was large, the writer may roll down the written calls as in a ratio write.*

Example: An investor has established the ratio write by buying an XYZ July 40 call and selling two July 60 calls with the stock near 60. He might have done this because the July 40 was selling at parity. If the underlying stock declines, this spreader could roll down to the 50's and then to the 45's, in the same manner as he would with a ratio write. *On the other hand, if the spread was initially set up with contiguous striking prices—the lower strike being just below the higher strike—no rolling-down action would be necessary.*

Reducing the Ratio

Upside follow-up action does not normally consist of rolling up as it does in a ratio write. Rather, one should usually buy in some more long calls to reduce the ratio in the spread. Eventually, he would want to reduce the spread to 1:1, or a normal bull spread. An example may help to illustrate this concept.

Example: In the initial example, one April 40 call was bought and two April 45's were sold, for a net credit of one point. Assume that the spreader is going to buy one more April 40 as a means of upside defensive action if he has to. When and if he buys this second long call, his total position will be a normal bull spread—long 2 April 40's and short 2 April 45's. The liquidating value of this bull spread would be 10 points if XYZ were above 45 at April expiration, since each of the two bull spreads would widen to its maximum potential—five points—with the stock above 45 in April. The ratio spreader originally brought in a one-point credit for the 2:1 spread. If he were later to pay 11 points to buy the additional long April 40 call, his total outlay would have been 10 points. This would represent a break-even situation at April expiration if XYZ were above 45 at that time, since it was just shown that the spread could be liquidated for 10 points in that case. So the ratio spreader could wait to take defensive action until the April call was selling for 11 points. This is a dynamic type of follow-up action, one that is dependent on the options' price, not the stock price per se.

This outlay of 11 points for the April 40 would leave a break-even situation as long as the stock did not reverse and fall in price below 45 after the call was bought. The spreader may decide that he would rather leave some room for upside profit rather than merely trying to break even if the stock rallies too far. He might thus decide to buy in the long call at 9 or 10 points rather than waiting for it to get to 11. Of course, this might increase the chances of a whipsaw occurring, but it would leave some room for upside profits if the stock continues to rise.

Where ratios other than 2:1 are involved initially, the same thinking can be applied. In fact, the purchase of the additional long calls might take place in a two-step process.

Example: If the spread was initially long 5 calls and short 10 calls, the spreader would not necessarily have to wait until the April 40's were selling at 11 and then buy in all five of the ones needed to make the spread a normal bull spread. He might decide to buy 2 or 3 at a lower price, thereby reducing his ratio somewhat. Then, if the stock rallied even further, he could buy in the remaining long calls. By buying in a few at a cheaper price, the spreader gives himself the leeway to wait considerably longer to the upside. In essence, all five additional long calls in this spread would have to be bought at an average price of 11 or lower in order for the spread to break even. However, if the first two of them are bought for 8 points, the spreader would not have to buy in the remaining 3 until they were selling around 13. Thus he could wait longer to the upside before reducing the spread ratio to 1:1 (a bull spread). There is a formula that can be applied to determine the price one would have to pay for the additional long calls, to convert the ratio spread into a bull spread. If the calls are bought in, such a bull spread would break even with the stock above the higher striking price at expiration:

$$\frac{\text{Break-even cost of}}{\text{long calls}} = \frac{\text{number of short calls} \times \text{difference in strikes} - \text{total debit to date}}{\text{number of naked calls}}$$

In the simple 2:1 example, the number of short calls was 2, the difference in the strikes was 5, the total debit was minus one (-1) (since it was actually a 1-point credit), and the number of naked calls is 1. Thus the break-even cost of the additional long call is $[2 \times 5 - (-1)]/1 = 11$. As another verification of the formula, consider the 10:5 spread at the same prices. The initial credit of this spread would be 5 points and the break-even cost of the five additional long calls is 11 points each. Assume that the spreader bought in two additional April 40's for 8 points each (16 debit). This would make the total debit to date of the spread equal to 11 points, and reduce the number of naked calls to 3. The break-even cost of the remaining 3 long calls that would need to be purchased if the stock continued to rally would be $(10 \times 5 - 11)/3 = 13$. This agrees with the observation made earlier. This formula can be used before actual follow-up action is implemented. For example, in the 10:5 spread, if the April 40's were selling for 8, the spreader might ask: "To what would I raise the purchase price of the remaining long calls if I buy 2 April 40's for 8 right now?" By using the formula, he could easily see that the answer would be 13.

Adjusting with the Delta

The theoretically oriented spreader can use the delta neutral ratio to monitor his spreads as well as to establish them. If the underlying stock moves up in price too far or down in price too far, the delta neutral ratio of the spread will change. The spreader can then readjust his spread to a neutral status by buying in some additional long calls on an upside movement by the stock, or by selling some additional short calls on a downward movement by the stock. Either action will serve to make the spread delta neutral again. The public customer who is employing the delta neutral adjustment method of follow-up action should be careful not to overadjust, because the commission costs would become prohibitive. A more detailed description of the use of the deltas as a means of follow-up action is contained in Chapter 30 under market-maker strategies, but the general concept is the same as that shown earlier for ratio writing. A brief example will explain the concept.

Example: Early in this chapter, when selection criteria were described, a neutral ratio was determined to be 16:10, with XYZ at 44. Suppose, after establishing the spread, that the common rallied to 48. One could use the current deltas to adjust. This information is summarized in Table 11-4. The current neutral ratio is approximately 14:10. Thus two of the short April 45's could be bought closing. In practice, one usually decreases his ratio by adding to the long side. Consequently, one would buy two April 40's, decreasing his overall ratio to 16:12, which is 1.33 and is close to the actual neutral ratio of 1.38. The position would therefore be delta neutral once more.

An alternative way of looking at this is to use the equivalent stock position (ESP), which, for any option, is the multiple of the quantity times the delta times the shares per option. The last three lines of Table 11-4 show the ESP for each call and for the position as a whole. Initially, the position has an ESP of 0, indicating that it is perfectly delta neutral. In the current situation, however, the position is delta short 140 shares. Thus, one could adjust the position to be delta neutral by buying 140 shares of XYZ. If he wanted to use the options rather than the stock, he could buy two April 45's which would add a delta long of 130 ESP ($2 \times .65 \times 100$) leaving the position delta short 10 shares, which is very near neutral. As pointed out in the above paragraph, the spreader probably should buy the call with the most intrinsic value—the April 40. Each one of these has an ESP of 90 ($1 \times .9 \times 100$). Thus, if one were bought the position would

TABLE 11-4.
Original and current prices and deltas.

	Original Situation	Current Situation
XYZ common	44	47
April 40 call	5	8
April 45 call	3	5
April 40 delta	.80	.90
April 45 delta	.50	.65
Neutral ratio	16:10 (.80/.50)	14:10 (.90/.65 = 1.38)
April 40 ESP	800 long (10 × .8 × 100)	900 long (10 × .9 × 100)
April 45 ESP	800 shrt (16 × .5 × 100)	1040 shrt (16 × .65 × 100)
Total ESP	0 (neutral)	140 shrt

be delta short 50 shares, or if two were bought, the total position would be delta *long* 40 shares. It would be a matter of individual preference for the spreader as to whether he wanted to be long or short the "odd lot" of 40 or 50 shares, respectively.

The ESP method is merely a confirmation of the other method. Either one works well. The spreader should become familiar with the ESP method because, in a position with many different options, it reduces the exposure on the entire position to a single number.

Taking Profits

In addition to defensive action, the spreader may find that he can close the spread early to take a profit or to limit losses. If enough time has passed and the underlying stock is close to the maximum profit point—the higher striking price—the spreader may want to consider closing the spread and taking his profit. Similarly, if the underlying stock is somewhere between the two strikes as expiration draws near, the writer will normally find himself with a profit as the long call retains some intrinsic value and the short calls are nearly worthless. If at this time one feels that there is little to gain (a price decline might wipe out the long call value), he should close the spread and take his profit.

SUMMARY

Ratio spreads can be an attractive strategy, similar in some ways to ratio writing. Both strategies offer a large probability of making a limited profit. The ratio spread has limited downside risk, or possibly no downside risk at all. In addition, if the long call(s) in the spread can be bought with little or no time value premium in them, the ratio spread becomes a superior strategy to the ratio write. One can adjust the ratio used to reflect his opinion on the underlying stock or to make a neutral profit range if desired. The ratio adjustment can be accomplished by using the deltas of the options. In a broad sense, this is one of the more attractive forms of spreading, since the strategist is buying mostly intrinsic value and is selling a relatively large amount of time value.

Chapter 12

Combining Calendar and Ratio Spreads

The previous chapters on spreading have introduced the basic types of spreads. The simplest forms of bull spreads, bear spreads, or calendar spreads can often be combined to produce a position with a more attractive potential. The butterfly spread, which is a combination of a bull spread and a bear spread, is an example of such a combination. The next three chapters will be devoted to describing other combinations of spreads, wherein the strategist not only mixes basic strategies—bull, bear, and calendar—but also uses varying expiration dates as well. Although these may seem overly complicated at first glance, they are combinations that are often employed by professionals in the field.

RATIO CALENDAR SPREAD

In this chapter, the *ratio calendar spread* will be described. It is a combination of the techniques used in the calendar and ratio spreads. Recall that one philosophy of the calendar spread strategy was to sell the near-term call and buy a longer-term call, with both being out-of-the-money. This is a bullish calendar spread. If the underlying stock never advances, the spreader loses the entire amount of the relatively small debit that he paid for the spread. However, if the stock advances after the near-term call expires worthless, large profits are possible. It was stated that this bullish calendar spread philosophy had a small probability of attaining large profits, and that the few profits could easily exceed the preponderance of small losses.

The ratio calendar spread is an attempt to raise the probabilities while allowing for large potential profits. *In the ratio calendar spread, one sells a number of near-term calls while buying fewer of the intermediate-term or long-term calls.* Since more calls are being sold than are being bought, naked options are involved. It is often possible to set up a ratio calendar spread for a credit, meaning that if the underlying stock never rallies above the strike, the strategist will still make money. However, since there are naked calls involved, the collateral requirements for participating in this strategy may be large.

Example: As in the bullish calendar spreads described in Chapter 9, the prices are:

XYZ common, 45;

XYZ April 50 call, 1; and

XYZ July 50 call, 1½.

In the bullish calendar spread strategy, one July 50 is bought for each April 50 sold. This means that the spread is established for a debit of ½ point and that the investment is $50 per spread, plus commissions. The strategist using the ratio calendar spread has essentially the same philosophy as the bullish calendar spreader—the stock will remain below 50 until April expiration and may then rally. The ratio calendar spread might be set up as follows:

Buy 1 XYZ July 50 call at 1½	1½ debit
Sell 2 XYZ April 50 calls at 1 each	2 credit
Net	½ credit

Although there is no cash involved in setting up the ratio spread since it is done for a credit, there is a collateral requirement for the naked April 50 call.

If the stock remains below 50 until April expiration, the long call—the July 50—will be owned free. After that, no matter what happens to the underlying stock, the spread cannot lose money. In fact, if the underlying stock advances dramatically after near-term expiration, large profits will accrue as the July 50 call increases in value. Of course, this is entirely dependent on the near-term call expiring worthless. If the underlying stock should rally above 50 before the April calls expire, the ratio calendar spread is in danger of losing a large amount of money because of the naked calls, and defensive action must be taken. Follow-up actions will be described later.

The collateral required for the ratio calendar spread is equal to the amount of collateral required for the naked calls less the credit taken in for the spread. Since naked calls will be marked to market as the stock moves up, *it is always best to allow enough collateral to get to a defensive action point*. In the example above, suppose that one felt he would definitely be taking defensive action if the stock rallied to 53 before April expiration. He should then figure his collateral requirement as if the stock were at 53, regardless of what the collateral requirement is at the current time. *This is a prudent tactic wherever naked options are involved, since the strategist will never be forced into an unwanted close-out before his defensive action point is reached*. The collateral required for this example would then be:

20% of 53		$1,060
Call premium	+	350
Less initial credit	−	50
Total collateral to set aside		$1,360

The strategist is not really "investing" anything in this strategy, because his requirement is in the form of collateral, not cash. That is, his current portfolio assets need not be disturbed to set up this spread, although losses would, of course, create debits in the account. Many naked option strategies are similar in this respect, and the strategist may earn additional money from the collateral value of his portfolio without disturbing the portfolio itself. However, he should take care to operate such strategies in a conservative manner since *any* income earned is "free," but losses may force him to disturb his portfolio. In light of this fact, it is always difficult to compute returns on investment in a strategy that requires only collateral to operate. One can, of course, compute computation because the collateral itself is making a return also. The large investor participating in such a strategy should be satisfied with any sort of positive return.

Returning to the example above, the strategist would make his $50 credit, less commissions, if the underlying stock remained below 50 until July expiration. It is not possible to determine the results to the upside so definitively. If the April 50 calls expire worthless and then the stock rallies, the potential profits are limited only by time. The case where the stock rallies before April expiration is of the most concern. If the stock rallies *immediately*, the spread will undoubtedly show a loss. If the stock rallies to 50 more slowly, but still before April expiration, it is possible that the spread will not have changed much. Again using the same example, suppose that XYZ rallies to 50 with only a few weeks of life remaining in the April 50 calls. Then the April 50 calls might be selling at 1½ while the July 50 call might be selling at 3. The ratio spread could be closed for even money at that point—the cost of buying back the 2 April 50's would equal the credit received from selling the one July 50. He would thus make ½ point, less commissions, on the entire spread transaction. Finally, at the expiration date of the April 50 calls, one can estimate where he would break even. Suppose one estimated that the July 50 call would be selling for 5½ points if XYZ were at 53 at April expiration. Since the April 50 calls would be selling for 3 at that time (they would be at parity), there would be a debit of ½ point to close the ratio spread. The two April 50 calls would be bought for 6 points and the July 50 call sold for 5½—a ½ debit. The entire spread transaction would thus have broken even, less commissions, at 53 at April expiration since the spread was put on for a ½ credit and was taken off for a ½ debit. *The risk to the upside depends clearly, then, on how quickly the stock rallies above 50 before April expiration.*

CHOOSING THE SPREAD

Some of the same criteria used in setting up a bullish calendar spread apply here as well. Select a stock that is volatile enough to move above the striking price in the allotted time—after the near-term expires, but before the long call expires. Do not use calls that are so far out-of-the-money that it would be virtually impossible for the stock to reach the striking price. Always set up the spread for a credit, commissions included. This will assure that a profit will be made even if the stock goes nowhere. However, if the credit has to be generated by using an extremely large ratio—greater than 3 short calls to every long one—one should be extremely selective in attempting to set up the spread, since the potential losses in an immediate rally would be large.

The *upside break-even point* prior to April expiration should be determined using a pricing model. Such a model, or the output from one, can generally be obtained from a data service or from some brokerage firms. It is useful to the strategist to know exactly how much room he has to the upside if the stock begins to rally. This will allow him to take defensive action in the form of closing out the spread before his break-even point is reached. Since a pricing model can estimate a call price for any length of time, the strategist can compute his break-even points at April expiration, 1 month before April expiration, 6 weeks before, and so on. When the long option in a spread expires at a different time than the short option, the break-even point is dynamic. That is, it changes with time. Table 12-1 shows how this information might be accumulated for the example spread used above. Since this example spread was established for a ½-point credit with the stock at 45, the break-even points would be at stock prices where the spread could be removed for a ½-point debit. Suppose the spread was initiated with 95 days remaining until April expiration. In each line of the table, the cost for buying 2 April 50's is ½ point more than the price of the July 50. That is, there would be a ½-point debit involved in closing the spread at those prices. Notice that *the break-even price increases as time passes*. Initially, the spread would show a loss if the stock moved up at all. This is to be expected, since an immediate move would not allow for any erosion in the time value premium of the near-term calls. As more and more time passes, time weighs more heavily on the near-term April calls than on the longer-term July call. Once the strategist has this information, he might then look at a chart of the underlying stock. If there is resistance for XYZ below 53, his eventual break-even point at April expiration, he could then feel more confident about this spread.

FOLLOW-UP ACTION

The main purpose of defensive action in this strategy is to limit losses if the stock should rally before April expiration. The strategist should be quick to close out the spread before any serious losses accrue. The long call quite adequately compensates for the losses on the short calls up to a certain point, a fact demonstrated in Table 12-1. However, the stock cannot be allowed to run. A rule of thumb that is often useful is to close the spread if the stock breaks out above technical resistance or if it breaks above the eventual break-even point at expiration. In the example above, the strategist would close the spread if, at any time, XYZ rose above 53 (before April expiration, of course).

If a significant amount of time has passed, the strategist might act even more quickly in closing the spread. As was shown earlier, if the

TABLE 12-1.
Break-even points changing over time.

Days Remaining Until April Expiration	Break-Even Point (Stock Price)	Estimated April 50 Price	Estimated July 50 Price
90	45	1	1½
60	48	1½	2½
30	51	2½	4½
0	53	3	5½

stock rallies to 50 with only a few weeks of time remaining, the spread may actually be at a slight profit at that time. It is often the best course of action to take the small profit, if the stock rises above the striking price.

The Probabilities Are Good

This is a strategy with a rather large probability of profit, provided that the defensive action described above is adhered to. The spread will make money if the stock never rallies above the striking price, since the spread is established for a credit. This in itself is a rather high-probability event, because the stock is initially below the striking price. In addition, the spread can make large potential profits if the stock rallies after the near-term calls expire. Although this is a much less probable event, the profits that can accrue add to the expected return of the spread. The only time that the spread loses is when the stock rallies quickly, and the strategist should close out the spread in that case to limit losses.

Although Table 12-2 is not mathematically definitive, it can be seen that this strategy has a positive expected return. Small profits occur more frequently than small losses do, and sometimes large profits can occur. These expected outcomes, when coupled with the fact that the strategist may utilize collateral such as stocks, bonds, or government securities to set up these spreads, demonstrate that this is a viable strategy for the advanced investor.

DELTA NEUTRAL CALENDAR SPREADS

The preceding discussion dealt with a specific kind of ratio calendar spread—the out-of-the-money call spread. A more accurate ratio can be constructed using the deltas of the calls involved, similar to the ratio spreads in the previous chapter. The spread can be created with either out-of-the-money calls or in-the-money calls. The former has naked calls,

TABLE 12-2.
Profitability of ratio calendar spreading.

Event	Outcome	Probability
Stock never rallies above strike	Small profit	Large probability
Stock rallies above strike in a short time	Small loss if defensive action employed	Small probability
Stock rallies above strike after near-term call expires	Large potential profit	Small probability

while the latter has extra long calls. Both types of ratio calendars will be described.

In either case, the number of calls to sell for each one purchased is determined by dividing the delta of the long call by the delta of the short call. This is the same for any ratio spread, not just calendars.

Example: Suppose XYZ is trading at 45 and one is considering using the July 50 call and the April 50 call to establish a ratio calendar spread. This is the same situation that was described earlier in this chapter. Furthermore assume that the deltas of the calls in question are .25 for the July and .15 for the April. Given that information, one can compute the neutral ratio to be 1.667 to 1 (.25/.15). That is, one would sell 1.667 calls for each one he bought; restated, he would sell 5 for each 3 bought.

This out-of-the-money neutral calendar is typical. One normally sells more calls than he buys to establish a neutral calendar when the calls are out-of-the-money. The ramifications of this strategy have already been described earlier in this chapter. Follow-up strategy is slightly different, though, and will be described later.

When the calls are in-the-money, the neutral spread has a distinctly different look. An example will help in describing the situation.

Example: XYZ is trading at 49, and one wants to establish a neutral calendar spread using the July 45 and April 45 calls. The deltas of these in-the-money calls are .8 for the April and .7 for the July. *Note that for in-the-money calls, a shorter-term call has a higher delta than a longer-term call.*

The neutral ratio for this in-the-money spread would be .875 to 1 (.7/.8). This means that .875 calls would be sold for each one bought; restated, 7 calls would be sold and 8 bought. Thus, the spreader is buying more calls than he is selling when establishing an in-the-money neutral calendar.

This type of position can be quite attractive. First of all, there is no risk to the upside as there is with the out-of-the-money calendar. Thus, if there were to be a large gap to the upside in XYZ—perhaps caused by a takeover attempt—the in-the-money calendar would make money. If, on the other hand, XYZ stays in the same area, then the spread will make money. Even though the extra call would probably lose some time value premium in that event, the other seven spreads would make a large enough profit to easily compensate for the loss on the one long call. The least desirable result would be for XYZ to drop precipitously, but then follow-up action can be taken. Even in the case of XYZ dropping, however, the loss is limited to the amount of the initial debit of the spread.

There are no naked calls to margin with this strategy, making it attractive to many smaller investors. In the above example, one would need to pay for the entire debit of the position, but there would be no further requirements.

FOLLOW-UP ACTION

If one decides to preserve a neutral strategy with follow-up action in either type of ratio call calendar, he would merely need to look at the deltas of the calls and keep the ratio neutral. Doing so might mean that one would switch from one type of spread to the other. For example, if XYZ started at 45, as in the first example, one would have sold more calls than he bought. If XYZ then rallied above 50, he would have to move his position into the in-the-money ratio and get long more calls than he is short.

While such follow-up action is strategically correct—maintaining the neutral ratio—it might not make sense practically, especially if the size of the original spread were small. If one had originally sold 5 and bought 3, he would be better to adhere to the follow-up strategy outlined earlier in this chapter. The spread is not large enough to dictate adjusting via the delta neutral ratios. If, however, a large trader had originally sold 500 calls and bought 300, then he has enough profitability in the spread to make several adjustments along the way.

In a similar manner, the spreader who had established a small in-the-money calendar might decide not to bother ratioing the spread if the stock dropped below the strike. He knows his risk is limited to his initial debit, and that would be small for a small spread. He might not want to introduce naked options into the position if XYZ declines. However, if the same spread were established by a large trader, it *should* be adjusted because of the greater tolerance of the spread to being adjusted, merely because of its size.

Chapter *13*

Reverse Spreads

In general, when a strategy has the term "reverse" in its name, the strategy is the opposite of a more commonly used strategy. The reader should be familiar with this nomenclature from the earlier discussions comparing ratio writing (buying stock and selling calls) with reverse hedging (shorting stock and buying calls). If the reverse strategy is sufficiently well-known, it usually acquires a name of its own. For example, the bear spread is really the reverse of the bull spread, but the bear spread is a popular enough strategy in its own right to have acquired a shorter, unique name.

REVERSE CALENDAR SPREAD

One type of reverse spread that is infrequently used is the *reverse calendar spread*. This strategy is not particularly attractive, but it is being included in this discussion to point out why it should *not* generally be used. In a reverse calendar spread, one would buy the near-term call and sell a longer-term call at the same strike. Note that this is exactly the opposite of the calendar spread. The reverse calendar spread would be established for a credit and the strategist would like the spread to shrink in value.

Again, this is opposite of the calendar spread, where the spread is initially put on for a debit and the strategist wants the spread to widen. For a calendar spread to shrink in value, the stock must move far away from the striking price before the near-term call expires. The spread cannot shrink to less than zero, however, so the reverse calendar spread has a limited profit potential equal to the net credit taken in initially. To demonstrate the profit potential of the reverse calendar spread, it is useful to look at the extreme cases. Suppose the stock falls dramatically in price. Then both options would be nearly worthless and the spread between the two would approach zero. On the other hand, if the stock rises dramatically in price, both options would trade at parity and again the spread would approach zero.

The risk would always be greater than the profit potential. The reverse calendar spread would have its greatest loss at near-term expiration if the underlying stock were exactly at the striking price. The near-term call, which is held long, would expire worthless, and the longer-term call, which is short, would have to be bought back. It has been demonstrated earlier that a calendar spread widens to its fullest extent if the stock is exactly at the striking price when the near-term call expires. Thus the reverse calendar spread would perform worst in that case. This would represent a limited loss, but it could possibly be two or three times the original credit.

The long-term call in the reverse calendar spread is a naked call. Recall that the margin definition of a spread requires that the long option have an expiration equal to or longer than the short option. This is not true in a reverse calendar spread, so the collateral requirement would be equal to the collateral required for the naked longer-term call, less the initial credit received, plus commission costs. Note that if the underlying stock advances substantially—representing a desirable event in the reverse calendar spread since the spread will be approaching zero differential—the collateral requirement will grow quite large as the naked call is marked to market. So even if the spread is shrinking, the increase in investment may become prohibitive.

No serious strategist employs this strategy by itself as a profit-making vehicle. For some reason, the strategy often appeals to the novice as "something to try," and is being included here to demonstrate that it is *not* something to try.

REVERSE RATIO SPREAD (BACKSPREAD)

A more sensible reverse strategy is *the reverse ratio call spread. In this type of spread one would sell a call at one striking price and then would buy several calls at a higher striking price.* This is exactly the opposite of the ratio spread described in Chapter 11. This position is also known as a *backspread. As in most reverse spreading strategies, the spreader wants the stock to move dramatically.* He does not generally care whether it moves up or down. Recall that in the reverse hedge strategy described in Chapter 4, the strategist had the potential for large profits if the stock moved either up or down by a great deal. In the reverse ratio spread, large potential profits exist if the stock moves up dramatically, but there is a limited profit potential to the downside.

Example: XYZ is selling for 43 and the July 40 call is at 4, with the July 45 call at 1. A reverse ratio spread would be established as follows:

Buy 2 July 45 calls at 1 each	2 debit
Sell 1 July 40 call at 4	4 credit
Net	2 credit

These spreads are generally established for credits. In fact, *if the spread cannot be initiated at a credit, it is usually not attractive.* If the underlying stock drops in price and is below 40 at July expiration, all the calls will expire worthless and the strategist will make a profit equal to his initial credit. The maximum *downside* potential of the reverse ratio spread is equal to the initial credit received. On the other hand, if the stock rallies substantially, the potential *upside* profits are unlimited, since the spreader owns more calls than he is short. *Simplistically, the investor is bullish and is buying out-of-the-money calls but is simultaneously hedging himself by selling another call.* He can profit if the stock rises in price, as he thought it would, but he also profits if the stock collapses and all the calls expire worthless.

This strategy has limited risk. *With most spreads, the maximum loss is attained at expiration at the striking price of the purchased call.* This is a true statement for reverse ratio spreads.

Example: If XYZ is at exactly 45 at July expiration, the July 45 calls will expire worthless for a loss of $200 and the July 40 call will have to be bought back for 5 points, a $100 loss on that call. The total loss would thus be $300, and this is the most that can be lost in this example. If the underlying stock should rally dramatically, this strategy has unlimited profit potential, since there are two long calls for each short one. In fact, one can always compute the upside break-even point at expiration. That break-even point happens to be 48 in this example. At 48 at July expiration, each July 45 call would be worth 3 points, for a net gain of $400 on the two of them. The July 40 call would be worth 8 with the stock at 48 at expiration, representing a $400 loss on that call. Thus the gain and the loss are offsetting and the spread breaks even, except for commissions, at

48 at expiration. If the stock is higher than 48 at July expiration, profits will result.

Table 13-1 and Figure 13-1 depict the potential profits and losses from this example of a reverse ratio spread. Note that the profit graph is exactly like the profit graph of a ratio spread that has been rotated around the stock price axis. Refer to Figure 11-1 for a graph of the ratio spread. There is actually a range outside of which profits can be made—below 42 or above 48 in this example. The maximum loss occurs at the striking price of the purchased calls—45—at expiration.

There are no naked calls in this strategy, so *the investment is relatively small*. The strategy is actually a long call added to a bear spread.

TABLE 13-1.
Profits and losses for reverse ratio spread.

XYZ Price at July Expiration	Profit on 1 July 40	Profit on 2 July 45's	Total Profit
35	+$ 400	−$ 200	+$ 200
40	+ 400	− 200	+ 200
42	+ 200	− 200	0
45	− 100	− 200	− 300
48	− 400	+ 400	0
55	− 1,100	+ 1,800	+ 700
70	− 2,600	+ 4,800	+ 2,200

FIGURE 13-1.
Reverse ratio spread (backspread).

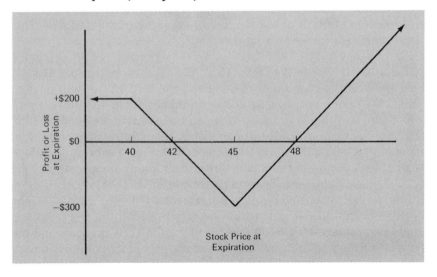

In this example, the bear spread portion is long the July 45 and short the July 40. This requires a $500 collateral requirement, because there are 5 points difference in the striking prices. The credit of $200 received for the spread can be applied against the initial requirement, so that the total requirement would be $300 plus commissions. There is no increase or decrease in this requirement since there are no naked calls.

Notice that *the concept of a delta neutral spread can be utilized in this strategy*, in much the same way that it was used for the ratio call spread. The number of calls to buy and sell can be computed mathematically by using the deltas of the options involved.

Example: The neutral ratio is determined by dividing the delta of the July 45 into the delta of the July 40.

	Prices		Delta
XYZ common:		43	
XYZ July 40 call:		4	.80
XYZ July 45 call:		1	.35

In this case, that would be a ratio of 2.29:1 (.80/.35). That is, if one sold five July 40's, he would buy 11 July 45's (or if he sold 10, he would then buy 23). By beginning with a neutral ratio, the spreader should be able to make money on a quick move by the stock in either direction.

The neutral ratio can also help the spreader to avoid being too bearish or too bullish to begin with. For example, a spreader would not be bullish enough if he merely used a 2:1 ratio for convenience, instead of using the 2.4:1 ratio. If anything, one might normally establish the spread with an extra bullish emphasis since the largest profits are to the upside. There is little reason for the spreader to have too little bullishness in this strategy. Thus, if the deltas are correct, the neutral ratio can aid the spreader in the determination of a more accurate initial ratio.

The strategist must be alert to the possibility of early exercise in this type of spread since he has sold a call that is in-the-money. Aside from watching for this possibility, there is little in the way of defensive follow-up action that needs to be implemented since the risk is limited by the nature of the position. He might take profits by closing the spread if the stock rallies before expiration.

This strategy presents a reasonable method of attempting to capitalize on a large stock movement with little tie-up of collateral. *Generally, the strategist would seek out volatile stocks* for implementation of this strategy, because he would want as much potential movement as possible by the time the calls expire. In Chapter 14, it will be shown that this strategy can become more attractive by buying calls with a longer maturity than the calls sold.

Chapter *14*

Diagonalizing a Spread

When one uses both different striking prices and different expiration dates in a spread, it is a diagonal spread. Generally, the long side of the spread would expire later than the short side of the spread. Note that this is within the definition of a spread for margin purposes: The long side must have a maturity equal to or longer than the maturity of the short side. With the exception of calendar spreads, all the previous chapters on spreads have described ones in which the expiration dates of the short call and the long call were the same. However, any of these spreads can be diagonalized—one can replace the long call in any spread with one expiring at a later date.

In general, *diagonalizing a spread in this manner makes it slightly more bearish at near-term expiration.* This can be seen by observing what would happen if the stock fell or rose substantially. If the stock falls, the long side of the spread will retain some value because of its longer maturity. Thus a diagonal spread will generally do better to the downside than will a regular spread. If the stock rises substantially, all calls will come to parity. Thus there is no advantage in the long-term call—it will be selling for approximately the same price as the purchased call in a normal spread. However, since the strategist had to pay more originally for the longer-term call, his upside profits would not be as great.

A diagonalized position has an advantage in that one can reestablish the position if the written calls expire worthless in the spread. Thus the increased cost of buying a longer-term call initially may prove to be a savings if one can write against it twice. These tactics will be described for various spread strategies.

THE DIAGONAL BULL SPREAD

A vertical call bull spread consists of buying a call at a lower striking price and selling a call at a higher striking price, both with the same expiration date. The *diagonal bull spread would be similar except that one would buy a longer-term call at the lower strike and would sell a near-term call at the higher strike.* The number of calls long and short would still be the same. By diagonalizing the spread, the position is hedged somewhat on the downside in case the stock does not advance by near-term expiration. Moreover, once the near-term option expires, the spread can often be reestablished by selling the call with the next maturity.

Example: The following prices exist:

	Strike	April	July	October	Stock Price
XYZ	30	3	4	5	32
XYZ	35	1	1½	2	32

A vertical bull spread could be established in any of the expiration series by buying the call with 30 strike and selling the call with 35 strike. A diagonal bull spread would consist of buying the July 30 or October 30 and selling the April 35. To compare a vertical bull spread with diagonal spread, the following two spreads will be used:

Vertical bull spread: buy the April 30 call, sell the April 35—2 debit

Diagonal bull spread: buy the July 30 call, sell the April 35—3 debit

The vertical bull spread has a 3-point potential profit if XYZ is above 35 at April expiration. The maximum risk in the normal bull spread is 2 points (the original debit) if XYZ is anywhere below 30 at April expiration. By diagonalizing the spread, the strategist lowers his potential profit slightly at April expiration, but also lowers the probability of losing 2 points in the position. Table 14-1 compares the two types of spreads at April expiration. The price of the July 30 call is estimated in order to derive the

TABLE 14-1.
Comparison of spreads at expiration.

XYZ Price at April Expiration	April 30 Price	April 35 Price	July 30 Price	Vertical Bull Spread Profit	Diagonal Spread Profit
20	0	0	0	− $200	− $300
24	0	0	½	− 200	− 250
27	0	0	1	− 200	− 200
30	0	0	2	− 200	− 100
32	2	0	3	0	0
35	5	0	5½	+ 300	+ 250
40	10	5	10	+ 300	+ 200
45	15	10	15	+ 300	+ 200

estimated profits or losses from the diagonal bull spread at that time. If the underlying stock drops too far—to 20, for example—both spreads will experience nearly a total loss at April expiration. However, the diagonal spread will not lose its entire value if XYZ is much above 24 at expiration, according to Table 14-1. The diagonal spread actually has a smaller dollar loss than the normal spread between 27 and 32 at expiration, despite the fact that the diagonal spread was more expensive to establish. On a percentage basis, the diagonal spread has an even larger advantage in this range. If the stock rallies above 35 by expiration, the normal spread will provide a larger profit. There is an interesting characteristic of the diagonal spread that is shown in Table 14-1. If the stock advances substantially and all the calls come to parity, the profit on the diagonal spread is limited to 2 points. However, if the stock is near 35 at April expiration, the long call will have some time premium in it and the spread will actually widen to more than 5 points. Thus *the maximum area of profit at April expiration for the diagonal spread is to have the stock near the striking price of the written call.* The figures demonstrate that the diagonal spread gives up a small portion of potential upside profits to provide a hedge to the downside.

Once the April 35 call expires, the diagonal spread can be closed. However, if the stock is below 35 at that time, it may be more prudent to then sell the July 35 call against the July 30 call that is held long. This would establish a normal bull spread for the 3 months remaining until July expiration. Note that if XYZ were still at 32 at April expiration, the July 35 call might be sold for 1 point if the stock's volatility was about the same. This should be true since the April 35 call was worth 1 point with the stock at 32 three months before expiration. Consequently, the strategist who had pursued this course of action would end up with a normal July bull spread for a net debit of 2 points—he originally paid 4 for the July 30 call, but then sold the April 35 for 1 point and subsequently sold the July 35 for 1 point. By looking at the table of prices for the first example in this chapter, the reader can see that it would have cost 2½ points to set up the normal July bull spread originally. Thus, by diagonalizing and having the near-term call expire worthless, the strategist is able to acquire the normal July bull spread at a cheaper cost than he could have originally. This is a specific example of how *the diagonalizing effect can prove beneficial if the writer is able to write against the same long call two times*—or three times if he originally purchased the longest-term call. In this example, if XYZ were anywhere between 30 and 35 at April expiration, the spread would be converted to a normal July bull spread. If the stock were above 35, the spread should be closed to take the profit. Below 30, the July 30 call would probably be closed or left outright long.

In summary, the diagonal bull spread may often be an improvement over the normal bull spread. The diagonal spread is an improvement when the stock remains relatively unchanged or falls, up until the near-term written call expires. At that time, the spread can be converted to a normal bull spread if the stock is at a favorable price. Of course, if at any time the underlying stock rises above the higher striking price at an expiration date, the diagonal spread will be profitable.

OWNING A CALL FOR "FREE"

Diagonalization can be used in other spread strategies to accomplish much the same purposes already described, but, in addition, it may also be possible for the spreader to wind up owning a long call at a substantially reduced cost, possibly even for free.

The easiest way to see this would be to consider a *diagonal bear spread.*

Example: XYZ is at 32 and the near-term April 30 call is selling for 3 points while the longer-term July 35 call is selling for 1½ points. A diagonal bear spread could be established by selling the April 30 and buying the July 35. This is still a bear spread, because a call with a lower striking price is being sold while a call at a higher strike is being purchased. However, since the purchased call has a longer maturity date than the written call, the spread is diagonalized.

This diagonal bear spread will make money if XYZ falls in price before the near-term, April call expires. For example, if XYZ is at 29 at expiration, the written call will expire worthless and the July 35 will still have some value, perhaps ½. Thus the profit would be 3 points on the April 30, less a 1-point loss on the July 35, for an overall profit of 2 points.

The risk in the position lies to the upside, just as in a regular bear spread. If XYZ should advance by a great deal, both options would be at parity and the spread would have widened to 5 points. Since the initial credit was 1½ points, the loss would be 5 minus 1½, or 3½ points in that case. As in all diagonal spreads, the spread will do slightly better to the downside because the long call will hold some value, but it will do slightly worse to the upside if the underlying stock advances substantially.

The reason that a strategist might attempt a diagonal bear spread would *not* be for the slight downside advantage that the diagonalizing effect produces. Rather it would be because he has a chance of *owning the July 35 call—the longer-term call—for a substantially reduced cost.* In the example, the cost of the July 35 call was 1½ points and the premium received from the sale of the April 30 call was 3 points. If the spreader can make 1½ points from the sale of the April 30 call, he will have completely covered the cost of his July option. He can then sit back and hope for a rally by the underlying stock. If such a rally occurred, he could make unlimited profits on the long side. If it did not, he loses nothing.

Example: If XYZ is at or below 31½ at April expiration, the April 30 call can be purchased for 1½ points or less. Since the call was originally sold for 3, this would represent a profit of at least 1½ points on the April 30 call. This profit on the near-term option covers the entire cost of the July 35. Consequently, the strategist owns the July 35 for free. If XYZ never rallies above 35, he would make nothing from the overall trade. However, if XYZ were to rally above 35 after April expiration—but before July expiration, of course—he could make potentially large profits. Thus *when one establishes a diagonal spread for a credit, there is always the potential that he could own a call for free.* That is, the profits from the sale of the near-term call could equal or exceed the original cost of the long call. This is, of course, a desirable position to be in, for if the underlying stock should rally substantially after profits are realized on the short side, large profits could accrue.

DIAGONAL BACKSPREADS

In an analogous strategy, one might buy more than one longer-term call against the short-term call that is sold. Using the foregoing prices, one might sell the April 30 for 3 points and buy 2 July 35's at 1½ points each. This would be an *even money spread.* The credits equal the debits when the position is established. If the April 30 call expires worthless, which would happen if the stock was below 30 in April, the spreader would own 2 July 35 calls for free. Even if the April 30 does not expire totally worthless, but if some profit can be made on the sale of it, the July 35's will be owned at a reduced cost. In Chapter 13, where reverse spreads were discussed, the strategy where one sells a call with a lower strike and then buys more calls at a higher strike was termed a reverse ratio spread, or backspread. The strategy just described is merely the *diagonalizing of a backspread. This is a strategy that is favored by some professionals*, because the short call reduces the risk of owning the longer-term calls if the underlying stock declines. Moreover, if the underlying stock advances, the preponderance of long calls with a longer maturity will certainly outdistance the losses on the written call. The worst situation that could result would be for the underlying stock to rise very slightly by near-term expiration. If this happened, it might be possible to lose money on both sides of the spread. This would have to be considered a rather low probability event, though, and would still represent a limited loss, so it does not substantially offset the positive aspects of the strategy.

Any type of spread may be diagonalized. There are some who prefer to diagonalize even butterfly spreads, figuring that the extra time to maturity in the purchased calls will be of benefit. Overall, the benefits of diagonalizing can be generalized by recalling the way in which the decay of the time value premium of a call takes place. Recall that it was determined that a call loses most of its time value premium in the last stages of its life. When it is a very long-term option, the rate of decay is small. Knowing this fact, it makes sense that one would want to sell options with a short life remaining, so that the maximum benefit of the decay could be obtained. Correspondingly, the purchase of a longer-term call would mean that the buyer is not subjecting himself to a substantial loss in time value premium, at least over the first 3 months of ownership. A diagonal spread encompasses both of these features—selling a short-term call to try to obtain the maximum rate of time decay, while buying a longer-term call to try to lessen the effect of time decay on the long side.

CALL OPTION SUMMARY

This concludes the description of strategies that utilize only call options. The call option has been seen to be a vehicle which the astute strategist can use to set up a wide variety of positions. He can be bullish or bearish, aggressive or conservative. In addition, he can attempt to be neutral, trying to capitalize on the probability that a stock will not move very far in a short time period.

The investor who is not familiar with options should generally begin with a simple strategy, such as covered call writing or outright call purchases. The simplest types of spreads are the bull spread, the bear spread, and the calendar spread. The more sophisticated investor might consider using ratios in his call strategies—ratio writing against stock or ratio spreading using only calls.

Once the strategist feels that he understands the risk and reward relationships between longer-term and short-term calls, between in-the-money and out-of-the-money calls, and between long calls and short calls, he could then consider utilizing the most advanced types of strategies. This might include reverse ratio spreads, diagonal spreads, and more advanced types of ratios, such as the ratio calendar spread.

A great deal of information, some of it rather technical in detail, has been presented in preceding chapters. The best pattern for an investor to follow would be to attempt only strategies that he fully comprehends. This does not mean that he merely understands the profitability aspects (especially the risk) of the strategy. One must also be able to readily understand the potential effects of early assignments, large dividend payments, striking price adjustments, and the like, if he is going to operate advanced strategies. Without a full understanding of how these things might affect one's position, one cannot operate an advanced strategy correctly.

PART THREE ————————————

PUT OPTION STRATEGIES

A *put option* gives the holder the right to *sell* the underlying security at the striking price at any time until the expiration date of the option. Listed put options are even newer than listed call options, having been introduced on June 3, 1977. The introduction of listed puts has provided a much wider range of strategies for both the conservative and aggressive investor. The call option is least effective in strategies where downward price movement by the underlying stock is concerned. The put option is a useful tool in that case.

All stocks with listed call options have listed put options as well. The use of puts or the combination of puts and calls can provide more versatility to the strategist.

When listed put options exist, it is no longer necessary to implement strategies involving long calls and short stock. Listed put options can be used more efficiently in such situations. There are many similarities between call strategies and put strategies. For example, put spread strategies and call spread strategies employ similar tactics, although there are technical differences of course. In certain strategies, the tactics for puts may appear largely to be a repetition of those used for calls, but they will be nevertheless spelled out in detail. The strategies that involve the use of both puts and calls together—straddles and combinations—have techniques of their own, but even in this case the reader will recognize certain similarities to strategies previously discussed. Thus the introduction of put options not only widens the realm of potential strategies, but also makes more efficient some of the strategies previously described.

Chapter *15*

Put Option Basics

Much of the same terminology that is applied to call options also pertains to put options. *Underlying security, striking price, and expiration date are all terms that have the same meaning for puts as they do for calls.* The expiration dates of listed put options agree with the expiration dates of the calls on the same underlying stock. In addition, puts and calls have the same striking prices. This means that if there are options at a certain strike, say on a particular underlying stock that has both listed puts and calls, *both* calls at 50 and puts at 50 will be trading, regardless of the price of the underlying stock. Note that it is no longer sufficient to describe an option as an "XYZ July 50." It must also be stated whether the option is a put or a call, for an XYZ July 50 call and an XYZ July 50 put are two different securities.

In many respects, the put option and its associated strategies will be very nearly the opposite of corresponding call-oriented strategies. However, *it is not correct to say that the put is exactly the opposite of a call.* In this introductory section on puts, the characteristics of puts will be described in an attempt to show where they are similar to calls and where they are not.

PUT STRATEGIES

In the simplest terms, *the outright buyer of a put is hoping for a stock price decline* in order for his put to become more valuable. If the stock were to decline well *below* the striking price of the put option, the put holder could make a profit. The holder of the put could buy stock in the open market and then exercise his put to sell that stock for a profit at the striking price, which is higher.

Example: If XYZ stock is at 40, an XYZ July 50 put would be worth at least 10 points, for the put grants the holder the right to sell XYZ at 50—10 points above its current price. On the other hand, if the stock price were *above* the striking price of the put option at expiration, the put would be worthless. No one would logically want to exercise a put option to sell stock at the striking price when he could merely go to the open market and sell the stock for a higher price. Thus, *as the price of the underlying stock declines, the put becomes more valuable.* This is, of course, the opposite of a call option's price action.

The meaning of in-the-money and out-of-the-money are altered when one is speaking of put options. *A put is considered to be in-the-money when the underlying stock is below the striking price of the put option; it is out-of-the-money when the stock is above the striking price.* This, again, is the opposite of the call option. If XYZ is at 45, the XYZ July 50 put is in-the-money and the XYZ July 50 call is out-of-the-money. However, if XYZ were at 55, the July 50 put would be out-of-the-money while the July 50 call would then be in-the-money. The broad definition of an in-the-money option as "an option that has intrinsic value" would cover the situation for both puts and calls. Note that a put option has intrinsic value when the underlying stock is below the striking price of the put. That is, the put has some "real" value when the stock is below the striking price.

The intrinsic value of an in-the-money put is merely the difference between the striking price and the stock price. Since the put is an option (to sell), it will generally sell for more than its intrinsic value when there is time remaining until the expiration date. This excess value over its intrinsic value is referred to as the *time value premium,* just as is the case with calls.

Example: XYZ is at 47 and the XYZ July 50 put is selling for 5, the intrinsic value is 3 points (50 − 47), so the time value premium must be 2 points. The time value premium of an in-the-money put option can always be quickly computed by the following formula:

$$\text{Time value premium} \atop \text{(in-the-money put)} = \text{put option price} + \frac{\text{stock}}{\text{price}} - \text{striking price}$$

This is not the same formula that was applied to in-the-money call options, although it is always true that the time value premium of an option is the excess value over intrinsic value.

$$\text{Time value premium} \atop \text{(in-the-money call)} = \text{call option price} + \frac{\text{striking}}{\text{price}} - \text{stock price}$$

If the put is out-of-the-money, the entire premium of the put is composed of time value premium, for the intrinsic value of an out-of-the-money option is always zero. The *time value premium of a put is largest when the stock is at the striking price of the put.* As the option becomes deeply in-the-money or deeply out-of-the-money, the time value premium will shrink substantially. These statements on the magnitude of the time value premium are true for both puts and calls. Table 15-1 will help to illustrate the relationship of stock price and option price for both puts and calls. The reader may want to refer to Table 1-1, which described the time value premium relationship for calls. Table 15-1 describes the prices of an XYZ July 50 call option and an XYZ July 50 put option.

Table 15-1 demonstrates several basic facts. As the stock drops, the actual price of a call option decreases while the value of the put option increases. Conversely, as the stock rises, the call option increases in value and the put option decreases in value. Both the put and the call have their

TABLE 15-1.
Call and put options compared.

XYZ Stock Price	XYZ July 50 Call Price	Call Intrinsic Value	Call Time Value Premium	XYZ July 50 Put Price	Put Intrinsic Value	Put Time Value Premium
40	½	0	½	9¾	10	−¼[a]
43	1	0	1	7	7	0
45	2	0	2	6	5	1
47	3	0	3	5	3	2
50	5	0	5	4	0	4
53	7	3	4	3	0	3
55	8	5	3	2	0	2
57	9	7	2	1	0	1
60	10½	10	½	½	0	½
70	19¾	20	−¼[a]	¼	0	¼

[a]A deeply in-the-money option may actually trade at a discount from intrinsic value in advance of expiration.

maximum time value premium when the stock is exactly at the striking price. However, *the call will generally sell for more than the put when the stock is at the strike.* Notice in Table 15-1 that, with XYZ at 50, the call is worth 5 points while the put is worth only 4 points. This is true, in general, except in the case of a stock that pays a large dividend. This phenomenon has to do with cost of carrying stock. More will be said about this effect later. Table 15-1 also describes an effect of put options that normally holds true—*an in-the-money put (stock is below strike) loses time value premium more quickly than an in-the-money call does.* Notice that with XYZ at 43 in Table 15-1, the put is 7 points in-the-money and has lost all its time value premium. But when the call is 7 points in-the-money—XYZ at 57—the call still has 2 points of time value premium. Again, this is a phenomenon that could be affected by the dividend payout of the underlying stock, but is true in general.

PRICING PUT OPTIONS

The same factors that determined the price of the call option also determine the price of the put option: price of the underlying stock, striking price of the option, time remaining until expiration, volatility of the underlying stock, dividend rate of the underlying stock, and the current risk-free interest rate (Treasury bill rate, for example). Also, market dynamics—supply, demand, and investor psychology—play a part as well.

Without going into as much detail as was shown in Chapter 1, the pricing curve of the put option can be developed. Certain facts remain true for the put option as they did for the call option. The rate of decay of the put option is not linear—that is, the time value premium will decay more rapidly in the weeks immediately preceding expiration. The more volatile the underlying stock, the higher will be the price of its options—both puts and calls. Moreover, the marketplace may at any time value options at a higher or lower volatility than the underlying stock actually exhibits. This is called implied volatility, as distinguished from actual volatility. Also, the put option is usually worth at least its intrinsic value at any time, and should be worth exactly its intrinsic value on the day that it expires. Figure 15-1 shows where one might expect the XYZ July 50 put to sell—for any stock price—if there are 6 months remaining until expiration. Compare this with the similar pricing curve for the call option (Figure 15-2). Note that the *intrinsic value line* for the put option faces in the opposite direction from the intrinsic value line for call options—that is, it gains value as the stock falls below the striking price. This put option pricing curve also demonstrates the effect mentioned earlier that a put option loses time value premium more quickly when it is in-the-money and also shows that an out-of-the-money put holds a great deal of time value premium.

FIGURE 15-1.
Put option price curve.

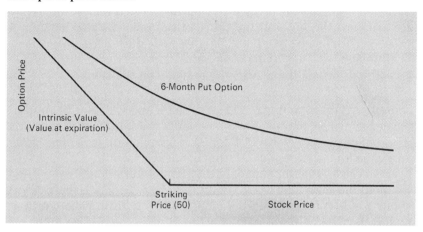

FIGURE 15-2.
Call option price curve.

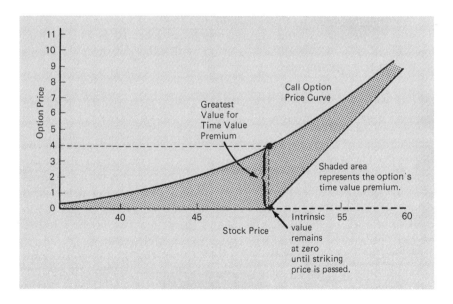

THE EFFECT OF DIVIDENDS ON PUT OPTION PREMIUMS

The dividend of the underlying stock is a negative factor on the price of its call options. The opposite is true for puts. *The larger the dividend, the more valuable the puts will be.* This is true because, as the stock goes ex-dividend, it will be reduced in price by the amount of the dividend. That is, the stock will decrease in price and therefore the put will become more valuable. Consequently, the buyer of the put will be willing to pay a higher price for the put and the seller of the put will also demand a high price. As with listed calls, listed puts are not adjusted for the payment of cash dividends on the underlying stock. However, the price of the option itself will reflect the dividend payments on the stock.

Example: XYZ is selling for $25 per share and will pay $1 in dividends over the next 6 months. Then a 6-month put option with strike 25 should automatically be worth at least $1, regardless of any other factor concerning the underlying stock. During the next 6 months, the stock will be reduced in price by the amount of its dividends—$1—and if everything else remained the same, the stock would then be at 24. With the stock at 24, the put would be 1 point in-the-money and would thus be worth at least its intrinsic value of 1 point. Thus, in advance, this large dividend payout of the underlying stock will help to increase the price of the put options on this stock.

On the day before a stock goes ex-dividend, the time value premium of an in-the-money put should be at least as large as the impending cash dividend payment. That is, if XYZ is 40 and is about to pay a $.50 dividend, an XYZ January 50 put should sell for at least 10½. This is true because the stock will be reduced in price by the amount of its dividend on the day of the ex-dividend.

EXERCISE AND ASSIGNMENT

When the holder of a put option exercises his option, he sells stock at the striking price. He may exercise this right at any time during the life of the put option. When this happens, *the writer of a put option with the same terms is assigned an obligation to* buy *stock at the striking price.* It is important to notice the difference between puts and calls in this case. The call holder exercises to *buy* stock and the call writer is obligated to *sell* stock. The reverse is true for the put holder and writer.

The method of assignment via the OCC and the brokerage firm are the same for puts and calls—many fair method of random or first-in/first-out assignment is allowed. Stock commissions are charged on both the purchase and sale of the stock via the assignment and exercise.

When the holder of a put option exercises his right to sell stock, he may be selling stock that he currently holds in his portfolio. Second, he may simultaneously go into the open market and buy stock for sale via the put exercise. Finally, he may want to sell the stock in his short stock account—that is, he may short the underlying stock by exercising his put option. He would have to be able to borrow stock and supply the margin collateral for a short sale of stock if he chose this third course of action.

The writer of the put option also has several choices in how he wants to handle the stock purchase that he is required to make. *The put writer who is assigned must receive stock* (the call writer who is assigned delivers stock). The put writer may currently be short the underlying stock, in which case he will merely use the delivery of stock from the assignment to cover his short sale. He may also decide to immediately sell stock in the open market to offset the purchase that he is forced to make via the put assignment. Finally, he may decide to retain the stock that is delivered to him—he merely keeps the stock in his portfolio. He would, of course, have to pay for (or margin) the stock if he decides to keep it.

The mechanics of which way the put holder wants to deliver the stock and the way in which the put writer wants to receive the stock are relatively simple. Each one merely notifies his brokerage firm of the way in which he wants to operate and, provided that he can meet the federal margin requirements, the exercise or assignment will be made in the desired manner.

Anticipating Assignment

The writer of a put option can anticipate assignment in the same way that the writer of a call can. *When the time value premium of an in-the-money put option disappears, there is a risk of assignment, regardless of the time remaining until expiration.* In Chapter 1, a form of arbitrage was described in which market-makers or firm traders, who pay little or no commissions, can take advantage of an in-the-money call selling at a discount to parity. Similarly, there is a method for these traders to take advantage of an in-the-money put selling at a discount to parity.

Example: XYZ is at 40 and an XYZ July 50 put is selling for $9\frac{3}{4}$— a $\frac{1}{4}$ discount from parity. That is, the option is selling for $\frac{1}{4}$ point below its intrinsic value. The arbitrageur could take advantage of this situation through the following actions:

1. Buy the July put at $9\frac{3}{4}$.
2. Buy XYZ common stock at 40.
3. Exercise the put to sell XYZ at 50.

The arbitrageur makes 10 points on the stock portion of the transaction, buying the common at 40 and selling it at 50 via exercise of his put. He paid $9\frac{3}{4}$ for the put option and he loses this entire amount upon exercise. However, his overall profit is thus $\frac{1}{4}$ point, the amount of the original discount from parity. Since his commission costs are minimal, he can actually make a net profit on this transaction.

As was the case with deeply in-the-money calls, this type of arbitrage with deeply in-the-money puts provides a secondary market where one might not otherwise exist. It allows the public holder of an in-the-money put to sell his option at a price near its intrinsic value. Without these arbitrageurs, there might not be a reasonable secondary market in which public put holders could liquidate.

Dividend payment dates may also have an effect on the frequency of assignment. For call options, the writer might expect to receive an assignment on the day the stock goes ex-dividend. The holder of the call is able to collect the dividend in this manner. Things are slightly different for the writer of puts. He might expect to receive an assignment on the day *after* the ex-dividend date of the underlying stock. Since the writer of the put is obligated to buy stock, it is unlikely that anyone would put the stock to him until after the dividend has been paid. In any case, the writer of the put can use a relatively simple gauge to *anticipate assignment near the ex-dividend date. If the time value premium of an in-the-money put is less than the amount of the dividend to be paid, the writer may often anticipate that he will be assigned immediately after the ex-dividend of the stock.* An example may show why this is true.

Example: XYZ is at 45 and it will pay a $.50 dividend. Furthermore, the XYZ July 50 put is selling at 5¼. Note that the time value premium of the July 50 put is ¼ point—less than the amount of the dividend, which is ½ point. An arbitrageur could take the following actions:

1. Buy XYZ at 45.
2. Buy the July 50 put at 5¼.
3. Collect the ½-point dividend (he must hold the stock until the ex-date to collect the dividend).
4. Exercise his put to sell XYZ at 50 (writer would receive assignment on the day after the ex-date).

The arbitrageur makes 5 points on the stock trades—buying XYZ at 45 and selling it at 50 via exercise of the put. He also collects the ½-point dividend, making his total intake equal to 5½ points. He loses the 5¼ points that he paid for the put but still has a net profit of ¼ point. Thus *as the ex-dividend date of a stock approaches, the time value premium of all in-the-money puts on that stock will tend to equal or exceed the amount of the dividend payment.*

This is quite different from the call option. It was shown in Chapter 1 that the call writer only needs to observe whether or not the call was trading at or below parity, regardless of the amount of the dividend, as the ex-dividend date approaches. The put writer must determine if the time value premium of the put exceeds the amount of the dividend to be paid. If it does, there is a much smaller chance of assignment because of the dividend. In any case, the put writer can anticipate the assignment if he carefully monitors his position.

Position Limits

Recall that the position limit rule states that one cannot have a position of more than the limit of options on the same side of the market in the same underlying security. The limit varies depending on the trading activity and volatility of the underlying stock and is set by the exchange on which the options are traded. The actual limits are 3,000, 5,500, or 8,000 contracts, depending on these factors. One cannot have more than 8,000 option contracts on the bullish side of the market—long calls and/or short puts—nor can he have more than 8,000 contracts on the bearish side of the market—short calls and/or long puts. He may, however, have 8,000 contracts on each side of the market—he could simultaneously be long 8,000 calls and long 8,000 puts.

For the following examples, assume that one is concerned with an underlying stock whose position limit is 8,000 contracts.

Long 8,000 calls, long 8,000 puts—no violation; 8,000 contracts bullish (long calls) and 8,000 contracts bearish (long puts)

Long 4,000 calls, short 4,000 puts—no violation; total of 8,000 contracts bullish

Long 4,100 calls, short 4,000 puts—violation; total of 8,100 contracts bullish

Money managers should be aware that these position limits apply to all "related" accounts, so that someone managing several accounts must total all the accounts' positions when considering the position limit rule.

CONVERSION

Many of the relationships between call prices and put prices relate to a process known as a *conversion*. This term dates back to the over-the-counter option days when a dealer who owned a put (or could buy one) was able to satisfy the needs of a potential call buyer by "converting" the put to a call. This terminology is somewhat confusing and the actual position that the dealer would take is little more than an arbitrage position. In the listed market, arbitrageurs and firm traders can set up the same position that the converter did.

The actual details of the conversion process, which must include the carrying cost of owning stock and the inclusion of all dividends to be paid by the stock during the time the position is held, will be described later. However, it is important for the put option trader to understand what the arbitrageur is attempting to do in order for him to fully understand the relationship between put and call prices in the listed option market.

A conversion position has no risk. The arbitrageur will do three things:

1. Buy 100 shares of the underlying stock.
2. Buy 1 put option at a certain striking price.
3. Sell 1 call option at the same striking price.

The arbitrageur has no risk in this position. If the underlying stock drops, he can always exercise his long put to sell the stock at a higher price. If the underlying stock rises, his long stock offsets the loss on his short call. Of course, the prices that the arbitrageur pays for the individual securities determine whether or not a conversion will be profitable. At times, a public customer may look at prices in the newspaper and see that he could establish a position similar to the foregoing one for a profit, even after commissions. However, unless prices are out of line, the public customer would not normally be able to make a better return than he could by putting his money into a bank or a Treasury bill, because of the commission costs that he would pay.

Without needing to understand, at this time, exactly what prices would make an attractive conversion, it is possible to see that it would not always be possible for the arbitrageur to do a conversion. The mere action of many arbitrageurs doing the same conversion would force the prices into line. The stock price would rise because arbitrageurs are buying the stock, as would the put price, and the call price would drop because of the preponderance of sellers.

When this happens, another arbitrage, known as a *reversal* (or *reverse conversion*), is possible. In this case, the arbitrageur does the opposite— he shorts the underlying stock, sells 1 put, and buys 1 call. Again, this is a position with no risk. If the stock rises, he can always exercise his call to buy stock at a lower price and cover his short sale. If the stock falls, his short stock will offset any losses on his short put.

The point of introducing this information, which is relatively complicated, at this place in the text is to demonstrate that *there is a rela-*

tionship between put and call prices. They are not independent of one another. If the put becomes "cheap" with respect to the call, arbitrageurs will move in to do conversions and force the prices back in line. On the other hand, if the put becomes expensive with relationship to the call, arbitrageurs will do reversals until the prices move back into line.

Because of the way in which the carrying cost of the stock and the dividend rate of the stock are involved in doing these conversions or reversals, two facts come to light regarding the relationship of put prices and call prices. First, a *put option will generally sell for less than a call option when the underlying stock is exactly at the striking price,* unless the stock pays a large dividend. In the older over-the-counter option market, it was often stated that the reason for this relationship was that the demand for calls was larger than the demand for puts. This may have been partially true, but certainly it is no longer true in the listed option markets, where a large supply of both listed puts and calls is available through the OCC. Arbitrageurs again serve a useful function in increasing supply and demand where it might not otherwise exist. The second fact concerning the relationship of puts and calls is that a *put option will lose its time value premium much more quickly in-the-money than a call option will* (and, conversely, a put option will generally hold out-of-the-money time value premium better than a call option will). Again, the conversion and reversal processes play a large role in this price action phenomenon of puts and calls.

In Chapter 31, exact details of conversions and reversals will be spelled out, with specific reasons why these procedures affect the relationship of put and call prices as stated above. However, at this time, it is merely sufficient for the reader to understand that there is an arbitrage process that is quite widely practiced that will, in fact, make true the foregoing relationships between puts and calls.

Chapter *16*

Put Option Buying

The purchase of a put option provides leverage in the case of a downward move by the underlying stock. In this manner, *it is an alternative to the short sale of stock*, much as the purchase of a call option is a leveraged alternative to the purchase of stock.

PUT BUYING VS. SHORT SALE

In the simplest case, when an investor expects a stock to decline in price, he must either short the underlying stock or buy a put option on the stock. Suppose that XYZ is at 50 and that an XYZ July 50 put option is trading at 5. If the underlying stock declines substantially, *the buyer of the put could make profits considerably in excess of his initial investment*. However, if the underlying stock rises in price, *the put buyer has limited risk*—he can only lose the amount of money that he originally paid for the put option. In this example, the most that the put buyer could lose would be 5 points, which is equal to his entire initial investment. Table 16-1 and Figure 16-1 depict the results, at expiration, of this simple purchase of the put option.

TABLE 16-1.
Results of put purchase at expiration.

XYZ Price at Expiration	Put Price at Expiration	Put Option Profit
20	30	+$2,500
30	20	+ 1,500
40	10	+ 500
45	5	0
48	2	− 300
50	0	− 500
60	0	− 500
70	0	− 500

The put buyer has limited profit potential since a stock can never drop in price below zero dollars per share. However, his potential profits can be huge, percentagewise. His loss—which normally would occur if the stock rises in price—is limited to the amount of his initial investment. *The simplest use of a put purchase is for speculative purposes when expecting a price decline in the underlying stock.*

FIGURE 16-1.
Put option purchase.

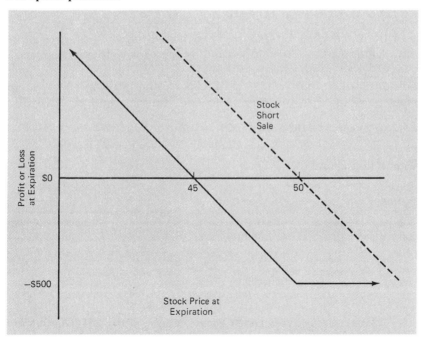

These results for the profit or loss of the put option purchases can be compared to a similar short sale of XYZ at 50 in order to observe the benefits of leverage and limited risk that the put option buyer achieves. In order to sell short 100 XYZ at 50, assume that the trader would have to use $2,500 in margin. Several points can be verified from Table 16-2 and Figure 16-1. If the stock drops in price sufficiently far, the percentage profits are much greater on the put option purchase than they are on the short sale of the underlying stock. This is the leveraging effect that an option purchase can achieve. If the underlying stock remains relatively unchanged, the short seller would do better because he does not risk losing his entire investment in a limited amount of time if the underlying stock changes only slightly in price. However, if the underlying stock should rise dramatically, the short seller can actually lose more than his initial investment. The short sale of stock has theoretically unlimited risk. Such is not true of the put option purchase, where the risk is limited to the amount of the initial investment. One other point should be made when comparing the purchase of a put and the short sale of stock. The short seller of stock is obligated to pay the dividends on the stock, but the put option holder has no such obligation. This is an additional advantage to the holder of the put.

SELECTING WHICH PUT TO BUY

Many of the same types of analyses that the call buyer goes through in deciding which call to buy can be used by the prospective put buyer as well. First, when approaching put buying as a speculative strategy, one should not place more than 15% of his risk capital in the strategy. Some investors participate in put buying to add some amount of downside

TABLE 16-2.
Results of selling short.

XYZ Price at Expiration	Short Sale	Put Option Purchase
20	+ $3,000 (+ 120%)	+ $2,500 (+ 500%)
30	+ 2,000 (+ 80%)	+ 1,500 (+ 300%)
40	+ 1,000 (+ 40%)	+ 500 (+ 100%)
45	+ 500 (+ 20%)	0 (0%)
48	+ 200 (+ 8%)	− 300 (− 60%)
50	0 (0%)	− 500 (− 100%)
60	− 1,000 (− 40%)	− 500 (− 100%)
75	− 2,500 (− 100%)	− 500 (− 100%)
100	− 5,000 (− 200%)	− 500 (− 100%)

protection to their basically bullishly oriented common stock portfolios. More will be said in Chapter 17 about buying puts on stocks that one actually owns.

The out-of-the-money put offers both higher reward potentials and higher risk potentials than does the in-the-money put. If the underlying stock drops substantially, the percentage returns from having purchased a cheaper, out-of-the-money put will be greater. However, should the underlying stock decline only moderately in price, the *in-the-money put* will often prove to be the better choice. In fact, since a put option tends to lose its time value premium quickly as it becomes an in-the-money option, there is an even greater advantage to the purchase of the in-the-money put.

Example: XYZ is at 49 and the following prices exist:

XYZ, 49;

XYZ July 45 put, 1; and

XYZ July 50 put, 3.

If the underlying stock were to drop to 40 by expiration, the July 45 put would be worth 5 points, a 400% profit. The July 50 put would be worth 10 points, a 233% profit over its initial purchase price of 3. Thus in a substantial downward move, the out-of-the-money put purchase provides higher reward potential. However, if the underlying stock drops only moderately, to 45 say, the purchaser of the July 45 put would lose his entire investment, since the put would be worthless at expiration. The purchaser of the in-the-money July 50 put would have a 2-point profit with XYZ at 45 at expiration.

The preceding analysis is based on holding the put until expiration. For the option buyer, this is generally an erroneous form of analysis, for the buyer generally tends to liquidate his option purchase in advance of expiration. When considering what happens to the put option in advance of expiration, it is helpful to remember that an in-the-money put tends to lose its time premium rather quickly. In the example above, the July 45 put is completely composed of time value premium. If the underlying stock begins to drop below 45, the price of the put will not increase as rapidly as would the price of a call that is going into-the-money.

Example: If XYZ fell by 5 points to 44, definitely a move in the put buyer's favor, he may find that the July 45 put has only increased in value to 2 or 2½ points. This is somewhat disappointing because, with call options, one would expect to do significantly better on a 5-point stock movement in his favor. Thus, when purchasing put options for specula-tion, *it is generally best to concentrate on in-the-money puts unless a very substantial decline in the price of the underlying stock is anticipated.*

Once the put option is in-the-money, the time value premium will decrease even in the longer-term series. Since this time premium is small in all series, the put buyer can often purchase a longer-term option for very little extra money, thus gaining more time to work with. Call option buyers are generally forced to avoid the longer-term series because the extra cost is not worth the risk involved, especially in a trading situation. However, the put buyer does not necessarily have this disadvantage. If he can purchase the longer-term put for nearly the same price as the near-term put, he should do so in case the underlying stock takes longer to drop than he had originally anticipated it would.

It is not uncommon to see such prices as the following:

XYZ common, 46:

XYZ April 50 put, 4;

XYZ July 50 put, 4½; and

XYZ October 50 put, 5.

None of these three puts have much time value premium in their prices. Thus the buyer might be willing to spend the extra 1 point and buy the longest-term put. If the underlying stock should drop in price immedi-ately, he will profit, but not as much as if he had bought one of the less expensive puts. However, should the underlying stock rise in price, he will own the longest-term put and will therefore suffer less of a loss, percentagewise. If the underlying stock rises in price, some amount of time value premium will come back into the various puts, and the longest-term put will have the largest amount of time premium. For example, if the stock rises back to 50, the following prices might exist:

XYZ common, 50;

XYZ April 50 put, 1;

XYZ July 50 put, 2½; and

XYZ October 50 put, 3½.

The purchase of the longer-term October 50 put would have suffered the least loss, percentagewise, in this event. Consequently, when one is pur-chasing an in-the-money put, he may often want to consider buying the longest-term put if the time value premium is small when compared to the time premium in the nearer-term puts.

In Chapter 3, the delta of an option was described as the amount by which one might expect the option will increase or decrease in price if the underlying stock moves by a fixed amount (generally considered to be one point, for simplicity). Thus if XYZ is at 49 and a call option is priced at 3 with a delta of ½, one would expect the call to sell for 3½ with XYZ at 50 and to sell at 2½ with XYZ at 48. In reality, the delta changes even on a fractional move in the underlying stock, but one generally assumes that it will hold true for a 1-point move. Obviously, put options have deltas as well. The delta of a put is a negative number, reflecting the fact that the put price and the stock price are inversely related. *As an approximation, one could say that the delta of the call option minus the delta of the put option with the same terms is equal to 1.* That is,

$$\text{delta of put} = \text{delta of call} - 1.$$

This is an approximation and is accurate unless the put is deeply in-the-money. It has already been pointed out that the time value premium behavior of puts and calls is different, so it is inaccurate to assume that this formula holds true exactly for all cases.

The delta of a put ranges between 0 and minus 1. If a July 50 put has a delta of $-\frac{1}{2}$, and the underlying stock *rises* by 1 point, the put will lose ½ point. The delta of a deeply out-of-the-money put is close to zero. It would decrease slowly at first as the stock declined in value, then would begin to decrease much more rapidly as the stock fell through the striking price, and would reach a value of minus 1 (the minimum) as the stock fell only moderately below the striking price. This is reflective of the fact that an out-of-the-money put tends to hold time premium quite well and an in-the-money put comes to parity rather quickly.

RANKING PROSPECTIVE PUT PURCHASES

In Chapter 3, a method of ranking prospective call purchases was developed that encompassed certain factors, such as the volatility of the underlying stock and the expected holding period of the purchased option. The same sort of analysis should be also applied to put option purchases.

The steps are summarized below. The reader may refer to the section entitled "Advanced Selection Criteria" in Chapter 3 for a more detailed description of why this method of ranking is superior.

1. Assume that each underlying stock can decrease in price in accordance with its volatility over a fixed holding period (30, 60, or 90 days).
2. Estimate the put option prices after the decrease.

3. Rank all potential put purchases by the highest reward opportunity for aggressive purchases.

4. Estimate how much would be lost if the underlying stock instead rose in accordance with its volatility, and rank all potential put purchases by best risk/reward ratio for a more conservative list of put purchases.

As was stated earlier, it is necessary to have a computer to make an accurate analysis of all listed options. The average customer is forced to obtain such data from a brokerage firm or data service. He should be sure that the list he is using conforms to the above-mentioned criteria. If the data service is ranking option purchases by how well the puts would do if each underlying stock fell by a fixed percentage (such as 5% or 10%), the list should be rejected because it is not incorporating the volatility of the underlying stock into its analysis. Also, if the list is based on holding the put purchase until expiration, the list should be rejected as well, because this is not a realistic assumption. There are enough reliable and sophisticated data services that one should not have to work with inferior analyses in today's option market.

For those readers who are more mathematically advanced and have the computer capability to construct their own analysis, the details of implementing an analysis similar to the one described above will be presented later, in Chapter 30. An application of put purchases, combined with fixed-income securities, is described in Chapter 27.

FOLLOW-UP ACTION

The put buyer can take advantage of strategies that are very similar to those the call buyer uses for follow-up action—either to lock in profits or to attempt to improve a losing situation. Before discussing these specific strategies, it should be stated again that it is rarely to the option buyer's benefit to exercise the option in order to liquidate. This precludes, of course, those situations where the call buyer actually wants to own the stock or the put buyer actually wants to sell the stock. If, however, the option holder is merely looking to liquidate his position, the cost of stock commissions makes exercising a prohibitive move. This is true even if he has to accept a price that is a slight discount from parity when he sells his option.

Locking in Profits

The reader may recall that there were four strategies—perhaps "tactics" is a better word—for the call buyer with an unrealized profit. These same four tactics can be used with only slight variations by the put option buyer. Additionally, there is a fifth strategy that can be employed as well when a stock has both listed puts and calls.

After an underlying stock has moved *down* and the put buyer has a relatively substantial unrealized gain, he might consider one of the following actions:

1. Sell the put and liquidate the position for a profit.
2. Do nothing and continue to hold the put.
3. Sell the in-the-money long put and use part of the proceeds to purchase out-of-the-money puts.
4. Create a spread by selling an out-of-the-money put against the one he currently holds.

These are the same four tactics that were discussed earlier with respect to call buying. In addition, the holder of a listed put who has an unrealized profit might consider buying a listed *call* to protect his position.

Example: A speculator originally purchased an XYZ October 50 put for 2 points when the stock was 52. If the stock has now fallen to 45, the put might be worth 6 points, representing an unrealized gain of 4 points and placing the put buyer in a position to implement one of these five tactics. After some time has passed, with the stock at 45, an at-the-money October 45 put might be selling for 2 points. Table 16-3 summarizes the situation. If the trader merely liquidates his position by selling out the October 50 put, he would realize a profit of 4 points. Since he is terminating the position, he can neither make more nor less than 4 points. This is the most conservative of the tactics, allowing no additional room for appreciation, but also eliminating any chance of losing back the accumulated profits.

If the trader does nothing, merely continuing to hold the October 50 put, he is taking an aggressive action. If the stock should reverse and rise back above 50 by expiration, he would lose everything. However, if the stock continues to fall, he could build up substantially larger profits. This is the only tactic that could eventually result in a loss at expiration.

TABLE 16-3.
Background table for profit alternatives.

Original Trade	Current Prices
XYZ common: 52	XYZ common: 45
Bought XYZ October 50 put at 2	XYZ October 50 put: 6
	XYZ October 45 put: 2

These two simple strategies—liquidating or doing nothing—are the easiest alternatives. The remaining strategies allow one to attempt to achieve a balance between retaining built-up profits and generating even more profits. The third tactic that the speculator could use would be to sell the put that he is currently holding and use some of the proceeds to purchase the October 45 put. *The general idea in this tactic is to pull one's initial investment out of the market* and then to increase the number of option contracts held by buying the out-of-the-money option.

Example: The trader would receive 6 points from the sale of the October 50 put. He should take 2 points of this amount and put it back into his pocket, thus covering his initial investment. Then he could buy 2 October 45 puts at 2 points each, with the remaining portion of the proceeds from the sale. He has no risk at expiration with this strategy, since he has recovered his initial investment. Moreover, if the underlying stock should continue to fall rapidly, he could profit handsomely because he has increased the number of put contracts that he holds.

The fourth choice that the put holder has is to create a spread by selling the October 45 put against the October 50 that he currently holds. This would create a bear spread, technically. This type of spread will be described in more detail later. For the time being, it is sufficient to understand what happens to the trader's risks and rewards by creating this spread. The sale of the October 45 put brings in 2 points, which covers the initial 2-point purchase cost of the October 50 put. Thus *his "cost" for this spread is nothing*—he has no risk, except for commissions. If the underlying stock should rise above 50 by expiration, all the puts would expire worthless (a put expires worthless when the underlying stock is above the striking price at expiration). This would represent the worst case—he would recover nothing from the spread. If the stock should be below 45 at expiration, he would realize the maximum potential of the spread, which is 5 points. That is, no matter how far XYZ is below 45 at expiration, the October 50 put will be worth 5 points more than the October 45 put, and the spread could thus be liquidated for 5 points. His maximum profit potential in the spread situation is 5 points. This tactic would be the best one if the underlying stock stabilized near 45 until expiration.

To analyze the fifth strategy that the put holder could use, it is necessary to introduce a call option into the picture.

Example: With XYZ at 45, there is an October 45 *call* selling for 3 points. The put holder could *buy* this call in order to limit his risk and still to retain the potential for large future profits. If the trader buys the call, he will have the following position:

$$\begin{array}{l} \text{Long 1 October 50 put} \\ \text{Long 1 October 45 call} \end{array} - \text{combined cost: 5 points}$$

The total combined cost of this put and call combination is 5 points—2 points were originally paid for the put, and now 3 points have been paid for the call. No matter where the underlying stock is at expiration, this combination will be worth at least 5 points. For example, if XYZ is at 46 at expiration, the put will be worth 4 and the call worth 1; or if XYZ is at 48, the put will be worth 2 and the call worth 3. If the stock is above 50 or below 45 at expiration, the combination will be worth more than 5 points. Thus the trader has no risk in this combination, since he has paid 5 points for it and will be able to sell it for at least 5 points at expiration. In fact, if the underlying stock continues to drop, the put will become more valuable and he could build up substantial profits. Moreover, if the underlying stock should reverse direction and climb substantially, he could still profit because the call will then become valuable. This tactic is the best one to use if the underlying stock does not stabilize near 45, but instead makes a relatively dramatic move—either up or down—by expiration. The strategy of simultaneously owning both a put and a call will also be discussed in much greater detail in a later chapter. It is being introduced here merely for the purposes of the put buyer wanting to obtain protection of his unrealized profits.

Each of these five strategies may work out to be the best one under a different set of circumstances. The ultimate result of each tactic is dependent on the direction that XYZ moves in the future. As was the case with call options, *the spread tactic never turns out to be the worst tactic*, although it is the best one only if the underlying stock stabilizes. Tables 16-4 and 16-5 summarize what results the speculator could expect from invoking each of these five tactics. The tactics are:

1. Liquidate—sell the long put for a profit and do not reinvest.
2. Do nothing—continue to hold the long put.

TABLE 16-4.
Comparison of each of the five tactics.

By expiration, if XYZ . . .	the best strategy was . . .	and the worst strategy was . . .
Continues to fall dramatically	"Roll down"	Liquidate
Falls moderately further	Do nothing	Combine
Remains relatively unchanged	Spread	Combine or "roll down"
Rises moderately	Liquidate	"Roll down" or do nothing
Rises substantially	Combine	Do nothing

TABLE 16-5.
Results of adopting each of the five tactics.

XYZ Price at Expiration	"Roll Down" Profit	Do-Nothing Profit	Spread Profit	Liquidate Profit	Combine Profit
30	+ $3,000 (B)	+ $1,800	+ $500	+ $400 (W)	+ $1,500
35	+ 2,000 (B)	+ 1,300	+ 500	+ 400 (W)	+ 1,000
41	+ 800 (B)	+ 700	+ 500	+ 400 (W)	+ 400
42	+ 600 (B)	+ 600 (B)	+ 500	+ 400	+ 300 (W)
43	+ 400	+ 500 (B)	+ 500 (B)	+ 400	+ 200 (W)
45	0 (W)	+ 300	+ 500 (B)	+ 400	0 (W)
46	0 (W)	+ 200	+ 400 (B)	+ 400 (B)	0 (W)
48	0 (W)	0 (W)	+ 200	+ 400 (B)	0 (W)
50	0	− 200 (W)	0	+ 400 (B)	0
54	0	− 200 (W)	0	+ 400 (B)	+ 400 (B)
60	0	− 200 (W)	0	+ 400	+ 1,000 (B)

3. "Roll down"—sell the long put, pocket the initial investment, and invest the remaining proceeds in out-of-the-money puts at a lower strike.

4. "Spread"—create a spread by selling the out-of-the-money put against the put already held.

5. "Combine"—create a combination by buying a call at a lower strike while continuing to hold the put.

Note that each tactic is the best one under one of the scenarios, but that the spread tactic is never the worst of the five. The actual results of each tactic, using the figures from the example above, are depicted in Table 16-5, where B denotes best tactic and W denotes worst one.

All the strategies are profitable if the underlying stock continues to fall dramatically, although the "roll down," "do nothing," and combinations work out best, because they continue to accrue profits if the stock continues to fall. If the underlying stock rises instead, only the combination outdistances the simplest tactic of all—liquidation.

If the underlying stock stabilizes, the "do-nothing" and "spread" tactics work out best. It would generally appear that the combination tactic or the "roll-down" tactic would be the most attractive, since neither one has any risk and both could generate large profits if the stock moved substantially. The advantage for the spread was substantial in call options, but in the case of puts, the premium received for the out-of-the-money put is not as large, and therefore the spread strategy loses some of its attractiveness. Finally, any of these tactics could be applied partially— for example, selling out half of a profitable long position in order to take some profits, and continuing to hold the remainder.

LOSS-LIMITING ACTIONS

The foregoing discussion concentrated on how the put holder could retain or increase his profit. However, it is often the case in option buying that the holder of the option is faced with an unrealized loss. The put holder may also have several choices of action to take in this case. His first, and simplest, course of action would merely be to sell the put and take his loss. Although this is advisable in certain cases, especially where the underlying stock seems to have assumed a distinctly bullish stance, it is not always the wisest thing to do. The put holder who has a loss may also consider either "rolling up" to create a bearish spread or may consider a calendar spread. Either of these actions could help him recover part or all of his loss.

The "Rolling-Up" Strategy

The "rolling-up" strategy will be described first. The reader may recall that a similar action, termed "rolling down," was available for call options held at a loss and was described in Chapter 3. The put buyer who owns a put at a loss may be able to create a spread that allows him to be able to break even at a more favorable price at expiration. Such action will inevitably limit his profit potential, but is generally useful in recovering something from a put that might otherwise expire totally worthless.

Example: An investor initially purchases an XYZ October 45 put for 3 points when the underlying stock was at 45. However, the stock rises to 48 at a later date and the put that was originally bought for 3 points is now selling for 1½ points. It is not unusual, by the way, for a put to retain this much of its value even though the stock has moved up and some amount of time has passed, since out-of-the-money puts tend to hold time value premium rather well. With XYZ at 48, an October 50 put might be selling for 3 points. The put holder could create a position designed to permit recovery of some of his losses by selling two of the puts that he is long—October 45's—and simultaneously buying one October 50 put. The net cost for this transaction would be only commissions, since he receives $300 from selling two puts at 1½ each, which completely covers the $300 cost of buying the October 50 put. The transactions are summarized in Table 16-6.

By selling two of the October 45 puts, the investor is now short an October 45 put. Since he also purchased an October 50 put, he has a spread (technically, a bear spread). He has spent no additional money, except commissions, to set up this spread, since the sale of the October 45's covered the purchase of the October 50 put. This strategy is most attractive when the debit involved to create the spread is small. In this example, the debit is zero.

TABLE 16-6.
Summary of rolling up transactions.

Original trade:	Buy 1 October 45 put for 3	
	with XYZ at 45	$300 debit
Later:	With XYZ at 48, sell 2	
	October 45's for 1½ each	$300 credit
	and buy 1 October 50 put for 3	$300 debit
Net position:	Long 1 October 50 put	
	Short 1 October 45 put	$300 debit

The effect of creating this spread is that *the investor has not increased his risk at all, but has raised the break-even point for his position.* That is, if XYZ merely falls a small distance, he will be able to get out even. Without the effect of creating the spread, the put holder would need XYZ to fall back to 42 at expiration in order for him to break even, since he originally paid 3 points for the October 45 put. His original risk was $300. If XYZ continues to rise in price and the puts in the spread expire worthless, the net loss will still be only $300 plus additional commissions. Admittedly, the commissions for the spread will increase the loss slightly, but they are small in comparison to the debit of the position ($300). On the other hand, if the stock should only fall back slightly to 47 by expiration, the spread will break even. At expiration, with XYZ at 47, the in-the-money October 50 put will be worth 3 points and the out-of-the-money October 45 put will expire worthless. Thus the investor will recover his $300 cost, except for commissions, with XYZ at 47 at expiration. His break-even point is raised from 42 to 47, a substantial improvement of his chances for recovery.

The implementation of this spread strategy reduces the profit potential of the position, however. The maximum potential of the spread is 2 points. If XYZ is anywhere below 45 at expiration, the spread will be worth 5 points, since the October 50 put will sell for 5 points more than the October 45 put. The investor has limited his potential profit to 2 points—the 5-point maximum width of the spread, less the 3 points that he paid to get into the position. He can no longer gain substantially on a large drop in price by the underlying stock. This is normally of little concern to the put holder faced with an unrealized loss and the potential for a total loss. He generally would be appreciative of getting out even or of making a small profit. The creation of the spread accomplishes this objective for him.

It should also be pointed out that he does not incur the maximum loss of his entire debit plus commissions unless XYZ closes above 50 at expiration. If XYZ is anywhere below 50, the October 50 will have some value and the investor will be able to recover something from the position.

This is distinctly different from the original put holding of the October 45, where the maximum loss would be incurred unless the stock were below 45 at expiration. Thus the introduction of *the spread also reduces the chances of having to realize the maximum loss.*

In summary, the put holder faced with an unrealized loss may be able to create a spread by selling twice the number of puts that he is currently long and simultaneously buying the put at the next higher strike. This action should only be used if the spread can be transacted at a small debit or, preferably, at even money (zero debit). The spread position offers a much better chance of breaking even and also reduces the possibility of having to realize the maximum loss in the position. However, the introduction of these loss-limiting measures reduces the maximum potential of the position if the underlying stock should subsequently decline in price by a significant amount. Using this spread strategy for puts would require a margin account, just as calls do.

The Calendar Spread Strategy

There is another strategy that is sometimes available to the put holder who has an unrealized loss. If the put that he is holding has an intermediate-term or long-term expiration date, he might be able to create a *calendar spread* by selling the near-term put against the put that he currently holds.

Example: An investor bought an XYZ October 45 put for 3 points when the stock was at 45. The stock rises to 48, moving in the wrong direction for the put buyer, and his put falls in value to 1½. He might, at that time, consider selling the near-term, July 45 put for 1 point. The ideal situation would be for the July 45 put to expire worthless, reducing the cost of his long put by 1 point. Then if the underlying stock declined below 45, he could profit after July expiration.

The major drawback to this strategy is that little or no profit will be made—in fact a loss is quite possible—if the underlying stock falls back to 45 or below before the near-term July option expires. Puts display different qualities in their time value premiums than calls do, as has been noted before. With the stock at 45, the differential between the July 45 put and the October 45 put might not widen much at all. This would mean that the spread has not gained anything, and the spreader has a loss equal to his commissions plus the initial unrealized loss. In the example above, if XYZ dropped quickly back to 45, the July 45 might be worth 1½ and the October worth 2½. At this point, the spreader would have a loss on both sides of his spread—he sold the July 45 put for 1 and it is now 1½; he bought the October 45 for 3 and it is now 2½, plus he has spent two commissions to date and would have to spend two more to liquidate the position.

At this point, the strategist may decide to do nothing and take his chances that the stock will subsequently rally so that the July 45 put will expire worthless. However, if the stock continues to decline below 45, the spread will most certainly become more of a loss as both puts come closer to parity.

This type of spread strategy is not as attractive as the "rolling-up" strategy. In the "rolling-up" strategy, one is not subjected to a loss if the stock declines after the spread is established, although he does limit his profits. The fact that the calendar spread strategy can lead to a loss even if the stock declines makes it a less desirable alternative.

EQUIVALENT POSITIONS

Before discussing other put-oriented strategies, the definition of an equivalent position will be presented. Two strategies, or positions, are equivalent when they have the same profit potential. They may have different collateral or investment requirements, but they have similar profit potentials. Many of the call-oriented strategies that were discussed in the first portion of the book have an equivalent put strategy. One such case has already been described: the "protected short sale"—shorting the common stock and buying a call—is equivalent to the purchase of a put. That is, both have a limited risk above the striking price of the option and relatively large profit potential to the downside. *An easy way to tell if two strategies are equivalent is to see if their profit graphs have the same shape.* The put purchase and the "protected short sale" have profit graphs with exactly the same shape. As more put strategies are discussed, it will always be mentioned if the put strategy is equivalent to a previously described call strategy. This may help to clarify the put strategies, which understandably may seem more complex to the reader who is not familiar with put options.

Chapter 17

Put Buying in Conjunction with Common Stock Ownership

Another useful feature of put options, in addition to their speculative leverage in a downward move by the underlying stock, is that *the put purchase can be used to limit downside loss in a stock that is owned.* When one simultaneously owns both the common stock and a put on that same stock, he has a position with limited downside risk during the life of the put. This position is also called a synthetic long call, because the profit graph is the same shape as a long call's.

Example: An investor owns XYZ stock, which is at 52, and purchases an XYZ October 50 put for 2. The put gives him the right to *sell* XYZ at 50, so the most that the stockholder can lose on his stock is 2 points. Since he pays 2 points for the put protection, his maximum potential loss until October expiration is 4 points, no matter how far XYZ might decline up until that time. If, on the other hand, the price of the stock should move up by October, the investor would realize *any* gain in the stock, less the 2 points that he paid for the put protection. *The put functions much like an insurance policy with a finite life.* Table 17-1 and Figure 17-1 depict the results at October expiration for this position—buying the October 50 put for 2 points to protect a holding in XYZ common

TABLE 17-1.
Results at expiration on a protected stock holding.

XYZ Price at Expiration	Stock Profit	Put Profit	Total Profit
30	− $2,200	+ $1,800	− $ 400
40	− 1,200	+ 800	− 400
50	− 200	− 200	− 400
54	+ 200	− 200	0
60	+ 800	− 200	+ 600
70	+ 1,800	− 200	+ 1,600
80	+ 2,800	− 200	+ 2,600

FIGURE 17-1.
Long common stock and long put.

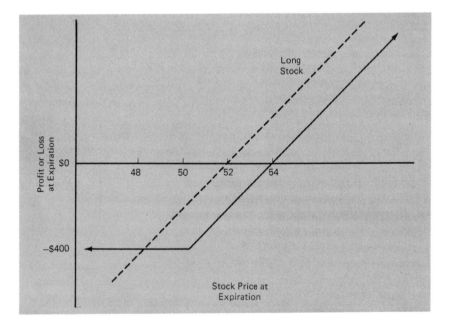

stock, which is selling at 52. The dashed line on the graph represents the profit potential of the common stock ownership by itself. Notice that if the stock were below 48 in October, the common stock owner would have been better off buying the put. However, with XYZ above 48 at expiration, the put purchase was a burden that cost a small portion of potential profits. This strategy, however, is not necessarily geared to maximizing one's profit potential on the common stock, but rather provides the stock owner with *protection*, eliminating the possibility of any devastating loss on the stock holding during the life of the put. In all the put buying strategies discussed in this chapter and Chapter 18, the put must be paid for in full. That is the only increase in investment.

Although any common stockholder may use this strategy, two general classes of stock owners find it particularly attractive. First, the long-term holder of the stock who is *not* considering selling the stock may utilize the put protection to limit losses over a short-term horizon. Second, the buyer of common stock who wants some "*insurance*" in case he is wrong may also find the put protection attractive.

The long-term holder who strongly feels that his stock will drop should probably sell that stock. However, his cost basis may make the capital gains tax on the sale prohibitive. He also may not be all that sure that the stock will decline—after all, he has owned it a long time—and wants to continue to hold the stock in case it *does* go up. In either case, the purchase of a put will limit the stockholder's downside risk while still allowing room for upside appreciation. There are a large number of individual and institutional investors who have holdings that they might find difficult to sell for one reason or another. The purchase of a low-cost put can often reduce the negative effects of a bear market on their holdings.

The second general class of put buyers for protection includes the investor who is *establishing* a position in the stock. He might want to buy a put at the same time that he buys the stock, thereby creating a position with a profitability as depicted in the previous profit graph. He immediately starts out with a position that has limited downside risk with large potential profits if the stock moves up. In this way, he can feel free to hold the stock during the life of the put without worrying when to sell it if it should experience a temporary setback. Some fairly aggressive stock traders use this technique because it eliminates the necessity of having to place a stop loss order on the stock. It is often frustrating to see a stock fall and touch off one's stop loss limit order, only to subsequently rise in price. The stock owner who has a put for protection need not overreact to a downward move. He can afford to sit back and wait during the life of the put, since he has built-in protection.

WHICH PUT TO BUY

The selection of which put the stock owner purchases will determine how much of his profit potential he is giving up and how much risk he is limiting. An out-of-the-money put will cost very little. Therefore, it will be less of a hindrance on profit potential if the underlying stock rises in price. Unfortunately, the put's protective feature is small until the stock falls to the striking price of the put. Therefore, *the purchase of the out-*

*of-the-money put will not provide as much downside protection as an at-
or in-the-money put would.* The purchase of a deeply out-of-the-money
put as protection is more like "disaster insurance"—it will prevent a
stock owner from experiencing a disaster in terms of a downside loss
during the life of the put, but will not provide much protection in the
case of a limited stock decline.

Example: XYZ is at 40 and the October 35 put is selling for ½. The
purchase of this put as protection for the common stock would not reduce
upside potential much at all—only by ½ point. However, the stock owner
could lose 5½ points if XYZ fell to 35 or below. That is his maximum
possible loss, for if XYZ were below 35 at October expiration, he could
exercise his put to sell the stock at 35—losing 5 points on the stock—
and he would have paid ½ of a point for the put, bringing his total loss
to 5½ points.

At the opposite end of the spectrum, the stock owner might buy an in-
the-money put as protection. This would quite severely limit his profit
potential, since the underlying stock would have to rise above the strike
and more for him to make a profit. However, the in-the-money put provides vast quantities of downside protection, limiting his loss to a very
small amount.

Example: XYZ is again at 40 and there is an October 45 put selling
for 5½. The stock owner who purchases the October 45 put would have
a maximum risk of ½ point, for he could always exercise the put to sell
stock at 45—giving him a 5-point *gain* on the stock—but he paid 5½
points for the put, thereby giving him an overall maximum loss of ½
point. He would have difficulty making any profit during the life of the
put, however. XYZ would have to rise by more than 5½ points (the cost
of the put) for him to make any total profit on the position by October
expiration.

*The deep in-the-money put purchase is overly conservative and is
usually not a good strategy.* On the other hand, it is not wise to purchase
a put that is too deeply out-of-the-money as protection. *Generally, one
should purchase a slightly out-of-the-money put as protection.* This attempts to achieve a balance between the positive feature of protection for
the common stock and the negative feature of limiting profits.

The reader may find it interesting to know that he has actually gone
through this analysis, back in Chapter 3. Glance again at the profit graph
for this strategy of using the put purchase to protect a common stock
holding (Figure 17-1). It has exactly the same shape as the profit graph of
a simple call purchase. *Therefore, the call purchase and the long put/*

long stock strategies are equivalent. Again, by equivalent it is meant that they have similar profit potentials. Obviously, the ownership of a call differs substantially from the ownership of common stock and a put. The stock owner continues to maintain his position for an indefinite period of time while the call holder does not. Also, the stockholder is forced to pay substantially more for his position than is the call holder, and he also receives dividends whereas the call holder does not. Therefore, "equivalent" does not mean *exactly* the same when comparing call-oriented and put-oriented strategies, but rather denotes that they have similar profit potentials.

In Chapter 3, it was determined that the slightly in-the-money call often offers the best ratio between risk and reward. When the call is slightly in-the-money, the stock is above the striking price. Similarly, the slightly out-of-the-money put often offers the best ratio between risk and reward for the common stockholder who is buying the put for protection. Again, the stock is slightly above the striking price. Actually, since the two positions are equivalent, the same conclusions *should* be arrived at—that is why it was stated that the reader has been through this analysis previously.

TAX CONSIDERATIONS

Although tax considerations will be covered in detail in Chapter 39, there is an important tax law concerning the purchase of puts against a common stock holding that should be mentioned at this time. If the stock owner is already a long-term holder of the stock at the time that he buys the put, the put purchase has no effect on his tax status. Similarly, if the stock buyer buys the stock at the time that he buys the put and identifies the position as a hedge, there is no effect on the tax status of his stock. However, *if one is currently a short-term holder of the common stock at the time that he buys a put, he eliminates any accrued holding period on his common stock. Moreover, the holding period for that stock does not begin again until the put is sold.*

Example: Assume the long-term holding period is 6 months. That is, a stock owner must own the stock for 6 months before it can be considered a long-term capital gain. An investor who bought the stock and held it for 5 months and then purchased a put would wipe out his entire holding period of 5 months. Suppose he then held the put and the stock simultaneously for 6 months, liquidating the put at the end of 6 months. His holding period would start all over again for that common stock. Even though he has owned the stock for 11 months—5 months prior to the put purchase and 6 months more while he simultaneously owned the put— his holding period for tax purposes is considered to be zero!

This law could have important tax ramifications and one should consult a tax advisor if he is in doubt as to the effect that a put purchase might have on the taxability of his common stock holdings. These tax consequences will be discussed more fully in Chapter 39.

PUT BUYING AS PROTECTION FOR THE COVERED CALL WRITER

Since put purchases afford protection to the owner of common stock, some investors naturally feel that the same protective feature could be used to limit their downside risk in the covered call writing strategy. Recall that the covered call writing strategy involves the purchase of stock and the sale of a call option against that stock. The covered write has limited upside profit potentials and offers protection, in the amount of the call premium to the downside. The covered writer will make money if the stock falls a little, remains unchanged, or rises by expiration. The covered writer can actually lose money only if the stock falls by more than the call premium received. He has potentially large downside losses. This strategy is sometimes called a "hedge wrapper."

The purchase of an out-of-the-money put option can eliminate the risk of large potential losses for the covered write, although the money spent for the put purchase will reduce the overall return from his covered write. He must therefore include the put cost in his initial calculations to determine if it is worthwhile to buy the put.

Example: XYZ is at 39 and there is an XYZ October 40 call selling for 3 points and an XYZ October 35 put selling for ½ point. A covered write could be established by buying the common at 39 and selling the October 40 call for 3. This covered write would have a maximum profit potential of 4 points if XYZ were anywhere above 40 at expiration. The write would lose money if XYZ were anywhere below 36, the break-even point, at October expiration. By also purchasing the October 35 put at the time the covered write is initiated, the covered writer will limit his profit potential slightly, but will also greatly reduce his risk potential. If the put purchase is added to the covered write, the maximum profit potential is reduced to 3½ points at October expiration. The break-even point moves up to 36½, and the writer will experience some loss if XYZ is below 36½ at expiration. However, the most that the writer could lose would be 1½ points if XYZ were below 35 at expiration. The purchase of the put option produces this loss-limiting effect. Table 17-2 and Figure 17-2 depict the profitability of both the regular covered write and the covered write that is protected by the put purchase.

TABLE 17-2.
Comparison of regular and protected covered writes.

XYZ Price at Expiration	Stock Profit	October 40 Call Profit	October 35 Put Profit	Total Profit
25	− $1,400	+ $300	+ $950	− $150
30	− 900	+ 300	+ 450	− 150
35	− 400	+ 300	− 50	− 150
36½	− 250	+ 300	− 50	0
38	− 100	+ 300	− 50	+ 150
40	+ 100	+ 300	− 50	+ 350
45	+ 600	− 200	− 50	+ 350
50	+ 1,100	− 700	− 50	+ 350

Commissions should be carefully included in the covered writer's return calculations as well as the cost of the put. It was demonstrated in Chapter 2 that the covered writer must include all commissions and margin interest expenses as well as all dividends received in order to produce an accurate "total return" picture of the covered write. Figure 17-2 shows that the break-even point is raised slightly and the overall profit potential is reduced by the purchase of the put. However, the *maximum risk is*

FIGURE 17-2.
Covered call write protected by a put purchase.

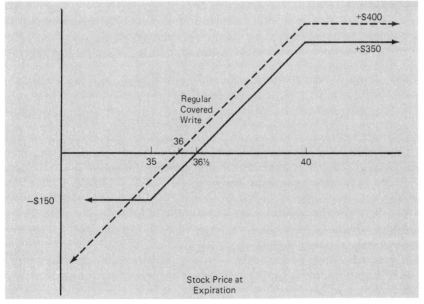

quite small and the writer need never be forced to roll down in a disadvantageous situation.

Recall that the covered writer who does not have the protective put in place is forced to roll down in order to gain increased downside protection. Rolling down merely means that he buys back the call that is currently written and writes another call, with a lower striking price, in its place. This rolling-down action can be helpful if the stock stabilizes after falling, but if the stock reverses and climbs upward in price again, the covered writer who rolled down would have limited his gains. In fact, he may have even *"locked in"* a loss. The writer who has the protective put need not be bothered with such things. He never has to roll down, for he has a limited maximum loss. Therefore, he should never get into a "locked-in" loss situation. This can be a great advantage, especially from an emotional viewpoint, because the writer is never forced to make a decision as to the future price of the stock, in the middle of the stock's decline. With the put in place, he can feel free to take no action at all since his overall loss is limited. If the stock should rally upward later, he will still be in a position to make his maximum profit.

The longer-term effects of buying puts in combination with covered writes are not easily definable, but it would appear that the writer reduces his overall rate of return slightly by buying the puts. This is because he gives something away if the stock falls slightly, remains unchanged, or rises in price. He only "gains" something if the stock falls heavily. Since the odds of a stock falling heavily are small in comparison to the other events—falling slightly, remaining unchanged, or rising—the writer will be gaining something in only a small percentage of cases. However, the put buying strategy may still prove useful in that it removes the emotional uncertainty of large losses. The covered writer who buys puts may often find it easier to operate in a more rational manner when he has the protective put in place.

This strategy is equivalent to one that has been described before— the bull spread. Notice that the profit graph in Figure 17-2 has the same shape as the bull spread profit graph (Figure 7-1). This means that the two strategies are equivalent. In fact, in Chapter 7 it was pointed out that the bull spread could sometimes be considered a "substitute" for covered writing. Actually, the bull spread is more akin to this strategy—the covered write protected by a put purchase. There are, of course, differences between the strategies. They are equivalent in profit and loss potential, but the covered writer could never lose all his investment in a short period of time, although the spreader could. In order to actually use bull spreads as substitutes for covered writes, one would invest only a small portion of his available funds in the spread and would place the remainder of his funds in fixed-income securities. Such a strategy was discussed in more depth in Chapter 7.

Chapter *18*

Buying Puts in Conjunction with Call Purchases

There are several ways in which the purchases of both puts and calls can be used to the speculator's advantage. One simple method is actually a follow-up strategy for the call buyer. If the stock has advanced and the call buyer has a profit, he might consider *buying a put as a means of locking in his call profits while still allowing for more potential upside appreciation*. In Chapter 3, four basic alternatives were listed for the call buyer who had a profit—he could liquidate the call and take his profit, he could do nothing, he could "roll up" by selling the call for a profit and using part of the proceeds to purchase more out-of-the-money calls, or he could create a bull spread by selling the out-of-the-money call against the profitable call that he holds. If the underlying stock has listed puts, he has another alternative—he could buy a put. This put purchase would serve to lock in some of the profits on the call and would still allow for room for further appreciation if the stock should continue to rise in price.

Example: An investor initially purchased an XYZ October 50 call for 3 points when the stock was at 48. Sometime later, after the stock had risen to 58, the call would be worth about 9 points. If there was an October 60 put, it might be selling for 4 points, and the call holder could buy this put to lock in some of his profits. His position, after purchasing the put, would be:

$$\left.\begin{array}{l}\text{Long 1 October 50 call at 3 points}\\\text{Long 1 October 60 put at 4 points}\end{array}\right\} \text{net cost: 7 points}$$

He would own a "*combination*"—any position consisting of both a put and call with differing terms—that is always worth at least 10 points. The combination will be worth exactly 10 points at expiration if XYZ is anywhere between 50 and 60. For example, if XYZ is at 52 at expiration, the call will be worth 2 points and the put will be worth 8 points. Alternatively, if the stock is at 58 at expiration, the put will be worth 2 points and the call worth 8 points. Should XYZ be above 60 at expiration, the combination's value will be equal to the call's value since the put will expire worthless with XYZ *above* 60. The call would have to be worth *more* than 10 points in that case, since it has a striking price of 50. Similarly, if XYZ were *below* 50 at expiration, the combination would be worth more than 10 points, since the put would be more than 10 points in-the-money and the call would be worthless.

The speculator has thus created a position in which he cannot lose money—that is because he only paid 7 points for the combination (3 points for the call and 4 points for the put). No matter what happens, the combination will be worth at least 10 points at expiration, and a 3-point profit is thus "locked in." If XYZ should continue to climb in price, the speculator could make more than 3 points of profit whenever XYZ is above 60 at expiration. Moreover, if XYZ should suddenly collapse in price, the speculator could make more than 3 points of profit if the stock was below 50 by expiration. The reader must realize the such a position can never be created as an initial position. This desirable situation only arose because the call had built up a substantial profit before the put was purchased. The similar strategy for the put buyer—who might buy a call to protect his unrealized put profits—was described in Chapter 16.

STRADDLE BUYING

A straddle purchase consists of buying both a put and a call with the same terms—same underlying stock, striking price, and expiration date. The straddle purchase allows the buyer to make large potential profits if the stock moves far enough in either direction. The buyer has a predetermined maximum loss, equal to the amount of his initial investment.

Example: The following prices exist:

XYZ common, 50;

XYZ July 50 call, 3; and

XYZ July 50 put, 2.

If one purchased both the July call and the July 50 put, he would be buying a straddle. This would cost 5 points, plus commissions. The investment required to purchase a straddle is the net debit. If the underlying stock is exactly at 50 at expiration, the buyer would lose all his investment since both the put and the call would expire worthless. If the stock were above 55 at expiration, the call portion of the straddle would be worth more than 5 points and the straddle buyer would make money, even though his put expired worthless. To the downside, a similar situation exists. If XYZ were below 45 at expiration, the put would be worth more than 5 points and he would have a profit despite the fact that the call expired worthless. Table 18-1 and Figure 18-1 depict the results of this example straddle purchase at expiration. The straddle buyer can immediately determine his break-even points at expiration—45 and 55 in this example. He will lose money if the underlying stock is between those break-even points at expiration. He has *potentially large profits* if XYZ should move a great distance away from 50 by expiration.

One would normally purchase a straddle on a relatively volatile stock which has the potential to move far enough to make the straddle profitable in the allotted time. This strategy is particularly attractive when option premiums are low, since low premiums will mean a cheaper straddle cost. Although *losses may occur in a relatively large percentage of cases that are held to expiration*, there is actually only a minute probability of losing one's entire investment. Even if XYZ should be at 50 at expiration, there would still be the opportunity to sell the straddle for a small amount on the final day of trading.

TABLE 18-1.
Results at expiration of straddle purchase.

XYZ Price at Expiration	Call Profit	Put Profit	Total Straddle Profit
30	− $ 300	+ $1,800	+ $1,500
40	− 300	+ 800	+ 500
45	− 300	+ 300	0
50	− 300	− 200	− 500
55	+ 200	− 200	0
60	+ 700	− 200	+ 500
70	+ 1,700	− 200	+ 1,500

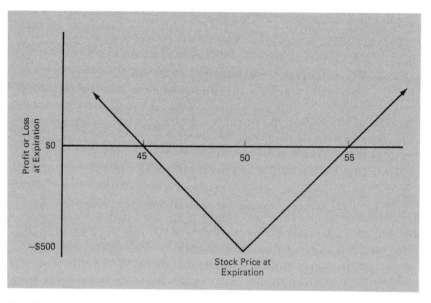

Equivalences

Straddle buying is equivalent to the reverse hedge — a strategy described in Chapter 4, in which one sells the underlying stock short and purchases two calls on the underlying stock. Both strategies have similar profit characteristics — a limited loss which would occur at the striking price of the options involved and potentially large profits if the underlying stock should rise or fall far enough in price. *The straddle purchase is superior to the reverse hedge*, however, and where listed puts exist on a stock, the reverse hedge strategy becomes obsolete. The reasons that the straddle purchase is superior are that dividends are not paid by the holder and that commission costs are much smaller in the straddle situation. As with many of these strategies where the put replaces a stock holding, one cannot invest a large sum of money in the straddle strategy since he could lose a significant portion of it in a short time period.

Example: The straddle purchase might require only $500 as investment but could involve a loss of up to $500. The reverse hedge strategy might require an investment of $3,000, but would involve the same $500 maximum loss. Thus, if one wants to operate with straddles instead of reverse hedges, he should invest the $500 in the straddle and place the remaining $2,500 in much more conservative investments. A similar strategy of dollar investment can be followed with any types of equivalent strategies.

Reverse Hedge with Puts

A third strategy is equivalent to both the straddle purchase and the reverse hedge. It consists of buying the underlying stock and buying two put options. If the stock rises substantially in price, large profits will accrue, for the stock profit will more than offset the fixed loss on the purchase of two put options. If the stock declines in price by a large amount, profits will also be generated. In a decline, the profits generated by 2 long puts will more than offset the loss on 100 shares of long stock. This form of the straddle purchase has limited risk as well. The worst case would occur if the stock were exactly at the striking price of the puts at their expiration date—the puts would both expire worthless. The risk is limited, per-centagewise and dollarwise, since the cost of two put options would normally be a relatively small percentage of the total cost of buying the stock. Furthermore, the investor may receive some dividends if the under-lying stock is a dividend-paying stock. Buying stock and buying two puts is superior to the reverse hedge strategy, but is still inferior to the straddle purchase—as long as the straddle buyer makes a more conservative in-vestment with the balance of his funds.

SELECTING A STRADDLE BUY

In theory, one could find the best straddle purchases by applying the analyses for best call purchases and best put purchases simultaneously. Then, if both the puts and calls on a particular stock showed attractive opportunity, the straddle could be bought. It is rare to find both the puts and calls simultaneously attractive. Rather, the straddle should be viewed as an entire position. A similar sort of analysis to that proposed for either put or call purchases could be used for straddles as well. First, one would assume the stock would move up or down in accordance with its volatility within a fixed time period, such as 60 or 90 days. Then, the prices of both the put and the call could be predicted for this stock movement. The straddles that offer the best reward opportunity under this analysis would be the most attractive ones to buy.

To demonstrate this sort of analysis, the previous example can be utilized again.

Example: XYZ is at 50 and the July 50 call is selling for 3 while the July 50 put is selling for 2 points. If the strategist is able to determine that XYZ has a 25% chance of being above 54 in 90 days and also a 25% chance of being below 46 in 90 days, he can then predict the option prices. A rigorous method for determining what percentage chance a stock has of making a predetermined price movement is presented in Chapter 28. For now, a general procedure of analysis is more important than its actual implementation. If XYZ were at 54 in 90 days, it might be reasonable to assume that the call would be worth 5½ and the put would be worth 1 point. The straddle would therefore be worth 6½ points. Similarly, if the stock were at 46 in 90 days, the put might be worth 4½ points, and the call worth 1 point, making the entire straddle worth 5½ points. It is fairly common for the straddle to be higher-priced when it is a fixed distance in-the-money on the call side (such as 4 points) than when it is in-the-money on the put side by that same distance. In this example, the strategist has now determined that there is a 25% chance that the straddle will be worth 6½ points in 90 days on an upside movement, and there is a 25% chance that the straddle will be worth 5½ points on a downside movement. The average price of these two expectations is 6 points. Since the straddle is currently selling for 5 points, this would represent a 20% profit. If all potential straddles are ranked in the same manner—allowing for a 25% chance of upside and downside movement by each underlying stock—the straddle buyer will have a common basis for comparing various straddle opportunities.

FOLLOW-UP ACTION

It has been mentioned frequently that there is a good chance that a stock will remain relatively unchanged over a short time period. This does not mean that the stock will *never* move much one way or the other, but that its *net* movement over the time period will generally be small.

    Example: If XYZ is currently at 50, one might say that its chances of being over 55 at the end of 90 days are fairly small, perhaps 30%. This may even be supported by mathematical analysis based on the volatility of the underlying stock. This does not imply, however, that the stock has only a 30% chance of *ever* reaching 55 during the 90-day period. Rather, it implies that it has only a 30% chance of being over 55 at the *end* of the 90-day period. These are two distinctly different events, with different probabilities of occurrence. Even though the probability of being over 55 at the *end* of 90 days might be only 30%, the probability of *ever* being 55 during the 90-day period could be amazingly high, perhaps as high as 80%. It is important for the straddle buyer to understand the differences between these events occurring, for he might often be able to take *follow-up action* to improve his position.

    Many times, after a straddle is bought, the underlying stock will begin to move strongly, making it appear that the straddle is immediately going to become profitable. However, just as things are going well, the stock reverses and begins to change direction—perhaps so quickly that it would now appear that the straddle will become profitable on the other side. These volatile stock movements often result in little net change, however, and at expiration the straddle buyer may have a loss. One might think that he would take profits on the call side when they became available in a quick upward movement, and then hope for a downward reversal so that he could take profits on the put side as well. *Taking small profits, however, is a poor strategy.* Straddle buying has limited losses and potentially unlimited profits. One might have to suffer through a substantial number of small losses before hitting a big winner, but the magnitude of the gain on that one large stock movement can offset many small losses. By taking small profits, the straddle buyer is immediately cutting off his chances for a substantial gain, and that is why it is a poor strategy to limit the profits.

This is one of those statements that sounds easier in theory than it is in practice. It is emotionally distressing to watch the straddle gain 2 or 3 points in a short time period, only to lose that and more when the stock fails to follow through. By using a different example, it will be possible to demonstrate the types of follow-up action that the straddle buyer might take.

Example: One had initially bought an XYZ January 40 straddle for 6 points when the stock was 40. After a fairly short time, the stock jumps up to 45 and the following prices exist:

XYZ common, 45:

XYZ January 40 call, 7;

XYZ January 40 put, 1; and

XYZ January 45 put, 3.

The straddle itself is now worth 8 points. The January 45 put price is included because it will be part of one of the follow-up strategies. What could the straddle buyer do at this time? First, he might do nothing, preferring to let the straddle run its course—at least for three months or so. Assuming that he is not content to sit tight, however, he might sell the call, taking his profit, and hope for the stock to then drop in price. This would be an inferior course of action since he is cutting off potential large profits to the upside.

In the older, over-the-counter option market, one might have tried a technique known as "*trading against the straddle.*" Since there was no secondary market for over-the-counter options, straddle buyers often traded the stock itself against the straddle that they owned. This type of follow-up action dictated that, if the stock rose enough to make the straddle profitable to the upside, one would sell short the underlying stock. This involved no extra risk, since if the stock continued up, the straddle holder could always exercise his call to cover the short sale for a profit. Conversely, if the underlying stock fell at the outset, making the straddle profitable to the downside, one would *buy* the underlying stock. Again this involved no extra risk if the stock continued down, since the put could always be exercised to sell the stock at a profit. The idea was to be able to capitalize on large stock price reversals with the addition of the stock position to the straddle. This strategy worked best for the brokers, who made numerous commissions as the trader tried to gauge the whipsaws in the market. In the listed options market, the same strategic effect can be realized (without as large of a commission expense) by merely selling out the long call on an upward move, and using part of the proceeds to buy a second put similar to the one already held. On a downside move, one could sell out the long put for a profit and buy a second call similar to the one he already owns. In the example above, the call would be sold for 7 points and a second January 40 put purchased for 1 point. This would allow the straddle buyer to recover his initial 6-point cost and would allow for large downside profit potential. This strategy is *not* recommended, however, since the straddle buyer is limiting his profit in the direction that the stock is moving. Once the stock has moved from 40 to 45, as in this example, it would be more reasonable to expect that it could continue up rather than experience a drop of more than 5 points.

A more desirable sort of follow-up action would be one where the straddle buyer could retain much of the profit already built up without limiting further potential profits if the stock continues to run. In the example above, the straddle buyer could use the January 45 put—the one at the higher price—for this purpose.

Example: Suppose that when the stock got to 45, he sold the put that he owned, the January 40, for 1 point, and simultaneously bought the January 45 put for 3 points. This transaction would *cost* 2 points, and would leave him in the following position:

> Long 1 January 40 call
> Long 1 January 45 put   — combined cost: 8 points

He now owns a combination at a cost of 8 points. However, no matter where the underlying stock is at expiration, this combination will be worth at least 5 points, since the put has a striking price 5 points higher than the call's striking price. In fact, if the stock is above 45 at expiration or is below 40 at expiration, the combination will be worth more than 5 points. This follow-up action has not limited the potential profits. If the stock continues to rise in price, the call will become more and more valuable. On the other hand, if the stock reverses and falls dramatically, the put will become quite valuable. In either case, the opportunity for large potential profits remains. Moreover, he has improved his risk exposure. The most that the new position can lose at expiration is 3 points, since the combination cost 8 points originally, and can be sold for 5 points at worst.

To summarize, *if the underlying stock moves up to the next strike, the straddle buyer should consider rolling his put up*—selling the one that he is long and buying the one at the next higher striking price. Conversely, *if the stock starts out with a downward move, he should consider rolling the call down*—selling the one that he is long and buying the one at the next lower strike. In either case, he reduces his risk exposure without limiting his profit potential—exactly the type of follow-up result that the straddle buyer should be aiming for.

BUYING A COMBINATION

A combination is any position that consists of both a put and a call on the same underlying stock, where the options have differing terms. They may have different striking prices and/or expiration dates. The most common combination position is one in which the put and call have the same expiration date but have different striking prices. The following example is a specific type of combination, often called a strangle.

Example: One might buy a combination consisting of an XYZ January 45 put and an XYZ January 50 call. Buying such a combination is quite similar to buying a straddle, although there are some differences, as the following discussion will demonstrate. Suppose the following prices exist:

XYZ common, 47;

XYZ January 45 put, 2; and

XYZ January 50 call, 2.

In this example, both options are out-of-the-money when purchased. This, again, is the most normal application of the combination purchase. If XYZ is still between 45 and 50 at January expiration, both options will expire worthless and the combination buyer will lose his entire investment. This investment—$400 in the example—is generally smaller than that required to buy a straddle on XYZ. If XYZ moves in either direction, rising above 50 or falling below 45, the combination will have some value at expiration. In this example, if XYZ is above 54 at expiration, the call will be worth more than 4 points (the put will expire worthless) and the buyer will make a profit. In a similar manner, if XYZ is below 41 at expiration, the put will have a value greater than 4 points and the buyer would make a profit in that case as well. *The potential profits are quite large, if the underlying stock should move a great deal before the options expire.* Table 18-2 and Figure 18-2 depict the potential profits or losses from this position at January expiration. The maximum loss is possible over a much wider range than that of a straddle. The straddle only achieves its maximum loss if the stock is exactly at the striking price of the options at

TABLE 18-2.
Results at expiration of a combination purchase.

XYZ Price at Expiration	Put Profit	Call Profit	Total Profit
25	+ $1,800	− $ 200	+ $1,600
35	+ 800	− 200	+ 600
41	+ 200	− 200	0
43	0	− 200	− 200
45	− 200	− 200	− 400
47	− 200	− 200	− 400
50	− 200	− 200	− 400
54	− 200	+ 200	0
60	− 200	+ 800	+ 600
70	− 200	+ 1,800	+ 1,600

FIGURE 18-2.
Strangle purchase.

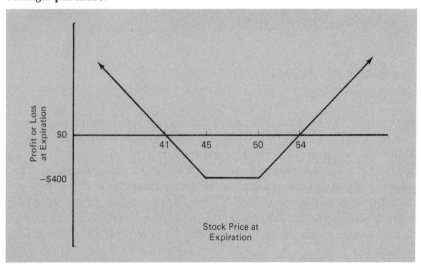

Stock Price at
Expiration

expiration. However, the combination has its maximum loss anywhere between the two strikes at expiration. The actual amount of the loss is smaller for the combination, and that is a compensating factor. The potential profits are large for both strategies.

The example above is one in which both options are out-of-the money. It is also possible to construct a very similar position by utilizing in-the-money options.

Example: With XYZ at 47 as before, the in-the-money options might have the following prices: XYZ January 45 call, 4, and XYZ January 50 put, 4. If one purchased this *in-the-money combination*, he would pay a total cost of 8 points. However, the value of this combination will always be at least 5 points, since the striking price of the put is 5 points higher than that of the call. The reader has seen this sort of position before— when protective follow-up strategies for straddle buying and for call or put buying were described. Because the combination will always be worth at least 5 points, the most that the in-the-money combination buyer can lose is 3 points in this example. His potential profits are still unlimited should the underlying stock move a large distance. Thus, even though it requires a larger initial investment, *the in-the-money combination may often be a superior strategy to the out-of-the-money combination, from a buyer's viewpoint.* The in-the-money combination purchase certainly involves less percentage risk—the buyer can never lose all his investment, since he can always get back 5 points, even in the worst case (when XYZ is between 45 and 50 at expiration). His percentage profits are lower with the in-the-money combination purchase since he paid more for the combination to begin with. These observations should come as no surprise, since when the outright purchase of a call was discussed, it was shown that the purchase of an in-the-money call was more conservative than the purchase of an out-of-the-money call, in general. The same was true for the outright purchase of puts—perhaps even more so, because of the smaller time value of an in-the-money put. Therefore, the combination of the two—an in-the-money call and an in-the-money put—should be more conservative than the out-of-the-money combination.

If the underlying stock moves quickly in either direction, the combination buyer may sometimes be able to take action to protect some of his profits. He would do so in a manner similar to that described for the straddle buyer. For example, if the stock moved up quickly, he could sell the put that he originally bought and buy the put at the next higher striking price in its place. This would then place him in a straddle, if he had started from an out-of-the-money combination position. The strategist should not blindly take this sort of follow-up action, however. It may be overly expensive to "roll up" the put in such a manner, depending on the amount of time that has passed and the actual option prices involved. Therefore, it is best to analyze each situation on a case-by-case basis to see whether it is logical to take any follow-up action at all.

As a final point, the out-of-the-money combinations may appear deceptively cheap—both options selling for fractions of a point as expiration nears. However, the probability of realizing the maximum loss equal to one's initial investment is fairly large with combinations. This is distinctly different from straddle purchases, where the probability of losing the entire investment is small. The aggressive speculator should *not* place a large portion of his funds in out-of-the-money combination purchases. The percentage risk is smaller with the in-the-money combination—being equal to the amount of time value premium paid for the options initially—but commission costs will be somewhat larger, and in either case the underlying stock still needs to move by a relatively large amount in order for the buyer to profit.

Chapter 19

The Sale of a Put

The buyer of a put stands to profit if the underlying stock drops in price. As might then be expected, the seller of a put will make money if the underlying stock increases in price. The uncovered sale of a put is a more common strategy than the covered sale of a put, and will therefore be described first. It is a bullishly oriented strategy.

THE UNCOVERED PUT SALE

Since the buyer of a put has a right to sell stock at the striking price, the writer of a put is obligating himself to buy that stock at the striking price. For assuming this obligation he receives the put option premium. If the underlying stock advances and the put expires worthless, the put writer will not be assigned and *he could make a maximum profit equal to the premium received*. He has large downside risk, since the stock could fall substantially, thereby increasing the value of the written put and causing large losses to occur. An example will aid in explaining these general statements about risk and reward.

Example: XYZ is at 50 and a 6-month put is selling for 4 points. The naked put writer has a fixed potential profit to the upside—$400 in this example—and a large potential loss to the downside (Table 19-1 and Figure 19-1). This downside loss is limited only by the fact that a stock cannot go below zero.

The collateral requirement for writing naked puts is the same as that for writing naked calls. The requirement is equal to 20% of the current stock price plus the put premium minus any out-of-the-money amount.

Example: If XYZ is at 50, the collateral requirement for writing a 4-point put with a striking price of 50 would be $1,000 (20% of 50) plus

TABLE 19-1.
Results from the sale of an uncovered put.

XYZ Price at Expiration	Put Price at Expiration (Parity)	Put Sale Profit
30	20	− $1,600
40	10	− 600
46	4	0
50	0	+ 400
60	0	+ 400
70	0	+ 400

FIGURE 19-1.
Uncovered sale of a put.

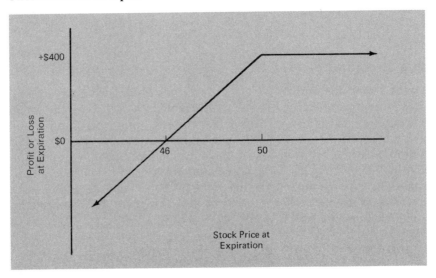

$400 for the put premium. If the stock were above the striking price, the striking price differential would be subtracted from the requirement. The minimum requirement is 15% of the stock price, even if the computation above yields a smaller result.

The uncovered put writing strategy is similar in many ways to the covered call writing strategy. Note that the profit graphs have the same shape—this means that the two strategies are equivalent. It may be helpful to the reader to describe the aspects of naked put writing by comparing it to similar aspects of covered call writing.

In either strategy, one needs to be somewhat bullish, or at least neutral, on the underlying stock. If the underlying stock moves upward, the uncovered put writer will make a profit, possibly profiting by the entire amount of the premium received. If the underlying stock should be unchanged at expiration—a neutral situation—the put writer will profit by the amount of the time value premium received when he initially wrote the put. This could represent the maximum profit if the put was out-of-the-money initially, since that would mean that the entire put premium was composed of time value premium. For an in-the-money put, however, the time value premium would represent something less than the entire value of the option. These are similar qualities to those inherent in covered call writing. If the stock moves up, the covered call writer can make his maximum profit. However, if the stock is unchanged at expiration, he will only make his maximum profit if the stock is above the call's striking price. So, *in either strategy, if the position is established with the stock above the striking price, there is a greater probability of achieving the maximum profit.* This represents the less aggressive application—writing an out-of-the-money put initially, which is equivalent to the covered write of an in-the-money call.

The more aggressive application of naked put writing is to write an in-the-money put initially. The writer will receive a larger amount of premium dollars for the in-the-money put and if the underlying stock advances far enough, he will thus make a large profit. By increasing his profit potential in this manner, he assumes more risk. If the underlying stock should fall, the in-the-money put writer will lose money more quickly than one who initially wrote an out-of-the-money put. Again, these facts were demonstrated much earlier with covered call writing. An in-the-money covered call write affords more downside protection but less profit potential than does an out-of-the-money covered call write.

It is fairly easy to summarize all of this by noting that in either the naked put writing strategy or the covered call writing strategy, *a less aggressive position is established when the stock is higher than the striking price of the written option. If the stock is below the striking price initially, a more aggressive position is created.*

There are, of course, some basic differences between covered call writing and naked put writing. First, the naked put write will generally require a smaller investment, since one is only collateralizing 20% of the stock price plus the put premium as opposed to 50% for the covered call write on margin. Also, the naked put writer is not actually investing cash — collateral is used, so he may finance his naked put writing through the value of his present portfolio, whether it be stocks, bonds, or government securities. However, any losses would create a debit and might therefore cause him to disturb a portion of this portfolio. The covered call writer receives the dividends on the underlying stock, but the naked put writer does not. In certain cases, this may be a substantial amount, but it should also be pointed out that the puts on a high-yielding stock will have more value and the naked put writer will thus be taking in a higher premium initially. From strictly a rate of return viewpoint, naked put writing is superior to covered call writing. Basically, there is a different psychology involved in writing naked puts than that required for covered call writing. The covered call write is a comfortable strategy for most investors, since it involves common stock ownership. Writing naked options, however, is a more foreign concept to the average investor, even if the strategies are equivalent. Therefore, it is relatively unlikely that the same investor would be a participant in both strategies.

FOLLOW-UP ACTION

The naked put writer would take protective follow-up action if the underlying stock drops in price. His simplest form of follow-up action is to merely close the position at a small loss if the stock drops. Since in-the-money puts tend to rapidly lose time value premium, he may find that his loss is often quite small if the stock goes against him. In the example above, XYZ was at 50 with the put at 4. If the stock falls to 45, the writer may be able to quite easily repurchase the put for 5½ or 6 points, thereby incurring a fairly small loss.

In the covered call writing strategy, it was recommended that the strategist roll down wherever possible. One reason for doing so, rather than closing the covered call position, was that stock commissions are quite large and one cannot generally afford to be moving in and out of stocks all the time. It is more advantageous to try to preserve the stock position and roll the calls down. This commission disadvantage does not exist with naked put writing. When one closes the naked put position, he merely buys in the put. Therefore, *rolling down is not as advantageous for the naked put writer.* For example, in the paragraph above, the put writer buys in the put for 5½ or 6 points. He could roll down by selling a put with striking price 45 at that time. However, there may be better put writing situations in other stocks and there should be no reason for him to continue to preserve a position in XYZ stock.

In fact, this same reasoning can be applied to any sort of rolling action for the naked put writer. It is extremely advantageous for the covered call writer to roll forward—that is, to buy back the call when it has little or no time value premium remaining in it and sell a longer-term call at the same striking price. By doing so, he takes in additional premium without having to disturb his stock position at all. However, the naked put writer has little advantage in rolling forward. He can also take in additional premium, but when he closes the initial uncovered put, he should then evaluate other available put writing positions before deciding to again write another put on the same underlying stock. His commission costs are the same if he remains in XYZ stock or if he goes on to a put writing position in a different stock.

EVALUATING A NAKED PUT WRITE

The computation of potential returns from a naked put write if not as straightforward as were the computations for covered call writing. The reason for this is that the collateral requirement changes as the stock moves up or down, since any naked option position is marked to the market. *The most conservative approach is to allow enough collateral in the position if the underlying stock should fall*, thus increasing the requirement. In this way, the naked put writer would not be forced to prematurely close a position because he cannot maintain the margin required.

Example: XYZ is at 50 and the October 50 put is selling for 4 points. The initial collateral requirement is 20% of 50 plus $400, or $1,400. There is no additional requirement, since the stock is exactly at the striking price of the put. Furthermore, let us assume that the writer is going to close the position should the underlying stock fall to 43. To maintain his put write, he should therefore allow enough margin to collateralize the position if the stock were at 43. The requirement at that stock price would be $1,560 (20% of 43 plus at least 7 points for the in-the-money amount). Thus the put writer who is establishing this position should allow $1,560 of collateral value for each put written. Of course, this collateral requirement can be reduced by the amount of the proceeds received from the put sale—$400 less commissions in this example. If we assume that the writer sells 5 puts, his gross premium inflow would be $2,000 and his commission expense would be about $75, for a net premium of $1,925.

Once this information has been determined, it is a simple matter to determine the maximum potential return and also the downside breakeven point. To achieve the maximum potential return, the put would expire worthless with the underlying stock above the striking price. Therefore, the maximum potential profit is equal to the net premium received. The return is merely that profit divided by the collateral used. In the example above, the maximum potential profit is $1,925. The collateral required is $1,560 per put (allowing for the stock to drop to 43) or $7,800 for 5 puts, reduced by the $1,925 premium received, for a total requirement of $5,875. The potential return is then $1,925 divided by $5,875, or 32.8%. Table 19-2 summarizes these calculations.

There are differences of opinion on how to compute the potential returns from naked put writing. The method presented above is a more conservative one in that it takes into consideration a larger collateral requirement than the initial requirement. Of course, since one is not really investing cash, but is merely using the collateral value of his present portfolio, it may even be correct to claim that one has no investment at all in such a position. This may be true, but it would be impossible to compare various put writing opportunities without having a return computation available.

TABLE 19-2.
Calculation of the potential return of uncovered put writing.

XYZ: 50	
XYZ January 50 put: 4	
Potential profit:	
Sell 5 puts	$2,000
Less commissions	− 75
Potential maximum profit (premium received)	$1,925
Break-even point:	
Striking price	$50.00
Less premium per put ($1,925/5)	− 3.85
Break-even stock price	46.15
Collateral required (allowing for stock to drop to 43):	
20% of 43	$ 860
Plus put premium	+ 700
	$1,560
	× 5
Requirement for 5 puts	$7,800
Less premium received	− 1,925
Net collateral	$5,875
Potential return:	
Premium divided by net collateral	$1,925/$5,875 = 32.8%

One other feature of return computations that is important is the return if unchanged. If the put is initially out-of-the-money, the return if unchanged is the same as the maximum potential return. However, if the put is initially in-the-money, the computation must take into consideration what the writer would have to pay to buy back the put when it expires.

Example: XYZ is 48 and the XYZ January 50 put is selling for 5 points. The profit that could be made if the stock were unchanged at expiration would be only 3 points, less commissions, since the put would have to be repurchased for 2 points with XYZ at 48 at expiration. Commissions for the buy-back should be included as well, to make the computation as accurate as possible.

As was the case with covered call writing, one can create several rankings of naked put writes. One list might be the *highest potential returns.* Another list would be the put writes that provided the *most downside protection*—that is, the ones that have the least chance of losing money. Both lists need some screening applied to them, however. When considering the maximum potential returns, one should take care to ensure at least some room for downside movement.

Example: If XYZ were at 50, the XYZ January 100 put would be selling at 50 also and would most assuredly have a tremendously large maximum potential return. However, there is no room for downside movement at all, and one would surely not write such a put. One simple way of allowing for such cases would be to reject any put that did not offer at least a 5% downside protection. Alternatively, *one could also reject situations in which the return if unchanged is below 5%.*

The other list—involving maximum downside protection—also must have some screens applied to it.

Example: With XYZ at 70, the XYZ January 50 put would be selling for ½ at most. Thus it is extremely unlikely that one would lose money in this situation—the stock would have to fall 20 points to do so. However, there is practically nothing to be made from this position, and one would most likely not ever write such a deeply out-of-the-money put.

A minimum acceptable level of return must accompany the items on this list of put writes. For example, one might decide that the return would have to be at least 12% on an annualized basis in order for the put write to be on the list of positions offering the most downside protection. Such a requirement would preclude an extreme situation as that shown above. Once these screens have been applied, the lists can then be ranked in a normal manner. The put writes offering the highest returns would be at the top of the more aggressive list, and those offering the highest percentage of downside protection would be at the top of the more conservative list. In the strictest sense, a more advanced technique to incorporate the volatility of the underlying stock should rightfully be employed. As mentioned previously, that technique will be presented in Chapter 30.

BUYING STOCK BELOW ITS MARKET PRICE

In addition to viewing naked put writing as a strategy unto itself, as was the case in the previous discussion, *some investors who actually want to acquire stock will often write naked puts as well.*

Example: XYZ is a $60 stock and an investor feels it would be a good buy at 55. He places an open buy order with a limit of 55. Three months later, XYZ has drifted down to 57 but no lower. It then turns and rises heavily, but the buy limit was never reached, and the investor misses out on the advance.

This hypothetical investor could have perhaps used a naked put to his advantage. Suppose that when XYZ was originally at 60, this investor wrote a naked three-month put for 5 points instead of placing an open buy limit order. Then, if XYZ is anywhere below 60 at expiration, he will have stock put to him at 60. That is, he will have to buy stock at 60. However, since he received 5 points for the put sale, his *net* cost for the stock is 55. Thus, even if XYZ is 57 at expiration and has never been any lower, the investor can still buy XYZ for a net cost of 55.

Of course, if XYZ rose right away and was above 60 at expiration, the put will not be assigned and the investor will not own XYZ. However, he will still have made $500 from selling the put, which is now worthless. The put writer thus assumes a more active role in his investments by acting rather than waiting. He at least receives some compensation for his efforts, even though he did not get to buy the stock.

If, instead of rising, XYZ fell considerably—say to 40—by expiration, the investor will be forced to purchase stock at a net cost of 55, thereby giving himself an immediate paper loss. He was, however, going to buy stock at 55 in any case, so the put writer and the investor using a buy limit have the same result in this case. Critics may point out that any buy order for common stock may be canceled if one's opinion changes about purchasing the stock. The put writer, of course, may do the same thing by closing out his obligation through a closing purchase of the put.

This technique is useful to many types of investors who are oriented toward eventually owning the stock. Large portfolio managers as well as individual investors may find the sale of puts useful for this purpose. *It is a method of attempting to accumulate a stock position at prices lower than today's market price.* If the stock rises and the stock is not bought, the investor will at least have received the put premium as compensation for his efforts.

THE COVERED PUT SALE

By definition, a put sale is covered only if the investor also owns a corresponding put with striking price equal to or greater than the strike of the written put. This is a spread. However, *for margin purposes, one is covered if he sells a put and is also short the underlying stock.* This creates a position with limited profit potential that is obtained if the underlying stock is anywhere *below* the striking price of the put at expiration. There is unlimited upside risk, since if the underlying stock rises, the short sale of stock will accrue losses, while the profit from the put sale is limited. This is really a position equivalent to a naked call write, except that the covered put writer must pay out the dividend on the underlying stock, if one exists. The naked sale of a call also has an advantage over this strategy in that commission costs are considerably smaller. In addition, the time value premium of a call is generally higher than that of a put, so that the naked call writer is taking in more time premium. The covered put sale is a little-used strategy that appears to be inferior to naked call writing. As a result, the strategy will not be described more fully.

RATIO PUT WRITING

A ratio put write would involve the short sale of the underlying stock plus the sale of 2 puts for each 100 shares sold short. This strategy has a profit graph exactly like that of a ratio call writing—achieving its maximum profit at the striking price of the written options, and having large potential losses if the underlying stock should move too far in either direction. The ratio call write is a highly superior strategy, however, for the reasons just outlined. The ratio call writer receives dividends while the ratio put writer would have to pay them out. In addition, the ratio call writer will generally be taking in larger amounts of time value premium because calls have more time premium than puts do. Therefore, the ratio put writing strategy is not a viable one.

Chapter *20* _____

The Sale of a Straddle

Selling a straddle involves selling both a put and call with the same terms. As with any type of option sale, the straddle sale may be either covered or uncovered. Both uses are fairly common. The covered sale of a straddle is very similar to the covered call writing strategy and would generally appeal to the same type of investor. The uncovered straddle write is more similar to ratio call writing, and is attractive to the more aggressive strategist who is interested in selling large amounts of time premium in hopes of collecting larger profits if the underlying stock remains fairly stable.

THE COVERED STRADDLE WRITE

In this strategy, *one owns the underlying stock and simultaneously writes a straddle on that stock.* This may be particularly appealing to investors who are already involved in covered call writing. In reality, this position is not totally covered—only the sale of the call is covered by the ownership of the stock. The sale of the put is uncovered. However, the name "covered" straddle is generally used for this type of position in order to distinguish it from the uncovered straddle write.

Example: XYZ is at 51 and an XYZ January 50 call is selling for 5 points while an XYZ January 50 put is selling for 4 points. A covered straddle write would be established by buying 100 shares of the underlying stock and simultaneously selling one put and one call. The similarity between this position and a covered call writer's position should be obvious. The covered straddle write is actually a covered write—long 100 shares of XYZ plus short one call—coupled with a naked put write. Since the naked put write has already been shown to be equivalent to a covered call write, *this position is quite similar to a 200-share covered call write.* In fact, all the profit and loss characteristics of a covered call write are the same for the covered straddle write. There is limited upside profit potential and potentially large downside risk.

The maximum profit is attained if XYZ is anywhere above the striking price of 50 at expiration. The amount of maximum profit in this example would be $800—the premium received from selling the straddle, less the 1-point loss on the stock if it is called away at 50. In fact, the maximum profit potential of a covered straddle write is quickly computed by the following formula:

Maximum profit = straddle premium + striking price—initial stock price

The break-even point in this example is 46. Note that the covered writing portion of this example—buying stock at 51 and selling a call for 5 points—has a break-even point of 46. Additionally, the naked put portion of the position has a break-even point of 46 as well, since the January 50 put was sold for 4 points. Therefore, the combined position—the covered straddle write—must have a break-even point of 46. Again, this observation is easily defined by an equation:

$$\text{Break-even price} = \frac{\text{stock price} + \text{strike price} - \text{straddle premium}}{2}$$

Table 20-1 and Figure 20-1 compare the covered straddle write to a 100-share covered call write of the XYZ January 50 at expiration.

The attraction for the covered call writer to become a covered straddle writer is that he may be able to increase his return without altering the parameters of his covered call writing position substantially. Using the prices in Table 20-1, if one had decided to establish a covered write by buying XYZ at 51 and selling the January 50 call at 5 points, he would have a position with its maximum potential return anywhere above 50 and with a break-even point of 46. By adding the naked put to his covered

TABLE 20-1.
Results at expiration of covered straddle write.

Stock Price	(A) 100-Share Covered Write	(B) Put Write	Covered Straddle Write (A + B)
35	− $1,100	− $1,100	− $2,200
40	− 600	− 600	− 1,200
46	0	0	0
50	+ 400	+ 400	+ 800
60	+ 400	+ 400	+ 800

FIGURE 20-1.
Covered straddle write.

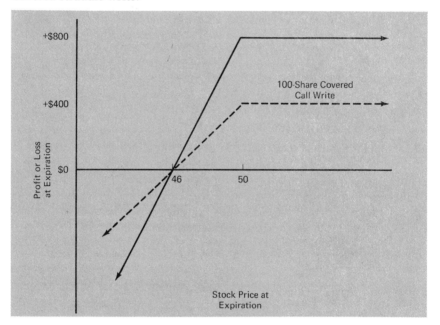

call position, he does not change the price parameters of his position—
he still makes his maximum profit anywhere above 50 and he still has a
break-even point of 46. Therefore, he does not have to change his outlook
on the underlying stock in order to become a covered straddle writer.

The investment is increased by the addition of the naked put, as are
the potential dollars of profit if the stock is above 50 and the potential
dollars of loss if the stock is below 46 at expiration. The covered straddle
writer loses money twice as fast on the downside, since his position is
similar to a 200-share covered write. Because the commissions are smaller

for the naked put write than for the covered call write, the covered call writer who adds a naked put to his position will generally be increasing his return somewhat.

Follow-up action can be implemented in much the same way that it would be for a covered call write. Whenever one would normally roll his call in a covered situation, he now rolls the entire straddle—rolling down for protection, rolling up for an increase of profit potential, and rolling forward when the time value premium of the straddle dissipates. Rolling up or down would probably involve debits, unless one rolled to a longer maturity.

Some writers might prefer to make a slight adjustment to the covered straddle writing strategy. Instead of selling the put and call at the same price, they prefer to sell an out-of-the-money put against the covered call write. That is, if one is buying XYZ at 50 and selling the call, he might then also sell a put at 45. This would increase his upside profit potential and would allow for the possibility of both options expiring worthless if XYZ were anywhere between 45 and 50 at expiration. Such action would, of course, increase the potential dollars of risk if XYZ fell below 45 by expiration, but the writer could always roll the call down to obtain additional downside protection.

One final point should be made with regard to this strategy. The covered call writer who is writing on margin and is fully utilizing his borrowing power for call writing will have to add additional collateral in order to write covered straddles. This is because the put write is uncovered. However, the covered call writer who is operating on a cash basis can switch to the covered straddle writing strategy without putting up additional funds. He merely needs to move his stock to a margin account and use the collateral value of the stock he already owns in order to sell the puts necessary to implement the covered straddle writes.

THE UNCOVERED STRADDLE WRITE

In an uncovered straddle write, *one sells the straddle without owning the underlying stock.* In broad terms, this is a neutral strategy with limited profit potential and large risk potential. However, the probability of making a profit is generally quite large and there are methods that can be implemented to reduce the risks of the strategy.

Since one is selling both a put and a call in this strategy, he is initially taking in large amounts of time value premium. If the underlying stock is relatively unchanged at expiration, the straddle writer will be able to buy the straddle back for its intrinsic value, which would normally leave him with a profit.

Example: The following prices exist:

XYZ common, 45;

XYZ January 45 call, 4; and

XYZ January 45 put, 3.

A straddle could be sold for 7 points. If the stock were above 38 and below 52 at expiration, the straddle writer would profit since the in-the-money option could be bought back for less than 7 points in that case, while the out-of-the-money option expires worthless (Table 20-2).

Notice that Figure 20-2 has a shape like a roof. *The maximum potential profit point is at the striking price at expiration, and large potential losses exist in either direction if the underlying stock should move too far.* The reader may recall that the ratio call writing strategy—buying 100 shares of the underlying stock and selling two calls—has the same profit graph. These two strategies, the naked straddle write and the ratio call write, are equivalent. The two strategies do have some differences, of course, as do all equivalent strategies, but they are similar in that both are highly probabilistic strategies that can be somewhat complex. In addition, both have large potential risks under adverse market conditions or if follow-up strategies are not applied.

The investment required for a naked straddle is the greater of the requirement on the call or the put. In general, this would mean that the margin requirement is equal to the requirement for the in-the-money option in a simple naked write. This requirement is 15% of the stock price plus the in-the-money option premium. *The straddle writer should allow enough collateral so that he can take whatever follow-up actions he deems*

TABLE 20-2.
The naked straddle write.

XYZ Price at Expiration	Call Profit	Put Profit	Total Profit
30	+$ 400	−$1,200	−$800
35	+ 400	− 700	− 300
38	+ 400	− 400	0
40	+ 400	− 200	+ 200
45	+ 400	+ 300	+ 700
50	− 100	+ 300	+ 200
52	− 300	+ 300	0
55	− 600	+ 300	− 300
60	− 1,100	+ 300	− 800

FIGURE 20-2.
Naked straddle sale.

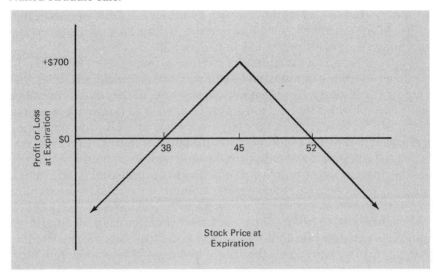

necessary without having to incur a margin call. If he is intending to close out the straddle if the stock should reach the upside break-even point—52 in the example above—then he should allow enough collateral to finance the position with the stock at 52. If, however, he is planning on taking other action that might involve staying with the position if the stock goes to 55 or 56, he should allow enough collateral to be able to finance that action. If the stock never gets that high, he will have excess collateral while the position is in place.

SELECTING A STRADDLE WRITE

Ideally, one would like to receive a premium for the straddle write that produces a profit range that is wide in relation to the volatility of the underlying stock. In the example above, the profit range is 38 to 52. This may or may not be extraordinarily wide, depending on the volatility of XYZ. This is a somewhat subjective measurement, although one could construct a simple straddle writer's index that ranked straddles based on the following simple formula:

$$\text{Index} = \frac{\text{straddle time value premium}}{\text{stock price} \times \text{volatility}}$$

Refinements would have to be made to such a ranking, such as eliminating cases in which either the put or the call sells for less than ½ point (or even 1 point, if a more restrictive requirement is desired) or where the in-the-money time premium is small. Furthermore, the index would have to be annualized to be able to compare straddles for different expiration months. More advanced selection criteria, in the form of an expected return analysis, will be presented in Chapter 30.

More screens can be added to produce a more conservative list of straddle writes. For example, one might want to ignore any straddles that are not worth at least a fixed percentage, say 10%, of the underlying stock price. Also, straddles that are too short-term, such as ones with less than 30 days of life remaining, might be thrown out as well. The remaining list of straddle writing candidates should be ones that will provide reasonable returns under favorable conditions, and also should be readily adaptable to some of the follow-up strategies to be discussed later. Finally, one would generally like to have some amount of technical support at or above the lower break-even price and some technical resistance at or below the upper break-even point. Thus, once the computer has generated a list of straddles ranked by an index such as the one listed above, the straddle writer can further pare down the list by looking at the technical pictures of the underlying stocks.

FOLLOW-UP ACTION

The risks involved in straddle writing can be quite large. When market conditions are favorable, one can make considerable profits, even with restrictive selection requirements, and even by allowing considerable extra collateral for adverse stock movements. However, in an extremely volatile market, especially a bullish one, losses can occur rapidly and follow-up action must be taken. Since the time premium of a put tends to shrink when it goes into-the-money, there is actually slightly less risk to the downside than there is to the upside. In an extremely bullish market, the time value premiums of call options will not shrink much at all and might even expand. This may force the straddle writer to pay excessive amounts of time value premium to buy back the written straddle, especially if the movement occurs well in advance of expiration.

The simplest form of follow-up action is to buy the straddle back when and if the underlying stock reaches a break-even point. The idea behind doing so is to limit the losses to a small amount, because the straddle should be selling for only slightly more than its original value when the stock has reached a break-even point. In practice, there are several flaws in this theory. If the underlying stock arrives at a break-even point well in advance of expiration, the amount of time value premium remaining in the straddle may be extremely large and the writer will be losing a fairly large amount by repurchasing the straddle. Thus a break-even point at expiration is probably a loss point prior to expiration.

Example: After the straddle is established with the stock at 45, there is a sudden rally in the stock and it climbs quickly to 52. The call might be selling for 9 points, even though it is 7 points in-the-money. This is not unusual in a bullish situation. Moreover, the put might be worth 1½ points. This is also not unusual, as out-of-the-money puts with a large amount of time remaining tend to hold time value premium very well. Thus the straddle writer would have to pay 10½ points to buy back this straddle, even though it is at the break-even point, 7 points in-the-money on the call side.

This example is included merely to demonstrate that *it is a misconception to believe that one can always buy the straddle back at the breakeven point and hold his losses to mere fractions of a point by doing so.* This type of buy-back strategy works best when there is little time remaining in the straddle. In that case, the options will indeed be close to parity and the straddle will be able to be bought back for close to its initial value when the stock reaches the break-even point.

Another follow-up strategy that can be employed, similar to the previous one, but with certain improvements, is to *buy back only the in-the-money option when it reaches a price equal to that of the initial straddle price.*

Example: Again using the same XYZ situation, suppose that when XYZ began to climb heavily, the call was worth 7 points when the stock reached 50. The in-the-money option—the call—is now worth an amount equal to the initial straddle value. It could then be bought back, leaving the out-of-the-money put naked. As long as the stock then remained above 45, the put would expire worthless. In practice, the put could be bought back for a small fraction after enough time had passed or if the underlying stock continued to climb in price.

This type of follow-up action does not depend on taking action at a fixed stock price, but rather is triggered by the option price itself. It is therefore a *dynamic* sort of follow-up action—one in which the same action could be applied at various stock prices, depending on the amount of time remaining until expiration. One of the problems with closing the straddle at the break-even points is that the break-even point is only a valid break-even point at expiration. A long time before expiration, this stock price will not represent much of a break-even point, as was pointed out in the last example. Thus buying back only the in-the-money option at a fixed price may often be a superior strategy. The drawback is that one does not release much collateral by buying back the in-the-money option, and he is therefore stuck in a position with little potential profit for what could amount to a considerable amount of time. The collateral release amounts to the in-the-money amount—the writer still needs to collateralize 20% of the stock price.

One could adjust this follow-up method to attempt to retain some profit. For example, he might decide to buy the in-the-money option when it has reached a value that is 1 point less than the total straddle value initially taken in. This would then allow him the chance to make a 1-point profit overall, if the other option expired worthless. In any case, there is always the risk that the stock would suddenly reverse direction and cause a loss on the remaining option as well. This method of follow-up action is akin to the ratio writing follow-up strategy of using buy and sell stops on the underlying stock.

Before describing other types of follow-up action that are designed to combat the problems described above, it might be worthwhile to address the method used in ratio writing—rolling up or rolling down. *In straddle writing, there is often little to be gained from rolling up or rolling down.* This is a much more viable strategy in ratio writing—one does not want to constantly be moving in and out of stock positions, because of the commissions involved. However, with straddle writing, once one position is closed, there is no need to pursue a similar straddle in that same stock. It may be more desirable to look elsewhere for a new straddle position.

There are two other very simple forms of follow-up action that one might consider using also, although neither one is for most strategists. *First, one might consider doing nothing at all,* even if the underlying stock moves by a great deal, figuring that the advantage lies in the probability that the stock will be back near the striking price by the time the options expire. This should be used only by the most diversified and well-heeled investors, for in extreme market periods, almost all stocks may move in unison, generating tremendous losses to anyone who does not take some sort of action. *A more aggressive type of follow-up action would be to attempt to "leg out" of the straddle,* by buying in the profitable side and then hoping for a stock price reversal in order to buy back the remaining side. In the example above, when XYZ ran up to 52, an aggressive trader would buy in the put at 1½, taking his profit, and then hope for the stock to fall back in order to buy the call in cheaper. This is a very aggressive type of follow-up action because the stock could easily continue to rise in price, thereby generating larger losses. This is a trader's sort of action, not that of a disciplined strategist, and it should be avoided.

In essence, follow-up action should be designed to do two things: first, to limit the risk in the position, and, second, to still allow room for a potential profit to be made. None of the above types of follow-up action accomplish both of these purposes. There is, however, a follow-up strategy that does allow the straddle writer to limit his losses while still allowing for a potential profit.

Example: After the straddle was originally sold for 7 points when the stock was at 45, the stock experiences a rally and the following prices exist:

XYZ common, 50;

XYZ January 45 call, 7;

XYZ January 45 put, 1; and

XYZ January 50 call, 3.

The January 50 call price is included because it will be part of the follow-up strategy. Notice that this straddle has a considerable amount of time value premium remaining in it, and thus would be rather expensive to buy back at the current time. Suppose, however, that the straddle writer does not touch the January 45 straddle that he is short, but instead buys the January 50 call for protection to the upside. Since this call costs 3 points, he will now have a position with a total credit of 4 points (the straddle was originally sold for 7 points credit and he is now spending 3 points for the call at 50). This action of buying a call at a higher strike than the striking price of the straddle has limited the potential loss to the upside, no matter how far the stock might run up. If XYZ is anywhere above 50 at expiration, the put will expire worthless and the writer will have to pay 5 points to close the call spread—short January 45, long January 50. This means that his maximum potential loss is 1 point plus commissions if XYZ is anywhere above 50 at expiration.

In addition to being able to limit the upside loss, this type of follow-up action still allows room for potential profits. If XYZ is anywhere between 41 and 49 at expiration—that is, less than 4 points away from the striking price of 45—the writer will be able to buy the straddle back for less than 4 points, thereby making a profit.

Thus the straddle writer has both limited his potential losses to the upside and has also allowed room for profit potential should the underlying stock fall back in price toward the original striking price of 45. Only a severe price reversal, with the stock falling back below 40, would cause a large loss to be taken. In fact, by the time that the stock could reverse its current strong upward momentum and fall all the way back to 40, a significant amount of time should have passed, thereby allowing the writer to purchase the straddle back with only a relatively small amount of time premium left in it.

This follow-up strategy has an effect on the margin requirement of the position. When the calls are bought as protection to the upside, the writer has—for margin purposes—a bearish spread in the calls and an uncovered put. The margin for this position would normally be less than that required for the straddle which is 5 points in-the-money.

A secondary move is available in this strategy.

Example: The stock continues to climb over the short term and the out-of-the-money put drops to a price of less than ½ of a point. The straddle writer might now consider buying back the put, thereby leaving himself with a bear spread in the calls. His net credit left in the position, after buying back the put at ½, would be 3½ points credit. Thus if XYZ should reverse direction and be within 3½ points of the striking price— that is, anywhere below 48½—at expiration, the position will produce a profit. In fact, if XYZ should be below 45 at expiration, the entire bear spread will expire worthless and the strategist will have made a 3½-point profit. Finally, this repurchase of the put releases the margin requirement for the naked put, and will generally free up excess funds so that a new straddle position can be established in another stock while the low-requirement bear spread remains in place.

In summary, this type of follow-up action is broader in purpose than any of the simpler buy-back strategies described earlier. It will limit the writer's loss, but not prevent him from making a profit. Moreover, he may be able to release enough margin to be able to establish a new position in another stock by buying in the uncovered puts at a fractional price. This would prevent him from tying up his money completely while waiting for the original straddle to reach its expiration date. The same type of strategy also works in a downward market. If the stock falls after the straddle was written, one can buy the put at the next lower strike to limit the downside risk, while still allowing for profit potential if the stock rises back to the striking price.

EQUIVALENT STOCK POSITION FOLLOW-UP

Since there are so many follow-up strategies that can be used with the short straddle, the one method that summarizes the situation best is again the equivalent stock position (ESP). Recall that the ESP of an option position is the multiple of the quantity times the delta times the shares per option. The quantity is a negative number if it is referring to a short position. Using the above scenario, an example of the ESP method follows:

Example: As before, assume that the straddle was originally sold for 7 points, but the stock rallied. The following prices and deltas exist:

XYZ common, 50;

XYZ Jan 45 call, 7, delta, .90;

XYZ Jan 45 put, 1, delta, −.10; and

XYZ Jan 50 call, 3, delta, .60.

Assume that 8 straddles were sold initially and that each option is for 100 shares of XYZ. The ESP of these 7 short straddles can then be computed:

Option	Position	Delta	ESP
Jan 45 call	short 8	0.90	short 720 ($-8 \times .9 \times 100$)
Jan 45 put	short 8	−0.10	long 80 ($-8 \times -.1 \times 100$)
Total ESP			short 640 shares

Obviously, the position is quite short. Unless the trader were extremely bearish on XYZ, he should make an adjustment. The simplest adjustment would be to buy 600 shares of XYZ. Another possibility would be to buy back 7 of the short January 45 calls. Such a purchase would add a delta long of 630 shares to the position ($7 \times .9 \times 100$). This would leave the position essentially neutral. As pointed out in the previous example, however, the strategist may not want to buy that option. If, instead, he decided to try to buy the January 50 call to hedge the short straddle, he would have to buy 10 of those to make the position neutral. He would buy this many because the delta of that January 50 is 0.60; a purchase of 10 would add a delta long of 600 shares to the position.

Even though the purchase of 10 is theoretically correct, since one is only short 8 straddles, he would probably only buy 8 January 50 calls as a practical matter.

STARTING OUT WITH THE PROTECTION IN PLACE

In certain cases, the straddle writer may be able to initially establish a position that has no risk in one direction—he can buy an out-of-the-money put or call at the same time that the straddle is written. This accomplishes the same purposes as the follow-up action described in the last few paragraphs, but the protective option will cost less since it is out-of-the-money when it is purchased. There are, of course, both positive and negative aspects involved in adding an out-of-the-money long option to the straddle write at the outset.

Example: Given the following prices:

XYZ, 45;

XYZ January 45 straddle, 7; and

XYZ January 50 call, 1½,

the upside risk will be limited. If one writes the January 45 straddle for 7 points and buys the January 50 call for 1½ points, his overall credit will be 5½ points. He has no upside risk in this position, for if XYZ should rise and be over 50 at expiration, he will be able to close the position by buying back the call spread for 5 points. The put will expire worthless. The out-of-the-money call has eliminated any risk above 50 on the position. Another advantage of buying the protection initially is that one is protected if the stock should experience a gap opening or a trading halt. If he already owns the protection, such stock price movement in the direction of the protection is of little consequence. However, if he was planning to buy the protection as a follow-up action, the sudden surge in the stock price may ruin his strategy.

The overall profit potential of this position is smaller than that of the normal straddle write, since the premium paid for the long call will be lost if the stock is below 50 at expiration. However, the automatic risk-limiting feature of the long call may prove to be worth more than the decrease in profit potential. The strategist has peace of mind in a rally and does not have to worry about unlimited losses accruing to the upside.

Downside protection for a straddle writer can be achieved in a similar manner by buying an out-of-the-money put at the outset.

Example: With XYZ at 45, one might write the January 45 straddle for 7 and buy a January 40 put for 1 point if he is concerned about the stock dropping in price.

It should now be fairly easy to see that the straddle writer could limit risk in either direction by initially buying both an out-of-the-money call and an out-of-the-money put at the same time that the straddle is written. The major benefit in doing this is that risk is limited in either direction. Moreover, the margin requirements are significantly reduced, since the whole position consists of a call spread and a put spread. There are no longer any naked options. The detriment of buying protection on both sides initially is that commission costs increase and the overall profit potential of the straddle write is reduced, perhaps significantly, by the cost of two long options. Therefore, one must evaluate whether the cost of the protection is too large in comparison to what is received for the straddle write. This completely protected strategy can be very attractive when available, and it will be described again when butterfly spreads are discussed in Chapter 23.

In summary, any strategy in which the straddle writer also decides to buy protection presents both advantages and disadvantages. Obviously, the risk-limiting feature of the purchased options is an advantage. However, the seller of options does not like to purchase pure time value premium as protection at any time. He would generally prefer to buy intrinsic value. The reader will note that, in each of the protective buying strategies discussed above, the purchased option has a large amount of time value premium left in it. Therefore, the writer must often try to strike a delicate balance between trying to limit his risk on one hand and trying to hold down the expenses of buying long options on the other hand. In the final analysis, however, the risk must be limited regardless of the cost.

COMBINATION WRITING

Recall that a combination is any position involving both puts and calls, where there is some difference in the terms of the options. Commonly, the puts and calls will have the same expiration date, but will have differing striking prices. *A combination write is usually established by selling both an out-of-the-money put and an out-of-the-money call with the stock approximately centered between the two striking prices.* This is also called a strangle write. In this way, the naked option writer can remain neutral on the outlook for the underlying stock, even when the stock is not near a striking price.

This is a strategy that is quite similar to straddle writing, except that *the strangle writer makes his maximum profit over a much wider range than the straddle writer does.* In this or any other naked writing strategy, the most money that the strategist can make is the amount of the premium received. The straddle writer has only a minute chance of making a profit of the entire straddle premium, since the stock would have to be exactly at the striking price at expiration in order for both the written put and call to expire worthless. The strangle writer will make his maximum profit potential if the stock is anywhere between the two strikes at expiration, for both options will expire worthless in that case. This strategy is equivalent to the variable ratio write, described in Chapter 6, in which two calls at two different striking prices were written against 100 shares of the underlying stock.

Example: Given the following prices:

XYZ common, 65;

XYZ January 70 call, 4; and

XYZ January 60 put, 3,

a combination write would be established by selling the January 70 call and the January 60 put. If XYZ is anywhere between 60 and 70 at January expiration, both options will expire worthless and the combination writer will make a profit of 7 points, the amount of the original credit taken in.

If XYZ is above 70 at expiration, the strategist will have to pay something
to buy back the call. For example, if XYZ is at 77 at expiration, the January
70 call will have to be bought back for 7 points, thereby creating a break-
even situation. To the downside, if XYZ were at 53 at expiration, the
January 60 put would have to be bought back for 7 points, thereby defining
that as the downside break-even point. Table 20-3 and Figure 20-3 outline
the potential results of this combination write. The profit range in this
example is quite wide, extending from 53 on the downside to 77 on the
upside. With the stock presently at 65, this is a relatively neutral position.

TABLE 20-3.
Results of a combination write.

Stock Price at Expiration	Call Profit	Put Profit	Total Profit
40	+ $ 400	− $1,700	− $1,300
50	+ 400	− 700	− 300
53	+ 400	− 400	0
57	+ 400	0	+ 400
60	+ 400	+ 300	+ 700
65	+ 400	+ 300	+ 700
70	+ 400	+ 300	+ 700
73	+ 100	+ 300	+ 400
77	− 300	+ 300	0
80	− 600	+ 300	− 300
90	− 1,600	+ 300	− 1,300

FIGURE 20-3.
Sale of a combination.

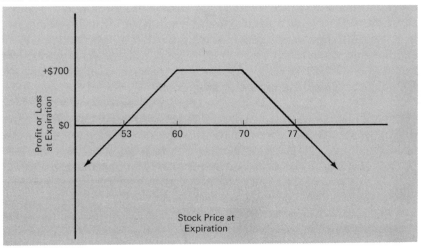

At first glance, this may seem to be a more conservative strategy than straddle writing because the profit range is wider and the stock needs to move a great deal to reach the break-even points. In the absence of follow-up action, this is a true observation. However, if the stock begins to rise quickly or to drop dramatically, the combination writer often has little recourse but to buy back the in-the-money option in order to limit his losses. This can, as has been shown previously, entail a purchase price involving excess amounts of time value premium, thereby generating a significant loss.

The only other alternative that is available to the combination writer (outside of attempting to trade out of the position) is to convert the position into a straddle if the stock reaches either break-even point.

Example: If XYZ rose to 70 or 71 in the previous example, the January 70 put would be sold. Depending on the amount of collateral available, the January 60 put may or may not be bought back when the January 70 put is sold. This action of converting the combination write into a straddle write will work out well if the stock stabilizes. It will also lessen the pain if the stock continues to rise. However, if the stock reverses direction, the January 70 put write will prove to be unprofitable. Technical analysis of the underlying stock may prove to be of some help in deciding whether or not to convert the combination write into a straddle. If there appears to be a relatively large chance that the stock could fall back in price, it is probably not worthwhile to roll the put up.

This example of a combination write is one in which the writer received a large amount of premium for selling the put and the call. Many times, however, an aggressive combination writer is tempted to sell two out-of-the-money options that have only a short life remaining. These options would generally be sold at fractional prices. This can be an extremely aggressive strategy at times, for if the underlying stock should move quickly in either direction through a striking price, there is little the combination writer can do. He must buy in the options to limit his loss. Nevertheless, this type of combination writing—selling short-term, fractionally priced, out-of-the-money options—appeals to many writers. This is a similar philosophy to the naked call writer, described in Chapter 5, who writes calls that are nearly restricted, figuring there will be a large probability that the option will expire worthless. It also has the same risk—a large price change or gap opening can cause such devastating losses that many profitable trades are wiped away. To sell fractionally priced combinations is a poor strategy and should be avoided.

Before leaving the topic of combination writing, it may be useful to define how the margin requirements apply to a combination write. Recall that the margin requirement for writing a straddle is 20% of the stock price plus the price of either the put or the call, whichever is in-the-money. In a combination write, however, both options may be out-of-the-money, as in the example above. When this is the case, the straddle writer is allowed to deduct the smaller out-of-the-money amount from his requirement. Thus, if XYZ were at 68 and the January 60 put and the January 70 call had been written, the collateral requirement would be 20% of the stock price, plus the call premium, less $200—the lesser out-of-the-money amount. The call is 2 points out-of-the-money and the put is 8 points out-of-the-money. Actually, the true collateral requirement for any write involving both puts and calls—straddle write or combination write—is *the greater of the requirement on the put or the call, plus the amount by which the other option is in-the-money.* The last phrase—the amount by which the other option is in-the-money—would apply to a situation in which a combination had been constructed by selling two in-the-money options. This is a less popular strategy, since the writer generally receives less time value premium by writing two in-the-money options. An example of an in-the-money combination would be to sell the January 60 call and the January 70 put with the stock at 65.

FURTHER COMMENTS ON UNCOVERED STRADDLE AND COMBINATION WRITING

When ratio writing was discussed, it was noted that it was a strategy with a high probability of making a limited profit. Since the straddle write is equivalent to the ratio write and the combination write is equivalent to the variable ratio write, the same statement applies to these strategies as well. The practitioner of straddle and combination writing must realize, however, that protective follow-up action is mandatory in limiting losses in a very volatile market. There are other techniques that the straddle writer can sometimes use to help reduce his risk.

  It has often been mentioned that puts lose their time value premium more quickly when they become in-the-money options than calls do. *One can often construct a neutral position by writing an extra put or two.* That is, if one sells 5 or 6 puts and 4 calls with the same terms, he may often have created a more neutral position than a straddle write. If the stock moves up and the call picks up time premium in a bullish market, the extra puts will help to offset the negative effect of the calls. On the other hand, if the stock drops, the 5 or 6 puts will not hold as much time premium as the 4 calls are losing—again a neutral, standoff position. If the stock begins to drop too much, the writer can always balance out the position by selling another call or two. The advantage of writing an extra put or two is that it counterbalances the straddle writer's most severe enemy—a quick, extremely bullish rise by the underlying stock.

Using the Deltas

This analysis, that adding an extra short put is a neutral position, can be substantiated more rigorously. Recall that a ratio writer or ratio spreader can use the deltas of the options involved in his position to determine a neutral ratio. The straddle writer can do the same thing, of course. It was stated that the difference in a call's delta and a put's delta is approximately one. Using the same prices as in the previous straddle writing example, and assuming the call's delta to be .60, a neutral ratio can be determined.

Prices		Deltas
XYZ common:	45	
XYZ January 45 call:	4	.60
XYZ January 45 put:	3	$-.40$ (.60 $-$ 1)

The put has a negative delta, to indicate that the put and the underlying stock are inversely related. A neutral ratio is determined by dividing the call's delta by the put's delta and ignoring the minus sign. The resultant ratio—1.5:1 (.60/.40) in this case—is the ratio of puts to sell for each call that is sold. Thus, one should sell 3 puts and sell 2 calls to establish a neutral position. The reader may wonder if the assumption that an in-the-money call has a delta of .60 is a fair one. It generally is, although very long-term calls will have higher at-the-money deltas, and very short-term calls will have a delta near .50. Consequently, a 3:2 ratio is often a neutral one. When neutral ratios were discussed with respect to ratio writing, it was mentioned that selling 5 calls and buying 300 shares of stock is often a neutral ratio. The reader should note that a straddle constructed by selling 3 puts and 2 calls is equivalent to the ratio write in which one sells 5 calls and buys 300 shares of stock.

If a straddle writer is going to use the deltas to determine his neutral ratio, he should compute each one at the time of his initial investment, of course, rather than relying on a generality such as that 3 puts and 2 calls is often neutral. The deltas can be used as a follow-up action, by adjusting the ratio to remain neutral after a move by the underlying stock.

Avoid Excess Trading

In any of the straddle and combination writing strategies described above, too much follow-up action can be detrimental because of the commission costs involved. Thus, although it is important to take protective action, the straddle writer should plan in advance to make the minimum number of strategic moves to protect himself. That is why buying protection is often useful, because not only does it limit the risk in the direction that the stock is moving, but it also involves only one additional option commission. In fact, if it is feasible, buying protection at the outset is often a better strategy than protecting as a secondary action.

An extension of this concept of trying to avoid too much follow-up action is that *the strategist should not attempt to anticipate movement in an underlying stock.* For example, if the straddle writer has planned to take defensive action should the stock reach 50, he should not anticipate by taking action with the stock at 48 or 49. It is possible that the stock could retreat back down and the writer would have taken a defensive action that not only cost him commissions, but reduced his profit potential. Of course, there is a little trader in everyone, and the temptation to anticipate (or wait too long, also) is always there. Unless there are very strong technical reasons for doing so, the strategist should resist the temptation to trade, and should operate his strategy according to his original plan. The ratio writer may actually have an advantage in this respect, because he can use buy and sell stops on the underlying stock to remove the emotion from his follow-up strategy. This technique was described in Chapter 6. Unfortunately, no such emotionless technique exists for the straddle or combination writer.

Using the Credits

In previous chapters, it was mentioned that the sale of uncovered options does not require any cash investment on the part of the strategist. He may use the collateral value of his present portfolio to finance the sale of naked options. Moreover, once he sells the uncovered options, he can take the premium dollars that he has brought in from the sales to buy fixed-income securities, such as Treasury bills. The same statements naturally apply to the straddle writing and combination writing strategies. However, the strategist should not be overly obsessed with continuing to maintain a credit balance in his positions, nor should he strive to hold onto the Treasury bills at all costs. If one's follow-up actions dictate that he must take a debit to avoid losses or that he should sell out his Treasury bills to keep a credit, he should by all means do so.

Chapter 21

Synthetic Stock Positions Created by Puts and Calls

It is possible for a strategist to establish a position that is essentially the same as a stock position, but he can do this using only options. The option position generally requires a smaller margin investment and may have other residual benefits over simply buying stock or simply selling stock short. In brief, the strategies are summarized by:

1. Buy call and sell put instead of buying stock.
2. Buy put and sell call instead of selling stock short.

SYNTHETIC LONG STOCK

When one buys a call and sells a put at the same strike he sets up a position that is equivalent to owning the stock. His position is sometimes called "synthetic" long stock.

Example: To verify that this option position acts much like a long stock position would, suppose that the following prices exist:

XYZ common, 50;

XYZ January 50 call, 5; and

XYZ January 50 put, 4.

If one were bullish on XYZ and wanted to buy stock at 50, he might consider the alternative strategy of buying the January 50 call and selling (uncovered) the January 50 put. By using the option strategy, the investor has nearly the same profit and loss potential as the stock buyer, as shown in Table 21-1. The two right-hand columns of the table compare the results of the option strategy with the results that would be obtained by merely owning the stock at 50.

The table shows that the result of the option strategy is exactly $100 less than the stock results for any price at expiration. Thus the "synthetic" long stock and the actual long stock have nearly the same profit and loss potentials. The reason that there is a difference in the results of the two equivalent positions lies in the fact that the option strategist had to pay 1 point of time premium in order to set up his position. This time premium represents the $100 by which the "synthetic" position underperforms the actual stock position at expiration. Note that, with XYZ at 50, both the put and the call are completely composed of time value premium initially. The synthetic position consists of paying out 5 points of time premium for the call and receiving in 4 points of time premium for the put. The net time premium is thus a 1-point payout.

The reason that one would consider using the synthetic long stock position rather than the stock position itself is that the synthetic position may require a much smaller investment than buying the stock would require. The purchase of the stock requires $5,000 in a cash account or $2,500 in a margin account (if the margin rate is 50%). However, the synthetic position requires only a $100 debit plus a collateral requirement—20% of the stock price, plus the put premium, minus the difference between the striking price and the stock price. The balance, invested in

TABLE 21-1.
Synthetic long stock position.

XYZ Price at Expiration	January 50 Call Result	January 50 Put Result	Total Option Result	Long Stock Result
40	− $500	− $600	− $1,100	− $1,000
45	− 500	− 100	− 600	− 500
50	− 500	+ 400	− 100	0
55	0	+ 400	+ 400	+ 500
60	+ 500	+ 400	+ 900	+ 1,000

short-term funds, would earn enough money, theoretically, to offset the $100 paid for the synthetic position. In this example, the collateral requirement would be 20% of $5,000, or $1,000, plus the $400 put premium, plus the $100 debit incurred by paying 5 for the call and only receiving 4 for the put. This is a total of $1,500 initially. There is no initial difference between the stock price and the striking price. Of course, this collateral requirement would increase if the stock fell in price, and would decrease if the stock rose in price, since there is a naked put. Also notice that buying stock creates a $5,000 debit in the account, whereas the option strategy's debit is $100—the rest is a collateral requirement, not a cash requirement.

The effect of this reduction in margin required is that some leverage is obtained in the position. If XYZ rose to 60, the stock position profit would be $1,000 for a return of 40% on margin ($1,000/$2,500). With the option strategy, the percentage return would be higher. The profit would be $900 and the return thus 60% ($900/$1,500). Of course, leverage works to the downside as well, so that the percent risk is also greater in the option strategy.

The synthetic stock strategy is generally not applied merely as an alternative to buying stock. Besides possibly having a smaller profit potential, *the option strategist does not collect dividends, whereas the stock owner does.* However, the strategist is able to earn interest on the funds that he did not spend for stock ownership. It is important for the strategist to understand that a long call plus a short put is equivalent to long stock. It thus may be possible for the strategist to substitute the synthetic option position in certain option strategies that normally call for the purchase of stock.

SYNTHETIC SHORT SALE

A position that is equivalent to the short sale of the underlying stock can be established by selling a call and simultaneously buying a put. This alternative option strategy, in general, offers significant benefits when compared with selling the stock short. Using the prices above—XYZ at 50, January 50 call at 5, and January 50 put at 4—Table 21-2 depicts the potential profits and losses at January expiration.

Both the option position and the short stock position have similar results—large potential profits if the stock declines and unlimited losses if the underlying stock rises in price. However, the option strategy does better than the stock position because the option strategist is getting the benefit of the time value premium. Again, this is because the call has more time value premium than the put, which works to the option strategist's advantage in this case, where he is selling the call and buying the put.

TABLE 21-2.
Synthetic short sale position.

XYZ Price at Expiration	January 50 Call Result	January 50 Put Result	Total Option Result	Short Stock Result
40	+ $500	+ $600	+ $1,100	+ $1,000
45	+ 500	+ 100	+ 600	+ 500
50	+ 500	− 400	+ 100	0
55	0	− 400	− 400	− 500
60	− 500	− 400	− 900	− 1,000

Leverage is a factor in this strategy also. The short seller would need $2,500 to collateralize this position, assuming that the margin rate is 50%. The option strategist only needs, initially, 20% of the stock price, plus the call price, less the credit received, for a $1,400 requirement. Moreover, one of the major disadvantages that was mentioned with the synthetic long stock position is not a disadvantage in the synthetic short sale strategy. The option trader does not have to pay out dividends on the options, but the short seller of stock would have to.

Because of the advantages of the option position in not having to pay out the dividend and also having a slightly larger profit potential from the excess time value premium, it may often be feasible for the trader who is looking to sell stock short to instead sell a call and buy a put. It is also important for the strategist to understand the equivalence between the short stock position and the option position. He might be able to substitute the option position in certain cases where the short sale of stock is called for normally.

SPLITTING THE STRIKES

The strategist may be able to use a slight variation of the synthetic strategy to set up an aggressive, but attractive position. Rather than using the same striking price for the put and call, he can use a lower striking price for the put and a higher striking price for the call. This action of splitting apart the striking prices gives him some room for error, while still retaining the potential for large profits.

Bullishly Oriented

If an out-of-the-money put is sold naked, and an out-of-the-money call is simultaneously purchased, an aggressive bullish position is established—often for a credit. If the underlying stock rises far enough, profits can be generated on both the long call and the short put. If the stock remains relatively unchanged, the call purchase will be a loss, but the put sale will be a profit. The risk occurs if the underlying stock drops in price, producing losses on both the short put and the long call.

Example: The following prices exist: XYZ is at 53, a January 50 put is selling for 2, and a January 60 call is selling for 1. An investor who is bullish on XYZ sells the January 50 put naked and simultaneously buys the January 60 call. This position brings in a credit of 1 point, less commissions. There is a collateral requirement necessary for the naked put. If XYZ is anywhere between 50 and 60 at January expiration, both options would expire worthless, and the investor would make a small profit equal to the amount of the initial credit received. If XYZ rallies above 60 by expiration, however, his potential profits are unlimited since he owns the call at 60. HIs losses could be very large if XYZ should decline well below 50 before expiration, since he has written the naked put at 50. Table 21-3 and Figure 21-1 depict the results at expiration of this strategy.

Essentially, the investor who uses this strategy is bullish on the underlying stock and is attempting to buy an out-of-the-money call for free. If he is moderately wrong and the underlying stock rallies only slightly or even declines slightly, he can still make a small profit. If he is correct, of course, large profits could be generated in a rally. He may lose heavily if he is very wrong and the stock falls by a large amount instead of rising.

TABLE 21-3.
Bullishly split strikes.

XYZ Price at Expiration	January 50 Put Profit	January 60 Call Profit	Total Profit
40	− $800	− $100	− $ 900
45	− 300	− 100	− 400
50	+ 200	− 100	+ 100
55	+ 200	− 100	+ 100
60	+ 200	− 100	+ 100
65	+ 200	+ 400	+ 600
70	+ 200	+ 900	+ 1,100

Bearishly Oriented

There is a companion strategy for the investor who is bearish on a stock. He could attempt to buy an out-of-the-money put, giving himself the opportunity for substantial profits in a stock price decline, and could "finance" the purchase of the put by writing an out-of-the-money call naked. The sale of the call would provide profits if the stock stayed below

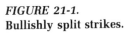

FIGURE 21-1.
Bullishly split strikes.

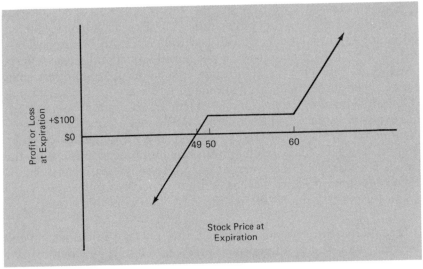

the striking price of the call, but could cost him heavily if the underlying stock rallies too far.

Example: With XYZ at 65, the bearish investor buys a February 60 put for 2 points, and simultaneously sells a February 70 call for 3 points. These trades bring in a credit of 1 point, less commissions. He must collateralize the sale of the call. If XYZ should decline substantially by February expiration, large profits are possible because the February 60 put is owned. Even if XYZ does not perform as expected, but still ends up anywhere between 60 and 70 at expiration, the profit will be equal to the initial credit because both options will expire worthless. However, if the stock rallies above 70, unlimited losses are possible because there is a naked call at 70. Table 21-4 and Figure 21-2 show the results of this strategy at expiration.

This is clearly an aggressively bearish strategy. The investor would like to own an out-of-the-money put for downside potential. In addition, he sells an out-of-the-money call, normally for a price greater than that of the purchased put. The call sale essentially lets him own the put for free. In fact, he can still make profits even if the underlying stock rises slightly or only falls slightly. His risk is realized if the stock rises above the striking price of the written call.

TABLE 21-4.
Bearishly split strikes.

XYZ Price at Expiration	February 60 Put Profit	February 70 Call Profit	Total Profit
50	+ $800	+ $300	+ $1,100
55	+ 300	+ 300	+ 600
60	− 200	+ 300	+ 100
65	− 200	+ 300	+ 100
70	− 200	+ 300	+ 100
75	− 200	− 200	− 400
80	− 200	− 700	− 900

FIGURE 21-2.
Bearishly split strikes.

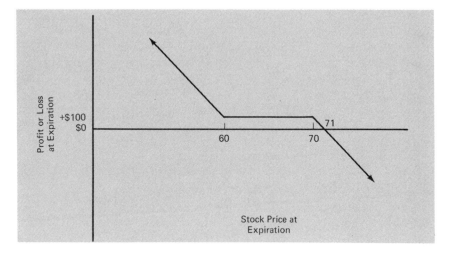

SUMMARY

In either of these aggressive strategies, *the investor must have a definite opinion about the future price movement of the underlying stock.* He buys an out-of-the-money option to provide profit potential for that stock movement. However, an investor can lose the entire purchase proceeds of an out-of-the-money option if the stock does not perform as expected. An aggressive investor, who has sufficient collateral, might attempt to counteract this effect by also writing an out-of-the-money option to cover the cost of the option that he bought. Then, he will not only make money if the stock performs as expected, but will also make money if the stock remains relatively unchanged. He will lose quite heavily, however, if the underlying stock goes in the opposite direction from this original anticipation. That is why he must have a definite opinion on the stock and also be fairly certain of his timing.

Chapter *22*

Basic Put Spreads

Put spreading strategies do not differ substantially in theory from their accompanying call spread strategies. Both bullish and bearish positions can be constructed with put spreads, as was also the case with call spreads. However, because puts are more oriented toward downward stock movement than calls are, some bearish put spread strategies are superior to their equivalent bearish call spread strategies.

The three simplest forms of option spreads are:

1. bull spread,
2. the bear spread, and
3. the calendar spread.

The same types of spreads that were constructed with calls can be established with puts, but there are some differences.

BEAR SPREAD

In a call bear spread, a call with a lower striking price was sold while a call at a higher striking price was bought. Similarly, *a put bear spread is* established by selling a put at a lower strike while buying a put at a higher strike. The put bear spread is a debit spread. This is true because a put with a higher striking price will sell for more than a put with a lower striking price. Thus on a stock with both puts and calls trading, one could set up a bear spread for a credit (using calls) or alternatively set one up for a debit (using puts):

Put Bear Spread	Call Bear Spread
Buy XYZ January 60 put	Buy XYZ January 60 call
Sell XYZ January 50 put	Sell XYZ January 50 call
(debit spread)	(credit spread)

The put bear spread has the same sort of profit potential as the call bear spread. There is a limited maximum potential profit and this profit would be realized if XYZ were below the lower striking price at expiration. The put spread would widen, in this case, to equal the difference between the striking prices. The maximum risk is also limited and would be realized if XYZ were anywhere above the higher striking price at expiration.

Example: The following prices exist:

XYZ common, 55;

XYZ January 50 put, 2; and

XYZ January 60 put, 7.

Buying the January 60 put and selling the January 50 would establish a bear spread for a 5-point debit. Table 22-1 will help verify that this is indeed a bearish position. The reader will note that Figure 22-1 has the same shape as the call bear spread's graph (Figure 8-1). The investment

TABLE 22-1.
Put bear spread.

XYZ Price at Expiration	January 50 Put Profit	January 60 Put Profit	Total Profit
40	− $800	+ $1,300	+ $500
45	− 300	+ 800	+ 500
50	+ 200	+ 300	+ 500
55	+ 200	− 200	0
60	+ 200	− 700	− 500
70	+ 200	− 700	− 500
80	+ 200	− 700	− 500

FIGURE 22-1.
Put bear spread.

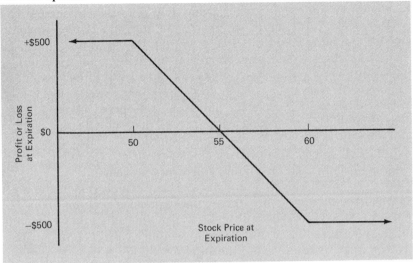

required for this spread is the net debit, and it must be paid in full. Notice that *the maximum profit potential is realized anywhere below 50 at expiration, and the maximum risk potential is realized anywhere above 60 at expiration.* The maximum risk is always equal to the initial debit required to establish the spread plus commissions. The break-even point is 55 in this example. The following formulae allow one to quickly compute the meaningful statistics regarding a put bear spread.

Maximum risk = initial debit

Maximum profit = difference between strikes − initial debit

Break-even price = higher striking price − initial debit

Put bear spreads have an advantage over call bear spreads. With puts, one is selling an out-of-the-money option when setting up the spread. Thus *one is not risking early exercise of his written option before the spread becomes profitable.* For the written put to be in-the-money, and thus in danger of being exercised, the spread would have to be profitable, because the stock would have to be below the lower striking price. Such is not the case with call bear spreads. In the call spread, one sells an in-the-money call as part of the bear spread, and thus could be at risk of early exercise before the spread has a chance to become profitable.

Besides this difference in the probability of early exercise, the put bear spread holds another advantage over the call bear spread. *In the put spread, if the underlying stock drops quickly, thereby making both options in-the-money, the spread will normally widen quickly as well.* This is because—as has been mentioned previously—put options tend to lose time value premium rather quickly when they go into-the-money. In the example above, if XYZ rapidly dropped to 48, the January 60 put would be near 12, retaining very little time premium. However, the January 50 put which is short would also not retain much time value premium, perhaps selling at 4 points or so. Thus the spread would have widened to 8 points. Call bear spreads often do not produce a similar result on a short-term downward movement. Since the call spread involves being short a call with a lower striking price, this call may actually pick up time value premium as the stock falls close to the lower strike. Thus, even though the call spread might have a similar profit *at expiration*, it often will not perform as well on a quick downward movement.

For these two reasons—less chance of early exercise and better profits on a short-term movement—the put bear spread is superior to the call bear spread. Some investors still prefer to use the call spread, since it is established for a credit and thus does not require a cash investment. This is a rather weak reason to avoid the superior put spread and should not be an overriding consideration. Note that the margin requirement for a call bear spread will result in a reduction of one's buying power by an amount approximately equal to the debit required for a similar put bear spread (the margin required for a call bear spread is the difference in the striking prices less the credit received from the spread). Thus the only accounts that gain any substantial advantage from a credit spread are those that are near the minimum equity requirement to begin with. For most brokerage firms, the minimum equity requirement for spreads is $2,000.

BULL SPREAD

A bull spread can be established with put options by buying a put at a lower striking price and simultaneously selling a put with a higher striking price. This, again, is the same way that a bull spread was constructed with calls—selling the higher strike and buying the lower strike.

Example: The same prices can be used:

XYZ common, 55;

XYZ January 50 put, 2; and

XYZ January 60 put, 7.

The bull spread is constructed by buying the January 50 put and selling the January 60 put. This would be a credit spread. The credit is five points in this example. If the underlying stock advances by January expiration, and is anywhere above 60 at that time, the maximum profit potential of the spread will be realized. In that case, with XYZ anywhere above 60, both puts would expire worthless and the spreader would make a profit of the entire credit—5 points in this example. Thus *the maximum profit potential is limited, and the maximum profit occurs if the underlying stock rises in price above the higher strike.* These are the same qualities that were displayed by a call bull spread (Chapter 7). The name "bull spread" is derived from the fact that this is a bullish position—that the strategist wants the underlying stock to rise in price.

The risk is limited in this spread. If the underlying stock should decline by expiration, the maximum loss will be realized with XYZ anywhere below 50 at that time. The risk is five points in this example. To see this, note that if XYZ were anywhere below 50 at expiration, the differential between the two puts would widen to 10 points, since that is the difference in their striking prices. Thus the spreader would have to pay 10 points to buy the spread back, or to close out the position. Since he initially took in a 5-point credit, this means his loss is equal to 5 points—the 10-point cost of closing out less the 5 points he initially received.

The investment required for a bullish put spread is actually a collateral requirement since the spread is a credit spread. The amount of collateral required is equal to the difference in the striking prices less the net credit received for the spread. In this example, the collateral requirement would be $500—the $1,000, or 10-point differential in the striking prices less the $500 credit received from the spread. Note that *the maximum possible loss is always equal to the collateral requirement in a bullish put spread.*

There is a break-even point in a bullish spread. In this example, the break-even point before commissions would be 55 at expiration. With XYZ at 55 in January, the January 50 put would expire worthless and the January 60 put would have to be bought back for 5 points. It would be 5 points in-the-money with XYZ at 55. Thus the spreader would break even since he originally received 5 points credit for the spread and would then pay out 5 points to close the spread. The following formulae allow one to quickly compute the details of a bullish put spread.

Maximum potential risk = initial collateral requirement
= difference in striking prices − net credit received

Maximum potential profit = net credit

Break-even price = higher striking price − net credit

CALENDAR SPREADS

In a calendar spread, a near-term option is sold and a longer-term option is bought, both with the same striking price. This definition applies to either a put or a call calendar spread. In Chapter 9, it was shown that there were two types of philosophies available for call calendar spreads, either a neutral strategy or a bullish one. Similarly, there are two philosophies available for put calendar spreads: neutral or bearish.

In a neutral calendar spread, one sets up the spread with the idea of closing the spread when the near-term call or put expires. In this type of spread, the maximum profit would be realized if the stock is exactly at the striking price at expiration. The spreader is merely attempting to capitalize on the fact that the time value premium disappears more rapidly from a near-term option than it does from a longer-term one.

Example: XYZ is at 50 and a January 50 put is selling for 2 points while an April 50 put is selling for 3 points. A neutral calendar spread can be established for a 1-point debit by selling the January 50 put and buying the April 50 put. The investment required for this position is the amount of the net debit, and it must be paid for in full. If XYZ is exactly at 50 at January expiration, the January 50 put will expire worthless and the April 50 put will be worth about 2 points, assuming other factors are the same. The neutral spreader would then sell the April 50 put for 2 points and take his profit. The profit in this case would be one point before commissions—he originally paid a 1-point debit to set up the spread and then liquidates the position by selling the April 50 put for 2 points. Since commission costs can substantially cut into available profits, spreads should be established in a large enough quantity to minimize the percentage cost of commissions. This would mean that at least ten spreads should be set up initially.

In any type of calendar spread, *the risk is limited to the amount of the net debit.* This maximum loss would be realized if the underlying stock moved substantially far away from the striking price by the time the near-term option expires. If this happened, both options would trade at nearly the same price and the differential would shrink to practically nothing, the worst case for the calendar spreader. For example, if the underlying stock drops very substantially, say to 20, both the near-term and the long-term put would trade at nearly 30 points. On the other hand, if the underlying stock rose substantially, say to 80, both puts would trade at a very low price—say $\frac{1}{16}$ or $\frac{1}{8}$—and again the spread would shrink to nearly zero.

Neutral call calendar spreads are generally superior to neutral put calendar spreads. Since the amount of time value premium is usually greater in a call option (unless the underlying stock pays a large dividend), the spreader who is interested in selling time value would be better off utilizing call options.

The second philosophy of calendar spreading is a more aggressive one. *With put options, a bearish strategy can be constructed using a calendar spread.* In this case one would establish the spread with out-of-the-money puts.

Example: With XYZ at 55, one would sell the January 50 put for 1 point and buy the April 50 put for 1½ points. He would then like the underlying stock to remain above the striking price until the near-term January put expires. If this happens, he would make the 1-point profit from the sale of that put, reducing his net cost for the April 50 put to ½ point. Then, he would become bearish, hoping for the underlying stock to decline in price substantially before April expiration in order that he might be able to generate large profits on the April 50 put that he holds.

Just as the bullish calendar spread with calls can be a relatively attractive strategy, so can the bearish calendar spread with puts. Granted, two criteria have to be fulfilled in order for the position to work to the optimum—the near-term put must expire worthless and then the underlying stock must drop in order to generate profits on the long side. Although these conditions may not occur frequently, one profitable situation can more than make up for several losing ones. This is true because the initial debit for a bearish calendar spread is small—½ point in the example above. Thus the losses will be small and the potential profits could be very large if things work out right.

The aggressive spreader must be careful not to "leg out" of his spread, since he could generate a large loss by doing so. The object of the strategy is to accept a rather large number of small losses, with the idea that the infrequent large profits will more than offset the sum of the losses. If one generates a large loss somewhere along the way, this may ruin the overall strategy. Also, if the underlying stock should fall to the striking price before the near-term put expires, the spread will normally have widened enough to produce a small profit, and that profit should be taken by closing the spread at that time.

Chapter 23

Spreads Combining Calls and Puts

Certain types of spreads can be constructed that utilize both puts and calls. One of these strategies has been discussed before—the butterfly spread. However, other strategies exist that uniquely offer potentially large profits to the spreader. These other strategies are all variations of calendar spreads and/or straddles that involve both put and call options.

THE BUTTERFLY SPREAD

This is a strategy that has been described previously, although its usage in Chapter 10 was restricted to constructing the spread with calls only. Recall that the butterfly spread is a neutral position that has limited risk as well as limited profits. The position involves three striking prices by utilizing a bull spread between the lower two strikes and also a bear spread between the higher two strikes. The maximum profit is realized at the middle strike at expiration, and the maximum loss is realized if the stock is above the higher strike or below the lower strike at expiration.

Since either a bull spread or a bear spread can be constructed with puts or calls, it should be obvious that a butterfly spread (consisting of both a bull spread and a bear spread) can be constructed in a number of ways. In fact, there are four ways in which the spread can be established. If option prices are fairly balanced—that is, the arbitrageurs are keeping prices in line—any of the four ways will have the same potential profits and losses at expiration of the options. However, because of the ways in which puts and calls behave prior to their expiration, there are certain advantages or disadvantages connected with some of the methods of establishing the butterfly spread.

Example: The following prices exist:

XYZ common:		60	
Strike:	50	60	70
Call:	12	6	2
Put:	1	5	11

The method using only the calls indicates that one would buy the 50 call, sell two 60 calls, and buy the 70 call. Thus there would be a bull spread in the calls between the 50 and 60 strikes, and a bear spread in the calls between the 60 and 70 strikes. In a similar manner, one could establish a butterfly spread by combining either type of bull spread between the 50 and 60 strikes with any type of bear spread between the 60 and 70 strikes. Some of these spreads would be credit spreads, while others would be debit spreads. In fact, one's personal choice between two rather equivalent makeups of the butterfly spread might be decided by whether there were a credit or debit involved.

Table 23-1 summarizes the four ways in which the butterfly spread might be constructed. In order to verify the debits and credits listed, the reader should recall that a bull spread consists of buying a lower strike

TABLE 23-1.
Butterfly spread.

Bull Spread (Buy Option at 50, . . . plus . . . sell at 60)	Bear Spread (Buy Option at 70, Sell at 60)	Total Money
Calls (6 debit)	Calls (4 credit)	2 debit
Calls (6 debit)	Puts (6 debit)	12 debit
Puts (4 credit)	Calls (4 credit)	8 credit
Puts (4 credit)	Puts (6 debit)	2 debit

and selling a higher strike, whether puts or calls are used. Similarly, bear spreads with either puts or calls consist of buying a higher strike and selling a lower strike. Note that the third choice—bull spread with puts and bear spread with calls—is a short straddle protected by buying the out-of-the-money put and call.

In each of the spreads above, the maximum potential profit at expiration is 8 points if the underlying stock is exactly at 60 at that time. The maximum possible loss in any of the four spreads is 2 points, if the stock is at or above 70 at expiration or is at or below 50 at expiration. For example, either the top line in the table, where the spread is set up only with calls, or the bottom line, where the spread is set up only with puts, has a risk equal to the debit involved—2 points. The large debit spread (second line of table) will be able to be liquidated for a minimum of 10 points at expiration, no matter where the stock is, so the risk is also 2 points (it cost 12 points to begin with). Finally, the credit combination (third line) has a maximum buy-back of 10 points, so it also has risk of 2 points. In addition, since the striking prices are 10 points apart, the maximum potential profit is 8 points (maximum profit = striking price differential minus maximum risk) in all the cases.

The factor that causes all these combinations to be equal in risk and reward is the arbitrageur. If put and call prices get too far out of line, the arbitrageur can take riskless action to force them back. This particular form of arbitrage, known as the box spread, is described in Chapter 29.

Even though all four ways of constructing the butterfly spread are equal at expiration, some are superior to others for certain price movements prior to expiration. Recall that it was previously stated that bull spreads are best constructed with calls, and bear spreads are best constructed with puts. Since the butterfly spread is merely the combination of a bull spread and a bear spread, the best way to set up the butterfly spread is to use calls for the bull spread and puts for the bear spread. This combination is the one listed on the second line of Table 23-1. This strategy involves the largest debit of the four combinations, and as a result, many investors shun this approach. However, all the other combinations involve selling an in-the-money put or call at the outset, a situation that could lead to early exercise. The reader may also recall that the credit combination, listed on the third line of Table 23-1, was previously described as a protected straddle position. That is, one sells a straddle and simultaneously buys both an out-of-the-money put and an out-of-the-money call with the same expiration month as protection for the straddle. Thus a butterfly spread is actually the equivalent of a completely protected straddle write.

Butterfly spreads are not an overly attractive strategy, although they may be useful from time to time. The commissions required are extremely high and there is no chance of making a large profit on the position. The limited risk feature is good to have in a position, but it alone cannot compensate for the less attractive features of the strategy. Essentially, the strategist is looking for the stock to remain in a neutral pattern until the options expire. If the potential profit is at least three times the maximum risk (and preferably four times) and the underlying stock appears to be in a trading range, the strategy is feasible. Otherwise, it is not.

THREE USEFUL, BUT COMPLEX STRATEGIES

The three strategies to be presented in this section are all designed to limit risk while allowing for large potential profits if correct market conditions develop. Each is a combination strategy—that is, it involves both puts and calls—and each is a calendar strategy, in which near-term options are sold and longer-term options are bought. A fourth strategy that is similar in nature to those about to be discussed will be presented in Chapter 24. Although all of these are somewhat complex, and are for the most advanced strategist, they do provide attractive risk/reward opportunities. In addition, they are strategies that are able to be employed by the public customer—they are not designed strictly for professionals. All three strategies will be described conceptually before specific selection criteria are presented in a later section.

A Two-Pronged Attack (The Calendar Combination)

A bullish calendar spread was shown to be a rather attractive strategy. A bullish call calendar spread is established with out-of-the-money calls for a relatively small debit. If the near-term call expires worthless and the stock then rises substantially before the longer-term call expires, the potential profits could be large. In any case, the risk is limited to the small debit required to establish the spread. In a similar manner, the bearish calendar spread which uses put options can be an attractive strategy as well. In this strategy, one would set up the spread with out-of-the-money puts. He would then want the near-term put to expire worthless, followed by a substantial drop in the stock price in order to profit on the longer-term put.

   Since both strategies are attractive by themselves, the combination of the two should be attractive as well. That is, *with a stock midway between two striking prices, one might set up a bullish out-of-the-money call calendar spread and simultaneously establish a bearish out-of-the-money put calendar spread.* If the stock remains relatively stable, both near-term options would expire worthless. Then a substantial stock price movement *in either direction* could produce large profits. With this strategy, the spreader does not care which direction the stock moves after the near options expire worthless—he only hopes that the stock becomes volatile and moves a large distance in either direction.

Example: Suppose that the following prices exist 3 months before the January options expire:

XYZ common:	65
January 70 call: 3	January 60 put: 2
April 70 call: 5	April 60 put: 3

The bullish portion of this combination of calendar spreads would be set up by selling the shorter-term January 70 call for 3 points and simultaneously buying the longer-term April 70 call for 5 points. This portion of the spread requires a two-point debit. The bearish portion of the spread would be constructed using the puts. The near-term January 60 put would be sold for 2 points while the longer-term April 60 put would be bought for 3. Thus the put portion of the spread is a 1-point debit. Overall, then, the combination of the calendar spreads requires a 3-point debit, plus commissions. This debit is the required investment—no additional collateral is required. Since there are four options involved, the commission cost will be large. Again, establishing the spreads in quantity can reduce the percentage cost of commissions.

Note that all the options involved in this position are initially out-of-the-money. The stock is below the striking price of the calls and is above the striking price of the puts. One has sold a near-term put and call combination and purchased a longer-term combination. For nomenclature purposes, this strategy is called a "calendar combination."

There are a variety of possible outcomes from this position. First, it should be understood that *the risk is limited to the amount of the initial debit*—three points in this example. If the underlying stock should rise dramatically or fall dramatically before the near-term options expire, both the call spread and the put spread will shrink to nearly nothing. This would be the least desirable result. In actual practice, the spread would probably have a small positive differential left even after a premature move by the underlying stock so that the probability of a loss of the entire debit would be small.

If the near-term options both expire worthless, a profit will generally exist at that time.

Example: If XYZ were still at 65 at January expiration in the prior example, the position should be profitable at that time. The January call and put would expire worthless with XYZ at 65, and the April options might be worth a total of 5 points. The spread could thus be closed for a profit with XYZ at 65 in January, since the April options could be sold for 5 points, and the initial "cost" of the spread was only 3 points. Although commissions would substantially reduce this 2-point gross profit, there would still be a good percentage profit on the overall position. If the strategist decides to take his profit at this time, he would be operating in a conservative manner.

However, the strategist may want to be more aggressive and hold onto the April combination in hope that the stock might experience a substantial movement before those options expire. Should this occur, *the potential profits could be quite large.*

Example: If the stock were to undergo a very bullish move and rise to 100 before April expiration, the April 70 call could be sold for 30 points (the April 60 put would expire worthless in that case). Alternatively, if the stock plunged to 30 by April expiration, the put at 60 could be sold for 30 points while the call expired worthless. In either case, the strategist would have made a substantial profit on his initial 3-point investment.

It may be somewhat difficult for the strategist to decide what he wants to do after the near-term options expire worthless. He may be torn between taking the limited profit that is at hand or holding onto the combination that he owns in hopes of larger profits. A reasonable approach for the strategist to take is to do nothing immediately after the near-term options expire worthless. He can hold the longer-term options for some time before they will decay enough to produce a loss in the position. Referring again to the previous example, when the January options expire worthless, the strategist then owns the April combination, which is worth 5 points at that time. He can continue to hold the April options for perhaps 6 or 8 weeks before they decay to a value of three points, even if the stock remains close to 65. At this point, the position could be closed for a net loss of the commission costs involved in the various transactions.

As a general rule, one should be willing to hold the combination, even if this means that he lets a small profit decay into a loss. The reason for this is that *one should give himself the maximum opportunity to realize large profits.* He will probably sustain a number of small losses by doing this, but by giving himself the opportunity for large profits, he has a reasonable chance of having the profits outdistance the losses.

There is a time to take small profits in this strategy. This would be when either the puts or the calls were slightly in-the-money as the near-term options expire.

Example: If XYZ moved to 71 just as the January options were expiring, the call portion of the spread should be closed. The January 70 call could be bought back for 1 point and the April 70 call would probably be worth about 5 points. Thus the call portion of the spread could be "sold" for 4 points, enough to cover the entire cost of the position. The April 60 put would not have much value with the stock at 71, but it should be held just in case the stock should experience a large price decline. Similar results would occur on the put side of the spread if the underlying stock were slightly in-the-money—say at 58 or 59—at January expiration. At no time does the strategist want to risk being assigned on an option that he is short, so he must always close the portion of the position that is in-the-money at near-term expiration. This is only necessary, of course, if the stock has risen above the striking price of the calls or has fallen below the striking price of the puts.

In summary, this is a reasonable strategy if one operates it over a period of time long enough to encompass several market cycles. The strategist must be careful not to place a large portion of his trading capital in the strategy, however, since even though the losses are limited, they still represent his entire net investment. A variation of this strategy, whereby one sells more options than he buys, is described in Chapter 24.

The Calendar Straddle

Another strategy that combines calendar spreads on both put and call options can be constructed by selling a near-term straddle and simultaneously purchasing a longer-term straddle. Since the time value premium of the near-term straddle will decrease more rapidly than that of the longer-term straddle, one could make profits on a limited investment. This strategy is somewhat inferior to the one described in the previous section, but is interesting enough to examine.

Example: Again, suppose that three months before January expiration, the following prices exist:

XYZ common: 40

January 40 straddle: 5   April 40 straddle: 7

A calendar spread of the straddles could be established by selling the January 40 straddle and simultaneously buying the April 40 straddle. This would involve a cost of 2 points, the debit of the transaction, plus commissions.

The risk is limited to the amount of this debit up *until the time the near-term straddle expires.* That is, even if XYZ moves up in price by a substantial amount or declines in price by a substantial amount, the worst that can happen is that the difference between the straddle prices shrinks to zero. This could cause one to lose an amount equal to his original debit, plus commissions. *This limit on the risk only applies until the near-term options expire.* If the strategist decides to buy back the near-term straddle and continue to hold the longer-term one, his risk then increases by the cost of buying back the near-term straddle.

Example: XYZ is at 43 when the January options expire. The January 40 call can now be bought back for 3 points. The put expires worthless; so the whole straddle was closed out for 3 points. The April 40 straddle might be selling for 6 points at that time. If the strategist wants to hold on to the April straddle, in hopes that the stock might experience a large price swing, he is free to do so after buying back the January 40 straddle. However, he has now invested a total of 5 points in the position—the original 2-point debit plus the 3 points that he paid to buy back the January 40 straddle. Hence his risk has increased to 5 points. If XYZ were to be at exactly 40 at April expiration, he would lose the entire 5 points. While the probabilities of losing the entire 5 points must be considered small, there is a substantial chance that he might lose more than 2 points—his original debit. Thus he has increased his risk by buying back the near-term straddle and continuing to hold the longer-term one.

This is actually a neutral strategy. Recall that when calendar spreads were discussed previously, it was pointed out that one establishes a neutral calendar spread with the stock near the striking price. This is true for either a call calendar spread or a put calendar spread. This strategy—a calendar spread with straddles—is merely the combination of a neutral call calendar spread and a neutral put calendar spread. Moreover, recall that the neutral calendar spreader generally establishes the position with the intention of closing it out once the near-term option expires. He is mainly interested in selling time in an attempt to capitalize on the fact that a near-term option loses time value premium more rapidly than a longer-term option does. The straddle calendar spread should be treated in the same manner. It is generally best to close it out at near-term expiration. If the stock is near the striking price at that time, a profit will generally result. To verify this, refer again to the prices in the preceding paragraph, where XYZ is at 43 at January expiration. The January 40 straddle can be bought back for 3 points and the April 40 straddle can be sold for 6. Thus the differential between the two straddles has widened to 3 points. Since the original differential was 2 points, this represents a profit to the strategist.

The maximum profit would be realized if XYZ were exactly at the striking price at near-term expiration. In this case, the January 40 straddle could be bought back for a very small fraction and the April 40 straddle might be worth about 5 points. The differential would have widened from the original 2 points to nearly 5 points in this case.

This strategy is inferior to the one described in the previous section (the "calendar combination"). In order to have a chance for unlimited profits, he must increase his net debit by the cost of buying back the near-term straddle. Consequently, this strategy should only be used in cases where the near-term straddle appears to be extremely overpriced. Furthermore, the position should be closed at near-term expiration unless the stock is so close to the striking price at that time that the near-term straddle can be bought back for a fractional price. This fractional buyback would then give the strategist the opportunity to make large potential profits with only a small increase in his risk. This situation of being able to buy back the near-term straddle at a fractional price will occur very infrequently—much more infrequently than the case where both the out-of-the-money put and call expire worthless in the previous strategy. Thus the "calendar combination" strategy will afford the spreader more opportunities for large profits, and also never forces him to increase his risk.

Owning a "Free" Combination (The "Diagonal Butterfly Spread")

The strategies described in the previous sections are established for debits. This means that even if the near-term options expire worthless, the strategist still has risk. The long options which he then holds could proceed to expire worthless as well, thereby leaving him with an overall loss equal to his original debit. There is another strategy involving both put and call options that gives the strategist the opportunity to own a "free" combination. That is, the profits from the near-term options could equal or exceed the entire cost of his long-term options.

This strategy consists of selling a near-term straddle and simultaneously purchasing both a longer-term, out-of-the-money call and a longer-term, out-of-the-money put. This differs from the protected straddle write previously described in that the long options have a more distant maturity than do the short options.

Example:

XYZ common:	40
April 35 put:	1½
January 40 straddle:	7
April 45 call:	2½

If one were to sell the short-term January 40 straddle for 7 points and simultaneously purchase the out-of-the-money put and call combination—April 35 put and April 45 call—*he would establish a credit spread.* The credit for the position is 3 points less commissions, since 7 points are brought in from the straddle sale and 4 points are paid for the out-of-the-money combination. Note that the position technically consists of a bearish spread in the calls—buy the higher strike and sell the lower strike—coupled with a bullish spread in the puts—buy the lower strike and sell the higher strike. The investment required is in the form of collateral since both spreads are credit spreads, and is equal to the differential in the striking prices, less the net credit received. In this example, then, the investment would be 10 points for the striking price differential (5 points for the calls and 5 points for the puts) less the 3-point credit received, for a total collateral requirement of $700, plus commissions.

The potential results from this position may vary widely. However, *the risk is limited before near-term expiration.* If the underlying stock should advance substantially before January expiration, the puts would be nearly worthless and the calls would both be trading near parity. With the calls at parity, the strategist would have to pay, at most, 5 points to close the call spread since the striking prices of the calls are 5 points apart. In a similar manner, if the underlying stock had declined substantially before the near-term January options expired, the calls would be nearly worthless and the puts would be at parity. Again, it would cost a maximum of 5 points to close the put spread since the difference in the striking prices of the puts is also 5 points. The worst result would be a 2-point loss in this example—3 points of credit were initially received and the most that the strategist would have to pay to close the position is 5 points. This is the theoretical risk. In actual practice, it is very unlikely that the calls would trade as much as 5 points apart, even if the underlying stock advanced by a large amount, because the longer-term call should retain some small time value premium even if it is deeply in-the-money. A similar analysis might apply to the puts. The risk can always be quickly computed as being equal to the difference in two contiguous striking prices (two strikes next to each other), less the net credit received.

The strategist's objective with this position is to be able to buy back the near-term straddle for a price less than the original credit received. If he can do this, he will own the longer-term combination for *free.*

Example: Near January expiration, the strategist is able to repurchase the January 40 straddle for 2 points. Since he initially received a 3-point credit and is then able to buy back the written straddle for 2 points, he is left with an overall credit in the position of 1 point, less commissions. Once he has done this, the strategist retains the long options, the April

35 put and April 45 call. *If the underlying stock should then advance substantially or decline substantially, he could make very large profits.* However, even if the long combination expires worthless, the strategist still makes a profit since he was able to buy the straddle back for less than the amount of the original credit.

In this example, the strategist's objective is to buy back the January 40 straddle for less than 3 points, since that is the amount of the initial credit. At expiration, this would mean that the stock would have to be between 37 and 43 for the buy-back to be made for 3 points or less. Although it is possible, certainly, that the stock will be in this fairly narrow range at near-term expiration, it is not probable. However, the strategist who is willing add to his risk slightly can often achieve the same result by "legging out" of the January 40 straddle. It has repeatedly been stated that one should not attempt to leg out of a spread, but this is an exception to that rule, since one owns a long combination and therefore is protected, so he is not subjecting himself to large risks by attempting to "leg out" of the straddle that he has written.

Example: XYZ rallies before January expiration and the January 40 put drops to a price of ½ during the rally. Even though there is time remaining until expiration, the strategist might decide to buy back the put at ½. This could potentially increase his overall risk by ½ point if the stock continues to rise. However, if the stock then reversed itself and fell, he could attempt to buy the call back at 2½ points or less. In this manner, he would still achieve his objective of buying the short-term straddle back for 3 points or less. In fact, he might be able to close both sides of the straddle well before near-term expiration if the underlying stock first moves quickly in one direction and then reverses direction by a large amount.

The maximum risk and the optimum potential objectives have been described, but there are also interim results that might occur in this strategy.

Example: XYZ is at 44 at January expiration. The January 40 straddle must be bought back for 4 points. This means that the long combination will not be owned free, but will have a cost of 1 point plus commissions. The strategist, at this time, must decide if he wants to hold on to the April options or if he wants to sell them, possibly producing a small overall profit on the entire position. There is no iron-clad rule in this type of situation. If the decision is made to hold on to the longer-term options, the strategist realizes that he has assumed additional risk by doing so. Nevertheless, he may decide that it is worth owning the long combination at a relatively low cost. The cost in this example would be 1 point, plus commissions, since he paid 4 points to buy back the straddle after only taking in a 3-point credit initially. The more expensive the buy-back of the near-term straddle is, the more the strategist should be readily willing to sell his long options at the same time. For example, if XYZ were at 48 at January expiration and the January 40 straddle had to be bought back for 8 points, there should be no question that he should simultaneously sell his April options as well. The most difficult decisions come when the stock is just outside the optimum buy-back area at near-term expiration. In this example, the strategist would have a fairly difficult decision if XYZ were in the 44 to 45 area or in the 35 to 36 area at January expiration.

The reader may recall that, back in Chapter 14, it was mentioned that one is sometimes able to own a call free by entering into a diagonal credit spread. A diagonal bear spread was given as an example. The same thing happens to be true of a diagonal bullish put spread, since that is a credit spread as well. The strategy being discussed in this section is merely a combination of a diagonal bearish call spread and a diagonal bullish put spread *and is known as a "diagonal butterfly spread."* The same concept that was described in Chapter 14—being able to make more on the short-term call than one originally paid for the long-term call—applies here as well. *One enters into a credit position with the hopes of being able to buy back the near-term written options for a profit greater than the cost of the long options.* If he is able to do this, he will own options for free and could make large profits if the underlying stock moves substantially in either direction. Even if the stock does not move after the buy-back, he still has no risk. *The risk occurs prior to the expiration of the near-term options, but this risk is limited.* As a result, this is an attractive strategy that, when operated over a period of market cycles, should produce some large profits. Ideally, these profits would offset any small losses that had to be taken. Since there are large commission costs involved in this strategy, the strategist is reminded that establishing the spreads in quantity can help to reduce the percentage effect of the commissions.

SELECTING THE SPREADS

Now that the concepts of these three strategies have been laid out, let us define selection criteria for them. The "calendar combination" is the easiest one of these strategies to spot. One would like to have the stock nearly halfway between two striking prices. The most attractive positions can normally be found where the striking prices are at least 10 points apart and the underlying stock is relatively volatile. The optimum time to establish the "calendar combination" is two or three months before the near-term options expire. Additionally, one would like the sum of the prices of the near-term options to be equal to at least one-half of the cost of the longer-term options. In the example given in the previous section on the "calendar combination," the near-term combination was sold for 5 points, where the longer-term combination was bought for 8 points. Thus the near-term combination was worth more than one-half of the cost of the longer-term combination. These five criteria can be summarized as follows:

1. Relatively volatile stock.
2. Stock price nearly midway between two strikes.
3. Striking prices at least 10 points apart.
4. 2 or 3 months remaining until near-term expiration.
5. Price of near-term combination greater than one-half the price of the longer-term combination.

Even though 5 criteria have been stated, it is relatively easy to find a position that satisfies all five conditions. The strategist may also be able to rely upon technical input. If the stock seems to be in a near-term trading range, the position may be more attractive, for that would indicate that the chances of the near-term combination expiring worthless are enhanced.

The "calendar straddle" is a strategy that looks deceptively attractive. As the reader should know by now, options do not decay in a linear fashion. Instead, options will tend to hold time value premium until they get quite close to expiration, when the time value premium disappears at a fast rate. Consequently, the sale of a near-term straddle and the simultaneous purchase of a longer-term straddle will often appear to be attractive because the debit seems small. Again, certain criteria can be set forth that will aid in selecting a reasonably attractive position. The stock should be at or very near the striking price when the position is established. Since this is basically a neutral strategy—one that offers the largest potential profits at near-term expiration—one should want to sell the most time premium possible. This is why the stock must be near the striking price initially. The underlying stock does not have to be a volatile one, although volatile stocks will most easily satisfy the next two criteria. The near-term credit should be at least two-thirds of the longer-term debit. In the example used to explain this strategy, the near-term straddle was sold for 5, while the longer-term straddle was bought for 7 points. Thus the near-term straddle was worth more than two-thirds of the longer-term straddle's price. Finally, the position should be established with two to four months remaining until near-term expiration. If positions with a longer time remaining are used, there is a significant probability that the underlying stock will have moved some distance away from the striking price by the time the near-term options expire. Summarizing, the three criteria for a "calendar straddle" are:

1. Stock near striking price initially.
2. 2 to 4 months remaining until near-term expiration.
3. Near-term straddle price at least two-thirds of longer-term straddle price.

The "diagonal butterfly" is the most difficult of these three types of positions to locate. Again, one would like the stock to be near the middle striking price when the position is established. Also, one would like the underlying stock to be somewhat volatile, since there is the possibility that long-term options will be owned for free. If this comes to pass, the strategist wants the stock to be capable of a large move in order to have a chance of generating large profits. The most restrictive criterion—one that will eliminate all but a few possibilities on a daily basis—is that the near-term straddle price should be at least one and one-half times that of the longer-term, out-of-the-money combination. By adhering to this criterion, one gives himself a reasonable chance of being able to buy the near-term straddle back for a price low enough to result in owning the longer-term options for free. In the example used to describe this strategy, the near-term straddle was sold for 7 while the out-of-the-money, longer-term combination cost 4 points. This satisfies the criterion. Finally, one should limit his possible risk before near-term expiration. Recall that the risk is equal to the difference in any two contiguous striking prices less the net credit received. In the example, the risk would be 5 minus 3, or 2 points. The risk should always be less than the credit taken in. This precludes selling a near-term straddle at 80 for 4 points and buying the put at 60 and the call at 100 for a combined cost of 1 point. Although the credit is substantially more than one and one-half times the cost of the long combination, the risk would be ridiculously high. The risk, in fact, is 20 points (the difference in two contiguous striking prices) less the 3 points crédit, or 17 points—much too high.

The criteria can be summarized as follows:

1. Stock near middle striking price initially.
2. Three to four months to near-term expiration.
3. Price of written straddle at least one and one-half times that of the cost of the longer-term, out-of-the-money combination.
4. Risk before near-term expiration less than the net credit received.

One way in which the strategist may notice this type of position is when he sees a relatively short-term straddle selling at what seems to be an outrageously high price. Professionals, who often have a good feel for a stock's short-term potential, will sometimes bid up straddles when the stock is about to make a volatile move. This will cause the near-term straddles to be very overpriced. When a straddle seller notices that a particular straddle looks too attractive as a sale, he should consider establishing a diagonal butterfly spread instead. He still sells the overpriced straddle, but also buys a longer-term, out-of-the-money combination as a hedge against large loss. Both factions can be right. Perhaps the stock will experience a very short-term volatile movement, proving that the professionals were correct. However, this will not worry the strategist holding a diagonal butterfly, for he has limited risk. Once the short-term move is over, the stock may drift back toward the original strike, allowing the near-term straddle to be bought back at a low price—the eventual objective of the strategist utilizing the diagonal butterfly spread.

These are admittedly three quite complex strategies and thus are not to be attempted by a novice investor. If one wants to gain experience in how he would operate such a strategy, it would be far better to operate a "paper strategy" for a while. That is, one would not actually make investments, but would instead follow prices in the newspaper and make day-to-day decisions without actual risk. This will allow the inexperienced strategist to gain a feel for how these complex strategies perform over a particular time period. The astute investor can, of course, obtain price history information and track a number of market cycles in this same way.

SUMMARY

These three various types of strategies that involve calendar combination of puts and calls may all be attractive. One should be especially alert for these types of positions when near-term calls are overpriced. Typically, this would be during, or just after, a bullish period in the stock market. For nomenclature purposes, these three strategies are called the "calendar combination," the "calendar straddle," and the "diagonal butterfly."

All three strategies offer the possibility of large potential profits if the underlying stock remains relatively stable until the near-term options expire. In addition, all three strategies have limited risk, even if the underlying stock should move explosively in either direction prior to near-term expiration. If an intermediate result occurs—for example, the stock moves a moderate distance in either direction before near-term expiration—it is still possible to realize a limited profit in any of the strategies, because of the fact that the time premiums will decay much more rapidly in the near-term options than they will in the longer-term options.

The three strategies have many things in common, but each one has its own advantages and disadvantages. The "diagonal butterfly" is the only one of the three strategies where the strategist has a possibility of owning free options. Admittedly, the probability of actually being able to own the options completely for free is small. However, there is a relatively large probability that one can substantially reduce the cost of the long options. The "calendar combination"—the first of the three strategies discussed—offers the largest probability of capturing the entire near-term premium. This is because both near-term options are out-of-the-money to begin with. The "calendar straddle" offers the largest potential profits at near-term expiration. That is, if the stock is relatively unchanged from the time the position was established until the time that the near-term options expire, the "calendar straddle" will show the best profit of the three strategies at that time.

Looking at the negative side, the "calendar straddle" is the least attractive of the three strategies, primarily because one is forced to increase his risk after near-term expiration, if he wants to continue to hold the longer-term options. It is often difficult to find a "diagonal butterfly" which offers enough credit to make the position attractive. Finally, the "calendar combination" has the largest probability of losing the entire debit eventually, because one may find that the longer-term options expire worthless also (they are out-of-the-money to begin with, just as the near-term options were).

The strategist will not normally be able to find a large number of these positions available at attractive price levels at any particular time in the market. However, since they are attractive strategies with little or no margin collateral requirements, the strategist should constantly be looking for these types of positions. A certain amount of cash or collateral should be reserved for the specific purpose of utilizing it for these types of positions—perhaps 15 to 20% of one's dollars.

Chapter 24

Ratio Spreads Using Puts

The put option spreader may want to sell more puts than he owns. This creates a ratio spread. Basically, there are two types of put ratio spreads that may prove to be attractive: the standard ratio put spread and the ratio calendar spread using puts. Both strategies are designed for the more aggressive investor, but, when operated properly, can both present attractive reward opportunities.

THE RATIO PUT SPREAD

The strategy is designed for a neutral to slightly bearish outlook on the underlying stock. In a ratio put spread, one buys a number of puts at a higher strike and sells more puts at a lower strike. This position involves naked puts, since one is short more puts than he is long. There is limited upside risk in the position, but the downside risk can be very large. The maximum profit can be obtained if the stock is exactly at the striking price of the written puts at expiration.

Example: Given the following:

XYZ common, 50;

XYZ January 45 put, 2; and

XYZ January 50 put, 4.

A ratio put spread might be established by buying one January 50 put and simultaneously selling two January 45 puts. Since one would be paying $400 for the purchased put and would be collecting $400 from the sale of the two out-of-the-money puts, the spread could be done for even money. There is no upside risk in this position. If XYZ should rally and be above 50 at January expiration, all the puts would expire worthless and the result would be a loss of commissions. However, there is downside risk. If XYZ should fall by a great deal, one would have to pay much more to buy back the two short puts than he would receive from selling out the one long put. The maximum profit would be realized if XYZ were at 45 at expiration, since the short puts would expire worthless, but the long January 50 put would be worth 5 points and could be sold at that price. Table 24-1 and Figure 24-1 summarize the position. Note that there is a range within which the position is profitable—40 to 50 in this example. If XYZ is above 40 and below 50 at January expiration, there will be some profit, before commissions, from the spread. Below 40 at expiration, losses will be generated, and, although these losses are limited by the fact that a stock cannot decline in price below zero, these losses could become very large. There is no upside risk, however, as was pointed out earlier. The following formulae summarize the situation for any put ratio spread:

Maximum upside risk = net debit of spread (no upside risk if done for a credit)

Maximum profit potential = striking price differential × number of long puts − net debit (or plus net credit)

Downside break-even price = lower strike price − maximum profit potential ÷ number of naked puts

TABLE 24-1.
Ratio put spread.

XYZ Price at Expiration	Long January 50 Put Profit	Short 2 January 45 Put Profit	Total Profit
20	+$2,600	−$4,600	−$2,000
30	+ 1,600	− 2,600	− 1,000
40	+ 600	− 600	0
42	+ 400	− 200	+ 200
45	+ 100	+ 400	+ 500
48	− 200	+ 400	+ 200
50	− 400	+ 400	0
60	− 400	+ 400	0

FIGURE 24-1.
Ratio put spread.

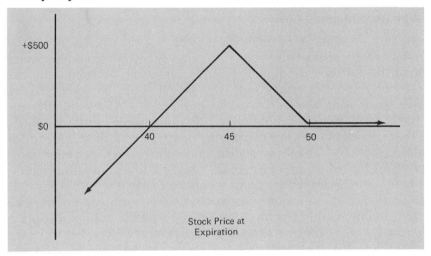

The investment required for the put ratio spread consists of the collateral requirement necessary for a naked put, plus or minus the credit or debit of the entire position. Since the collateral requirement for a naked option is 20% of the stock price, plus the premium, minus the amount by which the option is out-of-the-money, the actual dollar requirement in this example would be $700 (20% of $5,000, plus the $200 premium, minus the $500 by which the January 45 put is out-of-the-money). As with all types of naked writing positions, the strategist should allow enough collateral for an adverse stock move to occur. This will allow enough room for stock movement without forcing early liquidation of the position due to a margin call. If, in this example, the strategist felt that he might stay with the position until the stock declined to 39, he should allow $1,380 in collateral (20% of $3,900 plus the $600 in-the-money amount).

The ratio put spread is generally most attractive when the underlying stock is initially between the two striking prices. That is, if XYZ were somewhere between 45 and 50, one might find the ratio put spread used in the example attractive. If the stock is initially below the lower striking price, a ratio put spread is not as attractive, since the stock is already too close to the downside risk point. Alternatively, if the stock is too far above the striking price of the written calls, one would have to normally pay a large debit to establish the position. Although one could eliminate the debit by writing four or five short options to each put bought, large ratios have extraordinarily large downside risk and are therefore very aggressive.

Follow-up action is rather simple in the ratio put spread. There is very little that one need do, except for closing the position if the stock breaks below the downside break-even point. Since put options tend to lose time value premium rather quickly after they become in-the-money options, there is not normally an opportunity to roll down. Rather, one should be able to close the position with the puts close to parity if the stock breaks below the downside break-even point. The spreader may want to buy in additional long puts, as was described for call spreads in Chapter 11, but this is not as advantageous in the put spread because of the time value premium shrinkage.

This strategy may prove psychologically pleasing to the less experienced investor because he will not lose money on an upward move by the underlying stock. Many of the ratio strategies that involve call options have upside risk, and there is a large number of investors who do not like to lose money when stocks move up. Thus, although these investors might be attracted to ratio strategies because of the possibility of collecting the profits on the sale of multiple out-of-the-money options, they may often prefer ratio put spreads to ratio call spreads because of the small upside risk in the put strategy.

USING DELTAS

The "delta spread" concept can also be used for establishing and adjusting neutral ratio put spreads. The delta spread was first described in Chapter 11. A neutral put spread can be constructed by using the deltas of the two put options involved in the spread. The neutral ratio is determined by dividing the delta of the put at the higher strike by the delta of the put at the lower strike. Referring to the previous example, suppose that the delta of the January 45 put is $-.30$ and the delta of the January 50 put is $-.50$. Then a neutral ratio would be 1.67 ($-.50$ divided by $-.30$). That is, 1.67 puts would be sold for each put bought. One might thus sell 16 January 45 puts and buy 10 January 50 puts.

This type of spread would not change much in price for small fluctuations in the underlying stock price. However, as time passes, the preponderance of time value premium sold via the January 45 puts would begin to turn a profit. As the underlying stock moves up or down by more than a small distance, the neutral ratio between the two puts will change. The spreader can adjust his position back into a neutral one by selling more January 45's or buying more January 50's in order to produce a neutral position once more.

THE RATIO PUT CALENDAR SPREAD

The ratio put calendar spread consists of buying a longer-term put and selling a larger quantity of shorter-term puts, all with the same striking price. The position is generally established with out-of-the-money puts—

that is, the stock is above the striking price—so that there is a greater probability that the near-term puts will expire worthless. Also, the position should be established for a credit, where the money brought in from the sale of the near-term puts more than covers the cost of the longer-term put. If this is done and the near-term puts expire worthless, the strategist will then own the longer-term put free, and large profits could result if the stock subsequently experiences a sizable downward movement.

Example: If XYZ were at 55, and the January 50 put was at 1½ with the April 50 at 2, one could establish a ratio put calendar spread by buying the April 50 and selling two January 50 puts. This would be a credit position, for the sale of the two January 50 puts would bring in $300 while the cost of the April 50 put is only $200. If the stock remains above 50 until January expiration, the January 50 puts will expire worthless and the April 50 put will be owned for free. In fact, even if the April 50 put should then expire worthless, the strategist will make a small profit on the overall position in the amount of his original credit—$100—less commissions. However, after the Januarys have expired worthless, if XYZ should drop dramatically to 25 or 20, a very large profit would accrue on the April 50 put that is still owned.

The risk in the position could be very large if the stock should drop well below 50 before the January puts expire. For example, if XYZ fell to 30 prior to January expiration, one would have to pay $4,000 to buy back the January 50 puts and would receive only $2,000 from selling out his long April 50 put. This would represent a rather large loss. Of course, this type of tragedy can be avoided by taking appropriate follow-up action. *Normally, one would close the position if the stock fell more than 8 to 10% below the striking price before the near-term puts expire.*

As with any type of ratio position, there are naked options involved. This increases the collateral requirement for the position and also means that the strategist should allow enough collateral in order for the follow-up action point to be reached. In this example, the initial requirement would be $750 (20% of $5,500, plus the $150 January premium, less the $500 by which the naked January 50 put is out-of-the-money). However, if the strategist decides that he will hold the position until XYZ falls to 46, he should allow $1,320 in collateral (20% of $4,600 plus the $400 in-the-money amount). Of course, the $100 credit, less commissions, generated by the initial position can be applied against these collateral requirements.

This strategy is a sensible one for the investor who is willing to accept the risk of writing a naked put. Since the position should be established with the stock above the striking price of the put options, there is a reasonable chance that the near-term puts will expire worthless. This means that some profit will be generated, and that the profit could be large if the stock should then experience a large downward move before the longer-term puts expire. One should take care, however, to limit his losses before near-term expiration, since the eventual large profits will be able to overcome a series of small losses, but could not overcome a preponderance of large losses.

Ratio Put Calendars

Using the deltas of the puts in the spread, the strategist can construct a neutral position. If the puts are initially out-of-the-money, then the neutral spread generally involves selling more puts than one buys. Another type of ratioed put calendar can be constructed with in-the-money puts. As with the companion in-the-money spread with calls, one would buy more puts than he sells in order to create a neutral ratio.

In either case, the delta of the put to be purchased is divided by the delta of the put to be sold. The result is the neutral ratio, and is used to determine how many puts to sell for each one purchased.

Example: Consider the out-of-the-money case. XYZ is trading at 59. The January 50 put has a delta of 0.10 and the April 50 put has a delta of -0.17. If a calendar spread is to be established, one would be buying the April 50 and selling the January 50. Thus the neutral ratio would be calculated as 1.7 to 1 $(-0.17/-0.10)$. Seventeen puts would be sold for every 10 purchased.

This spread has naked puts and therefore has large risk if the underlying stock declines too far. However, follow-up action could be taken if the stock dropped in an orderly manner. Such action would designed to limit the downside risk.

Conversely, the calendar spread using in-the-money puts would normally have one buying more options than he is selling. An example using deltas will demonstrate this fact:

Example: XYZ is at 59. The January 60 put has a delta of -0.45 and the April 60 put has a delta of -0.40. It is normal for shorter-term, in-the-money options to have a delta that is larger (in absolute terms) than longer-term, in-the-money options.

The neutral ratio for this spread would be 0.889 $(-0.40/-0.45)$. That is, one would sell only 0.889 puts for each one he bought. Alternatively stated, he would sell 8 and buy 9.

A spread of this type has no naked puts and therefore does have large downside profit potential. If the stock should rise too far, the loss is limited to the initial debit of the spread. The optimum result would occur if the stock were at the strike at expiration because, even though the excess long put would lose money in that case, the spreads involving the other puts would overcome that small loss.

Another risk of the in-the-money put spread is that one might be assigned rather quickly if the stock should drop. In fact, one must be careful not to establish the spread with puts that are too deeply in-the-money for this reason. While being put will not necessarily change the profitability of the spread, it will mean increased commission costs and margin charges for the customer, who must buy the stock upon assignment.

A LOGICAL EXTENSION (THE RATIO CALENDAR COMBINATION)

The previous section demonstrated that ratio put calendar spreads can be attractive. The ratio call calendar spread was described earlier as a reasonably attractive strategy for the bullish investor. A logical combination of these two types of ratio calendar spreads (put and call) would be the *ratio combination*—buying a longer-term out-of-the-money combination and selling several near-term out-of-the-money combinations.

Example: The following prices exist:

XYZ common:	55
XYZ January 50 put: 1½	XYZ April 50 put: 2
XYZ January 60 call: 3½	XYZ April 60 call: 5

One could sell the near-term January combination (January 50 put and January 60 call) for 5 points. It would cost 7 points to buy the longer-term April combination (April 50 put and April 60 call). By selling more January combinations than April combinations bought, a ratio calendar combination could be established. For example, suppose that a strategist sold two of the near-term January combinations, bringing in 10 points, and simultaneously bought one April combination for 7 points. This would be credit position—a credit of 3 points in this example. If the near-term, out-of-the-money combination expires worthless, a guaranteed profit of 3 points will exist, even if the longer-term options proceed to expire totally worthless. *If the near-term combination expires worthless, the longer-term combination is owned for free, and a large profit could result on a substantial stock price movement in either direction.*

Although this is a superbly attractive strategy if the near-term options do, in fact, expire worthless, it must also be monitored closely so that large losses do not occur. These large losses would be possible if the stock broke out in either direction too quickly—before the near-term options expire. In the absence of a technical opinion on the underlying stock, one can generally compute a stock price where it might be reasonable to take follow-up action. This is a similar analysis to the one described for ratio call calendar spreads in Chapter 12. Suppose the stock in this example began to rally. There would be a point at which the strategist would have to pay 3 points of debit to close the call side of the combination. That would be his break-even point.

Example: With XYZ at 65 at January expiration (5 points above the higher strike of the original combination), the near-term January 60 call would be worth 5 points and the longer-term April 60 call might be worth 7 points. If one closed the call side of the combination, he would have to pay 10 points to buy back two January 60 calls and would receive 7 points from selling out his April 60. This closing transaction would be a 3-point debit. This represents a break-even situation up to this point in time, except for commissions, since a 3-point credit was initially taken in. The strategist would continue to hold the April 50 put (the January 50 put would expire worthless) just in case the improbable occurs and the underlying stock plunges below 50 before April expiration. A similar analysis could be performed for the put side of the spread in case of an early downside breakout by the underlying stock. It might be determined that the downside break-even point at January expiration is 46, for example. Thus the strategist has two parameters to work with in attempting to limit losses in case the stock moves by a great deal before near-term expiration: 65 on the upside and 46 on the downside. In practice, if the stock should reach these levels *before*, rather than *at*, January expiration, the strategist would incur a small loss by closing the in-the-money side of the combination. This action should still be taken, however, as the *objective of risk management of this strategy is to take small losses, if necessary.* Eventually, large profits may be generated that could more than compensate for any small losses that were incurred.

The foregoing follow-up action was designed to handle a volatile move by the underlying stock prior to near-term expiration. Another, perhaps more common, time that follow-up action is necessary is when the underlying stock is relatively unchanged at near-term expiration. If XYZ in the example above were near 55 at January expiration, a relatively large profit would exist at that time: the near-term combination would expire worthless for a gain of 10 points on that sale, and the longer-term combination would probably still be worth about 5 points, so that the unrealized loss on the April combination would only be 2 points. This represents a total (realized and unrealized) gain of 8 points. In fact, *as* long as the near-term combination can be bought back for less than the original 3-point credit of the position, the position will show a total unrealized gain at near-term expiration. Should the gain be taken or should the longer-term combination be held in hopes of a volatile move by the underlying stock? Although the strategist will normally handle each position on a case-by-case basis, the general philosophy should be to hold on to the April combination. A profit is already guaranteed at this time— the worst that can happen is a 3-point profit (the original credit). Consequently, the strategist should allow himself the opportunity to make large profits. The strategist may want to attempt to trade out of his long combination, since he will not risk making the position a losing one by doing so. Technical analysis may be able to provide him with buy or sell zones on the stock, and he would then consider selling out his long options in accordance with these technical levels.

In summary, *this strategy is very attractive and should be utilized by strategists who have the expertise to trade in positions with naked options.* As long as risk management principles of taking small losses are adhered to, there will be a large probability of overall profit from this strategy.

PUT OPTION SUMMARY

This concludes the section on put option strategies. The put option is useful in a variety of situations. First, it represents a more attractive way to take advantage of a bearish attitude with options. Second, the use of the put options opens up a new set of strategies—straddles and combinations—that can present reasonably high levels of profit potential. Many of the strategies that were described in Part II for call options have been discussed again in this part. Some of these strategies were described more fully in terms of philosophy, selection procedures, and follow-up action when they were first discussed. The second description—the one involving put options—was often shortened to a more mechanical description of how puts fit into the strategy. This format is intentional. The reader who is planning to employ a certain strategy that can be established with either puts or calls (a bear spread, for example) should familiarize himself with both applications by a simultaneous review of the call chapter and its analogous put chapter.

The combination strategies generally introduced new concepts to the reader. The combination allows the construction of positions that are attractive with either puts or calls (out-of-the-money calendar spreads, for example) to be combined into one position. The four combination strategies that involved selling short-term options and simultaneously buying longer-term options are complex, but are most attractive in that they have the desirable features of limited risk and large potential profits.

Chapter 25

LEAPS

Trading volume in equity options has dropped off in recent years as index options have moved to the forefront of activity. In an attempt to recapture some of that lost volume, as well as to provide customers with a broader range of derivative products, two new types of options—LEAPS (Long-term Equity Anticipation Securities) and CAPS—have been introduced. In addition, PERCS have debuted, not as a listed option, but as a listed security trading on the stock exchange. These are not really new types of securities, but are variations on preexisting options or strategies. Their attraction is partly their simplicity—for example, one may not have to execute a spread order if he trades CAPS. However, one still has to under-*stand* spreads in order to trade CAPS.

This chapter does a fair amount of reviewing basic option facts in order to explain the concepts behind LEAPS. The reader who has a knowledge of the preceding chapters—and therefore does not need the review—will be able to quickly skim through this chapter and pick out the strategically important points. However, if one encounters concepts here that don't seem familiar, he should review the previous chapter that discusses the pertinent strategy.

LEAPS is a wordy name for "long-term option." LEAPs are nothing more than a listed call or put option that is issued with two or more years of time remaining. It is a longer-term option than we are used to dealing with. Other than that, there is no material difference between LEAPS and the other calls and puts that have been discussed in the previous chapters.

LEAPS were first introduced by the CBOE in October 1990, and were offered on a handful of blue-chip stocks. Their attractiveness spurred listings on many underlying stocks on all option exchanges as well as on several indices (index options are covered in a later section of the book).

Strategies involving long-term options are not substantially different from those involving shorter-term options. However, the fact that the option has so much time remaining *seems* to favor the buyer and be a detriment to the seller. This is one reason why LEAPS have been popular. As a strategist, one knows that the length of time remaining has little to do with whether a certain strategy makes sense or not. Rather, it is the relative value of the option which dictates strategy. If an option is over-priced, it is a viable candidate for selling, whether it has two years of life remaining or two months. Obviously, follow-up action may become much more of a reality during the life of a two-year option, but that is a matter that will be discussed later in this chapter.

THE BASICS

Certain facets of LEAPS are the same as for other listed equity options, while others involve slight differences. The amount of standardization is considerably less, which makes the simple process of quoting LEAPS a bit more tedious. LEAPS are listed options that can be traded in a secondary market or can be exercised before expiration. As with other listed equity options, they do not receive the dividend paid by the underlying common stock.

Recall that four specifications uniquely describe any option contract:

1. The type (put or call),
2. The underlying stock name (and symbol),
3. The expiration date, and
4. The striking price.

Type. LEAPS are puts or calls. The LEAPS owner has the right to buy the stock at the striking price (LEAPS call) or sell it there (LEAPS put). This is exactly the same for LEAPS and for regular equity options.

Underlying Stock and Quote Symbol. The underlying stocks are the same for LEAPS as they are for equity options. The base symbol in an option quote is the part that designates the underlying stock. For equity options, the base symbol is the same as the stock symbol. However, until the Option Price Reporting Authority (OPRA) changes the way that all options are quoted, the *base symbols for LEAPS are not the same as the stock symbol*. For example, LEAPS options on stock XYZ might trade under the base symbol WXY. So it is possible that one stock might have listed options trading with different base symbols even though all the symbols refer to the same underlying stock. Check with your broker to determine the LEAPS symbol if you need to know it.

Expiration Date. LEAPS expire on the Saturday following the third Friday of the expiration month, just as equity options do. One must look in the newspaper or ask his broker to determine what the expiration months are, however, since they are also not completely standardized. When LEAPS were first listed, there were differing expiration months through December 1993. At the current time, LEAPS are issued to expire in January of each year, so some attempt is being made at standardization. However, there is no guarantee that varying expiration months won't reappear at some future time.

Striking Price. There is no standardized striking price interval for LEAPS as there is for equity options. If XYZ is a 95 dollar stock, there might be LEAPS with striking prices of 80, 95, and 105. Again, one must look in the newspaper or ask his broker to determine the actual LEAPS striking prices for any specific underlying stock. New striking prices can be introduced when the underlying stock rises or falls too far. For example, if the lowest strike for XYZ were 80 and the stock fell to 80, a new LEAPS strike of 70 might be introduced.

Other Basic Factors. LEAPS may be exercised at any time during their life, just as is the case with equity options. Note: this statement regarding exercise is *not* necessarily true for Index LEAPS or Index Options. See Part V of this book for discussions of index products.

Standard LEAPS contracts are for 100 shares of the underlying stock, just as equity options are. The number of shares would be adjusted for stock splits and stock dividends (leading to even more arcane LEAPS symbol problems). LEAPS are quoted on a per-share basis as are other listed options.

There are position and exercise limits for LEAPS just as there are for other listed options. These are currently 8,000 contracts for liquid stock, 5,500 for less liquid ones, and 3,000 for the least liquid ones. One must add his LEAPS position and his regular equity option position together in order to determine his entire position quantity. Exemptions may be obtained for bona fide hedgers of common stock.

As time passes, LEAPS eventually have less than 9 months remaining until expiration. When such a time is reached, the LEAPS are "renamed" and become an ordinary equity option on the underlying security.

Example: Assume LEAPS on stock XYZ were initially issued in January 1992 to expire in January 1994. Assume that one of these LEAPS is the XYZ Jan (1994) 90; that is, it has a striking price of 90 and expires in January, 1994. Its symbol is WXYAR (W for 1994, XY for the LEAPS base symbol, A for January, and R for 90).

15 months later, after April 1993 option expiration, the January 1994 LEAPS only have nine months of life remaining. The LEAPS symbol would be changed from WXYAR to XYZAR (a regular equity option), and the quotes would be listed in the regular equity option section of the newspaper instead of the LEAPS section.

PRICING LEAPS

Terms such as in-the-money, out-of-the-money, intrinsic value, time value premium, and parity all apply and have the same definition. The factors influencing the price of LEAPS are the same as those for any other option:

1. Underlying stock price
2. Striking price
3. Time remaining
4. Volatility
5. Risk-free interest rate
6. Dividend rate

The relative influence of these factors may be a little more pronounced for LEAPS than it is for shorter-term equity options. Consequently, the trader may think that a LEAPS is overly expensive or cheap by inspection, when in reality it is not. *One should be careful in his evaluation of LEAPS until he has acquired experience in observing how their prices relate to the shorter-term equity options with which he is experienced.*

It might prove useful to reexamine the option pricing curve with some LEAPS included. As always, the solid intrinsic value line is the bottom line—it is the same for any call option. The curves are all drawn with the same values for the pertinent variables: stock price, striking price, volatility, short-term interest rate, and dividends. Thus, they can be compared directly.

The most obvious thing to notice about the curves in Figure 25-1 is that the curve depicting the 2-year LEAPS is quite flat. It has the *general*

FIGURE 25-1.
LEAPS call pricing curve.

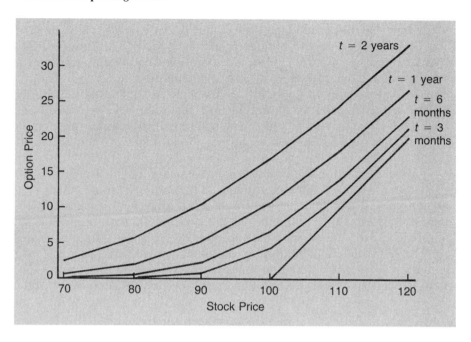

shape of the shorter-term curves, but there is so much time value at stock prices, even 25% in- or out-of-the-money, that the 2-year curve is much flatter than the others.

Other observations can be made as well. Notice the at-the-money options: the 2-year LEAPS sells for a little more than four times the 3-month option. As we shall see, this can change with the effects of interest rates and dividends, but it confirms something that was demonstrated earlier: time decay is not linear. Thus, the 2-year LEAPS, which has eight times the amount of time remaining as compared to the 3-month call, only sells for about four times as much. This LEAPS might appear cheap to the casual observer, but remember that these graphs depict the fair values for this set of input parameters. *Do not be deluded into thinking that a LEAPS looks cheap merely by comparing its price to a nearer-term option; use a model to evaluate it.* Or at least use the output of someone else's model.

The curves in Figure 25-1 depict the relationships between stock price, striking price, and time remaining. The most important remaining determinant of an option's price is the volatility of the underlying stock. Changes in volatility can greatly change the price of any option. This is especially true for LEAPS, since a long-term option's price will fluctuate greatly when volatility changes only a little. Some observations on the differing effects that volatility changes have on short- and long-term options are presented later.

Before that discussion, however, it may be beneficial to examine the effect that interest rates and dividends can have on LEAPS. These effects are much, much greater than those on conventional equity options. Recall that it was stated that interest rates and dividends are minor determinants in the price of an option, unless the dividend were large. That statement pertains mostly to short-term options. For longer-term options such as LEAPS, the cumulative effect of an interest rate or dividend over such a long period of time can have a magnified effect in terms of the absolute price of the option.

Figure 25-2 is the option pricing curve again, but the only option depicted is a 2-year LEAPS. The three curves represent option prices for risk-free interest rates of 3%, 6%, and 9%. All other factors (time to expiration, volatility, and dividends) are fixed. The difference between option prices caused merely by a shift in rates of 3% is very large.

The difference in LEAPS prices increases as the LEAPS becomes in-the-money. Note that in this figure, the distance between the curves gets wider as one scans them from left to right. The price difference for out-

FIGURE 25-2.
2-year LEAPS call pricing curve interest rate comparison.

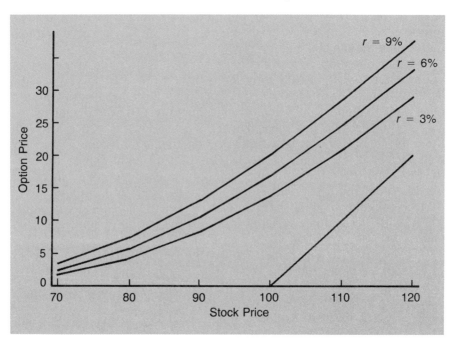

of-the-money LEAPS is large enough—nearly a point even for options fairly far out-of-the-money (that is, the points on the left-hand side of the graph). A shift of 3% in rates entails a larger price difference of over 2 points in the *at-the-money*, two-year LEAPS. The largest differential in option prices occurs *in-the-money!* This may seem somewhat illogical, but when LEAPS strategies are examined later, the reasons for this will become clear. Suffice it to say that the in-the-money LEAPS are changed in price by over four points when rates change by 3%. That is a monstrous differential and should cause any trader who is considering trading in-the-money LEAPS to consider what his outlook is for short-term interest rates.

There is always a substantial probability that rates can change by 3% in two years. Thus, it is difficult to predict with any certainty what risk-free rate to use in the pricing of two-year LEAPS. Moreover, one should be very careful when deciding LEAPS are "cheap" or "expensive" because, conventionally, the short-term interest rate is not usually considered as a significant factor in making such an analysis. For LEAPS, however, Figure 25-2 is obvious proof that interest rate considerations are important for LEAPS traders.

Now consider dividends. Figure 25-3 depicts the price of two-year LEAPS calls. The three curves on the graph are for different dividend rates—the top line representing the current rate, the middle line representing prices if the dividend were raised by $1 annually, and the bottom line showing what prices would be if the dividend were raised by $2 annually. All other factors (volatility, time remaining, and risk-free interest rates) are the same for each curve in this graph. The increase in dividends manifests itself by *decreasing* the LEAPS call price. The reason that this is true, of course, is that the stock will be reduced in price more when it goes ex-dividend by the larger amounts of the increased dividends.

The actual amount that the LEAPS calls lose in price increases slightly as the call is more in-the-money. That is, the curves are closer together on the left-hand (out-of-the-money) side than they are on the right-hand (in-the-money) side. For the in-the-money call, a $1 increase in dividends over two years can cause the LEAPS to be worth about 1½ points less in value.

Figure 25-3 is to the same scale as the previous two figures, so they can be compared directly in terms of magnitude. Notice that the effect of a $1 increase in dividends on the LEAPS call prices is much smaller than that of an increase in interest rates by 3%. Graphically speaking, one can observe this by noting that the spaces between the three curves in the previous figures are much wider than the spaces between the three curves on this figure.

Finally, note that dividend increases have the opposite effect on puts. That is, an increase in the dividend payout of the underlying common will cause a put to *increase* in price. If the put is a long-term LEAPS put, then the effect of the increase will be even larger.

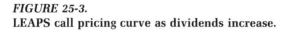

FIGURE 25-3.
LEAPS call pricing curve as dividends increase.

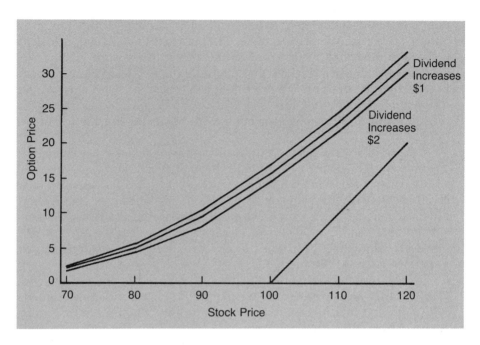

Lest one think that LEAPS are too difficult to price objectively, note the following. The prior figures of interest rate and dividend effects tend to magnify the effects on LEAPS prices for two reasons. First, they depict the effects on 2-year LEAPS. That is a large amount of life for LEAPS. Many LEAPS have less life remaining, so the effects would be diminished somewhat for LEAPS with 10 to 23 months of life left. Second, the figures depict the change in rates or dividends as being instantaneous. This is not completely realistic. If rates change, they will change by a little bit at a time—usually ¼% or ½% at a time, perhaps as much as 1%. If dividends are increased, that increase may be instantaneous, but it will not likely occur immediately after the LEAPS are purchased or sold. However, the intent that these figures are meant to convey is that interest rates and dividends have a much greater effect on LEAPS than on ordinary shorter-term equity options, and that is certainly a true statement.

COMPARING LEAPS AND SHORT-TERM OPTIONS

Table 25-1 will help to illustrate the problem in valuing LEAPS, either mentally or with a model. Each of the variables—stock price, volatility,

TABLE 25-1.
Comparing LEAPS and Short-Term Calls.

		Change in Price of the Options					
		20% out		at		20% in	
Variable	Increment	3-mo.	2-yr.	3-mo.	2-yr.	3-mo.	2-yr.
Stock Prc.	+1 pt	.03	.41	.54	.70	.97	.89
Volatility	+1%	.03	.43	.21	.48	.04	.33
Int. Rate	+1/2%	.01	.27	.08	.55	.14	.72
Dividend	+$.25/qtr	0	−.62	−.08	−1.18	−.14	−1.50

interest rates, and dividends—are incremented and the comparison is shown between 3-month equity options and 2-year LEAPS. There are three sets of comparisons: for options 20% out-of-the-money, options at-the-money, and options 20% in-the-money.

A few words are needed here to explain how volatility is shown in this table. Volatility is normally expressed as a percent. For example, the volatility of the stock market is about 15%. The table shows what would happen if volatility changed by 1% or 16%, for example. Of course, the table also shows what would happen if the other factors changed by a small amount.

Most of the discrepancies between the 3-month and the 2-year options are large. For example, if volatility increases by one percentage point, the 3-month out-of-the-money call will only increase in price by 3 cents (0.03 in the left-hand column) while the 2-year LEAPS call will increase by 43 cents, or almost ½ point. As another example, look at the bottom right-hand pair of numbers, where the effect of a dividend increase on the options that are 20% in-the-money is shown. The assumption is that the dividend will increase 25 cents this quarter (and will be 25 cents higher every quarter thereafter). This translates into a loss of 14 cents (about ⅛ of a point for the 3-month call, since there is only one ex-divided period that affects this call), but translates into a loss of 1½ for the 2-year LEAPS since the stock will go ex-dividend by an extra $2 over the life of that call.

This table also shows that only three of the discrepancies are not large. Two involve the stock price change. If the stock changes in price by 1 point, neither the at-the-money nor the in-the-money options behave all that differently, although the at-the-money LEAPS do jump by 70 cents. The observant reader will notice that the top line of the table depicts the *delta* of the options in question; it shows the change in option price for a one point change in stock price. The only other comparison that is not extremely divergent is that of volatility change for the at-the-money option. The 3-month call changes by 21 cents (¼ of a point) while the LEAPS changes by nearly ½ point. This is still a factor of two-to-one, but is much less than the other comparisons in the table.

Study the other comparisons in the table. The trader who is used to dealing with short-term options might ordinarily ignore the effect of a rise in interest rates of ½ of 1 percent, of a 25 cent increase in the quarterly dividend, of the volatility increasing by a mere 1%, or maybe even of the stock moving by one point (only if his option is out-of-the-money). The LEAPS option trader will gain or suffer substantially and immediately if any of these occur. In almost every case, his LEAPS call will gain or lose ½ point of value—a significant amount to be sure.

LEAPS STRATEGIES

Many of the strategies involving LEAPS are not significantly different from their counterparts that involve short-term options. However, as shown earlier, the long-term nature of the LEAPS can sometimes cause the strategist to experience a result different from that to which he has become accustomed.

As a general rule, one would want to be a buyer of LEAPS when interest rates were low and when the volatilities being implied in the marketplace are low. If the opposite were true (high rates and high volatilities), he would lean towards strategies in which the *sale* of LEAPS is used. Of course, there are many other specific considerations when it comes to operating a strategy, but since the long-term nature of LEAPS exposes one to interest rate and volatility movements for such a long time, one may as well attempt to position himself favorably with respect to those two elements when he enters a position.

LEAPS as Stock Substitute

Any in-the-money option can be used as a substitute for the underlying stock. Stock owners may be able to substitute a long in-the-money call for their long stock. Short sellers of stock may be able to substitute a long put for their short stock. This is not a new idea; it was briefly discussed back in Chapter 3 under reasons why people buy calls. It has been available as a strategy for some time with short-term options. Its attractiveness seems to have increased somewhat with the introduction of LEAPS, however. More and more people are examining the potential of selling the stock they own and buying long-term calls (LEAPS) as a substitute, or buying LEAPS instead of making an initial purchase in a particular common stock.

Substitution For Stock Currently Held Long. Simplistically, the strategy involves this line of thinking: if one owns stock and sells it, an investor could reinvest a small portion of the proceeds in a call option—thereby providing continued upside profit potential if the stock rises in price—

and invest the rest in a bank to earn interest. The interest earned would act as a substitute for the dividend, if any, to which he no longer is entitled. Moreover, he has less downside risk: if the stock should fall dramatically, his loss is limited to the initial cost of the call.

In actual practice, one should carefully calculate what he is getting and what he is giving up. For example, is the loss of the dividend too great to be compensated for by the investment of the excess proceeds? How much of the potential gain will be wasted in the form of time value premium paid for the call? The costs to the stock owner who decides to switch into call options as a substitute are commissions, the time value premium of the call, and the loss of dividends. The benefits are the interest that can be earned from freeing up a substantial portion of his funds, plus the fact that there is less downside risk in owning the call than in owning the stock.

Example: XYZ is selling at 50. There are one-year LEAPS with a striking price of 40 that sell for $12. XYZ pays an annual dividend of $0.50 and short-term interest rates are 5%. What are the economics that an owner of 100 XYZ common stock must calculate in order to see if it is viable to sell his stock and buy the one-year LEAPS as a substitute?

The call has time value premium of two points (40 + 12 − 50). Moreover, if the stock is sold and the LEAPS purchased, a credit of $3,800 less commissions would be generated. First, calculate the net credit generated:

Credit balance generated:		
Sale of 100 XYZ stock	$5,000	
Less stock commission	− 25	
Net sale proceeds:	$4,975 credit	
Cost of one LEAPS call		$1,200
Plus option commission		15
Net cost of call:		$1,215 debit
Total credit balance:	$3,760 credit	

Now the costs and benefits of making the switch can be computed:

Costs of switching:	
Time value premium	− $200
Loss of dividend	− $ 50
Stock commissions	− $ 25
Option commissions	− $ 15
Total cost:	− $290

Fixed Benefit from switching:
    Interest earned on
        credit balance of $3,760
        at 5% interest for one year = 0.05 × $3,760:   + $188

Net cost of switching   − $102

The stock owner must now decide if it is worth just over $1 per share in order to have his downside risk limited to a price of 39½ over the next year. The price of 39½ as his downside risk is merely the amount of the net credit he received from doing the switch ($3,760) plus the interest earned ($188), expressed in per-share terms. That is, if XYZ falls dramatically over the next year and the LEAPS expire worthless, this investor will still have $3,948 in a bank account. That is equivalent to limiting his risk to about 39½ on the original 100 shares.

If the investor decides to make the substitution, he should invest the proceeds from the sale in a 1-year CD or T-Bill for two reasons. First, he locks in the current rate—the one used in his calculations—for the year. Second, he is not tempted to use the money for something else, an action that might negate the potential benefits of the substitution.

The above calculations all assume that the LEAPS call or the stock would have been held for the full year. If that is known not to be the case, the appropriate costs or benefits must be recalculated.

Caveats. This ($102) *seems* like a reasonably small price to pay to make the switch from common stock to call ownership. However, if he were planning to sell the stock before it fell to 39½ in any case, he might not feel the need to pay for this protection (be aware, however, that he could accomplish essentially the same thing since he can sell his LEAPS call whenever he wants to). Moreover, when the year is up, he will have to pay another stock commission to repurchase his XYZ common if he still wants to own it (or he will have to pay two option commissions to roll his long call out to a later expiration date). One other detriment that might exist, although a relatively unlikely one, is that the underlying common might declare an increased dividend or, even worse, a special cash dividend. The LEAPS call owner would not be entitled to that dividend increase—in whatever form—while, obviously, the common stock owner would have been. If the company declared a stock dividend, it would have no effect on this strategy since the call owner *is* entitled to those. A change in interest rates is not a factor either since the owner of the LEAPS should invest in a 1-year Treasury Bill or a 1-year CD and therefore would not be subject to interim changes in short-term interest rates.

There may be other mitigating circumstances. Mostly these would involve tax considerations. If the stock is currently a profitable investment, the sale would generate a capital gain, and taxes might be owed. If the stock is currently being held at a loss, the purchase of the call would constitute a wash sale and the loss could not be taken at this time (see Chapter 39 for a broader discussion of the wash sale rule and option trading).

In theory, the calculations above could produce an overall credit, in which case the stock holder would normally want to substitute with the call unless he has overriding tax considerations, or suspects that a cash dividend increase is going to be announced. *Be very careful about switching if this situation should arise.* Normally, arbitrageurs—persons trading for exchange members and paying no commission—would take advantage of such a situation before the general public could. If they are letting the opportunity pass by, there must be a reason (probably the cash dividend), so be extremely certain of your economics and research before venturing into such a situation.

In summary, holders of common stock on which there exist in-the-money LEAPS should evaluate the economics of substituting the LEAPS call for the common stock. Even if arithmetic calculations call for the substitution, the stock holder should consider his tax situation as well as his outlook for the cash dividends to be paid by the common before making the switch.

Buying LEAPS As The Initial Purchase Instead of Buying a Common Stock

Logic similar to that used earlier—to determine whether a stockholder might want to substitute a LEAPS call for his stock—can be used by a prospective purchaser of common stock. In other words, *this* investor does not already own the common. He is *going* to buy it. This prospective purchaser might want to buy a LEAPS call and put the rest of the money he had planned to use in the bank instead of actually buying the stock itself.

His costs—real and opportunity—are calculated in a similar manner to those expressed earlier. The only real difference is that he has to spend the stock commission in this case, whereas he did not in the previous example (since he already owned the stock).

Example: As before, XYZ is selling at 50; there are 1-year LEAPS with a striking price of 40 that sell for $12; XYZ pays an annual dividend of $0.50 and short-term interest rates are 5%.

The *initial* purchaser of common stock would have these "opportunity" costs and savings if he decided instead to buy the LEAPS calls. First calculate the difference in investment required for the stock versus the LEAPS:

Prospective initial investment:	
Stock: $5,000 + $25 commission	= $5,025
LEAPS: $1,200 + $15 commission	= $1,215
Net difference:	$3,810

Now calculate the costs versus the savings:

Costs:	
Time value premium	−$200
Loss of dividend	−$ 50
Savings:	
Interest on $3,810 for one year at 5%:	+$190
Net opportunity cost:	−$ 60

In this case, it seems even more likely that the prospective stock purchaser would instead buy the LEAPS call. His net "cost" of doing so—provided he puts the difference in initial investment in a one-year CD or T-Bill—is only $60. For this small amount, he has all the upside appreciation (except $60 worth), but only has risk down to 40 (he will have $4,000 in his bank account at the end of one year even if the LEAPS expire worthless).

This strategy of buying in-the-money LEAPS and putting the difference between the LEAPS cost and the stock cost in an interest bearing instrument is an attractive one. It might seem it would be especially attractive if interest rates for the differential were high. Unfortunately, those high rates would present something of a "Catch-22" because, as was shown earlier, higher rates will cause the LEAPS to be more expensive.

In this margin strategy, one has the risk of not participating in cash dividends increases or specials as the stock holder who substitutes does. But the other concerns of the stock holder, such as taxes, are not pertinent here. Again, these specific calculations only apply if the stock were to be held for the entire year. Adjustments would have to be made if the holding period is envisioned to be shorter.

Using Margin. The same prospective initial purchaser of common stock might have been contemplating a purchase on margin. If he used the LEAPS instead, he could save the margin interest. Of course, he wouldn't have as much money to put in the bank, but he should also compare his costs against those of buying the LEAPS call instead:

Example: As before, XYZ is selling at 50; there are 1-year LEAPS with a striking price of 40 that sell for $12; XYZ pays an annual dividend of $0.50 and short-term interest rates are 5%. Furthermore, assume the margin rate is 8% on borrowed debit balances.

First, calculate the difference in prospective investments:

Cost of buying the stock:	
$5,000 + $25 commission:	$5,025
Amount borrowed (50%)	−2,512
Equity required	$2,513
Cost of buying LEAPS:	
$1,200 + $15 commission:	$1,215
Difference (available to be placed in bank account)	$1,298

Now the costs and opportunities can be compared, if it is assumed that he buys the LEAPS:

Costs:	
Time Value Premium	−$200
Dividend loss	− 50
Savings:	
Interest on $1,298 at 5%	+$ 65
Margin interest on $2,512 debit balance at 8% for one year	+ 201
Net Savings:	+$ 16

For the margin buyer, there is a real savings in this example. The fact that he does not have to pay the margin interest on his debit balance makes the purchase of the LEAPS call a cost-saving alternative.

In summary, a prospective purchaser of common stock may often find that if there is an in-the-money option available, that the purchase of that option is more attractive than buying the common stock itself. If he was planning to buy on margin, it is even more likely that the LEAPS purchase will be attractive. The main drawback is that he will not participate if cash dividends are increased or a special dividend is declared. Read on, however, for the next strategy may be better than the one above.

Protecting Existing Stock Holdings With LEAPS Puts

What was accomplished in the substitution strategy previously discussed? The stock owner paid some cost ($102 in the actual example) in order to limit the risk of his stock ownership to a price of 39½. What if he had just bought a LEAPS put instead? Forgetting the price of the put for a moment, concentrate on what the strategy would accomplish. He would be protected from a large loss on the downside since he owns the put, and he could participate in upside appreciation since he still owns the stock. Isn't this what the substitution strategy was trying to accomplish? *Yes, it is.* In this strategy, only one commission is paid—that being on a fairly cheap out-of-the-money LEAPS put—and there is no risk of losing out on dividend increases or special dividends.

The comparison between substituting a call or buying a put is a relatively simple one. First, do the calculations as they were performed in the initial example above. That example showed that the stock holder's cost would be $102 to substitute the LEAPS call for the stock, and such a substitution would protect him at a price of 39½. In effect, he is paying $152 for a LEAPS put with a strike of 40—the $102 cost plus the difference between 40 and the 39½ protection price. Now, if an XYZ one-year LEAPS put with strike 40 were available at 1½, he could accomplish everything he had initially wanted, by merely buying the put.

Moreover, he would save commissions and still be in a position to participate in increased cash dividends. These additional benefits should make the put worth even more to the stock holder, so that he might pay even slightly more than 1½ for the put. If the LEAPS put were available at this price, it would clearly be the better choice and should be bought instead of substituting the LEAPS call for the common stock.

Thus, any stock holder who is thinking of protecting his position can do it in one of two ways—sell the stock and substitute a call or continue to hold his stock and buy a put to protect it. LEAPS calls and puts are amenable to this strategy. Because of the LEAPS long-term nature, one does not have to keep reestablishing his position and pay numerous commissions as he would with short-term options. The stock holder should perform the simple calculations as shown above in order to decide if the move is feasible at all, and if it is, whether to use the call substitution strategy or the put protection strategy.

LEAPS Instead of Short Stock

Just as in-the-money LEAPS calls may sometimes be a smarter purchase than the stock itself, in-the-money puts may sometimes be a better purchase than *shorting* the common stock. Recall that either the put purchase or the short sale of stock is a bearish strategy, generally implemented by someone who expects the stock to decline in price. The strategist knows, however, that short stock is a component of many strategies and might reflect other opinions than pure bearishness on the common. In any case, an in-the-money put may prove to be a viable substitute for shorting the stock itself. The two main advantages that the put owner has are: he has limited risk (whereas the short seller of stock has theoretically unlimited risk); and he does not have to pay out any dividends on the underlying stock as the short seller would. Also, the commissions for buying the put would normally be smaller than those required to sell the stock short.

There is not much in the way of calculating that needs to be done in order to make the comparison between buying the in-the-money put and shorting the stock. If the time value premium spent is small in comparison with the dividend payout that is saved, then the put is probably the better choice.

Professional arbitrageurs and other exchange members, as well as some large customers, receive interest on their short sales. For these traders, the put would have to be trading with virtually no time premium at all in order for the comparison to favor the put purchase over the stock short sale. However, the public customer who is going to be shorting stock should be aware of the potential for buying an in-the-money put instead.

SPECULATIVE OPTION BUYING WITH LEAPS

Strategists know that buying calls and puts can have various applications. Witness the stock substitution strategies above. However, the most popular reason for buying options is for speculative gain. The leverage inherent in owning options, plus their limited risk feature make them attractive for this purpose as well. The risk, of course, can be 100% of the investment, and time decay works against the option owner as well. LEAPS calls and puts fit all of these descriptions—they just have longer maturities.

Time decay is the major enemy of the speculative option holder. Purchasing LEAPS options instead of the shorter-term equity options generally exposes the buyer to less risk of time decay on a daily basis. This is true because the extreme negative effects of time decay magnify as the option approaches its expiration. Recall that it was shown back in Chapter 3 that time decay is not linear—an option decays more rapidly at the end of its life than at the beginning. Eventually, a LEAPS put or call will become a normal short-term equity option and time will begin to take a more rapid toll. But, in the beginning of the life of LEAPS, there is so much time remaining that the short-term decay is not large in terms of price.

Table 25-2 and Figure 25-4 depict the rate of decay of two options: one is at-the-money (the lower curve) and the other is 20% out-of-the-money (the upper curve). The horizontal axis is months of life remaining until expiration. The vertical axis is the percent of the option price that is lost *daily* due to time decay. The options that qualify as LEAPS (more than 9 months of life remaining) are in the shaded area on the lower right-hand portion of the figure.

The upward sloping nature of both curves as time to expiration decreases shows the effect that time decay increases more rapidly as ex-

TABLE 25-2.
Daily Percent Time Value Decay.

Months Remaining	Percent Decay	
	At-the-money	20% Out-of-money
24,	.12	.18
18,	.14	.27
12,	.19	.55
9	.22	.76
6,	.27	1.18
3,	.60	3.57
2,	.73	4.43
1,	1.27	
2 wks	3.33	

FIGURE 25-4.
Daily percent time value decay.

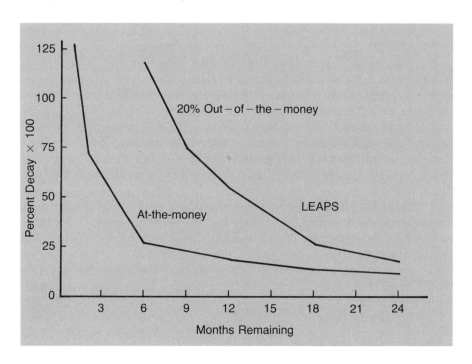

piration approaches. Notice how much more rapidly the out-of-the-money option decays, percentage wise, than the at-the-money. LEAPS, however, do not decay much at all compared to normal equity options. Most LEAPS, even the out-of-the-money ones, lose less than ¼ of one percent of their value daily. This is a pittance when compared with a 6-month equity option that is 20% out-of-the-money—that option loses well over 1% of its value daily and it still has six months of life remaining.

From the accompanying table, observe that the out-of-the-money two-month option loses over 4% of its value daily!

Thus, LEAPS do not decay at a rapid rate. This gives the LEAPS holder a chance to have his opinion about the stock price work for him without having to worry as much about the passage of time as the average equity option holder would. An advantage of owning LEAPS, therefore, is that one's timing of the option purchase does not have to be as exact as that for shorter-term option buying. This can be a great psychological advantage as well as a strategic advantage. The LEAPS option buyer who feels strongly that the stock will move in the desired direction has the luxury of being able to calmly wait for the anticipated move to take place. If it does not—even in perhaps as long as 6 months time—he may still be able to recoup a reasonable portion of his initial purchase price because of the slow percentage rate of decay.

Do not be deluded into believing that LEAPS don't decay at all. Although the *rate* of decay is slow (as shown previously), an option that is losing 0.15% of its value daily will still lose about 25% of its value in six months.

Example: XYZ is at 60 and there are 18-month LEAPS calls selling for $8. The daily decay of this call with respect to time will be minuscule—it will take about a week for even an eighth of a point to be lost due to time. However, if the option is held for six months and nothing else happens, the LEAPS call will be selling for about 6. Thus, it will have lost 25% of its value if the stock remained around 60 at the end of six months.

Those familiar with holding equity calls and puts are more accustomed to seeing an option lose 25% of its value in possibly as little as four or five weeks' time. Thus, the advantage of holding the LEAPS is obvious from the viewpoint of slower time decay.

This observation leads to the obvious question: "When is the best time to sell my call and repurchase a longer term one?" Referring again to the figure above may help answer the question. Note that for the at-the-money option, the curve begins to bend dramatically upward soon after the 6-month time barrier is passed. Thus, it seems logical that to minimize the effects of time decay—all other things being equal—one would sell his long at-the-money call when it has about 6 months of life left and simultaneously buy a 2-year LEAPS call. This keeps his time decay exposure to a minimum.

The out-of-the-money call is more radical. Figure 25-4 shows that the call that is 20% out-of-the-money begins to decay much more rapidly (percentage wise) at somewhere just before it reaches one year until expiration. The same logic would dictate, then, that if one is trading out-of-the-money options, he would sell his option held long when it has about one year to go and reestablish his position by buying a 2-year LEAPS option at the same time.

Advantages of Buying "Cheap"

It has been demonstrated that rising interest rates or rising volatility would make the price of a LEAPS call increase. Therefore, if one is attempting to participate in LEAPS speculative call buying strategies, he should be more aggressive when rates and volatilities are low.

A few sample prices may help to demonstrate just how powerful the effects of rates and volatilities are, and how they can be a friend to the LEAPS call buyer. Suppose that one buys a 2-year LEAPS call at-the-money when the following situation exists:

XYZ: 100
Jan (1994) 100 (i.e., 2-year LEAPS call with strike of 100): 14
Short-term Interest rates: 3%
Volatility: below average (historically)

For the purposes of demonstration, suppose that the current volatility is low for XYZ (historically) and that 3% is a low level for rates as well. If the stock moves up, there is no problem, for the LEAPS call will increase in price. But what if the stock drops or stays unchanged? Is all hope of a profit lost? Actually, no. If interest rates increase or the volatility that the calls trade at increases, we know the LEAPS call will increase in value as well. Thus, even though the direction in which the stock is moving may be unfavorable, it might still be possible to salvage one's investment. Table 25-3 shows where volatility would have to be or where short-term rates would have to go in order to keep the value of the LEAPS call at 14 even after the indicated amount of time had expired.

To demonstrate the usage of this table, consider if the stock price were 100 (unchanged) after one month. If interest rates had risen to 3.4% from their original level of 3% during that time, the call would still be worth 14 even though one month had passed. Alternatively, if rates were the same, but volatility had increased by only 5% from its original level,

TABLE 25-3.
Factors Necessary for Jan (1994) 100 to be = 14.

Stock Price	After 1 month	After 6 months
100 (unchanged)	r = 3.4% or v +5%	r = 6% or v +20%
95	r = 6% or v +20%	r = 9.4% or v +45%
90	r = 8.5% or v +45%	r = 12.6% or v +70%

then the call would also still be worth 14. Note that this means that volatility would have to increase only slightly (by ¹⁄₂₀th) from its original level, not by 5 percentage points.

Even if the stock were to drop to 90 and six months had passed, the LEAPS call holder would still be even if rates had risen to 12.6% (highly unlikely) or volatility had risen by 70%. It is often possible for volatilities to fluctuate to that extent in six months, but not likely for interest rates.

In fact, as interest rates go, only the top line of the table probably represents realistic interest rates—an increase of 0.4% in one month, or 3% in 6 months is possible. The others—where the stock drops in price— probably require too large of a jump in rates for rates alone to be able to salvage the call price. However, any increase in rates will be helpful. Volatility is another matter. It is often feasible for volatilities to change by as much as 50% from their previous level in a month, and certainly in six months. Hence, as has been stated before, the volatility factor is the more dominant one.

This table shows the power of rising interest rates and volatilities on LEAPS calls. It would be beneficial to the LEAPS call owner and, of course, detrimental to the LEAPS call seller. This is clear evidence that one should be aware of the general level of rates and volatility before using LEAPS options in a strategy.

The Delta

The delta of an option is the amount by which the option price will change if the underlying stock changes in price by one amount. In an earlier section of this chapter, comparing the differences between LEAPS and short-term calls, mention was made of delta. The subject will be explored in more depth here because it is such an important concept—not only for option buyers, but for most strategic decisions as well.

Figure 25-5 depicts the deltas of two different options: 2-year LEAPS and 3-month equity options. Their terms are the same except for their expiration date—striking price is 100, and volatility and interest rate

FIGURE 25-5.
Call delta comparison, 2-year LEAPS versus 3-month equity options.

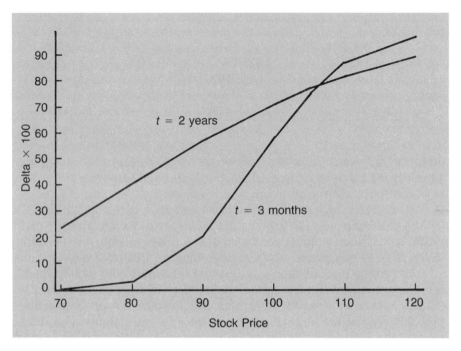

assumptions are equal. The horizontal axis displays the stock price while
the vertical axis shows the delta of the options.

Several relevant observations can be made. First, notice that the delta
of the at-the-money LEAPS is very large—nearly 0.70. This means that
the LEAPS call will move much more in line with the common stock than
a comparable short-term equity option would. Very short-term at-the-
money options have deltas of about ½, while slightly longer-term ones
have deltas ranging up to the 0.55–0.60 area. *What this implies is that
the longer the life of an at-the-money option, the greater its delta.*

In addition, the figure shows that the delta of the 3-month call and
the 2-year LEAPS call are about equal when the options are approximately
5% in-the-money. If the options are *more* in-the-money than that, then
the LEAPS call has a *lower* delta. This means that at- and out-of-the-
money LEAPS will move more in line with the common stock than comparable short-term options will. Restated, the LEAPS calls will move faster
than the ordinary short-term equity calls unless both options are more
than 5% in-the-money. Note that the movement referred to is in absolute
terms in change of price, not in percentage terms.

The delta of 2-year LEAPS does not change as dramatically when the stock moves as does the delta of the 3-month option (see Figure 25-5). Notice how the LEAPS curve is relatively flat on the chart—rising only slightly above horizontal. In contrast, the delta of the 3-month calls is very low out-of-the-money and very large in-the-money. What this means to the call buyer is that the amount by which he can expect the LEAPS call to increase or decrease in price is somewhat stable. This can affect his choice of whether to buy the in-the-money call or the out-of-the-money call. With normal short-term options, he can expect the in-the-money call to much more closely mirror the movement in the stock, so he might be tempted to buy that call if he expects a small movement in the stock. With LEAPS, however, there is much less discrepancy between the amount of option price movement that will occur.

Example: XYZ is trading at 82. There are 3-months calls with strikes of 80 and 90, and there are 2-year LEAPS calls at those strikes as well. The following table summarizes the available information:

XYZ: 82	Date: January, 1992		
Option		*Price*	*Delta*
Apr ('92) 80 call		4	⅝
Apr ('92) 90 call		1	⅛
Jan ('94) 80 LEAPS call		14	¾
Jan ('94) 90 LEAPS call		7	½

Suppose the trader expects a 3-point move by the underlying common stock, from 82 to 85.

If he were analyzing short-term calls he would see his potential as a gain of 1⅞ in the Apr 80 call versus a gain of ⅜ in the Apr 90 call. Each of these gains is projected by multiplying the call's delta times 3 (the expected stock move, in points). Thus, there is a large difference between the expected gain from these two options, particularly after commissions are considered.

Now observe the LEAPS. The Jan 80 would increase by 2¼ while the Jan 90 would increase by 1½ if XYZ moved higher by 3 points. This is not nearly as large of a discrepancy as the short-term options had. Observe that the Jan 90 LEAPS sells for half the price of the Jan 80. These movements projected by the delta indicate that the Jan 90 LEAPS will move by a larger *percentage* than the Jan 80 and therefore would be the better buy.

Put Deltas

Many of the previous observations regarding deltas of LEAPS calls can be applied to LEAPS puts as well. However, Figure 25-5 changes a little when the following formula is applied. Recall that the relationship between put deltas and call deltas, except for deeply in-the-money puts, is:

$$\text{put delta} = \text{call delta} - 1$$

This has the effect of *inverting* the relationships that have just been described. In other words, where the short-term calls didn't move as fast as the LEAPS, the *short-term puts move faster than the LEAPS puts in most cases.* Figure 25-6 shows the deltas of these options.

The vertical axis shows the puts' delta. Notice that out-of-the-money LEAPS puts and short-term equity puts don't behave all that differently in terms of price change (bottom right-hand section of figure).

In-the-money puts (where the stock is *below* the striking price) move faster if they are shorter-term. This fact is accentuated even more when

FIGURE 25-6.
Put delta comparison, 2-year LEAPS versus 3-month equity options.

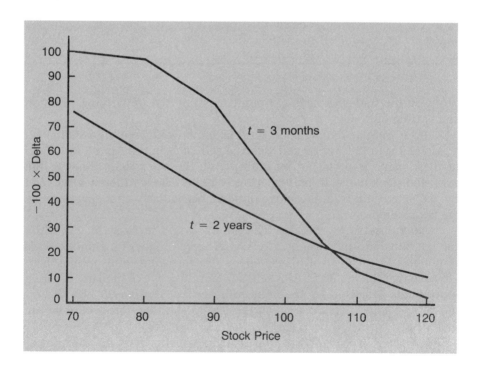

the puts are more deeply in-the-money. The left-hand side of the figure depicts this fact.

The LEAPS put delta curve is flat, just as the call delta curve was. Moreover, the delta is not very large anywhere across the figure. For example, at-the-money 2-year LEAPS puts only move about 30 cents for a one-point move in the underlying stock. *LEAPS put buyers who want to speculate on a stock's downward movement must realize that the leverage factor is not large*; it takes approximately a 3-point move by the underlying common for an at-the-money LEAPS put to increase in value by one point. Long-term puts don't mirror stock movement nearly as well as shorter-term puts do.

In summary, the option buyer who is considering buying LEAPS puts or calls as speculation should be aware of the different price action that LEAPS exhibit when compared to shorter-term options. Due to the large amount of time that LEAPS have remaining in their life, the time decay of the LEAPS options is smaller. For this reason, the LEAPS option buyer doesn't need to be as precise in his timing. In general, LEAPS calls move faster when the underlying stock moves, and LEAPS puts move more slowly. Other than that, the general reasons for speculative option buying apply to LEAPS as well: leverage and limited risk.

SELLING LEAPS

Strategies involving selling LEAPS options do not differ substantially from those involving shorter-term options. The discussions in this section will concentrate on the two major differences that seller of LEAPS will notice. First, the slow rate of time decay of LEAPS options means that option writers who are used to sitting back and watching their written options waste away will not experience the same effect with LEAPS. Second, follow-up action for writing strategies usually depends on being able to buy back the written option when it has little or no time value premium remaining. Since LEAPS retain time value even when substantially in- or out-of-the-money, follow-up action involving LEAPS may involve the repurchase of substantial amounts of time value premium.

Covered Writing

LEAPS options can be sold against underlying stock just as short-term options can. No extra collateral or investment is required to do so. The resulting position is again one with limited profit potential, but enhanced profitability (as compared to stock ownership) if the underlying stock remains unchanged or falls. The maximum profit potential of the covered write is reached whenever the underlying stock is at or above the striking price of the written option at expiration.

The LEAPS covered writer takes in substantial premium, in terms of price, when he sells the long-term option. He should compare the return that he could make from the LEAPS write with returns that can be made from repeatedly writing shorter-term calls. Of course, there is no guarantee that he will actually be able to repeat the short-term writes during the longer life of the LEAPS.

As an aside, the strategist who is utilizing the *incremental return* concept of covered writing may find LEAPS call writing quite attractive. This is the strategy wherein he has a higher target price at which he would be willing to sell his common stock, and he writes calls along the way to earn an incremental return (see Chapter 2 for details). Since this type of writer is only concerned with absolute levels of premiums being brought into the account and not with things like return if exercised, he should utilize LEAPS calls if available, since the premiums are the largest available. Moreover, if the incremental return writer is currently in a short-term call and is going to be called away, he might roll into a LEAPS call in order to retain his stock and take in more premium.

The rest of this section will discuss covered writing from the more normal viewpoint of the investor who buys stock and sells a call against it in order to attain a particular return.

Example: XYZ is selling at 50. The investor is considering a 500-share covered write and he is unsure whether to use the 6-month call or the 2-year LEAPS. The July 50 call sells for 4 and has 6 months of life remaining; the Jan (1994) 50 LEAPS call sells for 8½ and has two years of life. Further assume that XYZ pays a dividend of $0.25 per quarter.

As was done in Chapter 2, the net required investment is calculated, then the return (if exercised) is computed, and finally the downside break-even point is determined.

Net Investment Required		
	Jul 50 call	*Jan 50 LEAPS*
Stock cost (500 shares @ 50)	$25,000	$ 5,000
Plus stock commission	+ 300	+ 300
Less option premiums received	− 2,000	− 4,250
Plus option commissions	+ 50	+ 100
Net cash investment	$23,350	$21,150

Obviously, the LEAPS covered writer has a smaller cash investment since he is selling a more expensive call in his covered write. Note that the option premium is being applied against the net investment in either case, as is the normal custom when doing covered writing.

Now, using the net investment required, one can calculate the return (if exercised). That return assumes the stock is above the striking price of the written option at its expiration, and the stock is called away. The short-term writer would have collected two dividends of the common stock, while the LEAPS writer would have collected eight by expiration.

	Return If Exercised	
	Jul 50 call	Jan 50 LEAPS
Stock sale (500 @ 50)	$25,000	$25,000
Less stock commission	− 300	− 300
Plus dividends earned		
until expiration	+ 250	+ 1,000
Less net investment	− 23,350	− 21,150
Net profit if exercised	$ 1,600	$ 4,550
Return if exercised	6.9%	21.5%
(net profit/net investment)		

The LEAPS writer has a much higher net return if exercised, again because he wrote a more expensive option to begin with. However, in order to fairly compare the two writes, one must annualize the returns. That is, the Jul 50 covered write made 6.9% in six months, so it could make twice that in one year—*if it can be duplicated six months from now*. In a similar manner, the LEAPS covered writer can make 21.5% in two years if the stock is called away. However, on an annualized basis, he would only make half that amount.

Return If Exercised, Annualized	
Jul 50 call	Jan 50 LEAPS
13.8%	10.8%

Thus, on an annualized basis, the short-term write seems better. The shorter-term call will generally have a higher rate of return, annualized, than the LEAPS call. The problems with annualizing will be discussed in the following text.

Finally, the downside breakeven point can be computed for each write.

Downside Break-Even Calculation		
	Jul 50 call	Jan 50 LEAPS
Net Investment	$23,350	$21,150
Less Dividends Received	− 250	− 1,000
Total Stock Cost to Expirtn.	$23,100	$20,150
Divided by shares held (500), gives break-even price:	46.2	40.3

The larger premium of the LEAPS call that was written produces this dramatically lower break-even price for the LEAPS covered write.

Similar comparison could be made for a covered write on margin if the investor is using a margin account. The steps above are the mechanical ones that a covered writer should go through in order to see how the short-term write compares to the longer-term LEAPS write. Analyzing them is often a less routine matter. It would seem that the short-term write is better if one uses the *annualized* rate of return. However, the annualized return is a somewhat subjective number that depends on several assumptions.

The first assumption is that one will be able to generate an equivalent return six months from now when the July 50 call expires worthless or the stock is called away. If the stock were relatively unchanged, the covered writer would have to sell a 6-month call for 4 points again six months from now. Or, if the stock were called away, he would have to invest in an equivalent situation elsewhere. Moreover, in order to reach the 2-year horizon offered by the LEAPS write, the 6-month return would have to be regenerated *three* more times (six months from now, one year from now, and a year and a half from now). The covered writer cannot assume that such returns can be repeated with any certainty every six months.

The second assumption that was made when the annualized returns were calculated is that one-half the return, if exercised, on the LEAPS calls, would be made when one year had passed. But, as has been demonstrated repeatedly in this chapter, the time decay of an option is not linear. Therefore, one year from now, if XYZ were still at 50, the Jan (1994) 50 LEAPS call would not be selling for half its current price ($\frac{1}{2} \times 8\frac{1}{2} = 4\frac{1}{4}$). It would be selling for something more like $5\frac{3}{4}$, if all other factors remained unchanged. However, given the variability of LEAPS call premiums when interest rates, volatility, or dividend payouts change, it is extremely difficult to estimate the call price one year from now. Consequently, to say that the 21.5% 2-year return if exercised would be 10.8% after one year may well be a false statement.

Thus, the covered writer must make his decision on what he knows. He knows that with the short-term July 50 write, if the stock is called away in six months, he will make 6.9%, period. If he opts for the longer term, he will make 21.5% if he is called away in two years. Which is better? The question can only be answered by each covered writer individually. One's attitude towards long-term investing will be a major factor in making the decision. If he thinks XYZ has good prospects for the long term, and he feels conservative returns will be below 10% for the next couple of years, then he would probably choose the LEAPS write. However, if he feels that there is a temporary expansion of option premium in the short-term XYZ calls that should be exploited, and he would not really want to be a long-term holder of the stock, then he would choose the short-term covered write.

The actual downside breakeven point might enter into one's thinking as well. A downside breakeven point of 40.3 is available by using the LEAPS write and that is a known quantity. No matter how far XYZ might fall, as long as it can recover to slightly over 40 by expiration two years from now, the investment will at least break even. A problem arises if XYZ falls to 40 quickly. If that happened, the LEAPS call would still have a significant amount of time value premium remaining on it. Thus, if the investor attempted to sell his stock at that time and buy back his call, he would have a loss, not a break-even situation.

The short-term write offers downside protection only to a stock price of 46.2. Of course, repeated writes of 6-month calls over the next two years would lower the breakeven point below that level. The problem is that if XYZ declines and one is forced to keep selling six-month calls every six months, he may be forced to use a lower striking price, thereby locking in a smaller profit (or possibly even a loss) if premium levels shrink. The concepts of rolling down are described in detail in Chapter 2.

A further word about rolling down may be in order here. Recall that rolling down means to buy back the call that is currently written and sell another one with a lower striking price. Such action *always* reduces the profitability of the overall position, although it may be necessary to prevent further downside losses if the common stock keeps declining. Now that LEAPS are available, the short-term writer faced with rolling down may look to the LEAPS as a means of bringing in a healthy premium even though he is rolling down. It is true that a large premium could be brought into the account. But remember that by doing so, one is committing himself to sell the stock at a lower price than he originally had intended. This is why the rolling down reduces the original profit potential. *If he rolls down into a LEAPS call, he is reducing his maximum profit potential for a longer period of time.* Consequently, one should not always roll down into an option with a longer maturity. Instead, he should carefully analyze whether he wants to be committed for an even longer time to a position in which the underlying common stock is declining.

To summarize, the large absolute premiums available in LEAPS calls may make a covered write of those calls seem unusually attractive. However, one should calculate the returns available and see if a short-term write might not serve his purpose as well. The large amount of downside protection offered by the LEAPS call is real, but if the stock falls quickly, there would definitely be a loss at the calculated downside break-even point. Finally, one cannot always roll down into a LEAPS call if trouble develops, because he will be committing himself for an even longer period of time to sell his stock at a lower price than he had originally intended.

Selling Uncovered LEAPS

Uncovered option selling can be a viable strategy, especially if premiums are overpriced. LEAPS options may be sold uncovered with the same margin requirements as short-term options. Of course, the particular characteristics of the long-term option may either help or hinder the uncovered writer, depending on his objective.

Uncovered Put Selling. Naked put selling is being addressed first because, as a strategy, it is equivalent to covered writing, and covered writing was just discussed. Two strategies are equivalent if they have the same profit picture at expiration. Naked put selling and covered call writing are equivalent because they have the profit picture depicted in graph I, Appendix D. Both have limited upside profit potential and large loss exposure to the downside. In general, when two strategies are equivalent, one of the two has certain advantages over the other.

In this case, naked put selling is normally the more advantageous of the two because of the way margin requirements are set. One need not actually invest cash in the sale of a naked put; the margin requirement that is asked for may be satisfied with collateral. This means the naked put writer may use stocks, bonds, T-Bills, or money market funds as collateral. Moreover, the actual amount of collateral that is required is less than the cash or margin investment required to buy stock and sell a call. This means that one could operate his portfolio normally—buying stock, then selling it, putting the proceeds in a Treasury bill, or perhaps buying another stock—without disturbing his naked put position as long as he maintained the collateral requirement.

Consequently, the *strategist* who is buying stock and selling calls should probably be selling naked puts instead. This does not apply to covered writers who are writing against existing stock or who are using the incremental return concept of covered writing, for stock ownership is part of their strategy. However, the strategist who is looking to take in premium to profit if the underlying stock remains relatively unchanged or rises, while having a modicum of downside protection (which is the definition of both naked put writing and covered writing) should be selling naked puts. As an example of this, consider the LEAPS covered write discussed in the previous section.

Example: XYZ is selling at 50. The investor is debating between a 500-share covered write using 2-year LEAPS calls or selling 5 2-year LEAPS puts. The Jan (1994) 50 LEAPS call sells for 8½ and has two years of life, while the Jan (1994) 50 LEAPS put sells for 3½. Further assume that XYZ pays a dividend of $0.25 per quarter.

The net investment required for the covered write is calculated as it was before.

Net Investment Required—Covered Write	
Stock cost (500 shares @ 50)	$25,000
Plus stock commission	+ 300
Less option premiums received	− 4,250
Plus option commissions	+ 100
Net cash investment	$21,150

The collateral requirement for the naked put write is the same as that for any naked equity option: 20% of the stock price, plus the option price, less any out-of-the-money amount, with an absolute minimum requirement of 15% of the stock price.

Collateral Requirement—Naked Put	
20% of Stock Price (.20 × 500 × $50)	$5,000
Plus option premium	1,750
Less out-of-money amount	− 0
Total collateral requirement	$6,750

Note the actual premium received by the naked put seller is $1,750 less commissions of $100, for example, or $1,650. This net premium could be used to reduce the total collateral requirement.

Now one can compare the profitability of the two investments:

Return If Stock over 50 At Expiration	
	Cov. Write
Stock sale (500 @ 50)	$25,000
Less stock commission	− 300
Plus dividends earned until expiration	+ 1,000
Less net investment	− 21,150
Net profit if exercised	$ 4,550
	Naked Put Sale
Net Put premium received	$1,650
Dividends received	0
Net profit	$1,650

Now the returns can be compared, if XYZ is over 50 at expiration of the LEAPS:

Return if XYZ over 50
(net profit/net investment)
Naked put sale: 24.4%
Covered Write: 21.5%

The naked put write has a better rate of return, even before the following fact is considered. The strategist who is using the naked put write does not have to spend the $6,750 collateral requirement in the form of cash. That money can be kept in a Treasury Bill and earn interest over the two years that the put write is in place. Even if the T-Bill were earning only 4% per year, that would increase the overall two-year return for the naked put sale by 8%, to 32.4%. This should make it obvious that *naked put selling is more strategically advantageous than covered call writing.*

Even so, one might rightfully wonder if LEAPS put selling is better than selling shorter-term equity puts. As was the case with covered call writing, the answer depends on what the investor is trying to accomplish. Short-term puts will not bring as much premium into the account. So when they expire, one will be forced to find another suitable put sale to replace it. On the other hand, the LEAPS put sale brings in a larger premium and one does not have to find a replacement until the longer-term LEAPS put expires. The negative aspect to selling the LEAPS puts is that time decay won't help much right away and, even if the stock moves higher (which is ostensibly good for the position), the put won't decline in price by a large amount since the delta of the put is relatively small.

One other factor might enter in the decision regarding whether to use short-term puts or LEAPS puts. Some put writers actually are attempting to buy stock below the market price. That is, they would not mind being assigned on the put they sell, meaning that they would buy stock at a net cost of the striking price less the premium they received from the sale of the put. If they don't get assigned, they get to keep a profit equal to the premium they received when they first sold the put. Generally, a person would only sell puts in this manner on a stock that he had faith in, so that if he was assigned on the put, he would view that as a buying opportunity in the underlying stock. *This strategy does not lend itself well to LEAPS*. Since the LEAPS puts will carry a significant amount of time premium, there is little (if any) chance that the put writer will actually be assigned until the life of the put shortens substantially. This means that it is unlikely that the put writer will become a stock owner via assignment at any time in the near future. Consequently, if one is attempting to write puts in order to eventually buy the common stock when he is assigned, he would be better served to write shorter-term puts.

Uncovered Call Selling

There are very few differences between using LEAPS for naked call selling as opposed to using shorter-term calls, except for the ones that have been discussed already with regard to selling uncovered LEAPS: time value decay occurs more slowly and, if the stock rallies and the naked calls have to be covered, the call writer will normally be paying more time premium that he is used to when he covers the call. Of course, the reason that one is engaged in covered call writing might shed some more light on the use of LEAPS for that purpose.

The overriding reason that most strategists sell naked calls is to collect the time premium before the stock can rise above the striking price. These strategists generally have an opinion about the stock's direction, feeling that it is perhaps trapped in a trading range or even is headed lower over the short term. This strategy does not lend itself well to using LEAPS since it would be difficult to project that the stock would remain below the strike for so long of a period of time.

Short LEAPS Instead of Short Stock. Another reason that naked calls are sold is as a strategy akin to shorting the common stock. In this case, in-the-money calls are sold. The advantages are threefold:

1. The amount of collateral required to sell the call is less than that required to sell stock short
2. One does not have to borrow an option in order to sell it short, although one must borrow common stock in order to sell *it* short

3. An uptick is not required to sell the option, but one is required in order to sell stock short

For these reasons, one might opt to sell an in-the-money call instead of shorting stock.

The profit potentials of the two strategies are different. The short seller of stock has a very large profit potential if the stock declines substantially, while the seller of an in-the-money call can only collect the call premium no matter how far the stock drops. Moreover, the call's price decline will slow as the stock nears the strike. Another way to say this is to say that the delta of the call shrinks from a number close to 1—which means the call mirrors stock movements closely—to something more like 0.50 at the strike, which means that the call is only declining half as fast as the stock.

Another problem that may occur for the call seller is early assignment, a topic that will be addressed shortly. *One should not attempt this strategy if the underlying stock is not borrowable for ordinary short sales.* If the underlying stock is not available for borrowing, it generally means that extraneous forces are at work—perhaps there is a tender offer or exchange offer going on, or there is some form of convertible arbitrage taking place. In any case, if the underlying stock is not borrowable, one should not be deluded into thinking that he can sell an in-the-money call instead and have a worry-free position. In these cases, the call will normally have little or no time premium and may be subject to early assignment. If such assignment does occur, the strategist will become short the stock and, since it is not borrowable, will have to cover the stock. At the least, he will cost himself some commissions by this unprofitable strategy, and at worst, he will have to pay a higher price to buy back the stock as well.

LEAPS calls may help to alleviate this problem. Since they are such long-term calls, they are likely to have some time value premium in them. In-the-money calls that have time value premium are not normally assigned. As an alternative to shorting a stock that is not borrowable, one might try to sell an in-the-money LEAPS call, but *only if it has time value premium remaining.* Just because the call has a long time remaining until expiration does not mean that it *must* have time value premium, as will be seen in the following discussion. Finally, if one *does* sell the LEAPS call, he must realize that if the stock drops, the LEAPS call will not follow it completely. As the stock nears the strike, the amount of time value premium will build up to an even greater level in the LEAPS. Still, the naked call seller would make some profit in that case, and it presents a better alternative than not being able to sell the stock short at all.

Early Assignment. An American-style option is one that can be exercised at any time during its life. All listed equity options, LEAPS included, are of this variety. Thus, any in-the-money option that has been sold may become subject to early assignment. *The clue to whether early assignment is imminent is whether there is time value premium in the option.* If the option has no time value premium—i.e., is trading at parity or at a discount—then assignment may be close at hand. The option writer who does not want to be assigned would want to cover the option when it no longer carries time premium.

LEAPS may be subject to early assignment as well. It is possible, albeit far less likely, that a long-term option would lose all of its time value premium and therefore be subject to early assignment. This would certainly happen if the underlying stock were being taken over and a tender offer were coming to fruition. However, it may also occur because of an impending dividend payment—or more specifically, because the stock is about to go ex-dividend. Recall that the call owner, LEAPS calls included, is not entitled to any dividends paid by the underlying stock. So if the call owner wants the dividend, he exercises his call on the day *before* the stock goes ex-dividend. This makes him an owner of the common stock just in the nick of time to get the dividend.

What economic factors motivate him to exercise the call? If there is *any* time value premium at all in the call, the call holder would be better off selling the call in the open market and then purchasing the stock in the open market as well. In this manner, he would still get the dividend, but he would get a better price for his call when he sold it. If, however, there is no time premium in the call, he does not have to bother with two transactions in the open market—he merely exercises his call in order to buy stock.

All well and good, but what makes the call sell at parity before expiration? It has to do with the arbitrage that is available for any call option. In this case, the arbitrage is not the simple discount arbitrage that was discussed back in Chapter 1 when this topic was covered. Rather, it is a more complicated one that will be discussed in greater detail in Chapter 29. Suffice it to say that if the dividend is larger than the interest that can be earned from a credit balance equal to the striking price, then the time value premium will disappear from the call.

Example: XYZ is a $30 stock and about to go ex-dividend 50 cents. The prevailing short-term interest rate is 5% and there are LEAPS with a striking price of 20.

A 50-cent dividend on a striking price of 20 is an annual dividend rate (on the strike) of 10%. Since short-term rates are much lower than that, arbitrageurs economically cannot pay out 10% for dividends and earn 5% for their credit balances.

In this situation, the LEAPS call would lose its time value premium and would be a candidate for early exercise when the stock goes ex-dividend.

In actual practice, the situation is more complicated than this because the price of the puts comes into play, but this shows the general reasoning that the arbitrageur must go through.

Certain arbitrageurs construct positions that allow them to earn interest on a credit balance equal to the striking price of the call. His position involves being short the underlying stock and being long the call. Thus, when the stock goes ex-dividend, he will owe the dividend. If, however, the amount of the dividend is more than he will earn in interest from his credit balance, he will merely exercise his call to cover his short stock. This action will prevent him from having to pay out the dividend.

The arbitrageur's exercise of the call means that someone is going to be assigned. If you are a writer of the call, it could be you. It is not important to completely understand the arbitrage, for its effect will be reflected in the marketplace in the form of a call trading at parity or a discount. *Thus, even a LEAPS call with a substantial amount of time remaining may be assigned if it is trading at parity.*

Straddle Selling

Straddle selling is equivalent to ratio writing and is a strategy whereby one attempts to sell (overpriced) options in order to produce a range of stock prices within which the option seller can profit. The strategy often involves follow-up action as the stock moves around, and the strategist feels that he must adjust his position in order to prevent large losses. LEAPS puts and calls might be used for this strategy. However, their long-term nature is often not conducive to the aims of straddle selling.

First, consider the effect of time decay. One might normally sell a three-month straddle. If the stock "behaves" and is relatively unchanged after two months have passed, the straddle seller could reasonably expect to have a profit of about 40% of the original straddle price. However, if one had sold a 2-year LEAPS straddle, and the stock were relatively unchanged after two months, he would only have a profit of about 7% of the original sale price. This should not be surprising in light of what has been demonstrated about the decaying of long-term options. It should make the straddle seller somewhat leery of using LEAPS, however, unless he truly feels the options are overpriced.

Second, consider follow-up action. Recall that in Chapter 20, it was shown that the bane of the straddle seller was the whipsaw. A whipsaw occurs when one makes a follow-up protective action on one side (say he does something bullish because the underlying stock is rising and the short calls are losing money), only to have the stock reverse and come crashing back down. Obviously, the more time left until expiration, the more likely that a whipsaw will occur after any follow-up action, and the more expensive it will be since there will be a lot of time value premium left in the options that are being repurchased. This makes LEAPS straddle selling less than attractive.

LEAPS straddles may look expensive because of their large absolute price, and therefore may appear to be attractive straddle sale candidates. However, the price is often justified, and the seller of LEAPS straddles will be fighting sudden stock movements without getting much benefit from the passage of time. The best time to sell LEAPS straddles would be when short-term rates are high and volatilities are high as well (i.e., the options are overpriced). At least, in those cases, the seller will derive some real benefit if rates or volatilities should drop.

SPREADS USING LEAPS

Any of the spread strategies previously discussed can be implemented with LEAPS as well, if one desires. The margin requirements are the same for LEAPS spreads as they are for ordinary equity option spreads. One general category of spread lends itself well to using LEAPS—that of buying a longer-term option and selling a short-term one. Calendar spreads, as well as diagonal spreads, fall into that category.

The combinations are myriad, but the reasoning is the same. One wants to own the option that is not so subject to time decay while simultaneously selling the option that is quite subject to time decay. Of course, since LEAPS are so long-term and therefore so expensive, one is generally taking on a large debit in such a spread and may have substantial risk if the stock performs adversely. Other risks may be present as well. As a means of demonstrating these facts, let us consider a simple bull spread using calls.

Example: The following prices exist in January of 1992:

XYZ: 105
Apr 100 call: $10^1/_2$
Apr 110 call: $5^1/_2$
Jan (1994) 100 call: 26
Jan (1994) 110 call: $21^1/_2$

An investor is considering a bull spread in XYZ and is unsure of whether to use the short-term calls, the LEAPS calls, or a mixture. These are his choices:

Short-term bull spread:	Buy Apr 100 @ 10½
	Sell Apr 110 @ 5½
	Net Debit: $500
Diagonal bull spread:	Buy Jan ('94) 100 @ 26
	Sell Apr 110 @ 5½
	Net Debit: $2,050
LEAPS bull spread:	Buy Jan ('94) 100 @ 26
	Sell Jan ('94) 110 @ 21½
	Net Debit: $450

Notice that the debit paid for the LEAPS spread is slightly less than that of the short-term bull spread. This means that they have approximately the same profit potential at their respective expiration dates. However, the strategist is more concerned with how these compare directly with each other. The obvious point in time to do this comparison is when the short-term options expire.

Figure 25-7 shows the profitability of these three positions *at April 1992 expiration*. It was assumed that all of the following were the same

FIGURE 25-7.
Bull spread comparison at April 1992 expiration.

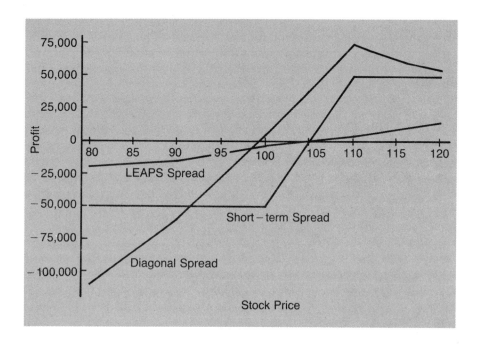

in April as they had been in January: volatility, short-term rates, and dividend payout.

Note that the short-term bull spread has the familiar profit graph from Chapter 7, making its maximum profit over 110 and taking its maximum loss below 100. (see Table 25-4.)

The LEAPS spread doesn't generate much of either a profit or loss in only three months time. Even if XYZ rises to 120, the LEAPS bull spread will only have a $150 profit. Conversely, if XYZ falls to 80, the spread only loses about $200. This price action is very typical for long-term bull spreads when both options have a significant amount of time premium remaining in them.

The diagonal spread is different, however. Typically, the maximum profit potential of a bull spread is the difference in the strikes less the initial debit paid. For this diagonal spread, that would be a $1,000 minus $2,050, a loss! Obviously this simple formula is not applicable to diagonal spreads because the purchased option still has time value premium when the written option expires. The profit graph shows that indeed the diagonal spread is the most bullish of the three. It makes its best profit at the strike of the written option—a standard procedure for any spread—and that profit is greater than either of the other two spreads *at April 1992 expiration* (under the significant assumption that volatility and interest rates are unchanged). If XYZ trades higher than 110, the diagonal spread will lose some of its profit, and, in fact, if XYZ were to trade at a *very* high price, the diagonal spread would actually have a loss (see Table 25-4). Whenever the purchased LEAPS call loses its time value premium, the diagonal spread will not perform as well.

If the common stock drops in price, the diagonal spread has the greatest risk in dollar terms but not in percentage terms, because it has the largest initial debit. If XYZ falls to 80 in three months, the spread will lose about $1,100, just over half the initial $2,050 debit. Obviously, the

TABLE 25-4.
Bull Spread Comparison At April '92 Expiration.

Stock Price	Short-Term	Diagonal	LEAPS
80	− 500	− 1,100	− 200
90	− 500	− 600	− 150
100	− 500	50	− 25
110	500	750	50
120	500	550	150
140	500	150	250
160	500	− 50	350
180	500	− 350	450

short-term spread would have lost 100% of its initial debit, which is only $500, at that same point in time.

The diagonal spread presents an opportunity to earn more money if the underlying common is near the strike of the written option when the written option expires. However, if the common moves a great deal in either direction, the diagonal spread is the worst of the three. This means that the diagonal spread strategy is a neutral strategy: one wants the underlying common to remain near the written strike until the near-term option expires. This is a true statement even if the diagonal spread is under the guise of a bullish spread, as in the previous example.

Many traders are fond of buying LEAPS and selling an out-of-the-money near-term call as a hedge. Be careful about doing this. If the under-lying common rises too fast and/or interest rates fall and/or volatility decreases, this could be a poor strategy. There is really nothing quite as psychologically damaging as being right about the stock, but being in the wrong option strategy and therefore losing money. Consider the above examples. Ostensibly, the spreader was bullish on XYZ—that's why he chose bull spreads. If XYZ became a wildly bullish stock and rose from 100 to 180 in three months, the diagonal spreader would have lost money. He couldn't have been happy—no one would be. This is something to keep in mind when diagonalizing a LEAPS spread.

Note that a diagonal spread could even be considered as a substitute for a covered write in some special cases. It was shown that LEAPS calls can sometimes be used as a substitute for the common stock, with the investor placing the difference between the cost of the LEAPS call and the cost of the stock in the bank (or in T-Bills). Suppose that an investor is a covered writer—buying stock and selling relatively short-term calls against it. If that investor were to make a LEAPS call substitution for his stock, he would then have a diagonal bull spread. Such a diagonal spread would probably have less risk than the one described above since the investor presumably chose the LEAPS substitution because it was "cheap." Still, the potential pitfalls of the diagonal bull spread would apply to this situation as well. Thus, if one is a covered writer, this does not necessarily mean that he can substitute LEAPS calls for the long stock without taking care. The resulting position may not resemble a covered write as much as he thought it would.

Backspreads. LEAPS may be applied to other popular forms of di-agonal spreads, such as the one in which *in-the-money, near-term options are sold, and a greater quantity of longer-term (LEAPS) at- or out-of-the-money calls are bought* (this was referred to as a diagonal backspread in Chapter 14). This is an excellent strategy, and LEAPS may be used as the long option in the spread. Recall that the object of the spread is for the stock to be volatile, particularly to the upside if calls are used. If that doesn't happen, and the stock declines instead, at least the premium captured from the in-the-money sale will be a gain to offset against the loss suffered on the longer-term calls that were purchased. The strategy can be established with puts as well, in which case the spreader would want the underlying stock to fall dramatically while the spread was in place.

Without going into as much detail as in the examples above, the diagonal backspreader should realize that he is going to have a significant debit in the spread and could lose a significant portion of it should the underlying stock fall a great deal in price. To the upside, his LEAPS calls will retain some time value premium and will move quite closely with the underlying common stock. Thus, he does not have to buy as many LEAPS as he might think, in order to have a neutral spread.

Example: XYZ is at 105 and a spreader wants to establish a backspread. Recall that the quantity of options to use in a neutral strategy is determined by dividing the deltas of the two options. The following prices and deltas exist:

XYZ: 105 in January 1992		
Option	*Price*	*Delta*
Apr 100	8	0.75
Jul 110	5	0.50
Jan (1994) 110	15	0.60

Two backspreads are available with these options. In the first, one would sell the April 100s and buy the July 110s. He would be selling a 3-month call and buying 6-month calls. The neutral ratio is 0.75/0.50 or 3 to 2; that is, 3 calls are to be bought for every two sold. Thus a neutral spread would be:

Buy 6 July 110 calls
Sell 4 April 100 calls

As a second alternative, he might use the LEAPS as the long side of the spread; he would still sell the April 100s as the short side of the spread. In this case, his neutral ratio would be 0.75/0.60 or 5 to 4. The resulting neutral spread would be:

| Buy 5 Jan (1994) LEAPS calls |
| Sell 4 April 100 calls |

Thus, a neutral backspread involving LEAPS involves buying fewer calls than a neutral backspread involving a 6-month option on the long side. This is because the delta of the LEAPS call is larger. The significant point here is that because of the time value retention of the LEAPS call, even when the stock moves higher, it is not necessary to buy as many. If one does not use the deltas, but merely figures that 3 to 2 is a good ratio for any diagonal backspread, then he will be overly bullish if he uses LEAPS. That could cost him if the underlying stock declines.

Calendar Spreads. LEAPS may also be used in calendar spreads— spreads in which the striking price of the longer-term option purchased and the shorter-term option sold are the same. The calendar spread is a neutral strategy, wherein the spreader wants the underlying stock to be as close as possible to the striking price when the near-term option expires. A calendar spread has risk if the stock moves too far away from the striking price (see Chapters 9 and 22). Purchasing a LEAPS call increases that risk in terms of dollars, not percentage, because of the larger debit that one must spend for the spread.

Simplistically, calendar spreads are established with equal quantities of options bought and sold. This is often not a neutral strategy in the true sense. As was shown in the chapter on call calendar spreads, one may want to use the deltas of the two options to establish a truly neutral calendar spread, particularly if the stock is not initially right at the striking price. Out-of-the-money, one would sell more calls than he is buying. Conversely, in-the-money, one would buy more calls than he is selling. Both strategies statistically have merit and are attractive. When using LEAPS deltas to construct the neutral spread, one need generally buy fewer calls than he might think because of the higher delta of a LEAPS call. This is the same phenomenon described in the previous example of a diagonal backspread.

SUMMARY

LEAPS are nothing more than long-term options. They are useable in a wide variety of strategies in the same way that any option would be. Their margin and investment requirements are similar to those of the more familiar equity options. Both LEAPS puts and calls are traded, and there is a secondary market for them as well.

There are certain differences between the prices of LEAPS and shorter-term options, but the greatest is the relatively large effect that interest rates and dividends have on the price of LEAPS because LEAPS are long-term options. Increases in interest rates will cause LEAPS to increase in price, while increases in dividend payout will cause LEAPS *calls* to decrease in price and LEAPS *puts* to increase in price. As usual, volatility has a major effect on the price of an option, and LEAPS are no exception. Even small changes in the volatility of the underlying common stock can cause large price differences in a two-year option. The rate of decay due to time is much smaller for LEAPS since they are long-term options. Finally, the delta of LEAPS calls is larger than for short-term calls; conversely, the delta of LEAPS puts is smaller.

Several common strategies lend themselves well to the usage of LEAPS. LEAPS may be used as a stock substitute if the cash not invested in the stock is instead deposited in a CD or T-Bill. LEAPS puts can be bought as protection for common stock. Speculative option buyers will appreciate the low rate of time decay of LEAPS. LEAPS calls can be written against common stock, thereby creating a covered write, although the sale of naked LEAPS puts is probably a better strategy in most cases. Spread strategies with LEAPS may be viable as well, but the spreader should carefully consider the ramifications of buying a long-term option and sell a shorter-term one against it. If the underlying stock moves a great distance quickly, the spread strategy may not perform as expected.

Overall, LEAPS are not really all that different from the shorter-term options to which traders and investors have become accustomed. Once these investors become familiar with the way these long-term options are affected by the various factors that determine the price of an option, they will consider LEAPS as an integral part of their strategic arsenal.

Chapter 26

PERCS

A Preferred Equity Redemption Cumulative Stock (PERCS) is not a listed option product but is rather a type of stock. It will be demonstrated that PERCS have an option imbedded within them, and as such are really very similar to a covered call write. PERCS are not currently available on very many stocks, although that may change as time passes.

A PERCS is a series of preferred stock issued by an existing corporation. At the time of issuance, the PERCS and the common stock are usually about the same price. The PERCS pays a higher dividend than the common stock, which may pay no dividend at all. If the underlying common should decline in price, the PERCS should decline by a lesser amount because the higher dividend payout will provide a yield floor, as any preferred stock does.

There is a limited life span with PERCS that is spelled out in the stock's prospectus at the time it is issued. Typically, that life span is about three years. At the end of that time, the PERCS becomes ordinary common stock. So far, this isn't too complicated, but it seems rather boring.

The tricky part is the following feature: A PERCS may be called at any time by the issuing corporation if the company's common stock exceeds a predetermined call price. In other words, this PERCS stock is callable. The call price is normally higher than the price where the common is trading when the PERCS is issued.

What one has then, if he owns a PERCS, is a position that will eventually become common stock unless it is called away. In order to compensate him for the fact that it might be called away, the owner receives a higher dividend. What if one substitutes the word "premium" for "higher dividend?" Then the last statement reads: *in order to compensate him for the fact that it might be called away, the owner receives a premium.* This is exactly the definition of a covered call option write. Moreover, it is an out-of-the-money covered write of a long-term call option, since the call price of the PERCS is akin to a striking price and is higher than the initial stock price.

Example: XYZ is selling at $35 per share. XYZ common stock pays $1 a year in dividends. The company decides to issue a PERCS.

The PERCS will have a three-year life and will be callable at $39. Moreover, the PERCS will pay an annual dividend of $2.50.

The PERCS annual dividend rate is 7% as compared to 2.8% for the common stock.

If XYZ were to rise to 39 in exactly three years, the PERCS would be called. The total return that the PERCS holder would have made over that time would be:

Stock price appreciation (39-35):	4
Dividends over 3 years:	7.50
Total gain	11.50
Total return:	11.50/25 = 32.9%
Annualized Return:	32.9%/3 = 11%

If the PERCS were called at an earlier time, the annualized return might be even higher.

CALL FEATURE

The company will most likely call the PERCS if the common is above the call price for a short period of time. The prospectus for the PERCS will describe any requirements regarding the call. A typical one might be that the common must close above the call price for five consecutive trading days. If it does, then the company may call the PERCS, although it does not have to. The decision to call or not is strictly the company's. The PERCS holder has no choice in the matter of when or if to call. This is the same situation in which the writer of a covered call finds himself. He cannot control when the exercise will occur, although there are often clues, including the disappearance of time value premium in the written listed call option. The PERCS holder is more in the dark, because he cannot actually see the separate price of the imbedded call within the PERCS. Still, as will be shown later, he may be able to use several clues to determine if a call is imminent.

Most PERCS may be called either for cash or common stock. This does not change the profitability from the strategist's standpoint. He either receives cash in the amount of the call price, or the same dollar amount of common stock. The only difference between the two is that, in order to completely close his position, he would have to sell out any common stock received via the call feature. If he had received cash instead, he wouldn't have to bother with this final stock transaction.

In the case of most PERCS the call feature is more complicated than that presented in the example above. Recall that the company that issued the PERCS can call it at any time during the three years as long as the common is above the call price. The holder of the XYZ PERCS in the example above would not be pleased to find that the PERCS was called before he had received any of the higher dividends that the PERCS pays. Therefore, in order to give a PERCS holder essentially the same return no matter when the PERCS is called, there is a "sliding scale" of call prices.

At issuance, the call price will be the highest. Then it will drop to a slightly lower level after some of the dividends have been paid (perhaps after the first year). This lowering of the call price continues as more dividends are paid, until it finally reaches the final call price at maturity. The PERCS holder should not be confused by this sliding scale of call prices. *The sliding call feature is designed to ensure that the PERCS holder is compensated for not receiving all his "promised" dividends if the PERCS should be called prior to maturity.*

Example: As before, XYZ issues a PERCS when the common is at 35. The PERCS pays an annual dividend of $2.50 per share as compared to $1 per share on the common stock. The PERCS has a final call price of 39 dollars per share in three years.

If XYZ stock should undergo a sudden price advance and rise dramatically in a very short period of time, it is possible that the PERCS could be called before any dividends are paid at all. In order to compensate the PERCS holder for such an occurrence, the *initial call price* would be set at 43½ per share. That is, the PERCS can't be called unless XYZ trades to a price over 43½ dollars per share. Notice that the difference between the eventual call price of 39 and the initial call price of 43½ is 4½ points, which is also the amount of additional dividends that the PERCS would pay over the three year period. The PERCS pays $2.50 per year and the common $1 per year, so the difference is $1.50 per year, or $4.50 over three years.

Once the PERCS dividends begin to be paid, the call price will be reduced to reflect that fact. For example, after one year, the call price would be 42, reflecting the fact that if the PERCS were not called until a year had passed, the PERCS holder would be losing $3 of additional dividends as compared to the common stock ($1.50 per year for the remaining two years). Thus the call price after one year is set at the eventual call price, 39, plus the $3 of potential dividend loss, for a total call price of 42.

This example shows how the company uses the sliding call price to compensate the PERCS holder for potential dividend loss if the PERCS is called before the three-year time to maturity has elapsed. Thus, the PERCS holder will make the same *dollars* of profit—dividends and price appreciation combined—no matter when the PERCS is called. In the case of XYZ PERCS in the above example, that total dollar profit is $11.50 (see the prior example). Notice that his annualized rate of return would be much higher if he were called prior to the eventual maturity date.

One final point: the call price slides on a scale as set forth in the prospectus for the PERCS. It may be every time a dividend is paid, but more likely it will be daily! That is, the present worth of the remaining dividends is added to the final call price to calculate the sliding call price daily. Do not be overwhelmed by this feature. Remember that it just a means of giving the PERCS holder his entire "dividend premium" if the PERCS is called before maturity.

For the remainder of this chapter, the call price of the PERCS will be referred to as the redemption price. Since much of the rest of this chapter will be concerned with discussing the fact that a PERCS is related to a call *option*, there could be some confusion when the word "call" is used. In some cases "call" could refer to the price at which the PERCS can be called; in other cases, it could refer to a call option—either listed or one that is imbedded within the PERCS. Hence, the word redemptional will be used to refer to the action and price at which the issuing company may call the PERCS.

A PERCS IS A COVERED CALL WRITE

It was stated earlier that a PERCS is like a covered write. However, that has not yet been proven. It is known that any two strategies are equivalent if they have the same profit potential. Thus, if one can show that the profitability of owning a PERCS is the same as that of having established a covered call write, then one can conclude that they are equivalent.

Example: For the purposes of this example, suppose that there is a 3-year listed call option with striking price 39 available to be sold on XYZ common stock. Also, assume that there is a PERCS on XYZ that has a redemption price of 39 in three years. The following prices exist:

XYZ common: 35
XYZ PERCS: 35
3-year call on XYZ common: 4½

First, examine the XYZ covered call write's profitability from buying 100 XYZ and selling one call. It was initially established at a debit of 30½ (35 less the 4½ received from the call sale). The common pays $1 per year in dividends, for a total of $3 over the life of the position.

XYZ Price in 3 Years	Price of a 3-Year Call	Pft/Loss on Securities	Tot Pft/Loss Incl. Dividend
25	0	− $550	− $250
30	0	− 50	+ 250
35	0	+ 450	+ 750
39	0	+ 850	+ 1,150
45	6	+ 850	+ 1,150
50	11	+ 850	+ 1,150

This is the typical picture of the total return from a covered write— potential losses on the downside with profit potential limited above the striking price of the written call.

Now look at the profitability of buying the PERCS at 35 and holding it for three years (assume that it is not called prior to maturity). The PERCS holder will earn a total of $750 in dividends over that time period.

XYZ Price in 3 years	Pft/loss on PERCS	Tot Pft/Loss incl. dividend
25	− $1,000	− $250
30	− 500	+ 250
35	0	+ 750
> = 39	+ 400	+ 1,150

This is exactly the same profitability as the covered call write. *Therefore, it can be concluded with certainty that a PERCS is equivalent to a covered call write.* Note that the PERCS potential early redemption feature does not change the truth of this statement. The early redemption possibility merely allows the PERCS holder to receive the same total dollars at an earlier point in time if the PERCS is demanded prior to maturity. The covered call writer could theoretically be facing a similar situation if the written call option were assigned before expiration: he would make the same total profit, only he would realize it in a shorter period of time.

The PERCS is like a covered write of a call option with striking price equal to the redemption price of the PERCS, except that the holder does not receive a call option premium, but rather receives additional dividends. In essence, the PERCS has a call option imbedded within it. The value of the imbedded call is really the value of the additional dividends to be paid between the current date and maturity.

The buyer of a PERCS is, in effect, selling a call option and buying common stock. He should have some idea of whether or not he is selling the option at a reasonably fair price. The next section of this chapter addresses the problem of valuing the call option that is imbedded in the PERCS.

PRICE BEHAVIOR

The way that a PERCS price is often discussed is with relationship to the common stock. One may hear that the PERCS is trading at the same price as the common or at a premium or discount to the common. As an option strategist who understands covered call writing, it should be a simple matter to picture how the PERCS price will relate to the common price.

First, consider the out-of-the-money situation. *If the underlying common declines in price, the PERCS will not decline as fast* because the additional dividends will provide yield support. The PERCS will therefore trade at a higher price than the common. However, as the maturity date nears and the remaining number of additional dividends dwindles to a small amount, then the PERCS price and the common price will converge.

The opposite effect occurs if the underlying common moves higher. *The PERCS will trade at a lower price than the common when the common trades above the issue price.* In fact, since there is a redemption price on the PERCS, it will not trade higher than the redemption price. The common, however, has no such restriction so it could continue to trade at prices significantly higher than the PERCS does.

These points are illustrated in Figure 26-1, which contains the price curves of two PERCS, one at issuance thus having three years remaining, and the other with just 6 months remaining until the maturity of the PERCS. For purposes of comparison, it was assumed that there is no sliding redemption feature involved. Several significant points can be made from the figure. First, notice that the PERCS and the common tend to sell at approximately the same price at the point labeled "I." This would

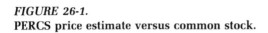

FIGURE 26-1.
PERCS price estimate versus common stock.

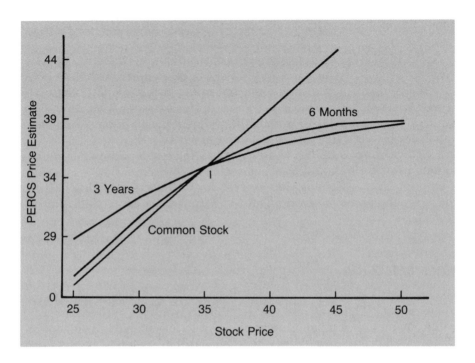

be the price at which the PERCS are issued. This issue price must be below the redemption price of the PERCS. More will be said later about how this price is determined.

Another observation that can be made from the figure is that the PERCS pricing curves level off at the redemption price. They cannot sell for more than that price.

Now look on the left hand side of the figure. Notice that the more time remaining until maturity, the more the PERCS will trade higher than the common stock. This is because of the extra dividends that the PERCS pay. Obviously, the PERCS with three years until maturity has the potential to pay more dividends than the one with three months remaining, so the 3-year PERCS will sell for more than the 6-month PERCS when the common is below the issue price. Since either PERCS pays more dividends than the common, they both trade for higher prices than the common.

When the common trades *above* the issue price (point "I"), the opposite is true. The 6-month PERCS trades for a slightly higher price than the 3-year PERCS, but both sell for significantly less than the common which has no limit on its potential price.

One other observation can be made regarding the situation where the common trades well below the issue price: after the last additional dividend has been paid by the PERCS, it will trade for the same price as the common in that situation.

Viewed strictly as a security, a PERCS may not appear all that attractive to some investors. It has much—but not all—of the downside risk of the common stock, and not nearly the upside potential. It does provide a better dividend, however, so if the common is relatively unchanged from the issue price when the PERCS matures, the PERCS holder will have come out ahead. If this description of the PERCS does not appeal to you, then neither should covered call writing, for it is the same strategy; a call option premium is merely substituted for the higher dividend payout.

PERCS STRATEGIES

Since the PERCS is equivalent to a covered write, strategies that have covered writes as part of their makeup are amenable to having PERCS as part of their makeup as well. Covered writing is part of ratio writing. Other modifications to the covered writing strategy itself, such as the protected covered write, can also be applied to the PERCS.

Protecting the PERCS with Listed Options

The safest way to protect the PERCS holding with listed options is to buy an out-of-the-money put. The resultant position—long PERCS and long put—is a protected covered write. The long put prevents large losses on the downside, but it costs the PERCS holder something. He won't make as much from his extra dividend payout because he is spending money for the listed put. Still, he may want the downside comfort.

Once one realizes that a PERCS is equivalent to a covered write, he can easily extend that equivalence to other positions as well. For example, it is known that a covered call write is equivalent to the sale of a naked put. Thus, *owning a PERCS is equivalent to the sale of a naked put.* Obviously, the easiest way to hedge a naked put is to buy another put, preferably out-of-the-money, as protection.

Do not be deluded into thinking that selling a listed call against the PERCS is a safe way of hedging. Such a call option sale does add a modicum of downside protection, but it exposes the upside to large losses and therefore introduces a potential risk into the position. It is really a ratio write. The subject is covered later in this chapter.

Removing the Redemption Feature

At issuance, the imbedded call is a three-year call, so it is not possible to exactly duplicate the PERCS strategy in the listed market. However, as the PERCS nears maturity there will be listed calls that closely approximate the call that is imbedded in the PERCS. Consequently one may be able to use the listed call or the underlying stock to his advantage.

If one were to buy a listed call with features similar to the imbedded call in a PERCS that he owned, he would essentially be creating long common stock. Not that one would necessarily need to go to all that trouble to create long common stock, but it might provide opportunities for arbitrageurs.

In addition, it might appeal to the PERCS holder if the common stock has declined and the imbedded call is now inexpensive. If one covers the equivalent of the imbedded call in the listed market, he would be able to more fully participate in upside participation if the common were to rally later. This is not always a profitable strategy, however. It may be better to just sell out the PERCS and buy the common if one expects a large rally.

Example: XYZ issued a PERCS some time ago. It has a redemption price of 39; the common pays a dividend of $1 per year, while the PERCS pay $2.50 per year.

XYZ has fallen to a price of 30 and the PERCS holder thinks a rally may be imminent. He knows that the imbedded call in the PERCS must be relatively inexpensive since it is 9 points out of the money (the PERCS is redeemable at 39, while the common is currently 30). If he could buy back this call, he could participate more fully in the upward potential of the stock.

Suppose that there is a 1-year LEAPS call on XYZ with a striking price of 40. If one were to buy that call, he would essentially be removing the redemption feature from his PERCS.

The following prices exist in January, 1992:

XYZ Common: 30
XYZ PERCS: 31
XYZ Jan (1993) 40 LEAPS call: 2

If one buys this LEAPS call and holds it until maturity of the PERCS one year from now, the profit picture of the long PERCS plus long call position will be the following:

XYZ Price in Jan 1993	PERCS Price	Jan 40 LEAPS	Total Value of long PERCS + long LEAPS
25	25	0	25
30	30	0	30
35	35	0	35
40	39	0	39
45	39	5	44
50	39	10	49

Thus, the PERCS + long call position is worth almost exactly what the common stock is after one year. The PERCS holder has regained his upside profit potential.

What did it cost him to reacquire his upside? He paid out 2 points for the call, thereby more than negating his $1.50 dividend advantage over the course of the year (the common pays a $1 dividend; the PERCS $2.50). Thus, it may not actually be worth the bother. In fact, notice that if the PERCS holder really wanted to reacquire his upside profit potential, he would have been better off selling his PERCS at 31 and buying the common at 30. If he had done this, he would have taken in 1 point from the sale and purchase, which is slightly smaller than the $1.50 dividend he is forsaking. In either case, he must relinquish his dividend advantage and then some in order to reacquire his upside profit potential. This seems fair, however, for there must be *some* cost involved with reacquiring the upside.

Remember that an arbitrageur might be able to find a trade involving these situations. He could buy a PERCS, sell the common short, and buy a listed call. If there were price discrepancies, he could profit. It is actions such as these that are required to keep prices in their proper relationship.

Changing the Redemption Price of the PERCS

When covered writing was discussed as a strategy, it was shown that the writer may want to buy back the call that was written and sell another one at a different strike. If the action results in a lower strike, it is known as "rolling down"; if it results in a higher strike, it is "rolling up."

This rolling action changes the profit potential of the position. If one rolls down, he gets more downside protection, but his upside is even more limited than it previously was. Still, if he is worried about the stock falling lower, this may be a proper action to take. Conversely, if the common is rallying, and the covered writer is more bullish on the stock, he can roll up in order to increase his upside profit potential. Of course, by rolling up, he creates more downside risk if the common stock should suddenly reverse direction and fall.

The PERCS holder can achieve the same results as the covered writer. He can effectively roll his redemption price down or up if he so chooses. His reasons for doing so would be substantially the same as the covered writer's. For example, if the common were dropping in price, the PERCS holder might become worried that his extra dividend income would not be enough to protect him in the case of further decline. Therefore, he would want to take in even more premium in exchange for allowing himself to be called away at a lower price.

Example: XYZ issued PERCS when both were trading at 35. Now, XYZ has fallen to 30 with only a year remaining until maturity and the PERCS holder is nervous about further declines. He could, of course, merely sell his stock, but suppose that he prefers to keep it and attempt to modify his position to more accurately reflect his attitude about future price movements.

The following prices exist in January 1992:

XYZ Common: 30
XYZ PERCS: 31
XYZ Jan (1993) 40 call: 2
XYZ Jan (1993) 35 call: 4

If he *Buys the Jan 40 call and sells the Jan 35 call* he will have accomplished his purpose. This is the same as selling a call bear spread. As shown in the previous example, buying the Jan 40 call is essentially the same as removing the redemption feature from the PERCS. Then selling the Jan 35 call will reinstate a redemption feature at 35. Thus, the PERCS holder has taken in a premium of two points and has lowered the redemption price.

If XYZ is below 35 when the options expire, he will have an extra $200 profit from the option trades. If XYZ rallies and is above 35 at expiration, he will be effectively called away at 35 instead of at the original demand price of 39.

The conclusion that can be drawn is that *in order to roll down the redemption feature of a PERCS, one must sell a vertical call* spread. In a similar manner, if he wanted to roll the strike *up*, he would *buy* a vertical call spread. Using the above example again, one would still buy the Jan 40 call (this effectively removes the redemption feature of the PERCS) and would then sell a Jan 45 call in order to raise the redemption price. Thus, *buying a vertical call spread raises the effective demand price of a PERCS.*

There is nothing magic about this strategy. Covered writers use it all the time. It merely evolves from thinking of a PERCS as a covered write.

Selling a Call Against a Long PERCS is a Ratio Write

It is obvious to the strategist that if one owns a PERCS and also sells a call against it, he does not have a covered write. The PERCS is *already* a covered write. What he has when he sells another call is a *ratio write*. His equivalent position is long the common and short two calls.

There is nothing inherently wrong with this, as long as the PERCS holder understands that he has exposed himself to potential large upside losses by selling the extra call. If the common stock were to rally heavily, the PERCS would stop rising when it reached its redemption price. However, the additional call that was sold would continue to rise in price, possibly inflicting large losses if no defensive action were taken.

The same strategies that apply to ratio writing or straddle writing would have to be used by someone who owns a PERCS and sells a call against it. He could buy common stock if the position were in danger on the upside, or he could roll the call(s) up.

A difference between ordinary ratio writing and selling a listed call option against a PERCS is that the imbedded call in the PERCS may be a very long-term call (up to three years). The listed call probably wouldn't be of that duration. So the ratio writer in this case has two different expiration dates for his options. This does not change the overall strategy, but it does mean that the imbedded long-term call will not diminish much in price due to the passage of time until the PERCS is nearer maturity.

Neutrality is normally an important consideration for a ratio writer. If one is long a PERCS and short a listed call he is by definition a ratio writer, so he should be interested in neutrality. The key to determining one's neutrality, of course, is to use the delta of the option. In the case of the PERCS stock, one would have to use the delta of the imbedded call.

Example: An investor is long 1,000 shares of XYZ PERCS maturing in two years. He thinks XYZ is stuck in a trading range and does not expect much volatility in the near future. Thus, a ratio write appeals to him. How many calls should he sell in order to create a neutral position against his 1,000 shares?

First, he needs to compute the delta of the imbedded option in the PERCS, and therefore the delta of the PERCS itself. *The delta of a PERCS is not 1.00, as is the delta of common stock.*

Assume the XYZ PERCS matures in two years. It is redeemable at 39 at that time. XYZ common is currently trading at 33. The delta of a two-year call with striking price 39 and common stock at 33 is can be calculated (the dividends, short-term interest rate, and volatility all play a part). Suppose that the delta of such an option is 0.30. Then the delta of the PERCS can be computed:

$$PERCS \ delta = 1.00 - delta \ of \ imbedded \ call$$

$$= 1.00 - 0.30 = 0.70 \ in \ this \ example.$$

Assume the following data is known:

Security	Price	Delta
XYZ Common	33	1.00
XYZ PERCS	34	0.70(!)
XYZ Oct 35 call	2	0.35

Being long 1,000 PERCS shares is the equivalent of being long 700 shares of common (ESP = 1,000 × 0.70 = 700). In order to properly hedge that ESP with the Oct 35 call, one would need to sell 20 Oct 35 calls.

$$Quantity \ to \ sell = ESP \ of \ PERCS/ESP \ of \ Oct \ 35 \ call$$

$$= 700/(100 \ shares \ per \ option \times 0.35)$$

$$= 700/35 = 20$$

Thus, the position—long 1,000 PERCS, short 20 Oct 35 calls—is a neutral one and it is a ratio write.

One may not want to have such a steep ratio since the result of this example is the equivalent of being long 1,000 common and short 30 calls in total (10 are imbedded in the long PERCS). Consequently, he could look at other options—perhaps writing in-the-money October calls—that have higher deltas and won't require so many to be sold in order to produce a neutral position.

To remain neutral, one would have to keep computing the deltas of the options—both listed and imbedded—as time passes because stock movements or the passage of time could change the deltas and therefore affect the neutrality of the position.

Hedging PERCS With Common Stock

Some traders may want to use the common stock to hedge the purchase of PERCS. These would normally be market makers or block traders who acquire the PERCS in order to provide liquid markets or because they think they are slightly mispriced. The simplest way for these traders to hedge their long PERCS would be with common stock.

This strategy might also apply to an individual who holds PERCS if he wants to hedge them from a potential price decline, but does not actually want to sell them (for tax reasons, perhaps).

In either case, *it is not correct to sell 100 shares of common against each 100 shares of PERCS owned.* That is not a true hedge. In fact, what one accomplishes by doing that is to create a naked call option. A PERCS is a covered write; if one sells 100 shares of common stock from a covered write, he is left with a naked call. This could cause large losses if the common rallies.

Rather, *the proper way to hedge the PERCS with common stock is to calculate the equivalent stock position of the PERCS* and hedge with the calculated amount of common stock. The above example showed how to calculate the ESP of the PERCS—one must calculate the delta of the imbedded call option, which may be a long-term one. Then the delta of the PERCS can be computed, and the equivalent stock position can be determined.

Example: Using the same prices from the example above, one can see how much stock he would have to sell in order to properly hedge his PERCS holding of 1,000 shares.

Assume XYZ is trading at 33, and the PERCS has two years until maturity. If the PERCS is redeemable at 39 at maturity, one can determine that the delta of the imbedded option is 0.30 (see previous example).

$$\text{Then the Delta of the PERCS} = 1 - \text{delta of imbedded call}$$

$$= 1 - 0.30$$

$$= 0.70$$

Hence, the equivalent stock position of 1,000 PERCS is 700 shares (1,000 × 0.70).

Consequently, one would sell short 700 shares of XYZ common in order to hedge this long holding of 1,000 PERCS.

This is not a static situation. If XYZ changes in price, the delta of the imbedded option will change as well, so that the proper amount of stock to sell as a hedge will change. The deltas will change with the passage of time as well. A change in volatility of the common stock can affect the deltas, too. Consequently, *one must constantly recalculate the amount of stock needed to hedge the PERCS.*

What one has actually created by selling some common stock against his long PERCS holding is another ratio write. Consider the fact that being long 1,000 PERCS shares is the equivalent of being long 1,000 common and short 10 imbedded, long-term calls. If one sells 700 common, he will be left with an equivalent position of long 300 common and short 10 imbedded calls—a ratio write.

The person who chooses to hedge his PERCS holding with a partial sale of common stock, as in the example above, would do well to visualize the resulting hedged position as a neutral ratio write. Doing so will help him to realize that there is both upside and downside risk if the underlying common stock should become very volatile (ratio writes have risk on both the upside and the downside). However, if the common remains fairly stable, the value of the imbedded call will decrease and he will profit. If it is a long-term imbedded call (that is, if there is a long time until maturity of the PERCS), the rate of time decay will be quite small, however, so the hedger should realize that fact as well.

In summary, the sale of some common against a long holding of PERCS is a viable way to hedge the position. When one hedges in this manner, he must continue to monitor the position and would be best served by viewing it is a ratio write at all times.

Selling PERCS Short

Can it make sense to sell PERCS short? The payout of the large dividend seems to be a deterrent against such a short sale. However, if one views it as the opposite of a long-term, out-of-the-money covered write, it may make some sense.

A covered write is long stock, short call; it is also equivalent to being long a PERCS. The opposite of that is short stock, long call—a synthetic put. Therefore *a long put is the equivalent of being short a PERCS*. Profit graph H in Appendix E shows the profit potential of being short stock and long a call. There is large downside profit potential, but the upside risk is limited by the presence of the long call. The amount of premium paid for the long call is a wasting asset. If the stock does not decline in price, the long call premium may be lost, causing an overall profit.

Shorting a PERCS would result in a position with those same qualities. The upside risk is limited by the redemption feature of the PERCS. The downside profit potential is large because the PERCS will trade down in price if the common stock does. The problem for the short seller of the PERCS is that he has to pay a lot for the imbedded call that affords him the protection from upside risk. The actual price that he has to pay is the dividends that he, as a short seller, must pay out. But this can also be thought of as having purchased a long-term call out-of-the-money as protection for a short sale of common stock. The long-term call is bound to be expensive since it has a great deal of time premium remaining; moreover, the fact that it is out-of-the-money means that one is also assuming the price risk from the current common price up to the strike of the call. Hence, this out-of-the-money amount plus the time value premium of the imbedded call can add up to a substantial amount.

This discussion mainly pertains to shorting a PERCS near its issuance price and date. However, one is free to short PERCS at any time. They may be a more attractive short when they have less time remaining until their maturity date, or when the underlying common is closer to the redemption price.

Overall, one would not normally expect the short sale of a PERCS to be vastly superior to a synthetic put constructed with listed options. Arbitrageurs would be expected to eliminate such a price discrepancy if one exists. However, if such a situation does present itself, the short seller of the PERCS should realize he has a position that is the equivalent of owning a put, and plan his strategy accordingly.

Determining the Issue Price

An investor might wonder how it is always possible for the PERCS and the common to be at the same price at the issue date. In fact, there are two variables that the issuing company has to work with that can ensure that the common price and the PERCS issue price are the same. One variable is the amount of the additional dividend that the PERCS will pay. The other is the redemption price of the PERCS. By altering these two items, the value of the covered write (i.e., the PERCS) can be made to be the same as the common on the issue date.

Figure 26-2 shows the values that are significant in determining the issue price of the PERCS. The line marked "final value" is the shape of the profit graph of a covered write at expiration. This is the PERCS' final value at its maturity. The curved line is the value of the covered write at the current time, well before expiration. Of course, these two are linked together.

The line marked "common stock" is merely the profit and loss of owning stock. The curved line (present PERCS value) crosses the "common stock" line at the issue price.

At the time of issuance, the difference between the current stock price and the eventual maturity value of the PERCS is the present value of all the additional dividends to be paid. That amount is marked as the vertical line on the graph. Therefore, anywhere out-of-the-money, the difference between the "final value" line and the "common stock" line is the present worth of the additional dividends to be paid between now and maturity of the PERCS.

Thus, on the day the PERCS are to be issued (or shortly before), the issuing corporation can alter the PERCS dividend or demand price in order to "move" the curved line (present PERCS value) so that it intersects the "common stock" line at today's stock price. The terms of the PERCS would then be set to those parameters.

FIGURE 26-2.
3-year PERCS issue price.

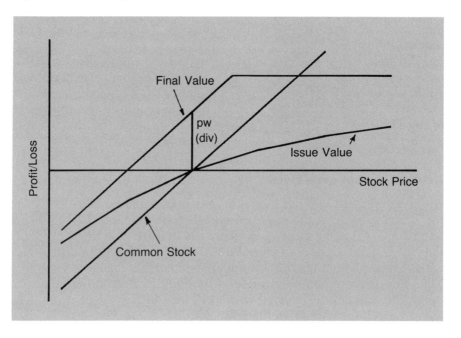

Pricing PERCS

The crucial factor in determining if a PERCS is fairly priced lies in valuing the imbedded call option within the PERCS. This may be a somewhat subjective task, especially if the PERCS has a long time until maturity. Recall that it was shown that small changes in the assumptions for LEAPS calls can seriously alter their theoretical values. The same holds true for valuing the call within the PERCS. If one trader is using a volatility assumption of 25%, say, for the common stock and another is using 28%, then they are going to arrive at different values for a 3-year call. In such a case, one trader may think the PERCS is expensive at its current price and another may think it is cheap.

Such discrepancies will be most notable when there is *not* a listed option that has terms near the terms of the PERCS' imbedded call. If there *is* such a listed option, then arbitrageurs should be able to use it and the common stock to bring the PERCS into line. However, if there is not any such listed option available, there may be opportunities for theoretical value traders.

Models used for pricing call options, such as the Black-Scholes model, are discussed in later chapters on mathematical applications. These models can be used to value the imbedded call in the PERCS as well. If the strategist determines the implied value of the imbedded call is out of line, he may be able to make a profitable trade. It is a fairly simple matter to determine the implied value of the imbedded call. The formula to be used is:

Imbedded call implies value = current stock price
                           + present value of dividends − current PERCS price

The validity of this formula can be seen by referring again to Figure 26-2. The difference between the "final value" (that is, the profit of the covered write at expiration) and the "issue value" or current value of the PERCS, is the imbedded call price. That is, the difference between the curved line and the line at expiration is merely the present time value of the imbedded call. Since this formula is describing an out-of-the-money situation, then the time value of the imbedded call is its entire price. It is also known that the "final value" line differs from the current stock price by the present value of all the additional dividends to be paid by the PERCS until maturity. Thus, the four variables are related by the above simple formula.

Example: XYZ has fallen to 32 after the PERCS was issued. The PERCS is currently trading at 34, and, as in previous examples, the PERCS pays an additional $1.50 per year in dividends. If there are two years remaining until maturity of the PERCS, what is the value of the imbedded call option?

First, calculate the present value of the additional dividends. One should calculate the present value of *each* dividend. Since they are paid quarterly, there will be eight of them between now and maturity.

Assume the short-term interest rate is 6%. Each additional quarterly dividend is $0.375 ($1.50 divided by 4). Thus the present value of the dividend to be paid in three months is

$$pw = 0.375/(1 + .06)^{1/4} = \$0.3696$$

While the present value of the dividend to be paid two years from now is

$$pw = 0.375/(1 + .06)^2 = \$0.338$$

Adding up all eight of these, it is determined that *the present worth of all the remaining additional dividends is $2.81*. Note that this is less than the actual amount that will eventually be paid over the two years, which is $3.00.

Now, using the simple formula above, the value of the imbedded call can be determined:

XYZ: 32
PERCS: 34
Present worth of additional dividends: 2.81

$$\text{Imbedded call} = \text{stock price} + pw \text{ divs} - \text{PERCS price}$$
$$= 32 + 2.81 - 34$$
$$= 0.81$$

Once this call value is determined, the strategist can use a model to see if this call appears to be cheap or expensive. In this case, the call looks cheap for a 2-year call option that is 7 points out-of-the-money. Of course, one would need to know how volatile XYZ stock is, in order to draw a definitive conclusion regarding whether the imbedded call is undervalued or not.

There is a basic relationship that can be drawn between the PERCS price and the calculated value of the imbedded call: *If the imbedded call is undervalued, then the PERCS is too expensive; if the imbedded call is overpriced, then the PERCS is cheap.* In this example, the value of the imbedded call was only 81 cents. If XYZ is a stock with average or above average volatility, then the call is certainly cheap. Therefore, the PERCS— trading at 34—is too expensive.

Once this determination has been made, the strategist must decide how to use the information. A buyer of PERCS will need to know this information to determine if he is paying too much for the PERCS; alternatively stated, he needs to know if he is selling the imbedded call too cheaply. A hedger might establish a true hedge by buying common and selling the PERCS, using the proper hedge ratio. It is possible for a PERCS to remain expensive for quite some time, if investors are buying it for the additional dividend yield alone and are not giving proper consideration to the limited profit potential. Nevertheless, both the outright buyer and the strategist should calculate the correct value of the PERCS in order to make rational decisions.

SUMMARY

A PERCS is a preferred stock with a higher dividend yield than the common, and it is demandable at a predetermined series of prices. The decision to demand is strictly at the discretion of the issuing company; the PERCS holder has no say in the decision. The PERCS is equivalent to a covered write of a long-term call option, which is imbedded in the PERCS value. Although there are not many PERCS trading at the current time, that number may grow substantially in the future.

Any strategies which pertain to covered writing will pertain to PERCS as well. Conventional listed options can be used to protect the PERCS from downside risk, to remove the limited upside profit potential, or to effectively change the price at which the PERCS is redeemable. Ratio writes can be constructed by selling a listed call. Shorting PERCS creates a security that is similar to a long put, which might be quite expensive if there is a significant amount of time remaining until maturity of the PERCS.

Neutral traders and hedgers should be aware that a PERCS has a delta of its own, which is equal to one minus the delta of the imbedded call option. Thus, hedging PERCS with common stock requires one to calculate the PERCS delta.

Finally, the implied value of the call option that is imbedded with the PERCS can be calculated quite easily. That information is used to determine if the PERCS is fairly priced or not. The serious outright buyer as well as the option strategist should make this calculation, since a PERCS is a security that is option-related. Either of these investors needs to know if he is making an attractive investment, and the valuation of the imbedded call is the only way to do so.

PART FOUR

ADDITIONAL
CONSIDERATIONS

Chapter 27

Buying Options and Treasury Bills

Numerous strategies have been described, ranging from the simple to the complex. Each one has advantages, but there are disadvantages as well. In fact, some of them may be too complex for the average investor to seriously consider implementing. The reader may feel that there should be an easier answer. Isn't there a strategy that might not require such a large investment or so much time spent in monitoring the position, but would still have a chance of returning a reasonable profit? In fact, there is a strategy that has not yet been described, a strategy considered by some experts in the field of mathematical analysis to be the best of them all. Simply stated, *the strategy consists of putting 90% of one's money in risk-free investments (such as short-term Treasury bills) and buying options with the remaining 10% of one's funds.*

It has been previously pointed out that some of the more attractive strategies are those that involve small levels of risk with the potential for large profits. Usually, these types of strategies inherently have a rather large frequency of small losses, and a small probability of realizing large gains. Their advantage lies in the fact that one or two large profits can conceivably more than make up for numerous small losses. This Treasury bill/option strategy is another strategy of this type.

HOW THE TREASURY BILL/OPTION STRATEGY OPERATES

Although there are certain details involved in operating this strategy, it is basically a simple one to approach. First, the most that one can lose is 10%, less the interest earned on the fixed-income portion of his portfolio (the remaining 90% of his assets), during the life of the purchased options. It is a simple matter to space out one's commitments to option purchases so that his overall risk in a one-year period can be kept down to nearly 10%.

Example: An investor might decide to put $2\frac{1}{2}\%$ of his money into three-month option purchases. Thus, in any one year, he would be risking 10%. At the same time he would be earning perhaps 6% from the overall interest generated on the fixed-income securities which make up the remaining 90% of his assets. This would keep his overall risk down to approximately 4.6% per year.

There are better ways to monitor this risk, and they will be described shortly. The potential profits from this strategy are limited only by time. Since one is owning options—say call options—he could profit handsomely from a large upward move in the stock market. As with any strategy in which one has limited risk and the potential of large profits, a small number of large profits could offset a large number of small losses. In actual practice, of course, his profits will never be overwhelming, since only approximately 10% of the money is committed to option purchases.

In total, *this strategy has greatly reduced risk with the potential of making above-average profits.* Since the 10% of the money that is invested in options gives great leverage, it might be possible for that portion to double or triple in a short time under favorable market conditions. This strategy is something like owning a convertible bond. A convertible bond, since it is convertible into the common stock, moves up and down in price with the price of the underlying stock. However, if the stock should fall a great deal, the bond will not follow it all the way down because eventually its yield will provide a "floor" for the price.

In fact, there is a strategy that is not used too often, called the "synthetic convertible bond." One buys a debenture and a call option on the same stock. If the stock rises in price, the call does too and so the combination of the debenture and the call acts much like a convertible bond would to the upside. If, on the other hand, the stock falls, the call will expire worthless, but the investor will retain most of his investment because he will still have the debenture plus any interest that the bond has paid.

The strategy of placing 90% of one's money into risk-free, interest-bearing certificates and buying options with the remainder is superior to the convertible bond or the "synthetic convertible bond" since there is no risk of price fluctuation in the largest portion of the investment.

The Treasury bill/option strategy is fairly easy to operate, although one does have to do some work every time that new options are purchased. Also, periodic adjustments need to be made to keep the level of risk approximately the same at all times. As for which options to buy, the reader may recall that specifications were outlined in Chapters 3 and 16 on how to select the best option purchases. These criteria can be briefly summarized as follows:

1. Assume that each underlying stock can advance or decline in accordance with its volatility over a fixed time period 30, 60, or 90 days).
2. Estimate the call prices after the advance, or put prices after the decline.
3. Rank all potential purchases by the highest reward opportunity.

The user of this strategy need only be interested in those option purchases which provide the highest reward opportunity under this ranking method. In the previous chapters on option buying, it was mentioned that one might want to look at the risk/reward ratios of his potential option purchases in order to have a more conservative list. However, that is not necessary in the Treasury bill/option strategy, since the overall risk has already been limited. A ranking of option purchases via the foregoing criteria will generally give a list of at- or slightly out-of-the-money options. These are not necessarily "underpriced" options, although if an option is truly underpriced, it will have a better chance of ranking higher on the selection list than one that is "overpriced."

A list of potential option purchases that is constructed with criteria similar to those outlined above is available from many data services and brokerage firms. The strategist who is willing to select his option purchases in this manner will find that he does not have to spend a great deal of time in his selection process. The reader should note that *this type of option purchase ranking completely ignores the outlook for the underlying stock.* If one would rather make his purchases based on an outlook for the underlying stock—preferably a technical outlook—he will be forced to spend more time in his selection process. Although this may be appealing to some investors, it will probably yield worse results in the long run than the previously described unbiased approach to option purchases unless the strategist is extremely adept at stock selection.

Keeping the Risk Level Equal

The second function that the strategist has to perform in this Treasury bill/option strategy is to keep his risk level approximately equal at all times.

Example: An investor starts the strategy with $90,000 in Treasury bills (T-bills) and $10,000 in option purchases. After some time has passed, the option purchases may have worked out well and perhaps he now has $90,000 in T-bills plus $30,000 worth of options, plus interest from the T-bills. Obviously, he no longer has 90% of his money in fixed-income securities and 10% in option purchases. The ratio is now 75% in T-bills and 25% in option purchases. This is too risky a ratio, and the strategist must consequently sell some of his options and buy T-bills with the proceeds. Since his total assets are $120,000 currently, he must sell out $18,000 of options to bring his option investment down from the current $30,000 figure to $12,000—10% of his total assets. If one fails to adhere to this readjustment of his funds after profits are made, he will eventually lose those profits. Since options can lose a great percentage of their worth in a short time period, the investor is always running the risk that the option portion of his investment may be nearly wiped out. If he has kept all his profits in the option portion of his strategy, he is constantly risking nearly all of his accumulated profits, and that is not wise.

One must also adjust his ratio of T-bills to options after losses occur.

Example: In the first year, the strategist loses all of the $10,000 he originally placed in options. This would leave him with total assets of $90,000 plus interest (possibly $6,000 of interest might be earned). He could readjust to a 90:10 ratio by selling out some of the T-bills and using the proceeds to buy options. If one follows this strategy, he will be risking 10% of his funds each year. Thus a series of loss years could depreciate the initial assets, although the net losses in one year would be smaller than 10% because of the interest earned on the T-bills. It is recommended that the strategist pursue this method of readjusting his ratios in both up and down markets in order to constantly provide himself with essentially similar risk/reward opportunities at all times.

The individual can blend the option selection process and the adjustment of the T-bill/option ratio to fit his individual portfolio. The larger portfolio can be diversified into options with differing holding periods, and the ratio adjustments can be made quite frequently, perhaps once a month. The smaller investor should concentrate on somewhat longer holding periods for his options, and would adjust the ratio less often. Some examples might help to illustrate the way in which both the large and small strategist might operate. It should be noted that this T-bill/option strategy is quite adaptable to fairly small sums of money, as long as the 10% that is going to be put into option purchases allows one to be able to participate in a reasonable manner. A tactic for the extremely small investor will also be described below.

Annualized Risk

Before getting into portfolio size, the concept of *annualized risk* will be described. One might want to purchase options with the intent of holding some of them for 30 days, some for 90 days, and some for 180 days. Recall that at any time he does not want his option purchases to represent more than 10% annual risk. In actual practice, if one purchases an option that has 90 days of life, but he is planning on holding the option only 30 days, he will most likely not lose 100% of his investment in the 30-day period. However, for purposes of computing annualized risk easily, the assumption that will be made is that the risk during any *holding period* is 100%, regardless of the length of time remaining in the life of the option. Thus a 30-day option purchase represents an annualized risk of 1,200% (100% risk every 30 days and there are twelve 30-day periods in one year). Ninety-day purchases have 400% annualized risk, and 180-day purchases have 200% annualized risk. There are multitudes of ways to combine purchases in these three holding periods so that the overall risk is 10% annualized.

   Example: An investor could put 2½% of his total money into 90-day purchases four times a year. That is, 2½% of his total assets are being subjected to a 400% annualized risk; 400 times 2½% equals 10% annualized risk on the total assets. Of course, the remainder of the assets would be placed in risk-free, income-bearing securities. Another of the many combinations might be to place 1% of the total assets in 90-day purchases and also place 3% of the total assets in 180-day purchases. Thus 1% of one's total money would be subjected to a 400% annual risk and 3% would be subjected to a 200% annual risk (.01 times 400 plus .03 times 200 equals 10% annualized risk on the entire assets). If one prefers a formula, annualized risk can be computed as:

$$\text{Annualized risk on entire portfolio} = \frac{\text{percent of total}}{\text{assets invested}} \times \frac{360}{\text{holding period}}$$

If one is able to diversify into several holding periods, the annualized risk is merely the sum of the risks for each holding period.

   With this information in mind, the strategist can then utilize option purchases of 1 month, 3 months, and 6 months—preferably each generated by a separate computer analysis similar to the one described earlier. He will know how much of his total assets he can place into purchases of each holding period because he will know his annualized risk.

   Example: A very large investor, or pool of investors, has $1 million committed to this T-bill/option strategy. Further, suppose ½ of 1% of the money is to be committed to 30-day option purchases with the idea of reinvesting every 30 days. Similarly, ½ of 1% is to be placed in 90-day purchases and 1% in 180-day purchases. The annualized risk is 10%:

$$\text{Total annualized risk} = 1/2\% \times \frac{360}{30} + 1/2\% \times \frac{360}{90} + 1\% \times \frac{360}{180}$$

$$= .06 \qquad + \qquad .02 \qquad + \qquad .02 = 10\%$$

With assets of $1 million, this means that $5,000 would be committed to 30-day purchases, $5,000 to 90-day purchases, and $10,000 to 180-day purchases. This money would be reinvested in similar quantities at the end of each holding period.

Risk Adjustment

The subject of adjusting the ratio to constantly reflect 10% risk must be addressed at the end of each holding period. Although it is correct for the investor to keep his percentage commitments constant, he must not be deluded into automatically reinvesting the same amount of dollars each time.

   Example: At the end of 30 days, the value of the entire portfolio, including potential option profits and losses, and interest earned, was down to $990,000. Then only ½ of 1% of *that* amount should be invested in the next 30-day purchase ($4,950).

   By operating in this manner—first computing the annualized risk and balancing it through predetermined percentage commitments to holding periods of various lengths, and second, readjusting the actual dollar commitment at the end of each holding period—the overall risk/reward ratios will be kept close to the levels described in the earlier, simple description of this strategy. This may require a relatively large amount of work on the part of the strategist, but large portfolios usually do.
   The smaller investor does not have the luxury of such complete diversification, but he also does not have to adjust his total position as often.

   Example: An investor decided to commit $50,000 to this strategy. Since there is a 1,200% annualized risk in 30-day purchases, it does not make much sense to even consider purchases that are so short-term for assets that are of this size. Rather, he might decide to commit 1% of his assets to a 90-day purchase and 3% to a 180-day purchase. In dollar amounts, this would be $500 in a 90-day option and $1,500 in 180-day options. Admittedly, this does not leave much room for diversification, but to risk more in the short-term purchases would expose the investor to too much risk. In actual practice, this investor would probably just invest 5% of his assets in 180-day purchases, also a 10% annualized risk. This would mean that he would only have to operate with one option buyer's analysis (the 180-day one) and could place $2,500 into selections from that list.

His adjustments of the assets committed to option purchases could not be done as frequently as the large investor, because of the commissions involved. He certainly would have to adjust every 180 days, but might prefer to do so more frequently—perhaps every 90 days—to be able to space his 180-day commitments over different option expiration cycles. It should also be pointed out that T-bills can only be bought and sold in amounts of at least $10,000 and in increments of $5,000 thereafter. That is, one could buy or sell $10,000 or $15,000 or $20,000 or $25,000, and so on, but could not buy or sell $5,000 or $8,000, or $23,000 T-bills. This is of little concern to the investor with $1 million, since it is only a fraction of a percentage of his assets to be able to round up to the next $5,000 increment for a T-bill sale or purchase. However, the medium-sized investor with a $50,000 portfolio might run into problems. While short-term T-bills do represent the best risk-free investment, the medium-sized investor might want to utilize—at least partially—one of the no-load, money market funds for part of his income-bearing assets. Such funds have only slightly more risk than T-bills and offer the ability to deposit and withdraw in any amount.

The truly small investor might be feeling somewhat left out. Could it be possible to operate this strategy with a very small amount of money, such as $5,000? Yes it could, but there are several disadvantages.

Example: It would be extremely difficult to keep the risk level down to 10% annually with only $5,000. For example, 5% of the money invested every 180 days is only $250 in each investment period. Since the option selection process that is described will tend to select at-or slightly out-of-the-money calls, many of these will cost more than $2\frac{1}{2}$ points for one option. The small investor might decide to raise his risk level slightly, although the risk level should never exceed 20% annually, no matter how small the actual dollar investment. To exceed this risk level would be to completely defeat the whole purpose of the fixed-income/option purchase strategy. Obviously, this small investor cannot buy T-bills, for his total investable assets are below the minimum $10,000 purchase level. He might consider utilizing one of the money market funds. Clearly, an investor of this small magnitude is operating at a double disadvantage—his small dollar commitment to option purchases may preclude him from buying some of the more attractive items, and his fixed-income portion will be earning a smaller percentage interest rate than that of the larger investor who is in T-bills or some other form of relatively risk-free, income-bearing security. Consequently, the *small investor should carefully consider his financial capability and willingness to adhere strictly to the criteria of this strategy before actually committing his dollars.*

It may appear to the reader that the actual dollars being placed at risk in each option purchase are quite small in these examples. In fact, they are rather small, but they have been shown to represent 10% annualized risk. An assumption was made in these examples that the risk in each option purchase was 100% for the holding period. This is a fairly restrictive assumption and, if it were lessened, would allow for larger dollar commitment in each holding period. It is difficult and dangerous, however, to assume that the risk in holding a call option is less than 100% in a holding period as long as 30 days. The strategist may feel that he is disciplined enough to sell out when losses occur and thereby hold the risk to less than 100%. Alternatively, mathematical analysis will generally show that the expected loss in a fixed time period is less than 100%. Adhering to either of these criteria can lead one to become too aggressive and therefore be too heavily committed to option purchases. It is far safer to stick to the simpler, more restrictive assumption that one is risking all his money—even over a fairly short holding period—when he buys an option.

Avoiding Excessive Risk

One final word of caution must be inserted. *The investor should not attempt to get "fancy" with the income-bearing portion of his assets.* T-bills may appear to be too "tame" to some investors, and they consider using GNMA's (Government National Mortgage Association certificates), corporate bonds, convertible bonds, or municipal bonds for the fixed-income portion. Although the latter securities may yield a slightly higher return than do T-bills, they may also prove to be less liquid and quite clearly involve more risk than a short-term T-bill does. Moreover, some investors might even consider placing the balance of their funds in other places, such as high-yield stock or covered call writing. While high-yield stock purchases and covered call writing are conservative investments, as most investments go, they would have to be considered very speculative in comparison to the purchase of a 90-day T-bill. In this strategy, the profit potential is represented by the option purchases. The yield on short-term T-bills will quite adequately offset the risks, and one should take great care not to attempt to generate much higher yields on the fixed-income portion of his investment, for he may find that he has assumed risk with the portion of his money that was not intended to have any risk at all.

A fair amount of rigorous, mathematical work has been done on the evaluation of this strategy. *The theoretical papers are quite favorable.* These scholars have generally considered only the purchase of call options as the risk portion of the strategy. Obviously, the strategist is quite free to purchase put options without harming the overall intent of the strategy. When only call options are purchased, both static and down markets harm the performance. If some puts are included in the option purchases, only static markets could produce the worst results.

There are trade-offs involved as well. If, after purchasing the options, the market has a substantial rally, that portion of the option purchase money that is devoted to put option purchases will be lost. Thus the combination of both put and call purchases would do better in a down market than a strategy of buying only calls, but would do worse in an up market. In a broad sense, it makes sense to include some put purchases— if one has the funds to diversify—since the frequency of market rallies is smaller than the combined frequency of market rallies and declines. The investor who owns both puts and calls will be able to profit from substantial moves in either direction, because the profitable options will be able to overcome the limited losses on the unprofitable ones.

SUMMARY

In summary, the T-bill/option strategy is attractive from several viewpoints. *Its true advantage lies in the fact that it has predefined risk and does not have a limit on potential profits.* Some theorists claim it is the best strategy available, if the options are "underpriced" when they are purchased. The strategy is also relatively simple to operate—it is not necessary to have a margin account or to compute collateral requirements for uncovered options. The strategy can be operated completely from a cash account. There are no spreads involved, nor is it necessary to worry about details such as early assignment (there are no short options in this strategy).

The investor who is going to employ this strategy must, however, not be deluded into thinking that it is so simple that it does not take any work at all. The concepts and application of annualized risk management are very important to the strategy. So are the mechanics of option buying— particularly a disciplined, rational approach to the selection of which calls and/or puts to buy. Consequently, this strategy is suitable only for the investor who has both the time and discipline to operate it correctly.

Chapter 28

The Best Strategy?

There is no one best strategy. Although this statement may appear to be unfair and disappointing to some, it is nevertheless the truth. Its validity lies in the fact that there are many types of investors, and no one strategy can be best for all of them. Knowledge and suitability are the keys to determining which strategy may be the best one for an individual. The previous chapters have been devoted to imparting much of the knowledge required to understand an individual strategy. This chapter will attempt to point out how the investor might incorporate his own risk/reward attitude and financial condition to select the most feasible strategies for his own use. The final section of this chapter describes which strategies have the better probabilities of success.

GENERAL CONCEPTS—MARKET ATTITUDE AND EQUIVALENT POSITIONS

A wide variety of strategies has been described. Certain ones are geared to capitalizing on one's (hopefully correct) outlook for a particular stock, or for the market in general. These tend to be the more aggressive strategies, such as outright put or call buying, and low-debit (high potential) bull and bear spreads. Other strategies are much more conservative, having as their emphasis the possibility of making a reasonable, but limited, return coupled with a decreased risk exposure. These would include covered call writing and in-the-money (large debit) bull or bear spreads. Even in these strategies, however, one has a general attitude about the market. He is bullish or bearish, but not overly so. If he is proven slightly wrong, he can still make money. However, if he is gravely wrong, relatively large percentage losses might occur. The third broad category of strategies is the one that is not oriented toward picking stock market direction, but is rather a neutral approach that allows one to earn time value premiums. If the net change in the market is small over a period of time—and there are historical indications that it is—these strategies should perform well. These strategies would include ratio writing, ratio spreading (especially "delta spreads"), straddle and combination writing, neutral calendar spreading, and butterfly spreads.

Certain other strategies overlap into more than one of the three broad categories. For example, the bullish or bearish calendar spread is initially a neutral position. It only assumes a bullish or bearish bias after the near-term option expires. In fact, any of the diagonal or calendar strategies whose ultimate aim is to generate profits on the sale of shorter-term options are similar in nature. If these near-term profits are generated, they can offset, partially or completely, the cost of long options. Thus one might potentially own options at a reduced cost and could profit from a definitive move in his favor at the right time. It was shown in Chapters 14, 23, and 24 that diagonalizing a spread can often be very attractive.

This brief grouping into three broad categories does not cover all the strategies that have been discussed. For example, some strategies are generally so poor that they are to be avoided by most investors—reverse calendar spreads, high-risk naked option writing (selling options for fractional prices), and covered or ratio put writing. In essence, the investor will normally do best with a position that has limited risk and the potential of large profits. Even if the profit potential is a low-probability event, one or two successful cases may be able to overcome a series of limited losses. Complex strategies that fit this description are the diagonal put and call combinations described in Chapters 23 and 24. The simplest strategy fitting this description is the T-bill/option purchase program.

Finally, many strategies may be implemented in more than one way. The method of implementation may not alter the profit potential, but the percentage risk levels can be substantially different. Equivalent strategies fit into this category.

Example: Buying stock and then protecting the stock purchase with a put purchase is an equivalent strategy in profit potential to buying a call. That is, both have limited dollar risk and large potential dollar profit if the stock rallies. However, they are substantially different in their structure. The purchase of stock and a put requires substantially more initial investment dollars than does the purchase, but the limited dollar risk of the strategy would normally be a relatively small percentage of the initial investment. The call purchase, on the other hand, involves a much smaller capital outlay, and while it also has limited dollar risk, the loss may easily represent the entire initial investment. The stockholder will receive cash dividends while the call holder will not. Moreover, the stock will not expire as the call will. This provides the stock/put holder with an additional alternative of choosing to extend his position for a longer period of time by buying another put or possibly by just continuing to hold the stock after the original put expires.

Many equivalent positions have similar characteristics. The straddle purchase and the reverse hedge (short stock and buy calls) have similar profit and loss potential when measured in dollars. Their percentage risks are substantially different, however. In fact, as was shown in Chapter 20, there is another strategy that is equivalent to both of these—buying stock and buying several puts. That is, buying a straddle is equivalent to buying 100 shares of stock and simultaneously buying two puts. The "buy stock and puts" strategy has a larger initial dollar investment, but the percentage risk is smaller and the stockholder will receive any dividends paid by the common stock.

In summary, the investor must know two things well—the strategy that he is contemplating using and his own attitude toward risk and reward. His own attitude represents suitability, a topic that will be discussed more fully in the following section. Every strategy has risk. It would not be proper for an investor to pursue the best strategy in the universe (such a strategy does not exist, of course) if the risks of that strategy violated the investor's own level of financial objectives or accepted investment methodology. On the other hand, it is also not sufficient for the investor to merely feel that a strategy is suitable for his investment objectives. Suppose an investor felt that the T-bill/option strategy was suitable for him because of the profit and risk levels. Even if he understands the philosophies of option purchasing, it would be proper for him to utilize the strategy unless he also understands the mechanics of buying Treasury bills and, more important, the concept of annualized risk.

WHAT IS BEST FOR ME MIGHT NOT BE BEST FOR YOU

It would be impossible to classify any one strategy as the best one. The conservative investor would certainly not want to be an outright buyer of options. For him, covered call writing might be the best strategy. Not only would it accomplish his financial aims—moderate profit potential with reduced risk—but it would be much more appealing to him psychologically. The conservative investor normally understands and accepts the risks of stock ownership. It is only a small step from that understanding to the covered call writing strategy. The aggressive investor would not consider covered call writing to be the best strategy, most likely, because he would consider the profit potential too small. He is willing to take larger risks for the opportunities of making larger profits. Outright option purchases might suit him best, and he would accept, by his aggressive nature, that he could lose nearly all his money in a relatively short time period. (Of course, one would hope that he only uses 15 to 20% of his assets for speculative option buying.)

Many investors fit somewhere in between the conservative description and the aggressive description. They might want to have the opportunity to make large profits, but certainly are not willing to risk a large percentage of their available funds in a short period of time. Spreads might therefore appeal to this type of investor—especially the low-debit bullish or bearish calendar spreads. He might also consider occasional ventures into other types of strategies—bullish or bearish spreads, straddle buys or writes and so on—but would generally not be into a wide range of these types of positions. The T-bill/option strategy might work well for this investor also.

The wealthy aggressive investor may be attracted by strategies that offer the opportunity of making money from credit positions, such as straddle or combination writing. Although ratio writing is not a credit strategy, it might also appeal to this type of investor because of the large amounts of time value premium that are gathered in. These are generally strategies for the wealthier investor because he needs the "staying power" to be able to ride out adverse cycles. If he can do this, he should be able to operate the strategy for a sufficient period of time in order to profit from the constant selling of time value premiums.

In essence, the answer to the question of "which strategy is best" again revolves around that familiar word *suitability. The financial needs and investment objectives of the individual investor are more important than the merits of the strategy itself.* It sounds nice to be able to say that one would like to participate in strategies with limited risk and potentially large profits. Unfortunately, if the actual mechanics of the strategy involve risk that is not suitable for the investor, he should not use the strategy—no matter how attractive it sounds.

Example: The T-bill/option strategy seems attractive: limited risk because only 10% of one's assets are subjected to risk annually; the remaining 90% of one's assets earn interest; and if the option profits materialize, they could be large. What if the worst scenario unfolds? Suppose that poor option selections are continuously made and there are three or four years of losses, coupled with a declining rate of interest earned from the Treasury bills (not to mention the commission charges for trading the securities). The portfolio might have lost 15 or 20% of its assets over those years. *A good test of suitability is for the investor to ask himself, in advance: "How will I react if this worst case occurs?"* If there will be sleepless nights, pointing of fingers, threats, and so forth, the strategy is unsuitable. If, on the other hand, the investor feels that he would be disappointed (because no one likes to lose money), but that he can withstand the risk, the strategy may indeed be suitable.

MATHEMATICAL RANKING

The discussion above demonstrates that it is not possible to ultimately define the best strategy when one considers the background—both financial and psychological—of the individual investor. However, the reader may be interested in knowing which strategies have the best mathematical chances of success, regardless of the investor's personal feelings. Not unexpectedly, *those strategies which take in large amounts of time value premium have high mathematical expectations.* These would include ratio writing, ratio spreading, straddle writing, and naked call writing (but only if the "rolling for credits" follow-up strategy is adhered to). The ratio strategies would have to be operated according to a delta neutral ratio in order to be mathematically optimum. Unfortunately, these strategies are not for everyone. All involve naked options, and also require that the investor have a substantial amount of money (or collateral) available to make the strategies work properly. Moreover, naked option writing in any form is not suitable for some investors, regardless of their protests to the contrary.

Another group of strategies that rank high on an expected profit basis are those that have limited risk with the potential of occasionally attaining large profits. The T-bill/option strategy is a prime example of this type of strategy. The strategies in which one attempts to reduce the cost of longer-term options through the sale of near-term options would fit in this broad category also, although one should limit his dollar commitment to 15 to 20% of his portfolio. Calendar spreads such as the combinations described in Chapter 23 (calendar combination, calendar straddle, and diagonal butterfly spread) or bullish call calendar spreads or bearish put calendar spreads are all examples of such strategies. These strategies may have a rather frequent probability of losing a small amount of money, coupled with a low probability of earning large profits. Still, a few large profits may be able to more than overcome the frequent, but small, losses.

Ranking behind these strategies would be the ones that offer limited profits with a reasonable probability of attaining that profit. Covered call writing, large debit bull or bear spreads (purchased option well in-the-money and possible written option as well), neutral calendar spreads, and butterfuly spreads would fit into this category. Unfortunately, all these strategies involve relatively large commission costs. Even though these are not normally strategies which require a large investment, the investor who wants to reduce the percentage effect of commissions must take larger positions and will therefore be advancing a sizable amount of money.

Speculative buying and spreading strategies rank the lowest on a mathematical basis. The T-bill/option strategy is not a speculative buying strategy. In-the-money purchases, including the in-the-money combination, generally outrank out-of-the-money purchases. This is because one has the possibility of making a large percentage profit but has decreased the chance of losing all his investment, since he starts out in-the-money. In general, however, the constant purchase of time value premiums—which must waste away by the time the options expire—will be a burdensome negative effect. The chances of large profits and large losses are relatively equal on a mathematical basis, and thus become subsidiary to the time premium effect in the long run. This mathematical outlook of course precludes those investors who are able to predict stock movements with an above-average degree of accuracy. Although the true mathematical approach holds that it is not possible to accurately predict the market, there are undoubtedly some who can and many who try.

SUMMARY

Mathematical expectations for a strategy do not make it suitable even if the expected returns are good, for the improbable may occur. Profit potentials also do not determine suitability—risk levels do. In the final analysis, one must determine suitability of a strategy by determining if he will be able to withstand the inherent risks if the worst scenario should occur. For this reason, no one strategy can be designated as the best one, because there are numerous attitudes as to the degree of risk that is acceptable.

Chapter 29

Arbitrage

Arbitrage in the securities market often connotes that one is buying something in one marketplace and selling it in another marketplace, for a small profit with little or no risk. For example, one might buy XYZ at 55 in New York and sell it at 55¼ in Chicago. Arbitrage—especially option arbitrage—involves a far wider range of tactics than this simple example. Many of the option arbitrage tactics involve buying one side of an equivalent position and simultaneously selling the other side. Since there is a large number of equivalent strategies—many of which have been pointed out in earlier chapters—a full-time option arbitrageur is able to construct a rather large number of positions, most of which have little or no risk. The public customer cannot generally operate arbitrage-like strategies because of the commission costs involved. Arbitrageurs are firm traders or floor traders who are trading through a seat on the appropriate securities exchange, and therefore have only minimal transaction costs.

The public customer can benefit from understanding arbitrage techniques, even if he does not personally employ them. The arbitrageurs perform a useful function in the option marketplace—often being the ones who make markets where a market might not otherwise exist (deeply in-the-money options, for example). This chapter is written in a tone directed at the strategist who is actually going to be participating in arbitrage. This should not be confusing to the public customer, for he will better understand the arbitrage strategies if he temporarily places himself in the arbitrageur's shoes.

It is virtually impossible to perform pure arbitrage on dually listed options; that is, to buy an option on the CBOE and sell it on the American Exchange in New York for a profit. Such discrepancies occur so infrequently and in such small size that an option arbitrageur could never hope to be fully employed in this type of simple arbitrage. Rather, the more complex forms of arbitrage described below are the ones on which he would normally concentrate.

BASIC PUT AND CALL ARBITRAGE ("DISCOUNTING")

The basic call and the basic put arbitrages are two of the simpler forms of option arbitrage. In these situations, *the arbitrageur attempts to buy the option at a discount while simultaneously taking an opposite position in the underlying stock.* He can then exercise his option immediately and make a profit equal to the amount of the discount.

The basic call arbitrage will be described first. This was also outlined in Chapter 1, under the section on anticipating exercise.

Example: XYZ is trading at 58 and the XYZ July 50 call is trading at $7\frac{3}{4}$. The call is actually at a discount from parity of $\frac{1}{4}$ point. Discount options are generally either quite deeply in-the-money or have only a short time remaining until expiration, or both. The call arbitrage would be constructed by:

1. Buying the call at $7\frac{3}{4}$.

2. Selling the stock at 58.

3. Exercising the call to buy the stock at 50.

The arbitrageur would make 8 points of profit from the stock—having sold it at 58 and bought it back at 50 via the option exercise. He loses the $7\frac{3}{4}$ points that he paid for the call option, but this still leaves him with an overall profit of $\frac{1}{4}$ point. Since he is a member of the exchange, or is trading the seat of an exchange member, the arbitrageur pays only a small charge to transact the trades.

In reality, the stock is not sold *short*, per se, even though it is sold before it is bought. Rather, the position is designated, at the time of its inception, as an "irrevocable exercise"—the arbitrageur is promising to exercise the call. As a result, no uptick is required to sell the stock.

The main goal in the call arbitrage is to be able to buy the call at a discount from the price at which the stock is sold. The differential is the profit potential of the arbitrage. *The basic put arbitrage is quite similar to the call arbitrage.* Again, the arbitrageur is looking to buy the put option at a discount from parity. The put arbitrage is completed with a stock *purchase* and option exercise.

Example: XYZ is at 58 and the XYZ July 70 put is at $11\frac{3}{4}$. With the put at a $\frac{1}{4}$ discount from parity, the arbitrageur might take the following action:

1. Buy put at $11\frac{3}{4}$.
2. Buy stock at 58.
3. Exercise put to sell stock at 70.

The stock transaction is a 12-point profit, since the stock was bought at 58 and is sold at 70 via the put exercise. The cost of the put—$11\frac{3}{4}$ points— is lost, but the arbitrageur stil makes a $\frac{1}{4}$-point profit. Again, *this profit is equal to the amount of the discount in the option when the position was established.* Generally, the arbitrageur would exercise his put option immediately because he would not want to tie up his capital to carry the long stock. An exception to this would be if the stock were about to go ex-dividend. Dividend arbitrage is discussed in the next section.

The basic call and put arbitrages may exist at any time, although they will be more frequent when there is an abundance of deeply in-the-money options or when there is a very short time remaining until expiration. After market rallies, the call arbitrage may be easier to establish, and after market declines, the put arbitrage will be easier to find. As an expiration date draws near, an option that is even slightly in-the-money on the last day or two of trading could be a candidate for discount arbitrage. The reason that this is true is that public buying interest in the option will normally wane. The only public buyers would be those who are short and want to cover. Many covered writers will elect to let the stock be called away, so that will reduce even further the buying potential of the public. This leaves it to the arbitrageurs to supply the buying interest.

The arbitrageur obviously wants to establish these positions in as large a size as possible, since there is no risk in the position if it is established at a discount. Usually, there will be a larger market for the stock than there will be for the options, so that the arbitrageur spends more of his time on the option position. However, there may be occasions when the option markets are larger than the corresponding stock quotes. When this happens, the arbitrageur has an alternative available to him— *he might sell an in-the-money option at parity rather than taking a stock position.*

Example: XYZ is at 58 and the XYZ July 50 call is at 7¾. These are the same figures as in the previous example. Furthermore, suppose that the trader is able to buy more options at 7¾ than he is able to sell stock at 58. If there were another in-the-money call that could be sold at parity, it could be used in place of the stock sale. For example, if the XYZ July 40 call could be sold at 18 (parity), the arbitrage could still be established. If he is assigned on the July 40 that he is short, he will then be short stock at a net price of 58—the striking price of 40, plus the 18 points that were brought in from the sale of the July 40 call. Thus *the sale of the in-the-money call at parity is equivalent to shorting the stock for the arbitrage purpose.*

In a similar manner, an in-the-money put can be used in the basic put arbitrage.

Example: With XYZ at 58 and the July 70 put at 11¾, the arbitrage could be established. However, if the trader is having trouble buying enough stock at 58, he might be able to use another in-the-money put. Suppose the XYZ July 80 put could be sold at 22. This would be the same as buying the stock at 58, for if the put were assigned the arbitrageur would be forced to buy stock at 80—the striking price—but his net cost would be 80 minus the 22 points he received from the sale of the put, for a net cost of 58. Again, the arbitrageur is able to use the sale of a deeply in-the-money option as a substitute for the stock trade.

The examples above assumed that the arbitrageur sold a deeper in-the-money option at parity. In actual practice, if an in-the-money is at a discount, an even deeper in-the-money option will generally be at a discount as well. The arbitrageur would normally try to sell, at parity, an option that was *less* deeply in-the-money than the one he is discounting.

In a broader sense, this technique is applicable to any arbitrage that involves a stock trade as part of the arbitrage, except where the dividend on the stock itself is important. *Thus any time that the arbitrageur is having trouble buying or selling stock as part of his arbitrage, he can always check to see if there is an in-the-money option that could be sold to produce a position equivalent to the stock position.*

DIVIDEND ARBITRAGE

There is a dividend arbitrage that is actually quite similar to the basic put arbitrage. The trader can lock in profits by buying both the stock and the put, then waiting to collect the dividend on the underlying stock before exercising his put. *In theory, on the day before a stock goes ex-dividend, all puts should have a time value premium at least as large as the dividend amount.* This is true even for deeply in-the-money puts.

Example: XYZ closes at 45 and is going to go ex-dividend by $1 tomorrow. Then a put with striking price of 50 should sell for at least 6 points—the in-the-money amount plus the amount of the dividend— because the stock will go ex-dividend and is expected to open at 44, six points in-the-money.

If, however, the put's time value premium should be less than the amount of the dividend, the arbitrageur can take a riskless position. Suppose the XYZ July 50 put is selling for $5\frac{3}{4}$, with the stock at 45 and about to go ex-dividend by $1. The arbitrageur can take the following steps:

1. Buy the put at $5\frac{3}{4}$.
2. Buy the stock at 45.
3. Hold the put and stock until the stock goes ex-dividend (1 point in this case).
4. Exercise the put to sell the stock at 50.

The trader makes 5 points from the stock trade—buying it at 45 and selling it at 50 via the put exercise—and also collects the one point dividend, for a total inflow of 6 points. Since he loses the $5\frac{3}{4}$ points he paid for the put, his net profit is $\frac{1}{4}$ point.

Far in advance of the ex-dividend date, a deeply in-the-money put may trade very close to parity. Thus it would seem that the arbitrageur could "load up" on these types of positions and merely sit back and wait for the stock to go ex-dividend. There is a flaw in this line of thinking, however, because *the arbitrageur has a carrying cost for the money that he must tie up in the long stock.* This carrying cost fluctuates with short-term interest rates.

Example: If the current rate of carrying charges were 6% annually, this would be equivalent to 1% every 2 months. If the arbitrageur were to establish this example position 2 months prior to expiration, he would have a carrying cost of .5075 point (his total outlay is $50\frac{3}{4}$ points, 45 for the stock and $5\frac{3}{4}$ for the options, and he would pay 1% to carry that stock and option for the two months until the ex-dividend date). This is more than $\frac{1}{2}$ point in costs—clearly more than the $\frac{1}{4}$-point potential profit. Consequently, the arbitrageur must be aware of his carrying costs if he attempts to establish a dividend arbitrage well in advance of the ex-dividend date. Of course, if the ex-dividend date is only a short time away, the carrying cost has little effect, and the arbitrageur can gauge the profitability of his position mostly by the amount of the dividend and the time value premium in the put option.

The arbitrageur should note that this strategy of buying the put and buying the stock to pick up the dividend might have a residual, rather profitable, side effect. If the underlying stock shall rally up to, or above, the striking price of the put, there could be rather large profits in this position. Although it is not likely that such a rally could occur, it would be an added benefit if it did. Even a rather small rally might cause the put to pick up some time premium, allowing the arbitrageur to trade out of his position for a profit larger than he could have made by the arbitrage discount.

This form of arbitrage lends itself occasionally to a limited form of risk arbitrage. Risk arbitrage is a strategy that is designed to lock in a profit, if a certain event occurs. If that event does not occur, there could be a loss (usually quite limited), and hence the position has risk. *This risk element differentiates a risk arbitrage from a standard, no-risk arbitrage.* Risk arbitrage will be described more fully in a later section, but the following example concerning a special dividend is one form of risk arbitrage.

Example: XYZ has been known to declare extra, or special, dividends with a fair amount of regularity. There are several stocks that do so—Eastman Kodak and General Motors, for example. In this case, assume that a hypothetical stock, XYZ, has generally declared a special dividend in the fourth quarter of each year, but that its normal quarterly rate is $1.00 per share. Suppose the special dividend in the fourth quarter has ranged from an extra $1.00 to $3.00 over the past five years. If the arbitrageur were willing to speculate on the size of the upcoming dividend, he might be able to make a nice profit. Even if he overestimates the size of the special dividend, he has a limited loss. Suppose XYZ is trading at 55 about two weeks before the company is going to announce their dividend for the fourth quarter. There is no guarantee that there will, in fact, be a special dividend, but assume that XYZ is having a relatively good year, profitwise, and that some special dividend seems forthcoming. Furthermore, suppose the January 60 put is trading at 7½. This put has 2½ points of time value premium. If the arbitrageur buys XYZ at 55 and also buys the January 60 put at 7½, he is setting up a risk arbitrage. He will profit—regardless of how far the stock falls or how much time value premium the put loses—if the special dividend is larger than $1.50. A special dividend of $1.50 plus the regular dividend of $1.00 would add up to $2.50, or 2½ points, thus covering his risk in the position. Note that $1.50 is in the low end of the $1.00 and $3.00 recent historical range for the special dividends, so the arbitrageur might be tempted to speculate a little by establishing this dividend risk arbitrage. Even if the company were to unexpectedly decide to declare no special dividend at all, it would most likely still pay out the $1.00 regular dividend. Thus the most that the arbitrageur would lose would be 1½ points (his 2½-point initial time value premium cost, less the 1 point dividend). In actual practice, the stock would probably not change in price by a great deal—it is a high-yield stock—over the next two weeks, and therefore the January 60 put would probably have some time value premium left in it after the stock goes ex-dividend. Thus the practical risk is even less than 1½ points.

While these types of dividend risk arbitrage are not frequently available, the arbitrageur who is willing to do some homework and also take some risk may find that he is able to put on a position with a small risk and a profitability quite a bit larger than the normal discount dividend arbitrage.

There is really not a direct form of dividend arbitrage involving call options. If a relatively high-yield stock is about to go ex-dividend, holders of the calls will attempt to sell. They do so because the stock will drop in price, thereby generally forcing the call to drop in price as well, because of the ex-dividend. However, the holder of a call does not receive cash dividends and therefore is not willing to hold the call if the stock is going to drop by a relatively large amount (perhaps ¾ point or more). The effect of these call holders attempting to sell their calls may often produce a discount option—and therefore a basic call arbitrage may be possible. The arbitrageur should be careful, however, if he is attempting to arbitrage a stock that is going ex-dividend on the following day. Since he must sell the stock to set up the arbitrage, he cannot afford to wind up the day being short any stock, for he will then have to pay out the dividend the following day (the ex-dividend date). Furthermore, his records must be accurate so that he exercises all his long options on the day before the ex-dividend date. If the arbitrageur is careless and is still short some stock on the ex-date, he may find that the dividend he has to pay out wipes out a large portion of the discount profits that he has established.

CONVERSIONS AND REVERSALS

In the introductory material on puts, it was shown that put and call prices are related through a process known as conversion. This is an arbitrage process whereby a trader may sometimes be able to lock in a profit at absolutely no risk. *A conversion consists of buying the underlying stock, and also buying a put option and selling a call option where both options have the same terms. This position will have a locked-in profit if the total cost of the position is less than the striking price of the options.*

Example: The following prices exist:

XYZ common, 55;

XYZ January 50 call, $6\frac{1}{2}$; and

XYZ January 50 put, 1.

The total cost of this conversion is $49\frac{1}{2}$—55 for the stock, plus 1 for the put, less $6\frac{1}{2}$ for the call. Since $49\frac{1}{2}$ is less than the striking price of 50, there is a locked-in profit on this position. To see that such a profit exists, suppose the stock is somewhere above 50 at expiration. It makes no difference how far above 50 the stock might be, for the result will be the same. With the stock above 50, the call will be assigned and the stock will be sold at a price of 50. The put will expire worthless. Thus the profit is $\frac{1}{2}$ point, since the initial cost of the position was $49\frac{1}{2}$ and it can eventually be liquidated for a price of 50 at expiration. A similar result occurs if XYZ is below 50 at expiration. In this case, the trader would exercise his put to sell his stock at 50, and the call would expire worthless. Again, the position is liquidated for a price of 50 and, since it only cost $49\frac{1}{2}$ to establish, the same $\frac{1}{2}$-point profit can be made. No matter where the stock is at expiration, this position has a locked-in-expiration of $\frac{1}{2}$ point.

This example is rather simplistic because it does not include two very important factors—the possible dividend paid by the stock and the cost of carrying the position until expiration. The inclusion of these factors complicates things somewhat, and its discussion will be deferred momentarily while the companion strategy, the reversal, is explained.

A reversal (or reverse conversion, as it is sometimes called) is exactly the opposite of a conversion. *In a reversal, the trader sells stock short, sells a put and buys a call.* Again, the put and call have the same terms. *A reversal will be profitable if the initial credit (sale price) is greater than the striking price of the options.*

Example: A different set of prices will be used to describe a reversal:

XYZ common, 55;

XYZ January 60 call, 2; and

XYZ January 60 put, $7\frac{1}{2}$.

The total credit of the reversal is $60\frac{1}{2}$—55 from the stock sale, plus $7\frac{1}{2}$ from the put sale, less the 2-point cost of the call. Since $60\frac{1}{2}$ is greater than the striking price of the options, 60, there is a locked-in-profit equal to the differential of $\frac{1}{2}$ point. To verify this, first assume that XYZ is anywhere below 60 at January expiration. The put will be assigned—stock is bought at 60—and the call will expire worthless. Thus the reversal position is liquidated for a cost of 60. A ½-point profit results since the original sale value (credit) of the position was 60½. On the other hand, if XYZ were above 60 at expiration, the trader would exercise his call, thus buying stock at 60, and the put would expire worthless. Again, he would liquidate the position at a cost of 60 and would make a ½-point profit.

Dividends and carrying costs are important in reversals, too, and these factors will now be addressed. The *conversion* involves buying stock and the trader will thus receive any dividends paid by the stock during the life of the arbitrage. However, the converter also has to pay out a rather large sum of money to set up his arbitrage, and must therefore deduct the cost of carrying the position from his potential profits. In the example above, the conversion position cost 49½ points to establish. If the trader's cost of money were 6% annually, he would thus lose .06/12 × 49½, or .2475 point per month for each month that he holds the position. This is nearly ¼ of a point per month. Recall that the potential profit in the example is ½ point, so that if he held the position for more than two months, his carrying costs would wipe out his profit. *It is extremely important that the arbitrageur compute his carrying costs accurately prior to establishing any conversion arbitrage.*

If one prefers formulae, the profit potentials of a conversion or a reversal can be stated as:

Conversion profit = striking price + call price − stock price − put price + dividends to be received − carrying cost of position

Reversal profit = stock + put − strike − call + carrying cost − dividends

Note that during any one trading day, the only items in the formulae that can change are the prices of the securities involved. The other items—*dividends and carrying cost—are fixed for the day.* Thus one could merely have a small computer program prepared that listed the fixed charges on a particular stock and all the strikes on that stock.

Example: It is assumed that XYZ stock is going to pay a ½-point dividend during the life of the position, and that the position will have to be held for three months at a carrying cost of 6% per year. If the arbitrageur were interested in a conversion with a striking price of 50, his fixed cost would be:

Conversion fixed cost = carrying rate × time held ×
striking price − dividend to be received
= .06 × ³⁄₁₂ × 50 − ½
= .75 − ½ = .25, or ¼ of a point

The arbitrageur would know that if the profit potential, computed in the simplistic manner using only the prices of the securities involved, was greater than ¼ of a point, he could establish the conversion for an eventual profit, including all costs. Of course, the carrying costs would be different if the striking price were 40 or 60, so a small computer printout of all the possible striking prices on each stock with both puts and calls would be useful in order for the trader to be able to quickly refer to a table of his fixed costs each day. To keep things workable for the trader, such a program should round the cost up to the nearest eighth of a point, so that the trader does not have to bother with decimal calculations during the trading day.

MORE ON CARRYING COSTS

The computation of carrying costs can be made more involved than the simple method used above. Simplistically, the carrying cost is computed by multiplying the debit of the position by the interest rate charged and by the time that the position will be held. That is, it could be formulated as:

$$\text{Carrying cost} = \text{strike} \times r \times t$$

where r is the interest rate and t is the time that the position will be held. Relating this formula for the carrying cost to the conversion profit formula given above, one would get:

Conversion profit = call − stock − put + div + strike − carrying cost

= call − stock − put + div + strike $(1 - rt)$

In an actuarial sense, the carrying cost could be expressed in a slightly more complex manner. The simple formula (strike × r × t) ignores two things: the compounding effect of interest rates and the "present value" concept—the present value of a future amount. The absolutely correct formula to include both present value and the compounding effect would necessitate replacing the factor strike $(1 - rt)$ in the profit formula by the factor

$$\frac{\text{strike}}{(1 + r)^t}$$

Is this effect large? No, not when r and t are small, as they would be for most option calculations. The interest rate per month would be normally less than 1% and the time would be less than 9 months. Thus it is generally acceptable, and is the common practice among many arbitrageurs, to use the simple formula for carrying costs. In fact, this is often a matter of convenience for the arbitrageur if he is computing the carrying costs on a hand calculator that does not do exponentiation. However, in periods of high interest rates when longer-term options are being analyzed, the arbitrageur who is using the simple formula should double-check his calculations with the correct formula to assure that his error is not too large.

For purposes of simplicity, the remaining examples will use the simple formula for carrying-cost computations. The reader should remember, however, that it is only a convenient approximation that works best when the interest rate and the holding period are small. Also, since the arbitrageur must round his calculations to the nearest eighth, most differentials between the approximation formula and the exact formula will be wiped away. This discussion of the compounding effect of interest rates also raises another interesting point: any investor using margin should, in theory, calculate his potential interest charge using the compounding formula. However, as a matter of practicality, extremely few investors do. An example of this compounding effect on a covered call write is presented in Chapter 2.

BACK TO CONVERSIONS AND REVERSALS

Profit calculation similar to the conversion profit formula is necessary for the reversal arbitrage. Since the reversal necessitates shorting stock, the trader must pay out any dividends on the stock during the time in which the position is held. However, he is now bringing in a credit when the position is established, and this money can be put to work to earn interest. In a reversal, then, the dividend is a cost and the interest earned is a profit.

Example: Use the same XYZ details described above—the stock is going to pay a ½-point dividend, the position will be held for three months, and the money will earn interest at a rate of ½ of 1% per month. If the trader were contemplating an arbitrage with a striking price of 30, the fixed cost would be:

$$\text{Reversal fixed cost} = \text{dividend to be paid} - \text{interest rate per month} \times$$
$$\text{months held} \times \text{striking price}$$

$$= \tfrac{1}{2} - .005 \times 3 \times 30$$

$$= \tfrac{1}{2} - .045 = .005 \text{ point}$$

The fixed cost in this reversal is extremely small. In fact, the reader should be able to see that it is often possible—even probable—that there will be a fixed profit, not a fixed cost, in a reversal arbitrage. To verify this, rework the example with a striking price of 50 or 60. As in a conversion, the fixed cost (or profit) in a reversal is a number that can be used for the entire trading day. It will not change.

Borrowing Stock to Sell Short

The above example assumes that the arbitrageur earns the full carrying rate on the short stock. Only certain arbitrageurs are actually able to earn that rate. When one sells stock short, he must actually borrow the stock from someone who owns it, and then the seller goes into the market to sell the stock. When customers of brokerage firms keep stock in a margin account, they agree to let the brokerage firm loan their stock out without the customer's specific approval. Thus, if an arbitrageur working for that brokerage firm wanted to establish a reversal, and if the stock to be sold short in the reversal were available in one of the margin accounts, the arbitrageur could borrow that stock and earn the full carrying rate on it. This is called "using box stock," since stock held in margin accounts is generally referred to as being in the "box."

There are other times, however, when an arbitrageur wants to do a reversal but does not have access to "box" stock. He must then find someone else from whom to borrow the stock. Obviously, there are people who own stock and would loan it to arbitrageurs for a fee. There are people who specialize in matching up investors with stock to loan and arbitrageurs who want to borrow stock. These people are said to be in the "stock loan" business. Generally, the fee for borrowing stock in this manner is anywhere from 10 to 20% of the prevailing carrying cost rate. For example, if the current carrying rate were 10% annually, then one would expect to pay 1 or 2% to the lender to borrow his stock. This reduces the profitability of the reversal slightly. Since small margins are being worked with, this cost to borrow the stock may make a significant difference to the arbitrageur.

These variations in the rates than an arbitrageur can earn on the credit balances in his account affect the marketplace. For example, a particular reversal might be available in the marketplace at a net profit of $\frac{1}{2}$-point, or 50 cents. Such a reversal may not be equally attractive to all arbitrageurs. Those who have "box" stock may be willing to do the reversal for 50 cents; those who have to pay 1% to borrow stock may want $\frac{9}{16}$ for the reversal; and those who pay 2% to borrow stock may need $\frac{5}{8}$ for the reversal. Thus, arbitrageurs who do conversions and reversals are in competition with each other not only in the marketplace, but in the stock loan arena as well.

Reversals are generally easier positions for the arbitrageur to locate than are conversions. This is because the fixed cost of the conversion is a rather burdensome effect. Only if the stock pays a rather large dividend that outweighs the carrying cost could the fixed portion of the conversion formula ever be a profit as opposed to a cost. In practice, the interest rate paid to carry stock is probably higher than the interest earned from being short stock, but any reasonable computer program should be able to handle two different interest rates.

The novice trader may find the term "conversion" somewhat illogical. In the over-the-counter option markets, the dealers create a position similar to the one shown here as a result of actually converting a put to a call.

Example: When someone owns a conventional put on XYZ with striking price of 60 and the stock falls to 50, there is often little chance of being able to sell the put profitably in the secondary market. The over-the-counter option dealer might offer to convert the put into a call. To do this, he would buy the put from the holder, then buy the stock itself, and then offer a call—at the original striking price of 60—to the holder of the put. Thus the dealer would be long the stock, long the put, and short the call—a conversion. The customer would then own a call on XYZ with a striking price of 60, due to expire on the same date that the put was destined to. The put that the customer owned has been converted into a call. To effect this conversion, the dealer pays out to the customer the difference between the current stock price, 50, and the striking price, 60. Thus the customer receives $1,000 for this conversion. Also, the dealer would charge the customer for costs to carry the stock, so that the dealer had no risk. If the stock rallied back above 60, the customer could make more money, because he owns the call. The dealer has no risk, as he has an arbitrage position to begin with. In a similar manner, the dealer can effect a reverse conversion—converting a call to a put—but will charge the dividends to the customer for doing so.

RISKS IN REVERSALS AND CONVERSIONS

Reversals and conversions are generally considered to be riskless arbitrage. That is, the profit in the arbitrage is fixed from the start and the subsequent movement of the underlying stock makes no difference in the eventual outcome. This is generally a true statement. However, there are some risks, and they are great enough that one can actually lose money in reversals and conversions if he does not take care. The risks are fourfold in reversal arbitrage: An extra dividend is declared, the interest rate falls while the reversal is in place, an early assignment is received, or the stock is exactly at the striking price at expiration. Converters have similar risks: a dividend cut, an increase in the interest rate, early assignment, or also the stock closing at the strike at expiration.

These risks will first be explored from the viewpoint of the reversal trader. If the company declares an extra dividend, it is highly likely that the reversal will become unprofitable. This is so because most extra dividends are rather large—more than the profit of a reversal. There is little the arbitrageur can do to avoid being caught by the declaration of a truly extra dividend. However, some companies have a track record of declaring extras with annual regularity. The arbitrageur should be aware of which companies these are and of the timing of these extra dividends. A clue sometimes exists in the marketplace. If the reversal appears overly profitable when the arbitrageur is first examining it (before he actually establishes it), he should be somewhat sceptical. Perhaps there is a reason why the reversal looks so tempting. An extra dividend that is being factored into the marketplace may be the answer.

The second risk is that of variation in interest rates while the reversal is in progress. Obviously rates can change over the course of the life of a reversal—normally 3 to 6 months. There are two ways to compensate for this. The simplest way is to leave some room for rates to move. For example, if rates are currently at 12% annually, one might allow for a movement of 2 to 3% in rates, depending on the length of time the reversal is expected to be in place. In order to allow for a 2% move, the arbitrageur would calculate his initial profit based on a rate of 10%, 2% less than the currently prevailing 12%. He would not establish any reversal that did not at least break even with a 10% rate. The rate at which a reversal breaks even is often called the "effective rate"—10% in this case. Obviously, if rates average higher than 10% during the life of the reversal, it will make money. Normally when one has an entire portfolio of reversals in place, he should know the effective rate of each set of reversals expiring at the same time. Thus, he would have an effective rate for his 2-month reversals, his 3-month ones, and so forth.

Allowing this room for rates to move does not necessarily mean that there will not be an adverse affect if rates do indeed fall. For example, rates could fall farther than the room allowed. Thus, a further measure is necessary in order to completely protect against a drop in rates: One should invest his credit balances generated by the reversals in interest-bearing paper that expires at approximately the same time the reversals do, and that bears interest at a rate that locks in a profit for the reversal account. For example, suppose that an arbitrageur has $5 million in 3-month reversals at an effective rate of 10%. If he can buy $5 million worth of 3-month Certificates of Deposit with a rate of $11\frac{1}{2}\%$, then he would lock in a profit of $1\frac{1}{2}\%$ on his $5 million. This method of using paper to hedge rate fluctuations is not practiced by all arbitrageurs—some feel it is not worth it. They feel that by leaving the credit balances to fluctuate at prevailing rates, they can make more if rates go up and that will cushion the effect when rates decline.

The third risk of reversal arbitrage is reception of an early assignment on the short puts. This forces the arbitrageur to buy stock and incurs a debit. Thus the position does not earn as much interest as was originally assumed. If the assignment is received early enough in the life of the reversal—recall that in-the-money puts can be assigned very far in advance of expiration—the reversal could actually incur an overall loss. Such early assignments normally occur during bearish markets. The only advantage of this early assignment is that one is left with unhedged long calls; these calls are well out-of-the-money and normally quite low-priced (¼ or less). If the market should reverse and turn bullish before the expiration of the calls, the arbitrageur may make money on them. There is no complete way to hedge against a market decline, but it does help if the arbitrageur tries to establish reversals with the call in-the-money and the put out-of-the-money. That, plus demanding a better overall return for reversals near the strike, should help cushion the effects of the bear market.

The final risk is the most common one—that of the stock closing exactly at the strike at expiration. This presents the arbitrageur with a decision to make regarding exercise of his long calls. Since the stock is exactly at the strike, he is not sure whether or not he will be assigned on his short puts at expiration. The outcome is that he may end up with an unhedged stock position on Monday morning after expiration. If the stock should open on a gap, he could have a substantial loss that wipes out the profits of many reversals. This risk of stock closing at the strike may seem minute, but it is not. In the absence of any real buying or selling in the stock on expiration day, the process of discounting will force a stock that is near the strike virtually right onto the strike. Once it is near the strike, this risk materializes.

There are two basic scenarios that could occur to produce this unhedged stock position. First, suppose one decides that he will not get put and he exercises his calls. However, he was wrong and he *does* get put. He has bought double the amount of stock—once via call exercise and again via put assignment. Thus he will be *long* on Monday morning. The other scenario produces the opposite effect. Suppose that he decides that he *will* get put and he decides not to exercise his calls. If he is wrong in this case, he does not buy any stock—he didn't exercise nor did he get put. Consequently, he will be *short* stock on Monday morning.

If one is truly undecided about whether or not he will be assigned on his short puts, he might look at several clues. First, has any late news come out on Friday evening that might affect the market's opening or the stock's opening on Monday morning? If so, that should be factored into the decision regarding exercising the calls. Another clue arises from the price at which the stock was trading during the Friday expiration day prior to the close. If the stock was below the strike for most of the day before closing *at* the strike, then there is a greater chance that the puts will be assigned. This is so because other arbitrageurs (discounters) have probably bought puts and bought stock during the day and will exercise to clean out their positions.

If there is still doubt, it may be wisest to exercise only half of the calls, hoping for a partial assignment on the puts (always a possibility). This halfway measure will normally result in some sort of unhedged stock position on Monday morning, but it will be smaller than the maximum exposure by at least ½.

There is another approach that the arbitrageur can take during the late trading of the options' life—during the last few days—if the stock is near the strike of the reversal. That is to roll the reversal to a later expiration or, failing that, to roll to another strike in the same expiration. First, let us consider rolling to another expiration. The arbitrageur knows the dollar price that equals his effective rate for a 3-month reversal. If the current options can be closed out and new options opened at the next expiration for at least the effective rate, then the reversal should be rolled. This is not a likely event, mostly due to the fact that the spread between the bid and asked prices on four separate options makes it difficult to attain the desired price. *Note:* this entire four-way order can be entered as a spread order; it is not necessary to attempt to "leg" the spread.

The second action—rolling to another strike in the same expiration month—may be more available. Suppose that one has the July 45 reversal in place (long July 45 call and short July 45 put). If the underlying stock is near 45, he might place an order to the exchange floor as a three-way spread: Sell the July 45 call (closing), buy the July 45 put (closing), and sell the July 40 call (opening) for a net credit of 5 points. This action costs the arbitrageur nothing except a small transaction charge, since he is receiving a 5-point credit for moving the strike by 5 points. Once this is accomplished, he will have moved the strike approximately 5 points away and will thus have avoided the problem of the stock closing at the strike.

Overall, these four risks are significant and reversal arbitrageurs should take care that they do not fall prey to them. The careless arbitrageur uses effective rates too close to current market rates, establishes reversals with puts in-the-money, and routinely accepts the risk of acquiring an unhedged stock position on the morning after expiration. He will probably sustain a large loss at some time. Since many reversal arbitrageurs work with small capital and/or have convinced their backers that it is a riskless strategy, such a loss may have the effect of putting them out of business. That is an unnecessary risk to take. There are countermeasures—as described above—that can reduce the effects of the four risks.

Let us consider the risks for conversion traders more briefly. The risk of stock closing near the strike is just as bad for the conversion as it is for the reversal. The same techniques for handling those risks apply equally well to conversions as to reversals. The other risks are similar to reversal risks, but there are slight nuances.

The conversion arbitrage suffers if there is a dividend cut. There is little the arbitrageur can do to predict this except to be aware of the fundamentals of the company before entering into the conversion. Alternatively, he might avoid conversions where the dividend makes up a major part of the profit of the arbitrage.

Another risk occurs if there is an early assignment on the calls before the ex-dividend date and the dividend is not received. Moreover, an early assignment leaves the arbitrageur with naked puts, albeit fractional ones since they are surely deeply out-of-the-money. Again, the policy of establishing conversions where the dividend is not a major factor would help to ease the consequences of early assignment.

The final risk is that interest rates increase during the time the conversion is in place. This makes the carrying costs larger than anticipated and might cause a loss. The best way to hedge this initially is to allow a margin for error. Thus, if the prevailing interest rate is 12%, one might only establish reversals that would break even if rates rose to 14%. If rates do not rise that far on average, a profit will result. The arbitrageur can attempt to hedge this risk by *shorting* interest-bearing paper that matures at approximately the same time as the conversions. For example, if one has $5 million worth of 3-month conversions, established at an effective rate of 14% and he shorts 3-month paper at 12½%, he locks in a profit of 1½%. This is not common practice for conversion arbitrageurs but it does hedge the effect of rising interest rates.

SUMMARY OF CONVERSION ARBITRAGE

The practice of conversion and reversal arbitrage in the listed option markets helps to keep put and call prices in line. If arbitrageurs are active in a particular option, the prices of the put and call will relate to the stock price in line with the formulae given earlier. Note that this is also a valid reason why puts tend to sell at a lower price than calls do. The cost of money is the determining factor in the difference between put and call prices. In essence, the "cost" (although it may sometimes be a credit) is subtracted from the theoretical put price. Refer again to the formula given above for the profit potential of a conversion. Assume that things are in perfect alignment. Then the formula would read:

$$\text{Put price} = \text{striking price} + \text{call price} - \text{stock price} - \text{fixed cost}$$

Furthermore, if the stock is at the striking price, the formula reduces to:

$$\text{Put price} = \text{call price} - \text{fixed cost}$$

So, whenever the fixed cost, which is equal to the carrying charge less the dividends, is greater than zero (and it usually is), the put will sell for less than the call if a stock is at the striking price. Only in the case of a large-dividend-paying stock, where the fixed cost becomes negative (that is, it is not a cost, but a profit), does the reverse hold true. This is supportive evidence for statements made earlier that at-the-money calls sell for more than at-the-money puts, all other things being equal. The reader can see quite clearly that it has nothing to do with supply and demand for the puts and calls—a fallacy that is sometimes proferred. This same sort of analysis can also be used to prove the broader statement that calls have a greater time value premium than puts do, except in the case of a large-dividend-paying stock.

One final word of advice should be offered to the public customer. He may sometimes be able to find conversions or reversals, by using the simplistic formula, that appear to have profit potentials that exceed commission costs. Such positions do exist from time to time, but the rate of return to the public customer will almost assuredly be less than the short-term cost of money. If it were not, arbitrageurs would be onto the position very quickly. The public option trader may not actually be thinking in terms of comparing the profit potential of a position with what he could get by placing the money into a bank, but he must do so to convince himself that he cannot feasibly attempt conversion or reversal arbitrages.

THE "INTEREST PLAY"

In the preceding discussion of reversal arbitrage, it is apparent that a substantial portion of the arbitrageur's profits may be due to the interest earned on the credit of the position. Another type of position is used by many arbitrageurs to take advantage of this interest earned. The arbitrageur sells the underlying stock short and simultaneously buys an in-the-money call that is trading slightly over parity. The actual amount over parity that the arbitrageur can afford to pay for the call is determined by the interest that he will earn from his short sale and the dividend payout before expiration. He does not use a put in this type of position. In fact, this "interest play" strategy is merely a reversal arbitrage without the short put. This slight variation has a residual benefit for the arbitrageur—if the underlying stock should drop dramatically in price, he could make large profits because he is short the underlying stock. In any case, *he will make his interest credit less the amount of time value premium paid for the call less any dividends lost.*

Example 1: XYZ is sold short at 60, and a January 50 call is bought for 10¼ points. Assume that the prevailing interest rate is 1% per month and that the position is established one month prior to expiration. XYZ pays no dividend. The total credit brought in from the trades is $4,975, so the arbitrageur will earn $49.75 in interest over the course of 1 month. If the stock is above 50 at expiration, he will exercise his call to buy stock at 50 and close the position. His loss on the security trades will be $25— the amount of time value premium paid for the call option (he makes 10 points by selling stock at 60 and buying at 50, but loses 10¼ points on the exercised call). His overall profit is thus $24.75.

Example 2: A real-life example may point out the effect of interest rates even more dramatically. In early 1979, IBM April 240 calls with about six weeks of life remaining were over 60 points in-the-money. IBM was not going to be ex-dividend in that time. Normally, such a deeply in-the-money option would be trading at parity or even a discount when the time remaining to expiration is so short. However, these calls were trading 3½ points over parity because of the prevailing high interest rates at the time. IBM was at 300, the April 240 calls were trading at 63½, and the prevailing interest rate was approximately 1% per month. The credit from selling the stock and buying the call was $23,700, so the arbitrageur earned $365.50 in interest for 1½ months, and lost $350—the 3½ points of time value premium that he paid for the call. This still left enough room for a profit.

In Chapter 1, it was stated that interest rates affect option prices. The above examples of the "interest play" strategy quite clearly show why. As interest rates rise, the arbitrageur can affort to pay more for the long call in this strategy, thus causing the call price to increase in times of high interest rates. If call prices are higher, so will put prices be, as the relationships necessary for conversion and reversal arbitrage are preserved. Similarly, if interest rates decline, the arbitrageur will make lower bids, and call and put prices will be lower. They are active enough to give truth to the theory that option prices are directly related to interest rates.

THE BOX SPREAD

An arbitrage consists of simultaneously buying and selling the same security or equivalent securities at different prices. For example, the reversal consists of selling a put and simultaneously shorting stock and buying a call. The reader should recall that the short stock/long call position was called a synthetic put. That is, shorting the stock and buying a call is equivalent to buying a pot. The reversal arbitrage therefore consists of selling a (listed) put and simultaneously buying a (synthetic) put. In a similar manner, the conversion is merely the purchase of a (listed) put and the simultaneous sale of a (synthetic) put. Many equivalent strategies can be combined for arbitrage purposes. One of the more common ones is the box spread.

Recall that it was shown that a bull spread or a bear spread could be constructed with either puts or calls. Thus if one were to simultaneously buy a (call) bull spread and buy a (put) bear spread, he could have an arbitrage. In essence, he is merely buying and selling equivalent spreads. If the price differentials work out correctly, a risk-free arbitrage may be possible.

Example: The following prices exist:

XYZ common, 55

XYZ January 50 call, 7

XYZ January 50 put, 1

XYZ January 60 call, 2

XYZ January 60 put, 5½

The arbitrageur could establish the box spread in this example by executing the following transactions:

Buy a call bull spread:		
Buy XYZ January 50 call	7 debit	
Sell XYZ January 60 call	2 credit	
Net call cost		5 debit
Buy a put bear spread:		
Buy XYZ January 60 put	5½ debit	
Sell XYZ January 50 put	1 credit	
Net put cost		4½ debit
Total cost of position		9½ debit

No matter where XYZ is at January expiration, this position will be worth 10 points. *The arbitrageur has locked in a risk-free profit of* ½ point, since he "bought" the box spread for 9½ points and will be able to "sell" it for 10 points at expiration. To verify this, the position will be evaluated at expiration, first with XYZ above 60, then with XYZ between 50 and 60, and finally with XYZ below 50. If XYZ is above 60 at expiration, the puts will expire worthless and the call bull spread will be at its maximum potential of 10 points—the difference between the striking prices. Thus the position can be liquidated for 10 points if XYZ is above 60 at expiration. Now assume that XYZ is between 50 and 60 at expiration. In that case, the out-of-the-money, written options would expire worthless—the January 60 call and the January 50 put. This would leave a long, in-the-money combination consisting of a January 50 call and a January 60 put. These two options must have a total value of 10 points at expiration with XYZ between 50 and 60 (for example, the arbitrageur could exercise his call to buy stock at 50 and exercise his put to sell stock at 60). Finally, assume that XYZ is below 50 at expiration. The calls would expire worthless if that were true, but the remaining put spread—actually a bear spread in the puts—would be at its maximum potential of 10 points. Again, the box spread could be liquidated for 10 points.

The arbitrageur must pay a cost to carry the position, however. In the prior example, if interest rates were 6% and he had to hold the box for 5 months, it would cost him an additional 14 cents (.06 × 9½ × 3/12). This still leaves room for a profit.

In essence, a bull spread (using calls) was purchased while a bear spread (using puts) was bought. The box spread was described in these terms only to illustrate the fact the the arbitrageur is buying and selling equivalent positions. The arbitrageur who is utilizing the box spread should *not* think in terms of bull or bear spread, however. Rather, he should be concerned with "buying" the entire box spread at a cost of less than the differential between the two striking prices. By "buying" the box spread, it is meant that both the call spread portion and the put spread portion are debit spreads. *Whenever the arbitrageur observes that a call spread and a put spread using the same strikes—and where both are debit spreads— can be bought for less than the difference in the strikes plus carrying costs, he should execute the arbitrage.*

Obviously, there is a companion strategy to the one just described. It might sometimes be possible for the arbitrageur to "sell" both spreads. That is, he would establish a credit call spread and a credit put spread, using the same strikes. *If this credit were greater than the difference in the striking prices, a risk-free profit would be locked in.*

Example: Assume that a different set of prices exists:

XYZ common, 75
XYZ April 70 call, 8½
XYZ April 70 put, 1

XYZ April 80 call, 3

XYZ April 80 put, 6

By executing the following transactions, the box spread could be "sold":

Sell a call (bear) spread:		
Buy April 80 call	3 debit	
Sell April 70 call	8½ credit	
Net credit on calls		5½
Sell a put (bull) spread:		
Buy April 70 put	1 debit	
Sell April 80 put	6 credit	
Net credit on puts		5 credit
Total credit of position		10½ credit

In this case, no matter where XYZ is at expiration, the position can be bought back for 10 points. This means that the arbitrageur has locked in a risk-free profit of ½ point. To briefly verify this statement, first assume that XYZ is above 80 at April expiration. The puts will expire worthless, and the call spread will have widened to 10 points—the cost to buy it back. Alternatively, if XYZ were between 70 and 80 at April expiration, the long, out-of-the-money options would expire worthless and the in-the-money combination would cost 10 points to buy back (for example, the arbitrageur could let himself be put at 80, buying stock there, and called at 70, selling the stock there—a net "cost" to liquidate of 10 points). Finally, if XYZ were below 70 at expiration, the calls would expire worthless and the put spread would have widened to 10 points. It could then be closed out at a cost of 10 points. In each case, the arbitrageur is able to liquidate the box spread by buying it back at 10.

In this, he would *earn* interest on the credit received while he holds the position.

There is an additional factor in the profitability of the box spread. Since the sale of a box generates a credit, the arbitrageur who sells a box will earn a small amount of money from that sale. Conversely, the purchaser of a box spread will have a charge for carrying cost. Since profit margins may be small in a box arbitrage, these carrying costs can have a definite effect. As a result, boxes may actually be sold for 5 points, even though the striking prices are 5 points apart, and the arbitrageur can still make money because of the interest earned.

These box spreads are not easy to find. If one does appear, the act of doing the arbitrage will soon make the arbitrage impossible. In fact, this is true of any type of arbitrage—it cannot be executed indefinitely because the mere act of arbitraging will force the prices back into line. Occasionally, the arbitrageur will be able to find the option quotes to his liking, especially in volatile markets, and can establish a risk-free arbitrage with the box spread. It can be evaluated at a glance. Only two questions need to be answered:

1. If one were to establish a debit call spread and a debit put spread, using the same strikes, would the total cost be *less than* the difference in the striking prices plus carrying costs? If the answer is yes, an arbitrage exists.
2. Alternatively, if one were to sell both spreads—establishing a credit call spread and a credit put spread—would the total credit received plus interest earned be *greater than* the difference in the striking prices? If the answer is yes, an arbitrage exists.

There are some risks to box arbitrage. Many of them are the same as those risks faced by the arbitrageur doing conversions or reversals. First, there is risk that the stock might close at *either* of the two strikes. This presents the arbitrageur with the same dilemma regarding whether or not to exercise his long options, since he is not sure if he will be assigned. Additionally, early assignment may change the profitability—assignment of a short put will incur large carrying costs on the resulting long stock; assignment of a short call will inevitably come just before an ex-dividend date, costing the arbitrageur the amount of the dividend.

There are not many opportunities to actually transact box arbitrage, but the fact that such arbitrage exists can help to keep markets in line. For example, if an underlying stock begins to move quickly and order flow increases dramatically, the specialist or market-markers in that stock's options may be so inundated with orders that they cannot be sure that their markets are correct. They can use the principles of box arbitrage to keep prices in line. For example, the most active options would be the ones at strikes nearest to the current stock price. The specialist can quickly add up the markets of the call and put at the nearest strike above the stock price and add to that the markets of the options at the strike just below. The sum of the four should add up to a price that surrounds the difference in the strikes. If the strikes are 5 points apart, then the sum of the four markets should be something like 4½ bid, 5½ asked. If, instead, the four markets add up to a price that allows box arbitrage to be established, then the specialist will adjust his markets.

VARIATIONS ON EQUIVALENCE ARBITRAGE

Other variations of arbitrage on equivalent positions are possible, although they are relatively complicated and probably not worth the arbitrageur's time to analyze. For example, one could buy a butterfly spread with calls and simultaneously sell a butterfly spread using puts. A listed straddle could be sold and a synthetic straddle could be bought—short stock and long 2 calls. Inversely, a listed straddle could be bought against a ratio write—long stock and short 2 calls. The only time that the arbitrageur should even consider anything like this is when there are more sizable markets in certain of the puts and calls than there are in others. If this were the case, he might be able to take an ordinary box spread, conversion, or reversal, and add to it, keeping the arbitrage intact by ensuring that he is, in fact, buying and selling equivalent positions.

THE EFFECTS OF ARBITRAGE

The arbitrage process serves a useful purpose in the listed options market because it may provide a secondary market where one might not otherwise exist. Normally, public interest in an in-the-money option dwindles as the option becomes deeply in-the-money or if the time remaining until expiration is very short. There would be few public buyers of these options. In fact, public selling pressure might increase because the public would rather liquidate in-the-money options held long then exercise them. The few public buyers of such options might be writers who are closing out. However, if the writer is covered—especially where call options are concerned—he might decide to be assigned rather than close out his option. This means that the public seller is creating a rather larger supply that is not offset by a public demand. The market created by the arbitrageur—especially in the basic put or call arbitrage—essentially creates the demand. Without these arbitrageurs, there could conceivably be no buyers at all, for those options which are short-lived and in-the-money, after public writers have finished closing out their positions.

Equivalence arbitrage—conversion, reversals, and box spreads—helps to keep the relative prices of puts and calls in line with each other and with the underlying stock price. This creates a more efficient and rational market for the public to operate in. The arbitrageur would help eliminate, for example, the case where a public customer buys a call, sees the stock go up, but cannot find anyone to sell his call to at higher prices. If the call were too cheap, arbitrageurs would do reversals, which involve call purchases, and would therefore provide a market to sell into.

Questions have been raised as to whether option trading affects stock prices, especially at or just before an expiration. If the amount of arbitrage in a certain issue becomes very large, it could appear to temporarily affect the price of the stock itself. For example, take the call arbitrage. This involves the sale of stock in the market. The corresponding stock purchase, via the call exercise, is not executed on the exchange. Thus, as far as the stock market is concerned, there may appear to be an inordinate amount of selling in the stock. If a large number of basic call arbitrages are taking place, they might thus hold the price of the stock down until the calls expire.

The put arbitrage has an opposite effect. This arbitrage involves buying stock in the market. The offsetting stock sale, via the put exercise takes place off the exchange. If a large amount of put arbitrage is being done, there may appear to be an inordinate amount of buying in the stock. Such action might temporarily hold the stock price up.

In a vast majority of cases, however, the arbitrage has no visible effect on the underlying stock price, because the amount of arbitrage being done is very small in comparison to the total number of trades in a given stock. Even if the open interest in a particular option is large, allowing for plenty of option volume by the arbitrageurs, the actual act of doing the arbitrage will force the prices of the stock and option back into line, thus destroying the arbitrage.

Rather elaborate studies, including doctoral theses, have been written which try to prove or disprove the theory that option trading affects stock prices. Nothing has been conclusively proven, and may never be, because of the complexity of the task. Logic would seem to dictate that arbitrage could temporarily affect a stock's movement if it has discount, in-the-money options shortly before expiration. However, one would have to reasonably conclude that the size of these arbitrages could almost never be large enough to overcome a directional trend in the underlying stock itself. Thus, in the absence of a definite direction in the stock, arbitrage might help to perpetuate the inertia, but if there were truly a preponderance of investors wanting to buy or sell the stock, these investors would totally dominate any arbitrage that might be in progress.

RISK ARBITRAGE USING OPTIONS

Risk arbitrage is a strategy that is well described by its name. It is basically an arbitrage—the same or equivalent securities are bought and sold. However, there is generally risk because the arbitrage usually depends on a future event occurring in order for the arbitrage to be successful. One form of a risk arbitrage was described earlier concerning the speculation on the size of a special dividend that an underlying stock might pay. That arbitrage consisted of buying the stock and buying the put, where the put's time value premium is less than the amount of the projected special dividend. The risk lies in the arbitrageur's speculation on the size of the anticipated special dividend.

Mergers

Risk arbitrage is an age-old type of arbitrage in the stock market. *Generally, it concerns speculation on whether a proposed merger or acquisition will actually go through as proposed.*

Example: XYZ, which is selling for $50 per share, offers to buy out LMN and is offering to swap one share of its (XYZ's) stock for every two shares of LMN. This would mean that LMN should be worth $25 per share if the acquisition goes through as proposed. On the day the takeover is proposed, LMN stock would probably rise to about $22 per share. It would not trade all the way up to 25 until the takeover was approved by the shareholders of LMN stock. The arbitrageur who feels that this takeover will be approved can take action. He would sell short XYZ and, for every share that he is short, he would buy 2 shares of LMN stock. If the merger goes through, he will profit. The reason that he shorts XYZ as well as buying LMN is to protect himself in case the market price of XYZ drops before the acquisition is approved. In essence, he has sold XYZ and also bought the equivalent of XYZ (two shares of LMN will be equal to one share of XYZ if the takeover goes through). This, then, is clearly an arbitrage. However, it is a risk arbitrage because if the stockholders of LMN reject the offer, he will surely lose money. His profit potential is equal to the remaining differential between the current market price of LMN (22) and the takeover price (25). If the proposed acquisition goes through, the differential disappears, and the arbitrageur has his profit.

The greatest risk in a merger is that it is canceled. If that happens, the stock being acquired (LMN) will fall in price, returning to its pre-takeover levels. In addition, the acquiring stock (XYZ) will probably rise. Thus, the risk arbitrageur can lose money on both sides of his trade. *If either or both of the stocks involved in the proposed takeover have options, the arbitrageur may be able to work options into his strategy.*

In merger situations, since large moves can occur in both stocks (they move in concert), option purchases are the preferable option strategy. If the acquiring company (XYZ) has in-the-money puts, then the purchase of those puts may be used instead of selling XYZ short. The advantage is that if XYZ rallies dramatically during the time it takes the merger to take effect, then the arbitrageur's profits will be increased.

Example: As above, assume that XYZ is at 50 and is acquiring LMN in a 2-for-1 stock deal. LMN is at 22. Suppose that XYZ rallies to 60 by the time the deal closes. This would pull LMN up to a price of 30. If one had been short 100 XYZ at 50 and long 200 LMN at 22, then his profit would be $600—a $1,600 gain on the 200 long LMN minus a $1,000 loss on the XYZ short sale.

Compare that result to a similar strategy substituting a long put for the short XYZ stock. Assume that he buys 200 LMN as before, but now buys an XYZ put. If one could buy an XYZ July 55 put with little time premium, say at 5½ points, then he would have nearly the same dollars of profit if the merger should go through with XYZ below 55.

However, when XYZ rallies to 60, his profit increases. He would still make the $1,600 on LMN as it rose from 22 to 30, but now would only lose $550 on the XYZ put—a total profit of $1,050 as compared to $600 with an all stock position.

The disadvantage to substituting long puts for short stock is that the arbitrageur does not receive credit for the short sale and, therefore, does not earn money at the carrying rate. This might not be as large a disadvantage as it initially seems, however, since it is often the case that it is very expensive—even impossible—to borrow the acquiring stock in order to short it. If the stock borrow costs are very large or if no stock can be located for borrowing, the purchase of an in-the-money put is a viable alternative. The purchase of an in-the-money put is preferable to an at- or out-of-the-money put because the amount of time value premium paid for the latter would take too much of the profitability away from the arbitrage if XYZ stayed unchanged or declined. This strategy may also save money if the merger falls apart, and XYZ rises. The loss on the long put may well be less than the loss would be on short XYZ stock.

Note also that one could sell the XYZ July 55 call short as well as buy the put. This would, of course, be synthetic short stock and is a pure substitute for shorting the stock. The use of this synthetic short is recommended only when the arbitrageur cannot borrow the acquiring stock. If this is his purpose, he should use the in-the-money put and out-of-the-money call, since if he were assigned on the call, he could not borrow the stock to deliver it as a short sale. The use of an out-of-the-money call lessens the chance of eventual assignment.

The companion strategy is to buy an in-the-money call instead of buying the company being acquired (LMN). This has advantages if the stock falls too far, either because the merger falls apart or because the stocks in the merger decline too far. Additionally, the cost of carrying the long LMN stock is eliminated, although that is generally built into the cost of the long calls. The larger amount of time value premium in calls as compared to puts makes this strategy often less attractive than that of buying the puts as a substitute for the short sale.

One might also consider selling options instead of buying them. Generally this is an inferior strategy, but in certain instances it makes sense. The reason that option sales are inferior is that they do not limit one's risk in the risk arbitrage, but they cut off the profit. For example, if one sells puts on the company being acquired (LMN) he has a bullish situation. However, if the company being acquired (XYZ) rallies too far, there will be a loss as the short puts will stop making money as soon as LMN rises through the strike. This is especially disconverting if a takeover bidding war should develop for LMN. The arbitrageur who is long LMN will participate nicely as LMN rises heavily in price during the bidding war. However, the put seller will not participate to nearly the same extent.

The sale of in-the-money calls as a substitute for shorting the acquiring company (XYZ) can be beneficial at certain times. It is necessary to have a plus tick in order to sell stock short. When many arbitrageurs are trying to sell a stock short at the same time, it may be difficult to sell much stock short. Morever, natural owners of XYZ may see the arbitrageurs holding the price down and decide to sell their long stock rather than suffer through a possible decline in the stock's price while the merger is in progress. Additionally, buyers of XYZ will become very timid, lowering their bid for the same reasons. All of this may add up to a situation in which it is very difficult to sell the stock short, even if it can be borrowed. The sale of an in-the-money call can overcome this difficulty. The call should be deeply in-the-money and not be too long-term, for the arbitrageur does not want to see XYZ decline below the strike of the call. If that happened, he would no longer be hedged; the other side of the arbitrage—the long LMN stock—would continue to decline but he would not have any remaining short against the long LMN.

Limits on the Merger

There is another type of merger for stock which is more difficult to arbitrage, but options may prove useful. In some merger situations, the acquiring company (XYZ) promises to give the shareholders of the company being acquired (LMN) an amount of stock equal to a set dollar price. This amount of stock would be paid even if the acquiring company rose or fell moderately in price. If XYZ falls too far, however, it cannot pay out an extraordinarily increased number of shares to LMN shareholders, so XYZ puts a limit on the maximum number of shares that it will pay for each share of LMN stock. Thus, the shareholders of XYZ are guaranteed that there will be some downside buffer in terms of dilution of their company in case XYZ declines, as is often the case for an acquiring company. However, if XYZ declines too far, then LMN shareholders will receive less. In return for getting this downside guarantee, XYZ will usually also stipulate that there is a *minimum* amount of shares that they will pay to LMN shareholders, even if XYZ stock rises tremendously. Thus, if XYZ should rise tremendously in price, then LMN shareholders will do even better than they had anticipated. An example will demonstrate this type of merger accord.

Example: Assume that XYZ is at 50 and it intends to acquire LMN for a stated price of 25 dollars per share, as in the previous example.

However, instead of merely saying that it will exchange two shares of LMN for one share of XYZ, the company says that they want the offer to be worth $25 per share to LMN shareholders as long as XYZ is between 45 and 55. Given this information, we can determine the maximum and minimum number of shares that LMN shareholders will receive: The maximum is the stated price, 25, divided by the lower limit, 45, or 0.556 shares; the minimum is 25 divided by the higher limit, 55, or 0.455.

This type of merger is usually stated in terms of how many shares of XYZ will be issued, rather than in terms of the price range that XYZ will be able to move in. In either case, one can be derived from the other so that the manner in which the merger deal is stated is merely a convention. In this case, for example, the merger might be stated as being worth 25 dollars per share, with each share of LMN being worth at least 0.455 shares of XYZ and at most 0.556 shares of XYZ. Note that these ratios make the deal worth 25 as long as XYZ is between 45 and 55: 45 times 0.556 equals 25, as does 0.455 times 55.

If the acquiring stock, XYZ, is between 45 and 55 at the time that merger is completed, then the number of shares of XYZ that each LMN shareholder will receive is determined in a preset manner. Usually, at the time the merger is announced, XYZ will say that its price on the closing date of the merger will be used to establish the proper ratio. As a slight alternative, sometimes the acquiring company will state that the price to be used in determining the final ratio is to be an average of the closing prices of the stock over a stated period of time. This stated period of time might be something like the 10 days prior to the closing of the merger.

Example: Suppose that the closing price of XYZ on the day that the merger closes is to be the price used in the ratio. Furthermore, suppose that XYZ closes at 51 on that day. It is within the prestated range, so a calculation must be done in order to determine how many shares of XYZ each LMN shareholder will get. This ratio is determined by dividing the stated price, 25, by the price in question, 51. This would give a final ratio of 0.490196. The final ratio is usually computed to a rather large number of decimal points in order to assure that LMN shareholders get as close to $25 per share as possible.

The above two examples explain how this type of merger works. A merger of this type is said to have "hooks"—the prices at which the ratio steadies. This makes it difficult to arbitrage. As long as XYZ roams around in the 45 to 55 range, the arbitrageur does not want to short XYZ as part of his arbitrage for the price of XYZ does not affect the price he will eventually receive for LMN—25. Rather, he would buy LMN and wait until the deal is near closing before actually shorting XYZ. By waiting, he will know approximately how many shares of XYZ to short for each share of LMN that he owns. The reason that he must short XYZ at the end of the merger is that there is usually a period of time before the physical stock is reorganized from LMN into XYZ. During that time, if he were long LMN, he would be at risk if he did not short XYZ against it.

Problems arise if XYZ begins to fall below 45 well before the closing of the merger, the lower "hook" in the merger. If it should remain below 45, then one should set up the arbitrage as being short 0.556 shares of XYZ for each share of LMN that is held long. As long as XYZ remains below 45 until the merger closes, this is the proper ratio. However, if, after establishing that ratio, XYZ rallies back above 45, the arbitrageur can suffer damaging losses. XYZ may continue to rise in price, creating a loss on the short side. However, LMN will not follow it, because the merger is structured so that LMN is worth 25 unless XYZ rises above too far. Thus, the long side stops following as the short side moves higher.

On the other hand, no such problem exists if XYZ rises too far from its original price of 50, going above the upper "hook" of 55. In that case, the arbitrageur would already be long the LMN and would not yet have shorted XYZ since the merger was not yet closing. LMN would merely follow XYZ higher after the latter had crossed 55.

This is not uncommon dilemma. Recall that it was shown that the acquiring stock will often fall in price immediately after a merger is announced. Thus, XYZ may fall close to, or below, the lower "hook." Some arbitrageurs attempt to hedge themselves by shorting a little XYZ as it begins to fall near 45 and then completing the short if it drops well below 45. The problem with handling the situation in this way is that one ends up with an inexact ratio. Essentially he is forcing himself to predict the movements of XYZ.

If the acquiring stock drops below the lower "hook," there may be an opportunity to establish a hedge without these risks if that stock has listed options. The idea is to buy puts on the acquiring company, and for those puts to have a striking price nearly equal to the price of the lower "hook." The proper amount of the company being acquired (LMN) is then purchased to complete the arbitrage. If the acquiring company subsequently rallies back into the stated price range, the puts will not lose money past the strking price and the problems described in the preceding paragraph will have been overcome.

Example: A merger is announced as described in the preceding example: XYZ is to acquire LMN at a stated value of 25 dollars per share, with the stipulation that each share of LMN will be worth at least 0.455 shares of XYZ and at most 0.556 shares. These share ratios equate to prices of 45 and 55 on XYZ.

Suppose that XYZ drops immediately in price after the merger is announced, and it falls to 40. Furthermore, suppose that the merger is expected to close sometime during July and that there are XYZ August

45 puts trading at 5½. This represents only a small ½ point time value premium. The arbitrageur could then set up the arbitrage by buying 10,000 LMN and buying 56 of those puts. Smaller investors might buy 1,000 LMN and buy 6 puts. Either of these is in approximately the proper ratio of 1 LMN to 0.556 XYZ.

Tender Offers

Another type of corporate takeover that falls under the broad category of risk arbitrage is the tender offer. In a tender offer, the acquiring company normally offers to exchange cash for shares of the company to be acquired. Sometimes the offer is for all of the shares of the company being acquired; sometimes it is for a fractional portion of shares. In the latter case, it is important to know what is intended to be done with the remaining shares. These might be exchanged for shares of the acquiring company, or they might be exchanged for other securities (bonds, most likely), or perhaps there is no plan for exchanging them at all. In some cases, a company tenders for part of its own stock, so that is in effect both the acquirer and the acquiree. Thus, tender offers can be complicated to arbitrage properly. The use of options can lessen the risks.

In the case where the acquiring company is making a cash tender for all the shares—called an "any and all" offer—the main use of options is the purchase of puts as protection. One would buy puts on the company being acquired at the same time that he bought shares of that company. If the deal fell apart for some reason, the puts could prevent a disastrous loss as the acquiring stock dropped. The arbitrageur must be judicious in buying these puts. If they are too expensive, or too far out-of-the-money, or if the acquiring company might not really drop too far if the deal falls apart, then the purchase of puts is a waste. However, if there is substantial downside risk, the put purchase may be useful.

Selling options in an "any and all" deal often seems like easy money, but there may be risks. If the deal is completed, the company being acquired will disappear and its options would be delisted. Therefore, it may often seem reasonable to sell out-of-the-money puts on the acquiring company. If the deal is completed, these expire worthless at the closing of the merger. However, if the deal falls through, these puts will soar in price and cause a large loss. On the other hand, it may also seem like easy money to sell naked calls with a striking price higher than the price being offered for the stock. Again, if the deal goes through, these will be delisted and expire worthless. The risk in this situation is that another company bids a higher price for the company on which the calls were written. If this happens, there might suddenly be a large upward jump in price and the written calls could suffer a large loss.

Options can play a more meaningful role in the tender offer that is for only part of the stock, especially when it is expected that the remaining stock might fall substantially in price after the partial tender offer is completed. An example of a partial tender offer might help to establish the scenario:

Example: XYZ proposes to buy back part of its own stock. It has offered to pay $70 per share for half the company. There are no plans to do anything further. Based on the fundamentals of the company, it is expected that the remaining stock will sell for approximately $40 per share. Thus, the average share of XYZ is worth 55 if the tender offer is completed (one-half can be sold at 70, and the other half will be worth 40). XYZ stock might sell for $52 or $53 per share until the tender is completed. On the day after the tender offer expires, XYZ stock will drop immediately to the $40-per-share level.

There are two ways to make money in this situation. One is to buy XYZ at the current price, say 52, and tender it. The remaining portion would be sold at the lower price, say 40, when XYZ reopened after the tender expired. This method would yield a profit of $3 per share if exactly 50% of the shares are accepted at 70 in the tender offer. In reality, a slightly higher percentage of shares is usually accepted because a few people make mistakes and don't tender. Thus, one's average net price might be $56 per share for a $4 profit from this method. The risk in this situation is that XYZ opens substantially below 40 after the tender at 70 is completed.

Theoretically, the other way to trade this tender offer might be to sell XYZ short at 52 and cover it at 40 when it reopens after the tender offer expires. Unfortunately, this method cannot be effected because there will not be any XYZ stock to borrow in order to sell it short. All owners will tender the stock rather than loan it to arbitrageurs. Arbitrageurs understand this and they also understand the risk they take if they try to short stock at the last minute—they might be forced to buy back the stock for cash or they may be forced to give the equivalent of $70 per share for half the stock to the person who bought the stock from them. For some reason, many individual investors feel that they can "get away" with this strategy. They short stock figuring that their brokerage firm will find some way to borrow it for them. Unfortunately, this usually costs the customer a lot of money.

The use of calls does not provide a more viable way of attempting to capitalize on the drop of XYZ from 52 to 40. In-the-money call options on XYZ will normally be selling at parity just before the tender offer expires. If one sells the call as a substitute for the short sale, he will probably receive an assignment notice on the day after the tender offer expires and therefore find himself with the same problems the short seller has.

The only safe way to play for this drop is to buy puts on XYZ. These puts will be very expensive. In fact, with XYZ at 52 before the tender offer expires, if the consensus opinion is that XYZ will trade at 40 after the offer expires, then puts with a 50 strike will sell for at least $10. This large price reflects the expected drop in price of XYZ. Thus, it is not beneficial to buy these puts as downside speculation unless one expects the stock to drop farther than to the $40 level. There is, however, an opportunity for arbitrage by buying XYZ stock and also buying the expensive puts.

Before giving an example of that arbitrage, a word about *short tendering* is in order. Short tendering is against the law. It comes about when one tenders stock into a tender offer when he does not really own that stock. There are complex definitions regarding what constitute ownership of stock during a tender offer. One must be *net long* all the stock that he tenders on the day the tender offer expires. Thus, he cannot tender the stock on the day before the offer expires, and then short the stock on the next day (even if he could borrow the stock). In addition, one must subtract the number of shares covered by certain calls written against his position: Any calls with a strike price less than the tender offer price must be subtracted. Thus, if he is long 1,000 shares and has written 10 in-the-money calls, he cannot tender any shares. The novice and experienced investor alike must be aware of these definitions and should not violate the short tender rules.

Let us now look at an arbitrage consisting of buying stock and buying the expensive puts.

Example: XYZ is at 52. As before, there is a tender offer for half the stock at 70, with no plans for the remainder. The July 55 puts sell for 15, and the July 50 puts sell for 10. It is common that both puts would be predicting the same price in the after-market: 40.

If one buys 200 shares of XYZ at 52 and buys one July 50 put at 10, he has a locked-in profit as long as the tender offer is completed. He only buys 1 put because he is assuming that 100 shares will be accepted by the company and only 100 shares be returned to him. Once the 100 shares has been returned, he can exercise the put to close out his position.

The following table summarizes these results:

Initial purchase	
Buy 200 XYZ at 52	$10,400 debit
Buy 1 July 50 put at 10	1,000 debit
Total Cost	$11,400 debit
Closing sale	
Sell 100 XYZ at 70 via tender	$ 7,000 credit
Sell 100 XYZ at 50 via put exercise	5,000 credit
Total proceeds	$12,000 credit
Total profit: $600	

This strategy eliminates the risk of loss if XYZ opens substantially below 40 after the tender offer. The downside price is locked in by the puts.

If more than 50% of XYZ should be accepted in the tender offer then a larger profit will result. Also, if XYZ should subsequently trade at a high-enough price that the July 50 put has some time value premium, then a larger profit would result as well (the arbitrageur would not exercise the put, but would sell the stock and the put separately in that case.)

Partial tender offers can be quite varied. The type described in the above example is called a "two-tier" offer because the tender offer price is substantially different from the remaining price. In some partial tenders, the remainder of the stock is slated for purchase at substantially the same price, perhaps through a cash merger. The above strategy would not be applicable in that case, since such an offer would more closely resemble the "any and all" offer. In other types of partial tenders, debt securities of the acquiring company may be issued after the partial cash tender. The net price of these debt securities may be different from the tender offer price. If so, the above strategy might work.

In summary, then, one should look at tender offers carefully. One should be careful not to take extraordinary option risk in an "any and all" tenders. Conversely, one should look to take advantage of any "two-tier" situation in a partial tender offer by buying stock and buying puts.

Profitability

Since the potential profits in risk arbitrage situations may be quite large— perhaps 3 or 4 points per 100 shares—the public can participate in this strategy. Commission charges will make the risk arbitrage less profitable for a public customer than it would be for an arbitrageur. The profit potential is often large enough, however, to make this type of risk arbitrage viable even for the public customer.

In summary, the risk arbitrageur may be able to use options in his strategy, either as a replacement for the actual stock position or as protection for the stock position. Although the public cannot normally participate in arbitrage strategies because of the small profit potential, risk arbitrages may often be exceptions. The profit potential can be large enough to overcome the commission burden for the public customer.

PAIRS TRADING

A stock trading strategy that has gained some adherents in recent years is called pairs trading. Simplistically, this strategy involves trading pairs of stocks—one held long, the other short. Thus it is a hedged strategy. The two stocks' price movement is related historically. The pairs trader would establish the position when one stock was expensive with respect to the other one, historically. Then when the stocks return to their historical relationship, a profit would result. In reality, some fairly complicated computer program search out the appropriate pairs.

The interest on the short sale offsets the cost of carry of the stock purchased. Therefore, the pairs trader doesn't have any expense except the possible differential in dividend payout.

The bane of pairs trading is a possible escalation of the stock sold short without any corresponding rise in price of the stock held long. A takeover attempt might cause this to happen. Of course, pairs traders will attempt to research the situation to ensure that they don't often sell short stocks which are perceived to be takeover candidates.

Pairs traders can use options to potentially reduce their risk if there are in-the-money options on both stocks. They would buy an in-the-money put instead of selling one stock short, and they would buy an in-the-money call on the other stock instead of buying the stock itself. In this option combination, they are paying very little time value premium, so that their profit potential is approximately the same as the pairs trading strategy using stocks (they would, however, have a debit since both options are purchased, so there would be a cost of carry in the option strategy).

If the stocks return to their historical relationship, the option strategy will reflect the same profit as the stock strategy, less any loss of time value premium. One added advantage of the option strategy, however, is that if a takeover occurs, the put has limited liability, and the trader's loss would be less.

Another advantage of the option strategy is that if both stocks should experience large moves, it could make money even if the pair doesn't return to historical norms. This would happen, for example, if both stocks dropped a great deal: the call has limited loss while the put's profits would continue to accrue. Similarly, to the upside, a large move by both stocks would make the put worthless, but the call would keep making money. In both cases, the option strategy could profit even if the pair of stocks didn't perform as predicted.

This type of strategy—buying in-the-money options as substitutes for both sides of a spread or hedge strategy—is discussed in more detail in Chapters 33 and 37.

FACILITATION (BLOCK POSITIONING)

Facilitation is the process whereby a trader seeks to aid in making markets for the purchase or sale of large blocks of stock. This is not really an arbitrage, and its description is thus deferred to Chapter 30.

Chapter *30*

Mathematical Applications

In previous chapters, many references have been made to the possibility of applying mathematical techniques to option strategies. Those techniques will be developed in this chapter. Although the average investor—public, institutional, or floor trader—normally has a limited grasp of advanced mathematics, the information in this chapter should still prove useful. It will allow the investor to see what sorts of strategy decisions could be aided by the use of mathematics. It will allow the investor to evaluate techniques of an information service. Additionally, if the investor is contemplating hiring someone knowledgeable in mathematics to do work for him, the information to be presented may be useful as a focal point for the work. The investor who does have a knowledge of mathematics and perhaps also has access to a computer will be able to directly use the techniques in this chapter.

THE BLACK-SCHOLES MODEL

Since an option's price is the function of stock price, striking price, volatility, time to expiration and short-term interest rates, *it is logical that a formula could be drawn up to calculate option prices* from these variables. Many models have been conceived since listed options began trading in 1973. Many of these have been attempts to improve on one of the first models introduced, the *Black-Scholes model.* This model was introduced in early 1973, very near to the time that listed options began trading. It was made public at that time and, as a result, gained a rather large number of adherents. The formula is rather easy to use in that the equations are short and the number of variables is small.

The actual formula is

$$\text{Theoretical option price} = pN(d_1) - se^{-rt}N(d_2)$$

$$\text{where } d_1 = \frac{\ln\left(\dfrac{p}{s}\right) + \left(r + \dfrac{v^2}{2}\right)t}{v\sqrt{t}}$$

$$d_2 = d_1 - v\sqrt{t}$$

The variables are:

p = stock price

s = striking price

t = time remaining until expiration, expressed as a percent of a year

r = current risk-free interest rate

v = volatility measured by annual standard deviation

$\ln$ = natural logarithm

$N(x)$ = cumulative normal density function

An important by-product of the model is the exact calculation of the delta—that is, the amount by which the option price can be expected to change for a small change in the stock price. The delta was described in Chapter 2, and is more formally known as the *hedge ratio.*

$$\text{Delta} = N(d_1)$$

The formula is so simple to use that it can fit quite easily on most programmable calculators. In fact, some of these calculators can be observed on the exchange floors as the more theoretical floor traders attempt to monitor the present value of option premiums. Of course, a computer can handle the calculations easily and with great speed. A large number of Black-Scholes computations can be performed in a very short period of time.

The cumulative normal distribution function can be found—in tabular form—in most statistical books. However, for computation purposes, it would be wasteful to repeatedly look up values in a table. Since the normal curve is a smooth curve (it is the "bell-shaped" curve used most commonly to describe population distributions), the cumulative distribution can be approximated by a formula:

$$x = 1 - z(1.330274y^5 - 1.821256y^4 + 1.781478y^3 - .356538y^2 + .3193815y)$$

$$\text{where } y = \frac{1}{1 + .2316419|\sigma|} \quad and \quad z = .3989423e^{-\sigma^2/2}$$

$$\text{Then } N(\sigma) = x \text{ if } \sigma > 0 \quad or \quad N(\sigma) = 1 - x \text{ if } \sigma < 0$$

This approximation is quite accurate for option pricing purposes, since one is not really interested in thousandths of a point where option prices are concerned.

Example: Suppose that a stock, XYZ, is trading at 45 and we are interested in evaluating the July 50 call, which has 60 days remaining until expiration. Furthermore, assume that the volatility of XYZ is 30% and that the risk-free interest rate is currently 10%. The theoretical value calculation will be shown in detail, in order that those readers who wish to program the model will have something to compare their calculations against.

Initially, determine t, d_1, and d_2, by referring to the formulae on the previous page:

$$t = 60/365 = .16438 \text{ years}$$

$$d_1 = \frac{\ln(45/50) + (.1 + .3 \times .3/2) \times .16438}{.3 \times \sqrt{.16438}}$$

$$= \frac{-.10536 + (.145 \times .16438)}{.3 \times .40544} = -.67025$$

$$d_2 = -.67025 - .3\sqrt{.16438} = -.67025 - (.3 \times .40544) = -.79189$$

Now calculate the cumulative normal distribution function for d_1 and d_2 by referring to the above formulae:

$$d_1 = -.67025$$

$$y = \frac{1}{1 + (.2316419 \mid -.67025 \mid)} = \frac{1}{1.15526} = .86561$$

$$z = .3989423e^{-(-.67025 \times -.67025)/2}$$

$$= .3989423e^{-.22462} = .31868$$

There are too many calculations involved in the computation of the fifth-order polynomial to display them here. Only the result is given:

$$x = .74865$$

Since we are determining the cumulative normal distribution of a negative number, the distribution is determined by subtracting x from 1.

$$N(d1) = N(-.67025) = 1 - x = 1 - .74865 = .25134$$

In a similar manner,

$$N(d2) = N(-.79179) = 1 - .78579 = .21421$$

Now, returning to the formula on the previous page, we can complete the calculation of the July 50 call's theoretical value, called value for short here:

$$\text{value} = 45 \times N(d_1) - 50 \times e^{-.1 \times .16438} \times N(d_2)$$

$$= 45 \times .25134 - 50 \times .9837 \times .21421$$

$$= .7746$$

Thus the theoretical value of the July 50 call is just slightly over $\frac{3}{4}$ of a point. Note that the delta of the call was calculated along the way as $N(d_1)$ and is equal to just over .25. That is, the July 50 call will change price about $\frac{1}{4}$ as fast as the stock for a small price change by the stock.

Hopefully this example will answer many of the questions that readers of the first edition have posed. The reader interested in a more in-depth description of the model, possibly including the actual derivation, should refer to the article "Fact and Fantasy in the Use of Options."[1] One of the less obvious relationships in the model is that option prices will

---

[1]Fisher Black, **Financial Analysts Journal**, July–August 1975, pp. 36–70.

increase as the risk-free interest rate increases. It may also be observed that the model correctly preserves relationships such as increased volatility, higher stock prices, or more time to expiration, which all imply higher option prices.

Characteristics of the Model

Several aspects of this model are worth further discussion. First, the reader will notice that *the model does not include dividends paid by the common stock*. As has been demonstrated, dividends act as a negative effect on call prices. Thus direct application of the model will tend to give inflated call prices, especially on stocks that pay relatively large dividends. There are ways of handling this. Fisher Black, one of the coauthors of the model, suggests the following method. Adjust the stock price to be used in the formula by subtracting, from the current stock price, the present worth of the dividends likely to be paid before maturity. Then calculate the option price. Second, assume that the option expires just prior to the last ex-dividend date preceding actual option expiration. Again adjust the stock price and calculate the option price. Use the higher of the two option prices calculated as the theoretical price. Another, less exact method would be to apply a weighting factor to call prices. The weighting factor would be based on the dividend payment, with a heavier weight being applied to call options on high-yielding stock. It should be pointed out that, in many of the applications that are going to be prescribed, it is not necessary to know the exact theoretical price of the call. Therefore, the dividend "correction" might not have to be applied for certain strategy decisions.

The model is based on a lognormal distribution of stock prices. Even though the normal distribution is part of the model, the inclusion of the exponential functions makes the distribution lognormal. For those less familiar with statistics, a normal distribution has a bell-shaped curve. This is the most familiar mathematical distribution. The problem with using a normal distribution is that it allows for negative stock prices, an impossible occurrence. Therefore, the lognormal distribution is generally used for stock prices, because it implies that the stock price can have a range only between zero and infinity. Furthermore, the upward (bullish) bias of the lognormal distribution appears to be logically correct, since a stock can only drop 100% but can rise in price by more than 100%. Many option pricing models that antedate the Black-Scholes model have attempted to use empirical distributions. An empirical distribution has a different shape than either the normal or the lognormal distribution. Reasonable empirical distributions for stock prices do not differ tremendously from the lognormal distribution, although they often assume that a stock has a greater probability of remaining stable than does the lognormal distribution. Critics of the Black-Scholes model claim that the model, largely because it uses the lognormal distribution, tends to overprice in-the-money calls and underprice out-of-the-money calls. This criticism is true, in some cases, but does not materially subtract from many applications of the model in strategy decisions. True, if one is going to buy or sell calls solely on the basis of their computed value, this would create a large problem. However, if strategy decisions are to be made on other factors that outweigh the overpriced/underpriced criteria, small differentials will not matter.

The computation of volatility is always a difficult problem for mathematical application. In the Black-Scholes model, volatility is defined as the annual standard deviation of the stock price. This is the regular statistical definition of standard deviation:

$$\sigma^2 = \frac{\displaystyle\sum_{i=1}^{n} (P_i - P)^2}{n - 1}$$

$$v = \sigma/P$$

where
P = average stock price of all P_i's
P_i = daily stock price
n = number of days observed
v = volatility

When volatility is computed using past stock prices, it is called a *historical volatility. The volatilities of stocks tend to change over time.* Certain predictable factors, such as a large stock split increasing the float of the stock, can reduce the volatility. The entry of a company into a more speculative area of business may increase the volatility. Other, less well defined factors can alter the volatility as well. Since the volatility is a very crucial element of the pricing model, it is important that the modeler be using a reasonable estimate of the current volatility. *It has become apparent that an annual standard deviation is not accurate because it encompasses too long of a period of time.* Recent efforts by many modelers have suggested that one should perhaps weight the recent stock price action more heavily than older price action in arriving at a current volatility. This is a possible approach, but the computation of such factors may introduce as much error as using the annual standard deviation does. The problem of accurately computing the volatility is critical, because the model is so sensitive to it.

Computing Lognormal Historical Volatility. The above calculation does not give the proper input for the Black-Scholes model because the model assumes that the *logarithms* of changes in price are normally distributed, not the prices themselves. That is, the term P_i in the above formula should be changed.

Example: XYZ closed at 51 today and at 50 yesterday. Thus its percentage change for the day is 51/50 = 1.02. The natural logarithm of 1.02 is then based on the volatility formula:

$$\ln(51/50) = \ln(1.02) = 0.0198$$

This is similar to saying that arithmetically the stock was up 2% today, but on a lognormal basis, it was only up 1.98%

If the stock is down, this method will yield a negative number. Suppose that on the following day, XYZ declined from 51 back to 50. The number to use in the volatility formula would then be:

$$\ln(50/51) = \ln(0.9804) = -0.0198$$

A new equation can now be formulated using this concept. It will yield volatilities that are consistent with the Black-Scholes model:

$$v = \sqrt{\frac{\sum_{i=1}^{n} (X_i - \overline{X})^2}{n - 1}}$$

where $X_i = \ln(P_i/P_{i-1})$; P_i = closing price on day i and $\overline{X}$ = the average of the X_i's over the desired number of days

So to compute a 10-day historical volatility, one would need 11 observations. In the following example, do not be concerned with the complete details if you do not plan to compute the volatilities yourself; they are provided for the mathematician or programmer who needs to check his work:

Day	XYZ Stock	P_i/P_{i-1}	$X_i = \ln(P_i/P_{i-1})$	$(X_i - \overline{X})^2$
1	153.875			
2	153.625	.9984	−.0016	.000020
3	151	.9829	−.0172	.000405
4	146	.9669	−.0337	.001336
5	144.125	.9872	−.0129	.000250
6	147.25	1.0217	.0215	.000345
7	146.25	.9932	−.0068	.000094
8	149.5	1.0222	.0220	.000365

9	152.5	1.0201	.0199	.000289
10	158.625	1.0402	.0394	.001332
11	158.375	0.9984	−.0016	.000020
			AVG: 0.00309	Σ: 0.004446

The average of the lns (4th column) over the 10 days is 0.00309.

The difference of each ln from the mean, squared is then summed (5th column). For example, for day 1 the term is $(−.0016 − .00309)2 = .00002$. This is the top number in the far right hand column. This process can be computed for each number in the "ln" column. The sum of all these terms is 0.004446.

$$\text{Now } v = \sqrt{(.004446/9)} = .0223$$

This is a 10-day volatility. To convert it into an annual volatility, we need to multiply by the square root of the number of trading days in a year. Since there are approximately 260 trading days in a year, the final volatility would be:

$$v = .0223 \times \sqrt{(260)} = .3589$$

Thus, one could say that the volatility of XYZ is 36% on an annualized basis.

This is then the proper way to calculate historic volatility. Obviously, the strategist can calculate 10-, 20-, and 50-day and annual volatilities if he wishes—or any other number for that matter. In certain cases, one can discern valuable information about a stock or future and its options by seeing how the various volatilities compare with one another.

There is, in fact, a way in which *the strategist can let the market compute the volatility for him.* This is called using the *implied volatility*— that is, the volatility that the market itself is implying. This concept makes the assumption that, for options with striking prices close to the current stock price and for options with relatively large trading volume, the market is fairly priced. This is something like an efficient market hypothesis. If there is enough trading interest in an option that is close to the money, that option will generally be fairly priced. Once this assumption has been made, a corollary arises: *If the actual price of an option is the fair price, it can be fixed in the Black-Scholes equation while letting volatility be the unknown variable.* The volatility can be determined by iteration. In fact, this process of iterating to compute the volatility can be done for each option on a particular underlying stock. This might result in several different volatilities for the stock. If one weights these various results by volume of trading and by distance in- or out-of-the-money, a single volatility can be derived for the underlying stock. This volatility is based on the closing price of all the options on the underlying stock for that given day.

Example: XYZ is 33 and the closing prices are given in Table 30-1. Each option has a different implied volatility as computed by determining what volatility in the Black-Scholes model would result in the closing price for each option: That is, if .34 were used as the volatility, the model would give 4½ as the price of the January 30 call. In order to rationally combine these volatilities, weighting factors must be applied before a voltility for XYZ stock itself can be arrived at.

The weighting factors for volume are easy to compute. The factor for each option is merely that option's daily volume divided by the total option volume on all XYZ options (Table 30-2). The weighting functions for distance from the striking price should probably not be linear. For example, if one option is 2 points out-of-the-money and another is 4 points out-of-the-money, the former option should not necessarily get twice as much weight as the latter. Once an option is too far in- or out-of-the-money, it should not be given much if any weight at all, regardless of its

TABLE 30-1.
Implied volatilities, closing price, and volume.

Option	Option Price	Volume	Implied Volatility
January 30	4½	50	.34
January 35	1½	90	.28
April 35	2½	55	.30
April 40	1½	5	.38
		200	

TABLE 30-2.
Volume weighting factors.

Option	Volume	Volume Weighting Factor
January 30	50	.25 (50/200)
January 35	90	.45 (90/200)
April 35	55	.275 (55/200)
April 40	5	.025 (5/200)

trading volume. Any parabolic function of the following form should suffice:

$$\text{Weighting factor} \begin{cases} = \dfrac{(x - a)^2}{a^2} & \text{if } x \text{ is less than } a \\ = 0 & \text{if } x \text{ is greater than } a \end{cases}$$

where x is the percentage distance between stock price and strike price and a is the maximum percentage distance at which the modeler wants to give any weight at all to the option's implied volatility.

Example: An investor decides that he wants to discard options from the weighting criterion which have striking prices more than 25% from the current stock price. The variable, a, would then be equal to .25. The weighting factors, with XYZ at 33, could thus be computed as shown in Table 30-3. To combine the weighting factors for both volume and distance from strike, the two factors are multiplied by the implied volatility for that option. These products are summed up for all the options in question. This sum is then divided by the products of the weighting factors, summed over all the options in question. As a formula, this would read:

$$\frac{\text{Implied}}{\text{volatility}} = \frac{\Sigma(\text{volume factor} \times \text{distance factor} \times \text{implied volatility})}{\Sigma(\text{volume factor} \times \text{distance factor})}$$

In our example, this would give an implied volatility for XYZ stock of 29.8% (Table 30-4). Note that the implied volatility, .298, is not equal to any of the individual option's implied volatilities. Rather, it is a composite figure that gives the most weight to the heavily traded, near-the-money options, and very little weight to the lightly traded (5 contracts), deeply out-of-the-money April 40 call. This implied volatility is still a form of standard deviation, and can thus be used whenever a standard deviation volatility is called for.

This method of computing volatility is quite accurate and proves to be sensitive to changes in the volatility of a stock. For example, as markets

TABLE 30-3.
Distance weighting factors.

Option	Distance from Stock Price	Distance Weighting Factor
January 30	.091 (3/33)	.41
January 35	.061 (2/33)	.57
April 35	.061 (2/33)	.57
April 40	.212 (7/33)	.02

TABLE 30-4.
Option's implied volatility.

Option	Volume Factor	Distance Factor	Option's Implied Volatility
January 30	.25	.41	.34
January 35	.45	.57	.28
April 35	.275	.57	.30
April 40	.025	.02	.38

$$\text{Implied volatility} = \frac{.25 \times .41 \times .34 + .45 \times .57 \times .28 + .275 \times .57 \times .30 + .025 \times .02 \times .38}{.25 \times .41 + .45 \times .57 + .275 \times .57 + .025 \times .02}$$

$$= .298$$

become bullish or bearish (generating large rallies or declines), most stocks will react in a volatile manner as well. Option premiums expand rather quickly, and this method of implied volatility is able to pick up the change quickly. One final bit of *fine tuning needs to be done* before the final volatility of the stock is arrived at. On a day-to-day basis, the implied volatility for a stock—especially one whose options are not too active— may fluctuate more than the strategist would like. A smoothing effect can be obtained by taking a moving average of the last 20 or 30 days' implied volatilities. An alternative, which does not require the saving of many previous days' worth of data, would be to use a momentum calculation on the implied volatility. For example, today's final volatility might be computed by adding 5% of today's implied volatility to 95% of yesterday's final volatility. This method requires saving only one previous piece of data—yesterday's final volatility—and still preserves a "smoothing" effect.

Once this implied volatility has been computed, it can then be used in the Black-Scholes model (or any other model) as the volatility variable. Thus one could compute the theoretical value of each option according to the Black-Scholes formula utilizing the implied volatility for the stock. Since the implied volatility for the stock will most likely be somewhat different than the implied volatility of this particular option, there will be a discrepancy between the option's actual closing price and the theoretical price as computed by the model. This differential represents the amount by which the option is theoretically overpriced or underpriced, *compared to other options on that same stock.*

EXPECTED RETURN

There are certain investors who will enter positions only when the historical percentages are on their side. When one enters into a transaction, he normally has a feeling as to the possibility of making a profit. For example, when he buys stock he may feel that there is a "good chance" that there will be a rally or that earnings will increase. The investor may consciously or unconsciously evaluate the probabilities, but, invariably, an investment is made based on a positive expectation of profit. Since options have fixed terms, they lend themselves to a more rigorous computation of expected profit than the aforementioned intuitive appraisal. This more rigorous approach consists of computing the expected return. *The expected return is nothing more than the return that the position should yield over a large number of cases.*

A simple example may help to explain the concept. The crucial variable in computing expected return is to outline what the chances are of the stock being at a certain price at some future time.

Example: XYZ is selling at 33, and an investor is interested in determining where XYZ will be in 6 months. Assume that there is a 20% chance of XYZ being below 30 in 6 months, and that there is a 40% chance that XYZ will be above 35 in 6 months. Finally, assume that XYZ has an equal 10% chance of being at 31, 32, 33, or 34 in 6 months. All other prices are ignored for simplification. Table 30-5 summarizes these assumptions.

Since the percentages total 100%, all the outcomes have theoretically been allowed for. Now suppose a February 30 call is trading at 4 and a February 35 call is trading at 2 points. A bull spread could be established by buying the February 30 and selling the February 35. This position would cost 2 points—that is, it is a 2-point debit. The spreader could make 3 points if XYZ were above 35 at expiration for a return of 150%, or he could lose 100% if XYZ were below 30 at expiration. The expected return for this spread can be computed by multiplying the outcome at expiration for each price by the probability of being at that price, and then summing the results. For example, if XYZ is below 30 at expiration, the spreader loses $200. It was assumed that there is a 20% chance of XYZ being below 30 at expiration, so the expected loss is 20% times $200, or $40. Table 30-6 shows the computation of the expected results at all the

TABLE 30-5.
Calculation of expected returns.

Price of XYZ in 6 Months	Chance of XYZ Being at That Price
Below 30	20%
31	10%
32	10%
33	10%
34	10%
Above 35	40%
	100%

TABLE 30-6.
Computation of expected profit.

XYZ Price Expiration	(A)	Chance of Being at That Price	(B)	Profit at That Price	Expected Profit: (A) × (B)
Below 30		20%		− $200	− $ 40
31		10%		− 100	− 10
32		10%		− 0	0
33		10%		+ 100	+ 10
34		10%		+ 200	+ 20
Above 35		40%		+ 300	+ 120
				Total expected profit	$100

prices. The total expected profit is $100. This means that the expected return (profit divided by investment) is 50% ($100/$200). This would appear to be an attractive spread, because the spreader could "expect" to make 50% of his money, less commissions.

What has really been calculated in this example is merely *the return that one would expect to make in the long run if he invested in the same position many times throughout history.* Saying that a particular position has an expected return of 8 or 9% is no different from saying that common stocks return 8 or 9% in the long run. Of course, in bull markets stock would do much better and in bear markets much worse. In a similar manner, this example bull spread with an expected return of 50% may do as well as the maximum profit or as poorly as losing 100% in any one case. It is the total return on *many* cases that has the expected return of 50%. *Mathematical theory holds that, if one constantly invests in positions with positive expected returns, he should have a better chance of making money.*

As is readily observable, the selection of what percentages to assign to the possible outcomes in the stock price is a *crucial* choice. In the example above, if one altered his assumption slightly so that XYZ had a 30% chance of being below 30 and a 30% chance of being above 35 at expiration, the expected return would drop considerably, to 25%. Thus *it is important to have a reasonably accurate and consistent method of assigning these percentages.* Furthermore, the example above was too simplistic, in that it did not allow for the stock to close at any fractional prices, such as 32½. A correct expected return computation must take into account all possible outcomes for the stock.

Fortunately, there is a straightforward method of computing the expected percentage chance of a given stock being at a certain price at a certain point in time. This computation involves using the distribution of stock prices. As mentioned earlier, the Black-Scholes model assumes a lognormal distribution for stock prices, although many modelers today are using nonstandard (empirical or heuristic) distributions. No matter what the distribution, *the area under the distribution curve between any two points gives the probability of being between those two points.*

Figure 30-1 is a graph of a typical lognormal distribution. The peak always lies at the "mean," or average, of the distribution. For stock price distributions, under the random walk assumption, *the "mean" is generally considered to be the current stock price.* The graph allows one to visualize the probability of being at any given price. Note that there is a fairly great chance that the stock will be relatively unchanged, there is no chance that the stock will be below zero, and there is a bullish bias to the graph— the stock could rise infinitely, although the chances of it doing so are extremely small.

The chance that XYZ will be below the mean at the end of the time period is 50% in a random walk distribution. This also means that 50% of the area under the graph lies to the left of the mean and 50% lies to the right of the mean. Note point A on the graph. Forty percent of the area under the distribution curve lies to the left of point A and 60% lies above point A. This means that there is a 40% chance that the stock will be below price A at the end of the time period and a 60% chance that the stock will be above point A. Consequently, the distribution curve can be used to determine the probabilities necessary for the expected return computation. The reader should take note of the fact that these probabilities apply to the *end of the time period.* They say nothing about the chances that XYZ might dip below price A at some time *during* the time period. To compute that percentage, an involved computation is necessary.

FIGURE 30-1.
Typical lognormal distribution.

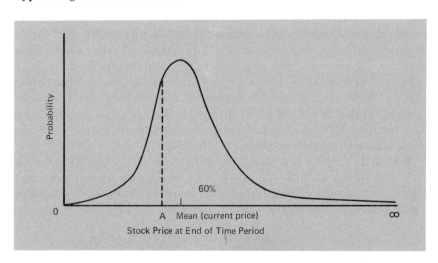

The height and width of the distribution graph are determined by the volatility of the underlying stock, when volatility is expressed as a standard deviation. This is consistent with the method of computing volatility described earlier in this chapter. Implied volatility can, of course, be used. Since the option modeler is generally interested in time periods other than one year, *the annual volatility must be converted into a volatility for the time period in question.* This is easily accomplished by the following formula:

$$v_t = v\sqrt{t}$$

Where
v = annual volatility

t = time, in years

v_t = volatility for time, t

As an example, a 3-month volatility wold be equal to one-half of the annual volatility. In this case, t would equal .25 (one fourth of a year), so $v_{.25} = v\sqrt{.25} = .5v$.

The necessary groundwork has been laid for the computation of the probability necessary in the expected return calculation. The following formula gives the probability of a stock, which is currently at price p, being below some other price, q, at the end of the time period. The log-normal distribution is assumed.

Probability of stock being below price q at end of time period, t:

$$P \text{ (below)} = N\left(\frac{\ln\left(\frac{q}{p}\right)}{v_t}\right)$$

Where
N = cumulative normal distribution

p = current price of the stock

q = price in question

$\ln$ = natural logarithm for the time period in question.

If one is interested in computing the probability of the stock being *above* the given price, the formula is

$$P \text{ (above)} = 1 - P \text{ (below)}$$

With this formula, the computation of expected return is quickly accomplished with a computer. One merely has to start at some price—

the lower strike in a bull spread, for example—and work his way up to a higher price—the high strike for a bull spread. At each eighth of a point in between, the outcome of the spread is multiplied by the probability of being at that price and a running sum is kept.

Simplistically, the following iterative equation would be used.

$$P \text{ (of being at price } x) = P \text{ (below } x) - P \text{ (below } y)$$

where y is close to but less than x in price. As an example:

$$P \text{ (of being at } 32\tfrac{3}{8}) = P \text{ (below } 32\tfrac{3}{8}) - P \text{ (below } 32\tfrac{1}{4})$$

Thus once the low starting point is chosen and the probability of being below that price is determined, one can compute the probability of being at prices that are successively higher merely by iterating with the preceding formula. In reality, one is using this information to integrate the distribution curve. Any method of approximating the integral that is used in basic calculus—such as the Trapezoidal Rule or Simpson's Rule—would be applicable here for more accurate results, if they are desired.

A partial example of an expected return calculation follows.

Example: XYZ is currently at 33 and has an annual volatility of 25%. The previous bull spread is being established—buy the February 30 and sell the February 35 for a 2-point debit—and these are 6-month options. Table 30-7 gives the necessary components for computing the expected return. Column (A), the probability of being below price q, is computed according to the previously given formula, where $p = 33$ and $v_t = .177$ ($v_t = .25\sqrt{\tfrac{1}{2}}$). The first stock price that needs to be looked at is 30, since all results for the bull spread are equal below that price—a 100% loss on the spread. The calculations would be performed for each eighth of a point

TABLE 30-7.
Calculation of expected returns.

Price at Expiration (q)	(A) P (below q)	(B) P (of being at q)	(C) Profit on Spread
30	.295	.295	−$200
30⅛	.301	.006	− 187.50
30¼	.308	.007	− 175
30⅜	.316	.008	− 162.50
.	.	.	.
.	.	.	.
.	.	.	.

up through a price of 35. The expected return is computed by multiplying the two right-hand columns, (B) and (C), and summing the results. Note that column (B) is determined by subtracting successive numbers in column (A). It would not be particularly enlightening to carry this example to completion, since the rest of the computations are similar and there is a large number of them.

In theory, if one had the data and computer power, he could evaluate a wide range of strategies every day and come up with the best positions on an expected return basis. He would probably get a few option buys (puts or calls), some bull spreads, some naked writes and ratio calendar spreads, fewer straddles, ratio writes, and a few covered call writes. This theory would be somewhat difficult to apply in practice because of the massive amounts of calculations involved and also because of the inaccuracy of closing price data. It was mentioned previously that a computer will assume that "bad" closing prices are actually attainable. By a "bad" closing price, it is meant that the option did not trade simultaneously with the stock later in the day, and that the actual market for the option is somewhat different in price than is reflected by the closing price for the option. A daily contract volume "screen" will help alleviate this problem—for example, one may want to discard any option from his calculations if that option did not trade a predetermined, minimum amount of contracts during the previous day. Data that give closing bids and offers for each option are more expensive but also more reliable and would alleviate the problem of "bad" closing prices. In addition to a volume screen, another way of reducing the calculations required is to limit oneself to strategies in which one has interest, or which one is reasonably certain will fit in well with his investment objectives. Regardless of the limitations that one places upon the quantity of computations, some computer power is necessary to compute expected return. A sophisticated programmable calculator may be able to provide a real-time calculation, but could never be used to evaluate the entire option universe and come up with a ranking of the preferable situations each day. On-line computer systems are also available that can provide these types of calculations using up-to-the-minute prices. While real-time prices may occasionally be useful, it is not an absolute necessity to have them.

One other by-product of the expected return calculation is that it could be used as another model for predicting the theoretical value of an option. All one would have to do is compute the probabilities of the stock being at each successive price above the striking price of the option by expiration and sum them up. The result would be the theoretical option value. These data are published by some services and generally give a different theoretical value than would the Black-Scholes model. The reason for the difference most readily lies in the inclusion of the risk-free interest rate in the Black-Scholes model and its omission in the expected return model.

APPLYING THE CALCULATIONS TO STRATEGY DECISIONS

Call Writing

One method of ranking covered call writes that was described in Chapter 2 was to rank all the writes that provided at least a minimal acceptable level of return by their probability of not losing money. If one were interested in safety, he might decide to use this approach. Suppose that he decided that he would consider any write that provided an annualized total return (capital gains, dividends, and commissions) of at least 12%. This would eliminate many potential writes but would leave him with a fairly large number of writing candidates each day. He knows the downside break-even point at expiration in each write. Therefore, the probability of the stock being below that break-even point at expiration can be quickly computed. His final list would rank those writes with the least chance of being below the break-even point at expiration as the best writes. Again, this ranking is based on an expected probability and is of course no guarantee that the stock will not, in reality, fall below the break-even point. However, over time, a list of this sort should provide the most conservative covered writes.

Example: XYZ is selling for 43 and a 6-month July 40 call is selling for 8 points. After including dividends and commission costs for a 500-share position, the downside break-even point at expiration is 36. If the annualized volatility of XYZ is 25%, the probability of making money at expiration can be computed. The 6-month volatility is 17.7% (25% times the square root of ½ year). The probability of being below 36 can be computed by using the formula given earlier in this section:

$$P \text{ (below 36 in 6 months)} = N\left(\frac{\ln\left(\frac{36}{43}\right)}{.177}\right) = N\left(\frac{-.178}{.177}\right) = 0.158$$

The expected probability of XYZ being below 36 in 6 months is 15.8%. Therefore, this would be an attractive write on a conservative basis, because it has a large probability of making money (nearly 65% chance of net being below the break-even point at expiration). The return if exercised in this example is approximately 20% annualized, so it should be acceptable from a profit potential viewpoint as well. It is a relatively easy matter to perform a similar calculation, with the aid of a computer, on all covered writing candidates.

The ability to measure downside protection in terms of a common denominator—volatility—can be useful in other types of covered call writing analyses. The writer interested in writing out-of-the-money calls, which generally have higher profit potential, is still interested in having an idea of what his downside protection is. He might, for example, decide that he wants to invest in situations in which the probability of making money is at least 60%. This is not an unusually difficult requirement to fulfill, and will leave many attractive covered writes with a high profit potential to choose from. A downside requirement stated in terms of probability of success removes the necessity of having to impose arbitrary requirements. Typical arbitrary requirements would be including only calls that sell for one point or more, or stating that the downside protection must be a certain percentage of the stock price. These obviously cannot suffice for stocks with different volatilities. Rather, the downside protection criterion should be stated in terms of "probabilty of down protection" or, alternatively, in terms of the volatility itself. In this manner, a uniform comparison can be made between volatile and nonvolatile stocks.

Call Buying

The option buyer can also constructively use the measurement of volatility to aid him in his option buying decisions. In Chapter 3, it was shown that *evaluating the profitability of calls based on the volatility of the underlying stock is the correct way to analyze an option purchase.* One specific method of analysis will be described. There are certain variables in this analysis that may be altered to fit the call buyer's individual preferences, but the general logic is applicable to all cases.

As a first step, *one should decide upon a uniform stock movement for ranking call purchases.* One might decide to rank all purchases by how they would perform if the underlying stock moved up in accordance with its volatility. The phrase "in accordance with its volatility" must be quantified. For example, one might decide to assume that every stock could move up one standard deviation, and then rank all call purchases on that basis. *The prospective call buyer must also fix the time period that he wants to use.* Generally, one looks at purchases to be held for 30 days, 60 days, and 90 days.

The exact steps to be followed in the analysis of profitability and risk can be listed as follows:

1. Specify the distance that underlying stock can move, up or down, in terms of its volatility.

2. Select the holding period over which the analysis is to take place.

Profitability

3. Calculate the stock price which the stock would move up to, when the foregoing assumptions are implemented.

4. Using a pricing model, such as the Black-Scholes model, estimate what the option price would become after the upward stock movement.

5. Calculate the percent profit, after deducting commissions.

6. Repeat steps 4 and 5 for each option on the stock.

A final ranking of all potential call buys can be obtained by performing steps 3 through 6 on all stocks, and ranking the purchases by their percentage reward.

Risk

7. Calculate the stock price that the stock could fall to, when the assumptions in steps 1 and 2 are applied.

8. With a model, price the option after the stock's decline.

9. Calculate the percentage loss after commissions.

10. Compute a reward/risk ratio: Divide the percentage profit from step 5 by the percentage risk from step 9.

11. Repeat steps 8 through 10 for each option on the stock.

A final ranking of less aggressive option purchases can be constructed by performing steps 7 through 11 on all stocks, and ranking the purchases by their reward/risk ratio.

The higher rofitability list of option purchases will tend to be at- or slightly out-of-the-money calls. The less aggressive list, ranked by reward/risk potential, will tend to be in-the-money options.

Example: Steps 1 and 2: Suppose an investor wants to look at option purchases for a 90-day holding period, under the assumption that each stock could move up by one standard deviation in that time. (There is only about a 16% chance that a stock will move more than one standard deviation in one direction in a given time period. Therefore, in actual practice, one might want to use a smaller stock movement in his ranking calculations). Furthermore, assume that the following data are known:

XYZ common, 41;

XYZ volatility, 30% annually;

XYZ January 40 call, 4; and

time to January expiration, 6 months

Step 3: Calculate upward stock potential. This is accomplished by the following formula:

$$q = pe^{av_t}$$

where
p = current stock price
q = potential stock price
v_t = volatility for the time period, t
a = a constant (see below)

The constants, a and t, are fixed under the assumptions in steps 1 and 2. The first constant, a, is the number of standard deviations of movement to be allowed. In our example, $a = 1$. That is, the analysis is being made under the assumption that the stock could move up by one standard deviation. The second constant, t, is .25, since the analysis is for a 90-day holding period, which is 25% of a year. In this example,

$$v_t = v\sqrt{t} = .30 \sqrt{.25} = .30 \times .50 = .15$$

so

$$q = 41e^{.15} = 41 \times 1.16 = 47.64$$

Thus this stock would move up to approximately 47⅝ if it moved one standard deviation in exactly 90 days.
Step 4: Using the Black-Scholes model, the XYZ January 40 call can be priced. It would be worth approximately 8⅛ if XYZ were at 47⅝ and there were 90 days' less life in the call.
Step 5: Calculate the profit potential. For this example, commissions will be ignored, but they should be included in a real-life situation.

$$\text{Percent profit} = \frac{8\frac{1}{8} - 4}{4} = \frac{4\frac{1}{8}}{4} = 103\%$$

Thus if XYZ stock moves up by one standard deviation over the next 90 days, this call would yield a projected profit of 103%. Recall again that there is only about a 16% chance of the stock actually moving at least this far. If all options on all stocks are ranked under this same assumption, however, a fair comparison of profitable options will be obtained.

Step 6 is omitted from this example—it would consist of performing a similar profit analysis (steps 4 and 5) on all other XYZ options, with the assumption that XYZ is at $47\frac{5}{8}$ after 90 days.

Step 7: Calculate the downside potential of XYZ. The formula for the downside potential of the stock is nearly the same as that used in step 3 for the upside potential:

$$q = pe^{-av_t}$$

$$= 41e^{-.15} = 41 \times .86 = 35.39$$

XYZ would fall to approximately $35\frac{1}{4}$ in 90 days if it fell by one standard deviation. Note that the actual distances that XYZ could rise and fall are not the same. The upward potential was $6\frac{5}{8}$ points, while the downward potential is about $5\frac{3}{4}$ points. This difference is due to the use of the lognormal distribution.

Step 8: Using the Black-Schoes model, one could estimate that the XYZ January 40 call would be worth about $1\frac{1}{8}$ if XYZ were at $35\frac{1}{4}$ in 90 days.

Step 9: The risk potential in the January 40 call would be

$$\text{Percent risk} = \frac{4 - 1\frac{1}{8}}{4} = \frac{2\frac{7}{8}}{4} = 72\%$$

Step 10: The reward/risk ratio is merely the percentage reward divided by the percentage risk:

$$\text{Reward/risk ratio} = \frac{103\%}{72\%} = 1.43$$

Step 11: This analysis would be repeated for all XYZ options, and then for all other optionable stocks. The less aggressive call purchases would be ranked by their reward/risk ratios, with higher ratios representing more attractive purchases. More aggressive purchases would be ranked by the potential rewards only (step 5).

   This completes the call buying example. Before leaving this section, it should be noted that the assumption of ranking the purchases after one full standard deviation movement by the underlying stock is probably excessive. A more moderate assumption would be that the stock might be able to move .7 standard deviation. There is about a 25% expected chance that a stock could move at least .7 standard deviation up at the end of a fixed time period.

Pricing a Put Option

Theoretical models for pricing put options have been derived—that is, ones which are separate from call pricing models. Black and Scholes presented such a model in their original paper. However, as has been demonstrated, there is a relationship between put and call prices in the listed option market due to the conversion and reversal strategies.

One could use the basic call pricing model for the purpose of predicting put prices if he assumes that arbitrageurs will efficiently influence the market via conversions. Theoreticians will argue that such a method of pricing puts assumes that the arbitrage process is always present and works efficiently, and that this is not true. The "conversion efficiency" assumption could be a serious fault if one were trying to determine the exact overpriced or underpriced nature of the put option. However, if one is merely comparing various put strategies under constant assumptions, the arbitrage model for pricing puts works quite well.

The listed put's price can be estimated by using the call pricing model and the arbitrage formula. Recall that the arbitrageur must include the cost of carrying the position as well as the dividends to be received.

$$\frac{\text{Theoretical}}{\text{put}} = \frac{\text{theoretical}}{\text{call price}} + \frac{\text{strike}}{\text{price}} - \frac{\text{stock}}{\text{price}} - \frac{\text{carrying}}{\text{cost}} + \text{dividends}$$

The "theoretical call price" is obtained from the Black-Scholes model. The carrying cost is the cost of money (interest rate) times the striking price multiplied by the time to expiration. Recall that this is the approximation formula for carrying cost (see Chapter 27 for comments on present value and compounding). Consequently, if XYZ were at 41 and a 6-month January 40 call option were valued at 4 points by the Black-Scholes model, the theoretical put price could be estimated. Assume that the cost of money interest rate is 10%, annually, and that the stock will pay $.50 in dividends in 6 months ($t = \frac{1}{2}$ year).

$$\text{Theoretical put price} = 4 + 40 - 41 - (.10 \times 40 \times \tfrac{1}{2}) + .50$$
$$= 3 - 2 + \tfrac{1}{2}$$
$$= 1\tfrac{1}{2}$$

This means that if the call could be sold for 4 points, the artibrageur would be willing to pay up to 1½ points for the put to establish a conversion. The arbitrageur's price is used as the theoretical listed put price estimate.

Put Buying

Put option purchases can be ranked in a manner very similar to that described for call option buying. Reward opportunities occur when the stock falls in accordance with its volatility. An upward stock movement represents risk for the put buyer. All of the 11 steps in the previous section on call buying would be applicable to put buying. The pricing of the put necessary for steps 4 and 8 would be done in accordance with the arbitrage model just presented.

   If an underlying stock does not have listed puts trading, the synthetic put can be considered. Recall that synthetic puts are created for customers by some brokerage houses. The brokerage sells the stock short and buys a call. The customer can purchase the synthetic put for the amount of the risk involved, plus any dividends to be paid by the underlying stock. The synthetic put pricing formula—which would be used in steps 4 and 8 of the option buying analysis—is exactly the same as the arbitrage model for listed puts, except that the carrying costs are omitted:

$$\begin{array}{c}\text{Theoretical synthetic} \\ \text{put price}\end{array} = \begin{array}{c}\text{theoretical} \\ \text{call price}\end{array} + \begin{array}{c}\text{strike} \\ \text{price}\end{array} - \begin{array}{c}\text{stock} \\ \text{price}\end{array} + \text{dividends}$$

   When the ranking analysis is performed, very few synthetic puts will appear as attractive put buys. This is because when the customer buys a synthetic put, he must advance the full cost of the dividend, but receives no offsetting cost reduction for the credit being earned by the short stock position. Consequently, synthetic puts are always more expensive, on a relative basis, than are listed puts. However, if one is particularly bearish on a stock that has no listed puts, a synthetic put may still prove to be a worthwhile investment. The recommended analysis can give him a feeling for the reward and risk potential of the investment.

Calendar Spreads

The pricing model can help in determining which neutral calendar spreads are most attractive. Recall that in a neutral calendar spread, one is selling a near-term call and buying a longer-term call, when the stock is relatively close to the striking price of the calls. The object of the spread is to capture the time decay differential between the two options. The neutral calendar spread is normally closed at the expiration of the near-term option. The pricing model can aid the spreader by estimating what the profit potential of the spread is, as well as aiding in the determination of the break-even points of the position at near-term expiration.

   To determine the maximum profit potential of the spread, assume that the near-term call expires worthless and use the pricing model to estimate the value of the longer-term call with the stock exactly at the striking price. Since commission costs are relatively large in spread transactions, it would be best to have the computations include commissions. A second profit potential is sometimes useful as well—*the profit if un-*

changed. To determine how much profit would be made if the stock were unchanged at near-term expiration, assume that the spread is closed with the near-term call equal to its intrinsic value (zero if the stock is currently below the strike, or the difference between the stock price and the strike if the stock is initially above the strike). Then use the pricing model to estimate the value of the longer-term call, which will then have three or six months of life remaining, with the stock unchanged. The resulting differential between the near-term call's intrinsic value and the estimated value of the longer-term call is an estimate of the price at which the spread could be liquidated. The profit, of course, is that differential minus the current (initial) differential, less commissions.

In the earlier discussion of calendar spreads, it was pointed out that there is both an upside break-even point and a downside break-even point at near-term expiration. These *break-even points can be estimated with the use of the pricing model*. One method of determination involves estimating the liquidating value of the spread at successive stock prices. When the liquidating value is found to be equal to the initial value, plus commissions, a break-even point has been located.

Example: If the spread in question is using options with a striking price of 30, one would begin his break-even point calculations at a price of 30. Estimate the liquidating value of the spread at 30, 29⅞, 29¾, 29⅝, and so forth until the break-even point is found. Once the downside break-even point has been determined in this manner, the iterations to locate the upside break-even point should begin again at the striking price. Thus one would evaluate the liquidating value at 30, 30⅛, 30¼, and so on. This is somewhat of a brute-force method, but with a large computer it is fairly fast. The number of calculations can be reduced by adopting a more complicated iteration process.

A final useful piece of information can be obtained with the aid of the pricing model—*the theoretical value of the spread*. Recompute the estimated value of both the near-term and longer-term calls at the current time and stock price, using the implied volatility for the underlying stock. The resultant differential between the two estimated call prices may differ substantially from the actual differential, perhaps highlighting an attractive calendar spread situation. One would want to establish spreads where the theoretical differential is *greater than* the actual differential (that is, he would want to buy a "cheap" calendar spread).

Once these pieces of information have been computed, the strategist can rank the spread possibilities by whatever criterion he finds most workable. *The logical method of ranking the spreads would be by their return if unchanged*. The spreads with the highest return if unchanged— at near-term expiration—would be those in which the stock price and striking price were close together initially, a basic requirement of the neutral calendar spread. More complicated ranking systems should try to include the theoretical value of the spread and possibly even the maximum potential of the spread. *A similar analysis can, of course, be worked out for put calendar spreads*, using the arbitrage pricing model for puts.

Ratio Strategies

Ratio strategies involve selling naked options. Therefore, the strategist has potentially large risk—either to the upside or to the downside or both. He should attempt to get a feeling for how probable this risk is. The formulae for determining the probability of a stock being above or below a certain price at some time in the future can give him these probabilities. For example, in a straddle writing situation, the strategist would want to compute such arithmetic quantities as maximum profit potential, return if unchanged, collateral required at upside break-even point or at upside action point (recall that the collateral requirement increases for naked options on an adverse stock movement), and the break-even points themselves. The probabilities of being above the upper break-even point at expiration and the probability of being below the lower break-even point should be computed as well. Moreover, an expected return analysis could be performed on the position to determine the general level of profitability of the position with respect to all other positions of the same type on other stocks. Such an expected return analysis need not assume that the position is held to expiration. Firm traders, paying little or no commissions, might be interested in seeing the expected results for a holding period as short as 30 days or less. Public customers might use a longer holding period, on the assumption that they would not trade the position as readily because of commission costs. Ratio positions should be ranked either by return if unchanged, or by expected return.

   The analyses described for calendar spreads and ratio positions should not be relied upon as gospel. In the proposed forms of analysis, one is projecting future option prices and stock prices under the assumption that the volatility of the underlying stock will remain the same. Although this may be true in some cases, there will also be many times when the volatility of the underlying stock will change during the life of the position. If the volatility decreases, the projected break-even points for a calendar spread will be too far away from the striking price. Thus a loss would result at some prices where the spreader expected to make money. If the volatility increases, the expected return of a ratio position will drop, because the probabilities of the stock moving outside the profit range will increase, thereby increasing the probability of loss.

   The effect of a changing volatility can be counteracted, in theory, by continuing to monitor the position daily after it has been established. In a straddle write, for example, if the stock begins to move dramatically, the expected return may become very low. If this happens, adjustments could be made to the position to improve it. Such monitoring is difficult to apply in practice for the public customer, because the commission costs involved in constant position adjustments would mount rapidly. There is no exact method that would allow for infrequent, periodic adjustments, but *by using a follow-up analysis the public customer may be able to get a better feeling for the timing of adjusting a position.* For example, suppose that one initially wrote a 5-point straddle when the stock was at 30. Sometime later, the stock is at 34. The expected return of writing a 5-point straddle with a strike of 30 when the stock is at 34 could be computed for the shorter time period remaining until expiration. If the expected return is negative, an adjustment needs to be made. Adopting this form of adjusting would keep the number of trades to a minimum, but would still allow the strategist to see when his position has become improperly balanced. Of course, the current volatility would be used in making these determinations. Another follow-up monitoring technique, using the deltas of the options involved, is presented later in this chapter, and has been described several times previously.

FACILITATION OR INSTITUTIONAL BLOCK POSITIONING

In this and the following section, *the advantages of using the hedge ratio will be outlined.* These strategies are primarily member firm, not public customer, strategies since they are best applied in the absence of commission costs. An institutional block trader may be able to use options to help him in his positioning, particularly when he is trying to help a client in a stock transaction.

Suppose that a block trader wants to make a bid for stock to facilitate a customer's sell order. If he wants some sort of a hedge until he can sell the stock that he buys, and the stock has listed options, he can sell some options to hedge his stock position. To determine the quantity of options to sell, he can use the hedge ratio. The exact formula for the hedge ratio was given earlier in this chapter in the section on the Black-Scholes pricing model. It is one of the components of the formula. Simply stated, the hedge ratio is merely the delta of the option—that is, the amount by which the option will change in price for small changes in the stock price. By selling the correct number of calls against his stock purchase, the block trader will have a neutral position. This position would, in theory, neither gain nor lose for small changes in the stock price. He is therefore buying himself time until he can unwind the position in the open market.

Example: A trader buys 10,000 shares of XYZ and a January 30 call is trading with a hedge ratio of .50. To have a neutral position, the trader should sell options against 20,000 shares of stock (10,000 divided by .50 equals 20,000). Thus, he should sell 200 of the January 30's. If the hedge ratio is correct—largely a function of the volatility estimate of the underlying stock—the trader will have greatly eliminated risk or reward on the position for small stock movements. Of course, if the block trader *wants* to assume some risk, that is a different matter. However, for the purposes of this discussion, the assumption is made that the block trader merely wants to facilitate the trade in the most risk-free manner possible. In this sample position, if the stock moves up by 1 point, the option should move up by ½ point. The trader would make $10,000 on his stock position and would lose $10,000 on his 200 short options—he has no gain or loss. Once the trader has the neutral position established, he can then begin to concentrate on unwinding the position.

In actual practice, this hedge ratio may not work exactly because of the fact that it tends to change constantly as the stock price changes. If the trader finds the stock moving more than fractionally, he may have to add more calls or buy some in, to maintain a neutral hedge ratio. This would expose him to some risk, but the risk is substantially smaller than if he had not hedged at all. Of course, there would also be certain cases in which he would profit by the stock price change as well. For example, implied volatility could decrease, making the calls cheaper.

A similar hedge can be established by the block trader who sells stock to accommodate a customer buy order. He could buy calls in accordance with the hedge ratio, to set up a neutral position.

This process of facilitation is quite widely practiced, especially by brokerage houses that are trying to attract the large business of the institutional customer. Since the introduction of listed call options and their applications for facilitating orders, many quotes for large blocks of stock have improved considerably. The block trader (who works for the brokerage house) is willing to make a higher bid or a lower offer if he can use options to hedge his position. This facilitation with options results in a better market (higher bid or lower offer) from the point of view of the institutional customer. Without the availability of such listed options, the block trader would probably make a bid or an offer that was substantially away from the prevailing market price in order to work out of his stock-only position with a lessened degree of risk. This would obviously present a poorer market for the institutional customer.

The Neutral Spread

The hedge ratios of two or more options may be used to determine a neutral spread. This strategy is especially useful to market makers on the options exchanges who may want to reduce the risk of options bought or sold in the process of providing a public market. If the hedge ratios of two options are known, *the neutral ratio is determined by dividing the two hedge ratios.*

Example: An XYZ January 35 has a hedge ratio of .25 and an XYZ January 30 has a hedge ratio of .50, so a neutral ratio would be 2:1 (.50 divided by .25). That is, one would sell 2 January 35's against one long January 30, or, conversely, would buy 2 January 35's against one short January 30. Thus a market-maker who has just bought 50 January 30's in an effort to provide a market for a public seller of that call could hedge his position by selling 100 January 35's. This should keep his risk small— for small stock price changes—until he can unwind the position. The ratio for the neutral spread is not as sensitive to the volatility estimate of the underlying stock as is the ratio concerning stock and options. This is because the same volatility estimate is applied to both options, and the resultant ratio for the spread would not tend to change greatly.

The risk trader can also use the neutral spread ratio to his advantage. This concept was illustrated several times in previous chapters describing ratio writing, ratio spreads, and straddle writes. Ratio spreads are quite popular with member firm traders and floor traders. Recall that a ratio spread consists of buying options at a certain strike, and selling more options further out-of-the-money. The hedge ratios can, of course, be used by the trader, or by a public customer, to initially establish a neutral position. Perhaps more important, the hedge ratio can also be used as a follow-up action to keep the position neutral after the stock changes in price. This strategy is the "delta spread" described in Chapter 11.

The risk trader is not attempting to establish the spread with the idea of minimizing risk for small stock movements. Rather, he is looking to make a profit, but would prefer to remain as neutral as possible on the underlying stock. He is implementing a risk strategy that has a neutral outlook on the underlying stock. He is selling much more time value premium than he is buying.

Example: The purchase of 15 January 30 calls and the sale of 30 January 35 calls—a ratio call spread—may be a position taken for profit potential. It would be a neutral position if the deltas were .60 and .30, for example. This spread would do best if the stock were at exactly 35 at expiration. However, if the stock rose quickly before expiration, the spread ratio would decrease from 2:1 to perhaps 3:2. That is, the neutral ratio between the January 30 call and the January 35 call should be 3 short January 35's to 2 long January 30's. If the trader wants to balance his position, he could buy 5 more January 30's, giving him a total of 20 long versus the 30 short January 35's that he originally sold. Conversely, if the stock dropped in price, the neutral spread ratio might increase, indicating that more calls should be sold. For example, if this stock declines, the neutral ratio might be 3:1. In that case, 15 more January 35's could be sold, making the position short 45 calls versus 15 long calls, which would produce the neutral 3:1 ratio.

It would not be proper to adjust the ratio constantly, because the frequent whipsaw losses on trading movements would wipe out the profit potential of the position. However, the trader may want to pick out points, in advance, at which he wants to reevaluate his position before something drastic goes wrong. For example, if the foregoing spread were established with the stock at a price of 30, the spreader might want to readjust at 33 or 27, whichever comes first.

By monitoring the spread using the hedge ratio, the trader may also be able to discern whether he has established too bullish or too bearish of a position.

Example: The trader starts with the example described above—long 15 January 30 calls and short 30 January 35 calls—when the hedge ratios were .60 and .30, respectively. Some later time, the stock falls to 27 and the trader needs to reevaluate his position. The hedge ratios may have become .42 for the January 30 and .14 for the January 35, indicating that a 3:1 ratio would be neutral (.42/.14 = 3). He now has a bullish position because his 2:1 ratio is *less than* the neutral 3:1 ratio. It is not mandatory that the trader act on this information. He may actually be bullish on the stock at this point and decide to remain with his position. The usefulness of the hedge ratio is that it allows him to see that his position is bullish and therefore he can make a correct judgment. Without this knowledge, he might still think his position to be neutral, a critical mistake if he indeed wants to be neutral. If the trader's ratio is greater than the neutral ratio (2:1 vs. 3:2, for example), he is bearishly positioned.

As a final point, it should be noted that the ratio can be adjusted by buying or selling either option.

Example: If the stock falls and it is desired that the ratio be increased to 3:1, one might sell more January 35's or might decide to sell out some of his January 30's. A bullish adjustment could be made by buying on either side of the spread in a similar manner. In general, one should adjust by selling time premium or buying intrinsic value. That is, out-of-the-moneys are usually sold and in-the-moneys are usually bought, when adjusting.

AIDING IN FOLLOW-UP ACTION

The computer can also be an invaluable aid to the strategist in that it can help him monitor his positions. It is generally necessary for the strategist to have some way of inputting his positions into an inventory data base and also to have some way of identifying different securities that are grouped within the same trading position. Once this has been done, *the computer can simultaneously read a pricing tape and the inventory data base to generate information concerning the current status of any position.*

A current mark to market (profit and loss) statement is of obvious use in that the trader can see how he is doing each day. The computer can also easily generate a set of warning flags that may be of interest to the trader and could print out a list summarizing possible positions that need action. In most of the strategies that were described, it was shown that the strategist should avoid early assignment if at all possible. It is a simple matter for the computer to calculate the remaining time value premium of any short options, and to warn the trader if there is only a small amount of time value premium remaining—perhaps ½ point or less. For similar reasons, the trader may want to have a daily list of positions that are nearing maturity—perhaps with less than 1 month of life remaining in the options. A flag indicating an approaching ex-dividend date might also be useful for this purpose. If the trader inputs another piece of information into the data base, the computer can help him in another follow-up action. In most strategies that were described, especially those involving uncovered options, the trader wants to take some sort of follow-up action based on the price movement of the underlying stock. If the stock rallies too far, he may want to cover short calls or buy other calls as protection. If the stock declines too far, similar maneuvers would apply to put options or to rolling down short calls. If the trader inputs the stock prices at which he would like to take action, the computer can monitor each day's closing price of the stock and generate a list of positions that have exceeded their upside or downside action points.

The computer can also do more sophisticated types of position monitoring. Recall that it was pointed out that the deltas of the options involved in a position can be compared to each other to tell whether the position is bullish or bearish. The Black-Scholes model can be used to calculate the deltas of the options in one's positions. Then the net position can be determined by the computer, thereby telling the trader whether his position has become "delta long" (bullish), "delta short" (bearish), or neutral. If he sees that a position is bearish and he does not want to be structured in that way, he can make bullish adjustments. The delta spread and neutral spread strategies very conveniently lend themselves to such types of follow-up action, although any of the more complicated straddle writing, and protected straddle writing positions can be monitored usefully in this way as well.

The computation of determining whether a position is net short or net long generally involves computing the "equivalent stock position" (ESP). If one owns 10 calls which have a delta of .45, his equivalent stock position from those calls is 10×100 shares per call $\times .45 = 450$. That is, owning those 10 calls is equivalent to owning 450 shares of the underlying stock, according to the delta. All puts and calls can be reduced to an ESP and can then, of course, be combined with any actual long or short stock in the position to produce an ESP for the entire strategy. The resultant ESP for each of the trader's positions can be printed out by the computer along with the items described above.

Further sophisticated measures can be taken. The computer can print out a table of results at expiration. If so desired, this could be presented as a graph, but that is not really necessary. A table suffices quite well, as shown by most of the examples in this book. Such a picture has meaning only if all options in the position expire at the same time. If they don't, one may instead want the computer to compose a table of results at *near-term expiration*. Thus, in a calendar spread, for example, one could see what sorts of profitability he would be looking at when it was time to remove the spread.

Finally, the computer can compute the expected return of a position already in place. This would give a more dynamic picture of the position, and this expected return is usually for a relatively short time period. That time period might be 30 days, or the time remaining until expiration, whichever is less. The expected return is calculated in much the same manner as the expected return computation described earlier in this chapter. First, one uses the stock's volatility to construct a range of prices over which to examine the position. Secondly, one uses the Black-Scholes model to calculate the values of the various options in the position at that future time and at the various stock prices. Some of the results should be printed in table form by the computer program. The expected profit is computed, as described earlier, by summing the multiples of the probabilities of the stock being at each price by the result of the position at that price. The expected return is then computed by dividing the expected profit by the expected investment. Since margin computations can require involved computer programs, it is sufficient to omit this last step and merely observe the expected profit. The following example shows how a sample position might look as the computer prints out the position itself, the ESP, the profit at expiration, and the expected profit in 30 days. A complex position will be assumed in order that the value of these analyses can be demonstrated.

Example: The following position exists when XYZ is at 31¾. It is essentially a backspread combined with a reverse ratio write. It resembles a long straddle in that there is increased profit potential in either direction if the stock moves far enough by expiration. Initially, the computer should display the position and the ESP.

Position		Delta	ESP	
Short	4,500 XYZ	1.00	Short	4,500 shares
Short	100 XYZ Apr 25 calls	0.89	Short	8,900 shares
Long	50 XYZ Apr 30 calls	0.76	Long	3,800 shares
Long	139 XYZ Jul 30 calls	0.74	Long	10,286 shares
Total ESP			Long	686 shares
Total money in position: $163,500 credit				

The advantage of using the ESP is that this fairly complex position is reduced to a single number. The entire position is equivalent to being long 686 shares of the common stock. Essentially, this is close to delta neutral for such a large position.

The next item that the computer should display is the total credit or debit in the position to date. With this information, an expiration picture can be drawn if it is applicable. In this position, since there is a mixture of April and July options, a strict expiration picture does not apply. Rather, the computer should draw a picture based on the position at April expiration or on a shorter time horizon.

Assume that April expiration is still some time away, so that the computer will instead draw the picture 30 days hence. In order to do so, the computer uses the stock's volatility to project stock prices 30 days in the future. Seven stock prices are shown in the next table—they represent points along the distribution curve of the stock, ranging from minus one and one-half standard deviations to plus one and one-half standard deviations movement from the current stock price. While these 7 points are certainly not the entire spectrum of possible stock moves, they are a representative sample.

Stock Price in 30 Days	Standard Deviations	Expected Results
35⅜	+1.5	+$15,847
34⅛	+1.0	+ 12,355
32⅞	+0.5	+ 10,097
31¾	0.0	+ 9,443
30⅝	−0.5	+ 10,743
29½	−1.0	+ 14,172
28½	−1.5	+ 19,605
Expected profit		+$11,426

Obviously this position has had some profitable adjustments made to it in the past. That is not important at this point, because the trader is interested only in the future. If the current mark to market of this position were in excess of $11,426 dollars, then he should consider removing the position since it would be more profitable than the expected profit.

IMPLEMENTATION

Many of the analyses described in this chapter can be obtained from a reliable data service or brokerage firm. The strategist who plans to prepare his own analysis—either by himself or by contracting the programming work out—should be aware that computer programs cannot be written in the COBOL language, for the mathematics are far too complicated for a business language. FORTRAN or ALGOL would suffice as programming languages, as would any higher-level language, such as PL/I, PASCAL, or "C." Reliable option pricing data that include dividend information on the underlying stock are also necessary. The larger programmable calculators can handle calculations such as the Black-Scholes model, computing the hedge ratio, and determining the probability of a stock being above or below a certain price at some future time. However, more involved calculations, such as computing the implied volatility or determining the expected return of a position, would require the use of a computer.

SUMMARY

Two basic mathematical aids have been presented—the pricing model and the ability to predict the probability of a stock's movement. The hedge ratio and the expected return analysis are extensions of the basic aids. Any strategy can be evaluated with these tools. Such an analysis should be able to give the trader or strategist some idea of the relative attractiveness of establishing the position and may also aid in follow-up adjustments to the position. All the analyses rely heavily on one's estimate of the volatility of the underlying stock. The implied volatility seems to be one of the best ways to obtain an accurate, current volatility estimate, since it is derived from the prices in the market itself. The applications presented here are not all-inclusive. The strategist who is, or becomes, familiar with the advantages of rigorous mathematical analysis will be able to construct many other aids for his trading, which utilize the basic mathematics that have been described in this chapter.

PART FIVE

INDEX OPTIONS
AND FUTURES

Chapter *31*

Introduction to Index Option Products and Futures

Since their introduction in 1981, listed index options have proved to be very popular. Index options are options whose underlying security is not a single stock but rather an index composed of many stocks. These include options on index futures contracts. Most popular types of cash settlement options are options on indices or subindices. The strategies employed in trading these options are not substantially different from those used in trading stock options, with a few notable exceptions. However, the options themselves tend to be priced differently and to trade differently. It is these differences between stock options and index options on which we will predominantly concentrate.

Index products—cash-based options, futures-based options, and index futures—will be the main topic of discussion in this section of the book. We will look at how indices are constructed, how to use these products to speculate, how to hedge, and how to spread one index against another. Both futures and options will be used in these strategies. The discussion of other futures options—currencies, grains, bonds, etc.—will be deferred to a later chapter.

In this chapter, we will be looking at introductory facts about index options and futures which differentiate them from the equity options that have encompassed the entire previous part of this book. First, however, we will take an in-depth look at stock indices and the methods of calculating them. Also in this chapter there will be a discussion of futures contracts and how trading them differs from trading stocks and stock options.

INDICES

Since many cash-based or futures options have an index of stocks underlying the option, it is useful to understand how indices are calculated, in order that one may be able to understand how an individual stock's movement within the index affects the overall value of the index. The indices on which options are traded are generally stock indices—that is, the items making up the index are stocks. There are two main ways of calculating a stock index: weighted by price or weighted by capital.

Capitalization-Weighted Indices

The capitalization of a stock is the total dollar value of its securities at current market prices: It is the multiple of the number of shares outstanding (the float) and the current stock price. In a capitalization-weighted index, the capitalizations of all stocks in the index are computed and added together to produce the total market value of the index. The price of each stock in the index is multiplied by the total number of shares of that stock that are outstanding (the "float"), and their sum is calculated. Finally, this total sum is divided by another number, termed the "divisor," to produce the final index value. An example will help to illustrate the concept of calculating the value of a capitalization-weighted index.

Example: Suppose that an index is composed of three stocks whose prices and floats are given in the following table. The multiple of price times float (capitalization) is also included in the table.

Stock	Price	Float	Capitalization
A	30	175,000,000	5,250,000,000
B	90	50,000,000	4,500,000,000
C	50	100,000,000	5,000,000,000
		Total capitalization:	14,750,000,000

Most indices use a divisor since it would be unwieldly to say that the index closed at 14,750,000,000 (for example, think of trying to quote the

Dow-Jones Industrial Average as such a large figure). The divisor is a generally arbitrary number that is initially used to reduce the index value to a workable number. When an index is initiated, the divisor might be set so that the index starts out at an even number. Suppose that in the sample index above, we wanted the initial value—as represented by the given prices and floats—to be 100.00. Then we would set the initial divisor to 147,500,000. Thus the total capitalization of the index divided by the divisor would give a value of 100.00.

The divisor of an index can be changed to provide continuity for the index's value when changes occur in the individual components. Note that the divisor does not have to be changed when a stock splits, because the price is adjusted downward automatically by an amount equal to the increase in the float of the stock that is splitting. Notice that in the above example, if stock B should split 2-for-1 then its price would be 45 (90 ÷ 2) and its float would double to 100 million shares from 50 million. Thus, the capitalization of stock B remains the same: $4,500,000,000.

However, if a stock should alter its capitalization in a manner that is not reflected by an automatic adjustment in its price, then the divisor must be changed. For example, a company might issue more stock in a secondary offering—something that would not cause the exchange where the stock is listed to automatically reduce the price of the stock. To produce continuity in the value of the index between the day the secondary is issued and the day after it is issued, the divisor is changed to keep the index value the same. Consider the following example.

Example: Using the same sample index as before, suppose that the following prices exist at the closing one day:

Stock	Price	Float	Capitalization
A	40	175,000,000	7,000,000,000
B	80	50,000,000	4,000,000,000
C	60	100,000,000	6,000,000,000
	Total capitalization:		17,000,000,000
	Divisor: 147,500,000		
	Index value: 115.25		

Now suppose that stock A issues a 2-million-share secondary that evening, giving that stock a total float of 177 million shares. Such an action would change the value of the index as follows:

Stock	Price	Float	Capitalization
A	40	177,000,000	7,080,000,000
B	80	50,000,000	4,000,000,000
C	60	100,000,000	6,000,000,000
	Total capitalization:		17,080,000,000
	Divisor: 147,500,000		
Index value: 115.80			

However, it makes no sense to change the value of the index from 115.25 to 115.80 when nothing actually changed in the marketplace. If investors deem it necessary to lower the price of stock A in the marketplace because of the secondary issue, so be it. But such a change in investor philosophy would be reflected in the price of the index as the stock drops. So, in order to keep the value of the index the same on the morning after the secondary is issued, the divisor must be changed to reflect the extra 2 million shares of stock A. The new divisor would be equal to the new total capitalization (17,080,000,000) divided by the old index value (115.2542373). This would give the new divisor:

New divisor: 148,194,117.6

As this example demonstrates, the divisor of a capitalization-weighted index can change quite often. Fortunately, there are organizations that are responsible for keeping the index current and for calculating the divisor every time it needs changing. Thus, an investor who needs to know the latest divisor can generally find it out by making a phone call. This is far easier than keeping track of everything by oneself.

In a capitalization-weighted index, the stocks with the largest market value have the most weight within the index. This means that indices that contain such largely capitalized stocks as IBM, AT&T, General Electric, Exxon, and General Motors will be dominated by those stocks. For example, the S&P 500 is one of the largest capitalization-weighted indices in terms of the number of stocks (500). However, IBM has such a large capitalization that it accounts for over 5% of the index. Obviously, there are many stocks in the S&P 500 that do not really have much weight at all. *In order to compute the percentage that a stock comprises of the index, it is merely necessary to divide that stock's capitalization by the total capitalization of the index.* Using the previous example, one can see how the percentage is computed.

Stock	Price	Float	Capitalization	Pct
A	40	177,000,000	7,080,000,000	41.5%
B	80	50,000,000	4,000,000,000	23.4%
C	60	100,000,000	6,000,000,000	35.1%
	Total capitalization:		17,080,000,000	100.0%

Another interesting statistic to know regarding any index is how many shares of each stock are in the index. In a capitalization-weighted index, *the number of shares of each stock is determined by dividing the stock's float by the divisor of the index.* In the same sample index, the following table shows how many shares of each stock are in the index.

Stock	Price	Float	Capitalization	Shares
A	40	177,000,000	7,080,000,000	1.20
B	80	50,000,000	4,000,000,000	0.34
C	60	100,000,000	6,000,000,000	0.68
		Total capitalization:	17,080,000,000	
		Divisor: 147,500,000		
		Index value: 115.80		

Thus if stock A goes up by one point, then the value of the index would increase by 1.20 points since there are 1.2 shares of stock A in the index. One can see the value of computing such a statistic—it readily allows him to see how any individual stock's movement will affect the index movement during a trading day. This is especially useful when a stock is halted, but the index itself keeps trading.

Example: Suppose that, in the above index, stock C has halted trading. There are 0.68 shares of stock C in the index. Suppose that stock C is indicated 3 points lower, but that the index is currently trading unchanged from the previous night's close due to the fact that both stocks A and B are unchanged on the day. If one were to try to price the options on the index, he would be wrong to use the current price of the index since that will soon change when stock C opens. However, there is not really a problem since one can readily see that if stock C opens 3 points lower, then the index will drop by 2.04 points (3 × 0.68). Thus one should price the options as if the index were already trading about 2 points lower. This kind of anticipation depends, of course, on knowing the number of shares of stock C in the index.

A similar type of analysis is useful when trying to predict longer-term effect of a stock on an index. If you thought stock C had a chance of rallying 30 points, then one can see that this would cause the index to rise over 20 points. Given this type of relationship, there are sometimes option spreads between the stock's options and the index's options that will be profitable based on such an assumption.

It should also be noted that the number of shares of stock in a capitalization-weighted index does not change on a daily basis since it does not depend on the price of the stocks in the index. However, *the percent that each stock comprises of the index does change each day as prices change*. Thus the number of shares is a more stable statistic to keep track of, and is also more directly usable to anticipate index value changes as stock prices change.

Capitalization-weighted indices are the most prevalent type, and most investors are familiar with several of them: the Standard and Poor's 500, the Standard and Poor's 400, the Standard and Poor's 100 (also called by its quote symbol, OEX), the New York Stock Exchange Index, and the American Stock Exchange Index.

Price-Weighted Indices

A price-weighted index contains an equal number of shares of each stock in the index. A price-weighted index is computed by adding together the prices of the various stocks in the index and then dividing that sum by the divisor to produce the index value. Again, the divisor is initially an arbitrary number that is used to produce a desired original index value— something like 100.00, for example. Let us use the same three stocks we were using above to construct an example of a price-weighted index. Assume the divisor at the time of this example is 1.65843.

Stock	Price
A	30
B	90
C	50
Price total:	170

Divisor: 1.65843
Index value: 102.51

Unlike the capitalization-weighted index, the divisor needs to be changed when a stock's price is adjusted by the exchange where it is listed (as in a stock split or stock dividend) but does not have to be adjusted when the company issues more stock. That is, the divisor in a price-weighted index is changed when the *price* of the stock is adjusted, but not when the stock's capitalization is changed.

If a certain stock issues new stock in a secondary offering, the exchange where its stock is listed will not automatically adjust the price of the stock downward. Hence, there is no change to the divisor of any price-weighted index containing that stock because the closing *price* of the stock was not adjusted by the exchange.

However, in the above example, if stock B should split 2-for-1, the exchange would change its closing from 90 to 45. Thus, the sum of the stocks in the price-weighted index would change without the market even being open. Consequently, the divisor would need to be changed to reflect the split. The following example sums up the situation after stock B splits 2-for-1.

Stock	*Price*
A	30
B	45
C	50
Price total:	125
Old divisor: 1.65843	
Previous closing index value: 102.51	
New divisor (i.e., the divisor necessary to keep the index value unchanged): 1.21943	

The new divisor is calculated by dividing the new sum of the prices, 125, by the old closing price, 102.51. Thus the divisor is reduced in order to produce the same index value—102.51—even though the sum of the prices of the stocks in the index is now 125 instead of the previous 170. Note that the new divisor is not dependent on the old divisor.

Another statistic that we looked at with capitalization-weighted indices was the number of shares of each stock in the index. In a price-weighted index each stock in the index has the same number of shares and that number is equal to 1 divided by the divisor of the index. In the last example above, with the divisor equal to 1.21943, there would be 1/1.21943 or 0.82 shares of each stock in the index. Thus any stock that was up by 1 point during a given day would be contributing an upward movement of 0.82 points in the index. Before the split there were 0.60 (1/1.65843) shares of each stock.

Another way to look at the revision of a price-weighted index following a split by one of its stocks is the following: If one stock splits, then to reestablish the fact that there are an equal number of shares of each stock in the index, part of the extra (split) shares should be sold off and used to buy an equal number of shares of each of the remaining stocks.

Note that before the split there were 0.60 shares of each stock, and 0.82 shares after. When stock B split 2-for-1, it increased its shares from 0.60 to 1.20, so to rebalance the index it was necessary to sell 0.38 shares of stock B and use the proceeds to buy 0.22 shares of each of stocks A and C.

A price-weighted index's divisor can be subject to fairly frequent revision, just as was the case with the capitalization-weighted index. These divisors are maintained by the organizations responsible for originating them, and they can be easily obtained just by calling the proper organization. The most popular price-weighted indices are the various Dow-Jones indices and the Major Market Index (XMI). Options are not traded on the Dow-Jones indices.

The stock with the most weight in a price-weighted index is the one with the highest price, which is substantially different from the capitalization-weighted index where the stock with the most weight is the one with the most market value. Thus, in the above examples, the stock with the greatest weight in the index would be stock B before the split and C after the split. Of course, the matter of a stock's volatility has something to do with which stock has the most weight in the change of the value of the index. Thus, if stock B was the highest-priced stock at $90 per share, but had a very low volatility, then its price changes would be small and it might consequently not have as great an influence on the changes in the price of the index as some lower-priced stock would.

In general, one is far less concerned with a stock's weight in a price-weighted index than he is in a capitalization-weighted index. That is, one might notice that four or five large stocks—IBM, AT&T, Exxon, General Motors, and General Electric, for example—might make up over 30% of the S&P 100 even though they represent only 5% of the stocks in the index. However, the same five stocks in a price-weighted index of 100 stocks would probably account for very nearly 5% of the index because their prices are not substantially different from those of the other 95 stocks (even though their capitalizations are). So if one were to notice a large change in the price of IBM, one might figure that capitalization-weighted indices that contained that stock would also be showing somewhat unusual price changes in the same direction that IBM is moving. A price-weighted index that contained IBM would, of course, also be affected by IBM's price change, but not extraordinarily so since IBM would have far less weight in the price-weighted index.

Subindices

Subindex is a term used to refer to an index of stocks in which all the stocks are members of the same industry group. Examples of groups on which subindices have been created—and on which options have traded—

are computers and technology, international oils, domestic oils, gold, transportation, airlines, and gaming and hotels. These indices are computed in the same ways as described above—either price-weighted or capitalization-weighted. They generally consist of fewer stocks than their major counterparts, however. Most subindices are comprised of between 20 and 30 stocks, since that is about all of the stocks in any one specific industry group. The large indices are usually referred to as "broad-based" indices, as opposed to the smaller subindices which are often referred to as "narrow-based" indices.

Options trade on these subindices. The intent of these options is to allow portfolio managers—who often are group-oriented—to be able to hedge off parts of their portfolio by industry group. The options on these subindices are usually cash-based options. Strategies will be discussed later, but there is not much difference in strategy between broad-based or narrow-based index options. One difference is that broad-based option writers receive more favorable margin treatment (that is, they are required to put up less collateral) than narrow-based option writers.

CASH-BASED OPTIONS

Now that the reader is familiar with indices, let us look at the most popular type of listed index option, the cash-based option.

Cash-based options do not have any physical entity underlying the option contract. Rather, if the option is exercised or assigned, the settlement is done with cash only—there is no equity involved. This type of option is generally issued on an index, such as the S&P 500, for which it would be virtually impossible to actually deliver the underlying securities in case of assignment or exercise.

Since many investors feel that it is easier to predict the market's movement rather than that of an individual stock, the cash-based index option has become very popular. Other indices that underlie cash-based option contracts are the New York Stock Exchange Index, the American Stock Exchange Index, the S&P 100 Index (OEX—an index introduced by the CBOE), the Major Market Index (XMI), the Pacific Exchange's Financial Composite Index (FNC), and several other indices. In all of these cases there are too many stocks in the index, and too many varying quantities of each of the stocks, to be able to handle the physical delivery of each of the stocks in the case of exercise or assignment. Some cash-based options are based on subindices (that is, subgroups of the larger indices such as the transportation group). Virtually all cash-based index options have options expiring every month, rather than every 3 months as is the case with stock options.

Exercise and Assignment

It is important to understand the ramifications of exercise and assignment when dealing with this type of option. *When a cash-based option is exercised, the owner receives cash equal to the difference between the index's closing price and the strike price of the option.* The option writer who is assigned must pay out an equal amount. The following example shows how a call exercise might work. In this and the following examples we will use a fictional index ZYX (index symbols normally end in X).

Example: Suppose an investor buys an ZYX September 160 call option. At a later date, the index has risen substantially in price and closes at 175.24 on a particular day. The investor decides it is time to take his profit by exercising his call option. Assume the ZYX contract is worth $100 per point, just as stock options are, he receives cash in the amount of $100 times the difference between the index closing price and the strike price: $100 × (175.24 − 160.00) = $1,524. He has no further position or rights—the option position disappears from his account by virtue of the exercise and he does not acquire any security by the exercise; he gets only cash.

An assignment would work in a similar manner, with the seller of an option having to pay out of his account cash equal to the difference between the index closing price and the option's striking price. As an example, suppose that a trader sells a put option on the ZYX Index—the October 165 put. Subsequently, the index drops in price, and one morning the writer of this put option finds that he has been assigned (as of the previous day, as is the case with stock options). If the index closed at 157.58 on the previous day, then the option writer's account will be debited an amount equal to $100 × (165.00 − 157.58) = $742.

European versus American Exercise

Before proceeding with more examples of index option exercise and the accompanying strategies, it is necessary to introduce two new definitions. *American exercise* means that an option may be exercised at any time; *European exercise* means that an option may only be exercised on its expiration day. Many of the cash-based index options have the European exercise feature. All stock options and some index options have the American exercise feature.

The European exercise feature was introduced because institutional investors who might tend to write calls against their portfolio of stocks wanted some assurance that their protection wouldn't be unexpectedly taken away from them. Thus several index option series became European exercise. Two major ones are the cash-based index options on the S&P

500 Index (SPX) and the cash-based options on the NYSE Index. OEX remains an American exercise.

In-the-money European put options will be cheaper than their American counterparts. This is because an arbitrageur would have to carry the position all the way to expiration; he could not exercise his puts and liquidate the position immediately. In fact, deeply in-the-money European puts will trade at a discount; the higher short-term interest rates are, the deeper the discount will be.

This can affect the full protective capability of long-term European puts. If a portfolio manager buys puts to protect his portfolio and the market crashes, the puts might be deeply in the money. If these puts have a European exercise feature, they would be selling at a deep discount and therefore would not have afforded all the price protection that the portfolio manager had been looking for.

American Exercise Consideration. The primary reason for the holder of an index option to exercise the option is to take his profit. One might think that, if the holder wanted to take a profit, he would merely sell his option in the open market. Of course, if he could, he would. However, many times the deeply in-the-money options sell at a substantial discount during the trading day. A deep discount is considered to be ½ to ¾ of a point, or more. Near the end of the day, these options tend to trade at only slight discounts. In either case, the holder of the option may decide to exercise rather than to sell at *any* discount. Of course, if one is the holder of a call option that is trading at a substantial discount in the morning of a particular day, and he decides to exercise, he may lose more by the end of the day (if the market trades down) than he would have if he had merely sold at the deep discount in the first place. In fact, some theoreticians feel that the "job" of a deeply in-the-money cash-based option during the trading day is to try to predict the market's close. This, of course, is not a "job" that can be consistently done with accuracy (if it could, the traders doing the predicting would be rich beyond their wildest dreams).

If the holder of a cash-based call option turned bearish, that would be another reason to exercise. That's right—if the holder of a cash-based call option is *bearish*, he should exercise because, by so doing, he liquidates his bullish position and takes his profit. This is somewhat opposite from an option that has a physical underlying security, such as a stock option. This presents an interesting scenario: If one turns bearish late in the day, even after the close, he might conceivably try to exercise his calls to liquidate his position. The exchanges recognize that such tactics might not be in everyone's best interest—for example, if one waited to see how the money supply numbers looked on a particular evening before exercising, he would definitely have an advantage over the writers of those same options. The writers could no longer viably hedge their positions after the market had closed. In order to prevent this, cash-based option exercise notices are only acceptable until 4:10 P.M. EST on any given trading day (except expiration, of course), in order to allow both holders and writers to be on somewhat equal footing.

There is one more fact regarding exercise of cash-based options that will interest brokerage customers, retail or institutional. Most brokerage firms will charge a commission for the cash-based option exercise or assignment. When index options were first traded, commissions were quite high. Currently, however, one should generally be paying a commission based upon the equivalent option price.

Example: In the previous example, one exercised a ZYX Sep 360 call at expiration when the index closed at 375.24. This is a differential of 15.24. One should pay a commission as if he had sold his long calls at a price of 15.24, not on anything more.

For writers of cash-based options, things are not so different from stock options. The writer is still warned of impending assignment by the fact that the option is trading at a discount. If it is not trading at a discount, it is probably not in danger of being assigned. Also, since there is no stock involved and therefore no dividends paid, the writer of a cash-based put option need only be concerned with whether the put is trading at a discount, not with whether it is trading at a discount to underlying price less the dividend, as is the case with stock options.

Traders doing spreads in cash-based options have special worries, however. *What may seem to be a limited-risk spread may acquire more risk than one initially perceived, due to early assignment of the short options in the spread.* Consider the following example.

Example: Suppose that an investor establishes a bearish call spread in ZYX options—he buys the November 160 call at a price of 1 and simultaneously sells the November 155 call at 3. His risk on the spread is $300 plus commissions if he has to pay the maximum, limited debit of $500 to buy back the spread, or so it appears. However, suppose that the index rises substantially in price and the spreader is assigned on the short side of his spread with the index at 175.24. He thus is charged a debit of $2,024 to "cover" each short call via the assignment: $100 times the in-the-money amount, 175.24 − 155.00, or 20.24. He receives this assignment notice in the morning before the next trading day begins. Note that he cannot merely exercise his long, since, if he did that, he would then receive the *next* night's closing price for his long. Under the worst scenario, suppose the market receives disappointing economic news the next day and opens sharply lower—with the index at 172. If he sells his long Nov

160 calls at parity ($1,200), he will have paid a debit of $824—larger than his initial, theoretically "limited" maximum debit of $500. Thus he loses $624 on this spread ($824 less the initial credit of $200)—over twice the theoretically limited loss of $300.

If the market should open sharply lower and trade down, he could lose more money than he thought because his long position is now exposed—there is no longer a spread in place after the short option is assigned. Of course, this could work to his advantage if the market rallied the next day. The point is, however, that a spread in cash-based options acquires more risk than the difference in the strikes (the maximum risk in stock options) if the short option in the spread becomes a deeply in-the-money option, ripe for assignment.

Naked Margin

When an index is designated as "broad-based," a lesser margin requirement applies to the writer of naked options. The SEC determines which indices are broad-based. A broad-based index receives more favorable margin treatment because the underlying index will not normally change in price as quickly as a stock or subindex. Thus, the naked writer theoretically has less of a risk with a naked broad-based index option.

The requirement for writing a broad-based index option naked is 15% of the index, plus the option premium, minus the amount, if any, that the option is out-of-the-money. There is a minimum requirement of 10% of the index for deeply out-of-the-money options.

Example: Suppose that the ZYX is at 168.00, with a Dec 170 call selling for 6 and a **Dec** 170 put selling for 5. The requirement for selling the call naked would be calculated as follows:

15% of index	$2,520
Plus call premium	+ 600
Less out-of-money amount	− 200
Naked call requirement	$2,920

The requirement for writing the Dec 170 put naked would be:

15% of index	$2,520
Plus put premium	+ 500
Naked put requirement	$3,020

Both of these requirements are above the minimum of 10% of the index.

Options on narrow-based indices are subject to the same naked requirements as stock options: 20% of the index plus the premium less an out-of-the-money amount, with a minimum requirement of 15% of the index.

Other margin requirements are similar to those for stock options. For example, if one wanted to write the Dec 170 straddle naked, using the same prices as in the last example, he would have a margin requirement equal to $3,020—the larger of the put or call requirement, just as he would for stock options. Spread requirements for index options work in exactly the same manner as they do for stock options.

LEAPS Index Options

LEAPS (Long-term Equity AnticiPation Securities) have been introduced on indices in recent years. Readers not familiar with LEAPS should review Chapter 25. Since LEAPS have become popular for stock options, it is only logical to think that they would become popular for indices as well.

The main problem was that a LEAPS could be a 2-year option on a 350 dollar underlying index. Such an option might cost 20 points. That is too expensive to attract the public customer. Just one option would cost $2,000. Therefore, the exchanges created mini-indices out of OEX, SPX, XMI, and others. These mini-indices that were created are exactly the same as the full indices, except that they are divided by 10. This means that instead of having the 2-year put with strike of 350 cost 20 points, a 2-year put with a strike of 35 costs 2 points. This is much more affordable for the individual trader.

The following example is of OEX options and the corresponding OAX LEAPS options on the same index. NOTE: OAX is *not* the universal symbol for this mini-index. OEX LEAPS are American exercise, while SPX LEAPS are European. A broker should be contacted for symbols, expiration dates, and other details.

Example: The following is a sample comparison of prices for OEX and for its companion index OAX, which is the OEX divided by 10.

OEX: 370.53	OAX: 37.05
	OAX 2-year LEAPS options:
	Jun 40 call: 1½
	Jun 37½ call: 4
	Jun 35 put: 2

Note that the striking prices of 35, 37½, and 40 for OAX correspond to 350, 375, and 400 for OEX itself. Also, if a 2-year OEX June 400 call existed, it would sell for 15 points (10 times 1½).

Warrants

Warrants are long-term options, with generally nonstandard characteristics. There have been warrants on stocks for decades. They entitle one to buy a certain number of shares (usually one) at a specified price (the exercise price) and they have an expiration date. Warrants trade like shares of stock; some are listed on the major stock exchanges.

Recently, however, a new category of index warrants has achieved some success. These are warrants on foreign stock indices. The first one listed—on the American Stock Exchange—was a put warrant on the Nikkei 225, representative of the Japanese stock market. The warrant was issued in early 1990 when the Japan market was very high. It was, at the time, the only way for Americans to easily short the Japanese market. The warrants were originally issued at a price of nearly 4 and eventually rose to over 30 by mid-1992.

Subsequently, many other index warrants were issued—both put and call warrants—on the Japanese market, the British stock market (Financial Times 100 Index), and the French stock market (Paris CAC 40).

The concept has now been extended to encompass other products: warrants on the foreign currency spread between Deutschemarks and Japanese yen; even warrants on the price of oil in 1995. The popularity of these warrants led to the introduction of LEAPS, according to some observors.

When a corporation issues a warrant, the warrant bears the corporation's name. These specialized index and commodity warrants, however, are not issued by a corporation. Rather, they may be issued by anyone with funds. The issuer is technically short the warrants, so he needs to hedge his position. This hedging is handled by a large brokerage firm who understands hedging techniques (e.g., using delta).

One example of these index warrants will be included because it is somewhat difficult to determine what parity is, since there is a foreign currency adjustment involved, as well as an artificially set divisor. That is, if the striking price of put warrant on the Japanese Nikkei 225 is 38,000 and the index is currently at 25,000, what is the intrinsic value of the warrant? It is 13,000 points on the Nikkei of course, but how does that translate into a price in dollars of the warrant trading on the American Stock Exchange? The following example will answer the question.

The general formula for determining the parity value of an in-the-money index warrant is as follows:

Parity = (strike − current index price)/(divisor × currency factor)

Example: The Kingdom of Denmark (!) issued the first put warrant on the Nikkei 225. Its issuance was handled by Goldman Sachs and the warrant was listed on the AMEX. It had a striking price of 37,516.77 (the price of the index above which the put warrant would be worthless at expiration). It expired on January 5, 1993. It also had a fixed currency adjustment of 145.325 yen to the dollar. Finally, there was a divisor of 5 (arbitrarily set by the issuer).

Using the formula above, we can determine what parity would be for the warrant listed on the AMEX if the Nikkei were at 25,000:

Parity = (37,516.77 − 25,000)/(5 × 145.325) = 17.23

Thus, the warrant's parity value would be about 17¼. Since it is so far in-the-money, it would indeed be trading at parity.

These warrants can be valued using the Black-Scholes model, but one must use the above formula to adjust the model's inputs. The strike price and the current index price would have to be adjusted to dollar terms before they could be input to the model.

Example: Another warrant—a call warrant—on the Nikkei, issued by Salomon Brothers, had a strike of 28,442.94 in terms of the Nikkei 225. The divisor was 2, and the currency adjustment factor was 158.80. With the Nikkei at 25,000, what terms would be input to the Black-Scholes model?

Strike price = nominal strike/(divisor × currency adjustment)

= 28,442.94/(2 × 158.80) = 89.56

Stock price = index value/(divisor × currency adjustment)

= 25,000/(2 × 158.80) = 78.715

Thus, at the current time, this call warrant is nearly 11 points out of the money.

Using the time to expiration, volatility, dividend estimate, and the current short-term interest rate one could calculate a Black-Scholes theoretical value for this call.

Warrants have a significant disadvantage compared to options: they must be borrowed before they can be sold short. Since the warrant is an actual security, one must borrow it to sell it short, just as he must do with stock. It is sometimes difficult to locate warrants to borrow. Options are contracts, not securities, so as long as someone is willing to agree to the buy side of the contract, a short seller can readily get short. This disadvantage means that warrants are not as versatile as options.

These warrants may prove to be a flash in the pan, or more issuers may come forth to replace expiring issues. In either case, the trader who is interested in the products offered—primarily foreign stock markets—should consider using these warrants as long as they are available. The trader must, of course, understand the above formula for parity conversion in order to be able to translate the warrant's nominal value into dollar terms.

FUTURES

We will now take a look at how futures contracts work. This section will be concerned only with cash-based index futures; futures for physical delivery are included in a later chapter. The ordinary stock investor might think that he will be able to employ index option strategies without getting involved in futures. While it may be *possible* to avoid futures, the *strategist* will realize that they are a necessary part of the entire index-trading strategy. Thus, in order to be completely prepared to hedge one's positions and to operate in an optimum manner, the use of index futures or index futures options is a necessary complement to nearly all index strategies.

A commodities futures contract is a standardized contract calling for the delivery of a specified quantity of a certain commodity at some future time. The older, more conventional types of commodities contracts were futures on grains, meats, and metals. In recent years, futures have expanded extensively and have encompassed financial securities—bonds, T-bills, Eurodollar Time Deposits, etc. Most recently, futures have been issued that are cash-based; that is, no actual commodity is deliverable. Rather, the contract settles for cash. Some of these cash-based futures contracts have stock market indices as their underlying "commodity." It is this latter type of future that will be the subject of the examples in this section, although the basic facts regarding futures are applicable to all futures contracts, cash-based or not.

Several types of traders or investors use futures contracts. One is the speculator: He is able to generate tremendous leverage with futures and may be able to capitalize on small swings in the price of the underlying commodity. Another is the true hedger: He is a dealer in the actual underlying commodity and uses futures to hedge his price risk. This is the more economic function of futures. Examples of hedges for physical commodities as well as stocks will be presented in later chapters. However, let us look at a simple example of how one might hedge a stock portfolio with stock index futures.

Example: Suppose that a stock mutual fund operates under the philosophy that investors cannot outperform a bullish market, so the best investment strategy when one is bullish is just to "buy the market." That is, this mutual fund actually buys all the stocks in the Standard & Poor's 500 Index and holds them.

If the manager of this fund turns bearish, he would want to sell out his positions. However, the commission costs for liquidating the entire portfolio would be large. Also, the act of selling so much stock might actually depress the market, thereby devaluing the remainder of his portfolio before he can sell it.

This manager might sell S&P 500 futures against his portfolio instead of selling his stocks. Such a futures contract would move up or down in line with the S&P 500 Index as it rises or falls. Suppose that he sold enough futures to hedge the entire dollar value of his stock portfolio. Then, even if the stock market declined, his futures contracts would decline also and would theoretically prevent him from having a loss. Of course, he couldn't make much of a gain if the market went up, since the futures would then lose money. What this money manager has accomplished is that he has effectively sold his stock portfolio without incurring stock commission costs (futures commissions are normally quite small).

If he turns bullish again at some later date, he can buy the futures back, and have his long stocks free to profit if the market rises. Again, he does not spend the stock commission nor does he have to go through the tedious process of placing 500 stock orders to "buy" the S&P 500—he merely places one order in futures contracts.

Futures contracts often trade at premiums to the underlying commodity, due to the fact that the investor who buys the future does not have to spend the money that one buys all the stocks would have to spend. Thus, he saves the carrying costs but forsakes any dividends. This savings is reflected by the marketplace in that a premium is placed on the price of the futures contract. As a consequence, longer-term contracts trade at a larger premium than do near-term contracts, much as is the case with options. In most cases, however, the index futures trader is concerned with the nearest-term contract, and perhaps the next one out in time.

Terms of the Contract

There are cash-based index futures on several indices, although some of these futures contracts are not heavily traded. The most heavily traded contract is the future on the S&P 500 Index. This contract trades on the Chicago Mercantile Exchange. It has contracts that expire every 3 months (March, June, September, December) and a 1-point move in the futures contract is worth $500. There is no particular reason *why* a 1-point move is worth $500, that is merely how the contract was defined when it was introduced.

Example: A futures trader buys 1 March S&P 500 contract at 401.00 (the smallest unit of trading is 0.05 points, a "nickel"). The contract rises in price to 403.30. The trader has a profit of 2.30 points, or $1,150 (2.30 points × $500 per point).

The terms of futures contracts can change as the exchanges on which they are traded attempt to adjust the contracts to be more competitive in the current trading environment. Consequently, the strategist should check with his broker to determine the exact terms of any contract before he begins trading it.

Another popular index futures contract is one trading on the New York Futures Exchange, using the New York Stock Exchange Index as its underlying index. Other cash-based index futures include one on the Value Line Index, traded on the Kansas City Futures Exchange, and a future on the Nikkei 225, the primary index of Japanese stocks. These contracts have the same terms as the S&P 500—quarterly expiration in the March cycle and 1 point is worth $500. There are also futures on "contrived" indices—ones invented in the last few years for the express purpose of giving the investor the opportunity to trade a certain segment of the marketplace. These include the Major Market Index (XMI) traded on the Chicago Board of Trade.

Thus, there are cash-based futures contracts available for various segments of the stock market. In the coming chapters, we will see how to use these various contracts in logical strategies.

Open Outcry

Futures contracts trade on listed commodity exchanges. However, the method of trading is different from that used for stocks and options. Futures trade by "open outcry" in rings or pits. Members of the exchange are the only ones allowed to trade on the exchange, of course, just as is the case with stocks and options. If the member is trying to execute a buy order, for example, he would announce his bid out loud (open outcry). Sellers would then respond by either showing him an offer or by selling to him at his bid price. This differs from stocks and options which use the specialist system, in that many people can be buying and selling at once, all over the pit. It also differs from the market-maker system used on some stock options exchanges because anyone can make the market in the commodity pit, not just a designated few traders.

This form of trading can produce some oddities not normally associated with stock or stock option trading. There may be slightly different markets at different places in a large, busy trading pit. Hence a buyer on one side of the pit may be trying to pay a price that is being offered on the other side of the pit, but the two do not trade with each other because of the size of the trading crowd. The buyer might buy on one side of the pit, but the seller on the other side does not sell. Then if the market trades lower, only one of the two will have received an execution even though they were trying to buy and sell at the same price. Thus, one cannot be certain that his futures order is executed unless the market trades through his price. That is, if one is bidding for futures at a price of 401.50 and a trade is printed at 401.45, then he can be certain that he has bought his contracts.

Futures exchange members who trade mainly for their own account from the ring or pit are known as "locals." They are somewhat akin to the stock option market-maker in that they may take the other side of public orders. Note, however, that they do not *have* to make a public market as market-makers do.

Margin, Limits, and Quotes

Futures contracts are traded on margin and are marked to market every day. Generally, the amount of margin required is small in comparison to the total size of the contract, so that there is tremendous leverage in trading futures. Anyone trading the futures must deposit the initial margin amount in his account on the day he initiates the trade. Then at the end of each day, the amount of gain or loss on the contract is computed, and the account is credited if there is a gain or debited if there is a loss. In case of a loss, the trader must add more cash to his account to cover the loss. This daily margin computation is known as maintenance margin. Treasury bills or other securities are good collateral for the initial margin, but the daily variation margin is required in cash.

Example: The S&P 500 futures contract is a cash-based futures contract that trades on the Chicago Mercantile Exchange. Since the contract is settled in cash, there is no actual physical commodity underlying the contract. Rather, the contract is based on the value of the S&P 500 stock index. At the expiration of the contract, each open contract is marked to market at the closing price of the S&P 500 stock index and disappears. All contracts are settled for cash on their final day and then they no longer exist—they expire. The terms of the contract specify that each point of movement is worth $500. Thus, if the S&P 500 Index itself is at 405, then the S&P futures contract is a contract on $500 × 405, or $202,500 worth of stocks comprising the index. Assume the initial margin for one of these contracts is $22,000, although it may vary at specific brokerage houses.

Suppose that a trader buys one December S&P futures contract for his account sometime in October. With the underlying index at 405.00, suppose he pays 407.40 for the futures contract. It is normal for the futures to trade at a premium to the actual index price. The reasons regarding this will be discussed in a later section. Initially, the customer puts up $22,000 as initial margin, and this may be in the form of T-bills. On the next day, however, the market declines and the futures close at 406.00. This represents a loss of 1.40 points from the purchase price. At $500 per point, the trader has a loss of $700 (500 × 1.40) at this time. He is required to add $700 in cash into the account.

If he continued to hold the contract until expiration, this process of adding his daily gain or subtracting his daily loss from the account would recur each day. Finally, on the last day, the futures contract is deemed to close at the exact opening price of the S&P 500 Index and the variation margin is calculated again at that price. Then the futures contract is expired, so it is "erased" from his account. He is then left with only the cash that he made or lost on the trade of his contract.

The leverage produced by small margin requirements (as a percent of the total value of the contract) is a major factor in making futures very volatile, in dollar terms. In the above example, a $22,000 margin investment controls $202,500 worth of stocks. Due to their volatility, many futures contracts trade with a limit. That is, the price can only fluctuate a fixed amount above or below the previous day's closing price. This concept is intended to prevent traders with large positions from being able to manipulate the market drastically in either direction.

S&P and NYSE Expiration. S&P 500 futures expiration occurs in a somewhat complex way, compared to those indices whose options and futures expire at the last sale on the final day of trading. Some years ago, in order to attempt to reduce the volatility that index futures and options expiration was causing in the stock market, the NYSE and the Chicago Mercantile Exchange (where the S&P 500 futures trade) agreed to change the expiration of their index products from the end of trading on the last Friday to the morning of that day. The effect of expiration on the stock market is discussed in Chapter 32.

As a result, the S&P futures and futures options as well as futures, futures options, and index options on the New York Stock Exchange Index settle in the following manner on their last day of trading. On expiration day—the third Friday of the month—the "final" price for purposes of settling futures and options is comprised of taking the *opening trade* of each stock and calculating an index price based on those opening prices. There is no actual trading in the futures and options on that last Friday; they cease trading at the close of trading on the previous day, Thurday.

The purpose of this change was to give the specialists on the New York Stock Exchange more time to line up the other side of trades to handle order imbalances. Under the new rules, index arbitrageurs are forced to enter their buy or sell orders as market on open orders on that last Friday before 9 am EST. The specialist can then take his time in opening the stock if he needs to; he can solicit orders if there is too much stock to buy or sell.

The effect of all this is that the "final" index price for settlement purposes is not known until all the stocks in the index have opened. It may take some time to open all 500 stocks in the S&P 500 Index if there is a volatile market that Friday morning (perhaps caused by news) or if there a severe order imbalances in many of the stocks (caused by index arbitrageurs). Index arbitrage is described in Chapter 32.

Limits. Originally, index futures traded without limits. However, the stock market crash of 1987 changed that. Certain parties felt that if the futures—which were leading the market down—had ceased trading for a while, the stock market could have stabilized. As a result, a series of trading limits now exists for stock index futures. These are designed to be "circuit breakers"—to prevent a stock market crash. They are not limits in the sense that other futures have limits, but they are similar.

The first circuit breaker is a 5-point limit on the S&P 500 futures. This is approximately a 38 point move in the Dow. This limit only applies to the opening of trading. If the S&P 500 futures open down 5 points, then they are not allowed to trade lower for 10 minutes. After that, the next circuit breaker on any trading day is a 12-point limit in the S&P futures. This is nearly a 90-point move on the Dow. Thus, if the S&P 500 futures were to trade down 12 points at any time during a trading day, they would not be allowed to trade down any lower (they could still trade higher) for one-half of an hour. At that point, trading would open again. The next, and final, circuit breaker is down 20 points on the S&P 500 futures. This is approximately down 150 points on the Dow. At that point, the S&P 500 futures would not be allowed to trade any lower on the day. They could trade lower the next day if need be. Similar limits exist on the XMI futures. Similar limits apply to upward price movements also.

There are actually other "circuit breakers" designed to prevent runaway stock markets, but they are not related to limits on futures trading. They will be described along with index arbitrage and program trading in Chapter 32.

Quotes. While stocks and stock options are always quoted in eighths, or sometimes sixteenths, such is not the case with futures. Some futures trade in fractions, while others trade in cents. S&P 500 futures trade in 5-cent increments, while the smaller contract on the Major Market Index trades in eighths. In the coming chapters, there will be many examples of the trading details of futures and options. However, the investor should familiarize himself with the details of an individual contract before beginning to trade it or its options. One's commodity broker can easily supply this information.

There are certain differences between the way futures trade and the way stocks trade. One difference that is extremely important to investors accustomed to dealing in stocks and stock options is that quotation vendors rarely show a bid and offer for futures. Thus, if one uses a quote machine to obtain the price of a stock he might see that the stock is currently 31 bid, 31⅛ asked, with a last sale of 31. An active futures contract (which is typically the type that one would want to trade) virtually never shows a bid and offer, but rather shows last sale only. In addition, each sale of a stock or stock option is recorded both as to its time of execution and ther quantity of execution. Such is not the case for futures. Only the price is recorded—one cannot tell how many contracts traded at the price, nor can he tell if there were repeated sales at that price.

OPTIONS ON INDEX FUTURES

As we saw earlier, futures contracts allow a person dealing in a commodity to minimize profit fluctuations in his commodity. The mutual fund manager who sold the futures largely removed any possibility of further upside profit or downside loss. Options, however, allow a little more leeway than futures do. With the option, a person can lock in one side of his position, but can leave room for further profits if conditions improve. For example, the mutual fund manager might buy put options on the S&P 500 Index to hedge his downside risk, but still leave room for upside profits if the stock market rises. This is different from the sale of a futures contract, which locks in his profit, but does not leave any room for further profits if the market moves favorably.

Options trade on many types of futures contracts. The security underlying the option is the *futures contract* having the same expiration month, not the entity underlying the futures contract itself. Thus, if one exercises a listed futures option, he receives a futures contract position, not the physical commodity.

Example: A trader owns the ZYX futures December 165 call option (165 is the striking price). Assume the ZYX December future closed at 171.20. Both the calls and the futures are worth $500 per point. If the call is exercised, the trader then owns one ZYX December (same expiration month as the option) futures contract at a price of 165. Since the current price is 171.20, there is a maintenance margin credit of $3,100 in his account (500 × 6.20 points). Note that even though the option is an option on a future which is cash-based, the exercise provides the holder of the option with a futures contract position, not with cash.

At the present time, there are futures options on all of the various index futures contracts.

Expiration Dates

Futures options have specifics much the same as stock options do: expiration month (agreeing with the expiration months of the underlying futures contract), striking price, etc. If a trader buys a futures option, he must pay for it in full, just as with stock options. Margin requirements vary for naked futures options, but are generally more lenient than stock options. Often, the naked requirement is based on the futures margin, which is much less than the 20% of the underlying stock price as is the case with listed stock options.

When the futures option has a cash-based futures contract underlying it, the option and the future generally expire on the same day. Thus, if one were to exercise a ZYX option on expiration day, one would receive the future in his account, which would in turn become cash because the future is cash-settled and expiring as well.

Example: Suppose that a trader owns a ZYX December 165 futures —worth $500 per point—call option and holds it through the last day of trading. On that last day, the ZYX Index closes at 174.00. He gives instructions to exercise the call, so the following sequence occurs:

1. Buy one ZYX future at 165.00 via the call exercise.
2. Mark the future at 174.00, the closing price. This is a variation margin profit of $4,500 = (174.00 − 165.00) × $500.
3. The option is removed from the account because it was exercised, and the future is removed as well because it expired.

Thus, the exercise of the option generates $4,500 in cash into the account and leaves behind no futures or option contracts. We do not know if this represents a profit or loss for this call holder, since we do not know if his original cost was greater than $4,500 or not.

Option Premiums

The dollar amount of trading of a futures option contract is normally the same as that of the underlying future. That is, since the S&P 500 future is worth $500 per point, so are the S&P 500 futures options. The same holds true for the New York Stock Exchange Index options.

Example: An investor buys a S&P 500 December 410 call for 4.20 with the index at 409.50. The cost of the call is $2,100 (4.20 × $500). The call must be paid for in full, as with equity options.

An interesting fact about futures options is that the longer-term options have a "double premium" effect. The option itself has time value premium and its underlying security, the future, also has a premium over the physical commodity. This phenomenon can produce some rather startling prices when looking at calendar spreads.

Example: The ZYX Index is trading at 162.00 sometime during the month of January. Suppose that the March ZYX futures contract is trading at 163.50 and the June futures contract at 167.50. These prices are reasonable in that they represent a premium over the index itself which is 162.00. These premiums are related to the amount of time remaining until the expiration of the futures contract.

Now, however, let us look at two options—the March 165 put and the June 165 put. The March 165 put might be trading at 3 with its underlying security, the March futures contract, trading at 163.50. The June 165 put option has as its underlying security the *June* futures contract. Since the June option has more time remaining until expiration, it will have more time value premium than a March option would. However, the underlying *June* future is trading at 167.50, so the June 165 put option is 2½ points out-of-the-money and therefore might be selling for 2½. This makes a very strange-looking calendar spread with the longer-term option selling at 2½ and the near-term option selling for 3. This is due to the fact, of course, that the two options have different underlying securities. One is in-the-money and the other is out-of-the-money. These two underlyings—the March and June futures—have a price differential of their own. So the option calendar spread is inverted due to this double premium effect.

Futures Option Margin

Most futures exchanges have gone to the new form of option margin called SPAN, which stands for Standard Portfolio ANalysis of Risk. This form of margining is very fair and attempts to base the margin requirement of an option position on the probability of movement by the underlying futures contract, as well as on the potential change of implied volatility of the options in question.

The older method of margining option positions is known as the "customer margin" method. The customer margin method generally results in higher margin requirements. The reader is referred to the chapter on futures and futures options for an in-depth discussion of SPAN and other option margin requirements.

Other Terms

Just as futures on differing physical commodities have differing terms, so do options on those futures. Some options have striking prices 5 points apart while others have strikes only 1 point apart, reflecting the volatility of the commodity. Specifically, for index futures options, the S&P 500 options have striking prices 5 points apart, and the NYSE options have striking prices 2 points apart.

There is no standard method for quoting futures on options as there is with stock options. In some cases, striking price symbols are similar to stock option symbols (B = 10, C = 15, etc.), while in others the letters are used incrementally (A = 1, B = 2, C = 3, etc.). Moreover, the method used may differ with each quote vendor. Since there is no standard method for quoting, one must obtain the symbols individually for futures options, a fact that makes quoting them extremely inconvenient.

There are position limits for some futures options, but they allow for very large positions. Check with your broker for exact limits in the various futures options.

Quotes

Most futures option quotes (bids and offers) are not displayed on quote-vending machines, as is also the case with futures. Options traded on the Chicago Mercantile Exchange are the exception. This can be somewhat distressing to the trader used to dealing in stock options, since options are normally far less liquid than the underlying security. It might be acceptable to trade off of last sales in a liquid futures contract, but not so with the options. As a result, futures options have not attracted many stock option traders into their fold.

The consequence of the inconsistencies in terms as well as the general unavailability of quotes has been that index futures options are generally traded by professionals, with the public largely ignoring them. This does not mean, however, that futures options are unworthy of the strategist's time and effort. In fact, just the opposite may be true—the lack of general information may produce some inefficiencies that the strategist can benefit from.

One factor concerning the trading of futures options can be of major concern to many customers and salesmen. Salesmen who are registered to sell stocks are not necessarily registered to sell futures—an additional test must be passed in order to sell many types of futures options. Similarly, many customers—primarily institutions—have received approval from their constituents to trade in stock options, but would need further approvals to trade futures or futures options. Neither of these things should stand in the way of the strategist—if there are opportunities in futures options, then the customer should find a broker who can trade them. Also if the strategist finds that he requires certain approvals from within his own institution before he can trade futures, then he should obtain those approvals.

STANDARD OPTIONS STRATEGIES USING INDEX OPTIONS

The stock option strategies described in the first 30 chapters of this book can be established with index options as well. The concepts are normally the same for index options as they would be for stock options. If one buys a call at one strike and sells a call at a higher strike, that is a bullish spread; if one sells both a put and a call at the same strike (a straddle), that is a neutral strategy. One uses deltas to determine how many options to sell against the ones that he buys in order to establish a delta neutral strategy. Likewise, he uses the deltas to tell, along the way, how his position is progressing and how to adjust it to keep it delta neutral.

We will not describe these same strategies over again. They have already been described in detail. The risk of early assignment removing one side of a position can alter some strategies. In some cases there are particular advantages or disadvantages with index options and futures. Thus, we will briefly go over some major option strategies, giving details pertaining to their usage as index option strategies.

Option Buying

The most common reason for wanting to buy index options is to take advantage of the diversification that they provide, in addition to the normal things that option purchasing provides: leverage and limited dollar risk. Many people feel that it is easier to predict the general market direction than it is to predict an individual stock's direction. This feeling, can, of course, be put to good advantage by buying index options. However, sometimes it is *not* better to buy the index options. In such cases, it may actually be smarter to purchase a package of individual stock options.

Due to a phenomenon known as volatility skewing, it is possible for index options to have implied volatilities that are out of line with projected index or stock price movements. This phenomenon is discussed in detail in Chapter 38.

For example, suppose that index puts are expensive, as they became after the 1987 stock market crash. When this happens it may actually be more profitable for a trader who is bearish on the market to buy a package of equity puts instead of buying index puts. The equity puts are forced to reflect the probability of stock price movement because arbitrage strategies will keep them in line. They will therefore be less expensive than index puts when this type of volatility skewing is present. Index puts can remain expensive for several reasons—primarily excessive demand and inflated margin requirements. In such situations, it is theoretically correct to buy a group of puts on stock options. In fact, one might even hedge this purchase by selling out-of-the money, excessive index puts.

Selling Index Options

In earlier chapters, we saw that many mathematically attractive strategies involve the sale of naked options—ratio writes, straddles, ratio spreads, etc. Index options present an even stronger case for these strategies. Recall that the greatest risk in these strategies with naked options is that the underlying security might move a great distance, thereby exposing the position to great loss if the movement is in the direction in which the naked options lie. That is, if one is naked calls and the underlying security rises dramatically, perhaps on a takeover bid, then large losses— potentially unlimited in the absence of follow-up action—could occur.

The strategist would, of course, never let the loss run uncontrolled. He would attempt to take some follow-up action to limit the loss or to neutralize the position. However, even the best strategist cannot hedge his position if the movement in the underlying occurs while the market is closed. For example, if the underlying security is a stock, certain news items might cause a large gap to occur between the closing price of a stock and its next opening price. Such news might be related to a takeover of the company or to a drastically negative earnings report, for example.

Index options do not have this particular drawback. An index— especially a broad-based index—is not as likely to open on a wide gap as a stock is. An index cannot be the subject of a takeover attempt. It cannot be severely depressed by bad earnings on one of its components. Thus, index options are more viable candidates for strategies involving naked option writing than stock options are. Index futures and options may often open on small gaps of a point or so, due to emotion or possibly due to the fact that a market that opens earlier (T-Bond futures, for example) has already made a rather large move by the time the futures open. Such a small gap is normally not extremely damaging to the naked writer.

One cannot assume that an index can *never* gap open widely—if something drastic were to happen in the marketplace that caused opening gaps in *many* stocks, then a gap could appear in the index itself. The worst case of such a gap was the stock market crash in 1987 when the major indices such as OEX and S&P 500 opened down over 20 points. Nothing has come close to that before or since, but the possibility always exists that it could happen again. Therefore, one cannot assume that naked option writing of index options is a low-risk strategy; however, it is generally less risky than naked option writing of equity options.

Handling Early Assignment of Cash-Based Options

The greatest problem that a spreader of index options has is the possibility of early assignment. This removes his hedge on one side of his position, exposing him to much more risk than he had wanted or anticipated.

One can often obtain a clue before early assignment occurs by observing the price of the in-the-money options. If they are trading at a discount, one can expect assignment to be more likely.

Example: ZYX is trading at 357 a few days before expiration of the January options. The stock market rallies heavily near the close, and the January 340 calls are trading with a market of $16\frac{1}{2}$ to $16\frac{3}{4}$ after 4 pm EST. Since parity is 17 for these calls, it is likely that a writer will receive an assignment notice in the morning.

The strategist who observes this situation taking place must make a rather quick decision. Since the market has rallied heavily on the close, it is likely that arbitrageurs or institutional accounts who are long index options are going to exercise them. The cynic among us would even think that they might be short stocks as well which they plan to cover in the morning. Notice that the effect of hedged call option sellers (i.e., spreaders) receiving assignment notices will be to make them all long the market. The short side of their spread will have been removed via assignment, and they will be left with only the long side. Therefore, in order to liquidate or hedge, they will have to sell stocks or index futures and options in the morning. This would force the market down temporarily and would be a boon to anyone who was short overnight.

The spreader's first potential choice of action is to notice what is happening near the close of trading and to try to exercise his long calls since he expects assignment of his short calls. The assignment, of course, is not certain—he is merely projecting it. Therefore, he could outfox himself and end up being very short if he did not receive an assignment notice on his short calls.

Assuming the strategist did not anticipate assignment and exercise his long calls, he has several choices after receiving an assignment notice the next morning. First, he could do nothing. This would be an overly aggressive bullish stance for someone who was previously in a hedged position, but it is sometimes done. The strategist who takes this aggressive tack is banking on the fact that the selling after the assignment will be temporary, and the market will rebound thereafter, giving him the opportunity to close out his remaining longs at favorable prices. This is an overly aggressive strategy and is not recommended.

The most prudent approach to take when one receives an early assignment on a cash-based option is to immediately try to do something to hedge the remaining position. The simplest thing to do is to buy or sell futures, depending on whether the assignment was on a put or call. If one was assigned on a put, a portion of the bullishness (short puts are bullish) of one's position has been removed. Therefore, one might buy futures to quickly add some bullishness to the remaining position. Generally, if one were assigned early on calls, part of the bearishness of his position would have been removed—short calls being bearish—and he might therefore sell futures to add bearishness to his remaining position. Once hedged, the position can be removed during that trading day, if desired, by trading out of the hedge established that morning.

The first opportunity to hedge is presented by the XMI futures, which began trading at 9:15 AM EST. If one does not avail himself of that opportunity, the next acceptable hedge is the S&P 500 futures, which begin trading at 9:30 AM EST. Finally, the OEX options, which open in a trading rotation, are probably available for free trading by 9:45 AM or so. One should be particularly careful about placing market orders in an opening rotation, especially on index options after a severe downside move has occurred the previous day. Market makers are very nervous and are not willing to sell puts as protection to the public in that situation. Consequently, puts are notoriously overpriced after a large down day in the stock market. One should refrain from buying put options in the opening rotation in such a case. In the future, it is possible that comparable situations may exist on the upside. To date, however, all gaps and severe mispricing anomalies have been on the bearish side of the market, the downside.

Conclusion

The introduction of index products has opened some new areas for option strategists. The ideas presented in this chapter form a foundation for exploring this new realm of option strategies. Many traders are lax to trade futures options because futures seem too foreign. Such should not be the case. By trading in futures options, one can avail himself of the same strategies available in stock options. Moreover, he may be able to take advantage of certain features of futures and futures options that are not available with stock options. For example, if one were to try to use options to construct a strategy based on his expectation of interest rate movements, he could use T-Bond futures and options, which is the easiest way. However, if he were to try to remain with stock options, he would probably be forced to do something with utility stocks or illiquid interest rate options—a clearly inferior alternative.

Trading in index options can be very profitable, but only if one understands the risks involved—especially the risk of early assignment in cash-based options. The advantages to being able to trade "the market" as opposed to trading one stock at a time are obvious: If one is right on the market, his index option strategies will be profitable. This is superior to stock-oriented buying whereby one might be right on the market, but not make any money because calls were bought on stocks that didn't follow the market.

The strategist should consider all of his alternatives when trading in these markets. If he is bullish, should he really be buying OEX calls? Maybe futures calls on the S&P 500 are better. Perhaps the OEX is expensive with respect to the NYSE and the NYA calls would be a better buy. In fact, perhaps all the calls are so expensive that stock options are the best buy. The ideas presented in this chapter lay the groundwork for the strategist to explore these questions and make the best decision for his investment strategy.

Finally, keep in mind that the index futures and options comprise a very diverse set of securities. They can be put to work for the investor, the trader, and the strategist in a multitude of ways. The only practical limit is in the mind of the user of these derivative securities.

PUT-CALL RATIO

Generally, we have not been concerned with technical trading systems in this book. Not that they aren't important, they are just in another category of investments other than option strategies. However, the put-call ratio system is so closely related to options that its inclusion is worthwhile.

The put-call ratio is simply the number of puts traded divided by the number of calls traded. It can be computed daily, weekly, or over any other time period. It can be computed for stock options, index options, or futures options. Sometimes it is computed using open interest instead of volume. If it is calculated daily, one usually averages several days' worth of figures to smooth out the fluctuations.

Example: The morning paper shows that yesterday the trading activity for OEX options was:

Total OEX Call Volume: 125,000 Contracts

Total OEX Put Volume: 135,000 Contracts

Therefore, the ratio is:

$$\text{Index Put-Call Ratio } = \frac{135,000}{125,000} = 1.08 \text{ for yesterday}$$

This technical indicator is a contrary one. The contrarian thinking is along these lines: if everyone is buying puts, then everyone must be bearish; if everyone is doing something, they can't all be right; therefore the contrarian must assume a bullish stance.

So, if the put-call ratio is high, too many traders are buying puts; a contrarian would interpret that as a bullish sign. Conversely, if the put-call ratio is low, too many traders are buying calls; the contrarian would consider that as a bearish indicator.

There are several typical put-call ratios that can be computed. Generally, one would not want to mix different types of options. For example, the equity put-call ratio uses the option trading volume of equity options only. The index put-call ratio uses index options only. Each futures contract put-call ratio is generally computed separately: gold, soybeans, currencies, etc. One might also attempt to screen his input a little further: for example, the index put-call ratio should only include index options on U.S. exchanges; the others can be computed separately.

Obviously, the more highly traded option contracts produce a more reliable put-call ratio: equity options and index options being very liquid. Gold futures options by themselves are not that active and may produce distorted results for a period of time.

The Ratio Itself. Traders and investors almost always buy more calls than puts where stock options are concerned. Therefore, the equity put-call ratio is normally a number far less than 1.00. If call buying is rampant, the equity put-call ratio may dip into the 0.30 range on a daily basis. Very bearish days may occasionally produce numbers of 1.00 or higher. An average day will generally produce a ratio of around 0.50.

Index options, however, produce much larger ratios. Many institutional and other investors are constantly looking to avail themselves of the protective capability of index puts. Therefore, far more index puts are purchased than are equity puts. An average day would produce a reading of about 1.00—an equal number of calls and puts being purchased. Bearish readings may approach 1.50 and bullish readings 0.50.

Interpreting The Ratio. There are several philosophies as to how to interpret the ratio once it has been calculated. All philosophies are of the contrarian variety, so the general comments made earlier that high ratios are bullish and low ratios are bearish still hold true. However, quantifying just what is "high" and what is "low" leaves room for interpretation.

One school believes that absolute ratios should be used. An example might be: "if the 10-day moving average of the equity put-call ratio is over 0.60, that is a buy signal." Unfortunately, applying absolute figures to any of the ratios can be counterproductive at times. If the market is in the grip of a prolonged bearish move, more and more puts will continue to be purchased, sending the ratio quite high before it can reverse and start coming back to normal levels. *Therefore, it is better to look for the ratios to make a high or a low before calling a buy or sell signal.* This is a more dynamic interpretation; it allows for buy and sell signals to come at different absolute levels of the put-call ratio.

Figure 31-1 shows the 50-day equity put-call ratio going back several years (the daily figures for the previous 50 trading days are averaged to produce the number plotted on the chart each day). One can see that at certain times, the put-call ratio reached extreme heights before finally generating a buy signal. Attempting to call a buy on the market at an absolute level would have been an error becuse the entry point came too early. Notice that the readings in late 1990—as the market bottomed in advance of Operation Desert Storm—were actually higher on an absolute basis than those made after the stock market crash in 1987. Similar observations can be made for sell signals after the ratio has reached low levels: don't anticipate—wait for the ratio to bottom out and turn up before declaring a sell signal or to roll over and turn down before declaring a buy signal.

The index put-call ratio is shown on the right in the figure. It tells a similar story to the equity ratio, although there are certainly differences—beyond the obvious one that the ratios have different absolute values. Note that this ratio averages about 1.00 while the equity ratio averaged about 0.50.

At times, index put buying becomes extensive even as the market climbs (see early 1992). This does not generally happen with equity options. It seems that institutional money managers, who are long stocks, are afraid that they will lose their profits after a quick stock market advance. However, rather than sell their stocks, they buy puts (possibly overpaying for them). Thus, they are really bullish (they own stocks), but they are buying puts as a hedge.

This is a difficult situation for the contrarian. What is the institutional manager's true bias? Is he bullish because he still owns stocks or is he bearish because he is buying puts? This is the bane of contrary analysis—attempting to accurately interpret the data that is being re-

FIGURE 31-1.
50-day equity put–call ratio: 1985–91.

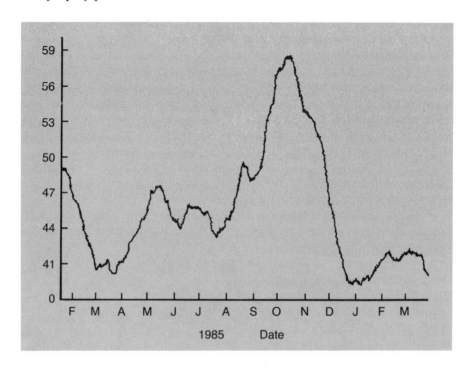

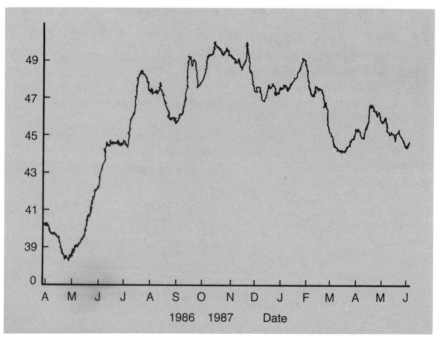

FIGURE 31-1.
(*Continued*)

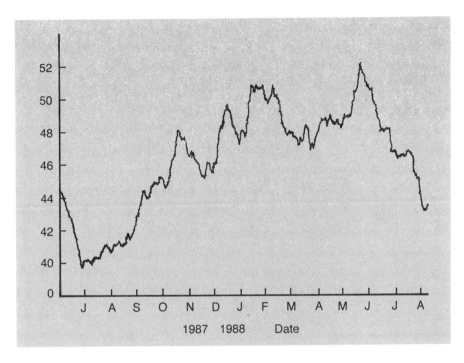

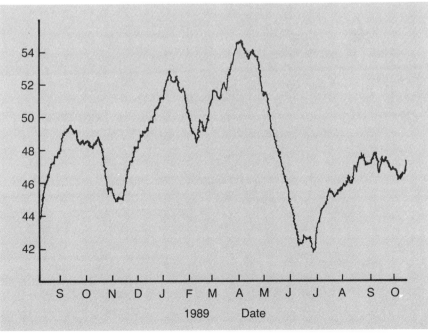

FIGURE 31-1.
(*Continued*)

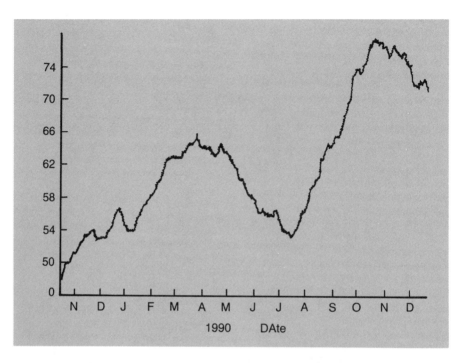

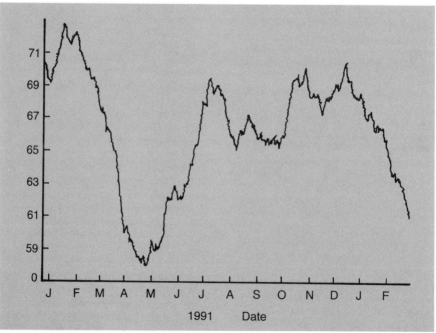

FIGURE 31-2.
50-day index put-call ratio: 1985–91.

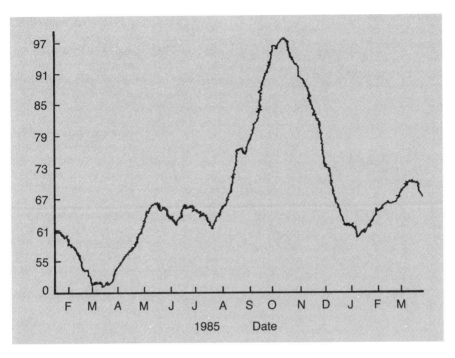

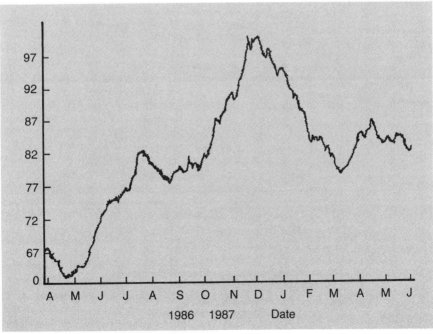

FIGURE 31-2.
(*Continued*)

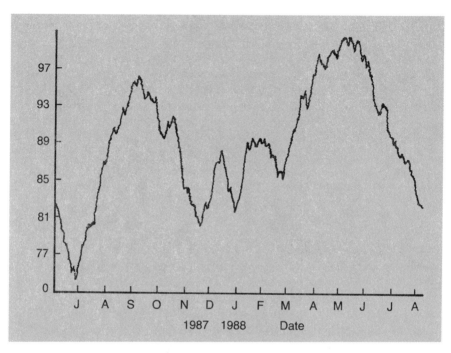

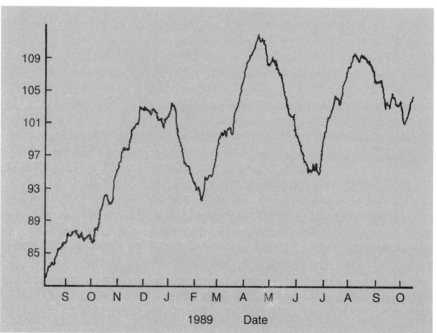

FIGURE 31-2.
(*Continued*)

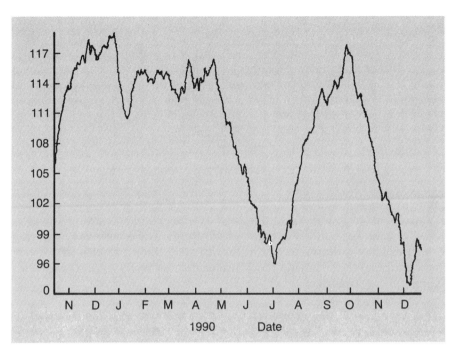

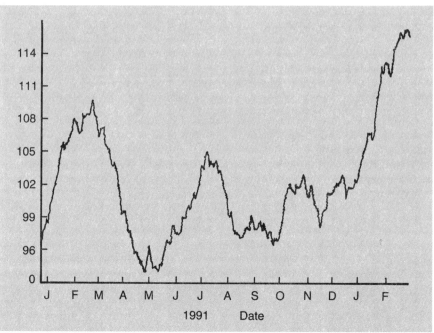

ceived. Figure 31-2 shows that the index put-call ratio is less reliable than the equity ratio, but is still helpful in determining market tops and bottoms.

In summary, the put-call ratio is an easily calculated one. Daily fluctuations can be smoothed out into 10-, 20-, or 50-day moving averages. The ratio should be interpreted bullishly when there is too much put buying and bearishly when there is too much call buying. The phrase "too much" is not easily interpreted, but looking for local maxima or local minima in the chart pattern is a reasonable way to approach the problem. When the put-call ratio moving average is increasing, a buy signal would not be given until the average rolls over and begins declining; a sell signal would be generated when the average which is declining bottoms out.

SUMMARY

There are several kinds of indices and several kinds of trading vehicles: cash-based options, futures options, and futures. These various underlying securities have differing terms in the way they trade and also in the way their options are designed. This variety creates many opportunities for astute option strategists.

Chapter 32

Stock Index Hedging Strategies

This chapter will be devoted primarily to examining the various ways that one might hedge a portfolio of stocks with index products. This portfolio might be a small one owned by an individual investor or it might be as large as the entire S&P 500 Index. We will explore this strategy from the various viewpoints of the individual investor, the institutional money manager, and the arbitrageur. This technique of hedging stocks with index products has become quite popular and has also drawn some attention because of the way that it can cause short-term movements in the entire stock market. The reasons why these movements occur will also be explained. Finally, we will look at ways of simulating a broad-based index by buying a group of stocks whose performance is geared to that of the index itself.

MARKET BASKETS

One of the most popular strategies using index futures and options has been the technique of buying stocks whose performance simulates the performance of a broader index and hedging that purchase with the sale of overpriced futures or options based on that index. The group of stocks that is purchased is commonly known as a "market basket" of stocks. This chapter will describe how these baskets can be used to trade against a very broad index, such as the S&P 500, or a far narrower index, such as the Major Market Index (XMI) of the American Stock Exchange, or even one as small as just a few stocks—perhaps a portfolio held by any investor.

The key to determining whether it will be profitable to trade some derivative security—options or futures—against a set of stocks is generally the level of premium in the futures contract itself. That is, if the S&P 500 Index is at 405.00 and the futures are trading at 408.00, then there is a premium of 3.00—the futures contract is trading 3.00 points higher than the index itself. The absolute level of the premium is not what is important, but rather the relationship between the premium and the fair value of the future. We will look at how to determine fair value shortly.

The futures are the leader among the derivative securities, especially the S&P 500 futures. Whenever these become overpriced, other derivative securities will generally follow suit. There are also futures on the NYSE Index, the Major Market Index (XMI), the Value Line Index, and the Japanese Nikkei 225 Index. Moreover, there are cash-based index options on the S&P 500 Index (as opposed to the futures options on that index) and the NYSE Index. These other securities would include the OEX (S&P 100) options, XMI options and futures, and NYSE futures and options. It follows as well that when the S&P 500 futures become underpriced, the other derivative securities quickly fall into line. If the other derivative securities don't follow suit, then there is an opportunity for spreading one market against another. That type of spreading can frequently be profitable, and will be discussed in the next chapter.

The normal scenario is for most of the derivative securities to follow the lead of the S&P 500 futures. When this happens, the only thing that is fairly priced is the index itself—that is, stocks. Consequently, the logical way to hedge the derivative security is to do it with stocks. The small investor might hedge his own individual portfolio, although that would not be a perfect hedge since his own portfolio is not composed of the exact same stocks as any index. If the index is small enough, such as the 20-stock XMI, then one might buy all 20 stocks and sell the futures when they are overpriced. This is a complete hedge and would, in fact, be an arbitrage. In the case of a larger index such as the S&P 500, it would be possible only for the most professional traders to buy all 500 stocks, so one might buy a smaller subset of the index in hopes that this smaller set of stocks will mirror the performance of the index well enough to simulate having bought the entire index. We will take in-depth looks at both types of hedging.

Even if the investor is not planning on using these hedging strategies, it is important for him to understand how they work. These strategies have certain ramifications upon the way that the entire stock market moves. In order to anticipate these movements, a working knowledge of these hedging strategies is necessary. The first thing that one must know in order to implement any of these hedging strategies is how to determine the fair value of a futures contract.

Futures Fair Value

The formula for calculating the fair value of the futures contract is extremely simple, although one of the factors is a little difficult to obtain information on. First, let's look at the simple futures fair value formula:

Simple Formula:

$$\text{Futures fair value} = \text{index} \times [1 + \text{time} \times (\text{rate} - \text{yield})]$$

where index is the current value of the index itself, rate is the current carrying rate (typically, the broker loan rate), yield is the combined annual yield of all the stocks in the index, and time is the time, in years, remaining until expiration of the contract.

Example: Suppose the ZYX Index is trading at 160.00, that the broker loan rate is 10%, that the yield on the 500 stocks is 5%, and there are exactly 3 months remaining until expiration of the futures contract. The time is .25, expressed in years, so the formula becomes

$$\text{Future fair value} = 160.00 \times [1 + .25 \times (.10 - .05)]$$

$$= 160.00 \times (1 + .0125) = 162.00$$

Thus the future should be trading at about 2 points above the value of the index itself. This premium of the future over the index represents the savings in not having to pay for and carry 500 stocks, less the loss of the dividends on the stocks (the future does not pay dividends). If the future should get very expensive—trading at 3.50 or 4 points over the index—then it would have to be considered very overvalued and an arbitrageur could move in to take advantage of that fact. Similarly, if the future should trade cheaply at less than a point over fair value, there might be an arbitrage available in that case as well.

The fair value is really only a function of four things: the value of the index itself, the time remaining until expiration, the current carrying rate, and the dividends being paid by the stocks in the index until expiration. Notice that "the dividends paid by the stock in the index until expiration" is not quite the same as the yield of the 500 stocks, which we used in the above simple formula. We will expand more on that difference shortly.

Before doing that, however, let us look at how changes in the variables in the formula affect the fair value of the futures contract. More importantly, we are interested in how changes in the variables affect the *premium* of the futures contract over the index value. This is what one is primarily concentrating on when trading market baskets.

As the index value itself rises, the fair value premium rises. For example, if 2 points is the fair premium when the index is at 160, as in the above example, then 4 points would be the fair premium if the index were at 320 and all the other variables remained the same. Conversely, as the index falls, the fair value of the premium shrinks.

The premium rises and falls in direct correlation with the carrying rate as well as with time remaining until expiration. Note that this statement is true for stock options also, and for the same reason: The savings in carrying costs are greater when rates are higher, or when one must hold for a longer time, or both. In the above example, if one were to assume there were 6 months to expiration instead of 3, the fair value of the premium would increase to 4 points from 2 points. Similarly, if the time were decreased, the fair value would be smaller.

Some investors, primarily institutional investors, use the short-term T-bill rate rather than the carrying rate in order to determine the futures fair value. The reason they do that is to determine if their money that they have in cash is better off in T-bills or in an arbitrage strategy such as this. More will be said about this use of the T-bill rate later.

Dividends Have An Inverse Correlation To The Premium Value. An increase in the overall yield of the index will shrink the fair value of the futures contract. This is because the futures holder does not get the dividends and therefore the future is not as valuable because of the loss of dividends. Conversely, if dividend yields fall, then the fair value of the premium increases. This is not the whole story on dividends, however.

Recall that a few paragraphs ago, it was pointed out that the yield and the amount of dividends are not exactly the same thing. This is because stocks don't pay their dividends in a uniform manner. Rather than paying a continuous yield as bonds do, stocks normally pay their dividends in four lump sums a year. This means that the yield variable in the simple formula shown above should be replaced by the actual amount of dividends remaining until expiration. This fact makes the computation of the fair value of the index a little more difficult. In order to do it accurately, one must know the dividend amounts and ex-dividend dates of each of the stocks in the index. Knowing all of this information is a far more formidable task than knowing the yield of the index, since the yield is published weekly in several places. In fact, the services of a computer are required in order to compute the actual dividend on the larger indices, where 100 or more stocks are involved.

As a result, the actual formula changes slightly from the simple formula shown above:

Actual Formula:

Futures fair value = index × (1 + time × rate) − dividends

In this formula, the *dividends are taken to be the present worth of all the dividends remaining until expiration of the future.*

Example: In an example similar to the one given for the simple formula, suppose the ZYX Index is trading at 160.00, that the broker loan rate is 10%, that the present worth of the dividends remaining until expiration is $1.89, and there are exactly 3 months remaining until expiration of the futures contract. The time is .25, expressed in years, so the formula becomes

$$\text{Future fair value} = 160.00 \times (1 + .25 \times .10) - 1.89$$
$$= 160.00 \times (1 + .025) - 1.89 = 162.11$$

In order to compute the present worth of the dividends of an index, it is necessary to know the amount of each stock's dividend as well as the payment date of the dividend. To compute the index's dividend, one computes the present worth of each dividend and multiplies that result by that stock's divisor in the index in order to give the dividend the proper weight. The index's total dividend is the sum of each of these individual stock computations. Each stock's divisor is merely the float of the stock divided by the divisor of the index. In a price-weighted index, it is not necessary to adjust the present worth of each dividend—merely add them together and divide by the divisor. As an example, we will look at a hypothetical index composed of three stocks in order to see how one computes the present worth of an index's dividends.

Example: Suppose a capitalization-weighted index is composed of three stocks: AAA, BBB, and CCC. Furthermore, suppose that the amount of each of the individual stocks' dividends and the time remaining until the dividend is paid are given in the following table, as well as each stock's float. Finally, assume the divisor for the index is 150,000,000.

Stock	Dividend Amount	Days until Dividend Payout	Float
AAA	1.00	135	50,000,000
BBB	0.25	60	35,000,000
CCC	0.60	8	120,000,000
Divisor: 150,000,000			

In order to compute the present worth of a future amount, one uses the formula:

$$\text{Present worth} = \frac{\text{future amount}}{(1 + \text{rate})^{\text{time}}}$$

where rate is the current short-term rate and time is expressed in years.

Assume that the current interest rate is 10%. Then the present worth of AAA's dividend would be:

$$\text{Present worth AAA} = \frac{1.00}{(1 + .10)^{(35/360)}}$$

$$= \frac{1.00}{(1.10)^{(.0972)}}$$

$$= \frac{1.00}{1.0093}$$

$$= 0.9908$$

The present worth of the dividend is always less than the actual dividend. The present worth of an amount is the amount of money that would have to be invested today at the stated rate (10% in this example) to produce the future amount. That is, 99.08 cents invested at 10% would be worth exactly 1.00 in 35 days.

The present worth of the other two dividends is .2461 for BBB and .5987 for CCC. The reader should verify for himself that these are indeed the correct amounts. Notice that the present worth of a dividend is not much less than the actual value of the dividend. However, in a larger index, where one is dealing with several hundred dividends the present worth may be significantly different from the actual sum of the dividends especially if short-term rates are high.

Since we made the assumption that this is a capitalization-weighted index, each of these figures must be adjusted for the capitalization of the stock in order to give each present worth the proper weight within the index. Thus for AAA, the adjusted dividend would be .9908 times 50,000,000 (AAA's float), divided by 150,000,000, the divisor of the index. This would result in an adjusted dividend of .3303 for AAA. When similar adjustments are made for BBB and CCC, their adjusted values become .0574 and .4790, respectively.

Thus the present worth of the dividend for the index would be the sum of the three individual adjusted present worths, or .3303 + .0574 + .4790 = $0.8667.

Note: If the index were a price-weighted index, the index's dividend would be the sum of these three present worths (.9908 + .2461 + .5987), divided by the divisor of that index.

The above fair value formula can be applied to options as well. For example, the OEX Index does not have futures. However, the fair value calculations can be done in the same manner and the synthetic index then constructed by using puts and calls can be compared with that fair value.

Example: Suppose that OEX is trading at 364.50 and a September OEX future—if one existed—would have a fair value of 367.10. That is, the future would command a premium of 2.60. Not only should a future trade with that theoretical premium, but so should the "synthetic OEX" composed of puts and calls at the same strike. Hence, the synthetic OEX constructed with options should trade at about 367.10 also.

That is, if the OEX Sep 365 call were selling for $4\frac{5}{8}$ and the Sep 365 put were selling for $2\frac{1}{2}$, then the synthetic OEX constructed by the use of these two options would be priced at $367\frac{1}{8}$. Recall that one determines the synthetic cost by adding the strike, 365, to the call price, $4\frac{5}{8}$, and then subtracting the put price: $365 + 4\frac{5}{8} - 2\frac{1}{2} = 367\frac{1}{8}$. This synthetic price of $367\frac{1}{8}$ is virtually the same as the theoretical futures price of 367.10.

The same calculations can be applied to any index with listed options trading. Let us now return to the broader subject at hand—trading market baskets of stocks against futures.

PROGRAM TRADING

Two terms that conjure up images of the stock market crash in 1987 and other severe price drops are "program trading" and "index arbitrage." Neither one by itself should affect the stock market since they are two-sided strategies—involving buying stocks and selling futures. This two-sided effect should have little affect on the market, theoretically. However, in practice, it is often the case that trades are not executed simultaneously, and the stock market takes a jump or a dive.

Program trading is nothing more than trading futures against a general stock portfolio. Index arbitrage is trading futures against the exact stocks that comprise an index.

Later discussions will assume that one is trying to create or simulate the index itself in order to hedge it with futures. This is the arbitrage approach. However, there are many other types of stock positions that may be hedged with the futures. These might include a portfolio of one's own construction containing various stocks, or might include a group of stocks from which one wants to remove "market risk." Normally, one would not own the makeup of any index, but rather would have a unique combination of stocks in his portfolio. Such an investor may want to use futures to hedge what he *does* own.

One reason why an investor who owned stocks would want to sell index products against them might be that he has turned bearish and would prefer to sell futures rather than incur the costs involved with selling out his stock portfolio (and repurchasing it later). Commission charges are quite small on futures transactions as compared to an equal dollar amount of stock. By selling the futures on an index—say the S&P 500—he removes the "market risk" from his portfolio (assuming the S&P 500 represents the "market"). What is left over after selling the futures is the "tracking error." The discrepancy between the movement of the general stock market and any individual portfolio is called "tracking error." This investor will still make money if his portfolio outperforms the S&P 500, but he will find that he did not completely eliminate his losses if his portfolio underperforms the index. Note that if the market goes up, the investor will not make any money except for possible tracking error in his favor.

Removing the Market Risk From a Portfolio

Stock portfolios are diverse in nature, not necessarily reflecting the composition of the index underlying the futures contracts. The characteristics of the individual stocks must be taken into account, for they may move more quickly or more slowly than "the market." Let us spend a moment to define what defines this characteristic of stocks that is so important.

Volatility versus Beta

Recall that when we originally defined volatility for use in the Black-Scholes model, we stated that Beta was not acceptable because it was strictly a measure of the correlation of a stock's performance to that of the stock market and was not a measure of how fast the stock changed in price. Now we are concerned with how the stock's movement relates to the market's as a whole. This is the Beta.

Unfortunately, Beta is not as readily available to the option strategist as is volatility. Many option traders merely have to punch a button on their quote machine and they can receive estimates of volatility. However, Beta estimates are more difficult to obtain, and the ones that are available are often for very long time periods, such as several years. These long-term Betas cannot be used for the purposes of the index hedging, which will be discussed in this chapter. Therefore, if one does not have access to shorter-term Beta calculations, then he can approximate Beta by comparing an individual stock's volatility with the market's volatility.

Example: XYZ is a relatively volatile stock, having both an implied and historical volatility of 36%. The overall stock market has a volatility of 15%. Therefore, one could approximate the Beta of XYZ as

$$\text{Beta approximation} = 36/15 = 2.40$$

There are certain situations where this approximation would not work well, and those are where the stock has little or no correlation to the overall stock market (e.g., gold or oil stocks). If one has a portfolio of stocks of that type, then he should make a serious attempt to attain their Betas, for the Beta estimate method just described will not be accurate. Such stocks may be volatile—that is, they change in price fairly rapidly— but they may go in totally different directions from the overall stock market: they would thus have high volatility, but low Beta. This is not conducive to the above short-cut for approximating Beta from volatility.

The remaining examples in this chapter will use the term Beta or *adjusted volatility* synonymously. Adjusted volatility is merely the approximation of Beta from volatility as described above: the stock's volatility divided by the market's volatility.

The Portfolio Hedge

In attempting to hedge a diverse portfolio, it is necessary to use the Beta or adjusted volatility because one does not want to sell too many or too few futures. For example, if the portfolio were composed of nonvolatile stocks and one sold too many futures against it, one could lose money if the market rallied even if his portfolio outperformed the market. This would happen because the general market, being more volatile, would rally farther than the nonvolatile portfolio. Ideally, one should sell only enough futures so that there would be no gain or loss if the market rallied. There would be only tracking error. Conversely, if one does not sell enough futures against a volatile portfolio, then there is risk of loss if the market declines since the portfolio would decline faster than the market.

The Beta or adjusted volatility of each stock is used in order to determine the proper number of futures to sell against the portfolio. The dollar value (capitalization) of each stock in the index is adjusted by that stock's volatility to give an "adjusted capitalization" for each stock. Then, when all these are added together, one will have determined how much "adjusted capitalization" must be hedged with futures. The suggested method, described in the following example, uses an adjusted volatility for each stock.

The steps to follow in determining how many futures to sell against a diverse portfolio of stocks are as follows:

1. If you don't know the Beta, divide each stock's volatility by the market's (S&P 500) volatility. This is the stock's adjusted volatility.
2. Multiply the quantity of each stock owned by its price and then multiply by the adjusted volatility from step 1. This gives the adjusted capitalization of the stock in the portfolio.
3. Add the results from step 2 together for each stock to get the total adjusted capitalization of the portfolio.
4. Divide the sum from step 3 by the index price of the futures to be used and the unit of trading for the futures ($500 per point for the S&P 500 futures) to determine how many futures to sell.

Example: Suppose that one owns a portfolio of three diverse stocks: 3,000 GOGO, an over-the-counter technology stock; 5,000 UTIL, a major public utility stock; and 2,000 OIL, a large oil company. The owner of this portfolio has become bearish on the market and would like to sell futures against the portfolio. He needs to determine how many futures to sell.

The prices and volatilities of these stocks are given in the following table. Assume that the volatility of the fictional ZYX Index is 15%. This is the "market's volatility" that is divided into each stock's volatility to get its adjusted volatility (step 1, above).

Stock	Volatility	Adjusted Volatility (Step 1)	Price	Quantity Owned	Adjusted Capitalization (Step 2)
GOGO	.60	4.00	25	3,000	$300,000
UTIL	.12	0.80	60	5,000	240,000
OIL	.30	2.00	45	2,000	180,000
Total adjusted capitalization:					$720,000 (step 3)

Now suppose that the ZYX Index is trading at 178.65 and a 1-point move in the futures is worth $500. Step 4 can now be calculated: $720,000 ÷

500 ÷ 178.65, or 8.06 futures contracts. Thus, the sale of 8 futures contracts would adequately hedge this diverse portfolio.

There is an important nuance in this simple example: *The price of the index should be used in all hedging calculations, as opposed to using the price of the future.* There will be many examples of hedging portfolios and market baskets with futures or options in this chapter and the next. Regardless of the situation, the value of the *index* should always be used to determine how much stock to buy or how much of the derivative security to sell.

Note that the actual capitalization of the above example portfolio was only $465,000 ($75,000 for GOGO, $300,000 for UTIL, and $90,000 for OIL). However, the portfolio is more volatile than the general market because of the presence of the two higher-volatility stocks. It is thus necessary to hedge $720,000 worth of "market," or adjusted capitalization, in order to compensate for the higher volatility of the portfolio.

A similar process can be used for far larger portfolios. The estimate of volatility is, of course, crucial in these calculations, but as long as one is consistent in the source from which he is extracting his volatilities, he should have a reasonable hedge. There is no way to judge the future performance of a portfolio of stocks vs. the ZYX Index. Thus one has to expect a rather large tracking error. In this type of hedge, one hopes to keep the tracking error down to a few *percent*, which could be several *points* in the futures contracts over a long enough period of time. Of course, the tracking error can work in one's favor also. The main point to recognize here is that the vast majority of the risk of owning the portfolios has been eliminated by selling the futures contracts. The upside profit potential of the portfolios has been eliminated as well, but the premise was that the investor was bearish on the market.

Note that if the futures are overpriced when one enacts his bearishly-oriented portfolio hedge, he will gain an additional advantage. This will act to offset some negative tracking error, should such tracking error occur. However, there is no guarantee that overpriced futures will be available at the time that the investor or portfolio manager decides to turn bearish. It is better to sell the futures and establish the hedge at the time one turns bearish, rather than to wait and hope that they will acquire a large premium before one sells them.

Hedging Portfolios With Index Options

As mentioned earlier, one could substitute options for futures wherever appropriate. If he were going to sell futures, he could sell and buy puts instead. In this section, we are also going to take a more sophisticated look at using index options against stock portfolios.

First, let us examine how the investor from the previous example might use index options to hedge his portfolio.

Example: Suppose that an investor owns the same portfolio as in the previous example: 3,000 GOGO, 5,000 UTIL, and 2,000 OIL. He decides to hedge with index UVX which has options worth $100 per point. Assume that the volatility of the UVX is 15%. This investor would then compute his total adjusted capitalization in the same manner as in the previous example, again arriving at a figure of $270,000.

Suppose that the UVX Index is at 175.60. This investor would want to hedge his $720,000 of adjusted capitalization with 4,100 "shares" of UVX ($720,000 ÷ 175.60). Since a 1-point move in UVX options is worth $100, this means that one would sell 41 UVX calls and buy 41 UVX puts. He would probably use the 175 strike or possibly the 180 strike, since those strikes are the ones whereby the calls have the least chance for early assignment.

Where short options are involved, as with the calls in the above example, one must be aware of the possibility of early assignment exposing the portfolio. Consequently, if the marketplace has an equal premium on the futures and the "synthetic" UVX, one should sell the futures in that case because there is no possibility of unwanted assignment. However, if the options represent a synthetic price that is more expensive than the futures, then using the options may be more attractive.

Example: Suppose that our same investor has decided to hedge his portfolio with its $720,000 of adjusted capitalization. He is indifferent as to whether to use the ZYX futures or the UVX options. He will use whichever one affords him the best opportunity. The following table depicts the prices of the securities that he is considering, as well as their fair values.

Security	Current Price	Fair Value	Index Price
ZYX Jun Future	180.50	180.65	178.65
UVX Jun 175 Call	5	5	175.60
UVX Jun 175 Put	2	2½	175.60
UVX Jun 180 Call	2½	2½	175.60
UVX Jun 180 Put	4½	5	175.60

This investor essentially has three choices: 1) to use the ZYX futures, 2) to use the UVX options with 175 strike, or 3) to use the UVX options with the 180 strike. Notice that the ZYX future is trading 15 cents below its fair value (180.50 vs. 180.65). The UVX Index fair value, as shown by the fair values of the options is 177.50. This can be computed by adding the call price to the strike and subtracting the put price. In the case of either strike, the fair values indicate an UVX Index fair value of 177.50.

However, the actual markets are slightly out of line. When using the actual prices, one sees that he can sell the UVX Index synthetically for 178.00 whether he uses the 175's or the 180's. Thus, by using the UVX options he can sell the UVX "future" synthetically for ½ point over fair value, while the ZYX futures would have to be sold at 15 cents under fair value. Thus, the options appear to be a better choice since 65 cents (the 50 cents that the UVX options are overvalued plus the 15 cents that the futures are undervalued) is probably enough of an edge to offset the possibility of early assignment.

With the futures having been eliminated as a possibility, the investor must now choose which strike to use. Since he will be selling calls and buying puts, and since either strike allows him to synthetically sell the UVX "future" at 178, he should choose the 180 strike. This should be his choice because the 180 calls are out-of-the-money and thus less likely to be the object of an early assignment.

Hedging with Index Puts

Let us now move on to discuss ways of hedging in which a complete hedge is not established, but rather some risk is taken. The main difference between options and futures is that futures lock in a price while options lock in a worst-case price (at greater cost) but leave room for further profit potential. To see this, consider a long stock portfolio hedged by short futures. In this case, one eliminates his upside profit potential except for positive tracking error. However, if he buys put options instead, he expends money—thereby incurring a greater cost to himself that if he had used futures—but he has profit potential if the market rallies.

One could hedge a long stock portfolio with options by either buying index puts or selling index calls. Buying the puts is generally the more attractive strategy, especially if the puts are cheap. In order to properly establish the hedge, it is not only necessary to adjust the dollars of stock in accordance with the Beta, but the deltas of the options must be taken into account as well. The following example will demonstrate the use of puts to hedge a portfolio of diverse stocks.

Example: Assume that an investor has the same portfolio of three stocks that was used in a previous example: 3,000 GOGO, 5,000 UTIL, and 2,000 OIL. He has become somewhat bearish on the market in general and would like to hedge some of his downside risk. However, he decides to use puts for the hedge just in case there is further rally in the market.

The table from that earlier example is reprinted below, showing the adjusted volatilities and capitalizations for each stock in the portfolio. The total adjusted capitalization of the portfolio is $720,000 as before.

Stock	Volatility	Adjusted Volatility (Step 1)	Price	Quantity Owned	Adjusted Capitalization (Step 2)
GOGO	.60	4.00	25	3000	$300,000
UTIL	.12	0.80	60	5000	240,000
OIL	.30	2.00	45	2000	180,000
Total adjusted capitalization:					$720,000 (step 3)

There are two ways that one might want to approach hedging this $720,000 portfolio with puts.

1. As disaster insurance: buy enough (out-of-the-money) puts so that the portfolio would be 100% hedged below the striking price of the puts.
2. As a hedge against current market movements: buy enough puts so that all current portfolio movements are hedged.

Example—Method 1: In this method, the portfolio manager is looking for disaster insurance. He is not so much concerned with hedging current market movements as he is with preventing a major loss if the market should collapse. The manager often uses an out-of-the-money put for disaster insurance.

Assume that he is going to use the UVX Index puts, which are worth $100 per point. The March 170 puts, trading at 1, are going to be used in the hedge. The index is currently at 178.00.

He would therefore divide his portfolio's adjusted capitalization ($720,000) by the value of the *striking price* of the puts to be used. In this case, the value of the striking price is $17,000 (100 × 170).

Puts to buy = $720,000 / $17,000 = 42.3

Cost of 42 puts: $4,200
Striking value of 42 puts: $714,000 (42 × $17,000)

The cost of buying 42 puts is $4,200. This can be thought of as an insurance premium, paid to buy $714,000 worth of insurance. He will have market risk on his portfolio between the current price of the index (178.00) and the striking price (170.00). The 42 puts would hedge a little of the drop in his portfolio during that 8 point drop in the index, but their full protective value would not be felt until they were in-the-money. It is not an exact hedge, of course, since the UVX Index may perform differently than the portfolio once UVX drops below 170. However, this put purchase will definitely remove a great deal of the market risk of further drops.

Example — Method 2: In this method, the portfolio manager is attempting to hedge the current value of his portfolio. He wants no further downside losses in his portfolio at all. He would generally buy at- or in-the-money puts in this case and would use the put's delta in order to construct a complete hedge.

Again assume that he is going to use the UVX Index puts, which are worth $100 per point. In this case, however, with the index at 178.00 he is considering the March 180 puts, trading at 4½, with a delta of −0.60 to be used in the hedge. The index is currently at 178.00.

In this case, the number of puts is determined by using the same formula as in the above example and then also dividing by the absolute value of the delta:

Puts to buy   = $720,000 / (100 × 180) / 0.60

                     = 67

Cost of protection: 67 × $450 = $30,150

In this case, the portfolio manager is spending much more for the puts, but for his additional expense, he acquires immediate protection for his portfolio. Furthermore, there is some intrinsic value to the puts he bought (2 points, or $13,400 on 67 of them). If the UVX Index drops at all, these puts will immediately begin to hedge his entire portfolio against loss. Of course, if the market rises, he loses his much more expensive insurance cost.

When one uses options instead of futures to hedge his position, he must make adjustments when the deltas of the options change. This was not the case when futures were used; perhaps with futures, one might recalculate the adjusted capitalization of the portfolio occasionally, but that would not be expected to affect the quantity of futures to any great degree. With put options, however, the changing delta can make the position delta short when the market declines, or can make it delta long if the market rises. This situation is akin to being long a straddle—the position becomes delta short as the market declines and becomes delta long as the market rises.

Basically, the adjustments would be same as those that a long straddle holder would make. If the market rallied, the position would be delta long because the delta of the puts would have shrunk and they would not be providing the portfolio with as much adjusted dollar protection as it needs. The investor might roll the puts up to a higher strike, a move which essentially locks in some of his stock profits. Alternatively, he could buy more puts at the current (low) strike to increase his protection.

Conversely, if the market had declined immediately after the position was established, the investor will find himself delta short. The delta of the long puts will have increased and there will actually be too much protection in place. His adjustment alternatives are still the same as those of a long straddle holder—he might sell some of the puts and thereby take a profit of them while still providing the required protection for the stock portfolio. Also he might roll the puts down to a lower strike, although that is a less desirable alternative.

Hedging with Index Calls

Another strategy to protect a stock portfolio is to establish a ratio write using short calls against the long stock. This is the opposite of using puts for protection, in that it is more equivalent to being short a straddle.

Example: In the last example, the March 180 put had a delta of -0.60. The March 180 call should then have a delta of 0.40. If the portfolio manager wanted to hedge his portfolio by ratio writing calls against it, he could use the same formula as in the previous example:

$$\text{Calls to sell} = \$720{,}000 \, / \, (100 \times 180) \, / \, 0.40 = 100$$

He would sell 100 calls to hedge his portfolio.

Adjustments would be made in much the same manner as those that a straddle seller would make. If the market rises, the delta of the calls will increase and the position will be delta short. One would probably buy calls in that case. Follow-up action for an actual short straddle might dictate buying in some of the underlying security rather than buying the calls, but that is not a realistic alternative in this case, since the sample portfolio is probably stable.

If, on the other hand, the market declined after the short calls were sold against the portfolio, the position would become delta long as the delta of the calls shrinks. The normal action in that case would be to roll the calls down and reestablish the proper amount of protection for the portfolio.

Overall, hedging the portfolio with short index calls does not present as attractive a position as hedging with long index puts. This is due mostly to the nature of what the portfolio manager is trying to accomplish, as opposed to the relative merits of long and short straddles. As was pointed out in previous chapters, straddle selling, while risky, is an excellent strategy on a statistical basis. However, in this section we are not dealing with a strategist who is going to go out and buy stocks and then write index calls against them. Rather, we have an existing portfolio and the portfolio manager is becoming bearish on the market. Thus, the stock portfolio is a fixed entity and the index options or futures are being built around it for protection.

Long puts serve the purpose of protection far better than short calls, for the following reasons. First, the types of adjustments that need to be made by a straddle seller often involve buying stock or at least buying relatively deeply in-the-money calls. A portfolio manager or investor holding a portfolio stock may not need to want to get involved in a multi-optioned position. Second, with calls there is large risk to the upside in case of a large market rally. Someone holding a portfolio of stocks might be willing to forego upside profits (as in the sale of futures), but generally would be quite upset to sustain large losses on the upside. Using puts, of course, leaves room for upside profit potential. Third, there is risk of early assignment with short index calls, although that is of minor significance in this case since the portfolio of stocks would have been long in any case. Other calls could be written immediately on the day after the assignment. The only real drawback to using the puts is that premium dollars are paid out and, if the market stabilizes, the time value decay will cause a loss on the puts. If one actually suspects that such a stabilization might occur, he should use futures against his position instead of puts or calls.

INDEX ARBITRAGE

As previously stated, index arbitrage consists of buying virtually all of the stocks in an index and selling futures against them, or vice versa. Whenever the futures on an index are mispriced, as determined by comparing their actual value with their fair value, there may be opportunities for arbitrage if the mispricing is large enough. When futures are extremely overpriced: buy stocks, sell futures; or when futures are underpriced: sell stocks, buy futures. In either case, the arbitrageur is attempting to capture the differential between the fair value price of the futures contract and the price at which he actually buys or sells the index. First, we will examine fully hedged situations—ones in which the entire index is bought or sold. After that, we will examine smaller sets of stocks which are designed to simulate the performance of the entire index.

Hedging indices with fewer stocks is easier than hedging larger indices. Hedging a price-weighted index is probably the simplest type of hedge. As examples, the same sample indices that were constructed in the previous chapter will be used.

Whenever futures or index options trade on an index, it is possible to set up market baskets for arbitrage. The trader should determine, in advance, how many shares of each stock he will buy or sell in order to duplicate the index. In a price-weighted index, of course, he will buy the same number of shares of each stock. In a capitalization-weighted index, he will be buying different numbers of shares of each stock. Let us first look at how the number of shares to buy is determined. Then we will discuss some of the nuances, such as monitoring bids and offers of the indices, order execution, and others.

How Many Shares to Buy

In advance of actually trading the stocks and futures or options, one should determine exactly how many shares of each stock he will be buying in each index he plans to arbitrage. Normally, one would decide in advance how many futures contracts or option contracts he will trade at one time. Then the number of shares of stock to be bought as a hedge can be determined as well. Essentially, one is going to hedge equal dollar amounts—that is, he will buy enough stocks to offset the total dollar amount represented by the index.

Example: Suppose that one decides he will set up his market baskets by using 50 ZYX futures at a time. How much stock should he buy against these 50 contracts? The futures contract has a trading unit of $500 per point. Assume the ZYX Index is trading at 168.89. Then the total dollar amount represented by 50 contracts is 50 × $500 × 168.89 = $422,225. The hedger would buy this much stock to hedge 50 futures contracts sold.

Again note that the index price, not the futures price, is used in order to determine how many futures to sell.

In a price-weighted index, one determines the number of *shares* to buy by determining the total dollar value of the index he plans to trade and then dividing that dollar amount by the divisor of the index. The resulting number is how many shares of each stock to buy in order to duplicate the price-weighted index.

Example: Suppose that we have a price-weighted index composed of three stocks, A, B, and C. The following data describe the index:

Stock	Price
A	30
B	90
C	50
Price total:	170
Divisor:	1.65843
Index value:	102.51

The number of shares of each stock that is in the index is 1 divided by the divisor, or $1/1.65843 = 0.60298$ shares. Thus if we were to buy .60298 shares of each of the three stocks, we would have created the index.

Suppose that futures exist on this index and that the trading unit in these futures is $250 per point. That is, the futures represent a total dollar value of the index times 250. With this information, it is easy to determine the number of shares of stock to buy to hedge one futures contract: 250 times the number of shares of each stock, .60298, for a total of 150.745 shares of each stock.

Normally, one would not merely sell one futures contract and hedge it with stock. Rather, he would employ larger quantities. Say that he decided to trade in lots of 100 futures contracts vs. the stocks. In that case, he would buy the following number of shares of each stock.

Number of shares = .60298 × $250/point × 100 futures contacts

= 15074.5 shares

Actually he would probably buy 15,100 shares of each stock against the index, and on every fourth "round" (100 futures vs. stock) would buy 15,000 shares. This would be a very close approximation without dealing in odd lots.

The trader might also use index options as his hedge instead of futures. The striking price of the options does not come into play in this situation. Typically, one would fully hedge his position with the index options—that is, if he bought stock, he would then sell calls *and* buy puts against that stock. Both the puts and the calls would have the same strike and expiration month. This creates a riskless position. This position is a conversion.

Example: Suppose that cash-based options trade on this index, and that these options are worth $100 per point as are normal stock options— that is, an option is essentially an option on 100 shares of the index. The trader is going to synthetically short the index by buying 100 June 105 puts and selling 100 June 105 calls. Assume that the index data is the same as in the previous example, that 0.60298 shares of each stock comprise the index. How many shares would one hedge these 100 option synthetics with?

Number of shares = .60298 × 100 contracts × 100 shares/contract

= 6029.8 shares

Note that in the case of a price-weighted index, neither the current index value nor the striking price of the options involved (if options are involved) affects the number of shares of stock to buy. Both of the above examples demonstrate this fact that the number of shares to buy is strictly a function of the divisor of the price-weighted index and the unit of trading of the option or future.

Hedging a capitalization-weighted index is more complicated, although the technique revolves around determining the makeup of the index in terms of shares of stock, just as the price-weighted examples above did. Recall that we could determine the number of shares of stock in a capitalization-weighted index by dividing the float of each stock by the divisor of the index. The general formula for the number of shares of each stock to buy is:

$$\begin{matrix} \text{Shares of stock N} \\ \text{to buy} \end{matrix} = \begin{matrix} \text{shares of N} \\ \text{in index} \end{matrix} \times \text{futures quantity} \times \begin{matrix} \text{futures unit} \\ \text{of trading} \end{matrix}$$

We will use the fictional capitalization-weighted index from the previous chapter to illustrate these points.

Example: The following table identifies the pertinent facts about the fictional index, including the important data: number of shares of each stock in the index.

Stock	Price	Float	Capitalization	Shares
A	40	177,000,000	7,080,000,000	1.20
B	80	50,000,000	4,000,000,000	0.34
C	60	100,000,000	6,000,000,000	0.68
	Total capitalization:		17,080,000,000	
	Divisor: 147,500,000			
	Index value: 115.80			

Thus if one were to buy 1.20 shares of A, .34 shares of B, and .68 shares of C, he would duplicate the index. Recall that one determines the number of shares of an individual stock in a capitalization-weighted index by dividing the float of the stock by the divisor of the index.

Suppose that a futures contract trades on this index, with one point being worth $500 in futures profit or loss. Then one would buy an amount of each stock equal to 500 times the number of shares in the index. Furthermore suppose that one decides to trade 5 futures at a time. Thus the number of shares of each stock that one would have to buy to hedge the 5-lot futures position would be:

Shares to buy = shares in index × 5 futures × $500/future

The following table lists that information, as well as totalling the dollar amount of stock represented by the total. We will verify that the dollar amount of stock purchased is equal to the dollar amount of index represented by the futures.

Stock	Shares in Index	Shares to Buy to Hedge 5 Futures	Price	$ Amount of Stock Bought
A	1.20	3,000	40	$120,000
B	0.34	850	80	68,000
C	0.68	1,700	60	102,000
				$290,000

Thus $290,000 worth of stock has been purchased. From an earlier example, we saw how to compute the total dollar worth of a futures trade. In this case, the index is at 115.80, 5 contracts were sold, and each point is worth $500. Thus the total dollar amount represented by the futures sale is $5 \times 500 \times 115.80 = \$289,500$. This verifies that our stock purchases hedge the futures sale adequately. Note that the slight difference in the stock purchase amount and the futures sale amount is due to the fact that the number of shares in the index is carried out to only two decimal points in this example.

There is an alternative method to determine how many shares to buy. In this method, one first determines how much stock he is going to buy in total dollars. For example, he might decide that he is going to buy 10 million dollars worth of the S&P 100 (OEX) Index. Next, one determines what percentage his dollar amount is of the total capitalization of the index. For example, 10 million dollars might be something like .02% of the total capitalization of the OEX. One would then buy .02% of the total number of shares outstanding of each of the stocks in the OEX. After the number of shares of each stock to buy has been determined, one would have to determine how many futures to sell against this stock—he would divide 10 million by the index price and also divide by the unit of trading for the futures. This procedure is demonstrated in the following example.

Example: Suppose that one wants to set up an arbitrage against the same index as in the previous example. For purposes of comparison with that example, we will suppose that this hedger wants to buy a total of $290,000 worth of stock. In reality, one would probably use a round number such as $300,000 or $500,000 worth of stock. However, by making a direct comparison, we will be able to more easily demonstrate that these two methods produce the same answer.

First, the hedger must determine the percent of the total capitalization that he is going to buy. In this case, he is buying $290,000 worth of stock and the total capitalization of the index is $17,080,000,000 (refer to table at the beginning of the previous example). This means that he is buying .0016979% of the total capitalization of the index.

Next, he uses this percentage and multiplies it by the float of each stock. That is, he is going to buy .0016979% of the total number of shares outstanding of each stock in the index. This results in purchases as shown in the following table:

Stock	Float	Shares to Buy
A	177,000,000	3,005
B	50,000,000	849
C	100,000,000	1,698

Compare these share purchases with the previous example. The number of shares to buy is the same, allowing for rounding off in the previous example. Thus these two methods of determining how many shares to buy are equivalent.

Before leaving this section, it should be pointed out that arbitrageurs can also establish an arbitrage when futures are underpriced. They can sell stocks short and buy the underpriced futures. This is a more difficult type of arbitrage to establish because short sales must be made on plus ticks. However, when futures are underpriced for an extensive period of time—perhaps during extreme pessimism on the part of speculators—it is possible to set up the arbitrage from this viewpoint.

Profitability of the Arbitrage

The key for many arbitrageurs and institutional investors is whether, after costs, there is enough of a return in this stock vs. futures strategy. The method in which we previously computed the fair value of the futures will be used in determining the overall incremental return of doing the arbitrage.

The major cost in executing the arbitrage is the cost of commissions. Since there are large quantities of stocks being bought or sold when an entire index is traded, the commission rate is generally quite low. For example, an institutional investor might pay 3 cents per share or even less. This still could be a substantial cost, especially when a large index such as the S&P 500 Index is being purchased. Even professional arbitrageurs may have to pay commission costs if they are using the services of a computer firm to buy stocks. These methods of trading stocks are described in the next section.

Once one's rate of commission charges is known, he can convert that into a number that represents a portion of the index price. He does so by multiplying his per-share commission rate by the current index value and then dividing that result by the average share price of the index. The following example describes that method of conversion.

Example: Suppose that one is going to buy the entire ZYX Index at a commission rate of 3 cents per share. The index is trading at 185.00. Furthermore, assume that the average price of a share in the index is 45 dollars per share. With this information, one can determine how much he is paying in commissions, in terms of the index itself.

$$\text{Commission in terms of index} = \frac{\dfrac{\text{commission rate}}{\text{per share}} \times \text{index value}}{\dfrac{\text{average price}}{\text{per share}}}$$

$$= \frac{.03 \times 185.00}{45}$$

$$= .123$$

Thus a commission rate of 3 cents per share translates into 12.3 cents of index value.

The most difficult factor to determine in the above equation is the average price per share for a capitalization-weighted index. There is a short cut that can be used. It is easy to determine the average price per share for a price-weighted index, such as XMI. The average price per share for large capitalization indices such as the OEX and S&P 500 is about 80% of that of the XMI.

Example: It is a simple matter to compute the average price per share for a price-weighted index. Merely divide the index value by the number of stocks comprising the index and then multiply that result by the divisor of the index. Suppose the XMI is trading at 352 and the divisor of the XMI is 4.4. Then, since there are 20 stocks in the XMI, we can quickly determine the average price per share of stocks in the XMI:

$$\frac{\text{Average price}}{\text{per share}} = \frac{\text{index price} \times \text{divisor}}{\text{number of stocks in index}}$$

$$= \frac{352 \times 4.4}{20}$$

$$= 77.44$$

Given this information, we can estimate that the average price per share for stocks in a broader-based index would be about 80% of that figure, or something like 62 or 63 dollars per share.

Now that the commission rate has been converted into an index value, one can determine hs net profit from trading the exact index against the futures. One must figure in his futures commission costs as well. The following example demonstrates the net profit from executing the arbitrage, including all costs. Once the net profit has been calculated, a rate of return can be computed.

Example: Suppose that the ZYX Index is trading at 185.00 and the futures, which expire in two months have a fair value premium of 2.00 points, but are trading at 188.50, a premium of 3.50. The futures are worth $500 per point. Thus, the futures are expensive and one might attempt to buy stocks and sell the futures. His net profit consists of the premium over fair value less all costs of entering and exiting the position.

As we saw in the previous example, at 3 cents per share stock commission, we pay an index value of .123 to enter the position. Similarly, we would pay .123 in index value to exit the position at a later date. Thus, the net round-turn stock commission is approximately 25 cents of index value.

Commissions on futures are generally charged only when the position is closed out. Generally, a futures commission on an S&P 500 contract might be reduced to something like $10 per contract for this type of hedging. Since 185.00, the index value, represents 1/500th of the value of the futures contract, we can reduce the futures commission to an index-related number by dividing the actual dollar commission by 500. Thus, the futures commission is, in index terms 10/500, or .02. The total commission for entering and exiting the position is thus .27 of index value, .123 each for the stocks and .02 for the futures.

$$\text{Net profit} = \frac{\text{futures}}{\text{price}} - \frac{\text{futures fair}}{\text{value}} - \frac{\text{commission}}{\text{costs}}$$

$$= 188.50 - 187.00 - 0.27$$

$$= 1.23$$

This absolute net profit number can be converted into a rate of return by annualizing the profit and dividing by the current index price. Suppose that there are two months exactly remaining until expiration. Then, the rate of return is computed as follows:

$$\begin{aligned} \frac{\text{Incremental}}{\text{rate of return}} &= \frac{\text{Net profit} \times (1/\text{time remaining})}{\text{index price}} \\ &= \frac{1.23 \times (12/2)}{185.00} \\ &= 3.99\% \end{aligned}$$

For the two month time period, his return is about ⅔ of one percent.

At first glance, a rate of return of almost 4% does not seem like much. But what we have computed here is an *incremental* rate of return. That is, this return is over and above whatever rate we used in determining the fair value of the futures. Thus, if an institution were going to invest their cash at the prevailing short-term rate, and that rate were used to determine the futures fair value in the above example, then they could earn an *additional* 4%, annualized, if they arbitraged the futures rather than put their money in the short-term money market.

Trade Execution

Most customers are not concerned with how the trades are executed, for they give the order to their broker and let him work out the details. However, for those are are interested in the actual trade execution, a short section dealing with that topic is in order.

Ideally, one should be able to monitor the progress of his index in terms of bid prices, offer prices, and last sales. There are several modern quote services that allow such monitoring. It is important to know the bids and offers because, when one actually executes the trades, he generally will be trading on the bid and offer, not the last sale.

Example: Suppose the fair value of the futures contract is represented by a premium of 1.25 points, but that the actual future is trading with a premium of 2.00 points: The index is at 176.75 and the futures are 167.75 (last sale). This might seem like enough "room" to execute a profitable arbitrage—buy the stocks in the index and sell the futures. However, the index value of 165.75 is the composite of the last sales of each of the individual stocks in the index. If one were to look at the offering prices of each stock and then recompute the index, he might end up with an index value that was 50 cents higher. This, then, would mean that he would be doing the arbitrage for 25 cents less costs, which is not enough of a margin to work with.

Similarly, when one is looking to sell out the stocks he has bought and simultaneously buy back the futures, he needs to know the bid value of the index in order to see what kind of premium he is paying to take his position off.

One normally executes the hedge by giving a series of stock orders to brokers on the floor of the exchange and simultaneously giving a futures order to the futures exchange. The actual trader controlling the order generally lets the stocks be executed at prevailing market prices, but might try to control the futures execution more closely.

There are two basic ways in which the actual stock order entry takes place. One is the conventional method of giving orders to brokers on the floor of the New York Stock Exchange. This method can be somewhat computerized by having a computer at the broker's main location send a series of orders to various locations of that brokerage firm on the floor of the exchange. The orders are then given to several brokers who quickly execute them. The quickness with which the executions must take place demonstrates why the price paid is usually the offering price and not the last sale—there merely isn't enough time for the broker to try to save an eighth of a point on one stock, since he has several other orders to execute.

The other method of order entry is completely computerized. The computer knows the quantity of each stock to buy and, when prompted, sends those buy orders via telecommunications lines to one of the automatic order execution systems on the exchange floor. The most common automatic system is the DOT system on the NYSE. The system guarantees the offering price for large quantities of stock. In this highly sophisticated method of order entry, the entire execution procedure may take place in about 1 minute for the entire index. This method of order entry is so quick and accurate that some brokerage firms with this capability offer it for a commission fee to other brokerage firms who do not have the capability.

Institutional Strategies

Holders of large portfolios of stocks can use futures and/or market basket strategies to their advantage. There are two basic strategies that can be easily used by these large traders. One is to buy futures instead of buying stocks and the other is to sell futures instead of selling stocks. Both of these strategies will be examined in more detail.

When one of these large institutions has money to invest in buying stocks, it might make more sense to buy Treasury bills and futures instead of buying stocks. Of course, this alternative strategy only makes sense for the institution if the stock purchase were going to be broad-based— something akin to duplicting the S&P 500 performance. The institution does not necessarily have to be intent on purchasing an exact index, but if the purchase were going to be diversified, the purchase of index features might help accomplish an equivalent result. If, however, the purchase were going to be quite specific, then this strategy would probably not apply.

This strategy works best when futures are underpriced. If the equivalent dollar amount of underpriced futures can be purchased instead of buying stocks, the entire amount intended for stock purchase can be put in Treasury bills instead. Recall that cash will have to be put into the futures account if the futures mark at a loss (maintenance margin). Even so, there can be a substantial savings to the institution if the futures are truly underpriced.

The second institutional strategy is applicable when futures are overpriced and the institution wants to sell stock. In such a case, it makes more sense to sell the futures than to sell the stock. First, there is a large savings in transaction costs (commissions). Second, the overpriced nature of the futures actually means that there is additional profitability in selling them as opposed to selling the stocks. Again, this strategy only makes sense if one were going to sell a diversified portfolio of stocks, something that is broad-based like the S&P 500 Index.

Of course, institutions may want to participate in the arbitrage regardless of their market stance. That is, if a money manager has a certain amount of money that he is going to put into short-term instruments (perhaps T-bills), he might instead decide to participate in this arbitrage of stocks vs. futures if the incremental return is high enough. Recall that we saw how to determine the incremental return in a previous section of this chapter. If he were going to get a $7\frac{1}{2}\%$ return from T-bills but could get a $11\frac{1}{2}\%$ return from futures arbitrage, he might opt for the latter.

FOLLOW-UP STRATEGIES

Once any hedge has been established, it must be monitored in case an adjustment needs to be made. The first and simplest type of monitoring is to take care of spinoffs or other adjustments in stocks in the market basket that is owned. Of a more serious nature, in terms of profitability, one also needs to monitor the hedge to see if it should be removed or if the futures should be rolled forward into a more distant expiration month.

Adjusting one's portfolio for stock spinoffs is a simple matter which we will address briefly. In many cases, one of the stocks in the index will spin off a division or segment of their business and issue stock to their shareholders. Such a spinoff is generally not included in the price of the index, so that the hedger should sell off such items as soon as he receives them, for they do not pertain to his hedge.

In a similar vein, in any portfolio certain stocks may occasionally be targets of tender offers or other reorganizations. If one does nothing in such a situation, he will not lose any money in terms of his portfolio vs. the underlying index. However, it is generally wise for one to tender his stock in such situations and replace it at a lower price after the tender. Sometimes, in fact, such a tender offer will entirely absorb an index component member. In that case, one must replace the disappearing stock with whatever stock is announced sa the new member of the index.

Technically, in an arbitrage hedge one should adjust his portfolio every time the divisor of the index changes. Thus, in a *capitalization-weighted* hedge he would be adjusting every time one of the components issues new common stock. This is really not necessary in most cases because the new issue is so small in comparison to the current float of the stock. Such a new issue does not include stock splits, for the divisor of the index does not change in that case. A more common case is for one of the stocks in a *price-weighted* index to split. In this case, one *must* adjust his portfolio. An example of such an adjustment was given in Chapter 31. In essence, one must sell off some of the split stock and buy extra shares of each of the other stocks in the price-weighted index.

Let us now take a look at follow-up methods of removing or preserving the hedge.

Rolling to Another Month

As expiration nears, the hedger is faced with a decision regarding taking off the market basket. If the futures premium is below fair value, he would probably unwind the entire position—selling the stocks and buying back the futures. However, if the futures remain expensive—especially the next series—then the hedger might roll his futures. That is, he would buy back the ones he is short and sell the next series of futures. For S&P 500 futures, this would mean rolling out 3 months, since that index has futures that expire every 3 months. For the XMI futures and OEX index options, there are monthly expirations, so one would only have to roll out 1 month if so desired.

It is a simple matter to determine if the roll is feasible—merely compare the fair value of the spread between the two futures in question. If the current market is greater than the theoretical value of the spread, then a roll makes sense if one is long stocks and short futures. If an arbitrageur had initially established his arbitrage when futures were underpriced, he would be short stocks and long futures. In that case he would look to roll forward to another month if the current market were less than the theoretical value of the spread.

Example: With the S&P 500 Index at 416.50, the hedger is short the March future which is trading at 417.50. The June future is trading at 421.50. Thus there is a 4-point spread between the March and June futures contracts.

Assume that the fair value formula shows that the fair value premium for the March series is 35 cents and for the June series is 3.25. Thus, the fair value of the spread is 2.90, the difference in the fair values.

Consequently, with the current market making the spread available at 4.00, one should consider buying back his March futures and selling the June futures. The rolling forward action may be accomplished via a spread order in the futures, much like a spread order in options. This roll would leave the hedge established for another 3 months at an overpriced level.

Another way to close the position is to hold it to expiration and then sell out the stocks as the cash-based index products expire. If one were to sell his entire stock holding at the time the futures expire, he would be getting out of his hedge at exactly parity. That is, he sells his stocks at exactly the last sale of the index and the futures expire, being marked also to the last sale of the index.

For S&P futures, the last sale is calculated from the *opening* prices on the last day of trading. For most others, the last sale is the *closing* price.

Example: In a normal situation if the S&P 500 Index is trading at 415, say, then that represents the index based on last sales of the stocks in the index. If one were to attempt to buy all the stocks at their current offering price, however, he would probably be paying approximately another 50 cents, or 415.50 for his market basket. Similarly, if he were to sell all the stocks at the current bid price, then he would sell the market basket at the equivalent of approximately 414.50.

However, on the last day of trading the cash-based index product will expire at the opening price of the index. If one were to sell out his entire market basket of stocks at the current bid prices at the exact opening of trading on that day, he would sell his market basket at the calculated last sale of the index. That is, he would actually be creating the last sale price of the index himself, and would thereby be removing his position at parity.

The problem with this is that it is correct theory, but difficult to put into practice. For example, if one has several million dollars of stocks to sell, he cannot expect the marketplace to absorb them easily when they are all being sold at the last minute on a Friday afternoon. We will discuss this more fully momentarily when we look at the impact of stock index arbitrage on the stock market in general.

There is another interesting facet of the arbitrage strategy that combines the spread between the near-term future and the next longest one with the idea of executing the stock portion of the arbitrage at the close of trading on the day the index products expire. Use of this strategy actually allows one to enter and to exit the hedge without having to lose the spread between last sale and bid or last sale and offer in either case. Suppose that one feels that he would set up the arbitrage for 3 months if he could establish it at a net price of 1.50 over fair value. Furthermore, if the fair value of the 3-month spread is 2.10, but it is currently trading at 3.60, then that represents 1.50 over fair value. One initiates the position by buying the near-term future and selling the longer-term future for a net credit of 3.60 points. At expiration of the near-term future, rather than close out the spread, one *buys* the index at the last sale of the trading day, thereby establishing his long stock position at the last sale price of the index at the same moment that his long futures expire. The resultant position is long stocks and short the futures that expire in 3 months at a premium of 3.60. Since the fair value of such a 3-month future should be 2.10, the hedge is established at 1.50 over fair value. The position can be removed at expiration in the same manner as described in the previous paragraph, again saving the differential between last sale and the bids of the stocks in the index. Note that this strategy creates buying pressure on the stock market at expiration of the near-term side of the spread and selling pressure at the latter expiration.

The final way to exit from one's position is to remove it before expiration. Sometimes, there are opportunities during the last 2 or 3 weeks before the futures expire. If one hedged with long stock and short futures, the opportunities to remove the hedge arise when the futures trade below fair value—perhaps even at an actual discount to parity. If the futures never trade below fair value, but instead continue to remain expensive, then rolling to the next expiration series is often warranted.

MARKET BASKET RISK

There are some uncertainties in this type of hedging, even though the entire index is being bought. Since one owns the actual index, there is no risk that the stocks one owns will fail to hedge the futures price movements properly. However there are other risks. One is the risk of execution. That is, it may appear that the futures are trading at a premium of 1.50 points when one enters the orders. However, if other hedgers are doing the same thing at the same time, one may pay more for the stocks than he thought when he entered his order and he may sell the futures for less as well. This "execution risk" is generally small, but if one is too slow in getting his stock orders executed, he may have set up a hedge that was not as attractive as he first thought.

One major risk is that interest rates might move against the arbitrageur while the position is in place. If he is long stocks and short the futures, then he would not want interest rates to rise. In the previous example, the incremental return for the 2-month time period that the position was going to be held was 2/3 of one percent. If short-term rates should rise by more than that, on average, for the 2-month period, the incremental strategy would be inferior. His carrying costs would have increased to the point of wiping out the profit from his arbitrage.

For institutional arbitrageurs who don't exactly have cost of carry, this situation would be viewed in the following manner. If rates increase, he may find that he would have been better off having his money invested in a money market fund at the prevailing short-term rate than in the incremental arbitrage strategy.

Conversely, if the arbitrage was originally established with short stocks and long futures, the arbitrageur would not want rates to *drop* for similar reasons.

One might leave a cushion against a movement in rates. If rates are currently 8%, then one might decide to use a 10% rate as a cushion. Hedges established that are profitable at the higher rate level will consequently be able to withstand rates moving up to 10%.

Example: Suppose that one would normally use a rate of $7\frac{1}{2}\%$ and would establish the stock vs. futures hedge at an incremental rate of return of $1\frac{1}{2}\%$. This is a relatively narrow cushion and if the hedge is on for a moderate length of time, rates could move up to such an extent that they advance to $9\frac{1}{2}\%$ or higher. Such a move would make the hedge position unprofitable. Instead, one might calculate the fair value of the futures using a rate equal to his current prevailing rate plus a cushion. That is, if his current rate is $7\frac{1}{2}\%$, he might use $8\frac{1}{2}\%$ and still demand an incremental return of $1\frac{1}{2}\%$. If he established the hedge at these levels, he could suffer a move of 1%, the cushion, against him and still earn his incremental rate of $1\frac{1}{2}\%$.

Another risk that the arbitrageur faces is that of changes in the dividend payout of the stocks in the index. Suppose that he is long stocks and short futures. If there are enough cuts in dividend payout, or dividend payments are delayed past the expiration date of the futures, then he will lose some of his return. Arbitrageurs who are short stocks and long futures would have similar problems if dividend payout were increased— especially if a large special dividend were declared by a stock that is a major component of the index—or payment dates were accelerated.

If one holds the arbitrage until expiration, he will be able to unwind it at parity. However, if he decides to remove the arbitrage before expiration, he might incur increased costs that would harm his projected return. Instead of selling his stocks at the last sale of the index, as he is able to do on expiration day, he would have to sell them on their bids, a fact which could cost him a significant portion of his profit.

In a later section, when we discuss hedging the futures with a market basket of stocks that does not exactly represent the entire index, we will be concerned with the greatest risk of all, "tracking error"—the difference between the performance of the index and the performance of the market basket of stocks being purchased.

IMPACT ON THE STOCK MARKET

The act of establishing and removing these hedge positions affects the stock market on a short-term basis. It is affected both before expiration and also at expiration of the index products. We will examine both cases and will also address how the strategist can attempt to benefit from his knowledge of this situation.

Impact Before Expiration

When bullish speculators drive the price of futures too high, arbitrageurs will attempt to move in to establish positions by buying stock and selling futures. This action will cause the stock market to jump higher, especially since positions are normally established with great speed and stocks are bought at offering prices. Such acceleration on the upside can move the market up 5 to 10 points in terms of the Dow-Jones Industrials in a matter of minutes.

Conversely, if futures become cheap there is also the possibility that arbitrageurs can drive the market downward. If positions are already established from the long side (long stock, short futures), then arbitrageurs might decide to unwind their positions if futures become too cheap. They would do this if futures were so cheap that it becomes more profitable to remove the position, even though stocks must be sold on their bid, rather than hold it to expiration or roll it to another series. When these long hedges are unwound in this manner, the stock market will decline quickly as stocks are sold on bids. In this case, the market can fall a substantial amount in just a few minutes.

Once long hedges are unwound, however, cheap futures will not cause the market to decline. If there is no more stock held long in hedges, then the only strategy that arbitrageurs can employ when futures become cheap is to sell stock short and buy futures. Since stock must be sold short on upticks, this action may put a "lid" on the market, but will not cause it to decline quickly.

Having long stock and short futures when these large discounts occur is so valuable to an arbitrageur, that some traders will establish the long stock/short futures hedge for no profit or even a loss. They hope that subsequent futures will plunge to a large discount and they can unwind their position for large profits. If that never occurs, they only lose a few cents of index value. Assume futures fair value is 3.50 over. Such arbitrageurs might buy stock and sell futures at a net cost of 3.45 over. That is, if they hold the position until expiration they will lose 5 cents, but if a large futures discount ever occurs, they will profit.

Regulatory bodies have become increasingly concerned over the years as to the effect that program trading and index arbitrage have on the stock market. In reality, when stocks and futures are executed more or less simultaneously, these strategies should not overly disturb the stock market. However, since they are not executed simultaneously (there are no rules in the futures markets against frontrunning), the New York Stock Exchange has imposed an arbitrary limit, called a "circuit breaker," on these activities. At the current time, if the Dow-Jones averages rise or fall more than 50 points at any time during a trading day, all computer-driven program order entry is prohibited for the rest of day, or until the Dow-Jones moves back to within 25 points of being unchanged on the day. This trading ban effectively shuts down program trading and index arbitrage, although it is still allowable to do it by having the trades executed by individual floor brokers. Some of the larger trading houses, trading for their own account, are therefore still able to execute index arbitrage if the discount in the futures is extremely wide, even when the trading ban is in effect.

The trading ban is really meant to halt declining markets, although in the interest of fairness, the ban goes into effect on days when the Dow-Jones rises by 50 points as well. Of the various measures that have been tried in order to stop a declining market from becoming a crash (e.g., circuit breaker trading limits on S&P 500 futures), this seems to be the most effective. There have been many times when the Dow-Jones will accelerate to the 50-point limit, and then once the trading ban goes into effect, the Dow-Jones will slide slowly back the other way, but at a much more leisurely pace.

Readers should remember, of course, that the stock market can move independently of the overpriced or underpriced nature of index products. That is, if futures are overpriced, the stock market can still decline. Perhaps there is a preponderance of natural sellers of stocks. Similarly, if futures are cheap, the stock market can still go up if enough traders are bullish. Thus one should be cautious about trying to link every movement of the stock market to index products.

Portfolio Insurance

Portfolio insurance is the generic name used to describe a strategy in which a portfolio manager uses the index derivatives market to protect his portfolio in case the market crashes. He could either sell futures or buy puts.

The generic concept was put into effect using futures in the mid 1980s. In the form of the strategy that was being practiced at the time, the portfolio manager did not sell futures against his entire portfolio right away. Rather, he only sold a few to begin with. This allowed him to retain a good deal of upside profit potential for his portfolio. If the market dropped further, then he would sell more. Eventually, if it dropped far enough, he would keep selling futures until his entire portfolio was properly hedged. There were computer programs that calculated when to sell the futures and how many to sell in order for the portfolio manager to eventually end up with the proper amount of insurance at the right price.

Unfortunately, the concept did not work properly in practice. In fact, it has often been identified as one of the major factors in the 500-point crash of October 19, 1987. What happened during the days leading up to that date was that the market was already going down fast. Futures, as a result, began to trade at a discount. The portfolio insurance strategy assumes futures are sold at fair value, more or less. Thus, the portfolio insurance managers did not sell their futures when they had originally intended; or they could not sell enough without driving the futures to tremendous discounts. In any case, the market kept going further down without any rebound (essentially from about mid-Afternoon on Thursday, October 15th, through the close on Monday, October 19th), a total of over 650 points on the Dow-Jones averages. As the market plunged, the portfolio insurance strategy kept demanding that more futures be sold, and they were, but often at prices well below where the strategy had originally dictated. This continued selling kept futures at a discount which triggered even more selling by other program traders and index arbitrageurs.

As a result, the portfolios were not completely protected—although it should be noted that they were somewhat protected since they had been selling some futures. Hence, the portfolio managers were not pleased. Stock market regulators were not pleased, either, although nothing illegal had been done. The strategy lost most of its adherents at that time and has not been resurrected in its previous form.

However, the concept is still a valid one, and it is now generally being practiced with the purchase of put options. The futures strategy was, in theory, superior to buying puts because the portfolio manager was supposed to be able to collect the premium from selling the futures. However, its breakdown came during the crash in that it was impossible to buy the insurance when it was most needed—similar to attempting to buy fire insurance when your house is burning down.

Currently, the portfolio manager buys puts to protect his portfolio. Many of these puts are bought directly over-the-counter from major banks or brokerage houses, for they can be tailored directly to the portfolio manager's liking. This practice somewhat concerns regulators because the major banks and brokerage houses that are selling the puts are taking some risk, of course. They hedge the sales (with futures or other puts), but regulators are concerned that, if another crash occurred, it would be the writers of these puts who would be in the market selling futures in a mad frenzy to protect their short put positions. Hopefully, the put sellers will be able to hedge their positions properly without disturbing the stock market to any great degree.

Impact at Expiration—The Rush to Exit

Some traders persist in attempting to get out of their positions on the last day at the last minute. These traders would not normally be professional arbitrageurs, but would be institutional clients who are large enough to practice market basket hedging. Moreover, they would have positions in indices whose options expire at the close of trading (OEX, XMI, etc.). If these hedgers have stock to sell, what generally happens is that some traders begin to sell before the close, figuring they will get better prices by beating the crowd to the exit. Thus, about an hour before the close the market may begin to drift down and then accelerate as the closing bell draws nearer. Finally, right on the bell that announces the end of trading for the day, whatever stock has not yet been sold will be sold on blocks—normally significantly lower than the previous last sale. These depressed sales will make the index decline in price dramatically at the last minute—when there is no longer an opportunity to trade against it.

    These blocks are often purchased by large trading houses who advance their own capital to take the hedgers out of their positions. The hedgers are generally customers of the block trading houses. Normally, on Monday, the market will rebound somewhat and these blocks of stock can be sold back into the market at a profit.

    Whatever happens on Monday, though, is of little solace to the trader trapped in the aftermath of the Friday action. For example, if one happened to be short puts and the index was near the strike as the close of trading was drawing near on Friday afternoon, he might decide to do nothing and merely allow the puts to expire, figuring that he would buy them back for a small cost when he was assigned at expiration. However, this flurry of block prints on the close might drive the index down by 2 or 3 points! This is an extremely large move for the index and the option trader has no recourse as the options cease trading. An index composed of only a few stocks, such as the XMI, will fall most dramatically when these events occur, although the OEX will drop heavily as well.

    We have also previously seen that the late market action on expiration day might be bullish. If institutional arbitrageurs have established the futures spread by being long the short-term futures and short the next series, then they will be buyers of stocks at the close of trading on expiration day. Additionally, if the only remaining arbitrage positions at expiration are short stocks vs. long futures, then there might also be buying pressure at expiration.

As might be expected, these events have not gone unnoticed and have caused some consternation among both regulators and traders. There have been accusations that some traders—particularly those with the foreknowledge of the block prints to come—buy very cheap index options on the last afternoon of trading and then force those options to become profitable by selling their clients' portfolios in the manner described above.

The strategist cannot be concerned with whether or not someone is acting irrationally or worse. Rather, he must decide how he will handle the situation should it occur. The key is to try to determine the direction that the market will move at the close of expiration day, if there is one that is discernible. If futures have had a large premium for a long period of time, then one must assume that many hedgers have long stock vs. short futures. Furthermore, even if futures subsequently trade below fair value, there will still be some hedgers who have stubbornly kept their positions, waiting to roll. The strategist should recognize that fact and take appropriate action late on the last day of trading—don't establish bullish positions at that time and don't allow positions that are expiring that day to become too bullish. That is, if one is short puts and the index is trading near the striking price of the puts, then buy them back.

Thus, *the strategist must be aware of how the futures have traded during their last 3 months in order to determine how he will address his positions on the last day.* Even with this information, there is no guarantee that one can exactly predict what will happen at expiration unless one is privy to the actual stock buy and sell orders. This order flow information is closely guarded and known only to the firms that will be executing the orders, generally on behalf of institutions. Consequently, it is a very risky strategy to attempt to apply this information for establishing positions on expiration day itself. That is, if one expects stock buy orders at expiration, he might decide to buy some cheap, expiring calls for himself on the last afternoon of trading. Conversely, if he expects stock selling, he might buy puts. Given the fact that such movements are hard to predict, such aggressive strategies are not warranted.

SIMULATING AN INDEX

The discussion in the previous section assumed that one bought enough stocks to duplicate the entire index. This is unfeasible for many investors for a variety of reasons, the most prominent being that the execution capability and capital required prevent one from being able to duplicate the indices. Still, these traders obviously would like to take advantage of theoretical pricing discrepancies in the futures contracts. The way to do this, in a hedged manner, would be to set up a market basket of a small number of stocks, in order to have some sort of hedge against the futures position.

In this section, we will demonstrate approaches that can be taken to hedge the futures position with a small number of stocks. This is different from when we looked at how to hedge individualized portfolios with index futures or options because we are now going to try to duplicate the performance of the entire index, but do it with a subset of stocks in the index. In either of these cases, there is a mathematical technique called regression analysis that can be used to measure the performance of these portfolios or small market baskets. However, we will take a simpler approach that does not require such sophisticated calculations, but will produce desired results.

Using the High-Capitalization Stocks

Recall that in a capitalization-weighted index, the stocks with the largest capitalizations (price times float) have the most weight. In many such indices, there are a handful of stocks that carry much more weight than the other stocks. Therefore, it is often possible to try to create a market basket of just those stocks as a hedge against a futures position. While this type of basket will certainly not track the index exactly, it will have a definite positive correlation to the index.

What one essentially tries to accomplish with the smaller market basket is to hedge dollars represented by the index with the same *dollar* amount of stocks. No hedge works in which the total dollars involved are not nearly equal. Listed below are the steps necessary to compute how many shares of each stock to buy in order to create a "mini-index" to hedge futures or options on a larger index:

1. Determine the percent of the large index to be hedged (OEX, NYSE, S&P 500, etc.) that each stock comprises. This information is readily available from the exchange on which the futures or options trade or can be calculated by the methods shown in Chapter 31.
2. Determine the percent of the mini-index to be constructed that each stock comprises, by inflating their relative percentages to total 100%.
3. Decide the total dollar amount of index to be traded at one time: index value times futures or option quantity times unit of trading in the futures.
4. Multiply the total dollar amount from step 3 by each individual percentage from step 2 to determine how many dollars of each stock to buy.
5. Divide the result from step 4 by the price of the stock in order to determine how many shares to buy.

These steps will result in the construction of a mini-index consisting of a small number of stocks, which are grouped together in relative proportion to their weights in the larger index, and have a total dollar amount sufficient to trade against the desired futures or options trading lot. This approach ignores volatility. Even without accounting for volatility, this approach is reasonable when using high-capitalization stocks to hedge a broad-based index.

Among the largest capitalization stocks are International Business Machines (IBM), Exxon (XON), General Electric (GE), and General Motors (GM). As a result, these four generally form the foundation of many small market baskets. All four are in the OEX (S&P 100), the S&P 500, and other major capitalization-weighted indices. As a first example, let us examine how one would hedge the futures using these four stocks only, according to the five steps outlined above.

Example: Suppose we are attempting to create a hedge for the UVX Index by using IBM, XON, GM, and GE. The following table gives certain information that will be necessary to use in computing how many shares of each stock to use in the small basket.

Stock	Float	Price	Shares in Index	Capitalization	Pct of Index (Step 1)
IBM	600,000	130	0.171	78,000,000	13.1%
XON	850,000	40	0.243	34,000,000	5.7%
GE	450,000	70	0.129	31,500,000	5.3%
GM	300,000	85	0.086	25,500,000	4.3%
					28.4%

OEX price: 170.25
Divisor: 3,500,000
Total capitalization: 595,875,000 (price times divisor)

Recall how these items are calculated: The number of shares of a stock in the index is that stock's float divided by the divisor of the index. Also, the percent of the index is the stock's capitalization (float times price) divided by the total capitalization of the index (this is step 1 above). Finally, the index value is the index's total capitalization divided by the index divisor.

With this information, we can now construct a mini-index that could be used to hedge the UVX itself. Notice that these four stocks alone comprise 28.4% of the entire UVX index. We would want each of these four stocks to have the same relative weight within our mini-index that they do within the UVX itself. The sum of the capitalizations of the four stocks

in the above table as well as their relative percentages are given in the
following table.

Stock	Capitalization	Pct of Index (Step 1)	Pct of Mini-Index (Step 2)
IBM	78,000,000	13.1%	46.2%
XON	34,000,000	5.7%	20.1%
GE	31,500,000	5.3%	18.6%
GM	25,500,000	4.3%	15.1%
Total:	169,000,000	28.4%	100.0%

The percent of the mini-index is each of the four stocks' capitalizations as a percent of the sum of their capitalizations (step 2 from above).
There are two ways to compute step 2. First, for IBM one would divide
78 million (its capitalization) by 169 million (the total capitalization).
Second, using the percentages from step 1, divide IBM's percent, 13.1, by
28.4, the total percent. Either method gives the answer of 46.2 percent.
We have now constructed the relative percentages of the mini-index that
each stock comprises. Note that they are in the same relationship to each
other as they are in the UVX itself. Now it is a simple matter to convert
that percent into shares of stock, once we decide how many futures contracts to trade against our mini-index.

When we know the total dollar amount of futures to hedge and we
know the percent of the mini-index that each stock comprises, we can
compute each stock's capitalization within the mini-index. Finally, we
divide by that stock's price to see how many shares of each stock to buy.
Assume that we are going to use UVX options, which are worth $100 per
point, in lots of 50 options. The total dollar amount of index with the
UVX at 170.25 would then be $851,250 (170.25 × 100 × 50). This ac-
complishes *step 3*. The following table shows the calculations necessary
to determine how many shares of stock to buy against these 50 option
contracts.

Stock	Pct of Mini-Index	Capitalization in Mini-Index (Step 4)	Price	Shares to Buy (Step 5)
IBM	46.2%	393,277	130	3,025
XON	20.1%	171,102	40	4,277
GE	18.6%	158,332	70	2,261
GM	15.1%	128,539	85	1,512
Total:	100.0%	851,250		

Note that the capitalization of each stock in the mini-index is determined
by multiplying the desired trading lot ($851,250) by the percent of the

mini-index that that stock comprises. This completes step 4, and step 5 follows: The number of shares of each stock to buy is then determined by dividing that number by the price of the stock. For example, the calculation for IBM in the above table would be $851,250 × .462 = $393,277; then $393,277/130 = 3,025.

Thus, one could attempt to hedge 50 UVX option contracts with the above amounts of each of the four stocks. As a matter of practicality, one would not buy the odd lots, but would probably round off each stock quantity to round lots: 3,000 IBM, 4,300 XON, 2,300 GE, and 1,500 GM.

As The Prices of The Stocks In The Mini-Basket Change, The Mini-Basket Needs To Be Recalculated. This is because the current prices of the stocks in the index were used to compute the mini-index. Thus, as the prices of the stocks change, the composition of our mini-index will begin to deviate from the composition of the UVX.

Example: Suppose that oil stocks do poorly and XON falls to 35 (it was 40 when we constructed the mini-index), while the other stocks are the same price as in the previous example. Finally, suppose that the overall UVX is unchanged at 170.25, even though Exxon has changed substantially. We must recalculate step 1: Determine the percent that each stock is of the UVX. Assume the divisor is unchanged and each stock's float is unchanged, so the percent is the price times the float divided by the total capitalization (595,875,000).

Stock	Price	Float (000s)	Capitalization (Millions)	Percent of Index (Step 1)	Percent of Mini-Index (Step 2)
IBM	130	600	78.00	13.1%	47.3%
XON	35	850	29.75	5.0%	18.1%
GE	70	450	31.50	5.3%	19.1%
GM	85	300	25.50	4.3%	15.5%
Total:			164.75	27.7%	100.0%

Note that the percent that Exxon comprises of the UVX as well as of the mini-index has fallen. All three of the other stock's percentages have increased proportionately. These percentage changes reflect the changes in the stock prices. Since we assumed the UVX is unchanged, the capitalization of the desired mini-index is still $851,250 (170.25 × $100 per point × 50 options). Now, if we complete steps 4 and 5, we will see how many shares of each stock make up the new version of the mini-index.

Stock	Capitalization in Mini-Index (Step 4)	Price	Shares to Buy (Step 5)
IBM	$402,641	130	3,097
XON	154,076	35	4,402
GE	162,589	70	2,323
GM	131,944	85	1,552
Total:	$851,250		

Compare the number of shares to be bought in this example with the number of shares to be bought in the previous example. Actually, we are buying more shares of each of the stocks. There are two reasons for this. In Exxon's case, we are buying more shares since the price has dropped more as a percentage of its previous price than its capitalization has dropped as a percentage. For the other stocks, we are buying more shares because the capitalization of each has increased within the mini-index and the price is unchanged.

This example serves to show that as the prices of the stocks in the mini-index change, the number of shares of each of the stocks might change. This means that the hedger using this type of hedge should re-calculate the makeup of the index rather frequently—at least once a week. In actual practice, the hedger will know which stocks are underperforming and which are outperforming. Hence, he will have some idea of what needs to be done in advance of actually computing it.

There are many methods of approaching these "mini-indices." Some traders who are extremely short-term oriented—possibly moving in and out of the futures one or more times *daily*—might attempt to hedge the futures with only *one* stock (generally IBM unless there is some reason to believe that the general market is moving in a substantially different direction from the largest of all stocks).

In other cases, hedgers with more capital and more resources—but unwilling to hedge the entire index—might try to use a larger mini-index to hedge with. In cases such as these, one is generally not interested in day-trading the futures and stocks, but rather in attempting to simulate the full hedge against fair value as described earlier. For example, the top 30 capitalization stocks in the OEX make up over 70% of the capitalization of the index. This provides very accurate tracking, but still does not overly tax the execution capabilities of even a small trading desk. Such a 30-stock mini-index can be calculated in exactly the same manner as in the previous examples. Since it represents over 70% of the index, it will track the index quite well, although not perfectly of course.

would still not own even 40% of the capitalization of the index. This does not provide as accurate tracking as one would hope after having bought fifty stocks. As a result, if one were trying to hedge the S&P 500 Index, he should use at least 200 stocks.

Tracking Error Risk

In any such simulated index portfolio, there is the largest risk of all with regard to index hedging, the *tracking error*. Tracking error is the difference in performance between the actual index and the simulated index portfolio. There are statistical ways to predict how closely a certain portfolio of stocks will simulate a given index. This is something akin to polltakers predicting the margin of victory of an election before the election is held. One may hear that a certain portfolio has a 98% correlation, say, to an index it is intended to simulate.

What does this measure represent? First, it must be understood that statistics cannot predict the exact performance of any set of stocks with respect to any other set, just as polls cannot exactly predict the outcome of an election. What the statistics do tell us is how probable it is that a certain portfolio will perform nearly the same as another one. The concept of expected return, which was described earlier in this book, is something like this. The statistical number does not guarantee that the portfolio will perform like the index 98% of the time or that it will never deviate from the index by more than 2%. It merely is a comparative measure that says that such a portfolio has a good correlation to the index.

The actual risk that one is taking by using the simulated index instead of the index itself is not completely measurable. If it were, then we could predict the exact performance of the simulated index, which we just showed we could not. However, assume an "average" performance—that the simulated index deviates from the real index by 2% over the course of 1 year. If we are speaking of the S&P 500 at 415, then 2% would be 9.30 points over a 1-year period, or 2.33 points over a 3-month period. That is a substantial amount of movement when one considers that most of our arbitrage examples were assuming profits of not much more than that. The compensating factor to this risk is that the simulated index may outperform the actual index and one could make more profits than would be available with arbitrage. If one had enough capital and enough time to constantly be participating in such a simulated-index strategy, he would, over time, have a tracking error that is relatively small if his simulated index has a high correlation to the index.

Monitoring the Hedge

Once the position has been established, the traders should have some way of monitoring the position. Ideally, he would have a computer system that could compute his mini-index in real time. This would allow accurate comparisons between the actual index movement and the mini-index. Tracking error can, of course, work for or against the trader.

It is not necessary to have a computer system built specifically for index hedging. Many computerized systems provide for real-time profit and loss calculations on a portfolio of the user's choosing. Any of these systems would be sufficient for computation of the relative value of the mini-index. In the course of computing the profit or loss on the portfolio, the program must compute the net value of the portfolio. As long as this is available, one can convert it into a mini-index value, suitable for comparison to the larger index. The "trick" is to use a mini-index multiplier that is a power of 10. That is, the futures unit of trading times the futures quantity is a power of 10. For example, if the futures unit of trading is $500 as with the S&P 500 fortunes, then a quantity of 20 would result in a power of 10 ($500 × 20 = 10,000). This means that the total capitalization of the mini-index portfolio should be able to be read as the "index value" with the mere adjustment of a decimal point.

Example: If one is trading against futures that have a trading move of $500 per point, then he might choose to use 20 futures against his mini-index. That is, the multiplier is 20 × $500 or $10,000. If he were hedging against an index trading at 170.25, he would then buy 10,000 × 170.25 or $1,702,500 worth of stock. The total value of the stocks in his mini-index would total $1,702,500 initially and he could therefore determine his mini-index value to be 170.2500 by moving the decimal point over four places. The following table summarizes how this might be constructed using the four stocks in the most recent example. Recall that in the previous example, the total capitalization of the four-stock mini-index was $851,250. In this example we would have had a total mini-index capitalization of twice that, or $1,702,500. Thus the capitalization and the number of shares to buy are doubled from the previous example.

Stock	Capitalization in Mini-Index (Step 4)	Price	Shares to Buy
IBM	$ 805,282	130	6,194
XON	308,152	35	8,804
GE	325,178	70	4,646
GM	263,888	85	3,104
Total:	$1,702,500		

Later, as the stocks change in value, one's computerized profit and loss system could readily compute the total capitalization of the mini-index and, by moving the decimal point over four places, have a "mini-index value" that could be compared against the actual index (UVX in this case) in order to determine tracking error.

Example: Suppose that the stocks in the mini-index were to increase to have a total value of $1,761,872 as shown in the following table.

Stock	Shares Owned	Price	Current Capitalization
IBM	6,194	135	$ 836,190
XON	8,804	37	325,748
GE	4,646	69	320,574
GM	3,104	90	279,360
Total:			$1,761,872

The mini-index value is now 176.1872 (moving the decimal point over four places), or 176.19. This means that our mini-index increased from a value of 170.25 to 176.19, an increase of 5.94. This could be compared to the UVX movement during the same period of time. For example, if the UVX had increased by 6.50 points over the time period, then it is easy to see that the mini-index underperformed the UVX by 56 cents. If, at some other time, our mini-index had increased faster than the UVX, then we would have tracking error in our favor.

Using Options Instead of Futures

As pointed out earlier, one could use options instead of futures when hedging these indices. Assuming one is creating a fully hedged situation, he would have positions similar to conversions when he uses options to hedge a long stock market basket position. He would both sell calls and buy puts with the same striking price in order to create the hedge. This is similar to a conversion arbitrage.

When attempting to hedge the S&P 500, one could use the S&P 500 futures options or the S&P 500 cash options, but that would not necessarily present a more attractive situation than using the futures. On the other hand, there is not a liquid S&P 100 (OEX) futures contract, so that when hedging that contract, one generally uses the OEX options. As mentioned earlier, inter-index option spreads between various indices, including the S&P 100 and 500, will be discussed in the next chapter.

Those hedgers attempting to use the Major Market Index (XMI) have a choice of either the futures or the options. There is not normally much difference as to which of the two is better at any one time. However, since a full option hedge requires two executions (both selling the call and buying the put), the futures probably have a slight advantage since they involve only a single execution.

In order to substitute options for futures in any of the examples in these chapters on indices, one merely has to use the appropriate number of options as compared to the futures. If one were going to sell OEX calls instead of S&P 500 futures, he would multiply the futures quantity by 5. Five is the multiple since S&P 500 futures are worth $500 per point while OEX options are worth $100 per point. Thus, if an example calls for the sale of 20 S&P 500 futures, then an equivalent hedge with OEX options would require 100 short calls and 100 long puts.

One could attempt to create less fully hedged positions by using the options instead of the futures. For example, he might buy stocks and just write in-the-money calls instead of selling futures. This would create a covered call write. He would still use the same techniques to decide how much of each stock to buy, but he would have downside risk if he decided not to buy the puts. Such a position would be most attractive when the calls are very overpriced.

Similarly, one might try to buy the stocks and buy slightly in-the-money puts without selling the calls. This position is a synthetic long call and would have upside profit potential and would lose if the index fell, but would have limited risk. Such a position might be established when puts are cheap and calls are expensive.

TRADING THE TRACKING ERROR

Another reason that one might sell futures against a portfolio of stocks is to actually attempt to capture the tracking error. If one were bullish on oil drilling stocks, for example, and expected them to outperform the general market, he might buy several drillers and sell S&P 500 futures against them. The sale of the futures essentially removes "the market" from the package of drilling stocks. What would be left is a position that will reflect how well the drillers perform against the general stock market. If they outperform, the investor will make money. In this section, we are going to look at ways of implementing these hedging strategies. This investor is not particularly concerned with predicting whether the market will go up or down; all he wants to do is remove the "market" from his set of stocks. Then he hopes to profit if these stocks do, indeed, outperform the broad market. Again, we will not use regression analysis, but instead will concentrate on methods that are more simply implemented.

Often, investors or portfolio managers think in terms of industry groups. That is, one may think that the oil drilling stocks will outperform the market, or that the auto stocks will underperform, for example. In either case, one sells futures to attempt to remove the market action and capitalize on the performance differential. In some sense, one is creating a hedge in which he hopes to profit from tracking error. In previous discussions tracking error has not been a particularly desirable thing. In this situation, however, one is going to attempt to profit by predicting the direction of the tracking error and trading it.

The technique for establishing this hedge is exactly the same as in the examples at the beginning of this chapter when we looked at hedging a specific stock portfolio. The exception is that now one must decide which stocks to buy. Once that is decided, he can use the four steps outlined previously to decide how many futures to sell against them.

Step 1: Compute each stock's adjusted volatility by dividing its volatility by that of the market. Use Beta if the group's movement does not correlate well with the general market.

Step 2: Multiply by the quality and price of each stock to get an adjusted capitalization.

Step 3: Add these to get the total capitalization for the portfolio.

Step 4: Determine how many futures to sell by dividing the index price into the total adjusted capitalization.

Example: Suppose that an investor feels that oil drilling stocks will outperform the market. He decides to invest $500,000 to buy equal dollar amounts of five drilling stocks. Normally one would buy an equal dollar amount of each stock in this situation. The stocks are Hughes Tool (HT), Fluor Corp (FLR), Schlumberger (SLB), Kaneb (KAB), and Halliburton (HAL). The first table shows the price of each stock and how many shares of each will be purchased: $100,000 is invested in each stock.

Stock	Price	Quantity Purchased
FLR	20	5,000
HAL	50	2,000
HT	25	4,000
KAB	10	10,000
SLB	40	2,500

Now, if one obtains the volatilities of these stocks, he can perform the necessary computations. These computations will tell him how many futures to sell against the portfolio of drilling stocks. The volatilities and computations are given in the following table, assuming the market volatility is 15%. First, dividing the stock's volatility by the market's volatility gives the adjusted volatility (step 1). That result multiplied by the price and quantity of the stock gives the adjusted capitalization (step 2) and adding these together gives the total adjusted capitalization (step 3).

Stock	Vola-tility	Adjusted Volatility (Step 1)	Price	Quantity Owned	Adjusted Capitalization (Step 2)
FLR	.46	3.07	20	5,000	$ 306,667
HAL	.30	2.00	50	2,000	200,000
HT	.21	1.67	25	4,000	166,667
KAB	.50	3.33	10	10,000	333,333
SLB	.35	2.33	40	5,000	233,333
Total adjusted capitalization:					$1,240,000 (step 3)

ZYX futures are worth $500 per point. If the ZYX Index is selling at 175, then one would sell 14 futures against this portfolio of drilling stocks: $1,240,000 ÷ $500 per point ÷ 175 is approximately equal to 14 (step 4).

In a situation such as this, one does not have to be bullish or bearish on the market in order to establish the hedge. He is rather attempting to time the performance of the group in question. Similarly, the decision as to when to remove the position is not a matter of market opinion. Perhaps one has an unrealized profit and decides to take it, or perhaps something changes fundamentally within the group that leads the investor to believe that the group no longer has the potential to outperform the market.

If the futures are underpriced when one begins to investigate this strategy, he should not establish the position. What is gained in tracking error could be lost in theoretical value of the futures. Since one is establishing both sides of the hedge (stocks and futures) at essentially the same time, he can afford to wait until the futures are attractively priced. This is not to say that the futures must be *overpriced* when the position is established, although that fact would be an enhancement to the position.

If one thinks that a particular group will *underperform* the market, he merely needs to decide how many shares of each stock to sell short and then can determine how many futures to *buy* against the short sales in order to try to capture the tracking error. If one decides to capture the negative tracking error in this manner, he must be careful *not* to buy overpriced futures. Rather, he should wait for the futures to be near fair value in order to establish the position.

Collateral Requirements

In any of the portfolio hedging strategies that we have discussed in this section, there is no reduction in margin requirements for either the futures or the options. That is, the stocks must be paid for in full or margined as if they had no protection against them, and the hedging security—the futures or options—must be margined fully as well. Long puts would have to be paid for in full, short futures would require their normal margin and would be marked to the market via variation margin, and short calls would have to be margined as naked and would also be marked to the market. If one has not margined his stocks, he could use them as collateral for the naked call requirements if he so desired.

SUMMARY

There have been two major impacts of index futures and options. One is that they allow a trader to "buy the market" without having to select individual stocks. This is important because many traders have some idea of the direction in which the market is heading, but may not be able to pick individual stocks well. The other, perhaps more major, impact is that large holders of stocks can now hedge their portfolios without nearly as much difficulty. The use of these futures and options against actual stocks indices—real or simulated—has introduced a strategy into the market-place that did not previously exist. The versatility of these derivative securities is evidenced by the various strategies that were described in this chapter—hedging an actual index or a simulated one, trading the tracking error, selling the futures instead of the entire portfolio when one turns bearish, or buying the futures when they are cheap instead of buying stocks. The owner of a stock portfolio—be he an individual or a large institution—should understand these strategies because they often are preferable to merely buying or selling stock.

Chapter 33

Index Spreading

In this chapter, we will look at strategies oriented toward spreading one index against another. This may be done with either futures or options. In some cases, this is almost an arbitrage because the indices track each other quite well. In others, it is a high-risk venture because the indices bear little relationship to each other. In any case, if the futures relationship between the two indices is out of line, one may have an extra advantage.

INTER-INDEX SPREADING

There are general relationships between many stock indices, both in the United States and worldwide. The idea behind inter-index spreading is often to capitalize on one's view of the relationships between the two indices without having to actually predict the direction of the stock market. Note that this is often the philosophy behind many option spreads as well.

Sometimes an analyst will say that he expects small-cap stocks to outperform large-cap stocks. This analyst should consider using an inter-index spread between the S&P 500 Index and the Value Line Index (which contains many small stocks), or perhaps between the S&P and an Over-the-counter Index. If he buys the index, which is comprised of smaller stocks and sells the S&P 500 Index, he will make money if his analysis is right, regardless of whether the stock market goes up or down. All he wants is for the index he is long to outperform the index he is short.

Occasionally, the futures or options on these indices will be mispriced in comparison to the way the indices are priced. When this happens, one may be able to capitalize on the pricing discrepancy. At times, the spread between the index products on two indices can trade at significantly different price levels than the spread between the two indice themselves. When this happens, an inter-index spread becomes feasible.

The margin requirements for these spreads are often reduced because margin rules recognize that futures on one index can be hedged by futures on another index.

The general rule of thumb as far as selecting a futures spread to establish between two indices is to compare the price difference in the respective futures to the actual price difference in the indices themselves. If the difference in the futures is substantially different than the difference in the cash prices of the indices, then one would sell the more expensive future and buy the cheaper one. Several specific spreads will be discussed in this chapter.

Regardless of whether one is entering into the spread because he is trying to predict the relationships between the cash indices, or because he knows the two respective futures are out of line, he must decide in what ratio he wants to establish the spread. There are two lines of thinking on this subject. The first is to merely buy one future and sell one future (on two different indices, of course). Many chart books and spread history charts are graphed in this manner—they compare one index to another index on a one-for-one basis.

Example: A spreader wants to buy the ZYX Index futures and sell ABX futures against them. They are both trading in units of $500 per point, but ZYX is currently at 175.00 while ABX is at 130.00. Thus, the current differential is 45.00 points. This spreader would want the spread to widen to something larger in order to make money. The following profit table shows how he could make a $2,500 profit if the spread widens to 50.00 points, no matter which way the market goes.

Market Direction	ZYX Price	ZYX Profit	ABX Price	ABX Profit	Total Profit
up	185.00	+$5,000	135.00	−$2,500	+$2,500
neutral	177.00	+ 1,000	127.00	+ 1,500	+ 2,500
down	160.00	− 7,500	110.00	+10,000	+ 2,500

Notice that in each case, the difference in the prices of the indices ZYX and ABX is 50.00 points. The profit is the same regardless of whether the general stock market rose, was relatively unchanged, or fell.

The $2,500 profit is the five points of profit that the spreader makes by buying the spread of 45.00 and selling it at 50.00 (5.00 points × $500 per point = $2,500).

The second approach to index spreading is to use a ratio of the two indices. This approach is often taken when the two indices trade at substantially different prices. For example, if one index sells for twice the price of the other, and if both indices have similar volatilities, then a one-to-one spread gives too much weight to the higher-priced index. A two-to-one ratio would be better, for that would give equal weighting to the spread between the indices.

Example: UVX is an index of stock prices that is currently priced at 100.00. ZYX, another index, is priced at 200.00. The two indices have some similarities and, therefore, a spreader might want to trade one against the other. They also display similar volatilities.

If one were to buy one UVX future and sell one ZYX future, his spread would be too heavily oriented to ZYX price movement. The following table displays that, showing that if both indices have similar percentage movements, the profit of the one-by-one spread is dominated by the profit or loss in the ZYX future. Assume both futures are worth $500 per point.

Market Direction	ZYX Price	ZYX Profit	UVX Price	UVX Profit	Total Profit
up 20%	240	− $20,000	120	+ $10,000	− $10,000
up 10%	220	− 10,000	110	+ 5,000	− 5,000
down 10%	180	+ 10,000	90	− 5,000	+ 5,000
down 20%	160	+ 20,000	80	− 10,000	+ 10,000

This is not much of a hedge. If one wanted a position that merely reflected the movement of the ZYX index, he could merely trade the ZYX futures and not bother with a spread.

If, however, one had used the ratio of the indices to decide how many futures to buy and sell, he would have a more neutral position. In this example, he would buy *two* UVX futures and sell one ZYX future.

Proponents of using the ratio of indices are attempting strictly to capture any performance difference between the two indices. They are not trying to predict the overall direction of the stock market.

Technically, the proper ratio should also include the volatility of the two indices because that is also a factor in determining how fast the move in relationship to each other.

$$\text{Ratio} = \frac{v_1}{v_2} \times \frac{p_1}{p_2} \times \frac{u_1}{u_2}$$

where

p_1 and p_2 are the prices of the indices

v_1 and v_2 are the respective volatilities

and u_1 and u_2 are the units of trading ($500 per point, for example)

Including the volatility ensures that one is spreading essentially equal "volatility dollars" of each index. Moreover, if the two futures don't have the same unit of trading, that should be factored in as well.

Example: The ZYX Index is not very volatile, having a volatility of 15%. A trader is interested in spreading it against the ABX Index, which is volatile, having a historical volatility of 25%. The following data sum up the situation:

Price		Volatility	Unit of Trading
ZYX Futures	175.00	15%	$250/pt
ABX Futures	225.00	25%	$500/pt

$$\text{Ratio} = \frac{.25}{.15} \times \frac{225.00}{175.00} \times \frac{500}{250}$$

$$= 4.286$$

In round numbers, one would probably trade four ZYX futures against one ABX future.

S&P 500 versus NYSE Index

Perhaps the most consistent relationships between any two indices is that between the S&P 500 and the New York Stock Exchange Index (NYSE) (see Figure 33-1 and 33-2). If one were to look at charts of the two, he would immediately see that they move in almost perfect synchronization. This might seem somewhat surprising since the S&P 500 is composed of only 500 stocks, while the NYSE is composed of all the stocks listed on the New York Stock Exchange—around 1,800 stocks. In any case, the two indices mirror each other so well that one can attempt to capitalize on even small differentials in the relative values of the futures that trade on the two indices. Therefore, these two indices are traded by the ratio method.

The ratio of these two indices is usually in the neighborhood of 1.75 to 1 to 1.80 to 1. This is usually implemented as a 7 to 4 ratio of NYSE futures traded against S&P 500 futures.

Since these two indices mirror each other so well, one would only want to attempt this spread when the futures on the two indices are out of line with each other. Perhaps the S&P 500 futures are trading at a premium and the NYSE futures are trading at parity, for example.

To determine if there is a potentially profitable spread, one would first calculate the ratio between the two indices. Then he would apply the ratio to the futures prices to determine their differential. If there is a discrepancy of more than 50 cents between the adjusted futures premiums, then a spread is feasible. These steps are summarized as follows:

r = S&P 500 Index/NYSE Index

X = (r × S&P 500 future − NYSE future)

If $X > .50$, then buy 4 S&P futures and sell 7 NYSE futures

If $X < -.50$, then buy 7 NYSE futures and sell 4 S&P futures

Whenever X, as determined by the above equation is positive, that means that the NYSE future is correspondingly more expensive than the S&P 500 future, so we would sell the NYSE futures and buy the S&P futures. The NYSE future would be considered cheap with respect to the S&P 500 futures if X were negative, so in that case we would buy the NYSE futures and sell the S&P futures.

Example: Suppose that the following prices exist:

	Index Price	Futures Price
S&P 500	411.69	413.65
NYSE	228.72	230.20

According to the above formula, we would get a value of 0.71 for X:

$$r = 411.69/228.72 = 1.8$$

$$X = (1.8 \times 230.20 - 413.65)$$

$$= .71$$

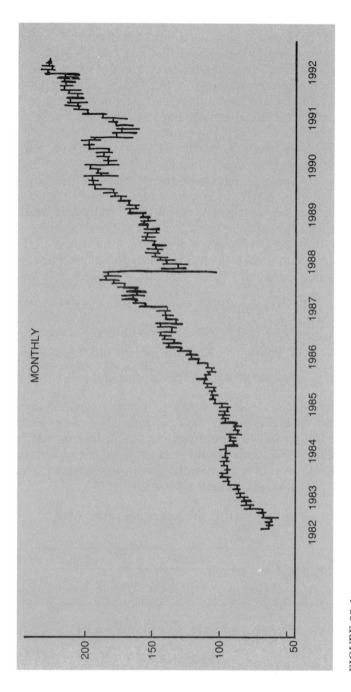

FIGURE 33-1.
NYSE monthly.

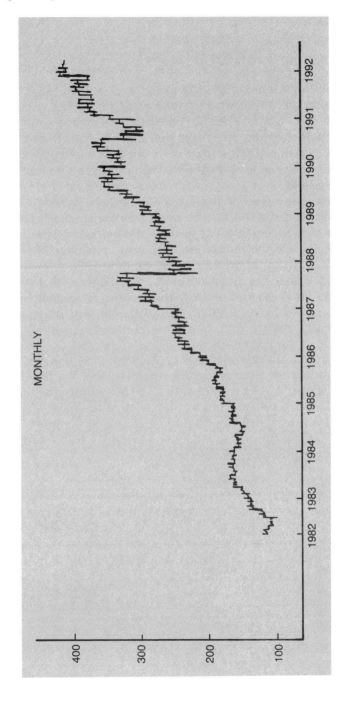

FIGURE 33-2.
S&P 500 monthly.

Since X is larger than 0.50, this is telling us that the NYSE future is too expensive with respect to the S&P 500 future. Thus we should sell 7 NYSE futures and buy 4 S&P 500 futures.

This inter-index spread is recognized as a spread for margin purposes, although the contract requirement for spread margin is slightly different than the number of contracts used in the actual spread. The spread margin requirement says that 2 NYSE futures can be hedged by one S&P 500 future. This is close to, but not exactly equal to, our 7-to-4 spread. In any case, the 7-to-4 spread benefits by this lessened requirement to some extent.

This spread position is not an arbitrage because one might lose money even if the indices and futures return to comparatively fair values (that is, even if X becomes equal to zero at some later date). One normally would hope that the futures would return to comparable values quickly so that a profit could be realized. If the futures do not converge quickly as expected, then the indices could move slightly so that even though the futures and the case indices are in their correct relationships to each other, one would not have profited. Two examples will illustrate these price movements.

Example: In this example, we will suppose that the futures return to an appropriate pricing quickly—that is, that the NYSE future is no longer expensive with respect to the S&P 500 future, and the cash indices are in the same relationship as they were at the onset. Assume that the position was established at the prices shown in the previous example—selling 7 NYSE futures at 230.20 and buying 4 S&P futures at 413.65—and that the following prices are now current:

	Index Price	*Futures Price*
S&P 500	412.13	415.20
NYSE	228.96	230.70

With these new prices, we can calculate X = 0.06. Thus, one would remove the position since X has become small indicating that the cash indices and their futures are "in line." The profit in this example would be calculated as follows: There is a loss of 50 cents on the NYSE futures originally sold at 230.20 and bought back at 230.70. Since 7 contracts were sold, and a 1-point move is worth $500, the total dollar loss on the NYSE future is $1,750. However, the S&P 500 future shows a profit of 80 cents (bought at 413.65 and sold at the current price of 415.20). Since 4 contracts were owned, the total dollar profit on the S&P 500 futures is $3,100. Thus the spread earned a total profit of $1,350 before transaction costs.

The previous example shows how one might realize a profit if the future relationship returns to the same relationship as the cash indices while the indices remain stable relative to each other. Now let us look at a less desirable situation, in which the cash indices do not remain stable relative to each other:

Example: Suppose again that the original 7-by-4 spread was established: selling 7 NYSE futures at 230.20 and buying 4 S&P 500 futures at 413.65. Assume that some time has passed and the following prices exist.

	Index Price	*Futures Price*
S&P 500	412.02	414.00
NYSE	229.29	230.60

With these prices we can calculate $X = .37$. Since X is small it indicates that the futures prices have no real discrepancy with the cash prices. However, note that the NYSE cash index has moved up more than the S&P 500 Index and, even though X is small, there is no profit in the futures spread. There is a current loss of 40 cents, or $1,400, on the NYSE futures, but only a gain of 35 cents, or $1,100, on the 4 long S&P futures. Thus, the spread shows a total loss of $300 in this case.

What has happened is that the cash indices' relationship widened out and caught up to where the futures relationship originally was.

The trader should take the spread off whenever X becomes small: $-0.15 \leq X \leq 0.15$. He should do this regardless of whether he has a profit or a loss at the time, because he originally set out to capture a pricing differential in the futures with respect to the cash. When X becomes small, that differential is gone, and the position should be removed. If one does not remove the position when X becomes small, he has changed the objective of his position from trying to capture a pricing discrepancy between futures and cash to trying to predict the way in which the two cash indices will move in relationship to each other. That is, he would be trying to predict the value of r in the previous equation. This may be quite difficult to predict. The spreader should not be stubborn and try to hang onto a losing position if X has become small. He should recognize the fact that occasionally the indices will move apart and cause a loss. We will discuss predicting the relative movements of two indices later, but that prediction is not the purpose of this futures spread.

Fortunately, most of the time, the futures will return to a proper relationship fairly quickly and the spreader will have a profit. This is true because the futures should reflect the current cash price differential, more or less. When they do not, it is usually an aberration rather than an attempt by the futures to predict a movement of the cash spread.

The key to setting up a potentially profitable situation is speed of execution. The trader actually executing the spread should have simultaneous contact with both commodity exchanges (the S&P 500 futures trade on the Chicago Merc and the NYSE futures trade on the New York Futures Exchange, called the NYFE). Thus, a customer who is attempting to trade this spread should enter his orders through a brokerage firm that offers the ability for simultaneous communication with both futures exchange floors.

The concept of this S&P/NYSE spread extends beyond just its simple use as a spread vehicle. In effect, the two indices are interchangeable and, at any time, one may be better to use for a certain result than the other. Thus, when one is trading market baskets as described in the previous chapter, he may ordinarily buy stocks and sell S&P 500 futures. However, the NYSE futures may at times actually be a better sale based on the calculations described in the above spread examples. Thus one should look at this S&P 500/NYSE relationship whenever he is considering using the S&P 500 futures in a hedged situation. It is not unusual to have two potentially profitable situations existing simultaneously: the market basket and this spread. Often, when the stock market gets volatile and speculators drive the futures out of line with respect to their fair value, many hedge strategies are attractive at the same time.

It is possible to do a similar spread using the options on these two indices. One would merely use a synthetic long position (long call, short put) instead of the long futures and vice versa for the short futures. Near expiration, in-the-money options can be used as well. In general, the liquidity of the futures is greater than that of the options, so that one is better off with the futures when one wants to trade the absolute spread differential as described above. However, knowing that the two indices have this 7-to-4 relationship can lead to some interesting spread concepts.

The spread relationships between other indices are not so well-defined as the S&P 500/NYSE spread. We will discuss several other types of inter-index spreads. Note that whenever the S&P 500 or the NYSE is used in the following discussions, one could easily substitute one for the other merely by using the 7-to-4 ratio.

Index Characteristics

Before discussing specific spreads, it might be constructive to describe how the makeup of the various indices which have listed options affects their price movements. The Value Line Index is composed of 1,600 stocks, some of which are traded over the counter. The Value Line Index move-ment is much more closely related to how small stocks perform, while the NYSE Index will reflect more heavily the performance of the large capitalization stocks. In fact, it has been said that a chart of the Value Line Index looks almost like the advance-decline line (the running daily total of advances minus declines). The S&P 500, on the other hand, looks much more like the Dow-Jones 30 Industrials because of the heavy weight-ing given the large capitalization stocks.

The S&P 100 (OEX) contains 100 stocks, but is capitalization-weighted and the stocks are generally the largest ones with listed options trading on the CBOE. Thus its performance is much more like the S&P 500 and NYSE indices. The OEX is slightly more volatile than these two larger indices, and also has more technology and less basic industry such as steel and chemicals. The OEX movement definitely has some correlation to the S&P 500, but it is not nearly as perfect as the NYSE/S&P 500 re-lationship. For both the S&P 500 and the OEX, a 1-point move is approx-imately equal to a move of 7 or $7\frac{1}{2}$ points in the Dow-Jones Industrial Average.

The Major Market Index (symbol: XMI) is composed of 20 of the largest companies in America, price-weighted. It has the most "blue chips" of the indices that have listed options. Its performance probably more closely mirrors that of the Dow-Jones 30 Industrials than any other index. A 1-point move in the XMI is approximately equal to a 10 or $10\frac{1}{2}$ point move in the Dow-Jones Industrial Average.

As we look at various ways of spreading these indices, one against the other, it will be beneficial to remember the individual characteristics. Often, one has an idea of how various market sectors are going to perform and, if there are indices that reflect that performance, then an inter-index spread might make sense.

In general, it is easier to spread the indices by using futures rather than options. One reason for this is liquidity—the index futures markets have large open interest. Another reason is tightness of markets. Futures markets are normally 5 or 10 cents wide, while option markets are an eighth or more. Moreover, an option position that is a full synthetic re-quires both a put and a call. Thus, the spread in the option quotes comes into play twice.

Futures are traded on the Value Line, the Major Market indices, and several other indices in addition to the two used in the above examples (S&P 500 and NYSE). Inter-index spreads involving the OEX must use options. We will look at the other spreads using futures before considering option spreads.

The Japanese stock market can be spread against the U.S. markets by spreading any of the above against Nikkei futures or futures options, traded on the Chicago Merc, or against JPN options, traded on the AMEX.

Spreads Against the Value Line Index

The Value Line futures trade on the Kansas City Board of Trade and a 1-point move is worth $500, as is the case with the S&P and NYSE futures.

There are two approaches to trading the Value Line versus other indices. In the first approach, one is attempting to predict the movements of the indices—he feels that the Value Line (i.e., smaller stocks) will either underperform or outperform an index composed of larger stocks.

The second approach is to attempt to capture large futures pricing differentials. Since the Value Line Index is composed of significantly different stocks than the other major indices, one cannot establish this spread at narrow margins—such as the 50 cent threshold used for the S&P 500/NYSE spread. At times, the premium on Value Line futures will be vastly different than the premium on S&P 500 futures—sometimes 6 points difference or more!

Value Line vs. S&P 500. The most popular spread against the Value Line futures involves the S&P 500 futures, although other futures can be used as we will show later. The S&P 500 Index contains less speculative stocks and is less volatile than the Value Line Index. In a bull market, the spread between the two will widen as the Value Line moves up faster than the S&P 500. In bearish markets the spread will shrink as the Value Line declines more rapidly than the S&P 500. In short periods of time, however, the relationship between the two may not necessarily follow that general pattern.

Figure 33-3 shows the historical relationship between the Value Line Index and the S&P 500. In 1982, the two indices were almost the same price. During the rest of the 1980s, large capitalization stocks clearly outperformed small cap stocks, as evidenced by this chart. By the end of 1990, the spread between the two had widened to a historical high of over 90 points! Since then, there has been more interest in small-cap stocks, so the price differential between the two indices has shrunk. Obviously, there is a lot of room for profit if one gauges the movement between these two indices correctly.

The other method for trading the Value Line versus the S&P is not concerned with predicting long-range movements between the indices, as shown in Figure 33-3. Rather, it is an attempt to capture the premium differential between the futures.

Figure 33-4 shows the closing price differential of the S&P 500 futures *premium* and the Value Line futures *premium*. The near-term futures contracts are used in both cases. Notice that this differential varies quite widely, sometimes inflating to 5.00 points (S&P futures premium is 5.00 higher than Value Line futures premium), or at others, falling to -6.00 points (S&P premium is 6 points less than Value Line).

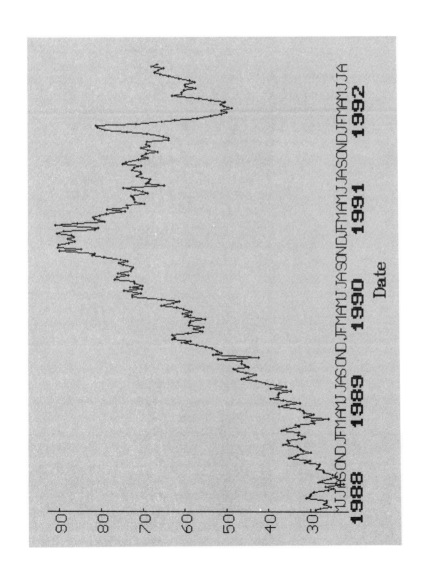

FIGURE 33-3.
Historical price spread.

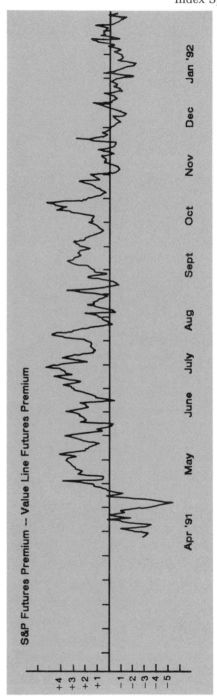

FIGURE 33-4.
Closing futures premium differential: S&P 500 vs. value line.

The actual formula used to plot the points in this Figure is:

(S&P 500 future price − SPX) − (Value Line future price − XVA)

where

SPX is the S&P 500 cash index value
and XVA is the Value Line cash index value

The reason that this relationship gets so far out of line is mostly due to the Value Line futures. Since the S&P futures are the subject of heavy arbitrage trading, they don't deviate from their fair value by tremendously wide margins. However, the Value Line futures may. The points on the upper portion of the figure represent S&P futures overpriced relative to Value Line futures. In extreme cases—near +5.00 on the chart—what typically happens is that the S&P futures are a little expensive with respect to fair value and the Value Line futures might be trading at a discount.

Points on the lower side of the Figure represent cases where the Value Line futures have a larger premium than the S&P futures. Extreme cases—near −6.00—are the result of S&P futures being a little cheap and Value Line futures trading at tremendous premiums, sometimes as large as 7 or 8 points!

The spread to capture this differential is generally traded on a one-to-one basis: one S&P 500 future versus one Value Line future.

Example: The following prices exist:

SPX : 410.00
XVA : 360.00

S&P March futures: 411.00
Value Line March futures: 364.00

The formula yields the following results:

Differential = (411.00 − 410.00) − (364.00 − 360.00)

= −3.00

This is a fairly large differential, and a spreader might decide to try to capture the premium difference. The Value Line futures are carrying a 4 point premium—too wide in comparison to the 1-point S&P futures premium.

He would buy one S&P future at 411.00 and sell one Value Line future at 364.00, a differential of 53 points.

At a later time, prices return to levels more in line with the fair values:

SPX : 408.00
XVA: 359.00

S&P March futures: 410.00
Value Line March futures: 362.00

Differential = (410.00 − 408.00) − (362.00 − 359.00)

= −1.00

The actual profit on the spread is one point, or $500, since the purchase of the S&P future lost one point, but the sale of the Value Line future made two points.

As with the NYSE/S&P spread, there is no guarantee that a profit will be made merely because the differential goes back to zero. If the cash indices move in an adverse manner, the spread could still lose money. Some of that adverse movement can be countered, of course, by trading the futures in a ratio rather than on a one-to-one basis. However, the strategy is a reasonable one because the spreader is selling a future that is clearly overpriced with respect to the future that he is buying.

This spread can be used by individual investors since the profitability is larger than the few cents generally available in the NYSE/S&P 500 spread. The individual should recognize, however, that this spread has both large risk and large reward due to the unpredictability of the Value Line vs. the S&P.

Some further comments regarding trading of this spread are necessary. Even though the futures trade on different exchanges, the spread can be placed as a spread order. The customer should be willing to give a little leeway to the broker in terms of entering the spread order. If the customer in the above example gave an order to establish the spread at 53.00 points (the last sale differential in the futures), he might not be able to get many spreads executed. If, however, he were to give the broker an extra 20 cents to work with—entering the spread order at 52.80 points—he would probably increase his chances of getting a reasonable number of spreads executed.

This spread, as described above, is intended for short-term trading. It might be established one day and removed within 2 to 4 days. There is no guarantee, of course, that the spread will shrink in that quick a time. It depends on what has caused the initial distortion. If a short-term illiquidity in the futures or a short-term volatility in the stock market caused the initial spread to widen, then it will probably shrink back closer to normal in a matter of days or hours. However, if the spread is wide because of a major move in the stock market, the cash indices may begin to widen as well, and the spread would not be profitable (at least not as quickly). In this latter case, *one may counter the effect of a move in the cash indices by using differing quantities of futures.* That is, utilize the ratio strategy.

Value Line versus Other Index Futures. As mentioned earlier, other indices can be spread against the Value Line. Obviously, the NYSE futures can be substituted, using the 7-to-4 ratio as described for the NYSE/S&P spread. That is, if one were normally going to buy 4 S&P futures and sell 4 Value Line futures, he could—if the earlier formula showed it was warranted—buy 7 NYSE futures and sell 4 Value Lines. He would do this if the NYSE were cheap with respect to the S&P (that is, X is negative in the formula given in the description of the NYSE/S&P spread). Value Line could be spread against OEX as well.

Spreading the Value Line against the XMI (Major Market Index) is a little trickier. These two indices represent the opposite ends of the spectrum with the Value Line representing small stocks and the XMI representing the largest stocks. Since there are futures on both indices, it is possible to find a substantial differential between the futures spread and the cash spread. This is similar to what was described earlier regarding the S&P and the Value Line. However, in this case, there can be substantial cash moves in a single day. The XMI, since it consists of only 20 stocks, can show extreme short-term volatility if institutions decide to move into or out of the major stocks. The Value Line, consisting of 1,600 stocks, will not show that short-term volatility. On a slightly longer-term horizon (perhaps a matter of days or weeks), it is possible for these two indices to move substantially apart as stock investors reevaluate their positions in the top-tier stocks vs. the secondary stocks. In either case, the risk of adverse cash price movements in the cash spread is too great and it is therefore not recommended as a viable hedge strategy to spread the Value Line *premium* against the XMI *premium.*

Such a spread may be set up for speculative reasons, of course. Whenever it is, the same logic used for the Value Line/S&P spread is applied as to when to establish the spread, when to take it off, and whether or not to use a ratio of futures as opposed to the same quantity on both sides of the spread.

S&P 500 vs. XMI

Another index futures spread that has not yet been discussed is the one between the S&P 500 and the XMI. These two indices do not move nearly as much in tandem as the NYSE and the S&P 500. In fact, there can be large discrepancies in their movements, especially when large (institutional) investors rush to buy or sell the large capitalization stocks which comprise the XMI. However, there still may be times when the spread between the futures on the two indices is substantially out of line with the cash spread between the indices. At those times, one might consider establishing a futures spread. As with any futures spread which one attempts to trade by looking at its relationship to the cash spread, one compares the absolute values of the two spreads and looks to take advantages of large differences. Figure 33-5 shows the historic relationship of these two indices.

Inter-Index Spreads Using Options

These indices all have options, either cash-based index options or futures options. As mentioned before, it may not be as efficient to try to use options in lieu of the actual futures spreads since the futures are more liquid. However, there are still many applications of the inter-index strategy using options.

OEX versus S&P 500. One major index that was not included in the above discussions of inter-index spreading was the OEX (also known as the S&P 100). This was because there are no OEX futures. However, the OEX cash-based index options are the *most* liquid option contract. Thus, any inter-index spread involving the OEX and other indices must include the OEX options.

First, let us take a look at how the cash indices behave. Figure 33-6 depicts the history. The S&P 100 was first introduced in 1982 by the CBOE. It was originally intended to be a S&P 500 look-alike whose characteristics would allow investors who did not want to trade futures (S&P 500 futures) the opportunity to be able to trade a broad index by offering options on the OEX. Initially, the index was known as the CBOE 100, but later the CBOE and Standard and Poor's Corp. reached an agreement whereby the index would be added to S&P's array of indices. It was then renamed the S&P 100.

Initially, the two indices traded at about the same price. The OEX was the more expensive of the two for a while in the early 1980s. As the bull market of the 1980s matured, the S&P 500 ground its way higher, eventually reaching a price nearly 30 points higher than OEX. As one can see, there is ample room for movement in the spread between the cash indices.

The S&P 500 has more stocks, and while both indices are capitalization-weighted, 500 stocks include many smaller stocks than the 100-stock index. Also, the OEX is more heavily weighted by technology issues and is therefore slightly more volatile. Finally, the OEX does not contain several stocks that are heavily weighted in the S&P 500 because those stocks

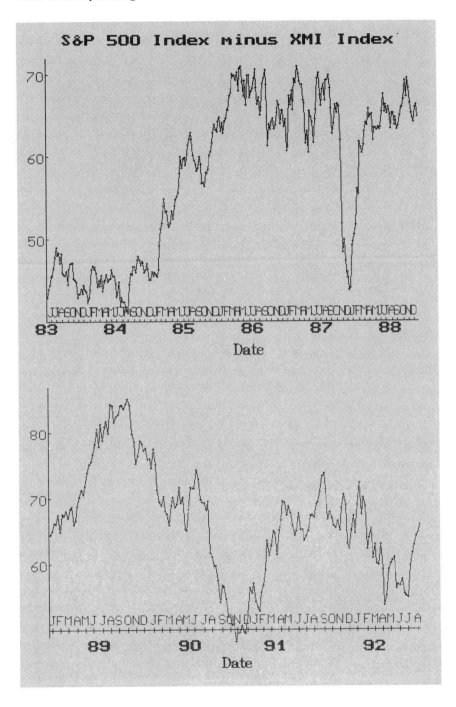

FIGURE 33-5.
Historical price spread.

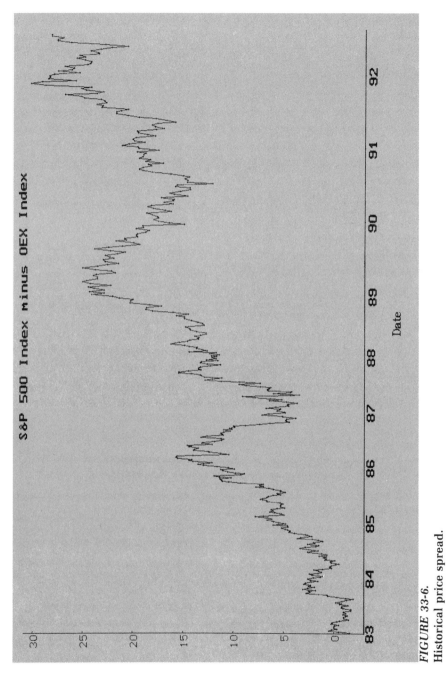

FIGURE 33-6.
Historical price spread.

do not have options listed on the CBOE: Procter and Gamble, Philip Morris, and Royal Dutch to name a few. There are two ways to approach this spread—either from the perspective of the derivative products differential or by attempting to predict the cash spread.

In actual practice, most market-makers in the OEX use the S&P 500 futures to hedge with. Therefore if the futures have a larger premium—are overpriced—then the OEX calls will be expensive and the puts will be cheap. Thus, there is not as much of an opportunity to establish an inter-index spread in which the derivative products (futures and options in this case) spread differs significantly from the cash spread. That is, the derivative products spread will generally follow the cash spread very closely because of the number of people trading the spread for hedging purposes.

Nevertheless, the application does arise, albeit infrequently, to spread the premium of the derivative products in two indices on strictly a hedged basis without trying to predict the direction of movement of the cash indices. In order to establish such a spread, one would take a position in futures and an opposite position in both the puts and calls on OEX. Due to the way that options must be executed, one cannot expect the same speed of execution that he can with the futures, unless he is trading from the OEX pit itself. Therefore, there is more of an execution risk with this spread. Consequently, most of this type of inter-index spreading is done by the market-makers themselves. It is much more difficult for upstairs traders and customers.

Using Options in Index Spreads

Whenever both indices have options, as most do, the strategist may find that he can use the options to his advantage. This does not merely mean that he can use a synthetic option position as a substitute for the futures position (long call, short put at the same strike instead of long futures, for example). There are at least two other alternatives with options. First, he could use an in-the-money option as a substitute for the future. Second, he could use the options' delta to construct a more leveraged spread. These alternatives are best used when one is interested in trading the spread between the cash indices—they are not really amenable to the short-term strategy of spreading the *premiums* between the futures.

Using in-the-money options as a substitute for futures gives one an additional advantage: if the cash indices move far enough in either direction, the spreader could still make money, even if he was wrong in his prediction of the relationship of the cash indices.

Example: The following prices exist:

ZYX: 175.00

UVX: 150.00

ZYX Dec 185 put: 10½

UVX Dec 140 call: 11

Suppose that one wants to buy the UVX index and sell the ZYX index. He expects the spread between the two—currently at 25 points—to narrow. He could by the UVX futures and sell the ZYX futures. However, suppose that instead he buys the ZYX *put* and buys the UVX *call*.

The time value of the Dec 185 put is ½ point and that of the Dec 140 call is 1 point. This is a relatively small amount of time value premium. Therefore, the combination would have results very nearly the same as the futures spread, as long as both options remain in-the-money; the only difference would be that the futures spread would outperform by the amount of the time premium paid.

Even though he pays some time value premium for this long option combination, he has the opportunity to make larger profits than he would with the futures spread. In fact, he could even make a profit if the cash spread *widens*, if the indices are volatile. To see this, suppose that after a large upward move by the overall market, the following prices exist:

ZYX: 200.00

UVX: 170.00

ZYX Dec 185 put: 0 (virtually worthless)

UVX Dec 140 call: 30

The combination that was originally purchased for 21½ points is now worth 30, so the spread has made money. But observe what has happened to the cash spread: it has widened to 30 points, from the original price of 25. This is a movement in the opposite direction from what was desired, yet the option position still made money.

The reason that the option combination in the example was able to make money, even though the cash spread moved unfavorably, is because both indices rose so much in price. The puts that were owned eventually became worthless, but the long call continued to make money as the market rose. This is a situation that is very similar to owning a long strangle (long put and call with different strikes), except that the put and call are based on different underlying indices. This concept is discussed in more detail in the chapter on futures spreads.

The second way to use options in index spreading is to use options that are less deeply in-the-money. In such a case, one must use the deltas of the options in order to accurately compute the proper hedge. He would calculate the number of options to buy and sell by using the previous formula for the ratio of the indices, which incorporates both price and volatility, and then multiplying by a factor to include delta.

$$\text{Option Ratio} = \frac{v_1}{v_2} \times \frac{p_1}{p_2} \times \frac{u_1}{u_2} \times \frac{d_1}{d_2}$$

where

v_i is the volatility of index i

p_i is the price of index i

u_i is the unit of trading

and d_i is the delta of the selected option on index i

Example: The following data is known:

ZYX: 175.00, volatility $= 20\%$
UVX: 150.00, volatility $= 15\%$

ZYX Dec 175 put: 7, delta $= -.45$, worth $500/pt.
UVX Dec 150 call: 5, delta $= .52$, worth $100/pt

Suppose that one decides that he wants to set up a position that will profit if the spread between the two cash indices shrinks. Rather than use the deeply in-the-money options, he now decides to use the at-the-money options. He would use the option ratio formula to determine how many puts and calls to buy (ignore the put's negative delta for the purposes of this formula).

$$\text{Option Ratio} = \frac{.20}{.15} \times \frac{175.00}{150.00} \times \frac{500}{100} \times \frac{.45}{.52} = 6.731$$

He would buy nearly 7 UVX calls for every ZYX put purchased.

In the previous example, using in-the-money options, one had a very small expense for time value premium and could profit if the indices were volatile, even if the cash spread did not shrink. This position has a great deal of time value premium expense, but could make profits on smaller moves by the indices. Of course, either one could profit if the cash indices moved favorably.

Volatility Differential. A theoretical "edge" that sometimes appears is that of volatility differential. If two indices are supposed to have essentially the same volatility, or at least a relationship in their volatilities, then one might be able to establish an option spread if that relationship gets out of line. In such a case, the options might actually show up as fair-valued on both indices, so that the disparity is in the volatility differential, and not in the pricing of the options.

OEX and XMI options trade with essentially the same implied volatility—approximately 14% to 15% as an average volatility. Thus, if one index's options are trading with a higher implied volatility than the other's, a potential spread might exist. Normally, one would want the differential in implied volatilities to be at least 2% apart before establishing the spread for volatility reasons.

In any case, whether establishing the spread because one thinks the cash index relationship is going to change, or because the options on one index are expensive with respect to the options on the other index, or because of the disparity in volatilities, the spreader must use the deltas of the options and the price ratio and volatilities of the indices in setting up the spread.

Striking Price Differential. The index relationships can also be used by the option trader in another way. When an option spread is being established with options whose strikes are not near the current index prices—that is, they are relatively deeply in- or out-of-the-money—one can use the ratio between the indices to determine which strikes are equivalent.

Example: ZYX is trading at 250 and the ZYX July 270 call is overpriced. An option strategist might want to sell that call and hedge it with a call on another index. Suppose that he notices that calls on the UVX Index are trading at approximately fair value with the UVX Index at 175. What UVX strike should he buy to be equivalent to the ZYX 270 strike?

One can multiply the ZYX strike, 270, by the ratio of the indices to arrive at the UVX strike to use:

$$\text{UVX strike} = 270 \times (175/250)$$

$$= 189.00$$

So he would buy the UVX July 190 calls to hedge. The exact number of calls to buy would be determined by the previous formula for option ratio.

SUMMARY

This concludes the discussion of index spreading. The above examples are intended to be an overview of the most usable strategies in the complex universe of index spreading. The multitude of strategies involving inter-index and intra-index spreads cannot all be fully described. In fact, one's imagination can be put to good use in designing and implementing new strategies as market conditions change and as the emotion in the marketplace drives the premium on the futures contracts.

Often one can discern a usable strategy by observation. Watch how two popular indices trade with respect to each other and observe how the options on the two indices are related. If, at a later time, one notices that the relationship is changing, perhaps a spread between the indices is warranted. The key point to remember is that the index option and futures world is more diverse than that of stock options. Stock option strategies, once learned or observed, apply equally well to all stocks. Such is not the case with index spreading strategies. The diversification means that there are more profit opportunities that are recognized by fewer people than is the case with stock options. The reader is thus challenged to build upon the concepts described in this part of the book.

Chapter *34*

CAPS

CAPS are relatively new option securities that resemble bull or bear spreads. The reader should be familiar with the concepts of vertical spreads discussed in Chapters 7 (call bull spreads), 8 (call bear spreads), and 22 (put bear and bull spreads). These types of spreads have limited risk and limited reward. Understanding the nuances of CAPS is important for the strategist because other similar products, or at least products with similar features, may be introduced in the future.

In general, a call CAPS is like a call bull spread if it is purchased. A put CAPS is like a put bear spread if purchased. Moreover, there is a unique automatic exercise feature to the CAPS. Currently, CAPS only exist on index options so that one uses them to capitalize on market movements, but if they prove popular, they may be issued as stock options as well. As with index options, CAPS are cash settlement options.

CALL CAPS

Call CAPS provide the owner with the right to participate in all upward movement between two specified striking prices. If the index should trade above the higher of those two striking prices, the owner of the CAPS cannot participate any further in the appreciation of the index. Moreover, his risk is limited to his initial investment. No matter how far the index falls in price, he cannot lose more than he paid for the call CAPS to begin with. Furthermore, he would break even at a price equal to the lower striking price plus the cost of the call CAPS. So far, this sounds exactly like a call bull spread. Graph K in Appendix D shows the general shape of a call bull spread or a call CAPS.

An example will demonstrate these points.

Example: OEX is selling at 390. The CBOE issues 4-month call CAPS, expiring in April, with a lower strike of 390 and a higher strike of 420. The contract, called the *OEX CAPS April 390 call*, sells for 15. A buyer would pay $1,500 for one of these call CAPS. If the OEX Index declines substantially and is below 390 at April expiration, the call CAPS will be worthless and the holder would lose his entire $1,500. However, if OEX rises and is above 420, the call CAPS holder is only entitled to the appreciation up to 420—not beyond. Hence, he would make $1,500 in that case. *The higher strike, 420 in this case, is called the cap price.* Note: the discussion following this example amplifies on the ramifications if OEX trades above the cap price of 420 during a trading day.

If OEX is somewhere in between 390 and 420 at April expiration, the call CAPS will have some value, and the holder will be able to recover something, or possibly even profit. In this example, his breakeven point is 405 (the lower strike of 390 plus the 15 that he paid for the call CAPS).

Table 34-1 shows the profit potential at various prices.

Note that the simple arithmetic formulae that were previously used for determining significant points regarding call bull spreads still apply.

TABLE 34-1.
Call CAPS profit and loss at April expiration.

OEX Price At April Exprtn	Call CAPS Option Price	Profit
390 or lower	0	− 1,500
395	5	− 1,000
400	10	− 500
405	15	0
410	20	+ 500
415	25	+ 1,000
420 or higher	30	+ 1,500

For call CAPS:

Maximum Risk = initial cost of call CAPS

Breakeven Point = Lower strike + Maximum Risk

Maximum Profit Potential =

Upper Strike − Breakeven point =

(Cap Price − breakeven point =)

Difference of strikes − Maximum Risk

Using the numbers from the above example, one obtains:

Maximum Risk = 15 ($1,500)

Breakeven Point = 390 + 15 = 405

Maximum Potential = 420 − 405 = 15 ($1,500)

or   = 30 − 15 = 15 ($1,500)

Automatic Exercise

There is an additional consideration—and this is a truly new concept in listed options: if the underlying index *closes* above the higher of the two specified striking prices—the cap price—of a call CAPS, automatic exercises occurs. That is, if the differential between the two striking prices were 30 points, then the holder would be credited with $3,000 credit upon automatic exercise. In the above example, that would result in an immediate profit of $1,500, since he originally paid 15 for the call CAPS. When this automatic exercise happens, all open contracts of this series are wiped off the books and this call CAPS series would cease to exist—even if there were a substantial amount of time remaining until the nominal expiration date!

Note that the underlying index must *close* above the highest strike, not just trade there. This means that during a trading day, if the index trades over the cap price but then sells off and closes below there, no automatic exercise would occur.

This automatic exercise feature is a definite benefit to the holder of CAPS. Therefore, it makes CAPS more expensive than regular call bull spreads, as buyers are willing to pay something extra in order to have this desirable feature. More will be said later about the value of this feature. In order to see that it is desirable for the CAPS holder, note that he reaches his maximum profit potential even if there were a great deal of time remaining until expiration. In a normal call bull spread, when the index reaches the higher strike, it is at the maximum point of time value premium for the short option in the spread. Hence, the holder of a normal call bull spread could never hope to close the spread at its maximum value prior to expiration with the index right at the higher striking price. Since automatic exercise allows the CAPS holder to do so, that is a clear advantage.

CAPS are the first listed option to have an early termination feature based on the price of the underlying common stock, although it is a common practice in many over-the-counter options. Over-the-counter options are not options on over-the-counter stocks, but are option contracts that are bought and written privately, not on a listed exchange. Therefore, there is a direct link between the buyer and seller. Such contracts often have unusual terms. In recent years, there have been may unique styles of over-the-counter options that have been created to fill a particular hedging need. Some of these have automatic exercise features or other features that are "triggered" when the stock reaches a particular point. One common type of option that has this feature is the "down and out" call option: if, after you buy the call, the underlying stock goes "down" to a certain point, your option becomes automatically worthless and you are therefore "out." It would not be particularly surprising in coming years to see more listed options have these somewhat unusual features. This is because there is always a hunger on the part of the option exchanges to introduce new products for the purpose of attracting new and more business.

European Exercise

CAPS are European-style options. This means that the holder cannot exercise them prior to expiration. European exercise has become a popular form for index options because the seller knows exactly when he can be removed from his position. This, of course, does not prevent the automatic exercise from taking place. But, when it does, the seller knows he is being assigned; it does not come as a surprise to him the next morning when an assignment notice is received.

PUT CAPS

Put CAPS trade also. The put CAPS buyer is establishing the equivalent of a put bear spread. In this case, the holder is entitled to participate, to a limited extent, in downward market movements. Again, two strikes are specified. If the index closes above the higher strike at expiration, the put CAPS expire worthless and the holder loses his original investment; he cannot lose more than that, however. If the index drops substantially and trades below the lower strike at any time, the automatic exercise feature comes into play and the holder receives a credit equal to the difference

in the striking prices. For a put CAPS, *the lower strike is the cap price.*
Finally, if the index is somewhere between the two strikes at expiration,
the CAPS will have some value. The holder can compute his breakeven
point; it is the higher strike minus the cost of the put CAPS. Graph L in
Appendix **D** shows the general shape of the profit graph for put bear
spreads and put CAPS.

Example: Again OEX is at 390. There are put CAPS expiring in April
with 390 as the higher striking price and 360 as the lower striking price,
or cap price. These puts, referred to as the *OEX CAPS Apr 390 puts,* are
selling for 12. Table 34-2 depicts the profit potential of this put CAPS.

Note that the breakeven point, 378, is equal to the higher strike minus
the cost of the put CAPS (390 − 12). Below the cap price, the put CAPS
makes its maximum profit of $1,800; above the higher strike, the entire
investment is lost. In between the two strikes, varying results occur, with
losses above the breakeven point and profits below.

For those who prefer formulae, here are the pertinent ones for put
CAPS, (they are the same as for put bull spreads):

For put CAPS:

Maximum Risk = initial cost of put CAPS

Breakeven point = higher strike − maximum risk

Maximum profit = breakeven point − lower strike (cap price)

= difference in strikes − maximum risk.

TABLE 34-2.
Put CAPS Profit and Loss at April Expiration.

OEX Price At April Exprtn	Put CAPS Price	Profit
360 or lower	30	+ $1,800
365	25	+ 1,300
370	20	+ 800
375	15	+ 300
378	12	0
380	10	− 200
385	5	− 700
390 or higher	0	− 1,200

In the above example, these formulae compute as follows:

$$\text{Maximum risk} = 12 \ (\$1{,}200)$$

$$\text{Breakeven point} = 390 - 12 = 378$$

$$\text{Maximum profit} = 378 - 360 = 18(\$1{,}800)$$

$$\text{or} \qquad\qquad = 30 - 12 = 18 \ (\$1{,}800)$$

Other Details

Pricing. While much more will later be said about pricing, it is important to realize that CAPS have a very important pricing feature: *CAPS will never sell for more than the difference between the striking prices.* If one did, there would be a guaranteed profit for the seller and a guaranteed loss for the buyer, and no buyer would be so uneconomical as to guarantee himself a loss.

Striking Prices. CAPS are referred to by the striking price that was at-the-money when the CAPS was issued (for example, OEX April 390 call or April 390 put). This is the lower strike for calls or the higher strike for puts. The other striking price is the *cap price.*
The striking price intervals are determined by the exchange listing the underlying index. It is incumbent upon the investor to check the details of CAPS with his broker before trading them. However, the concepts are the same — limited risk and limited reward — no matter what the striking price interval is, or on what underlying instruments CAPS are listed.

Cash Account. Since a CAPS is a single security, not a spread, it can be bought and sold in a cash account. This has made spreading techniques available to some institutional investors for the first time. Some of these investors are not allowed to have margin accounts, and since traditional spreads must be done in a margin account, they could not trade spreads. Of course, they can only do vertical spreads now, but that is better than nothing.

Symbols. The symbols for CAPS are different than the symbols for the indices themselves. Again, the investor must check with his broker if he needs to know the symbol.

Position Limits. CAPS options are aggregated in with all other standard options on the index and the total is subject to position and exercise limits.

SELLING CAPS

CAPS may be either bought or sold as the opening transaction. CAPS sellers would expect the index to move in the opposite direction that the CAPS buyer does. That is, call CAPS sellers would want the index to move down in price; put CAPS sellers would want the index to rise. The seller of call CAPS has established a bear spread with calls; the seller of put CAPS has a bull spread with puts. As with regular options, these vertical spreads have limited risk. One reaches the following conclusions that these two spreads are each equivalent to one of the spreads presented previously.

Bull spread = buy call CAPS = sell put CAPS

These two strategies both have limited loss to the downside and limited profit potential to the upside.

Bear spread = sell call CAPS = buy put CAPS

These two strategies both have limited loss to the upside and limited profit potential to the downside.

The formulae for computing these are the inverses of the ones presented for buying put and call CAPS presented above:

	Selling put CAPS	Selling call CAPS
Maximum profit:	Credit received	Credit received
Breakeven point:	Higher strike − maximum point	Lower strike + maximum profit
Maximum risk:	Breakeven point − lower strike (cap price) or Difference in strikes − maximum profit	Higher Strike (cap price) − breakeven point or Difference in strikes − maximum profit

Of course, the automatic exercise feature still applies. This means that although the risk is limited, it might be realized before expiration if the index trades through the farthest strike. As such, this is a detriment to the seller, but he receives some compensation for this by the fact that CAPS are sold at higher prices than normal bear spreads could be.

Some exchange literature trumpets CAPS selling as a limited and known risk, as compared to the sale of traditional options. This is comparing "apples and oranges," of course, since limited risk bear spreads have always been available for sale. CAPS' risk and reward properties should not be compared to traditional options. Rather, they should be compared to vertical spreads.

Initial Requirement. The CAPS seller must advance the risk. That is, if he sells the put CAPS for 12 and there is a 30-point difference in the striking prices of the put CAPS, then his risk is $1,800, and he must put that amount up as margin. Technically, his requirement is the difference in the striking prices ($3,000 in this case), but he may apply the premium received against the requirement, thereby reducing it to $1,800. There is also a clause in the definition of the requirements that states that if the margin required for margining a naked index option at the strike is less than the requirement stated above, the smaller requirement would apply. The index would have to be substantially out-of-the-money for that to occur, so for all intents and purposes, the requirement is the risk. Note that an opening sale of CAPS can be made in a cash account; a margin account is not required.

CAPS STRATEGIES

Most strategies involving CAPS are the same as they would be for normal bull and bear spreads. However, the automatic exercise feature introduces a few new wrinkles. The following discussions are going to be conducted with call CAPS as examples. The reader should realize that the same points apply to put CAPS as well.

Risk and Reward

A CAPS buyer would be taking an aggressive position if he bought the option at a very low price when the underlying index was substantially below the lower strike in a call CAPS, thereby necessitating a large move by the index in order to make the CAPS profitable at expiration. For example, if XMI (the Major Market Index, whose options trade on the American Exchange) were at 360, and there were call CAPS with strike of 380 (and a cap price of 400), then the call CAPS would be quite inexpensive. However, this is considered an aggressive purchase, because the buyer will lose his entire investment unless the index advances 20 points by expiration.

In a similar manner, selling an inexpensive CAPS is also an aggressive strategy, because one could lose several times more than he could make.

Example: XMI is at 360, and the March 380 call CAPS is selling for 2. If the trader sells this call CAPS, the most he could make is $200. However, his maximum risk is many times larger:

Maximum risk (selling a call CAPS)

$$= \text{Difference in strikes} - \text{maximum profit} = 20 - 2 = 18 \ (\$1,800)$$

Thus he could lose as much as $1,800, if XMI rose above 400 at any time between now and expiration. Obviously, the probability of that happening is small, since XMI is only at 360 now—but the fact that it could happen would make this trade an aggressive one.

Thus, if one is trading in low-priced CAPS, he is trading aggressively, although from two different viewpoints. The buyer is being aggressive because there is a significant chance that he could lose his entire investment. The seller is being aggressive in another manner: although the probabilities of making money are with him (they are the opposite of the probabilities that are hindering the low-cost call CAPS buyer), he could lose several times his initial investment, even though his risk is limited.

A better blend of risk and reward for both buyers and seller is offered when the index is slightly above the lowest strike. The buyer would not need a large move to make money, and the seller could make some money, even if the index were unchanged at expiration. Overall, one must be correct on his prediction of market movement to make money with CAPS, but he need not take an overly aggressive stance in order to profit.

Trades Near The Cap Price. In earlier chapters it was shown that a call vertical spread was most conservative when the underlying was above both strikes in the spread. This is impossible with CAPS since the automatic exercise feature prevents this from ever happening. So, the choices for more conservative situations must arise when the index is between the two strikes.

There are two schools of thought on how to approach a call CAPS when the underlying index is trading near, but not over, the cap price. Obviously, the CAPS will be quite expensive at that point in time—being nearly equal to the difference in the strikes—since automatic exercise is near. Should one sell the expensive call CAPS, hoping for a drop in price and a chance to make large profits? Or should he buy the expensive CAPS, figuring that the chances of automatic exercise are so large that there is a virtual certainty that he will realize a small profit? Trading near the cap price is an extremely aggressive practice and is not recommended, but this chapter will include a discussion of it so that one may understand the ramifications of trying such a trade.

Example: OEX is trading at 419, and there are 390 call CAPS available. OEX has been rallying lately, and the call CAPS are selling for 29. The reason that they are so expensive is that if OEX closes only one point higher (at 420), automatic exercise will occur and the CAPS will be "cashed in" for 30 points. See the later section on pricing CAPS for a further discussion of why CAPS are so expensive when the index is near the higher strike.

If one buys this call CAPS, he needs a mere move of 1 point on this $419 index to make his profit. Furthermore that profit could come as soon as the same trading day, mere hours from the time the trade was established. Of course, if something unforeseen happened to the stock market and it began heading down, one could lose up to $2,900—all for having tried to make $100, less commissions.

On the other hand, the *seller* of this call CAPS advances $100 in risk capital. He could literally lose it all in hours. In fact, there is probably a good chance that he will. But if fate is kind and the market drops quickly, he would have a large profit potential.

There is no one answer as to which is the better of these two strategies. If the buyer tries this every time the index is within one point of the cap price, he may make money over time. For example, if the index closes above 420 29 times out of 30, he should make a profit from this strategy no matter what happens on the thirtieth time: he makes $100 29 times ($2,900 total), so even if he loses his entire investment of $2,900 the thirtieth time, he would still be even. Moreover, if he is astute enough to take a smaller loss on the thirtieth time, then he would have an overall profit.

However, he must assess the actual probabilities. They are surely not as high as 29 out of 30. In reality, if the index is one point below the cap price and is rallying towards it (note that it can't be declining down from the cap price or the automatic exercise feature would have been invoked on the previous day's close), there is probably a reasonably high chance that it will actually close above it (perhaps as high as 2 times out of 3). This means that on 20 times out of 30, the call CAPS buyer will make $100 in this strategy. That is a total profit of $2,000. He will, however, *lose* the other 10 times. In order to at least break even overall, he would have to limit his average loss on those 10 losers to $200 each, because 10 × $200 = $2,000, the amount of his gain.

Similar but opposite prospects face the seller, except that he knows he can never lose more than $100. Therefore, this must be considered the better of the two strategies. He must realize that he often *will* lose the $100. If he loses the $100 too often, he will not be able to recoup his losses on the one time that he gets lucky and finds the index decline substantially down from the cap price without ever closing above it. Thus, while it seems attractive to sit back and risk $100 to see if one can make $2,900, in the long run, there may be so many $100 losses that the selling strategy is not worthwhile.

Using Futures. Be careful about attempting to trade futures as a hedge against CAPS. There is no limit on the movement of futures as there is with CAPS. Consequently, there could be substantial risk past the automatic exercise point.

A call CAPS holder would be pleased to see the index trade above the cap price of his CAPS during the trading day. However, if he is worried about the fact that the index may fall back below the strike before the close, he should sell out his call CAPS, *not sell futures against it.*

Example: SPX has just traded up to 441 around noon on a particular trading day. This places all 410 call CAPS in jeopardy of automatic exercise if the index can close above 440. In order to hedge his profit, the call CAPS owner decides to sell S&P futures against his CAPS in case the SPX trades down below 440.

This is a poor strategy, for if SPX goes *up* instead, there is no protection. The call CAPS cannot appreciate any further, while the short future can cause substantial losses.

At the time (noon) the call CAPS is trading at 29. The call CAPS holder, if he is nervous about losing his profit, should merely sell out his CAPS and leave the final $100 of profit to someone willing to take the risk. This is his only true hedge against the index falling back below 440 before the closing bell.

The purpose of including this is that there is often an offhanded comment that futures can be used as a hedge against expensive CAPS. They may be, but not as an absolute way to lock in the maximum profit on a CAPS that is nearing automatic exercise.

The true way to hedge in this situation, if one doesn't want to merely sell out his long call CAPS, is to use the ordinary index options to establish a spread that hedges his call CAPS. If one is long a call CAPS and the index is trading above the cap price, he could establish a bear call spread with ordinary index options on the same index. Then, if the index fell back, his newly acquired bear spread would protect his call CAPS profits. Alternatively, if the index continued higher, the bear spread has a limited risk feature and, while it may cost him a small loss, would certainly not cause a loss anywhere near as large as the futures might.

Example: As above, SPX is at 441 at noon. The 410-440 call CAPS is nearing automatic exercise, and a call CAPS holder wants to hedge his position in case the market collapses later in the day. Assume the following data exist:

Date: February 1st

SPX: 441

Mar 410 call CAPS: 29

SPX Mar 410 call: 33
SPX Mar 440 call: 10

Note that the ordinary call bull spread is only worth 23, since there are still 1½ months until March expiration. Suppose the call CAPS holder decides to sell the ordinary call bear spread as a hedge. Table 34-3 shows how he would fare by the end of the trading day.

The column labeled "Hedge Result" is the net profit or loss on the hedge: the difference between 29 and the "Call CAPS" column plus the difference between the "Ordinary Bear Spread" and 23, the sale price.

Consider the row of figures at 435: the ordinary bear spread would have shrunk to 20, so there would be a $300 profit from the sale at 23; also the CAPS would have fallen to 27, so there would be a loss of $200 from its noon price of 29. Together, these add up to a $100 gain.

Notice that the bear spread protects the call CAPS quite nicely if the index should fall in price during the afternoon. In fact, the hedge costs very little unless the index rallies substantially. Even in that case, with SPX rising all the way to 450 in the same afternoon, the hedge only costs $200.

The holder of a call CAPS must decide for himself whether it is worth going through the problem and commission expense of establishing such a hedge, as opposed to just selling his long call CAPS out at a price slightly less than 30.

Butterfly Spreads

The butterfly spread was first discussed in Chapters 10 and 23. It is a spread which has both limited profit potential and limited risk. It can be constructed with either puts or calls, or both. Three striking prices are involved. One owns options at the highest and lowest strikes, and sells two options at the middle strike. The resultant position has the profit

TABLE 34-3.
Hedging a long call CAPS with a call bear spread near the CAP price.

SPX Price	Ordinary Bear Spread	Call CAPS	Hedge Result
435	20	27	+100
439	22	29	+100
441	23	30	+100
443	24	30	0
445	24½	30	− 50
450	26	30	−200

potential shown in the profit picture on graph N in Appendix D—it looks something like a butterfly. The maximum profit potential is attained at the middle strike at expiration. The worst results occur if the stock is above the highest strike or below the lowest strike at expiration. This worst result, however, is limited to a predetermined amount. Once this predetermined risk is known, it is also a simple matter to calculate the maximum profit potential, for it is merely the difference in striking prices minus the risk.

With conventional options, these are the three ways that a butterfly spread can be established, as shown in the following table:

Three Ways to Construct A Butterfly Spread

	1	2	3
Lowest strike:	Buy call	Buy put	Buy put
+	+	+	+
Middle strike:	Sell 2 calls	Sell put & sell call	Sell 2 puts
+	+	+	+
Highest strike	Buy call	Buy put	Buy put

Notice that the second spread (2) is the sale of a straddle, surrounded by buying out-of-the-money options on either side to limit the risks. Since these three constructions all have the same profit graph, it means they are all equivalent.

There is another way to visualize these components, however: *A butterfly spread is merely a combination of a bull spread and a bear spread.* A bull spread *always* involves buying an option (put or call) at a lower strike and selling the same type of option at a higher strike. Notice that in each of the above constructions, there is a *bull* spread between the two lower strikes. It is either long call at lowest strike and short call at middle strike, or is long put at lowest strike and short put at middle strike. Both of these are bull spreads.

In addition, in each construction above, there is a *bear* spread between the two *higher* strikes. A bear spread *always* involves buying an option (put or call) at a higher strike and selling the same type of option at a lower strike. So, in each of the above constructions, there is a bear spread between the middle and highest strikes. Constructions 1 and 2 have call bear spreads, while the third construction has a put bear spread.

Now that it has been established that a butterfly spread is merely a combination of a bull spread and a bear spread, where the middle striking price overlaps both spreads, it is possible to see that CAPS can easily be used to construct a butterfly spread. Selling a call CAPS is essentially a bear spread, and selling a put CAPS is a bull spread. This was demonstrated earlier. So, if one combines the two in the proper way, he should get a butterfly spread.

Example: The OEX index is at 390 and there is a 390 put CAPS available for trading as well as a 390 call CAPS. The following prices exist:

OEX: 390

Mar 390 put CAPS: 12

Mar 390 call CAPS: 14

If one *sells* the put CAPS he will have a bull spread between the lower strikes (360 and 390). If he also *sells* the call CAPS he will have added a bear spread involving the higher strikes (390 and 420). This is one of the definitions of a butterfly spread.

If he sells both CAPS, he takes in a credit of 26 points. Consider the profit potential at March expiration, if automatic exercise does not occur:

OEX Price	Put CAPS Price	Call CAPS Price	Net Profit/ Loss
360	30	0	− $ 400
364	26	0	0
370	20	0	+ 600
380	10	0	+ 1,600
390	0	0	+ 2,600
400	0	10	+ 1,600
410	0	20	+ 600
416	0	26	0
420	0	30	− 400

The maximum risk and profit potential are easily calculated:

Maximum profit potential = Initial credit received
= $2,600 in the above example
Maximum risk if carried to expiration =
Difference in strikes − max. profit potential
= $3,000 − 2,600 = $400 in the example

Note: Automatic exercise introduces extra risk before expiration. This is examined in the following discussion.

There are two breakeven points at expirations:

Upside breakeven = middle strike + maximum profit potential
                 = 390 + 26 = 416 (verify in above table)

Downside breakeven = middle strike − maximum profit potential
                   = 390 − 26 = 364 (verify in above table)

Thus, this position of selling both a put CAP and call CAPS with a common middle strike is a butterfly spread. Well, almost. Automatic exercise complicates the analysis slightly. First, consider it simplistically: if OEX closes below 360, the put CAPS will be automatically exercised, debiting the account 30 points, or $3,000. If OEX then remains below 390 until March expiration, the call CAPS will expire worthless, and the entire position's loss would be just $400. The problem arises if OEX rallies after automatic exercise occurs on the puts. Of course, the same problem could occur on the upside as well if OEX first closes over 420, causing automatic exercise, and then drops suddenly to below 360.

This means that *there is potential for a devastating whipsaw in the CAPS butterfly.* Theoretically, one could be automatically assigned on *both* sides of the spread if he did nothing and OEX had an extremely large trading range before March expiration. The best remedy for this is to have a predetermined point in mind at which one is willing to take his loss and close the entire position. This point would probably be somewhere that allows for a slight reversal of price by OEX, but not a devastating one.

Example: A spreader has established the CAPS butterfly spread as in the previous example, for a credit of 26 points. Some time thereafter, OEX goes into a downtrend and closes below 360, causing automatic assignment on the put CAPS spread that was sold.

At this point in time, the call CAPS would still be worth something, depending on how much time is left until expiration. Obviously, that value won't be extremely large, since the call CAPS is at least 30 points out-of-the-money, with OEX closing below 360.

Suppose that the call CAPS is selling for 2. Then, the spreader could buy it back, thereby closing out the entire position for a total loss of $600 (he initially took in $2,600 and then would pay out $3,000 on the automatic assignment plus another $200 to buy back the call CAPS).

His alternative would be to do nothing, hoping for OEX to remain below 390 until March expiration, thereby allowing him to close out the position without actually having to buy back the call CAPS that he is short. This could be a dangerous strategy if OEX had a large rally, so he should have a "mental stop" point in mind. For example, if OEX should rally back to about 370, he might decide to close the position at that time in order to avoid larger losses later. Once the mental stop is set, the trader should adhere to it and not change his mind later. It is often best to take small losses at an early date rather than agonize as large ones approach, when there is little that can be done at that late date to avoid them.

Possible whipsaws not withstanding, the sale of CAPS butterfly spreads has some inherent attraction. For some time after issuance, the combination of the put and call CAPS often will sell for between 25 and 28 points *when the underlying index is near the middle strike*. It was 26 in the above example. This means that one is risking a small amount in hopes of making the entire credit. Of course, he cannot allow himself to be completely whipsawed, but that is a matter of discipline.

If one were able to sell the CAPS butterfly spread for 28 points, it would seem worthwhile. If some time passes, the spread will become cheaper and he can repurchase it at a profit before expiration. Even if the index movement causes automatic exercise on one side, the other side of the spread should be able to be repurchased at a relatively low cost. If automatic exercise occurs near expiration, his loss would be only slightly more than $200. His potential profits are up to $2,800. This certainly is an attractive risk-reward ratio.

The requirement needed to sell a CAPS butterfly would be the sum of the requirements for the two CAPS sold separately. That is, the requirement for the put CAPS must be added to the requirement for the call CAPS, even though the risk in the entire spread is less than that.

Example: Use the same prices as in the previous examples:

OEX: 390

Mar 390 put CAPS: 12

Mar 390 put CAPS: 14

If one sells both the CAPS in order to create a CAPS butterfly spread, his requirements would be:

Put CAPS risk	$3,000
Less premium received	− 1,200
Plus:	
Call CAPS risk	+ 3,000
Less premium received	− 1,400
Total requirement	$3,400

The CAPS butterfly might be more expensive—perhaps even exceeding 30 points when the index is very near to automatic exercise on one side or the other. Selling it there is not a guaranteed winner, however, for if one receives automatic assignment immediately, he may have to purchase the other side back as well, thereby expending a debit of more than 30 points. Thus, it seems that the best selling strategy is to establish the butterfly spread when the index is near the middle strike.

Buying Butterflies. This entire discussion has concentrated on *selling* CAPS butterflies. They can, of course, be bought as well. The problem with buying the butterfly is that the profit potential is so small compared with the risk potential. The buyer cannot count on a large whipsaw occurring in his favor. The best result for him would be for the index movement to cause automatic exercise on one side or the other. If he can recover something from the then out-of-the-money portion of his butterfly, so much the better.

The buyer's motivation would be to make a profit as long as the underlying index is volatile. If he buys the butterfly, he does not have to predict the direction of market movement. He merely hopes for movement, period. Given this goal, he would normally want to establish the butterfly spread when the stock were near the strike of the CAPS.

The buyer would not normally buy the longer-term CAPS that are so expensive (that is, those that sell for 25 to 28 points when the striking price differential is 30 points). Rather, he would buy a shorter-term one that sells for significantly less than the difference in the strikes, so that he has a chance of making money on a smaller movement in the index.

Example: The following prices exist two months from expiration:

OEX: 390
OEX Mar 390 put CAPS: 6
OEX Mar 390 call CAPS: 8

The total cost of this CAPS is 14 points. If one were to buy it, he could make money if the index moved more than 14 points in either direction before expiration. This is about 100 points on the Dow-Jones Industrials, so there is certainly no guarantee that such a move will happen in only two months' time, but the buyer has limited risk if it does not. His profit potential is outlined in Table 34-4.

The buyer has a true butterfly, and then some. The automatic exercise feature works to his advantage, since if the index goes through one of the outer strikes, he may still be able to sell the remaining out-of-the-money CAPS for something and actually collect slightly more than 30 points for liquidating his position. Furthermore, if a large whipsaw occurred, it is

TABLE 34-4.
Profit and loss from buying CAPS butterfly.

OEX Price	Put CAPS Price	Call CAPS Price	Net Profit /Loss At Expiration
< = 360	30	0	+ $1,600
370	20	0	+ 600
376	14	0	0
380	10	0	− 400
390	0	0	− 1,400
400	0	10	− 400
404	0	14	0
410	0	20	+ 600
> = 420	0	30	+ 1,600

theoretically possible for both CAPS to be automatically exercised. This is not a realistic probability, but it is a theoretical one.

Summary. Butterfly spreads have limited risk and limited proft potential both for the buyer and seller. The seller views it as a neutral strategy, while the buyer wants the underlying stock to move through one of the outer strikes. Trading butterflies with CAPS is better from a commission standpoint (only two commissions are involved, not four as with conventional options). CAPS butterflies have the added feature of automatic exercise, which is a benefit to the buyer and a detriment to the seller. However, the seller collects a higher price to begin with, thereby compensating him to a certain extent for the automatic exercise feature. The CAPS butterfly seller would normally want to sell them at a high price, hoping to profit from time decay before automatic exercise can occur. The buyer would normally buy cheaper butterflies, hoping for a large move in the underlying index before expiration. The limited risk feature really only applies to the buyer, but the seller can take follow-up action to protect himself. Overall, the strategy using CAPS is a moderately interesting one, depending on the strategist's objectives. If one has been trading butterflies using ordinary options, he may find the alternative strategy using CAPS an attractive one.

Calendar Spreads

A calendar spread involves buying a longer-term option and selling a near-term option with similar terms (i.e., same type of option—put or call—and same striking price). The idea is to be able to capture the faster rate of decay of the short-term option while being protected by owning a longer-term option.

Typically, one buys and sells an equal number of options in a calendar spread, but neutral traders will vary the ratio of options bought sold to those sold. The strategy has limited risk (as long as naked options are not involved) equal to the initial debit paid for the spread.

As a true "spread strategy," the calendar spread is removed at expiration of the near-term option. As such, it makes its maximum profit if the stock is near the striking prices of the options involved in the spread. This strategy, then, is a neutral one, as the strategist prefers the stock remain near the striking price of the options. If the stock moves too far away from the strike in either direction, the calendar spreader is in danger of losing the entire debit that was paid for the spread as the time value premium disappears from both options in the spread. Consider a call calendar spread in order to understand this risk. If the stock falls a lot, both calls will become nearly worthless, although the longer-term one may retain a little value. On the other hand, if the stock rises too fast, both options may lose their time value premium, again shrinking the spread and causing a loss. Profit graph M in Appendix D shows the general shape of a calendar spread at expiration of the near-term call.

If automatic exercise has not wiped out a particular series of CAPS options, it may be possible to execute CAPS calendar spreads. First, look at an example of a call CAPS calendar spread:

Example: OEX is at 390. Both March and June call CAPS exist. A calendar spread could be established by buying the longer-term June CAPS and selling the near-term March CAPS.

> Call CAPS calendar: Buy Jun 390 call CAPS at 12
>   Sell Mar 390 call CAPS at 9
>   Net Debit: 3 points

If OEX is below 390 at March expiration, the Mar 390 call CAPS will expire worthless and the Jun 390 CAPS will remain. If it can be sold for more than 3, the initial debit of the spread, a profit will result. Obviously, it would be best for the spreader if OEX were at 389.99 at March expiration, since the March would expire worthless and the June would hopefully be worth a good deal.

If OEX is *above* 390 at March expiration, the entire spread would have to be closed. If the time value premium remaining in the Jun 390 CAPS is more than 3 points, then the spreader will profit. If it is not, he will lose money.

Automatic exercise is the bane of this strategy. If OEX should trade up to 420 at any time prior to March expiration, both options would be automatically exercised and assigned, and the position would be removed, leaving the spreader with a 3 point loss! *Thus, automatic exercise makes this strategy achieve its worst possible result.* In a regular calender spread, if the underlying security should rally a great deal and then fall back to the original strike, one would have a chance to profit. With CAPS calendars, once the large rally occurs, the spread is finished as automatic exercise occurs; there is no chance to allow the index to fall back towards the original strike.

Figure 34-1 compares a calendar spread with ordinary options and one with CAPS. The following prices are used in constructing the graph:

OEX: 390
June 390 call: 17
Mar 390 call: 12
Jun 390 call CAPS: 12
Mar 390 call CAPS: 9

Calendar spreads can be established by buying June 390 calls and selling March 390 calls. An ordinary calendar spread can be established with the 390 calls for a 5 point debit. Alternatively, a call CAPS calendar spread can be established for a 3 point debit. The CAPS spread will,

FIGURE 34-1.
Calendar spreads at March expiration.

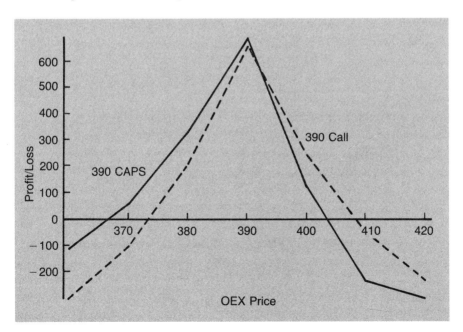

however, always remain cheaper than the ordinary call spread for reasons outlined below. Notice the profit graph in Fig. 34-1 comparing these two strategies at March expiration. Somewhat surprisingly, they both have about the same dollars of maximum profit potential with OEX at 390 at March expiration; this fact favors the CAPS calendar, since one only had to put up 3 points to establish it, as opposed to 5 points for the ordinary calendar.

What happens as OEX moves away from 390 is quite interesting. If OEX is below the strike, the CAPS calendar holds more relative value than the ordinary call calendar. Hence, the CAPS calendar is much superior, with OEX below 390 at March expiration. However, above 390, the ordinary calendar performs best, and the closer to 420 (the cap price) that OEX rises, the bigger the discrepancy between the ordinary calendar and the CAPS calendar.

Of course, it is the automatic exercise feature that is causing this to happen; as OEX approaches the cap price, the CAPS calendar dwindles to nearly 0, while the ordinary calendar retains some time value premium in the long June 390 calls.

Consequently, *the call CAPS calendar is a slightly bearish strategy when compared to the ordinary call calendar*. The profit graph is evidence of this: the CAPS calendar outperforms below 390 at expiration and underperforms above 390. For puts the opposite would be true: *the put CAPS calendar is more bullish that an ordinary put calendar*.

The CAPS calendar seemingly has a poor strategy imbedded within it. Recall that a call CAPS is like a bull spread with calls. Breaking a call CAPS calendar into its "compenent" parts would mean that one's position would be equivalent to the following:

> Long Jun 390 call CAPS = long Jun 390 call
> short Jun 420 call

and

> Short Mar 390 call CAPS = short Mar 390 call
> long Jun 420 call

> Restated, the component parts could be viewed this way:
> Long Jun 390 call, short Mar 390 call (a calendar)

and

> Long Mar 420 call, Short Jun 420 call (a *reverse* calendar)

In other words, being long a call CAPS calendar is like having a regular calendar at the 390 strike and *reverse* calendar at the 420 strike. Reverse calendar spreads were discussed in Chapter 13, and it was shown that this is a poor strategy with little profit potential. What this imbedded reverse calendar spread does is to limit the amount by which the CAPS calendar can widen. This is why the CAPS spread is cheaper than the ordinary call spread.

One might attempt to factor his outlook for the index into the way he establishes CAPS calendar spreads. If he has a slightly bearish bias, he would favor call CAPS calendars over ordinary call calendars. If he has a positive bias, he would favor put CAPS calendars over ordinary put calendars.

Trading near the CAP price. One could even use the CAPS for a short-term, aggressive trade. When the index is near the cap price, the calendar spread will be very low-priced, since automatic exercise is forcing the price towards zero. Both CAPS options in a calendar spread would be very expensive, since they are both deeply in-the-money, but they would both be nearly the same price because of automatic exercise.

One might attempt to establish the spread—buy the call CAPS calendar—with the index just below the strike, hoping for a large downward move.

If the index is uncooperative, however, and proceeds on up through the cap price during the trading day, one may attempt to leg out of the spread in order to profit. The following strategy works the same whether the spread was already in place or was just recently bought with the index near the cap price.

For example, if OEX is over 420 during a trading day, one could sell the long side of his CAPS calendar spread out for nearly 30 points and then hope for the market to collapse by the close of trading that day, thereby allowing him to profit on the remaining short side of his spread. Legging out of a spread is not usually recommended because of the unlimited exposure that one creates by doing so. However, in this case, the maximum loss is limited by the automatic exercise feature, so it might be a worthwhile attempt to make money. That is, if he sells out the long side of his spread for $29\frac{1}{2}$ points, the worse that can happen is that automatic exercise occurs and he is forced to cover the short side of his spread for 30 points. Thus, he has incurred an extra $\frac{1}{2}$ point of risk, plus some commissions, in return for the opportunity to make larger profits if OEX should fall back below the cap price by the end of the trading day.

In summary, CAPS calendar spreads might be viable alternatives to ordinary calendar spreads. Both are an attempt to capture the faster rate of time decay of near-term options as opposed to longer-term ones. The CAPS calendar is inferior if the underlying index moves towards the cap price, but may be otherwise superior. Consequently, the calendar spread strategist should probably factor his view of the market into the type of spread he wants to establish. For example, if he is slightly bullish and wants to do call calendars, he should do ordinary call calendars. Finally, the calendar spread affords one the opportunity to try to maneuver near the cap price for very little additional risk.

Vertical CAPS Spreads

It might be possible, from time to time, to have CAPS expiring in the same month with different striking prices. Hence, a vertical spread could be established with CAPS. Since CAPS themselves are equivalent to vertical spreads, one would actually have a vertical spread between vertical spreads.

Generally, when CAPS are listed, they are listed at only the at-the-money strike (for example, OEX June 390 call CAPS and OEX June 390 put CAPS). That strike would stay in effect until expiration or until automatic exercise wipes it out. At that point, another CAPS might be issued with a different strike but the same expiration date as the original CAPS:

Example: It is February, OEX is at 390, and June 390 call CAPS (with strikes of 390 and 420) are listed, as well as are June 390 put CAPS (with strikes of 390 and 360).

Subsequently, OEX trades up to 420 in March and the June 390 call CAPS are automatically exercised.

At that time, the exchange might list June 420 call CAPS and June 420 put CAPS. The new put CAPS would have strikes of 420 and 390.

Since there are now two put CAPS expiring in June with different strikes, vertical spreads are possible.

Note: There is no definite procedure regarding new listings of CAPS after automatic exercise has eliminated an existing series. The new CAPS issued at that time or after an expiration might have different expiration dates. Thus, although there would then be CAPS with different striking prices, they might have different *expiration dates* as well. For the purposes of the following discussions, it will be assumed that CAPS with the same expiration dates exist. The more complicated case of different expiration dates and different strikes will be addressed later.

Once automatic exercise occurs and the new series are listed, a vertical spread is possible. In the above example, it would consist of buying the June 420 put CAPS and selling the June 390 put CAPS. The resulting position is just another butterfly spread. The following example will describe the profit potential of such a position:

Example: The following prices exist after the automatic exercise has occurred, and the new CAPS series have been listed:

OEX: 420

OEX June 420 put CAPS: 11

OEX June 390 put CAPS: 3

A vertical CAPS spread is bought for 8 debit: buying the June 420 put CAPS and selling the June 390 put CAPS. The profitability of this vertical spread, at expiration, can be seen in Table 34-5.

The profit picture for this example is shown in Figure 34-2. It is equivalent to selling a butterfly spread, as can be seen by the shape of the graph. Recall that all butterfly spreads and equivalent strategies have profit graphs with the same shape.

Note that automatic exercise cannot whipsaw this strategy, since the long side of the vertical spread (the June 420 put CAPS in this example) is subject to automatic exercise first—that is, before the short side is. This is a plus, since when the sale of a butterfly spread was first examined, automatic exercise made the position subject to whipsaw. What happens when automatic exercise occurs is that vertical spread turns into a short put CAPS as the long side of the spread is removed via the exercise. Since a short put CAPS is certainly different from a vertical CAPS spread, the spreader may elect to close the remaining portion of his position when automatic exercise first occurs. Of course, he will have to spend a debit to buy back the short, but he should still be realizing a profit at that time.

Margin requirements allow this CAPS spread to be treated as such for margin purposes. In the above example, then, one would only have to expend the net debit of the spread ($800) in order to establish the position.

In this type of butterfly spread, one is establishing the position when the index is initially at or near one of the wings of the butterfly. In the above example, OEX is at 420, the highest strike involved in the put CAPS

TABLE 34-5.
Profit and loss of vertical put CAPS spread at June expiration.

OEX	June 420 Put CAPS	June 390 Put CAPS	Net Profit/Loss At Expiration
> = 420	0	0	−$ 800
412	8	0	0
400	20	0	+ 1,200
390	30*	0	+ 2,200
380	30*	10	+ 1,200
368	30*	22	0
< = 360	30*	30*	− 800

*Automatic exercise occurs.

FIGURE 34-2.
Vertical CAPS spread using put CAPS.

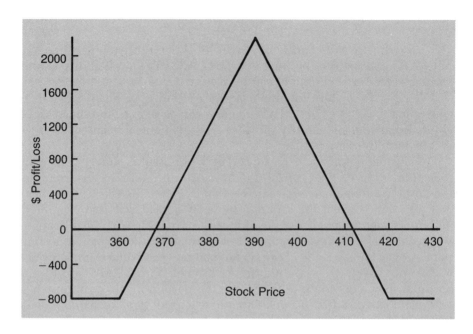

butterfly. This means that a movement by the underlying stock (down, in this example) is necessary in order to make money. Thus, the vertical spread butterfly strategy is not as neutral as those previously discussed, where the index was initially near the middle strike when the position was established.

Different Expiration Months in The Vertical Spread. In a sense, one might view this vertical CAPS spread strategy as a way to reduce the cost of a CAPS by selling an out-of-the-money CAPS against it. In the above example, one is buying the at-the-money June 420 put CAPS. It costs 11. In order to reduce his cost, he sells the out-of-the-money June 390 put CAPS against it, thereby reducing his cost by 3 points, to 8 net. Keep this thought in mind as CAPS vertical spreads with different expiration months are discussed.

It will often be the case that when automatic exercise or expiration causes one CAPS series to cease to exist, the new CAPS that are listed will *not* have the same expiration month as the other out-of-the-money CAPS that remain. Again, consider an example using puts. This is similar to the above example, but expiration dates have changed.

Example: Suppose that automatic exercise has just occurred, and that new CAPS series are being listed, expiring in August. The existing put CAPS that remain have a June expiration. The following prices exist:

OEX: 420

OEX August 420 put CAPS: 14

OEX June 390 put CAPS: 3

A vertical CAPS spread is bought for 11 debit: buying the August 420 put CAPS and selling the June 390 put CAPS.

One must look at the results of this spread at June expiration. In a diagonal spread (one involving different expiration months and striking prices), the strategist is interested in the profitability of the spread at the expiration of the short-term options. Table 34-6 estimates the price of the August 420 put CAPS for the purpose of drawing a profit graph.

In essence, one still has a butterfly spread of sorts, but the different expiration dates of the CAPS make this a sort of diagonal vertical spread. If OEX should fall to 390 or below at June expiration, the results are definitively known, since automatic exercise will have occurred. The maximum profit of $1,900 would be reached if OEX were at exactly 390 at June expiration. However, if OEX remains above 390 until then, the June 390 put CAPS will expire worthless and the spreader will be left holding the August 420 put CAPS. The amount of money that he originally collected from the sale of the out-of-the-money put CAPS (3 points in this example) becomes a realized profit and can be viewed as having reduced the cost of the put CAPS that are owned.

TABLE 34-6.
Profit and Loss of Diagonal CAPS Spread.

OEX	August 420 Put CAPS	June 390 Put CAPS	Net Profit/Loss At Expiration
440	6e	0	− $ 500
430	8e	0	− 300
420	11e	0	0
410	15e	0	+ 400
400	21e	0	+ 1,000
390	30*	0	+ 1,900
380	30*	10	+ 9,00
371	30*	19	0
360	30*	30*	− 1,100

*Automatic exercise has occurred.
eEstimated price at June expiration.

In the above example, it is also important to notice that the automatic exercise feature cannot hurt the vertical spreader. In fact, he may want to close the entire position if OEX falls to 390 before June expiration. It will obviously cost him something to buy back the short June 390 put CAPS, but he will have maximized the profit from the 420 put CAPS held long when automatic exercise occurs. This action would avoid the worst result of seeing OEX fall substantially to 360, thereby causing automatic assignment of the short side, and making the overall strategy a loser of $1,100.

Again, spread margin treatment is available for the CAPS spread as long as the purchased side of the spread expires at a later time that the side of the spread that is sold. In this example, one would have to put up $1,100—the initial debit—to establish the spread.

There is one more "twist" that the market can apply in terms of different expiration dates and striking prices, and that is that the strikes of the CAPS may not be spaced apart by the same interval as the automatic exercise interval. That is, for OEX, where the automatic exercise interval is 30 points, it might often be the case that CAPS have strikes that are 10 or 20 points apart.

Example: In February, the CBOE issues CAPS expiring in June with a strike of 390. In April, OEX is at 400 and the CBOE issues 4-month CAPS expiring in August with a strike of 410. Thus, the striking prices of the CAPS are 10 points apart, and they each have different expiration dates.

One could still establish a vertical put CAPS spread using the following prices:

OEX: 410

August 400 put CAPS: 14

June 390 put CAPS: 6

By buying the August 400 put CAPS for 14 and selling the June 390 put CAPS for 6, a vertical spread (of sorts) will have been established for 8 points debit. The profitability of this spread, again calculated at near-term June expiration, can be estimated as follows:

OEX	August 420 Put CAPS	June 390 Put CAPS	Net Profit/Loss At Expiration
430	5e	0	−$300
420	6e	0	− 200
410	8e	0	0
400	11e	0	+ 400
390	15e	0	+ 800
380	21e	10	+ 300
370	30*	20	+ 200
368	30*	22	0
<= 360	30*	30*	−$800

This spread is not much different from the previous one, except that the striking prices being only 10 points apart means that the maximum profit that the spread can make ($800 at 390 in this example) is less than when the strikes are farther apart ($1,900 at 390 in the previous example). In either case, the maximum profit point is still the automatic exercise point of the CAPS held long.

The sale of the out-of-the-money 390 CAPS acts as a cushion against loss if OEX rises in price. Note that the 6 points of premium that were taken in from the sale protects the position up to 410 at June expiration. In the above example, it is estimated that the entire position would break even with OEX at 410 at that time.

In summary, vertical CAPS spreads should be viewed as modified butterfly spreads. The sale of the out-of-the-money CAPS will reduce the cost of the CAPS that is being bought (the at-the-money CAPS). However, the sale limits the maximum profit potential, as it will have some time value or intrinsic value if the index falls quickly and causes automatic exercise of the long side of the spread. The vertical spread is a viable way to attempt to reduce the cost of a purchased CAPS, although there might not always be an out-of-the-money CAPS to utilize.

Reversing the vertical spread strategy is not practical for a couple of reasons. The reverse spread would involve *selling* the at-the-money CAPS and *buying* an out-of-the-money CAPS as "protection." First, protection is not needed for a CAPS that is sold, since it has its own brand of built-in protection—the automatic exercise. Second, if automatic exercise occurs in the reverse spread, the maximum loss is incurred at a point where the long side of the spread might not have much value. Hence, larger losses are certainly possible. Third, spread margin treatment is not available in the reverse situation. Vertical CAPS spreading should be kept to the strategies discussed in the previous examples: buy the at-the-money CAPS and reduce its cost by selling an out-of-the-money CAPS.

Pricing CAPS

The theoretical pricing of CAPS is an interesting topic. The inclusion of automatic exercise makes pricing them somewhat difficult. The simplest way to approach the pricing problem is to consider what is known for certain:

1. At the point where automatic exercise will occur, the CAPS must be fully valued;
2. A CAPS must cost less than a normal option because of its spread feature;
3. A CAPS must cost more than a normal vertical spread because it includes the automatic exercise feature, which is a benefit to the buyer and a detriment to the seller.

So there are some conditions to limit the range in which the price of a CAPS may fall. These conditions are known as *boundary conditions*, and their use is common in pricing options with early termination features such as automatic exercise. Once one has a feeling as to the range in which the price of the CAPS must fall, it is much easier to attempt to price the CAPS itself.

Some short examples will verify the truthfulness of the three boundary conditions set forth above.

Example: An OEX June 390 call CAPS exists. The cap price is 420. If OEX is trading at or above 420 during the trading day, the call CAPS must be worth nearly 30, since automatic exercise is imminent. Thus, the first boundary condition is true: *at the point where automatic exercise will occur (420), the CAPS must be fully valued.* That is, it must be equal to 30 for this OEX CAPS.

The second boundary condition compares the value of a CAPS and that of an ordinary index option, where the ordinary index option has the same strike and expiration date as the CAPS. Since the profit potential of the ordinary option is unlimited, it will sell for a higher price than the CAPS. Stated another way, the spread-like feature of the CAPS reduces its cost, as compared to an ordinary index option with the same strike.

Example: OEX is at 390. There is a June 390 call CAPS as well as a plain June 390 call. The June 390 call sell for 12. The June 390 CAPS will sell for approximately 10. *Thus, the call CAPS costs less than an ordinary call option with the same strike and expiration date.* The second boundary condition is verified.

The third and final boundary condition states that the CAPS must be more valuable than an ordinary bull spread (call CAPS) or bear spread (put CAPS) because of the automatic exercise feature. That is, automatic exercise *adds* something to the value of an ordinary bull spread because it allows the CAPS holder to realize his maximum profit at the cap price, *even if there is a significant amount of time remaining to expiration when the index closes there.* Obviously, this is a penalty to the CAPS seller, so he demands a higher price when he sells a CAPS in order to compensate for granting the automatic exercise feature to the buyer.

Example: OEX is again at 390. There is a June 390 call CAPS available for trading with a cap price of 420. In addition, there are ordinary index options expiring in June with strikes of 390 and 420. Their prices are as follows:

OEX: 390

June 390 call CAPS: 10

June 390 call: 12

June 420 call: 3

A bull spread constructed with the June 390 and June 420 ordinary index calls would cost 9 (12 − 3). The call CAPS, however, costs 10. The extra point of price is the value of the automatic exercise feature when OEX is at 390. *The call CAPS sells for more than an ordinary call bull spread.* This is the third boundary condition.

Figure 34-3 depicts that the three boundary conditions for a hypothetical OEX 6-month call and a corresponding 6-month bull spread. The point marked "A" is the automatic exercise point. The value of the CAPS must fall somewhere between these two curves and must also wind up at point A when OEX is at 420. The distance between the two curves will vary with such variables as volatility, short-term interest rates, and dividends remaining to be paid until expiration. However, the relative shapes of the curves will remain the same. The reader should also convince

FIGURE 34-3.
CAPS boundary conditions, six months left.

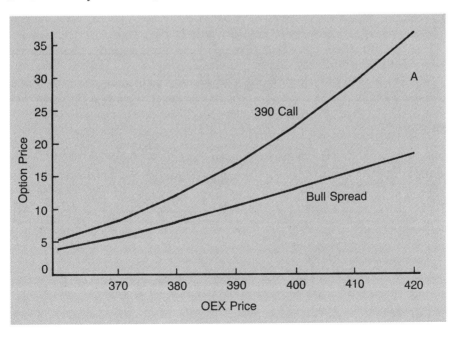

himself that the top curve can never pass *below* point A, for the call would be trading at a discount if it did. Similarly, the lower curve can never pass *above* point A because the 390–420 ordinary call spread would have to be worth more than the difference in the striking prices prior to expiration—a situation which cannot occur.

So now that one knows the general area in which the price of the CAPS must fall, how can he actually predict the CAPS price itself? The following discussion gives a general rule of thumb that will be close to the theoretical price of the CAPS. Figure 34-4 depicts a CAPS pricing curve laid between the two pricing curves from Figure 34-3. These are the boundary condition curves. Notice that the CAPS pricing curve is very close to the bull spread pricing curve when the options are far out-of-the-money (that is, when OEX is below 370 on this Figure 34-4). As OEX climbs in price, the automatic exercise feature becomes more valuable as there is a greater and greater chance that it will actually happen. Thus, the CAPS curve begins to rise faster than the bull spread curve, as it must eventually meet up with point "A" when OEX gets to 420. The middle curve on this graph is the way a pricing curve for a call CAPS option looks. Obviously, a put CAPS pricing curve could be constructed as well by applying the similar boundary conditions for puts.

FIGURE 34-4.
CAPS price estimate, six months left.

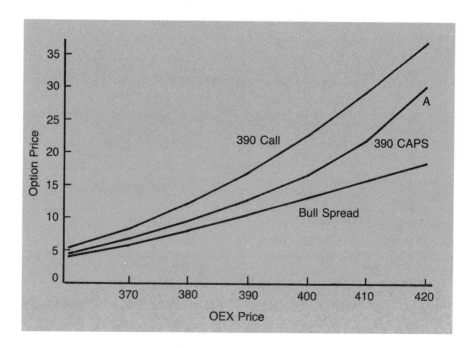

Figures 34-5 and 34-6 amplify on the call CAPS pricing curve by showing how it would look as expiration draws nearer. The curve in Figure 34-6 shows the situation with three months remaining until expiration and all variables the same as in the previous two figures. The curve in Figure 34-5 depicts the situation with only one month to go. The reader can see that the general shape of the CAPS curve is the same in all cases. The automatic exercise feature in the one-month case is not worth nearly as much in terms of price even with OEX at 410. However, the CAPS must still meet up with point A, so the last 10 points of OEX movement for a short-term CAPS make it accelerate quite dramatically in price.

The value of the automatic exercise feature is directly linked with the probability of the index arriving at the cap price. Thus, the key to pricing a CAPS is to be able to quantify that probability. There is a strict mathematical way to do that, but the average trader is looking for something quicker to use as an estimate. Two suggestions follow. The first is to create an artificial constant that is used to price the CAPS a certain distance between the two boundary curves shown in the figures above. For values of OEX far out-of-the-money, the constant would be small: 0.1 to 0.2, possibly. This means that the CAPS value would lie only 10 to 20 percent of the way between the lower curve (the bull spread) and the

FIGURE 34-5.
CAPS price estimate, one month left.

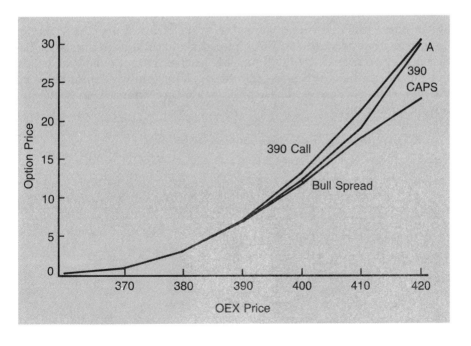

FIGURE 34-6.
CAPS price estimate, three months left.

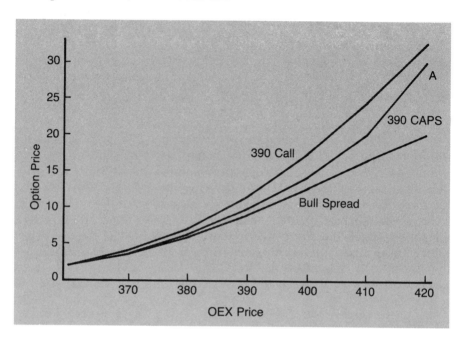

higher curve (the call value). However, at the strike of the CAPS (390 in the above examples), the CAPS is priced about 30% of the distance between the two curves. By the time OEX reaches 410, or one strike below the cap price, the CAPS price should be about midway (50%) between the two boundary curves. These observations are summarized in the following simple model.

The simple CAPS pricing model is as follows:

$$\text{Call CAPS theoretical price} = SP + a \times HCP$$

Where

   SP = price of ordinary bull spread

   HCP = price of ordinary call with strike equal to cap price

and "a" is a constant between 0 and 1, that grows larger as the underlying
   index price nears the cap price.

The constant "a" would have values something like this:

Index Price	Price	Value of "a"
Well below CAPS strike	370	0.1
Slightly below CAPS strike	380	0.2
CAPS strike	390	0.3
⅓ between CAPS strike and cap price	400	0.4
⅔ between CAPS strike and cap price	410	0.5

Example: Given the following OEX call prices, the simple CAPS model can be used to predict the June 390 call CAPS price. As an example of the model, look at the prices when OEX is at 390: the ordinary call spread is 9 (June 390 call is 12 and June 420 call is 3) and the call with strike equal to the caps price is the June 420 call, which is 3.

Therefore, SP = 9 and HCP = 3. With OEX at the strike of the CAPS, the above table shows that the constant "a" should be 0.3.

So, CAPS Price = 9 + 0.3 * 3 = 9.9, with OEX at 390.

The CAPS price values for various OEX prices are calculated in Table 34-7.

Obviously, this is a rough approximation of the preceding figures, but it should be good enough to give one an approximate value for the CAPS.

A little more accuracy can be introduced into this rough model if one has access to calculations of the options' delta. Recall that delta is generally defined as the amount by which an option's price will change

TABLE 34-7.
Estimated value of call CAPS.

OEX	June 390 Call Prc	June 420 Call Prc	'a'	Predicted June 390 Call CAPS Price
360	2	¼	0.1	1.78
370	4	½	0.1	3.55
380	7	1	0.2	6.20
390	12	3	0.3	9.90
400	18	5	0.4	15.00
410	25	8	0.5	21.00

when the underlying stock moves by one point. *However, another definition of call delta—a slightly more mathematical one—is that the delta of an option is approximately the probability of the stock being above the option's strike at the time the option expires.* Look at the following table of OEX prices and deltas and envision the delta in light of this alternative definition.

OEX: 390

Option	Delta
June 360 call	0.90
June 370 call	0.80
June 380 call	0.60
June 390 call	0.55
June 400 call	0.40
June 410 call	0.30
June 420 call	0.20

The normal definition of delta means that the June 420 call would rise in price about 20 cents if OEX rose in price by 1 point. Under the alternative definition of delta, one could say that there is a 20% chance of OEX being over 420 at June expiration.

Recall that the value of the automatic exercise feature is directly linked with the probability of the index arriving at the cap price. The alternative definition of delta is very close to the piece of information that one needs to know in order to price the automatic exercise feature. It is not quite the complete information needed, but it is close. In order to properly evaluate the automatic exercise feature, one needs to know the probability of the index closing above the cap price at *any* time between now and expiration. This latter probability would be larger than the probability of closing above the cap price *at expiration*, which is what the delta is. Still, this concept is the basis of a new definition of the third boundary condition:

The third boundary condition is now:

$$\text{CAPS} >= \text{SP} + \text{HCP} \times \text{delta of HCP}$$

where SP and HCP are defined as before:

   SP = price of ordinary bull spread

   HCP = price of ordinary call with strike equal to cap price

Spreads Against Ordinary Index Options

It might be possible from time to time to create positions in which one buys or sells CAPS and also buys or sells an opposite equivalent position in index options. At first glance, this might seem like an arbitrage—a box spread of sorts. But it is not because the automatic exercise features makes the CAPS sufficiently different from the ordinary index options spreads.

One's objectives in establishing such spreads would be to buy the CAPS and have automatic exercise occur, while the short side of the spread has not expanded as much. This type of position can easily by constructed with call CAPS: buy the CAPS and sell the corresponding same vertical spread with index options.

Example: OEX is at 390. The following prices exist, as they have in previous examples:

OEX: 390

June 390 call CAPS: 10

June 390 call: 12

June 420 call: 3

If one were to buy the call CAPS for 10 points debit and simultaneously sell the 390–420 bear spread using the ordinary index options for nine points credit, he would have a position with one point of risk. So, this is the initial position:

Buy 1 June 390 call CAPS	10 db
Buy 1 June 420 call	3 db
Sell 1 June 390 call	12 cr
Total Position	1 db

There is no favorable margin treatment for this spread. The long call CAPS would have to be paid for ($1,000), and the bear spread margined as usual ($3,000 − $900 = $2,100).

If OEX never approaches the cap price of 420, the spread between the two will never widen, and the position will lose the initial debit of 1 point. However, if the index *does* trade up to the cap price, the CAPS that are held long will approach 30 points, but the bear spread in the index options will not widen out nearly that much. In fact, if there is a lot of time remaining until June expiration, the profit potential of this strategy could be quite large.

Table 34-8 shows the potential profitability of this position at various times before expiration, with OEX at a price of nearly 420.

Thus, even if OEX doesn't approach the cap price until there is only one month left until expiration, the bear spread will still not widen out to completely 30 points because of the excess time value premium re-

TABLE 34-8.
Hedging a call CAPS with an ordinary call bear spread (OEX: 420).

Time Remaining Until Expire	CAPS Price	Bear Spread Price	Total Profit/Loss
6 months	29	20	+$800
3 months	29	23	+ 500
1 month	29	25	+ 300

maining in the June 420 call. Thus, this is a low-risk strategy that could offer a high return if the index becomes bullish.

Notice that this spread attempts to take advantage of the difference between the lower boundary condition curve and CAPS pricing curve. Review the previous option pricing graph that showed these curves. Notice that OEX would not have to trade all the way to 420 in order for the two curves to begin spreading apart. Even if it trades up to 415 or so, this spread should begin producing a nice profit if there is still sufficient time remaining until June expiration.

In some cases, the spreader may even want to try to be right twice. Suppose that OEX closes over 420 and automatic exercise occurs. The strategist who has the above position would be left with a bear spread in ordinary index options. He could close out his bear spread and take his profit. However, if OEX were to decline from that point, he could make even more money on his bear spread. It would be a large mistake to waste the profit that he already has, but he may want to risk a portion of it in order to see if OEX might drop in price. Thus, he could close out a good portion of his bear spreads, retaining a few to see if the index drops in price.

A potential risk of this strategy would occur if OEX is above 390 but well below 420, and early assignment of the short June 390 call in the bear spread occurs. This would leave the position exposed to a quick downside move in OEX. Thus, if early assignment appears imminent, all portions of this spread should be closed. A slight variation can sometimes be made to the original spread in order to avoid this early assignment problem. That would be to establish the bear spread in ordinary index options with puts instead of calls. That is, one would buy the June 420 put and sell the June 390 put instead of using calls. This initially requires a large debit, and thus ties up more actual dollars while the position is in place. Furthermore, one may have to pay too much for such a put bear spread, since the June 420 point is 30 points in the money and probably would not have a liquid market. Nevertheless, the put bear spread alternative should be checked out before establishing this type of spread.

Using Puts. A similar strategy can be attempted with puts if one is bearish on the index itself. He would buy the put CAPS and establish a bull spread with ordinary index options. A similar philosophy is behind this spread. If OEX drops to 360, the put cap price, then the CAPS is automatically exercised. However, the bull spread will still have some time value premium in it, and the entire position can be closed at a profit.

The bull spread portion involving ordinary index options can be constructed by either selling a put spread for a credit or by buying a call spread for a large debit. Again, note that the call spread would involve a deeply in-the-money call, and therefore might not be feasible for purchase. However, the advantage of the call spread is that it would not be subject to early assignment as June expiration nears.

SUMMARY

CAPS are substitutes for vertical spreads, with the addition of an automatic exercise feature. That feature makes CAPS more expensive than the corresponding spreads constructed with ordinary options. Since CAPS may be traded in cash accounts, margin accounts are not required, and therefore institutional investors may be able to participate in vertical spread strategies.

These strategies include the outright purchase of CAPS, and may include call CAPS or put CAPS. In all cases, risk and reward are both limited. The automatic exercise feature works to the benefit of the CAPS buyer and to the detriment of the CAPS seller. Spread strategies are also available with CAPS. The most promising is the CAPS vertical spread, wherein one attempts to reduce the cost of a CAPS that he is buying by selling an out-of-the-money CAPS against it. Butterfly spreads may also be constructed with similar put and call CAPS (and in other ways as well). The strategy has some merit, but there are dangers of whipsaws. Calendar spreads may also be attractive if one is willing to factor his viewpoint of the market into the spread strategy. Finally, one will surely be tempted to try some maneuvers if the index trades over the cap price during any one trading day. The best way to attempt to profit from such a position would be to merely sell an in-the-money CAPS, or to sell out the long side of a CAPS calendar spread.

It is likely that, in the future, two things may occur. First, CAPS may be listed on other underlying instruments besides indices. Second, other listed option products may be introduced that have early termination features such as automatic exercise. It thus behooves the strategist to understand CAPS now so that he may be able to fully take advantage of similar products to come in the future.

Chapter 35

Mathematical Considerations for Index Products

In this chapter, we will look at some riskless arbitrage techniques as they apply to index options. Then a summary of mathematical techniques, especially modeling, will be presented.

ARBITRAGE

Most of the normal arbitrage stategies have been described previously. We will review them here, concentrating on specific techniques not described in previous chapters on hedging (market baskets) and index spreading.

Discounting

We saw that discounting in cash-based options is done with in-the-money options as it is with stock options. However, since the discounter cannot exactly hedge the cash-based options, he will normally do his discounting near the close of the day so that there is as little time as possible between the time the option is bought and the close of the market. This reduces the risk that the underlying index can move too far before the close of trading.

Example: The OEX is trading at 373.53. The June 380 puts are offered at a discount; one can buy them for 6¼. Since parity is 6.47, this represents a 22-cent discount. Is this enough of a discount?

If it quite near closing time for the market, it probably is enough of a discount. For the market to move 22 cents on the OEX would be roughly equal to 1½ to 2 points on the Dow-Jones Industrials (1 OEX or S&P point is about 7½ Dow points). Obviously, this is not a lot of cushion, but it is probably sufficient if there are only a few minutes of trading left, except on a expiration day.

However, if this situation were presented to the discounter at an earlier time in the trading day, he might defer. If there were several hours of trading left, he would probably want to buy the puts at a discount of ½ to ¾ of a point. With that larger cushion, he could set up a hedge to protect himself. He might, for example, buy futures, buy OEX calls, or sell puts on an another index. At the end of the day, he could exercise the puts he bought at a discount and reverse the hedging position in the open market.

Conversions and Reversals

Conversions and reversals in cash-based options are really the market basket hedges (index arbitrage) described in an earlier chapter. That is, the underlying security is actually all the stocks in the index. However, the more standard conversion and reversals can be executed with futures and futures options.

Since there is no credit to one's account for selling a future and no debit for buying one, most futures conversions and reversals trade very nearly at a net price equal to the strike. That is, the value of the out-of-the-money futures option is equal to the time premium of the in-the-money option that is its counterpart in the conversion or reversal.

Example: An index future is trading at 179.00. If the December 180 call is trading for 5.00, then the December 180 put should be priced near 6.00. The time value premium of the in-the-money put is 5.00 (6.00 + 170.00 − 180.00), which is equal to the price of the out-of-the-money call at the same strike.

If one were to attempt to do a conversion or reversal with these options, he would have a position with no risk of loss but no possibility of gain: A reversal would be established, for example, at a "net price" of 180. Sell the future at 179, add the premium of the put, 6.00, and subtract the cost of the call, 5.00: 179 + 6.00 − 5.00 = 180.00. As we know from the earlier chapter on arbitrage, one unwinds a conversion or reversal for a "net price" equal to the strike. Hence there would be no gain or loss from this futures reversal.

For index futures options, there is no risk when the underlying closes near the strike since they settle for cash. One is not forced to make a choice as to whether or not to exercise his calls (see the earlier chapter on arbitrage for a description of risks at expiration when trading reversals or conversions).

In actual practice, floor traders may attempt to establish conversions in futures options for small increments—perhaps 5 or 10 cents in S&P futures, for example. The arbitrageur should note that futures *options* do actually create a credit or debit in the account. That is, they are like stock options in that respect, even though the underlying instrument is not. This means that if one is using a deep in-the-money option in the conversion, there will actually be some carrying cost involved.

Example: An index future is trading at 179.00 and one is going to price the December 190 conversion, assuming that December expiration is 50 days away. Assume that the current carrying cost of money is 10% annually. Finally, assume that the December 190 call is selling for 1.00, and the December 190 put is selling for 11.85. Note that the put has a time value premium of only 85 cents, less than the premium of the call. The reason for this is that one would have to pay a carrying cost to do the December 190 conversion.

If one established the 190 conversion, he would buy the futures (no credit or debit to the account), buy the put (a debit of 11.85), and sell the call (a credit of 1.00). Thus, the account actually incurs a debit of 10.85 from the options. The carrying cost for 10.85 at 10% for 50 days is $10.85 \times 10\% \times 50/365 = 0.15$. This indicates that the converter is willing to pay 15 cents less time premium for the put (or conversely that the reversal trader is willing to sell the put for 15 cents less time premium). Instead of the put trading with a time value premium equal to the call price, the put will trade with a premium of 15 cents less. Thus, the time premium of the put is 85 cents, rather than being equal to the price of the call, 1.00.

Box Spreads

Recall that a "box" consists of a bullish vertical spread involving two striking prices, and a bearish vertical spread using the same two strikes. One spread is constructed with puts and the other with calls. The profitability of the box is the same regardless of the price of the underlying security at expiration.

Box arbitrage with equity options involves trying to buy the box for less than the difference in the striking prices. For example, trying to buy a box in which the strikes are 5 points apart for 4¾. Selling the box for more than 5 points would represent arbitrage as well. In fact, even selling the box at exactly 5 points would produce a profit for the arbitrageur since he earns interest on the credit from the sale.

These same strategies apply to options on futures. However, boxes on cash-based options involve another consideration. It is often the case with cash-based options that the box sells for more than the difference in the strikes. For example, a box in which the strikes are 10 points apart might sell for 10½, a substantial premium over the striking price differential. The reason that this happens is because of the possibility of early assignment. The seller of the box assumes that risk and, as a result, demands a higher price for the box.

If he sells the box for a half point more than the striking price differential, then he has a built-in cushion of ½ point of index movement if he were to be assigned early. In general, box strategies are not particularly attractive. However, if the premium being paid for the box is excessively high, then one should consider selling the box. Since there are four commissions involved, this is not normally a retail strategy.

MATHEMATICAL APPLICATIONS

The following material is intended to be a companion to Chapter 30 on mathematical applications. Index options have a few unique properties which must be taken into account when trying to predict their value via a model.

The Black-Scholes model is still the model of choice for options, even for index options. Other models have been designed, but the Black-Scholes model seems to give accurate results without the extreme complications of most of the other models.

Futures

Modeling the fair value of most futures contracts is a difficult task. The Black-Scholes model is not usable for that task. Recall that we saw earlier that the fair value of a future contract on an index could be calculated by computing the present value of the dividend and also knowing the savings in carrying cost of the futures contract vs. buying the actual stocks in the index.

Cash-Based Index Options

The futures fair value model for a capitalization weighted index requires knowing the exact dividend, dividend payment date and capitalization of each stock in the index (for price-weighted indices, the capitalization is unnecessary). This is the only way of getting the accurate dividend for use in the model. The same dividend calcuation must be done for any other index before the Black-Scholes formula can be applied.

In the actual model, the dividend for cash-based index options is used in much the same way that dividends are used for stock options:

The present value of the dividend is subtracted from the index price and the model is evaluated using that adjusted stock price. With stock options, there was a second alternative—shortening the time to expiration to be equal to the ex-date—but that is not viable with index options since there are numerous ex-dates.

Let's look at an example using the same fictional dividend information and index that were used in Chapter 32.

Example: Assume that we have a capitalization-weighted index composed of three stocks: AAA, BBB, and CCC. The following table gives the pertinent information regarding the dividends and floats of these three stocks:

Stock	Dividend Amount	Days until Dividend	Float
AAA	1.00	35	50,000,000
BBB	0.25	60	35,000,000
CCC	0.60	8	120,000,000
Divisor:	150,000,000		

One first computes the present worth of each stock's dividend, multiplies that amount by the float, and then divides by the index divisor. The sum of these computations for each stock gives the total dividend for the index. Refer to the example in Chapter 32 for the exact computation that the present worth of the dividend for this index is $0.8667.

Assume that the index is currently trading at 175.63 and that we want to evaluate the theoretical value of the July 175 call. Then, using the Black-Scholes model from Chapter 30, we would perform the following calculations:

1. Subtract the present worth of the dividend, 0.8667, from the current index price of 175.63, giving an adjusted index price of 174.7633.
2. Evaluate the call's fair value using 174.7633 as the stock price. All other variables are as they are for stocks, including the risk-free interest rate at its actual value (10%, for example).

The theoretical value for puts is computed in the same way as for equity options, by using the arbitrage model. This is sufficient for cash-based index options because it is possible—albeit difficult—to hedge these options by buying or selling the entire index. Thus, the options should reflect the potential for such arbitrage. The put value should, of course, reflect the potential for dividend arbitrage with the index. The arbitrage valuation model presented in the early chapter on modeling called for the dividend to be used. For these index puts, one would use the present worth of the dividend on the index—the same one that was used for the call valuation, as in the last example.

European Exercise

To account for European exercise, one basically ignores the fact that an in-the-money put option's minimum value is its intrinsic value. European exercise puts can trade at a discount to intrinsic value. Consider the situation from the viewpoint of a conversion arbitrage. If one buys stock, buys puts, and sells calls, he has a conversion arbitrage. In the case of a European exercise option, he is forced to carry the position to expiration in order to remove it: he cannot exercise early, nor can he be called early. Therefore, his carrying costs will always be the maximum value to expiration. These carrying costs are the amount of the discount of the put value.

For a deeply in-the-money put, the discount will be equal to the carrying charges required to carry the striking price to expiration,

$$\text{carry} = s\left[1 - \frac{1}{(1 + r)^t} \right]$$

Less deeply in-the-money puts, that is, those with deltas less than -1.00, would not require the full discounting factor. Rather, one could multiply the discounting factor by the absolute value of put's delta to arrive at the appropriate discounting factor.

Futures Options

A modified Black-Scholes model, called the Black Model, can be used to evaluate futures options. See the chapter on futures for a futures discussion. Essentially, the adjustment is as follows: use 0% as the risk-free rate in the Black-Scholes model and obtain a theoretical call value; then discount that result.

Black model:

Call value $= e^{-rt} \times$ Black-Scholes Call Value [using $r = 0\%$]

where

r is the risk-free interest rate

and t is the time to expiration in years

The relationship between a futures call theoretical value and that of a put can also be discussed from the model:

$$\text{Call} = \text{Put} + e^{-rt}(f - s)$$

where

    f is the futures price
and s is the striking price

    Example: The following prices exist:

            ZYX Cash Index: 174.49
            ZYX December future: 177.00

    There are 80 days remaining until expiration, the volatility of ZYX is 15%, and the risk-free interest rate is 6%.

    In order to evaluate the theoretical value of a ZYX Dec 185 call, the following steps would be taken:

1. evaluate the regular Black-Scholes model using 185 as the strike, 177.00 as the stock price, 15% as the volatility, 0.22 as the time remaining (80/365), *and 0% as the interest rate.* Note that the *futures price,* not the Index price, is input to the model as stock price.

    Suppose that this yields a result of 2.05

2. discount the result from step 1:

$$\text{Black model call value} = e^{-(.06 \times 0.22)} \times 2.05$$

$$= 2.02$$

    In this case, the difference between the Black model and the Black-Scholes model is small (2 cents). However, the discounting factor can be large for longer-term or deeply in-the-money options.

    The other items of a mathematical nature that were discussed in Chapter 30 are applicable, without change, to index options. Expected return and implied volatility have the same meaning. Implied volatility can be calculated by using the Black-Scholes formulas as specified above.

    Neutral positioning retains its meaning as well. Recall that any of the above theoretical value computations gives the delta of the option as a by-product. These deltas can be used for cash-based and futures options just as they are used for stock options to maintain a neutral position. This is done, of course, by calculating the equivalent stock position (or equivalent "index" or "futures" position, in these cases).

Follow-up Action

The various types of follow-up action that were applicable to stock options are available for index options as well. In fact, when one has spread options on the same underlying index, these actions are virtually the same.

However, when one is doing inter-index spreads, there is another type of follow-up picture that is useful. The reason for this is that the spread will have different outcomes based not only on the price of one index, but also based on that index's relationship to the other index.

It is possible, for example, that a mildly bullish strategy implemented as an inter-index spread might actually lose money even if one index rose. This could happen if the other index performed in a manner that was not desirable. If one could have his computer "draw" a picture of several different outcomes, he would have a better idea of the profit potential of his strategy.

Example: Assume a put spread between the ZYX and the ABX indices was established. An ABX June 180 put was bought at 3.00 and a ZYX June 175 put was sold at 3, when the ZYX was at 175 and the ABX Index was at 178.00. This spread will obviously have different outcomes if the price of the ZYX and the ABX move in dramatically different patterns.

On the surface, this would appear to be a bearish position—long a put at a higher strike and short a put at a lower strike. However, the position could make money even in a rising market if the indices move appropriately: If, at expiration, the ZYX and ABX are both at 179.00, for example, then the short option expires worthless and the long option is still worth 1.00. This would mean that a 1-point profit, or $500, was made in the spread ($1,500 profit on the short ZYX puts less a $1,000 loss on the one ABX put).

Conversely, a downward movement doesn't guarantee profits either. If the ZYX falls to 170.00 while the ABX declines to 175.00, then both puts would be worth 5 at expiration and there would be no gain or loss in the spread.

What the strategist needs in order to better understand his position is a "sliding scale" picture. That is, most follow-up pictures gives the outcome (say at expiration) of the position at various stock or index prices. That is still needed: One would want to see the outcome for ZYX prices of, say, 165 up to 185 in the example. However, in this spread something else is needed: The outcome should also take into account how the ZYX matches up with the ABX. Thus, one might need three (or more) tables of outcomes, each of which depicts the results as ZYX ranges from 165 up to 185 at expiration: One might first show how the results would look if ZYX were, say, 5 points below ABX; then another table would show ZYX and ABX unchanged from their original relationship (a 3-point differential); finally, another table would show the results if ZYX and ABX were equal at expiration.

If the relationship between the two indices were at 3 points at expiration, such a table might look like this:

	Price of Expiration				
ZYX	165	170	175	180	185
ABX	168	173	178	183	188
ZYX Jun 175P	10	5	0	0	0
ABX Jun 180P	12	7	2	0	0
Profit	+$1,000	+$1,000	+$1,000	0	0

This picture indicates that the position is neutral to bearish, since it makes money even if the indices are unchanged. However, contrast this with the situation in which the ZYX falls to a level 5 points below the ABX by expiration.

	Price at Expiration				
ZYX	165	170	175	180	185
ABX	170	175	180	185	190
ZYX Jun 175P	10	5	0	0	0
ABX Jun 180P	10	5	0	0	0
Profit	0	0	0	0	0

In this case, the spread has no potential for profit at all, even if the market collapses. Thus, even a bearish spread like this might not prove profitable if there is an adverse movement in the relationship of the indices.

Finally, observe what happens if the ZYX rallies so strongly that it catches up to the ABX.

	Price at Expiration				
ZYX	165	170	175	180	185
ABX	165	170	175	180	185
ZYX Jun 175P	10	5	0	0	0
ABX Jun 180P	15	10	5	0	0
Profit	+$2,500	+$2,500	+$2,500	+$2,500	+$2,500

These tables can be called "sliding scale" tables, because what one is actually doing is showing a different set of results by sliding the ABX scale over slightly each time while keeping the ZYX scale fixed. Note that in the above two tables, the ZYX results are unchanged, but the ABX has been slid over slightly to show a different result. Tables like this are necessary for the strategist who is doing spreads in options with different underlying indices or trader inter-index spreads.

This concludes the chapter on riskless arbitrage and mathematical modeling. Recall that arbitrage in stock options can affect stock prices. The arbitrage techniques outlined here do not affect the indices themselves. That is done by the market basket hedges. It was also known that no new models are necessary for evaluation. For index options, one merely has to properly evaluate the dividend for usage in the standard Black-Scholes model. Future options can be evaluated by setting the risk-free interest rate to 0% in the Black-Scholes model and discounting the result, which is the Black model.

Chapter *36*

Futures and Futures Options

In the previous chapters on index trading, a particular type of futures option—the index option—was described in some detail. In this chapter, some background information on futures themselves will be spelled out, and then the broad category of futures options will be investigated. In recent years, options have been listed on many types of futures as well as some physical entities. These include options on things as diverse as gold futures and cattle futures, as well as options on currency and bond futures.

Much of the information in this chapter will be concerned with describing the ways that futures options are similar to, or different from, ordinary equity and index options. There are certain strategies that can be developed specifically for futures options as well. However, it should be noted that once one understands an option strategy, it is generally applicable no matter what the underlying instrument is. That is, a bull spread in gold options entails the same general risks and rewards as does a bull spread in any stock's options—limited downside risk and limited upside profit potential. The gold bull spread would make its maximum profit if gold futures were above the higher strike of the spread at expiration, just as an equity option bull spread would do if the stock were above the higher strike at expiration. Consequently, it would be a waste of time and space to go over the same strategies again, substituting soybeans or orange juice futures, say, for XYZ stock in all the examples that have been given in the previous chapters of this book. Rather, the concentration will be on areas where there is truly a new or different strategy that futures options provide.

Before beginning, it should be pointed out that futures contracts and futures options have far less standardization than equity or index options do. Most futures trade in different units. Most options have different expiration months, expiration times, and striking price intervals. All the different contract specificatiors will not be spelled out here. One should contact his broker or the exchange where the contracts are traded in order to receive complete details. However, whenever examples are used, full details of the contracts used in those examples will be given.

FUTURES CONTRACTS

Before getting into options on futures, a few words about futures contracts themselves may prove beneficial. Recall that a futures contract is a standardized contract calling for the delivery of a specified quantity of a certain commodity at some future time. Future contracts are listed on a wide variety of commodities and financial instruments. In some cases, one must make or take delivery of a specific quantity of a physical commodity (50,000 bushels of soybeans, for example). These are known as futures on physicals. In others, the futures settle for cash as do the S&P 500 Index futures described in previous chapter; there are other futures that have this same feature (Eurodollar time deposits, for example). These types of futures are cash-based, or cash settlement, futures.

In terms of total number of contracts listed on the various exchanges, the more common type of futures contract is one with a physical commodmodity underlying it. These are sometimes broken down into sub-categories, such as agricultural futures (those on soybeans, oats, coffee, or orange juice) and financial futures (those on U.S. Treasury bonds, bills, and notes).

Hedging

The primary economic function of futures markets is hedging—taking a futures position to offset the risk of actually owning the physical commodity. The physical commodity or financial instrument is known as the "cash." For index futures, this hedging was designed to remove the risk from owning stocks (the "cash market" that underlies index futures). A portfolio manager who owned a large quantity of stocks could sell index futures against them to remove much of the price risk of that stock ownership. Moreover, he is able to establish that hedge at a much smaller commission cost and with much less work than would be required to sell thousands of shares of stock. Similar thinking applies to all the cash markets that underlie futures contracts. The ability to hedge is important for people who must deal in the "cash" market because it gives them price protection as well as allowing them to be more efficient in their pricing and profitability. A general example may be useful to demonstrate the hedging concept.

Example: An international businessman based in the United States obtains a large contract to supply a Swiss manufacturer. The manufacturer wishes to pay in Swiss francs, but the payment is not due until the goods are delivered 6 months from now. The U.S. businessman is obviously delighted to have the contract, but perhaps is not so delighted to have the contract paid in francs 6 months from now. If the U.S. dollar becomes stronger relative to the Swiss franc, the U.S. businessman will be receiving fewer dollars for his contract than he originally thought he would. In fact, if he is working on a narrow profit margin, he might even suffer a loss if the Swiss franc becomes too weak with respect to the dollar.

A futures contract on the Swiss franc may be appropriate for the U.S. businessman. He is "long" Swiss francs via his contract (that is, he will get francs in 6 months, so he is exposed to their fluctuations during that time). He might sell short a Swiss franc futures contract that expires in 6 months in order to lock in his current profit margin. Once he sells the future he locks in a profit no matter what happens.

The future's profit and loss is measured in dollars since it trades on a U.S. exchange. If the Swiss franc becomes stronger over the 6-month period, he will lose money on futures sale, but will receive more dollars for the sale of his products. Conversely, if the franc becomes weak, he will receive less dollars from the Swiss businessman, but his futures contract sale will show a profit. In either case, the futures contract enables him to lock in a future price (hence the name "futures") that is profitable to him at today's level.

The reader should note that there are certain specific factors that the hedger must take into consideration. Recall that the hedger of stocks faces possible problems when he sells futures to hedge his stock portfolio. First, there is the problem of selling futures below their fair value; changes in interest rates or dividend payouts can affect the hedge as well. The U.S. businessman who is attempting to hedge his Swiss Francs may face similar problems. Certain items such as short-term interest rates, which affect the cost of carry, and other factors may cause the Swiss Franc futures to trade at a premium or discount to the cash price. That is, there is not necessarily a complete one-to-one relationship between the futures price and the cash price. However, the point is that the businessman is able to substantially reduce the currency risk, since in six months there could be a large change in the relationship of the U.S. dollar and the Swiss Franc. While his hedge might not eliminate every bit of the risk, it will certainly get rid of a very large portion of it.

Speculating

While the hedgers provide the economic function of futures, speculators provide the liquidity. The attraction for speculators is leverage. One is able to trade futures with very little margin. Thus, large percentages of profits and losses are possible.

Example: A futures contract on cotton is for 50,000 pounds of cotton. Assume the March cotton future is trading at 60 (that is 60 cents per pound). Thus one is controlling $30,000 worth of cotton by owning this contract ($0.60 per pound × 50,000 pounds). However, assume the exchange minimum margin is $1,500. That is, one only has to initially have $1,500 to trade this contract. This means that one can trade cotton on 5% margin ($1,500/$30,000 = 5%).

What is the profit or risk potential here? A one cent move in cotton, from 60 to 61, would generate a profit of $500. One can always determine what a one-cent move is worth as long as he knows the contract size. For cotton the size is 50,000 pounds, so a one cent move is 0.01 × 50,000 = $500.

Consequently, if cotton were to fall three cents, from 60 to 57, this speculator would lose 3 × $500, or $1,500—his entire initial investment. Alternatively, a 3-cent move to the upside would generate a profit of $1,500, a 100% profit.

This example clearly demonstrates the large risks and rewards facing a speculator in futures contracts. Certain brokerage firms may require the speculator to place more initial margin than the exchange minimum. Usually, the most active customers who have a sufficient net worth are allowed to trade at the exchange minimum margins; other customers may have to put up two or three times as much initial margin in order to trade. This still allows for a lot of leverage, but not as much as the speculator who is trading with exchange minimum margins. Initial margin requirements can be in the form of cash or Treasury Bills. Obviously, if one uses Treasury Bills to satisfy his initial margin requirements, he can be earning interest on that money while it serves as collateral for his initial margin requirements. If he uses cash for the initial requirement, he will not earn interest (note: some large customers do earn credit on the cash used for margin requirements in their futures accounts, but most customers do not).

A speculator will also be required to keep his account current daily through the use of maintenance margin. His account is marked to market daily, so unrealized gains and losses are taken into account as well as are realized ones. If his account loses money, he must add cash into the account or sell out some of his Treasury Bills in order to cover the loss, on a daily basis. However, if he makes money, that unrealized profit is available to be withdrawn or used for another investment.

Example: The cotton speculator from the above example sees the price of the March cotton futures contract he owns fall from 60.00 to 59.20 on the first day he owns it. This means there is a $400 unrealized loss in his account, since his holding went down in price by 0.80 cents and a one cent move is worth $500. He must add $400 to his account, or sell out $400 worth of T-Bills.

The next day, rumors of a drought in the growing areas send cotton prices much higher. The March future closes at 60.90, up 1.70 from the previous day's close. That represents a gain of $850 on the day. The entire $850 could be withdrawn, or used as initial margin for another futures contract, or transferred to one's stock market account to be used to purchase another investment there.

Without speculators, a futures contract would not be successful, for the speculators provide liquidity. Volatility attracts speculators. If the contract is not trading and open interest is small, the contract may be delisted. The various futures exchanges can delist futures just as stocks can be delisted by the New York Stock Exchange. However, when stocks are delisted, they merely trade over-the-counter, since the corporation itself still exists. When futures are delisted, they disappear—there is no "over-the-counter futures market". Futures exchanges are generally more aggressive in listing new products, and delisting them if necessary, than are stock exchanges.

Terms

Futures contracts have certain standardized terms associated with them. However, trading in each separate commodity is like trading an entirely different product. The standardized terms for soybeans are completely different than those for cocoa, for example, as might well be expected. The size of the contract (50,000 pounds in the cotton example) is often based on the historical size of commodity delivered to market; at other times it is merely a contrived number ($100,000 face amount of U.S. Treasury bonds, for example).

Also, futures contracts have expiration dates. For some commodities, crude oil and its products—heating oil and unleaded gasoline—there is a futures contract for every month of the year. Other commodities may have expirations in only 5 or 6 calendar months of the year. These items are listed along with the quotes in a good financial newspaper, so they are not difficult to discover.

The number of expiration months listed at any one time varies from one commodity to another. Eurodollar Time Deposits and U.S. Treasury bonds have futures contracts expiring every three months for the next three or four years; soybean contracts have expirations reaching just over one year from the current date; S&P 500 futures expirations are always all less than one year.

Moreover, the day of the expiration month on which trading ceases is different for each commodity as well. It is not standardized, as the third Friday is for stock and index options.

Trading hours are different, even for different commodities listed on the same futures exchange. For example, U.S. Treasury Bond futures, which are listed on the Chicago Board of Trade, have very long trading hours (currently 8:20 a.m. to 3 p.m. and also 7 p.m. to 10:30 p.m. every day, Eastern time). But, on the same exchange, soybean futures trade a very short day (10:30 a.m. to 2:15 p.m., Eastern time). Some markets alter their trading hours occasionally, while others have been fixed for years. For example, as the foreign demand for U.S. Treasury Bond futures increases, the trading hours might expand even further. However, the grain markets have been using these trading hours for decades, and there is little reason to expect them to change in the future.

Units of trading vary for different futures contracts as well. Grain futures trade in eighths of a point, 30 year bond futures trade in thirty-seconds of a point, while the S&P 500 futures trade in 5 cent increments (0.05). Again, it is the responsibility of the trader to familiarize himself with the units of trading in the futures market if he is going to be trading there.

Each futures contract has its own margin requirements as well. These conform to the type of margin that was described with respect to the cotton example above. An initial margin may be advanced in the form of collateral, and then daily mark-to-market price movement are paid for in cash or by selling some of the collateral. Recall that maintenance margin is the term for the daily mark to market.

Finally, futures are subject to position limits. This is to prevent any one entity from attempting to corner the market in a particular delivery month of a commodity. Different futures have different position limits. This is normally only of interest to hedgers or very large speculators. The exchange where the futures trade defines the position limit.

Trading Limits

Most futures contracts have some limit on their maximum daily price change. For index futures, it was shown that the limits are designed to act like circuit breakers to prevent the stock market from crashing. Trading limits exist in many futures contracts in order to help ensure that the market cannot be manipulated by someone forcing the price to move tremendously in one direction or the other. Another reason for having trading limits is ostensibly to allow only a fixed move, approximately equal to or slightly less than the amount covered by the initial margin requirement, so that maintenance margin can be collected if need be. However, limits have been applied to all futures, some which don't really seem to warrant a limit—U.S. Treasury Bonds, for example. The bond issue is too large to manipulate, and there is a liquid "cash" bond market to hedge with.

Regardless, limits are a fact of life in futures trading. Each individual commodity has its own limits, and those limits may change depending on how the exchange views the volatility of that commodity. For example, when gold was trading wildly at a price of more than $700 per ounce, gold futures had a larger daily trading limit than they do at more stable levels of $300 to $400 an ounce (the current limit is a $15 move per day). If a commodity reaches its limit repeatedly for two or three days in a row, the exchange will usually increase the limit to allow for more price movement. The Chicago Board of Trade automatically increases limits by 50% if a futures contract trades at the limit three days in a row.

Whenever limits exist there is always the possibility that they can totally destroy the liquidity of a market. The actual commodity underlying the futures contract is called the "spot" and trades at the "spot price." The spot trades without a limit, of course. Thus it is possible that the spot commodity can increase in price tremendously while the futures contract can only advance the daily limit each day. This scenario means that the futures could trade "up or down the limit" for a number of days in a row. As a consequence, no one would want to sell the futures if they were trading up the limit, since the spot was much higher, and therefore there is no trading in the futures—they are merely quoted as bid up the limit and no trades take place. This is disastrous for short sellers. They may be wiped out without ever having the chance to close out their positions. This sometimes happens to orange juice futures when an unexpected severe freeze hits Florida. Options can help alleviate the illiquidity caused by limit moves. That topic will be covered later in this chapter.

Delivery

Futures on physical commodities can be assigned, much like stock options can be assigned. When a futures contract is assigned, the *buyer* of the contract is called upon to receive the full contract. Delivery is at the seller's option, meaning that the owner of the contract is informed that he must take delivery. Thus, if a corn contract is assigned, one is forced to receive

5,000 bushels of corn. The old adage about this being dumped in your yard is untrue. One merely receives a warehouse receipt and is charged for storage. His broker makes the actual arrangements. Futures contracts cannot be assigned at any time during their life, as options can. Rather, there is a short period of time before they expire during which one can take delivery. This is generally a 4- to 6-week period and is called the "notice period"—the time during which one can be notified to accept delivery. The first day upon which the futures contract may be assigned is called the "first notice day," for logical reasons. Speculators close out their positions before the first notice day, leaving the rest of the trading up to the hedgers. Such considerations are not necessary for cash-based futures contracts (the index futures), since there is no physical commodity involved.

It is always possible to make a mistake, of course, and receive an assignment when you didn't intend to. Your broker will normally be able to reverse the trade for you, but it will cost you the warehouse fees and generally at least one commission.

The terms of the futures contract specify exactly what quantity of the commodity must be delivered, and also specify what form it must be in. Normally this is straightforward, as is the case with gold futures: That contract calls for delivery of 100 Troy ounces of gold that is at least 0.995 fine, cast either in one bar or in three one-kilogram bars.

However, in some cases, the commodity necessary for delivery is more complicated, as is the case with Treasury-Bond futures. The futures contract is stated in terms of a nominal 8% interest rate. However, at any time, it is likely that the prevailing interest rate for long-term Treasury Bonds will not be 8%. Therefore, the delivery terms of the futures contract allow for delivery of bonds with other interest rates.

Notice that the delivery is at the *seller's option*. Thus, if one is short the futures and doesn't realize that first notice day has passed, he has no problem, for delivery is under his control. It is only those traders holding long futures who may receive a surprise delivery notice.

One must be familiar with the specific terms of the contract and its methods of delivery if he expects to deal in the physical commodity. Such details on each futures contract are readily available from both the exchange and one's broker. However, most futures traders never receive or deliver the physical commodity—they close out their futures contract before the time at which they can be called upon to make delivery.

Pricing of Futures

It is beyond the scope of this book to describe futures arbitrage versus the cash commodity. Suffice it to say that this arbitrage is done—more in some markets (U.S. Treasury bonds, for example) than others (soybeans).

Therefore, futures can be overpriced or underpriced as well. The arbitrage possibilities would be calculated in a manner similar to that described for index futures—the futures premium versus cash being the determining factor.

OPTIONS ON FUTURES

The reader is somewhat familiar with options on futures, having seen many examples of index futures options. The commercial use of the option is to lock in a worst case price as opposed to a future price. The U.S. businessman from the earlier example sold Swiss franc futures to lock in a future price. However, he might decide instead to buy Swiss franc futures put options to hedge his downside risk, but still leave room for upside profits if the currency markets move in his favor.

Description

A futures option is an option on the futures contract, not the cash commodity. Thus if one exercises or assigns a futures option, he buys or sells the futures contract. The options are always for one contract of the underlying commodity. Splits and adjustments do not apply in the futures markets as they do for stock options. Futures options generally trade in the same denominations as the future itself (there are a few exceptions to this rule, such as the T-Bond options, which trade in sixty-fourths while the futures trade in thirty-seconds).

Example: Soybean options will be used to describe the above features of futures options.

Suppose that March soybeans are selling at 575.

Soybean quotes are in cents. Thus, 575 is $5.75—soybeans cost $5.75 per bushel. A soybean contract is for 5,000 bushels of soybeans, so a one cent move is worth $50 (5,000 × .01).

Suppose the following option prices exist. The dollar cost of the options is also shown (one cent is worth $50).

Option	Price	Dollar Cost
March 525 put	5	$250
March 550 call	35½	$1,775
March 600 call	8¼	$412.50

The actual dollar cost is not necessary for the option strategist to determine the profitability of a certain strategy. For example, if one buys the March 600 call, he needs March soybean futures to be trading at $608\frac{1}{4}$ or higher at expiration in order to have a profit at that time. This is the normal way in which a call buyer views his breakeven point at expiration: strike price plus cost of the call. It is not necessary to know that soybean options are worth $50 per point in order to know that $608\frac{1}{4}$ is the breakeven price at expiration.

If the future is a cash settlement future (Eurodollar, S&P 500, and other indices), then the options and futures generally expire simultaneously at the end of trading on the last trading day. (Actually, the S&P's expire on the next morning's opening). However, options on physical futures will expire before the first notice day of the actual futures contract in order to give traders time to close out their positions before receiving a delivery notice. The fact that the option expires in advance of the expiration of the underlying future has a slightly odd effect: the option often expires in the month *preceding* the month used to describe it.

Example: Options on March soybean futures are referred to as "March options." They do not actually expire in March—however, the soybean *futures* do.

The rather arcane definition of the last trading day for soybean options is "the last Friday preceding the last business day of the month prior to the contract month by at least 5 business days"!

Thus, the March soybean options actually expire in February. Assume that the last Friday of February is the 23rd. If there is no holiday during the business week of February 19th to 23rd, then the soybean options will expire on Friday, February 16th, which is 5 business days before the last Friday of February.

However, if President's Day happened to fall on Monday, February 19th, then there would only be four business days during the week of the 19th to the 23rd, so the options would have to expire one Friday earlier, on February 9th.

Not too simple, right? The best thing to do is to have a futures and options expiration calendar that one can refer to. *Futures Magazine* publishes a yearly calendar in its December issue, annually, as well as monthly calendars which are published each month of the year. Alternatively, your broker should be able to provide you with the information.

In any case, the March soybean futures options expire in February, well in advance of the first notice day for March soybeans, which is the last business day of the month preceding the expiration month (February 28th in this case). The futures option trader must be careful not to assume that there is a long time between option expiration and first notice day of the futures contract. In certain commodities, the futures first notice day is the day after the options expire (live cattle futures, for example).

Thus, *if one is long calls or short puts and, therefore, acquires a long futures contract via exercise or assignment, respectively, he should be aware of when the first notice day of the futures is; he could receive a delivery notice on his long futures position unexpectedly if he is not paying attention.*

Other Terms

Striking Price Intervals. Just as futures on differing physical commodities have differing terms, so do options on those futures. Striking price intervals are a prime example. Some options have striking prices 5 points apart, while others have strikes only 1 point apart, reflecting the volatility of the futures contract. Specifically, S&P 500 options have striking prices 5 points apart, while soybean options striking prices are 25 points (25 cents) apart, and gold options are 10 points ($10) apart. Moreover, as is often the case with stocks, the striking price differential for a particular commodity may change if the price of the commodity itself is vastly different:

Example: Gold is quoted in dollars per ounce. Depending on the price of the futures contract, the striking price interval may be changed. The current rules are:

Striking Price Interval	Price of Futures
$10	below $500/oz.
$20	between $500 and $1,000/oz.
$50	above $1,000/oz.

Thus, when gold futures are more expensive, the striking prices are farther apart. Note that gold has never traded above $1,000/oz., but the option exchanges are all set if it does.

This variability in the striking prices is common for many commodities. In fact, some commodities alter the striking price interval depending on how much time is remaining until expiration, possibly in addition to the actual price of the futures themselves. Sugar is one such contract:

Example: Sugar futures are quoted in cents per pound. Not only do the sugar futures options have different striking price intervals based on the actual price of sugar futures, but the intervals are also changed, based on the time remaining until expiration of the futures.

At any one time there are options listed on six different futures expirations. Suppose that, at the current time, there are options on sugar futures that expire in March, April, May, July, October, and December. The rules for striking price intervals on these options state that the two nearby months may have narrower stiking price intervals than the longer term contracts.

| Striking Price Interval: | | Price of |
Two Near Months	Other Months	Sugar Futures
$.005	$.01	below $.10/lb
$.01	$.01	between $.10 and $.16/lb
$.01	$.02	between $.16 and $.40/lb
$.02	$.04	above $.40/lb

Hence, if sugar is currently trading at 8 cents/lb., then there would be March options with strikes of 7, 7½, 8, 8½, 9, etc. But the *May* options would have strikes of 7, 8, 9, etc., since May is the third month out, while March is one of the two nearby months.

Realizing that the striking price intervals may change—that is, that new strikes will be added when the contract nears maturity—may help to plan some strategies, as it will give more choices to the strategist as to which options he can use to hedge or adjust his position.

Automatic Exercise. Most futures options are *not* subject to automatic exercise as are stock options. This is an unfair practice, for an option holder may lose a great deal of money merely because he made a mistake and forgot it was an expiration day. However, it is the way the rules are currently made. Thus, *a futures option holder must be sure to issue specific exercise notices if he has an in-the-money option and is planning on exercising it.* Your broker should clearly warn you beforehand that you have an option that is expiring, but that is not a foolproof safeguard, like automatic exercise. Your broker can also tell you, of course, which futures options *do* have automatic exercise privileges.

Expiration Series. Futures options may not be listed for every contract that exists within a particular commodity. For example, it was stated earlier that Eurodollar Time Deposit futures expirations can carry nearly four years out—they expire every 3 months for 16 expirations (Mar '92, June '92, . . . , Sep '95, Dec '95). However, of those 16 Eurodollar futures, there are listed options trading only on the nearest 8 expirations.

Serial Options

In addition to the expiration series that match futures expirations, there are other options series that may be listed as well. These are called serial options and they are futures options whose expiration month is *not* the same as their corresponding underlying futures.

Example: Gold futures expire in February, April, June, August, October, and December. There are options that expire in those months as well. Notice that these expirations are spaced two months apart. Thus, when one gold contract expires, there are two months remaining until the next one expires.

Most option traders recognize that the heaviest activity in an option series is in the nearest-term option. If the nearest-term option has two months remaining until expiration, it will not draw the trading interest that a shorter-term option would.

Recognizing this fact, the exchange has decided that *in addition to the regular expiration, there will be an option contract that expires in the nearest non-cycle month.* That is, in the nearest month that does not have an actual gold future expiring. So, if it were currently January 1st, there might be gold options expiring in February, *March*, April, etc.

Thus, the March option would be a *serial option.* There is no actual March gold future. Rather, the March options would be exercisable into April futures.

Serial options are exercisable into the nearest actual futures contract that exists after the options' expiration date. The number of serial option expirations depends on the underlying commodity. For example, gold will always have at least one serial option trading, per the definition highlighted in the example above. Certain futures whose expirations are three months apart (S&P 500 and all currency options) have serial options for the nearest *two* months that are not represented by an actual futures contract. Sugar, on the other hand, has only one serial option expiration per year—in December—to span the gap that exists between the normal October and March sugar futures expirations.

Strategists trading in options that may have serial expirations should be careful in how they evaluate their strategy. For example, June S&P 500 futures options strategies can be planned with respect to where the underlying S&P 500 Index of stocks will be at expiration, for the June options are exercisable into the June futures, which settle at the same price as the Index itself on the last day of trading. However, if one is trading *April* S&P 500 options, he must plan his strategy on where the *June* futures contract is going to be trading at *April* expiration. The April options are exercisable into the June futures at April expiration. Since the June futures contract will still have some time premium in it in April, the strategist cannot plan his strategy with respect to where the actual S&P 500 Index will be in April.

Example: The S&P 500 Stock Index (symbol SPX) is trading at 410.50. The following prices exist:

	Options	
Cash (SPX): 410.50	April 415 call: 5.00	
June futures: 415.00	June 415 call: 10.00	

If one buys the June 415 call for 10.00, he knows that the SPX Index will have to rise to 425.00 in order for his call purchase to break even at June expiration. Since the SPX is currently at 410.50, a rise of 14.50 by the cash index itself will be necessary for breakeven at June expiration.

However, a similar analysis will not work for calculating the break-even price for the April 415 call at April expiration. Since 5.00 points are being paid for the 415 call, the breakeven at April expiration is 420. But exactly what needs to be at 420? The *June* future, since that is what the April calls are exercisable into.

Currently, the June futures are trading at a premium of 4.50 to the cash Index (415.00 − 410.50). However, by April expiration, the fair value of that premium will have shrunk. Suppose that fair value is projected to be 3.50 premium at April expiration. Then the SPX would have to be at 416.50 in order for the June futures to be fairly valued at 420.00 (416.50 + 3.50 = 420.00).

Consequently, the SPX cash Index would have to rise 6 points, from 410.50 to 416.50, in order for the June futures to trade at 420 at April expiration. If this happened, the April 415 call purchase would breakeven at expiration.

Quote symbols for futures options are, simply stated, a nightmare. Whereas stock options are standardized, and plans are being made to put even more standardization in stock and index option quotes, futures option quote symbols are not. The expiration *month* symbol of futures and futures options is not the difficult part of quoting futures options. Table 36-1 provides the month symbols for futures or futures options.

Determining quote symbols for striking prices is where things begin to break down. In some cases, striking price symbols are similar to those used for stock options (B = 10, C = 15, etc.). In others, letters are used incrementally (A = 1, B = 2, C = 3, etc.), so that a striking price of 45 might be quoted as "DE." To make matters worse, different quote vendors

TABLE 36-1.
Month symbols for futures or futures options.

Futures or Futures Options Expiration Month	Month Symbol
January	F
February	G
March	H
April	J
May	K
June	M
July	N
August	Q
September	U
October	V
November	X
December	Z

often have different methods of quoting options. The more user friendly quote vendors have gone to a system of using numbers instead of letters for the striking price (Silver March 500 calls would be quoted as SVHC500—"SV" for silver, "H" for March, "C" for call, and 500 for the striking price). This method will, hopefully, be adopted throughout the industry.

If a strategist is going to be repeatedly requesting quotes on different futures options, he would best be served using a quote vendor that displays an entire page of quotes without needing each one requested separately by symbol. He could therefore see many futures options quotes on one screen of his quote machine.

Bid-Offer Spread. Even if one goes through the tedious process to find the quote symbol for an individual option, it is likely that all he will be able to see when he quotes it is the last sale price. The actual markets—bids and offers—for most futures options are not generally available from quote vendors (options traded on the Chicago Merc are usually a pleasant exception). The same is true for futures contracts themselves. One can always request a market from the trading floor, but that is a time-consuming process and is impractical if one is attempting to analyze a large number of options. Strategists who are used to dealing in stock or index options will find this to be a major inconvenience. The situation has persisted for years and shows no sign of improving.

Commissions. Futures traders generally pay a commission only on the closing side of a trade. If a speculator first buys gold futures, he pays no commissions at that time. Later, when he sells what he is long—closes his position—he is charged a commission. This is referred to as a "round turn" commission for obvious reason. However, futures *option* commissions are charged on every buy and sell.

In either case, commissions are negotiated to a flat rate by many traders. Discount futures commission merchants (i.e., brokerage houses) often attract business this way.

Example: A customer works out an agreement with his broker to pay commissions of $30 per round turn on futures, and $15 "per side" on futures option trades. It is typical for the option commission to be one-half the round turn commission, essentially equalizing the two, since option commissions are paid on both the opening and closing transaction.

A customer buys corn at 265 ($2.65 per bushel). Later, he sells it at 275, making 10 cents, or $500 (corn profits and losses are $50 per cent, as are soybeans). When he sells the corn futures, he will also be charged the $30 commission, resulting in a net profit of $470 on this trade.

In general, this method of paying commissions is to the customer's benefit. However, it does have a hidden effect that the option trader should pay attention to. This effect makes it potentially more profitable to trade options on some futures than on others.

Example: The same customer pays $15 in option commissions per side. Since option commissions are $15 and corn options are worth $50 per cent, he is paying 0.30 of a point every time he trades a corn option (15/50 = .30).

Now, consider the same customer trading options on the S&P 500 futures. The S&P 500 futures and options are worth $500 per point. So, he is paying only 0.03 of a point to trade S&P 500 options. (15/500 = .03)

He clearly stands a much better chance of making money in an S&P 500 option than he does in a corn option. He could buy an S&P option at 5.00 and sell it at 5.10 and make .04 points profit. However, with corn options, if he buys an option at 5, he needs to sell it at $5\frac{5}{8}$ to make money— a substantial difference between the two contracts. In fact, if he is participating in spread strategies and trading many options, the differential is even more important.

Position limits exist for futures options. While the limits for financial futures are generally large, other futures—especially agricultural ones— may have small limits. A large speculator who is doing spreads might inadvertently exceed a smaller limit. Therefore, one should check with his broker for exact limits in the various futures options before acquiring a large position.

Cessation of Trading. Futures options do not necessarily *cease trading* at uniform times. Most futures options on physicals do not expire at the end of the trading day as do stock and index options. The reader may recall that, initially, stock options—on their last trading day—used to cease trading 1 hour before the close of the stock market. The initial purpose of this rule was to allow option buyers and sellers time to tally their final position and hedge it, if necessary, in the stock market. This rule was eliminated for stocks some time ago. Stock and index options now trade until the close of the stock market even on their last trading day.

As mentioned earlier, options on cash settlement futures (indices and Eurodollars) generally cease trading at the same time on the last day of the futures contract. However, most other futures options—those on physical commodities—expire during the trading day, in the same way that stock options once did. Moreover, recall that this last trading day for options on physicals is generally well in advance of the actual futures expiration.

This early cessation of trading in the options may be unfamiliar to some traders. It means that the option strategist must still pay close attention to the underlying market until it closes on that trading day. He cannot ignore the futures trading merely because the options have ceased trading. An example may help to demonstrate how the strategist might deal with a large trading move after the options have stopped trading, but before the underlying future closes for the day.

Example: An option holder owns 10 calls on soybean futures, and today is the last day of trading in the options. The calls have a striking price of 600, which, for soybeans, actually means 6 dollars per bushel. These calls are on November soybeans, and the November soybean futures contract is currently trading at 590.

Soybean options cease trading more than one hour before the futures close for the day. So, one hour before the close, suppose that November soybeans were still trading at 590. It thus appears that the calls are going to expire worthless and the option holder will lose his entire investment in them.

However, during the last hour of trading in the futures—after the options have ceased trading—a rally occurs in the grain markets. There are many fundamental factors that could cause such a rally: foreign buying of grain, for example. In any case, November soybeans rally to 603. What should the option holder do?

Since the options have ceased trading, the option holder must trade the futures against his call holding. Note that he still owns the calls and can still exercise them. They haven't expired yet, they have just ceased trading. The safest tack to take is to sell short enough November soybean futures to hedge the long call holding. By doing so, the option holder recoups something—3 points in this case—for his calls which appeared to be expiring worthless. At the close of trading in the futures, the calls would be exercised. This exercise would buy back—at 600—the short sale of the futures and the position would be closed. This strategy locks in a price of 3 for the calls. Note that when one approaches the situation in this manner, he could benefit substantially if the November soybean futures suddenly fell after he had shorted them, and they dropped back below 600, the striking price of the calls.

A more aggressive stance would be for the call holder to merely let the November soybeans run to the upside and exercise his calls without hedging them. He would then be long November soybeans. This presents large risk if November soybeans should open down dramatically on the next trading day.

Option Margins

Futures option margin requirements are generally more logical than equity or index option requirements. For example, if one has a conversion or reversal arbitrage in place, his requirement would be nearly zero for futures options, while it could be quite large for equity options. Moreover, futures exchanges have recently introduced a new, better way of margining futures and futures option portfolios.

SPAN Margin. The newest form of futures option margin—which is now used by nearly all of the exchanges—is the SPAN system (Standard Portfolio ANalysis of Risk). SPAN is designed to determine the entire risk of a portfolio, including all futures and options. It is a unique system in that it bases the option requirements on projected movements in the futures contracts as well as potential changes in implied volatility of the options in one's portfolio. This creates a more realistic measure of the risk than the somewhat arbitrary requirements that were previously used (called the "customer margin" system) or than those used for stock and index options.

Not all futures clearing firms automatically put their customers on SPAN margin. Some use the older customer margin system for most of their option accounts. As a strategist, it would be beneficial to be under SPAN margin. Thus, one should deal with a broker who will grant SPAN margin.

The main advantages of SPAN margin to the strategist are twofold. First, naked option margin requirements are generally less, and second, certain long option requirements are reduced as well. This second point may seem somewhat unusual—margin on long options? SPAN calculates the amount of a long option's value that is at risk for the current day. Obviously, if there is time remaining until expiration, a call option will still have some value even if the underlying futures trade down the limit.

SPAN attempts to calculate this remaining value. If that value is less than the market price of the option, the excess can be applied toward any other requirement in the portfolio! Obviously, in-the-money options would have a greater excess value under this system.

   How SPAN Works. Certain basic requirements are determined by the futures exchange, such as the amount of movement by the futures contract that must be margined (maintenance margin). Once that is known, the exchange's computers generate an array of potential gains and losses for the next day's trading, based on futures movement within a range of prices and based on volatility changes. These results are stored in a "risk array." There is a different risk array generated for *each* futures contract and each option contract. The clearing member (your broker) or you do not have to do any calculations other than to see how the quantities of futures and options in your portfolio are affected under the gains or losses in the SPAN risk array. The exchange does all the mathematical calculations needed to project the potential gains or losses. The results of those calculations are presented in the risk array.

   There are 16 items in the risk array: for seven different futures prices, SPAN projects a gain or loss for both increased and decreased volatility — that makes 14 items — plus SPAN also projects a profit or loss for an "extreme" upward move and an "extreme" downward move. The futures exchange determines the exact definition of "extreme," as well as defines "increased" or "decreased" volatility.

   SPAN "margin" applies to futures contracts as well, although volatility considerations don't mean anthing in terms of evaluating the actual futures risk. As a first example, consider how SPAN would evaluate the risk of a futures contract.

   Example: The S&P 500 futures will be used for this example. Suppose that the Chicago Mercantile Exchange determines that the required maintenance margin for the futures is $10,000, which represents a 20-point move by the futures (recall that S&P futures are worth $500 per point). Moreover, the exchange determines that an "extreme" move is 14 points, or $7,000 of risk.

Scenario	Long 1 Future Potential Pft/Loss
Futures unchanged; volatility up	0
Futures unchanged; volatility down	0
Futures up one-third of range; volatility up	+ 3,330

Futures up one-third of range; volatility down	+ 3,330
Futures down one-third of range; volatility up	− 3,330
Futures down one-third of range; volatility down	− 3,330
Futures up two-thirds of range; volatility up	+ 6,670
Futures up two-thirds of range; volatility down	+ 6,670
Futures down two-thirds of range; volatility up	− 6,670
Futures down two-thirds of range; volatility down	− 6,670
Futures up three-thirds of range; volatility up	+10,000
Futures up three-thirds of range; volatility down	+10,000
Futures down three-thirds of range; volatility up	**−10,000**
Futures down three-thirds of range; volatility down	−10,000
Futures up "extreme" move	+ 7,000
Futures down "extreme" move	− 7,000

The 16 array items are always displayed in this order. Note that since this array is for a futures contract, the "volatility up" and "volatility down" scenarios are always the same, since the volatility that is referred to is the one that is used as the input to an option pricing model.

Notice that the actual price of the futures contract is not needed in order to generate the risk array. *The SPAN requirement is always the largest potential loss from the array.* Thus if one were long one S&P 500 futures contract, his SPAN margin requirement would be $10,000, which occurs under the "futures down three-thirds" scenarios. This will always be the maintenance margin for a futures contract.

Now let us consider an option example. In this type of calculation, the exchange uses the same moves by the underlying futures contract and calculates the option theoretical values as they would exist on the next trading day. One calculation is performed for volatility increasing and one for volatility decreasing.

Example: Using the same S&P 500 futures contract, the following array might depict the risk array for a long December 410 call. One does not need to know the option or futures price in order to use the array — the exchange incorporates that information into the model used to generate the potential gains and losses.

Scenario	Long 1 Dec 410 call Potential Pft/Loss
Futures unchanged; volatility up	+ 460
Futures unchanged; volatility down	− 610
Futures up one-third of range; volatility up	+2,640

Futures up one-third of range; volatility down	+1,730
Futures down one-third of range; volatility up	−1,270
Futures down one-third of range; volatility down	−2,340
Futures up two-thirds of range; volatility up	+5,210
Futures up two-thirds of range; volatility down	+4,540
Futures down two-thirds of range; volatility up	−2,540
Futures down two-thirds of range; volatility down	−3,430
Futures up three-thirds of range; volatility up	+8,060
Futures up three-thirds of range; volatility down	+7,640
Futures down three-thirds of range; volatility up	−3,380
Futures down three-thirds of range; volatility down	**−3,990**
Futures up "extreme" move	+3,130
Futures down "extreme" move	−1,500

The items in the risk array are all quite logical: upward futures movements produce profits and downward futures movements produce losses in the long call position. Moreover, worse results are always obtained by using the lower volatility as opposed to the higher one. In this particular example, the SPAN requirement would be $3,990 ("futures down three-thirds; volatility down"). That is, the SPAN system predicts that you could lose $3,990 of your call value if futures fell by their entire range and volatility decreased—a "worst case" scenario. Therefore, that is the amount of margin one is required to keep for this long option position.

While the exchange does not tell us how much of an increase or decrease they use in terms of volatility, one can get something of a feel for the magnitude by looking at the first two lines of the table. The exchange is saying that if the futures are unchanged tomorrow, but volatility "increases," then the call will increase in value by $460 (92 cents); if it "decreases," however, the call will lose $610 (1.22 points) of value. These are large price changes, so one can assume that the volatility assumptions are significant.

The real ease of use of the SPAN risk arrays is when it comes to evaluating the risk of a more complicated position, or even a portfolio of options. All one needs to do is to combine the risk array factors for each option or future in the position in order to arrive at the total requirement.

Example: Using the above two examples, one can see what the SPAN requirements would be in for a covered write: long the S&P future and short the Dec 410 call.

Scenario	Long 1 S&P Future	Short 1 Dec 410 call Potential Pft/Loss	Cov'd Write
Futures unchanged; vol. up	0	− 460	− 460
Futures unchanged; vol. down	0	+ 610	+ 610
Futures up ⅓ of range; vol. up	+ 3,330	− 2,640	+ 690
Futures up ⅓ of range; vol. down	+ 3,330	− 1,730	+ 1,600
Futures down ⅓ of range; vol. up	− 3,330	+ 1,270	− 2,060
Futures down ⅓ of range; vol. down	− 3,330	+ 2,340	− 990
Futures up ⅔ of range; vol. up	+ 6,670	− 5,210	+ 1,460
Futures up ⅔ of range; vol. down	+ 6,670	− 4,540	+ 2,130
Futures down ⅔ of range; vol. up	− 6,670	+ 2,540	− 4,130
Futures down ⅔ of range; vol. down	− 6,670	+ 3,430	− 3,240
Futures up ³⁄₃ of range; vol. up	+ 10,000	− 8,060	+ 1,940
Futures up ³⁄₃ of range; vol. down	+ 10,000	− 7,640	+ 2,360
Futures down ³⁄₃ of range; vol. up	**− 10,000**	**+ 3,380**	**− 6,620**
Futures down ³⁄₃ of range; vol. down	− 10,000	+ 3,990	− 6,010
Futures up "extreme" move	+ 7,000	− 3,130	+ 3,870
Futures down "extreme" move	− 7,000	+ 1,500	− 5,500

As might be expected, the worst case projection for a covered write is for the stock to drop, but for the implied volatility to increase. The SPAN system projects that this covered writer would lose $6,620 if that happened. Thus, "futures down 3/3rds of range; volatility up" is the SPAN requirement, $6,620.

As a means of comparison, under the older "customer margin" option requirements, the requirement for a covered write was the futures margin, plus the option premium, less one-half the out-of-the-money amount. In the above example, assume the futures were at 408 and the call was trading at 8. The "customer" covered write margin would then be more than twice the SPAN requirement:

Futures margin	$10,000
Option premium	+ 4,000
¹⁄₂ out-of-money amount	− 1,000
	$13,000

Obviously, one can alter the quantities in the use of the risk array quite easily. For example, if he had a ratio write of long 3 futures and short 5 Dec 410 calls, he could easily calculate the SPAN requirement by multiplying the projected futures gains and losses by 3, multiplying the projected option gains and losses by 5, and adding the two together to obtain the total requirement. Once he had completed this calculation, his SPAN requirement would be the worst expected loss, as projected by SPAN for the next trading day.

In actual practice, the SPAN requirements are even more sophisticated: they take into account a certain minimum option margin (for deeply out-of-the-money options); they account for spreads between futures contracts on the same commodity (different expiration months); they add a delivery month charge (if you are holding a position past the first notice day); and they even allow for slightly reduced requirements for related, but different, futures spreads (T-Bills versus T-Bonds, for example).

Calculating SPAN For Yourself. The procedures for the actual calculation of SPAN requirements are too complicated for the individual clearing member or customer to bother with. However, the risk arrays are available to everyone if they want them. As a private customer, one can buy a simple computer program from the Chicago Mercantile Exchange. This program, called PC-SPAN, makes all the required calculations and prints them out in a fair amount of detail. The program only costs $100. The user inputs his positions into the program and the program does all the rest of the work.

In addition to running the program, one must be able to get the risk array data from the exchange when he wants it. This is easily accomplished since the exchanges have worked out an arrangement with Compuserve to place the risk arrays on that system each night. Then, it is a matter of using the modem on your computer to place a local telephone call (in most cases) to access the risk array data. An additional program, called Intro-Pak, costs $15 and is required in order to be able to load the risk arrays from Compuserve.

The real advantage to having this program is not so much to calculate the SPAN requirements on your present position (although you may occasionally want to check your broker to make sure he's doing the calculations correctly). Rather, its main use for the strategist is to be able to tell what the margin requirements would be for a new position that is being considered. Without the risk array data, one cannot predict his SPAN margin requirement for a proposed new position, since he does not have a simple formula to rely on like stock or equity option traders do.

Disagreement Between the Futures and Options Contracts. In virtually every case but one, the unit of trading of an option is the same as the unit of trading of the entity underlying the option. For example, a stock option is an option on 100 shares of stock, and the basic unit of trading in the stock market is 100 shares of stock; a T-Bond option is an option on $100,000 face amount of bonds and the T-Bond future is a contract on $100,000 face amount of bonds.

However, the grain options and futures are the exception to the rule. Historically, a grain *contract* consisted of 5,000 bushels, but the unit of *trading* in grain futures is 1,000 bushels. Reporting of grain trades, even including confirmation of trades to customer's account, normally includes the number of bushels traded, not the number of contracts. Thus, if one tells his broker to buy 5 November soybean futures, he would normally buy 5,000 bushels of November soybean futures, since the future is on 1,000 bushels. This would normally be reported on the customer's statement in a manner like the following: "Bought 5M Nov soybean at 592¼." The concept of a *contract* is not normally used when trading in grain futures—the number of bushels traded is what is important.

The problem arises when trading grain options because the option is an option on a grain *contract*, or 5,000 bushels. Thus, if one exercises a soybean call, for example, he would buy "5M Nov soybeans." Then, if he wanted to dispose of what he acquired through exercise, he would sell 5 November soybeans, even though he only exercised one option contract. If one is not aware of this anomaly, he could acquire a soybean futures position when he didn't mean to. The strategist, then, should be aware of what terms are being used—bushels or contracts—whenever he enters a grain order. An example will illustrate this point.

Example: In the above example, the trader owned 10 calls on November soybeans and, after the options ceased trading, the November soybean futures rallied to 603, higher than the 600 strike of the calls. The trader decides that he wants to sell soybeans short in order to recapture something for his calls. He must sell futures on 50,000 bushels of soybeans since each of his 10 calls is a call on 5,000 bushels.

Physical Currency Options

Another type of listed option on a physical is the currency options that trade on the Philadelphia Stock Exchange (PHLX). In addition, there is an even larger over-the-counter market in foreign currency options. Since the physical commodity underlying the option is currency, in some sense of the word, these are cash-based options as well. However, the cash that the options are based in is not dollars, but rather may be Deutschmarks, Swiss francs, British pounds, Canadian dollars, French francs, or Japanese yen. Futures trade in these same currencies on the Chicago Mercantile Exchange. Hence, many traders of the physical options use the Chicago-based futures as a hedge for their positions.

Unlike stock options, these currency options do not have standardized terms—the amount of currency underlying the option contract is not the same in each of the cases. The striking price intervals and units of trading are not the same either. However, since there are only the six different contracts and since their terms correspond to the details of the futures contracts, these options have had much success. The foreign currency markets are some of the largest in the world, and that size is reflected in the liquidity of the futures on these currencies.

The Swiss franc contract will be used to describe the workings of the foreign currency options. The other types of foreign currency options work in a similar manner, although they are for differing amounts of foreign currency. The amount of foreign currency controlled by the foreign currency contract is the unit of trading, just as 100 shares of stock is the unit of trading for stock options. The unit of trading for the Swiss franc option on the PHLX is 62,500 Swiss francs. Normally, the currency itself is quoted in terms of U.S. dollars. For example, a Swiss franc quote of 0.50 would mean that one Swiss franc is worth 50 cents in U.S. currency.

Note that when one takes a position in foreign currency options (or futures also), he is simultaneously taking an opposite position in U.S. dollars. That is, if one owns a Swiss franc call, he is long the franc (at least delta long) and is by implication therefore short U.S. dollars.

Striking prices in Swiss options are assigned in 1-cent increments and are stated in cents, not dollars. That is, if the Swiss franc is trading at 50 cents then there might be striking prices of 48, 49, 50, 51, and 52. Given the unit of trading and the striking price in U.S. dollars, one can compute the total dollars involved in a foreign currency exercise or assignment.

Example: Suppose the Swiss franc is trading at 0.50 and there are striking prices of 48, 50, and 52—representing U.S. cents per Swiss franc. If one were to exercise a call with a strike of 48, then the dollars involved in the exercise would be 125,000 (the unit of trading) times 0.48 (the strike in U.S. dollars), or $60,000.

Option premiums are stated in U.S. cents. That is, if a Swiss franc option is quoted at 0.75, its cost is $.0075 times the unit of trading, 125,000, for a total of $937.50. Premiums are quoted in hundredths of a point. That is, the next "tick" from 0.75 would be 0.76. Thus, for the Swiss franc options, each tick or hundredth of a point is equal to $12.50 (.0001 × 125,000).

Actual delivery of the security to satisfy an assignment notice must occur within the country of origin. That is, the seller of the currency must make arrangements to deliver the currency in its country of origin. On exercise or assignment, sellers of currency would be put holders who exercise or call writers who are assigned. Thus, if one were short Swiss franc calls and he were assigned, he would have to deliver Swiss francs into a bank in Switzerland. This essentially means that there have to be agreements between your firm or your broker and foreign banks if you expect to exercise or be assigned. The actual payment for the exercise or assignment takes place between the broker and the Options Clearing Corporation (OCC) in U.S. dollars. The OCC then can receive or deliver the currency in its country of origin since OCC has arrrangements with banks in each country.

Exercise & Assignment

The currency options that trade on the PHLX (Philadelphia Exchange) have exercise privileges similar to those for all other options that we have studied—they can be exercised at any time during their life.

Even though PHLX currency options are "cash" options in the most literal sense of the word, they do not expose the writer to the same risks of early assignment that cash-based index options do.

Example: Suppose that a currency trader has established the following spread on the PHLX: long Swiss franc December 50 puts, short Swiss franc December 52 puts—a bullish spread. As in any one-to-one spread, there is limited risk. However, the dollar rallies and the Swiss franc falls, pushing the exchange rate down to 48 cents (U.S.) per Swiss franc. Now, the puts that were written—the December 52 contracts—are deeply in-the-money and might be subject to early assignment as would any deeply in-the-money put if it were trading at a discount.

Suppose that the trader learns that he has indeed been assigned on his short puts. He still has a hedge, for he is long the December 50 puts and he is now long Swiss francs. This is still a hedged position, and he still has the same limited risk as he did when he started (plus possibly some costs involved in taking physical delivery of the francs). This situation is essentially the same as stock or futures options, where the spreader would still be hedged after an assignment because he would have acquired the stock or future. Contrast this to the cash-based index option, where there is no longer a hedge after an assignment.

FUTURES OPTION TRADING STRATEGIES

The strategies that will be described here are those which are unique to futures option trading. Although there may be some general relationships to stock and index option strategies, for the most part these strategies apply only to futures options. It will also be shown—in the backspread and ratio spread examples—that one can compute the profitability of an option spread in the same manner, no matter what the underlying instrument is (stocks, futures, etc.) by breaking everything down into "points" and not "dollars."

Before getting into specific strategies, it might prove useful to observe some relationships about futures options and their price relationships to each other and to the futures contract itself. Carrying cost and dividends are built into the price of stock and index options because the underlying instrument pays dividends and one has to pay cash to buy or sell the stock. Such is not the case with futures. The "investment" required to buy a futures contract is not initially a cash outlay. Note that the cost of carry associated with futures generally refers to the carrying costs of owning the cash commodity itself. That carrying cost has no bearing on the price of a futures option other than to determine the futures price itself. Moreover, the future has no dividends or similar payout. This is even true for something like U.S. Treasury bond options, because the interest rate payout of the cash bond is built into the *futures* price; thus the option, which is based on the futures price and not on the cash price directly, does not have to allow for carry, since the *future* itself has no initial carrying costs associated with it.

Simplistically, it can be stated that:

Futures Call = Futures Put + Futures Price − Strike Price

Example: April crude oil futures closed at 18.74 ($18.74 per barrel). The following prices exist:

Strike Price	April Call Price	April Put Price	Put + futures − strike
17	1.80	0.06	1.80
18	0.96	0.22	0.96
19	0.35	0.61	0.35
20	0.10	1.36	0.10

Note that, at every strike, the above formula is true. Call = put + futures − strike. These are not theoretical prices; they were taken from actual settlement prices on a particular trading day.

In reality, where deeply in-the-money or longer-term options are involved, this simple formula is not correct. However, for most options on a particular nearby futures contract, it will suffice quite well. Examine the quotes in today's newspaper to verify that this is a true statement.

A subcase of this observation is that *when the futures contract is exactly at the striking price, the call and put with that strike will both trade at the same price.* Note that in the above formula, if one sets the futures price equal to the striking price, the last two terms cancel out and one is left with: call price = put price.

One final observation before getting into strategies:

For a put and a call with the same strike,

Net change call − net change put = net change futures.

This is a true statement for stock and index options as well, and is a useful rule to remember. Since futures options bid and offer quotes are not always disseminated by quote vendors, one is forced to use last sales. If the last sales don't conform to the rule above, then at least one of the last sales is probably not representative of the true market in the options.

Example: April crude oil is up 50 cents to 19.24. A trader punches up the following quotes on his machine and sees the following prices:

Option	Last Sale	Net Change
April 19 call:	0.55	+0.20
April 19 put:	0.31	−0.30

These options conform to the above rule:

$$\text{Net change futures} = \text{net change call} - \text{net change put}$$
$$= +0.20 - (-0.30)$$
$$= +0.50$$

The net changes of the call and put indicate the April future should be up 50 cents, which it is.

Suppose that one also priced a less active option on his quote machine and saw the following:

Option	Last Sale	Net Change
April 17 call:	2.10	+0.30
April 17 put:	0.04	−0.02

In this case, the formula yields an incorrect result:

$$\text{Net change futures} = +0.30 - (-0.02) = +0.32$$

Since the futures are really up 50 cents, one can assume that one of the last sales is out of date. It is obviously the April 17 call, since that is the in-the-money option; if one were to ask for a quote from the trading floor, that option would probably be indicated up about 48 cents on the day.

Delta

While we are on the subject of pricing, a word about delta may be in order as well. The delta of a futures option has the same meaning as that of a stock option—it is the amount by which the option is expected to increase in price for a one point move in the underlying futures contract. As we also know, it is an instantaneous measurement that is obtained by taking the first derivative of the option pricing model.

In any case, the delta of an at-the-money stock or index option is greater than 0.50; the more time remaining to expiration, the higher the delta is. In a simplified sense, this has to do with the cost of carrying the value of the striking price until the option expires. But part of it is also due to the distribution of stock price movements—there is an upward bias—and with a long time remaining until expiration, that bias makes call movements more pronounced than put movements.

Options on futures do not have this carrying cost feature to deal with. But they do have the positive bias in their price distribution. A futures contract, just like a stock, can increase by more than 100%—but cannot fall more than 100%. Consequently, deltas of at-the-money futures calls will be slightly larger than 0.50. The more time remaining until expiration of the futures option, the higher the at-the-money call delta will be.

Many traders erroneously believe that the delta of an at-the-money futures option is 0.50, since there is no carrying cost involved in the futures conversion or reversal arbitrage. That is not a true statement, since the distribution of futures prices affects the delta as well.

As always, for futures options—as well as for stock and index options, *the delta of a put is related to the delta of a call with the same striking price and expiration date:*

$$\text{Delta of put} = 1 - \text{delta of call}$$

Finally, the concept of equivalent stock position applies to futures option strategies—except, of course, it is called the *equivalent futures position* (EFP). The EFP is calculated by the simple formula:

$$\text{EFP} = \text{delta of option} \times \text{option quantity}$$

Thus, if one is long 8 calls with a delta of 0.75, then that position has an EFP of 6 (8 × 0.75). This means that being long those 8 calls is the same as being long 6 futures contracts.

Note that in the case of stocks, the equivalent stock position formula has another factor—shares per option. That concept does not apply to futures options, since they are always options on one futures contract.

Mathematical Considerations

This brief section discusses modeling considerations for futures options and options on physicals.

Futures Options. The Black Model (see chapter on Mathematical Considerations for index options) is used to price futures options. Recall that futures don't pay dividends, so there is no dividend adjustment necessary for the model. In addition, there is no carrying cost involved with futures, so the only adjustment that one needs to make is to use 0% as the interest rate input to the Black-Scholes model. This is an oversimplification, especially for deeply in-the-money options. One is tying up some money in order to buy an option. Hence, the Black model will discount the price from the Black-Scholes model price. Therefore, the actual pricing model to be used for theoretical evaluation of futures options is the Black model, which is merely the Black-Scholes model, using 0% as the interest rate, and then discounted:

Call Theoretical Price $= e^{-rt} \times$ Black-Scholes formula [$r = 0$]

Recall that it was stated above that

Futures call = Futures put + Future price − Strike price

The actual relationship is

Futures call = Futures put + e^{-rt} (Futures price − Strike price)

where

$r =$ the short-term interest rate

$t =$ the time to expiration in years and

$e^{-rt} =$ the discounting factor.

The short-term interest rate has to be used here because when one pays a debit for an option, he is theoretically losing the interest that he could earn if he had that money in the bank instead, earning money at the short-term interest rate.

The difference between these two formulae is so small for nearby options that are not deeply in-the-money that it is normally less than the bid-asked spread in the options, and the first equation can be used.

Example: The table below compares the theoretical values computed with the two formulae, where $r = 6\%$ and $t = 0.25$ (¼ of a year). Furthermore, assume the futures price is 100. The strike price is given in the first column, and the put price is given in the second column. The predicted call prices—according to each formula—are then shown in the next two columns.

Strike	Put Price	Formula 1 (Simple)	Formula 2 (Using e^{-rt})
70	0.25	30.25	29.80
80	1.00	21.00	20.7
90	3.25	13.25	13.10
95	5.35	10.35	10.28
100	7.50	7.50	7.50
105	10.70	5.70	5.77
110	13.90	3.90	4.05
120	21.80	1.80	2.10

For options that are 20 or 30 points in- or out-of-the-money, there is a noticeable differential in these three-month options. However, for options closer to the strike, the differential is small.

If the time remaining to expiration is shorter than that used in the example above, the differences are smaller; if the time is longer, the differences magnify.

Options on Physicals. Determining the fair value of options on physicals such as currencies is more complicated. The proper way to calculate the fair value of an option on a physical is quite similar to that used for stock options. Recall that in the case of stock options, one first subtracts the present worth of the dividend from the current stock price before calculating the option value. A similar process is used for determining the fair value of currency or any other options on physicals. In any of these cases, the underlying security bears interest continuously instead of quarterly as stocks do. Therefore, all one needs to do is to subtract from the underlying price, the amount of interest to be paid until option expiration and then add the amount of accrued interest to be paid. All other inputs into the Black-Scholes model would remain the same, including the risk-free interest rate being equal to the 90-day T-bill rate.

Again the practical option strategist has a short cut available to him. If one assumes that the various factors necessary to price currencies have been assimilated into the futures markets in Chicago, then one can merely use the *futures* price as the price of the underlying for evaluating the physical delivery options in Philadelphia. This will not work well near expiration, since the future expires one week prior to the PHLX option. In addition, it ignores the early exercise value of the PHLX options. However, except for these small differentials, the short cut will give theoretical values that can be used in strategy-making decisions.

Example: It is sometime in April and one desires to calculate the theoretical values of the June Deutschmark physical delivery options in Philadelphia. Assume that one knows four of the basic items necessary for input to the Black-Scholes formula: 60 days to expiration, strike price of 68, interest rate of 10%, and volatility of 18%. But what should be used as the price of the underlying Deutschmark? Merely use the price of the June Deutschmark futures contract in Chicago.

Strategies Regarding Trading Limits

The fact that trading limits exist in most futures contracts could be detrimental to both option buyers and option writers. At other times, however, the trading limit may present a unique opportunity. The following section will focus on who might benefit from trading limits in futures and who would not.

Recall that a trading limit in a futures contract limits the absolute amount of points that the contract can trade up or down from the previous close. Thus, if the trading limit in T-Bonds is 3 points and they closed last night at $74^{21}/_{32}$, then the highest they can trade on the next day is $77^{21}/_{32}$, regardless of what might be happening in the cash bond market. Trading limits exist in many futures contracts in order to help ensure that the market cannot be manipulated by someone forcing the price to move tremendously in one direction or the other. Another reason for having trading limits is ostensibly to allow only a fixed move, approximately equal to the amount covered by the initial margin, so that maintenance margin can be collected if need be. However, limits have been applied in cases where they are unnecessary. For example, in T-Bonds, there is too much liquidity for anyone to be able to manipulate the market. Moreover, it is relatively easy to arbitrage the T-Bond futures contract against cash bonds. This also increases liquidity and would keep the future from trading at a price substantially different from its theoretical value.

Sometimes the markets actually *need* to move far quickly and cannot because of the trading limit. Perhaps cash bonds have rallied 4 points, when the limit is 3 points. This makes no difference—when a futures contract has risen as high as it can go for the day, it is bid there (a situation called "limit bid") and usually doesn't trade again as long as the underlying commodity moves higher. It is, of course, possible for a future to be limit bid, only to find that later in the day, the underlying commodity becomes weaker, and traders begin to sell the future, driving it down off the limit. Similar situations can also occur on the downside, where, if the future has traded as low as it can go, it is said to be "limit offered."

As was pointed out earlier, futures *options* sometimes have trading limits imposed on them as well. This limit is of the same magnitude as the futures limit. Most of these are on the Chicago Board of Trade (all grains, U.S. Treasury bonds, Municipal Bond Index, Nikkei stock index, and silver), although currency options on the Chicago Merc are included as well. In other markets, options are free to trade, even though futures have effectively halted because they are up or down the limit. However, even in the situations where futures options themselves have a trading limit, there may be out-of-the-money options available for trading that have not reached their trading limit.

When options are still trading, one can use them to imply the price where the futures would be trading, were they not at their trading limit.

Example: August Soybeans have been inflated in price due to drought fears, having closed on Friday at 650 ($6.50 per bushel). However, over the weekend it rains heavily in the Midwest, and it appears that the drought fears were overdone. Soybeans open down 30 cents—to 620— down the allowable 30 cent limit. Furthermore, there are no buyers at that level and the August bean contract is locked limit down. No further trading ensues.

One may be able to use the August soybean options as a price discovery mechanism to see where August soybeans would be trading if they were open.

Suppose that the following prices exist, even though August soybeans are not trading because they are locked limit down:

Option	Last Sale Price	Net Change For the Day
August 625 call	19	−21
August 625 put	31	+16

An option strategist knows that synthetic long futures can be created by buying a call and selling a put, or vice versa for short futures. Knowing this, one can tell what price futures are projected to be trading at:

Implied Futures Price = Strike Price + Call Price − Put Price

$$= 625 + 19 - 31 = 613$$

With these options at the prices shown, one can create a synthetic futures position at a price of 613. Therefore, the implied price for August soybean futures in this example is 613.

Note that this formula is merely another version of the one previously presented in this chapter.

In the example above, neither of the options in question had moved the 30-point limit, which applies to soybean options as well as to soybean futures. If they had, they would not be useable in the formula for implying the price of the future. *Only options that are freely trading—not limit up or down—can be used in the above formula.*

A more complete look at soybean futures options on the day they opened and stayed down the limit would reveal that some of them are not tradeable either:

Example: Continuing the above example, August soybeans are locked limit down 30 cents on the day. The following list shows a wider array of option prices. Any option that is either up or down 30 cents on the day has also reached its trading limit, and therefore could not be used in the process necessary to discover the implied price of the August futures contract.

Option	Last Sale Price	Net Change For the Day
August 550 call	71	− 30
August 575 call	48	− 30
August 600 call	31	− 26
August 625 call	19	− 21
August 650 call	11	− 15
August 675 call	6	− 10
August 550 put	4	+ 3
August 575 put	9	+ 6
August 600 put	18	+ 11
August 625 put	31	+ 16
August 650 put	48	+ 22
August 675 put	67	+ 30

The deeply in-the-money calls, August 550's and August 575's, and the deeply in-the-money August 675 puts are all at the trading limit. All other options are freely trading and could be used for the above computation of the August future's implied price.

One may ask how the market makers are able to create markets for the options when the future is not freely trading. They are pricing the options off of cash quotes. Knowing the cash quote, they can imply the price of the future (613 in this case), and they can then make option markets as well.

The real value in being able to use the options when a future is locked limit up or limit down, of course, is to be able to hedge one's position. Simplistically, if a trader came in long the August soybean futures and they were locked limit down as in the example above, he could use the puts and calls to effectively close out his position.

Example: As before, August soybeans are at 620, locked down the limit of 30 cents. A trader has come into this trading day long the futures and he is very worried. He cannot liquidate his long position, and if soybeans should open down the limit again tomorrow, his account will be wiped out. He can use the August options to close out his position.
Recall that it has been shown that the following is true:

Long put + short call is equivalent to short stock.

It is also equivalent to short futures, of course. So if this trader were to buy a put and short a call at the same strike, then he would have the equivalent of a short futures position to offset his long futures position.
Using the following prices—which are the same as before—one can see how his risk is limited to the effective futures price of 613. That is, buying the put and selling the call is the same as selling his futures out at 613, down 37 cents on the trading day.
Current prices:

Option	Last Sale Price	Net Change For the Day
August 625 call	19	− 21
August 625 put	31	+ 16

Position:

Buy August 625 put for 19

Sell August 625 call for 31

August Futures at Option Expiration	Put Price	Put Pft/loss	Call Price	Call P/L	Net Profit or Loss on Position
575	50	+ $1,900	0	+ $1,900	+ $3,800
600	25	− 600	0	+ 1,900	+ 1,300
613	12	− 1,900	0	+ 1,900	0
625	0	− 3,100	0	+ 1,900	− 1,200
650	0	− 3,100	25	− 600	− 3,700

This profit table shows that selling the August 625 call at 19 and buying the August 625 put at 31 is equivalent to—that is, it has the same profit potential as—selling the August future at 613. So, if he buys the put and sells the call, he will effectively have sold his future at 613 and taken his loss.

His resultant position after buying the put and selling the call would be a conversion (long futures, long put, and short call). The margin required for a conversion or reversal is zero in the futures market. The margin rules recognize the riskless nature of such a strategy. Thus, any excess money that he has after paying for the unrealized loss in the futures will be freed up for new trades.

The futures trader does not have to completely hedge off his position if he does not want to. He might decide to just buy a put to limit the downside risk. Unfortunately, to do so after the futures are already locked limit down may be too little, too late. There are many kinds of partial hedges that he could establish—buy some puts, sell some calls, utilize different strikes, etc.

The same or similar strategies could be used by a naked option seller who cannot hedge his position because it is up the limit. He could also utilize options that are still in free trading to create a synthetic futures position.

Futures options generally have enough out-of-the-money striking prices listed that some of them will still be free trading—even if the futures are up or down the limit. This fact is a boon to anyone who has a losing position that has moved the daily trading limit. Knowing how to use just this one option trading strategy should be a worthwhile benefit to many futures traders.

COMMONPLACE MISPRICING STRATEGIES

Futures options are sometimes prone to severe mispricing. Of course, any product's options may be subject to mispricing from time to time. However, it seems to appear in futures options more often than it does in stock options. The following discussion of strategies will concentrate on a specific pattern of futures options mispricing that occurs with relative frequency. It generally manifests itself in that out-of-the-money puts are too cheap, and out-of-the-money calls are too expensive. The proper term for this phenomenon is "volatility skewing" and it is discussed further in the chapter on advanced concepts. In this chapter we will concentrate on how to spot it and how to attempt to profit from it.

Occasionally, stock options will exhibit this trait to a certain extent. Generally, it occurs in stocks when speculators have it in their minds that a stock is going to experience a sudden, substantial rise in price. They will then bid up the out-of-the-money calls, particularly the near-term ones, as they attempt to capitalize on their bullish expectations. When takeover rumors abound, stock options will display this mispricing pattern. Mispricing is, of course, a statistically related term; it does not infer anything about the possible validity of takeover rumors.

A significant amount of discussion is going to be spent on this topic, because *the futures option trader* will *have ample opportunities to see and capitalize on this mispricing pattern*; it is *not* something that just comes along rarely. He should therefore be prepared to make it work to his advantage.

Example: January soybeans are trading at 583 ($5.83 per bushel). The following prices exist:
January beans: 583

Strike	Call Price	Put Price
525		½
550		3¼
575	19½	12
600	11	28
625	5¾	
650	3½	
675	2¼	

Suppose one knows that, according to historic patterns, the "fair values" of these options are the prices listed in the following table.

Strike	Call Price	Call Theo. Value	Put Price	Put Theo. Value
525			½	1.6
550			3¼	5.4
575	19½	21.5	12	13.7
600	11	10.4	28	27.6
625	5¾	4.3		
650	3½	1.5		
675	2¼	0.7		

Notice that the out-of-the-money puts are priced well below their theoretical value, while the out-of-the-money calls are priced above. The options at the 575 and 600 strikes are much closer in price to their theoretical values than are the out-of-the-money options.

There is another way to look at this data, and that is to view the options' implied volatility. Implied volatility was discussed in the chapter on mathematical applications. It is basically the volatility that one would have to plug into his option pricing model in order for the model's theoretical price to agree with the actual market price. Alternatively, it is the volatility that is being implied by the actual marketplace. The options in this example each have different implied volatilities, since their mispricing is so distorted. Table 36-2 gives those implied volatilities. The deltas of the options involved are shown as well, for they will be used in later examples.

These implied volatilities tell the same story: the out-of-the-money puts have the lowest implied volatility, and therefore are the cheapest options; the out-of-the-money calls have the *highest* implied volatilities, and are therefore the most expensive options.

So, no matter which way one prefers to look at it—through comparison of the option price with theoretical price or by comparing implied volatilities—it is obvious that these soybean options are out of line with one another.

This sort of pricing distortion is prevalent in many commodity options. Soybeans, sugar, coffee, gold, and silver are all subject to this distortion from time to time. The distortion is endemic to some—soybeans, for example—or may be present only when the speculators turn extremely bullish.

This precise mispricing pattern is so prevalent in futures options that strategists should constantly be looking for it. There are two major ways to attempt to profit from this pattern. Both are attractive strategies, since one is buying options that are relatively less expensive than the options that are being sold. Such strategies, when implemented when the options are mispriced, tilt the odds in the strategist's favor, creating a positive expected return for the position.

TABLE 36-2.
Volatility skewing of soybean options.

Strike	Call Price	Put Price	Implied Volatility	Delta Call/Put
525		½	12%	/−0.02
550		3¼	13%	/−0.16
575	19½	12	15%	0.59/−0.41
600	11	28	17%	0.37/−0.63
625	5¾		19%	0.21
650	3½		21%	0.13
675	2¼		23%	0.09

The two theoretically attractive strategies are:

1. Buy out-of-the-money puts and sell at-the-money puts; or
2. Buy at-the-money calls and sell out-of-the-money calls.

One might just buy one cheap and sell one expensive option—a bear spread with the puts, or a bull spread with the calls. However, it is better to implement these spreads with a ratio between the number of options bought and the number sold. That is, the first strategy involving puts would be a backspread, while the second strategy involving calls would be a ratio spread. By doing the ratio, each strategy is a more neutral one. Each strategy will be examined separately.

Backspreading the Puts

The backspread strategy works best when one expects a large degree of volatility. Implementing the strategy with puts means that a large drop in price by the underlying futures would be most profitable, although a limited profit could be made if futures rose. Note that a moderate drop in price by expiration would be the worst result for this spread.

Example: Using prices from the above example, suppose that one decides to establish a backspread in the puts. Assume that a neutral ratio is obtained in the following spread:

Buy 4 Jan bean 550 puts 3¼	13 DB
Sell 1 Jan bean 600 put at 28	28 CR
Net positions:	15 Credit

The deltas (see Table 36-2) of the options are used to compute this neutral ratio.

Figure 36-1 shows the profit potential of this spread. It is the typical picture for a put backspread—limited upside potential with a great deal of profit potential for large downward moves. Note that the spread is initially established for a credit of 15 cents. If January soybeans have volatile movements in either direction, the position should profit. Obviously, the profit potential is larger to the downside, where there are extra long puts. However, if beans should rally instead, the spreader could still make up to 15 cents ($750), the initial credit of the position.

Note that one can treat the prices of soybean options in the same manner as he would treat the prices of stock options in order to determine such things as breakeven points and maximum profit potential. The fact that soybean options are worth $50 per point (which is *cents* when re-

FIGURE 36-1.
January soybean, backspread.

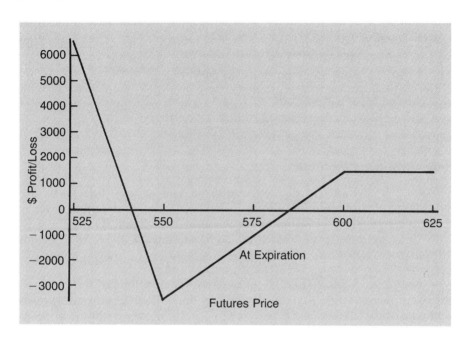

ferring to soybeans) and stock options are worth $100 per point does not alter these calculations for a put backspread.

$$\text{Maximum upside profit potential} = \text{initial debit or credit of position}$$

$$= 15 \text{ points}$$

$$\text{Maximum risk} = \text{maximum upside} - \text{distance between strikes}$$

$$\times \text{ number of puts sold short}$$

$$= 15 - 50 \times 1$$

$$= -35 \text{ points}$$

$$\text{Downside breakeven point} = \text{lower strike}$$

$$- \text{points of risk/number of excess puts}$$

$$= 550 - 35/3$$

$$= 538.3$$

Thus, one is able to analyze a futures option position or a stock option position in the same manner—by reducing everything to be in *terms of points, not dollars.* Obviously, one will eventually have to convert to dollars in order to calculate his profits or losses. However, note that referring to everything in "points" works very well—later, one can use the "dollars per point" to obtain actual dollar cost. "Dollars per point" would be $50 for soybeans options, $100 for stock or index options, $400 for live cattle options, $375 for coffee options, $1,120 for sugar options, etc. In this way, one does not have to get hung up in the nomenclature of the futures contract; he can approach everything in the same fashion for purposes of analyzing the position. He will, of course, have to use proper nomenclature to enter the order, but that comes after the analysis is done.

Ratio Spreading the Calls

Returning to the subject at hand—spreads that capture this particular mispricing phenomenon of futures options—recall that the other strategy that is attractive in such situations is the ratio call spread. It is established with the maximum profit potential being somewhat above the current futures price, since the calls that are being sold are out-of-the-money.

Example: Again using the January soybean options of the previous few examples, suppose that one establishes the following ratio call spread. Using the calls' deltas (see previous table) the following ratio is approximately neutral to begin with:

Buy 2 Jan bean 600 calls at 11	22 DB
Sell 5 Jan bean 650 calls at 3½	17½ CR
Net positions:	4½ Debit

Figure 36-2 shows the profit potential of the ratio call spread. It looks fairly typical for a ratio spread: limited downside exposure, maximum profit potential at the strike of the written calls, and unlimited upside exposure.

Since this spread is established with both options out-of-the-money, one needs some upward movement by January soybean futures in order to be profitable. However, too much movement would not be welcomed (although follow-up strategies could be used to deal with that). Consequently, this is a moderately bullish strategy; one should feel that the underlying futures have a chance to move somewhat higher before expiration.

Again, the analyst should treat this position in terms of points—not dollars or cents of soybean movement—in order to calculate the significant profit and loss points. Refer to Chapter 11 for the original explanation of these formulae for ratio call spreads:

FIGURE 36-2.
January soybean, ratio spread.

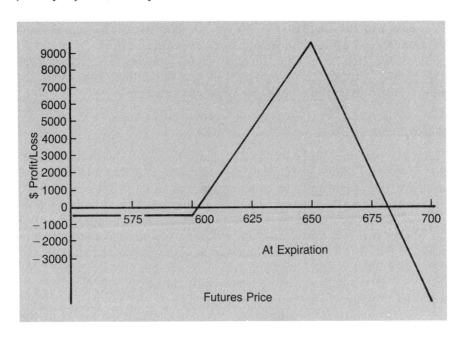

$$\text{Maximum downside loss} = \text{initial debit or credit}$$
$$= -4\tfrac{1}{2} \text{ (it is a debit)}$$
$$\text{Points of maximum profit} = \text{maximum downside loss}$$
$$+ \text{ difference in strikes}$$
$$\times \text{ number of calls owned}$$
$$= -4\tfrac{1}{2} + 50 \times 2$$
$$= 95\tfrac{1}{2}$$
$$\text{Upside breakeven price} = \text{higher striking price}$$
$$+ \text{ maximum profit/net number of naked calls}$$
$$= 650 + 95\tfrac{1}{2}/3$$
$$= 681.8$$

These are the significant points of profitability at expiration. One does not care what the unit of trading is (for example, cents for soybeans) or how many dollars are involved in one unit of trading ($50 for soybeans and soybean options). He can conduct his analysis strictly in terms of "points," and he *should* do so.

Before proceeding into the comparisons between the backspread and the ratio spread as they apply to mispriced futures options, it should be pointed out that the serious strategist should analyze how his position will perform over the short term as well as at expiration. These analyses are presented in a later chapter on advanced concepts.

Which Strategy To Use

The profit potential of the put backspread is obviously far different from that of the call ratio spread. They are similar in that they both offer the strategist the opportunity to benefit from spreading mispriced options. Choosing which one to implement (assuming liquidity in both the puts and calls) may be helped by examining the technical picture (chart) of the futures contract. Recall that futures traders are often more technically oriented than stock traders, so it pays to be aware of basic chart patterns, because others are watching them as well. If enough people see the same thing and act on it, the chart pattern will be correct, if only from a "self-fulfilling prophecy" viewpoint if nothing else.

Consequently, if the futures are locked in a (smooth) downtrend, the put strategy is the strategy of choice because it offers the best downside profit. Conversely, if the futures are in a smooth uptrend, the call strategy is best.

The worst result will be achieved if the strategist has established the call ratio spread, and the futures have an explosive rally. In certain cases, there will be very bullish rumors around—weather predictions such as drought or El Nino, foreign labor unrest in the fields or mines, Russian buying of grain—that will produce this mispricing phenomenon. The strategist should be leery of using the call ratio spread strategy in such situations, even though the out-of-the-money calls look and are ridiculously expensive. If the rumors prove true, or if there are too many shorts being squeezed, the futures can move too far too fast and seriously hurt the spreader who has the ratio call spread in place. His margin requirements will escalate quickly as the futures price moves higher. The option premiums will remain high or possibly even expand if the futures rally quickly, thereby overriding the potential benefit of time decay. Moreover, if the fundamentals change immediately—it rains; the strike is settled; no grain credits are offered to the Russians—or rumors prove false, the futures can come crashing back down in a hurry.

Consequently, *if rumors of fundamentals have introduced volatility in the futures market, implement the strategy with the put backspread.* The put backspread is geared to taking advantage of volatility—and this fundamental situation as described is certainly volatile. It may seem that because the market is exploding to the upside, it is a waste of time to establish the put spread. Still, it is the wisest choice in a volatile market, and there is always the chance that an explosive advance can turn into a quick decline, especially when the advance is based on rumors or fundamentals that could change overnight.

There are a few "don'ts" associated with the ratio call spread. Do not be tempted to use the ratio spread strategy in volatile situations such as those just described—it works best in a slowly rising market. Also, do not implement the ratio spread with ridiculously far out-of-the-money options, as one is wasting his theoretical advantage if the futures do not have a realistic chance to climb to the striking price of the written options. Finally, *do not attempt to use overly large ratios in order to gain the most theoretical advantage.* This is an important concept, and the next example illustrates it well.

Example: Assume the same pricing pattern for January soybean options that has been the basis for this discussion. January beans are trading at 583. The (novice) strategist sees that the slightly in-the-money Jan 575 call is the cheapest and the deeply out-of-the-money Jan 675 call is the most expensive. This can be verified from either of two previous tables— the one showing the actual price as compared to the "theoretical" price or the one showing the implied volatilities.

Again, one would use the deltas (see previous table) to create a neutral spread. A neutral ratio of these two would involve selling approximately six calls for each one purchased.

Buy 1 Jan bean 575 call at 19½	19½ DB
Sell 6 Jan bean 675 calls at 2¼	13½ CR
Net position:	6 Debit

Figure 36-3 shows the possible detrimental effects of using this large ratio. While one could make 94 points of profit if beans were at 675 at January expiration, he could lose that profit quickly if beans shot on through the upside breakeven point, which is only 693.8. The previous formulae can be used to verify these maximum profit and upside breakeven point calculations. The upside breakeven point is too close to the striking price to allow for reasonable follow-up action. Therefore, this would not be an attractive position from a practical viewpoint, even though at first glance it looks attractive theoretically.

It would seem that neutral spreading could get one into trouble if it "recommends" positions like the 6-to-1 ratio spread. In reality, it is the

FIGURE 36-3.
January soybean, heavily ratioed spread.

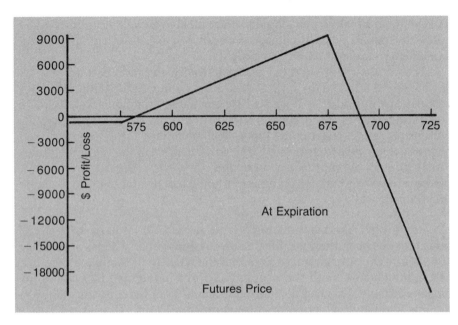

strategist who is getting into trouble if he doesn't look at the whole picture. The statistics are just an aid—a tool. The strategist must use the tools to his advantage. It should be pointed out as well that there is a tool missing from the toolkit at this point. There are statistics that will clearly show the risk of this type of a high ratio spread. In this case, that tool is the *gamma* of the option. Chapter 38 covers the use of gamma and other more advanced statistical tools. This same example is expanded in that chapter to include the gamma concept.

Follow-up Action

The same follow-up strategies apply to these futures options as did for stock options. They will not be rehashed in detail here; refer to earlier chapters for broader explanations. This is a summary of the normal follow-up strategies:

Ratio call spread:
    Follow-up action in strategies with naked options, such as this, generally
        involves taking or limiting losses. A rising market will produce a
        negative EFP.
    Neutralize a negative EFP by:
        Buying futures
        Buying some calls

Limit upside losses by placing buy stop orders for futures at or near the
  upside breakeven point.
Put backspread:
  Follow-up action in strategies with an excess of long options generally
    involves taking or protecting profits. A falling market will produce a
    negative EFP.
  Neutralize a negative EFP by:
    Buying futures
    Selling some puts

The reader has seen these follow-up strategies earlier in the book.
However, there is one new concept that is important: *the mispricing continues to propagate itself no matter what the price of the underlying
futures contract.* The at-the-money options will always be about fairly
priced; they will have the average implied volatility.

Example: In the above examples, January soybeans were trading at
583 and the implied volatility of the options with striking price 575 was
15%, while those with a 600 strike were 17%. One could, therefore, conclude that the at-the-money January soybean options would exhibit an
implied volatility of about 16%.

This would still be true if beans were at 525 or 675. The mispricing
of the other options would extend out from what is now the at-the-money
strike. Table 36-3 shows what one might expect to see if Jan soybeans
rose 75 cents in price, from 583 to 658.

Note that the same mispricing properties exist in both the old and
new situations—the puts that are 58 points out-of-the-money have an
implied volatility of only 12%, while the calls that are 92 points out of
the money have implied volatilities of 23%.

TABLE 36-3.
Propagation of volatility skewing.

Original Situation		New Situation
Jan beans: 583		Jan beans: 658
Strike	Implied Volatility	Strike
525	12%	600
550	13%	625
575	15%	650
600	17%	675
625	19%	700
650	21%	725
675	23%	750

This example is not meant to infer that the volatility of an at-the-money soybean futures option will always be 16%. It could be anything, depending on the historical and implied volatility of the futures contract itself. However, the volatility skewing will still persist even if the futures rally or decline.

This fact will affect how these strategies behave as the underlying futures contract moves. It is a benefit to both strategies. First, look at the put backspread when the stock falls to the striking price of the purchased puts.

Example: The put backspread was established under the following conditions:

Strike	Put Price	Theoretical Put Price	Implied Volatility
550	3¼	5.4	13%
600	28	27.6	17%

If January soybean futures should fall to 550, one would expect the implied volatility of the Jan 550 puts that are owned to be about 16% or 17%, since they would be at-the-money at that time. This makes the assumption that the at-the-money puts will have about a 17% implied volatility, which is what they did when the position was established.

Since the strategy involves being long a large quantity of these Jan 550 puts, this increase in implied volatility as the futures drop in price will be of benefit to the spread.

Note that the implied volatility of the Jan 600 puts would increase as well, which would be a small negative aspect for the spread. However, since there is only one put short and it is so deeply in the money with the futures at 550, this negative cannot outweigh the positive effect of the expansion of volatility on the long Jan 550 puts.

In a similar manner, the call spread would benefit. The implied volatility of the written options would actually drop as the futures rallied, since they would be *less* far out-of-the-money than they originally were when the spread was established. While the same can be said of the long options in the spread, the fact that there are extra, naked, options means the spread will benefit overall.

In summary, the futures option strategist should be alert to mispricing situations like those described above. They occur frequently in a few commodities and occasionally in others. The put backspread strategy has limited risk and might therefore be attractive to more individuals; it is best used in downtrending and/or volatile markets. However, if the futures are in a smooth uptrend—not a volatile one—a ratio call spread would be better. In either case, the strategist has established a spread that is statistically attractive because he has sold options that are expensive in relation to the ones that he has bought.

SUMMARY

This chapter presented the basics of futures and futures options trading. The basic differences between futures options and stock or index options were laid out. In a certain sense, a futures option is easier to utilize than is a stock option because the effects of dividends, interest rates, stock splits, and so forth do not apply to futures options. However, the fact that each underlying physical commodity is completely different from most other ones means that the strategist is forced to familiarize himself with a vast array of details involving striking prices, trading units, expiration dates, first notice days, etc.

More details mean there could be more opportunities for mistakes, most of which can be avoided by visualizing and analyzing all positions in terms of "points" and not in dollars. Also, the fact that there is no automatic exercise for most futures options could be costly, so the futures option traders must be particularly alert to exercise his long options on the expiration date if he wants to acquire a futures position, either long or short.

Futures options do not create new option strategies. However, they may afford one the opportunity to trade when the futures are locked limit up. Moreover, the volatility skewing that is present in futures options will offer opportunities for put backspreads and call ratio spreads that are not normally present in stock options.

The following chapter will discuss futures spreads and how one can use futures options with those spreads. Calendar spreads will be discussed as well. Calendar spreads with futures options are different from calendar spreads using stock or index options. These are important concepts in the futures markets—distinctly different from an option spread—and are therefore significant for the futures option trader.

Chapter 37

Futures Option Strategies for Futures Spreads

A spread with futures is not really the same as a spread with options, except that one item is bought while another is simultaneously sold. In this manner, one side of the spread hedges the risk of the other. This chapter will describe futures spreading and will offer ways to use options as an adjunct to those spreads.

The concept of calendar spreading with futures options is covered in this chapter as well. This is the one strategy that is very different when using futures options, as opposed to using stock or index options.

FUTURES SPREADS

Before getting into option strategies, it is necessary to define futures spreads and to examine some common futures spreading strategies.

Futures Pricing Differentials

It has already been shown that, for any particular physical commodity, there are, at any one time, several futures that expire in different months. Oil futures have monthly expirations; sugar futures expire only in five months of any one calendar year. The frequency of expiration months depends on which futures contract one is discussing.

Futures on the same underlying commodity will trade at different prices. The differential is due to several factors, not just time, as is the case with stock options. A major factor is carrying costs—how much one would spend to buy and hold the physical commodity until futures expiration. However, other factors may enter in as well, including supply and demand considerations. In a normal carrying cost market, futures that expire later in time are more expensive than those that are nearer-term.

Example: Gold is a commodity whose futures exhibit forward or normal carry. Suppose it is March 1st and spot gold is trading at 351. Then, the futures contracts on gold and their respective prices might be as follows:

Expiration Month	Price
April	352.50
June	354.70
August	356.90
December	361.50
June	369.10

Notice how each successive month is more expensive than the previous one. There is a 2.20 differential between each of the first three expirations, equal to 1.10 per month of additional expiration time. However, the differential is not quite that great for the December, which expires in 9 months, or for the June contract which expires in 15 months. The reason for this might be that longer-term interest rates are slightly lower than the short-term rates, and so the cost of carry is slightly less.

However, prices in all futures don't line up this nicely. In some cases, different months may actually represent different products, even though both are on the same underlying physical commodity. For example, wheat is not always wheat. There is a summer crop and a winter crop. While the two may be related in general, there could be a substantial difference between the July wheat futures contract and the December contract, for example, that has very little to do with what interest rates are.

Sometimes short-term demand can dominate the interest rate effect, and a series of futures contracts can be aligned such that the *short-term* futures are more expensive. This is known as a reverse carrying charge market, or contango.

Intramarket Futures Spreads

Some futures traders attempt to predict the relationships between various expiration months on the same underlying physical commodity. That is, one might buy July soybean futures and sell September soybean futures. *When one both buys and sells differing futures contracts, he has a spread. When both contracts are on the same underlying physical commodity, he has an intramarket spread.*

The spreader is not attempting to predict the overall direction of prices. Rather, he is trying to predict the *differential* in prices between the July and September contracts. He doesn't care if beans go up or down— as long as the spread between July and September goes his way.

Example: A spread trader notices that historic price charts show that if September soybeans get too expensive with respect to July soybeans, the differential usually disappears in a month or two. The opportunity for establishing this trade usually occurs early in the year—February or March.

Assume it is February 1st, and the following prices exist:

July soybean futures: 600 ($6.00/bushel)

Sept soybean futures: 606

The price differential is 6 cents. It rarely gets worse than 12 cents, and often reverses to the point where July futures are more expensive than soybean futures—some years as much as 100 cents more expensive.

If one were to trade this spread from a historical perspective, he would thus be risking approximately 6 cents, with possibilities of making over 100 cents. Certainly a good risk/reward ratio—if historic price patterns hold up in the current environment.

Suppose that one establishes the spread:

Buy one July future @ 600

Sell one Sept future @ 606

At some later date, the following prices and, hence, profits and losses, exist.

Futures Price	Profit/Loss
July: 650	+50 cents
Sept: 630	−24 cents
Total Profit:	26 cents ($1,300)

The spread has inverted, going from an initial state where Sept was 6 cents more expensive than July, to a situation where July is 20 cents more expensive. The spreader would thus make 26 cents, or $1,300, since 1 cent in beans is worth $50.

Notice that the same profit would have been made at any of the following pairs of prices, because the price differential between July and September is 20 cents in all cases (with July being the more expensive of the two).

July Futures	Sept Futures	July Profit	Sept Profit
420	400	− 180	+ 206
470	450	− 130	+ 156
550	530	− 50	+ 76
600	580	0	+ 26
650	630	+ 50	− 24
700	680	+ 100	− 74
800	780	+ 200	− 174

Therefore, the same 26 cent profit can be made whether soybeans are in a severe bear market, in a rousing bull market, or even somewhat unchanged. The spreader is only concerned with whether the spread widens from a 6 cent differential or not.

Charts, some going back years, are kept of the various relationships between one expiration month and another. Spread traders often use these historical charts to determine when to enter and exit intramarket spreads. These charts display the seasonal tendencies that make the relationships between various contracts widen or shrink. Analysis of the fundamentals that cause the seasonal tendencies could also be motivation for establishing intramarket spreads.

The margin required for intramarket spread trading (and some other types of futures spreads) is smaller than that required for speculative trading in the futures themselves. The reason for this is that spreads are considered less risky than outright positions in the futures. However, one can still make or lose a good deal of money in a spread—percentage-wise as well as in dollars—so it cannot be considered conservative; it's just less risky than outright futures speculation.

Example: Using the soybean spread from the example above, assume the speculative initial margin requirement is $1,700. Then, the spread margin requirement might be $500. That is considerably less than one would have to put up as initial margin if each side of the spread had to be margined separately, a situation which would require $3,400.

In the previous example, it was shown that the soybean spread had the potential to widen as much as 100 points ($1.00), a move which would be worth $5,000 if it occurred. While it is unlikely that the spread would actually widen to historic highs, it is certainly possible that it could widen 25 or 30 cents, a profit of $1,250 to $1,500.

That is certainly high leverage on an $500 investment over a short time period, so one must classify spreading as a risk strategy.

Intermarket Futures Spreads

Another type of futures spread is one in which one buys futures contracts in one market and sells futures contracts in another, probably related, market. When the futures spread is transacted in two different markets, it is known as an intermarket spread. Intermarket spreads are just as popular as intramarket spreads.

One type of intermarket spread involves directly related markets. Examples include spreads between currency futures on two different international currencies; between financial futures on two different bond, note, or bill contracts; or between a commodity and its products—oil, unleaded gasoline, and heating oil, for example.

Example: Interest rates have been low in both the United States and Japan. As a result, both currencies are depressed with respect to the European currencies, where interest rates remain high. A trader feels that interest rates will become more equal worldwide, causing the Japanese Yen to appreciate with respect to the German Mark.

However, since he is not sure whether Japanese rates will move up or German rates will move down, he is reluctant to take an outright position in either currency. Rather, he decides to utilize an intermarket spread to implement his trading idea.

Assume he establishes the spread at the following prices:

Buy 1 Jun Yen future: 77.00

Sell 1 Jun Mark future: 60.00

This is an initial differential of 17.00 between the two currency futures. He is hoping for the differential to get larger. The dollar trading terms are the same for both futures: one point of movement (from 60.00 to 61.00, for example) is worth $1,250. His profit and loss potential would therefore be:

Spread Differential at a Later Date	Profit/Loss
14.00	− $3,750
16.00	− $1,250
18.00	+ 1,250
20.00	+ 3,750

In some cases, the exchanges recognize frequently traded intermarket spreads as being eligible for reduced margin requirements. That is, the exchange recognizes that the two futures are a hedge against one another if one is sold and the other is bought.

These spreads between currencies, called cross-currency spreads, are so heavily traded that there are other specific vehicles—both futures and warrants—that allow the speculator to trade them as a single entity. Regardless, they serve as a prime example of an intermarket spread when the two futures are used.

In the example above, assume the outright speculative margin for a position in either currency future is $1,700 per contract. Then, the margin for this spread would probably be nearly $1,700 as well—equal to the speculative margin for one side of the spread. This position is thus recognized as a spread position for margin purposes. The margin treatment isn't as favorable as the intramarket spread (see the soybean example above), but the spread margin is still only one-half of what one would have to advance as initial margin if both sides of the spread had to be margined separately.

Other intermarket spreads are also eligible for reduced margin requirements, although at first glance they might not seem to be as direct of a hedge as the two currencies above were.

Example: A common intermarket spread is the TED spread, which consists of Treasury Bill futures on one side and Eurodollar futures on the other. Treasury Bills represent the safest investment there is; they are guaranteed. Eurodollars, however, are not insured, and therefore represent a less safe investment. Consequently, Eurodollars yield more than Treasury Bills. But *how much more* is the key. For as the yield differential expands or shrinks, the spread between the prices of T-Bill futures and Eurodollar futures expands or shrinks as well. In essence, the yield differential is small when there is stability and confidence in the financial markets, because uninsured deposits and insured deposits are not that much different in times of financial certainty. However, in times of financial uncertainty and instability, the spread widens because the uninsured depositors require a comparatively higher yield for the higher risk they are taking.

Assume the outright initial margin for either the T-Bill future or the Eurodollar future is $800 per contract. The margin for the TED spread, however, is only $400. Thus, one is able to trade this spread for only one fourth of the amount of margin that would be required to margin both sides separately.

The reason that the margin is more favorable is that there is not a lot of volatility in this spread. Historically, it has ranged between about 0.30 and 1.70. In both futures contracts, one cent (0.01) of movement is worth $25. Thus, the entire 140 cent historic range of the spread only represents $3,500 (140 × $25).

More will be said later about the TED spread when the application of futures options to intermarket spreads is discussed. Since there is a liquid option market on both futures, it is sometimes more logical to establish the spread using options instead of futures.

One other comment should be made regarding the TED spread: it has "carrying cost." That is, if one buys the spread and holds it, the spread will shrink as time passes, causing a small loss to the holder. When interest rates are low, the carrying cost is small (about 0.05 for 3 months). It would be larger if short-term rates rise. The prices in Table 37-1 show how the spread is more costly for longer-term contracts:

Many intermarket spreads have some sort of carrying cost built into them, so the spreader should be aware of that fact, for it may figure into his profitability.

One final, and more complex, example of an intermarket spread is the crack spread. There are two major areas where a basic commodity is traded, as well as two of its products: crude oil, unleaded gasoline, and heating oil; or soybeans, soybean oil, and soybean meal. A crack spread involves trading all three—the base commodity and both byproducts.

Example: The crack spread in oil consists of buying two futures contracts of crude oil and selling one contract each of heating oil and unleaded gasoline.

TABLE 37-1.
Carrying costs of the TED spread.

Month	T-Bill Future	Eurodollar Future	TED Spread
Mar	96.27	95.86	0.41
Jun	96.15	95.69	0.46
Sep	95.90	95.39	0.51

   The units of trading are not the same for all three. The crude oil future is a contract for 1,000 barrels of oil; it is traded in units of dollars per barrel, so a $1 increase in oil prices—from $18.00 to $19.00, say—is worth $1,000 to the futures contract. Heating oil and unleaded gasoline futures contracts have similar terms, but they are different from crude oil. Each of these futures is for 42,000 gallons of the product, and they are traded in cents. So, a one cent move—gasoline going from 60 cents a gallon to 61 cents a gallon—is worth $420. This information is summarized in Table 37-2 by showing how much a unit change in price is worth.
   The following formula is generally used for the oil crack spread:

$$\text{Crack} = \frac{(\text{unleaded gasoline} + \text{heating oil}) \times 42 - 2 \times \text{crude}}{2}$$

$$= \frac{(.6000 + .5500) \times 42 - 2 \times 18.00}{2}$$

$$= (48.3 - 36)/2$$

$$= 6.15$$

   Some traders don't use the divisor of 2 and, therefore, would arrive at a value of 12.30 with the above data.
   In either case, the spreader can track the history of this spread and will attempt to buy oil and sell the other two—or vice versa—in order to attempt to make an overall profit as the three products move. Suppose that a spreader felt that the products were too expensive with respect to crude oil prices. He would then implement the spread in the following manner:

Buy 2 Mar crude oil futures @ 18.00

Sell 1 Mar heating oil future @ 0.5500

Sell 1 Mar unleaded gasoline future @ 0.6000

TABLE 37-2.
Terms of oil production contract.

Contract	Initial Price	Subsequent Price	Gain in Dollars
Crude Oil	18.00	19.00	$1,000
Unleaded Gasoline	.6000	.6100	$ 420
Heating Oil	.5500	.5600	$ 420

Thus, the crack spread was at 6.15 when he entered the position. Suppose that he was right, and futures prices changed as shown below. The profit is also shown in Table 37-3.

One can calculate that the crack spread at the new prices has shrunk to 5.965. Thus, the spreader was correct in predicting that the spread would narrow, and he profited.

Margin requirements are also favorable for this type of spread, generally being slightly less than the speculative requirement for two contracts of crude oil.

The above examples demonstrate some of the various intermarket spreads that are heavily watched and traded by futures spreaders. They often provide some of the most reliable profit situations without requiring one to predict the actual direction of the market itself. Only the differential of the spread is important.

One should not assume that all intermarket spreads receive favorable margin treatment. Only those that have traditional relationships do. For example, one might decide that the Japanese stock market is going to fare far worse than the U.S. stock markets. There are futures on major indices in both markets—the Nikkei 225 futures and the S&P 500 futures. Consequently, one might short the Nikkei futures and buy the S&P futures as a hedge. While this may be a logical hedge, it does not qualify for reduced margin requirements (at the current time).

USING FUTURES OPTIONS IN FUTURES SPREADS

After viewing the above examples, one can see that futures spreads are not the same as what we typically know as option spreads. However, option contracts may be useful in futures spreading strategies. They can often provide an additional measure of profit potential for very little additional risk. This is true for both intramarket and intermarket spreads.

TABLE 37-3.
Profit and loss of crack spread.

Contract	Initial Price	Subsequent Price	Gain in Dollars
2 Mar Crude	18.00	18.50	+$1,000
1 Mar Unleaded	.6000	.6075	−$ 315
1 Mar Heating Oil	.5500	.5575	−$ 315
Net Profit (before commissions)			+$ 370

The futures option calendar spread will be discussed first. The calendar spread with futures options is not the same as the calendar spread with stock or index options. In fact, it may best be viewed as an alternative to the intramarket futures spread rather than as an option spread strategy.

Calendar Spreads

A calendar spread with futures options would still be constructed in the familiar manner—buy the May call, sell the March call with the same striking price. However, there is a major difference between the futures option calendar spread and the stock option calendar spread. That difference is that a *calendar spread using futures options involves two separate underlying instruments, while a calendar spread using stock options does not.* When one buys the May soybean 600 call and sells the March soybean 600 call, he is buying a call on the May soybean futures contract and selling a call on the March soybean futures contract. Thus, the futures option calendar spread involves two separate, but related, underlying futures contracts. However, if one buys the IBM May 100 call and sells the IBM March 100 call, both calls are on the same underlying instrument— IBM. This is a major difference between the two strategies, although both are called "calendar spread."

To the stock option trader who is used to visualizing calendar spreads, the futures option variety may confound him at first. For example, a stock option trader may feel that if he can buy a four month call for 5 points and sell a two month call for 2 points, that he has a good calendar spread possibility. Such an analysis is meaningless with futures options. If one can buy the May soybean 600 call for 5 and sell the Mar soybean 600 call for 3, is that a good spread or not? It's impossible to tell, unless you know the relationship between May and March soybean *futures* contracts. Thus, *in order to analyze the futures option calendar spread, one must not only analyze the options' relationship, but the two futures contracts' relationship as well.* Simply stated, when one establishes a futures option calendar spread, he is not only spreading time—as he does with stock options— he is also spreading the relationship between the underlying futures.

Example: A trader notices that near-term options in soybeans are relatively more expensive than longer-term options. He thinks a calendar spread might make sense, as he can sell the overpriced near-term calls and buy the relatively cheaper longer-term calls. This is a good situation, considering the theoretical value of the options involved. He establishes the spread at the following prices:

Soybean Contract	Initial Price	Trading Position
March 600 call	14	Sell 1
May 600 call	21	Buy 1
March future	594	none
May future	598	none

The May/March 600 call calendar spread is established for 7 points debit. March expiration is two months away. At the current time, the May futures are trading at a four point premium to March futures. The spreader figures that if March futures are approximately unchanged at expiration of the March options, he should profit handsomely, because the March calls are slightly overpriced at the current time, plus they will decay at a faster rate than the May calls over the next two months.

Suppose that he is correct and March futures are unchanged at expiration of the March futures. This is still no guarantee of profit, because one must also determine where May futures are trading. If the spread between May and March futures behaves poorly (May declines with respect to March), then he might still lose money. Look at the following table to see how the *futures* spread between March and May futures affects the profitability of the calendar spread. The calendar spread cost 7 debit when the futures spread was +4 initially.

Futures Prices March/May	Futures Spread Price	May 600 Call Price	Calendar Spread Profit/Loss
594/570	−24	4	−3 cents
594/580	−14	6½	−½
594/590	−4	10	+3
594/600	+6	14½	+7½

Thus, the calendar spread could lose money even with March futures unchanged—top two lines of table. It also could do better than expected if the futures spread widens—bottom line of table.

The profitability of the calendar spread is heavily linked to the futures spread price. In the above example, it was possible to lose money even though the March futures contract was unchanged in price from the time the calendar spread was initially established. This would never happen with stock options. If one placed a calendar spread on IBM and the stock were unchanged at the expiration of the near-term option, the spread would make money virtually all of the time (unless implied volatility had shrunk dramatically).

The futures option calendar spreader is therefore trading two spreads at once. The first one has to do with the relative pricing differentials (implied volatilities, for example) of the two options in question, as well as the passage of time. The second one is the relationship between the two underlying futures contracts. As a result, it is difficult to draw the ordinary profit picture. Rather, one must approach the problem in this manner:

1. Use the horizontal axis to represent the *futures spread price* at the expiration of the near-term option.

2. Draw several profit curves, one for each price of the near-term future at near-term expiration.

Example: Expanding on the above example, this method will be demonstrated.

Figure 37-1 shows how to approach the problem. The horizontal axis depicts the spread between March and May soybean futures at the expi-

FIGURE 37-1.
Soybean futures calendar spreads, at March expiration.

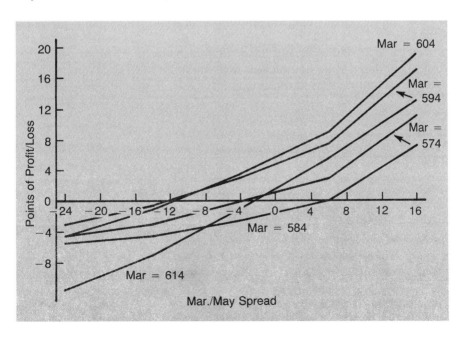

ration of the March futures options. The vertical axis represents the profit and loss to be expected from the calendar spread, as it always does.

The major difference between this profit graph and standard ones is that there are now several sets of profit curves. A separate one is drawn for each price of the *March futures* that one wants to consider in his analysis. The previous example showed the profitability for only one price of the March futures—unchanged at 594. However, one cannot rely on the March futures to remain unchanged, so he must view the profitability of the calendar spread at various March futures prices.

The data that is plotted in the Figure is summarized in Table 37-4.

Several things are readily apparent. First, if the futures spread improves in price, the calendar spread will generally *make* money. These are the points on the far right of the figure and on the bottom line of the table below. Second, if the futures spread behaves miserably, the calendar spread will almost certainly *lose* money (points on the left hand side of the figure, or top line of table).

Third, if March futures rise in price too far, the calendar spread could do poorly. In fact, if March futures rally *and* the futures spread worsens, *one could lose more than his initial debit* (bottom left hand point on figure). This is partly due to the fact that one is buying the March options back at a loss if March futures rally, and may also be forced to sell his May options out at a loss if May futures have fallen at the same time.

Fourth, as might be expected, best results are obtained if March futures rally slightly or remain unchanged and the futures spread also remains relatively unchanged (points in the upper right hand quadrant of the figure).

In Table 37-4, the far right hand column shows how a futures spreader would have fared if he had bought May and sold March at 4 points May over March, not using any options at all.

TABLE 37-4.
Profit and loss from soybean call calendar.

Futures Spread (May-Mar)	Mar Future Price:	Calendar Spread Profit					Future Spread Profit
		574	584	594	604	614	
− 24		− 5.5	− 4.5	− 3	− 4.5	− 11.5	− 28
− 14		− 4.5	− 3	− 0.5	− 1	− 7	− 18
− 4		− 2.5	0	+ 3	+ 3.5	− 1	− 8
6		0	+ 3	+ 7.5	+ 9	+ 5.5	+ 2
16		+ 7	+ 11	+ 17	+ 19	+ 13	+ 12

All Prices at March Option Expiration

This example demonstrates just how powerful the influence of the *futures* spread is. The calendar spread profit is predominantly a function of the futures spread price. Thus, even though the calendar spread was attractive from the theoretical viewpoint of the option's prices, its result does not seem to reflect that theoretical advantage, due to the influence of the futures spread. Another important point for the calendar spreader used to dealing with stock options to remember is that *one can lose more than his initial debit in a futures calendar spread* if the spread between the underlying futures inverts.

There is another way to view a calendar spread in futures options, however, and that is as a substitute or alternative to an intramarket spread in the futures contracts themselves. Look at the above table again and notice the far right-hand column. This is the profit or loss that would be made by an intramarket soybean spreader who bought May and sold March at the initial prices of 598 and 594, respectively. The calendar spread generally outperforms the intramarket spread for the prices shown in this example. This is where the true theoretical advantage of the calendar spread comes in. So, *if one is thinking of establishing an intramarket spread, he should check out the calendar spread in the futures options first.* If the options have a theoretical pricing advantage, the calendar spread may clearly outperform the standard intramarket spread.

Study the previous table for a moment. Note that the intramarket spread is only better when prices drop—but the spread widens (lower left corner of table). In all other cases, the calendar spread strategy is better. One could not always expect this to be true, of course; the results in the example are partly due to the fact that the March options that were sold were relatively expensive when compared with the May options that were bought.

In summary, the futures option calendar spread is more complicated when compared to the simpler stock or index option calendar spread. As a result, calendar spreading with futures options is a less popular strategy than its stock option counterpart. However, this does not mean that the strategist should overlook this strategy. As the strategist knows, he can often find the best opportunities in seemingly complex situations because there may be pricing inefficiencies present. For this strategy, its main application may be for the intramarket spreader who also understands the usage of options.

Long Combinations

Another attractive use of options is as a substitute for two instruments that are being traded one against the other. Since intermarket and intramarket futures spreads involve two instruments being traded against each other, futures options may be able to work well in these types of spreads. You may recall that a similar idea was presented with respect to "pairs trading," as well as certain risk arbitrage strategies and index futures spreading.

In any type of futures spread, one might be able to substitute options for the actual futures. He might buy calls for the long side of the spread instead of actually buying futures. Likewise, he could sell calls or buy puts instead of selling futures for the other side of the spread. In using options, however, he wants to avoid two problems. First, he does not want to increase his risk. Second, he does not want to pay a lot of time value premium that could waste away, costing him the profits from his spread.

Let's spend a short time to discuss these two points. First, he does not want to increase his risk. In general, selling options instead of utilizing futures increases one's risk. If he sells calls instead of selling futures, and sells puts instead of buying futures, he could be increasing his risk tremendously if the futures prices moved a lot. If the futures rose tremendously, the short calls would lose money, but the short puts would cease to make money once the futures rose through the striking price of the puts. *Therefore, it is not a recommended strategy to sell options in place of the futures in an intramarket or intermarket spread.* The next example will show why not.

Example: A spreader wants to trade an intramarket spread in live cattle. The contract is for 40,000 pounds, so a one cent move is worth $400. He is going to sell April and buy June futures, hoping for the spread to narrow between the two contracts.

The following prices exist for live cattle futures and options:

April future: 78.00

June future: 74.00

April 78 call: 1.25

June 74 put: 2.00

He decides to use the options instead of futures to implement this spread. He sells the April 78 call as an alternative to selling the April future; he also sells the June 74 put as an alternative to buying the June future.

Sometime later, the following prices exist:

April future: 68.00

June future: 66.00

April 78 call: 0.00

June 74 put: 8.05

The futures spread has indeed narrowed as expected—from 4.00 points to 2.00. However, this spreader has no profit to show for it; in fact he has a loss. The call that he sold is now virtually worthless and has therefore earned a profit of 1.25 points; however, the put that was sold for 2.00 is now worth 8.05—a loss of 6.05 points. Overall, the spreader has a net loss of 4.80 points since he used short options instead of the 2.00 point gain he could have had if he had used futures instead.

The second thing that the futures spreader wants to ensure is that he does not pay for a lot of time value premium that is wasted, costing him his potential profits. If he buys at- or out-of-the-money calls instead of buying futures, and if he buys at- or out-of-the-money puts instead of selling futures, he could be exposing his spread profits to the ravages of time decay. *Do not substitute at- or out-of-the-money options for the futures in intramarket or intermarket spreads.* The next example will show why not.

Example: A futures spreader notices that a favorable situation exists in Wheat. He wants to buy July and sell May. The following prices exist for the futures and options:

May futures: 410
July futures: 390
May 410 put: 20
July 390 call: 25

This trader decides to buy the May 410 put instead of selling May futures; he also buys the July 390 call instead of buy July futures.
Later, the following prices exist:

May futures: 400
July futures: 400
May 410 put: 25
July 390 call: 30

The futures spread would have made 20 points, since they are now the same price. At least this time, he has made money in the option spread. He has made 5 points on each option for a total of 10 points overall— only half the money that could have been made with the futures themselves. Note that these sample option prices still show a good deal of time value premium remaining. If more time had passed and these options were trading closer to parity, the result of the option spread would be worse.

It might be pointed out that the option strategy in the above example would work better if futures price were volatile and rallied or declined substantially. This is true to a certain extent. If the market had moved a lot, one option would be very deeply in-the-money and the other deeply out-of-the-money. Neither one would have much time value premium and he would therefore have wasted all the money spent for the initial time premium. So, unless the futures moved so far as to out-distance that loss of time value premium, the futures strategy would still outrank the option strategy.

However, this last point of volatile futures movement helping an option position is a valid one. It leads to the reason for the only favorable option strategy that is a substitute for futures spreads—that is using in-the-money options. *If one buys in-the-money calls instead of buying futures, and buys in-the-money puts instead of selling futures, he can often create a position that has an advantage over the intramarket or intermarket futures spread.* In-the-money options avoid most of the problems described in the two previous examples. There no increase of risk since the options are being bought, not sold. In addition, the amount of money spent on time value premium is small since both options are in-the-money. In fact, one could buy them so far in the money as to virtually eliminate any expense for time value premium. However, that is not recommended, for it would negate the possible advantage of using moderately in-the-money options: *if the underlying futures behave in a volatile manner, it might be possible for the option spread to make money, even if the futures spread does not behave as expected.*

In order to illustrate these points, the TED spread, an intermarket spread will be used. Recall that in order to buy the TED spread, one would buy T-Bill futures and sell an equal quantity of Eurodollar futures.

Options exist on both T-Bill futures and Eurodollar futures. If T-Bill calls were bought instead of T-Bill futures, and if Eurodollar puts were bought instead of selling Eurodollar futures, a similar position could be created that might have some advantages over buying the TED spread using futures. The advantage is that if T-Bills and/or Eurodollars change in price by a large enough amount, the option strategist can make money, even if the TED spread itself does not cooperate.

One might not think that short-term rates could be volatile enough to make this a worthwhile strategy. However, they can move substantially in a short period of time, especially if the Federal Reserve is active in lowering or raising rates. For example, suppose the Fed continues to lower rates and both T-Bills and Eurodollars substantially rise in price. Eventually, the puts that were purchased on the Eurodollars will become worthless, but the T-Bill calls that are owned will continue to grow and grow in value. Thus, one could make money, even if the TED spread was unchanged or shrunk, as long as short-term rates dropped far enough.

Similarly, if rates were to rise instead, the option spread could make money as the puts gained in value (rising rates mean T-Bills and Eurodollars will fall in price) and the calls eventually became worthless.

Example: The following prices for June T-Bill and Eurodollar futures and options exist in January. All of these products trade in units of 0.01, which is worth $25. So, a whole point is worth $2,500.

June T-Bill futures: 94.75

June Euro$ futures: 94.15

June T-Bill 9450 calls: 0.32

June Euro$ 9450 puts: 0.40

The TED spread, basis June, is currently at 0.60 (the difference in price of the two futures). Both futures have in-the-money options with only a small amount of time value premium in them.

The June T-Bill calls with a striking price of 94.50 are 0.25 in the money and are selling for 0.32. Their time value premium is only 0.07 points. Similarly, the June Eurodollar puts with a striking price of 94.50 are 0.35 in the money and are selling for 0.40. Hence, their time value premium is 0.05.

Since the total time value premium—0.12 ($300)—is small, the strategist decides that the option spread may have an advantage over the futures intermarket spread, so he establishes the following position:

	Cost
Buy one June T-Bill call @ 0.40	$1,000
Buy one June Euro$ put @ 0.32	$ 800
Total cost:	$1,800

Later, financial conditions in the world are very stable and the TED spread begins to shrink. However, at the same time, rates are being lowered in the United States, and T-Bill and Eurodollar prices begin to rally substantially. In May, when the June T-Bill options expire, the following prices exist:

June T-Bill futures: 95.50

June Euro$ futures: 95.10

June T-Bill 9450 calls: 1.00

June Euro$ 9450 puts: 0.01

The TED spread has *shrunk* from 0.60 to only 0.40. Thus, any trader attempting to buy the TED spread using only futures would have lost $500 as the spread moved against him by 0.20.

However, look at the option position. The options are now worth a combined value of 1.01 points ($2,525), and they were bought for 0.72 points ($1,800). Thus, the option strategy has turned a profit of $725, while the futures strategy lost money.

Any traders who used this option strategy instead of using futures would have enjoyed profits, because as the Federal Reserve lowered rates time after time, the prices of both T-Bills and Eurodollars rose far enough to make the option strategist's calls more profitable than the loss in his puts. This is the advantage of using in-the-money options instead of futures in futures spreading strategies.

In fairness, it should be pointed out that if the futures prices had remained relatively unchanged, the 0.12 points of time value premium ($300) could have been lost, while the futures spread may have been relatively unchanged. However, this does not alter the reasoning behind wanting to use this option strategy.

Another consideration that might come into play is the margin required. Recall that the initial margin for implementing the TED spread was $400. However, if one uses the option strategy, he must pay for the options in full—$1,800 in the above example. This could conceivably be a deterrent to using the option strategy. Of course, if by investing $1,800, one can *make* money instead of *losing* money with the smaller investment, then the initial margin requirement is irrelevant. Therefore, the profit potential must be considered the more important factor.

Follow-Up Considerations

When one uses long option combinations to implement a futures spread strategy, he may find that his position changes from a spread to more of an outright position. This would occur if the markets were volatile and one option became deeply in-the-money, while the other one was nearly worthless. The TED spread example above showed how this could occur as the call wound up being worth 1.00, while the put was virtually worthless.

As one side of the option spread goes out-of-the-money, the spread nature begins to disappear and a more outright position takes its place. One can use the deltas of the options in order to calculate just how much exposure he has at any one time. The following examples will go through a series of analyses and trades that a strategist might have to face. The first example concerns establishing an intermarket spread in oil products.

Example: In late summer, a spreader decides to implement an intermarket spread. He feels that the coming winter may be severely cold;

furthermore, he feels that gasoline prices are too high, being artificially buoyed by the summer tourist season, and the high prices are being carried into the future months by inefficient market pricing.

Therefore, he wants to buy heating oil futures or options and sell unleaded gasoline futures or options. He plans to be out of the trade, if possible, by early December, when the market should have discounted the facts about the winter. Therefore, he decides to look at January futures and options. The following prices exist:

Future or Option	Price	Time Value Premium
Jan heating oil futures:	.6550	
Jan unleaded gasoline futures:	.5850	
Jan heating oil 60 call:	6.40	0.90
Jan unleaded gas 62 put:	4.25	0.75

The differential in futures prices is .07, or 7 cents per gallon. He thinks it could grow to 12 cents or so by early winter. However, he also feels that oil and oil products have the potential to be very volatile, so he considers using the options. One cent is worth $420 for all these items.

The time value premium of the options is 1.65 for the put and call combined. If he pays this amount ($693) per combination, he can still make money if the futures widen by 5.00 points, as he expects. Moreover, the option spread gives him the potential for profits if oil products are volatile, even if he is wrong about the futures relationship.

Therefore, he decides to buy five combinations:

Position	Cost
Buy 5 Jan heating oil 60 calls @ 6.40	$13,440
Buy 5 Jan unleaded 62 puts @ 4.25	8,925
Total cost:	$22,365

This initial cost is substantially larger that the initial margin requirement for five futures spreads, which would be about $7,000. Moreover, the option cost must be paid for in cash, while the futures requirement could be taken care of with Treasury Bills, which continue to earn money for the spreader. Still, the strategist feels that the option position has more potential, so he establishes it.

Notice that in this analysis, *the strategist compared his time value premium cost to the profit potential he expected from the futures spread itself.* This is often a good way to evaluate whether or not to use options or futures. In this example, he felt that, even if futures prices remained relatively unchanged, thereby wasting away his time premium, he could still make money—as long as he was correct about heating oil outper-forming unleaded gasoline.

Some follow-up actions will now be examined. If the futures rally, the position becomes "long". Some profit might have accrued, but the whole position is subject to losses if the futures fall in price. The strategist can calculate the extent to which his position has become long by using the delta of the options in the strategy. He can then use futures or other options in order to make the position more neutral, if he wants to.

Example: Suppose that both unleaded gasoline and heating oil have rallied some and that the futures spread has widened slightly. The fol-lowing information is known:

Future or Option	Price	Net Change	Profit/Loss
Jan heating oil futures:	.7100	+ .055	
Jan unleaded gasoline futures:	.6300	+ .045	
Jan heating oil 60 call:	11.05	+4.65	+$9,765
Jan unleaded gas 62 put:	1.50	-2.75	- 5,775
Total profit:			+$3,990

The futures spread has widened to 8 cents. If the strategist had es-tablished the spread with futures, he would now have a one cent ($420) profit on five contracts, or a $2,100 profit. The profit is larger in the option strategy.

The futures have rallied as well. Heating oil is up 5½ cents from its initial price, while unleaded is up 4½ cents. This rally has been large enough to drive the puts out-of-the-money. When one has established the intermarket spread with options, and the futures rally this much, the profit is usually greater from the option spread. Such is the case in this example, as the option spread is ahead by almost $4,000.

This example shows the most desirable situation for the strategist who has implemented the option spread. The futures rally enough to force the puts out-of-the-money, or alternatively fall far enough to force the calls to be out-of-the-money. If this happens in advance of option expiration, one option will generally have almost all of its time value premium dis-appear (the calls in the above example). The other option, however, will still have some time value (the puts in the example).

This represents an attractive situation. However, there is a potential negative, and that is that the position is too long now. It is not really a spread anymore. If futures should drop in price, the calls will lose value quickly. The puts will not gain much, though, because they are out-of-the-money and will not adequately protect the calls. At this juncture, the strategist has the choice of taking his profit—closing the position—or making an adjustment to make the spread more neutral once again. He could also do nothing, of course, but a *strategist* would normally want to protect a profit to some extent.

Example: The strategist decides that, since his goal was for the futures spread to widen to 12 cents, he will not remove the position when the spread is only 8 cents as it is now. However, he wants to take some action to protect his current profit, while still retaining the possibility to have the profit expand.

As a first step, the equivalent futures position (EFP) is calculated. The pertinent data is shown in Table 37-5.

Overall, the position is long the equivalent of about three futures contracts. The position's profitability is mostly related to whether the futures rise or fall in price, not to how the spread between heating oil futures and unleaded gas futures behaves.

The strategist could easily neutralize the long delta by selling three contracts. This would leave room for more profits if prices continue to rise (there are still two extra long calls). It would also provide downside protection if prices suddenly drop, since the 5 long puts plus the 3 short futures would offset any loss in the 5 in-the-money calls.

Which futures should the strategist short? That depends on how confident he is in his original analysis of the intermarket spread widening. If he still thinks it will widen farther, then he should sell unleaded gasoline futures against the deeply in-the-money heating oil calls. This would give him an additional profit or loss opportunity based on the relationship of the two oil products. However, if he decides that the intermarket spread

TABLE 37-5.
EFP of long combination.

Future or Option	Price	Delta	EFP
Jan heating oil futures:	.7100		
Jan unleaded gasoline futures:	.6300		
Jan heating oil 60 call:	11.05	0.99	+4.95
Jan unleaded gas 62 put:	1.50	−0.40	−2.00
		Total EFP:	+2.95

should have widened more than this by now, perhaps he will just sell 3 heating oil futures as a direct hedge against the heating oil calls.

Once one finds himself in a profitable situation, as in the above example, *the most conservative course is to hedge the in-the-money option with its own underlying future.* This action lessens the further dependency of the profits on the intermarket spread. There is still profit potential remaining from futures price action. Furthermore, if the futures should fall so far that both options return to in-the-money status, then the intermarket spread comes back into play. Thus, in the above example, the conservative action would be to sell three heating oil futures against the heating oil calls.

The more aggressive course is to hedge the in-the-money option with the future underlying the other side of the intermarket spread. In the above example, that would entail selling the unleaded gasoline futures against the heating oil calls.

Suppose that the strategist in the previous example decides to take the conservative action, and he therefore shorts three heating oil futures at .7100, the current price. This action preserves large profit potential in either direction. It is better than selling out-of-the-money options against his current position.

He would consider removing the hedge if futures prices dropped—perhaps when the puts returned to an in-the-money status with a put delta of at least -0.75 or so. At that point, the position would be at its original status, more or less, except for the fact that he would have taken a nice profit in the three futures that were sold and covered.

Prologue: The above examples are taken from actual price movements. In reality, the futures fell back, not only to their original price, but far below it. The fundamental reason for this reversal was that the weather was warm, hurting demand for heating oil, and gasoline supplies were low. By the option expiration in December, the following prices existed:

January heating oil futures: .5200

January unleaded gas futures: .5200

Not only had the futures prices virtually crashed, but the intermarket spread had been decimated as well. The spread had fallen to zero! It had never reached anything near the 12 cent potential that was envisioned. Any spreader who had established this spread with futures would have almost certainly lost money; he probably would not have held it until it reached this lowly level, but there was never much opportunity to get out at a profit.

The strategist who established the spread with options, however, most certainly would have *made* money. One could safely assume that he covered the three futures sold in the previous example at a nice profit—possibly seven points or so. One could also assume that as the puts became in-the-money options, he established a similar hedge and *bought* three unleaded gasoline futures when the EFP reached −3.00. This probably occurred with unleaded gasoline futures around .5700—5 cents in the money.

Assuming that these were the trades, the following table shows the profits and losses.

Position	Initial Price	Final Price	Net Profit/ Loss
Bot 5 calls	6.40	0	− $13,440
Bot 5 puts	4.25	10.00	+ 12,075
Sold 3 htg oil futures	.7100	.6400	+ 8,820
Bot 3 unleaded futures	.5700	.5200	− 6,300
Total profit:			+ $ 1,155

In the final analysis, the fact that the intermarket spread collapsed to zero actually aided the option strategy, since the puts were the in-the-money option at expiration. This was not planned, of course, but by being long the options, the strategist was able to make money when volatility appeared.

Intramarket Spread Strategy

It should be obvious that the same strategy could be applied to an intra-market spread as well. If one is thinking of spreading two different soybean futures, for example, he could substitute in-the-money options for futures in the position. He would have the same attributes as shown for the intermarket spread: large potential profits if volatility occurs. Of course, he could still make money if the intramarket spread widens, but he would lose the time value premium paid for the options.

SUMMARY

Futures spreading is a very important and potentially profitable endeavor. Utilizing options in these spreads can often improve profitability to the point where an original mistaken assumption can be overcome by volatility of price movement.

Futures spreads fall into two categories—intermarket and intramarket. They are an important strategy because many futures exhibit historic and/or seasonal tendencies that can be traded without regard to the overall movement of futures prices.

Options can be used to enhance these futures spreading strategies. The futures calendar spread is closely related to the intramarket spread. It is distinctly different from the stock or index option calendar spread.

Using in-the-money long option combinations in lieu of futures can be a very attractive strategy for either intermarket or intramarket spreads. The option strategy also affords the strategist the opportunity for follow-up action based on the equivalent futures position that accumulates as prices rise or fall.

Traders who utilize futures spreads as part of their trading strategy should give serious consideration to substituting options where applicable. Such an alternative strategy will often improve the chances for profit.

Chapter *38* _____

Advanced Concepts

As the option markets have matured, strategists have been forced to rely more on mathematics in order to select new positions as well as to discern how their positions will behave in fluctuating markets. These techniques can be used on simple strategies, such as bull spreads or ratio spreads, or on far more complex portfolios of options.

First, the concept of implied volatility will be examined in more detail, primarily as an aid in choosing new positions that have a positive expected return. Then, the concept of risk management will be explored. In effect, one can reduce his option position into several components of risk measurement that can be readily understood. This chapter will describe the techniques used to evaluate one's position, and will show how to use this information to reduce the risk in the position. The actual mathematical calculations required to perform these analyses are included at the end of this chapter.

USING IMPLIED VOLATILITY

The concept of volatility was discussed in some detail in the chapter on mathematical applications. This section will expand on those definitions with a concentration on using the volatility in order to help operate a neutral strategy.

In review, volatility is a measure of how quickly a stock's price changes. It is an important input to any option pricing model; probably the most important input. When one computes volatility by using past stock prices, the result is called the *historic volatility*. Using the historic volatility can present some problems to the option strategist, because current events in the market may change the stock's current volatility, rendering the usage of historic volatility ineffective. These events might include such things as takeover rumors or large revisions in a company's earnings estimate. When the current market volatility rises dramatically due to such events, all options will appear to be overpriced (according to any option pricing model that is using historical volatility). This fact could lead the strategist to sell options heavily. But, if the actual volatility of the stock has changed, the strategist may be making a big mistake if he sells options. In effect, the option prices may be based on a projection of future volatility, not on the past performance of stock prices.

Thus, many traders prefer another measure of volatility—one that is able to cope with current changes in the marketplace. This volatility would be the one that is being implied by the marketplace itself. That is, one only need ask the question, "What volatility would I need to plug into the Black-Scholes model in order to arrive at the current price of the option?" The answer is called the *implied volatility*.

Example: with XYZ at 49, the Jan 50 call is trading at 3½. If one uses 32% as his volatility input to the Black-Scholes model, the model gives 3.46 as the value of the call. This result is very close to the actual trading price of the Jan 50 call, thus the implied volatility of the Jan 50 call is 32%.

Note that this definition could apply to any model, not just the Black-Scholes. For convenience, the remaining discussions will refer to models as the Black-Scholes model, but the reader should understand that the concepts could apply to any other model just as easily. In addition, futures option strategists can freely substitute the word 'future' for 'stock.'

Using the implied volatilities of its options in order to deduce an overall implied volatility for the underlying stock may be tricky. Each individual option has its own implied volatility. In a perfect world, of course, each option would have the *same* implied volatility. Then, the strategist could use that implied volatility as the volatility of the underlying stock itself. In the real world, unfortunately, things rarely work out so well. In fact, it is possible that no two options on the same underlying stock will have the exact same implied volatility. The strategist needs to average them in some fashion in order to be able to get a composite implied volatility for the underlying stock. Generally, one would give more weight to the options which have the highest trading volume, are closest to the striking price, and have the least time to expiration. Furthermore, since the implied volatility may jump around from day to day, especially if the underlying stock is being buffeted by rumors, the strategist needs to use a moving average of the daily implieds. A formula for combining the individual implied volatilities was presented in the chapter on mathematical applications.

How can this information help the strategist? It can alert him to options that are theoretically mispriced, allowing him to establish a position with favorable expected returns. There are two basic ways that the implied volatility can be used to establish or adjust positions. First, if the implied volatility of the stock is significantly different from the historical volatility, an opportunity may exist. Second, if the implied volatilities of individual options on the same underlying stock are significantly different from each other, then an opportunity surely exists. In either case, the strategist would attempt to establish a neutral position, preferring not to predict market movement, but to merely let the favorable mathematical relationships work for him. Let us discuss these two concepts in more detail.

Historical Volatility Differs From Implied Volatility

One way of using volatility to establish a theoretically favorable position is to compare the historical volatility with the current volatility that is being implied in the market. If there is a substantial difference between the two, there *may* be an opportunity to profit.

Example: XYZ stock has a historical volatility of 23%. This reflects the trading pattern of past stock prices, averaged over some reasonable time—perhaps 20 or 30 trading days. However, assume XYZ has been in a tight trading range and has not advanced or declined much in the last six weeks. Note that the fact that a stock is in a trading range does not necessarily mean that its historical volatility will decrease substantially.

This stagnant price performance has discouraged option buyers, and they have disappeared, or at least have lowered their bids. As a result of the hesitancy on the part of option buyers, option premiums have lowered to the point where the *implied volatility* of XYZ is only 14%.

This situation might be exemplified by the following data, where the "theoretical" option price is based on the *historical* volatility of 23%:

XYZ Common: 65   Historical Volatility: 23%

Averaged Implied Volatility: 14%

Option	Actual Price	Implied Volatility	"Theoretical" Price
Jan 65 call	1½	14%	2.32
Jan 70 call	¼	17%	0.62
Feb 65 call	2	13%	3.17
Mar 70 call	¾	16%	1.74
Jan 65 put	1	13%	1.92
Feb 65 put	1⅜	14%	2.47

Note how cheap the options appear. Their actual prices are very much below their theoretical prices. This is because the theoretical prices are computed using a volatility of 23% as the input to the Black-Scholes model, whereas one can easily see that the *implied volatilities* of the options are each well below 23%.

If one believes that XYZ will exhibit price changes that reflect the 23% volatility, then he should do some option buying, preferably in a neutral position. The easiest position would be to buy a straddle — perhaps the Feb 65 straddle for 3⅜ (its "theoretical" value at 23% volatility is 5.64, so one would be buying it substantially under "theoretical" value).

There are two ways to profit. If XYZ does actually have price swings in line with the 23% volatility, then odds favor the stock moving far enough to make the straddle profitable. However, the straddle buyer can profit in another way: if the marketplace decides to value the XYZ options at a higher implied volatility, then he will also profit. That is, if option buyers perceive that XYZ is going to be more volatile, they would bid more for options, thus producing a profit for the Feb 65 straddle buyer, *even if XYZ does not change in price.*

Clearly, the purchase of the cheap straddle in this example does not guarantee a profit. XYZ may never make enough of a move to produce a profit in the Feb 65 straddle, and buying interest may never appear in the options (that is, the implied volatilities may never rise). If neither of these things happened, the straddle buyer would surely lose money.

So, is this a good position or not? The answer does not necessarily lie in whether the position eventually makes a profit. It is always possible that an excellent position (theoretically) fails to produce a profit. Rather, the answer lies in whether the historical volatility estimate of 23% can be trusted, or should one be using the implied volatility estimate of 14%? Each is a known quantity — it can be computed easily. But the real question that one must ask is, "*Is the future volatility of XYZ going to be 14% or 23%?*"

Now, no one knows what the *future* volatility of XYZ is going to be for sure, but obviously that is what is going to be a major factor in determining if this is a profitable position or not. All one can do is try to decide if the historical volatility is a better estimate of future volatility than is implied volatility. Making that decision is more of an art than a science, but there are clues that may help.

If the historical volatility is distorted for some reason, then one should view it with caution. For example, when the market crashes or has a tremendously volatile period (generally to the downside), price swings magnify and historical volatilities increase. However, as time passes, these price swings diminish on a daily basis. The historical volatility is generally calculated over a specific historical period (50 trading days, for example). If the volatile price behavior is encompassed in that historical period, the historical volatility may be inflated. In such a case, one should not buy the options, for the implied volatility is probably more accurate than the historical.

However, if the underlying security has not experienced any particularly abnormal price movements in the recent past, then the historical volatility can be relied upon. Therefore, a situation such as the one presented in the above example would lead one to option buying because he feels that the historical volatility can be trusted.

Inflated implied volatility. In the reverse situation, where the historical volatility is *lower* than the implied volatility, one would be led toward selling options. Since at least some of these options would be sold naked, the strategist must exercise great care to be certain that he can rely upon the historical volatility:

Example: XYZ is at 45. The stock's historical volatility is 30%, but the options have suddenly gotten quite expensive and are exhibiting an implied volatility of nearly 45%. Again, the "theoretical" price column is computed using the historical volatility of 30%.

XYZ Common: 45   Historical Volatility: 30%

Averaged Implied Volatility: 45%

Option	Actual Price	Implied Volatility	"Theoretical" Price
Jan 45 call	3	46%	2.00
Jan 50 call	1⅛	44%	0.45
Jan 55 call	½	48%	0.06
Feb 45 call	3¾	42%	2.74
Feb 55 call	⅞	43%	0.28

Notice that the actual price is much higher than the "theoretical" price in each case. Does this mean that one can blithely sell these options? Not unless he has great faith in the historical volatility estimate, since that is what was used to determine that the options are now "expensive."

If he did, indeed, decide to establish a position, it again should be something neutral: the sale of the Jan 45 straddle, perhaps, or the sale of both out-of-the-money calls and puts.

He could profit from such a strategy in two ways: either XYZ remains in a relatively narrow trading range and the options lose value as time passes, or the implied volatility of the options decreases and the options lose value because of the volatility decrease.

Again, the strategist must attempt to determine which of the two volatilities—historical or implied—is more accurate. When the implied is inflated, as in this example, he needs to be extremely careful, for he will almost certainly be establishing a position that contains naked options if he decides to sell premium. In many cases, the implied increases dramatically when there are rumors in the market concerning the underlying stock: takeover rumors, rumors of a dramatic change in earnings, or the supposed announcement of a new product discovery or approval. If the strategist feels that such rumors are the reason for inflated implied volatility, then he should probably *avoid* selling the options, because other people may have better information regarding the fundamentals of the company than the strategist does. Stated in another way, the implied volatility is probably a better predictor of future volatility because, if the rumor proves to be true, then the stock will be more volatile. Of course, even rumors based on facts which eventually prove to be true can get overdone. If the strategist feels that the implied is *so* inflated that it has discounted even the most extreme rumors, then he could feel safer about selling premium.

In summary, when there is a large discrepancy between historical volatility and implied volatility, the strategist may have an opportunity to establish a theoretically profitable position. However, he must decide which of the volatilities is the better predictor of *future volatility*. If he decides that the historical volatility is the better predictor, then he has the opportunity to do something—buy options if the historical is less than the implied; sell options if the opposite is true.

If he is led towards buying options, then his risk will be limited. It is often easier to trust the historical volatility in this case. Can the implied volatility really be expected to predict that a security will become dull? That is a hard prediction to make, especially if there is no unusual activity (such as a crash) in the makeup of the historical volatility.

On the other hand, if the implied volatility is expensive, then someone may have better fundamental information than the strategist does. In this case, the strategist should be extremely careful about taking on a position that involves naked options. In fact, he should probably avoid doing so.

Some traders feel that the market is efficient enough that the current implied volatility should almost always be trusted with respect to the historical volatility. *In other words, the options will always be the correct predictor of future volatility.* If this is the case, then one would not even bother with attempting to establish positions based on discrepancies between the two volatilities. Does this mean he would not use volatility at all? No, it merely means he would rather look for large discrepancies between the implied volatilities of individual options on the same underlying security.

Differing Implied Volatilities on the Same Underlying Security

As explained earlier, the implied volatility of an option is the volatility that one would have to use as input to the Black-Scholes model in order for the result of the model to be equal to the current market price of the option. Each option on a security will thus have its own implied volatility. Generally, they will be fairly close to each other, although not exactly the same. However, in some cases, there will be large enough discrepancies between the individual implied volatilities to warrant the strategist's attention. It is this latter condition of large discrepancies that will be addressed in this section.

Example: XYZ is trading at 45. The following option prices exist, along with their implied volatilities:

Option	Actual Price	Implied Volatility
Jan 45 call	2¾	41%
Jan 50 call	1¼	47%
Jan 55 call	⅝	53%
Feb 45 call	3½	38%
Feb 50 call	4	45%

Note that the implied volatilities of the individual options range from a low of 38% to a high of 53%. This is a rather large discrepancy for options on the same underlying security, but it is useful for exemplary purposes.

A neutral strategy could be established by buying options with lower implied volatilities and simultaneously selling ones with higher volatilities, such as buy 10 Feb 45 calls and sell 20 Jan 50 calls. Examples of neutral spreads will be expanded upon in a later section, when more exact measures for determining how many calls to buy and sell are discussed.

Before just jumping into such a position, the strategist should ask himself if there is a valid reason why the different options have such different implied volatilities. As a generalization, it might be fair to say that out-of-the-money options have slightly higher implieds than at-the-money ones, and that longer-term options have lower implieds than short-term ones. But there are many instances where such is not the case, so one must be careful not to over-generalize.

Speculators often desire the lowest dollar cost option available. Thus, in a takeover rumor situation, they would buy the out-of-the-moneys as opposed to the higher-priced at- or in-the-moneys. If the out-of-the-moneys are extremely expensive because of a takeover rumor, then the strategist must be careful, because the neutral strategy concept may lead him into selling naked calls. This is not to say he should avoid the situation altogether; he may be able to structure a position with enough upside room to protect himself, or he may feel the rumors are false. The discussion of specific positions will be deferred to a later section, where the concepts of delta and gamma will be used to establish a neutral strategy.

Returning to the general topic of differing implied volatilities on the same underlying stock, the strategist might ask how he is to determine if the discrepancies between the individual options are significantly large to warrant attention. A mathematical approach is presented at the end of this chapter in a section on advanced mathematical concepts. Suffice it to say that there is a way that the differences of the various implieds can be reduced to a single number—a sort of "standard deviation of the implieds," which is easy for the strategist to use. A list of these numbers can be constructed, comparing which stocks or futures might be candidates for this type of neutral spreading. On a given day, the list is usually quite short—perhaps 20 stocks and 10 futures contracts will qualify.

Using Implied Volatility In Follow-Up Action

The profit picture is one of the more important tools that the strategist can use in order to see how his position is going to behave. In order to draw the profit picture at some time prior to expiration, a model must be used to predict the prices of the options involved. What volatility should one use in the model in order to fairly predict the profitability of a position? If he uses the historical volatility, it may distort the potential profits and lead him to a false conclusion.

Example: As in the above example, a situation exists in which the individual options on a security have differing implied volatilities:

XYZ: 44; historical volatility = 35%

Option	Price	Implied Volatility
July 45 call	2½	45%
July 50 call	1½	55%

Suppose one were to buy 10 July 45 calls and sell 20 July 50 calls. Figure 38-1 shows how this position would look 14 days after it was established. It is no problem to draw the straight lines that depict a position's profit picture at expiration. The problem arises in deciding which volatility to plug into the model to draw the profit picture 14 days from

FIGURE 38-1.
XYZ ratio spread, in 14 days.

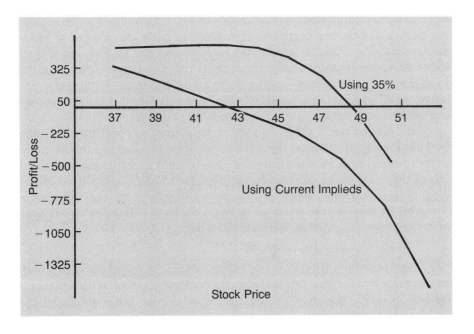

now. The higher curved line is drawn using 35% as the volatility for XYZ as well as for each of the options. This is probably an *incorrect* assumption. There is little likelihood that all pricing discrepancies would correct themselves in just two weeks. The lower curved line is drawn using each option's current implied volatility as the input to the model. That is, one is assuming that the options will still bear the same distorted relationship to each other in two weeks that they have right now. For some index and futures options, that is the best assumption to make, for the distorted relationships between individual implied volatilities often persist for a long time.

Notice that the lower curve offers a less rosy profit picture. It is, however, probably the more correct one. Thus, the strategist should use the current implied volatilities when projecting profits over the short term.

This concept of the implied volatilities of various options on the same underlying stock remaining out of line with each other is one that needs more discussion. In the following section, the idea of semi-permanent distortion between the volatilities of different striking prices is discussed.

Volatility Skewing

After the stock market crashed in 1987, index options experienced what has since proven to be a permanent distortion: puts have remained more expensive than calls. Futhermore, out-of-the-money puts are more expensive than at-the-money puts; out-of-the-money calls are cheaper than at-the-money calls. This distorted effect is due to several factors, but it is so deep-seated that it has remained through all kinds of up and down markets since then. Other markets—particularly futures markets—have also experienced a long-lasting distortion between the implied volatilities at various strikes.

The proper name given to this phenomenon is *volatility skewing: the long-lasting effect whereby options at different striking prices trade with differing implied volatilities.* It should be noted that the calls and puts at the *same* strike must trade for the same implied volatility—otherwise, conversion or reversal arbitrage would eliminate the difference. However, there is no true arbitrage between different striking prices. Hence, arbitrage cannot eliminate volatility skewing.

Example: Volatility skewing exists in OEX index options. Assume the "average" volatility of OEX and its options is 16%. With volatility skewing present, the implied volatilities at the various striking prices might look like this:

OEX: 380

Strike	Implied Volatility of Both Puts & Calls
350	22%
360	19%
370	17%
380	16%
390	15%
400	14%
410	13%

In this form of volatility skewing, the out-of-the-money puts are the most expensive options; the out-of-the-money calls are the cheapest.

The causes of this effect stem from the stock market's penchant to crash occasionally. Investors who want protection buy index puts; they don't sell index futures as much as they used to because of the failure of the portfolio insurance strategy during the 1987 crash. In addition, margin requirements for selling naked index puts have increased, especially for market makers, who are the main suppliers of naked puts. Consequently, demand for index puts is high and supply is low. Therefore, out-of-the-money index puts are overly expensive.

This does not entirely explain why index calls are so cheap. Part of the reason for that is that there is no restrictive margin treatment on the sale of index calls for market makers. In addition, institutional traders can help finance the cost of those expensive index puts by selling some out-of-the-money index calls. Such sales would essentially be covered calls if the institution owned stocks, which it most certainly would.

This distortion in volatilities is not in accordance with the probability distribution of stock prices. These distorted implied volatilities define a different probability curve for stock movement. They seem to say that there is more chance of the market dropping than there is of it rising. This is not true; in fact, just the opposite is true. Refer to the reasons for using lognormal distribution to define stock price movements. Consequently, there are opportunities to profit from volatility skewing, if one is able to hold the position until expiration.

It was shown in previous examples that one would attempt to sell the options with higher implied volatilities and buy ones with lower implieds as a hedge. Hence, for OEX traders, two strategies seem relevant:

1. Buy OEX puts and sell a larger number of out-of-the-money puts—a ratio write of put options.
   Example: Buy 10 OEX June 360 puts
             Sell 20 OEX June 350 puts

2. Sell OEX calls and buy a larger number of out-of-the-money calls—a backspread of call options.
   Example: Buy 20 OEX June 390 calls
           Sell 10 OEX June 380 calls

In either case, one is selling the higher implied volatility and buying options with lower implied volatilities. The first strategy would be best suited for moderately bearish investors, although a crash might drive the index so low that the additional puts that were sold could cause some risk. However, *statistically* this is an attractive strategy. At expiration, the volatility skewing must disappear; the markets will have moved in line with their real probability distribution, not the false one being implied by the skewed options. This makes for a potentially profitable situation for the strategist.

The backspread strategy would work best for bullish investors, although some backspreads can be created for credits, so a little money could also be made if the index fell. In theory, a strategist could implement both strategies simultaneously, which would give him an "edge" over a wide range of index prices. Again, this does not mean that he cannot lose money; it merely means that his strategy is statistically superior because of the way the options are priced. That is, the odds are in his favor.

Another interesting thing happens in these strategies that may be to their benefit: the volatility skewing that is present propagates itself throughout the striking prices as OEX moves around. It was shown in the previous section's example that one should probably continue to project his profits using the distorted volatilities that were present when he establishes a position. This is a conservative approach, but a correct one. In the case of these OEX spreads, it may be a benefit.

Assuming that the skewing is present wherever OEX is trading means that the at-the-money strike will have 16% as its implied volatility regardless of the absolute price level; the skewing will then extend out from that strike. So, if OEX rises to 400, then the 400 strike would have a volatility of 16%, or if it fell to 360, then the 360 puts and calls would have a volatility of 16%. Of course, 16% is just a representative figure; the "average" volatility of OEX can change as well. For illustrative purposes, it is convenient to assume that the at-the-money strike keeps a constant volatility.

Example: Initially, a trader establishes a call backspread in OEX options in order to take advantage of the volatility skewing:

Initial situation: OEX: 380

Option	Implied Volatility	Delta
Jun 390 call	15%	0.40
Jun 400 call	14%	0.20

A neutral spread would be:

Buy 2 June 400 calls

Sell 1 June 390 call

since the deltas are in the ratio of 2-to-1.

Now, suppose that OEX rises to 400 at a later date, but well before expiration. This is not a particularly attractive price for this position. Recall that, at expiration, a backspread has its worst result at the striking price of the purchased options. Even prior to expiration, one would not expect to have a profit with the index right at 400.

However, the statistical advantage that the strategist had to begin with might be able to help him out. The present situation would probably look like this:

Present situation: OEX: 400

Option	Implied Volatility
Jun 390 call	17%
Jun 400 call	16%

The June 400 call is now the at-the-money call since OEX has risen to 400. As such, its implied volatility will be 16% (or whatever the "average" volatility is for OEX at that time—the assumption is made that it is still 16%). The June 390 call has a slightly higher volatility (17%) because volatility skewing is still present.

Thus, the options that are long in this spread have had their implied volatility *increase*; that is a benefit. Of course, the options that are short had theirs increase as well, but the overall spread should benefit for two reasons:

1. Twice as many options are owned as were sold.
2. The effect of increased volatility is greatest on the at-the-money option; the in-the-money will be affected to a lesser degree.

All index options exhibit this volatility skewing. Volatility skewing exists in other markets as well. The other markets where volatility skewing is prevalent are usually futures option markets. In particular, gold, silver, sugar, soybeans, and coffee options will from time to time display a form of volatility skewing that is the opposite of that displayed by index options. In these futures markets, the cheapest options are out-of-the-money puts, while the most expensive options are out-of-the-money calls.

Example: January soybeans are trading at 580 ($5.80 per bushel). The following table of implied volatilities shows how volatility skewing that is present in the soybean market is the opposite from that shown by the OEX market in the previous examples:

January beans: 580

Strike	Implied Volatility
525	12%
550	13%
575	15%
600	17%
625	19%
650	21%
675	23%

Notice that the calls are now the more expensive items, while puts are the cheapest.

The distribution of soybean prices implied by these volatilities is just as incorrect as the OEX one was for the stock market. This soybean implied distribution is too bullish. It implies that there is a much larger probability of the soybean market rising 100 points than there is for it to fall 50 points. That is incorrect, considering the historical price movement of soybeans.

A strategist in this market would attempt to establish backspreads with *puts* (this allows him to buy more of the cheaper volatilities while selling higher volatilities); he also might attempt to set up ratio spreads in the calls for essentially the same reason.

Summary

Whenever volatility skewing exists—no matter what market—opportunities arise for the neutral strategist to establish a position that has advantages. These advantages arise out of the fact that normal market movements are different from what the options are implying. Moreover, the options are wrong when there is skewing at all strikes, from the lowest to the highest. The strategist should be careful to project his profits, prior to expiration, using the same skewing, for it may persist for some time to come. However, at expiration, it must of course disappear. Therefore, the strategist who is planning to hold the position to expiration will find that volatility skewing has presented him with an opportunity for a positive expected return.

NEUTRALITY

In the preceding examples, it was generally assumed that one would take a "neutral" position in order to capture the pricing or volatility differential. Why this concentration on neutrality? Neutrality, as it applies to option positions, means that one is non-committal with respect to at least one of the factors that influence an option's price. Simply put, this means that one can design an option position in which he can profit, no matter which way the underlying security moves.

Most option strategies fall into one of two categories: as a hedge to a stock or futures strategy (for example, buying puts to protect a portfolio of stocks), or as a profit venture unto itself. This latter category is where most traders find themselves, and they often approach it in a fairly speculative manner—either by buying options or by being a premium seller (covered or uncovered). In such strategies, the trader is taking a view of the market; he needs certain price action from the underlying security in order to profit. Even covered call writing, which is considered to be a "conservative" strategy, is subject to large losses if the underlying stock drops drastically.

It doesn't have to be that way. Strategies can be devised that will have a chance to profit regardless of price changes in the underlying stock, as well as *because* of them. Such strategies are *neutral strategies* and they always require at least two options in the position—a spread, straddle, or other combination. Often, when one constructs a neutral strategy, he is neutral with respect to price changes in the underlying security. It is also possible, and often wise, to be neutral with respect to the *rate of price change of the underlying security*, with respect to the *volatility* of the security, or with respect to *time decay*. This is not to imply that any option spread that is neutral will automatically be a money-maker; rather, one looks for an opportunity—perhaps an overpriced series of options— and attempts to capture that overpricing by constructing a neutral strategy around it. Then, regardless of the movement of the underlying stock, the strategist has a chance of making money if the overpricing disappears.

Note that the neutral approach is distinctly different from the speculator's, who, upon determining that he has discovered an underpriced call, would merely buy the call, hoping for the stock to increase in price. He would not make money if XYZ fell in price unless there was a huge expansion in implied volatility—not something to count on. The next section of this chapter deals with how one determines his neutrality. In effect, if he is not neutral, then he has risk of some sort. The following sections outline various measures of risk, which the strategist can use to establish a new position or manage an existing one.

The most important of these risk measurements is how much market exposure the position currently has. This has been previously described as the "delta." Of nearly equal importance to the strategist is how much the option strategy will change with respect to the rate of change in the price of the underlying security. Also of interest are how changes in volatility, in time remaining until expiration, or even in the risk-free interest rate will affect the position. Once the components of the option position are defined, the strategist can then take action to reduce the risk associated with any of the factors, should he so desire.

THE "GREEKS"

These risk measurements have generally been given names of actual or contrived Greek letters. For example, "delta" is one that was discussed in previous chapters. It has become common practice to refer to the exposure of an option position merely by describing it in terms of this "Greek" nomenclature. For example, "delta long 200 shares" means that the entire option position behaves as if the strategist were merely long 200 shares of the underlying stock. In all, there are six components, but only four are heavily used.

Delta

The first risk measurement that concerns the option strategist is *how much current exposure his option position has as the underlying security moves. This is called the "delta."* In fact, the term delta is commonly used in at least two different contexts: to express the amount by which an option changes for a 1-point move in the underlying security, or to describe the *equivalent stock position* of an entire option portfolio.

Reviewing the definition of the delta of an individual option (first described in Chapter 3), recall that the delta is a number that ranges between 0.0 and 1.0 for calls, and between −1.0 and 0.0 for puts. It is the amount by which the option will move if the underlying stock moves one point; or stated another way, it is the percentage of any stock price change that will be reflected in the change of price of the option.

Example: Assume an XYZ Jan 50 call has a delta of 0.50 with XYZ at a price of 49. This means that the call will move 50% as fast as the stock will move. So, if XYZ jumps to 51, a gain of 2 points, then the Jan 50 call can be expected to increase in price by 1 point (50% of the stock increase).

In another context, the delta of a call is often thought of as the probability of the call being in-the-money at expiration. That is, if XYZ is 50 and the Jan 55 call has a delta of 0.40, then there is a 40% probability that XYZ will be over 55 at January expiration.

Put deltas are expressed as negative numbers to indicate that puts prices move in the opposite direction from the underlying security. Recall that deltas of out-of-the-money options are smaller numbers, tending towards 0 as the option becomes very far out-of-the money. Conversely, deeply in-the-money calls have deltas approaching 1.0, while deeply in-the-money puts have deltas approaching -1.0. Note: mathematically, the delta of an option is the partial derivative of the Black-Scholes equation (or whatever formula one is using) with respect to stock price. Graphically, it is the slope of a line that is tangent to the option pricing curve.

Let us now take a look at how both volatility and time affect the delta of a call option. Much of the data to be presented in this chapter will be in both tabular and graphical form, since some readers prefer one style or the other.

The volatility of the underlying stock has an effect on delta. If the stock is not volatile, then in-the-money options have a higher delta, and out-of-the-money options have a lower delta. Figure 38-2 and Table 38-1 depict the delta of various calls on two stocks with differing volatilities. The deltas are shown for various strike prices, with the time remaining to expiration equal to 3 months and the underlying stock at a price of 50 in all cases. Note that the graph confirms the fact that a low-volatility stock's in-the-money options have the higher delta. The opposite holds true for out-of-the-money options: the high-volatility stock's options have the higher delta in that case. Another way to view this data is that a higher-volatility stock's options will always have more time value premium than the low-volatility stock's. In-the-money, these options with more time value will not track the underlying stock price movement as closely as ones with little or no time value. Thus, in-the-money, the low-volatility stock's options have the higher delta since they track the underlying stock price movements more closely. Out-of-the-money, the entire price of the option is composed of time value premium. The ones with

FIGURE 38-2.
Delta comparison, with XYZ = 50.

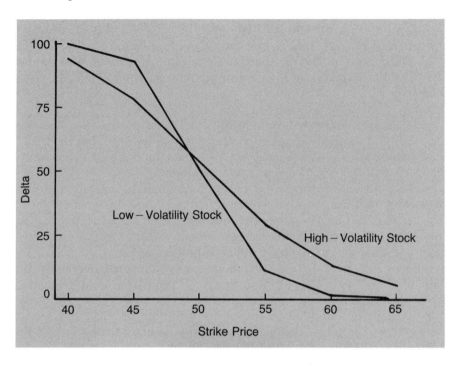

TABLE 38-1.
Delta comparison for different volatilities with XYZ = 50 and time = 3 months.

	Delta	
Strike Price	Low Volatility Stock	High Volatility Stock
40,	100	94
45,	93	78
50,	51	53
55,	11	29
60,	1	13
65,	0	5

higher time value (the ones on the high volatility stock) will move more since they have a higher price. Thus, out-of-the-money, the higher-volatility stock's options have the greater delta.

Time also affects delta. Figures 38-3 (see Table 38-2) and 38-4 show the relationships between time and delta. Figure 38-3's scales are similar

FIGURE 38-3.
Delta comparison, with XYZ = 50.

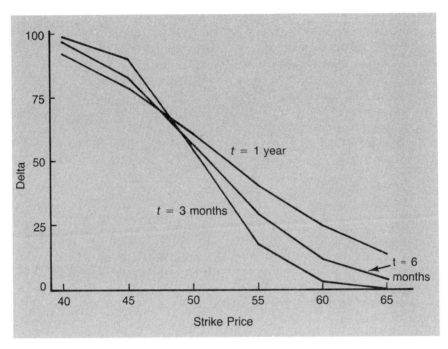

TABLE 38-2.
Delta comparison—varying time remaining with XYZ = 50.

	Delta		
Strike Price	t = 1 year	t = 6 months	t = 3 months
40,	92	97	99
45,	79	83	90
50,	61	57	55
55,	41	30	18
60,	25	12	3
65,	14	4	0

to those on Figure 38-2, delta vs. volatility: the deltas are shown for various striking prices with XYZ assumed to be equal to 50 in all cases. Notice that in-the-money, the shorter-term options have the higher delta. Again, this is because they have the least time value premium. Out-of-the-money, the opposite is true: the longer-term options have the higher deltas, since these options have the most time value premium.

FIGURE 38-4.
Delta as a function of time.

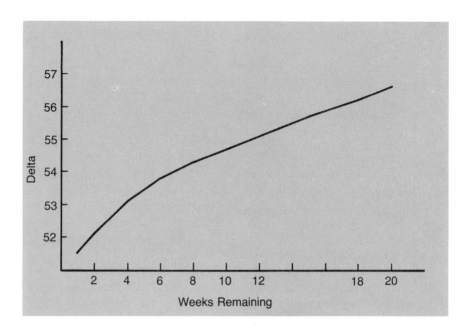

TABLE 38-3.
Delta as a function of time.

Weeks Remaining	Delta
20	.566
18	.562
15	.557
13	.553
10	.547
8	.543
6	.538
4	.531
2	.521
1	.515

Figure 38-4 (see Table 38-3) depicts the delta for an XYZ Jan 50 call with XYZ equal to 50. The horizontal axis in this graph is "weeks until expiration." Note that the delta of a longer-term at-the-money option is larger than that of a shorter-term option. In fact, the delta shrinks more rapidly as expiration draws nearer. Thus, even if a stock remains unchanged and its volatility is constant, the delta of its options will be altered as time passes. This is an important point to note for the strategist, since he is constantly monitoring the risk characteristics of his position. He cannot assume that his position is the same just because the stock has remained at the same price for a period of time.

POSITION DELTA

Another usage of the term "delta" is what has been previously referred to as the equivalent stock position (ESP) or, for futures options, it would be referred to as EFP (equivalent futures position). To differentiate between the two terms, the delta of the option is generally referred to as "option delta," while the ESP or EFP is called "position delta." Recall that the position delta is computed according to the following simple equation:

Position delta = option's delta × shares per option × option quantity.

For futures options, the term "shares per option" would be replaced by "shares per contract," which is always 1. This is the risk measurement of how much market exposure the option position has. Whether called "position delta," "ESP" or "EFP," one uses the deltas of the individual options in his portfolio to calculate the overall exposure. By summing the calculations for each item in a position, or even in an entire option portfolio, one can approximate how much market exposure the entire option position has. The following example, reprinted from the chapter on mathematical applications, shows how one computes the net exposure of a complicated position.

Example: The following position exists when XYZ is at 31¾. It resembles a long straddle (or backspread), in that there is increased profit potential in either direction if the stock moves far enough by expiration. Many market makers and professional traders attempt to structure these types of positions, if possible, in order to take advantage of the sudden volatility that is inherent in today's markets.

Position	*Delta*	*Position Delta*
Short 4500 XYZ	1.00	− 4,500
Short 100 XYZ Apr 25 calls	0.89	− 8,900
Long 50 XYZ Apr 30 calls	0.76	+ 3,800
Long 139 XYZ Jul 30 calls	0.74	+10,286
	Total ESP:	+ 686

This position, even though complicated to the naked eye, reduces to only being long approximately 700 shares of XYZ. This is commonly referred to as being "delta long 700 shares." Thus, the terms "delta," when referring to the sum of deltas of a whole position, and "equivalent stock position" are synonymous.

This position has some exposure to the market since it is "delta long." If the position delta were zero, it would be referred to as being delta neutral and would, theoretically, have no exposure to the market at this time.

Note that one can derive some general characteristics of his delta by just examining his portfolio by eye: short calls or long puts will introduce negative delta into the position; long calls or short puts will introduce positive delta. Furthermore, it is obvious that being long the underlying security adds to the long delta of the position, while being short the underlying security places more negative delta in the position. The use of this information to adjust the delta of one's position will be discussed in a later section of this chapter.

Obviously, the delta of this entire position will change as the stock price moves up or down as time passes. The above figure is merely an instantaneous look at how the position is structured. It is the need to know how the position will change when other factors change that have led strategists to employ the following concepts.

Gamma

Simply stated, *the gamma is how fast the delta changes* with respect to changes in the underlying stock price. It is known that the delta of a call increases as the call moves from out-of-the-money to in-the-money. The "gamma" is merely a precise measurement of how fast the delta is increasing.

Example: with XYZ at 49, assume the Jan 50 call has a delta of 0.50 and a gamma of 0.05. If XYZ moves up one point to 50, the delta of the call will increase by the amount of the gamma: it will increase from 0.50 to 0.55.

As with the delta, the gamma can also be expressed as a percentage. Only in this case, the increase or decrease applies to the delta.

Example: Again, with XYZ at 49, assume the Jan 50 call has a delta of 0.50 and a gamma of 0.05. If XYZ moves up 2 points to 51, the delta of the call will increase by 5% *of the stock move*, because the gamma is 0.05, or 5 percent. Five percent of the *stock move* is 0.05×2, or 0.10. Thus, the delta will increase by 0.10, from 0.50 to 0.60.

Obviously, the delta cannot keep increasing by 0.05 each time XYZ gains another point in price, for it will eventually exceed 1.00 by that calculation, and it is known that the delta has a maximum of 1.00. Thus, it is obvious that the gamma changes. In general, *the gamma is at its maximum point when the stock is near the strike of the option.* As the stock moves away from the strike in either direction, the gamma decreases, approaching its minimum value of zero.

Conceptually, this means that a deeply in-the-money or deeply out-of-the-money option has a *gamma* of nearly zero. This makes sense—it implies that the *delta* of a deep in- or deep out-of-the-money option does not change very much at all, even if the stock moves by one point.

Example: Assume XYZ is 25, and the Jan 50 call has a delta of virtually zero. If XYZ moves up one point to 26, the call is still so far out-of-the-money, that the delta will still be zero. Thus, the gamma of this call is zero, since the delta does not change when the stock increases in price by a point.

In a similar manner, the Jan 45 put on XYZ would have a delta of −1.0 with XYZ at 25. If XYZ moved up one point to 26, the put's delta would not change; it is still so far in-the-money that it would still be −1.0. Thus, the gamma of this deeply in-the-money option is also zero, since the delta remains unchanged in the face of a one point rise in the underlying security.

Note that the gamma of any option is expressed as a positive number, whether it be a put or a call.

Other properties of gamma are useful to know as well. As expiration nears, the gamma of at-the-money options increases dramatically. Consider an option with a day or two of life remaining. If it is at-the-money, the delta is approximately 0.50. However, if the stock were to move 2 points higher, the delta of the option would jump to nearly 1.00 because of the short time remaining until expiration. Thus, the gamma would be roughly 0.25 (the delta increased by 0.50 when the stock moved 2 points), as compared to much smaller values of gamma for at-the-money options with several weeks or months of life remaining. The same 2-point rise in the underlying stock would not result in much of an increase in the delta of longer-term options at all.

Out-of-the-money options display a different relationship between gamma and time remaining. An out-of-the-money option that is about to expire has a very small delta, and hence a very small gamma. However, if the out-of-the-money option has a significant amount of time remaining, then it will have a larger gamma than the option that is close to expiration.

Figure 38-5 (see Table 38-4) depicts the gammas of three options with varying amounts of time remaining until expiration. The properties

FIGURE 38-5.
Gamma comparison, with XYZ = 50.

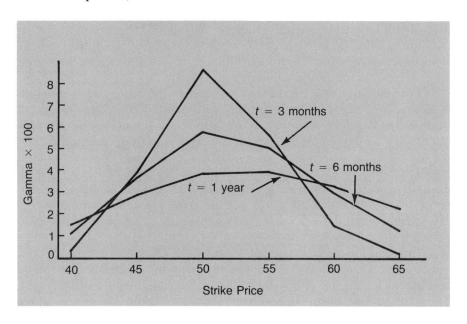

TABLE 38-4.
Gamma comparison—various amounts of time remaining (with XYZ = 50).

Time Remaining	Strike Price					
	40	45	50	55	60	65
1 year	.015	.029	.039	.04	.033	.023
6 months	.011	.037	.058	.051	.030	.013
3 months	.003	.039	.086	.057	.015	.002
2 months			.108			
1 month			.166			
1 week			.288			

regarding the relationship of gamma and time can be observed here. Notice that the short term options have very low gammas deeply in- or out-of-the-money, but have the highest gamma at-the-money (at 50). Conversely, the longest-term, one year option has the highest gamma of the three time periods for deeply in- or out-of-the-money options. The data is presented in Table 38-4. This table contains a slight amount of additional data: the gamma for the at-the-money option at even shorter periods of time remaining until expiration. Notice how the gamma explodes as time decreases, for the at-the-money option. With only one week remaining, the gamma is over 0.28, meaning that the delta of such a call would, for example, jump from 0.50 to 0.78 if the stock merely moved up from 50 to 51.

Gamma is dependent on the volatility of the underlying security as well. At-the-money options on less volatile securities will have higher gammas than similar options on more volatile securities. The following example demonstrates this fact.

Example: Assume XYZ is at 49, as is ABC. Moreover, XYZ is a more volatile stock (30% implied) as compared to ABC (20%). Then, similar options on the two stocks would have significantly different gammas.

Option	XYZ Gammas (Volatility = 30%)	ABC Gammas (Volatility = 20%)
Jan 50	.066	.097
Jan 55	.045	.039
Jan 60	.019	.0053
Feb 50	.055	.081
Feb 60	.024	.011

Note that the at-the-money options (Jan 50's and Feb 50's) on ABC, the less volatile stock, have larger gammas than do their XYZ counterparts. However, look one strike higher (Jan 55's), and notice that the more volatile options have a slightly higher gamma. Look two strikes higher and the more volatile options have a vastly higher gamma, both for the Jan 60's and the Feb 60's.

This concept makes sense if one thinks about the relationship of volatility and delta. On non-volatile stocks, one finds the delta of even a slightly in-the-money option increases rapidly. This is because, since the stock is not volatile, buyers are not willing to pay much time premium for the option. As a result, the gamma is high as well, because as the stock moves into-the-money, the *increase* in delta will be more dramatic than it would be for a non-volatile stock. Out-of-the-money options are an entirely different story. Since the non-volatile stock will have difficulty moving fast enough to reach an out-of-the-money striking price, the delta of the out-of-the-money option is small and it will not change quickly (that is, the gamma is small also).

These concepts are summarized in Figure 38-6 (see Table 38-5), which depicts the gammas for similar options on stocks with differing volatilities. For the purposes of these graphs, XYZ is equal to 50 and there are three months remaining until expiration.

FIGURE 38-6.
Gamma comparison, with XYZ = 50, t = three months.

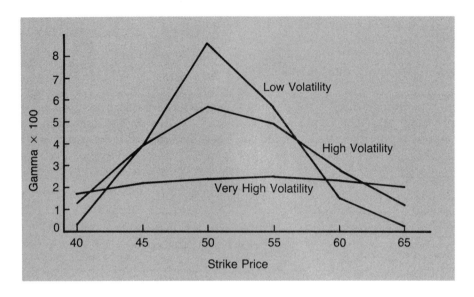

TABLE 38-5.
Gamma comparison for varying volatilities (XYZ = 50, t = 3 months).

| | | Gamma | |
Strike	Low Volatility	Med Volatility	High Volatility
40	.003	.013	.017
45	.039	.039	.022
50	.086	.057	.024
55	.057	.049	.025
60	.015	.028	.023
65	.002	.012	.020

Notice that for a very volatile stock, the gamma is quite stable over nearly all striking prices when there are 3 months remaining until expiration. This means that the deltas of all options on such a volatile stock will be changing quite a bit for even a one-point move in the underlying stock. This is an important point for neutral strategists to note, because a position that starts out as delta neutral may quickly change if the underlying stock is very volatile. As this table implies, the deltas of the options in that "neutral" spread may be altered quickly, thereby rendering the spread quite un-neutral. This concept will be discussed in greater detail later in this chapter.

As delta was used to construct the equivalent stock position of an entire option position or portfolio, gamma can be used in a similar manner. An example of this follows below, using the same securities from the above example on the delta of a position. An important point to note is that *the gamma of the underlying security itself is zero.* This is true because the *delta* of the underlying security (which is always 1.0) never changes—hence the gamma is zero. The gamma is measuring the amount of change of the delta; if the delta of the underlying security never changes, the gamma of the underlying security must be zero.

Example: The following position exists when XYZ is at $31\frac{3}{4}$. Recall that it resembles a long straddle (or backspread) in that there is increased profit potential in either direction if the stock moves far enough by expiration. In addition to the delta previously listed, the gamma is now shown as well. Note that since gamma is a small absolute number, it is sometimes calculated out to three or four decimal places.

Position	Option Delta	Position Delta	Option Gamma	Position Gamma
Short 4,500 XYZ	1.00	− 4,500	0.0000	0
Short 100 XYZ Apr 25 calls	0.89	− 8,900	0.0100	− 100
Long 50 XYZ Apr 30 calls	0.76	+ 3,800	0.0300	+ 150
Long 139 XYZ Jul 30 calls	0.74	+10,286	0.0200	+ 278
Totals:		+ 686		+ 328

As before, the position still has a delta long of almost 700 shares. In addition, one can now see that it has a *positive gamma* of over 300 shares.This means that the delta can be expected to change by 328 shares for each point that XYZ moves: if it moves up one point, the delta will increase to + 1,014 (the current delta, 686, plus the gamma of 328). However, if XYZ moves *down* by one point, then the delta will decrease to + 358 (the current delta, 686. less the gamma of 328).

Note that, in the above example, if XYZ continues higher, the gamma will remain positive (although it will eventually shrink some), and the delta will continue to increase. This means the position is getting longer and longer—a fact which makes sense when one notes that there are extra long calls and they would be getting deeper in-the-money as the stock moves up. Conversely, if XYZ continues to move lower, the delta will continue to decrease and will quickly become negative, meaning that the position would become short overall. Hence, the position does indeed resemble a long straddle—it gets longer as the market moves up and it gets shorter as the market moves down.

Long options, whether puts or calls, have positive gamma, while short options have negative gamma. Thus, a strategist with a position that has positive gamma has a net long option position and is generally hoping for large market movements. Conversely, if one has a position with negative gamma, it means he has shorted options and wants the market to remain fairly stable.

Note that it is possible to be delta neutral, but to have a significant gamma (for example, if one owns puts and calls with offsetting deltas, he would be delta neutral, but would have positive gamma since both options are long). If he is delta neutral, he knows he has no market exposure at this time, but his gamma will show him what exposure his position will acquire as the market moves. These concepts will be discussed in greater detail later in this chapter.

Vega or Tau

There is no letter in the Greek alphabet called "vega." Thus, some strategists, being purists, prefer to use a real Greek letter, "tau," to refer to this risk measurement. The term "vega" will be used in this book, but the reader should note that "tau" means the same thing. *Vega is the amount by which the option price changes when the volatility changes.* Vega is always expressed as a positive number, whether it refers to a put or a call.

It is known that more volatile stocks have more expensive options. Thus, as volatility increases, the price of an option will rise. If volatility falls, the price of the option will fall as well. The vega is merely an attempt to quantify how much the option price will increase or decrease as the volatility moves, all other factors being equal.

Before considering an example, a review of the term "volatility" is in order. Volatility is a measure of how quickly the underlying security moves around. Statistically, it is usually calculated as the standard deviation of stock prices over some period of time, generally annualized. This statistical measure is expressed as a percent, although relating that percent to actual stock movements can be complicated. Suffice it to say that a stock that has a 50% volatility is more volatile than a stock with 30% volatility. The stock market generally has a volatility of about 15% overall, although that may change from time to time (crashes, for example).

Example: Again, assume XYZ is at 49, and the Jan 50 call is selling for 3½. The vega of the option is 0.25, and the current volatility of XYZ is 30%.

If the volatility increases by one "point" or 1% to 31%, then the vega indicates that the option will increase in value by 0.25, to 3¾.

If the volatility had instead decreased by one percent to 29%, then the Jan 50 call would have decreased to 3¼ (a loss of 0.25, the amount of the vega).

Recall that the use of historical price movements to calculate a volatility for XYZ results in a number called the "historical volatility." In actual use, the other volatility that enters the picture is the implied volatility—that is, the volatility that the market itself is implying. This is merely the volatility that one would plug into the Black-Scholes model so that the model's result would be the current market price of the option. The concept was discussed previously in the chapter on mathematical applications and in this chapter as well.

If the implied volatility of an option increases, the option price will increase as well. Consequently, even though XYZ stock may be exhibiting the same historic movement that it always has, and therefore its (historical) volatility would be unchanged, if option buyers appear in sufficient quantity, they may drive the implied volatility of XYZ's options higher. Likewise, an excess of option sellers could drive the implied volatility lower, even though the historical volatility does not change. So, it must be concluded that *vega measures how much the option price changes as implied volatility changes.*

Vega is related to time. Figure 38-7 (see Table 38-6) shows the vegas for options with differing times remaining until expiration. The underlying stock is assumed to be 50 in all cases. Notice that the more time that remains, the higher the vega is. It is interesting to note that, for very

FIGURE 38-7.
Vega comparison, XYZ = 50.

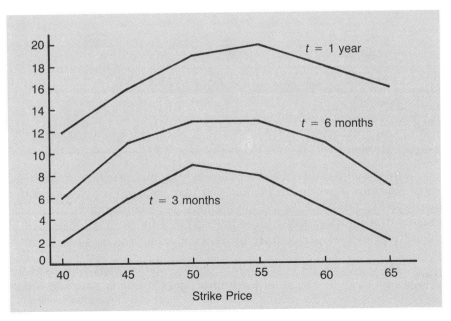

TABLE 38-6.
Vega comparison for different time periods (with XYZ = 50).

	Vega		
Strike Price	t = 1 Year	t = 6 Months	t = 3 Months
40	0.12	0.06	0.02
45	0.16	0.11	0.06
50	0.19	0.13	0.09
55	0.20	0.13	0.08
60	0.18	0.11	0.05
65	0.16	0.07	0.02

long term options, the vega of the slightly out-of-the-money calls (strike = 55) is actually higher than that of the at-the-money. However, this discrepancy disappears as time passes. Not shown, but equally true, is that the vega of a slightly out-of-the-money option on a very volatile stock may be higher than that of the at-the-money.

As with the measurements of risk discussed above, vega can refer to the option itself ("option vega") or to the position as a whole ("position vega"). Since vega is expressed as a positive number, if one is long options, then his position vega will be positive. This means he has exposure if volatilities decrease, or can make money if volatilities increase.

Example: Again, assume that we have the same backspread position as before, with XYZ at $31\frac{3}{4}$.

Position	Option Vega	Position Vega
Short 4,500 XYZ	0.00	0
Short 100 XYZ Apr 25 calls	0.02	− 200
Long 50 XYZ Apr 30 calls	0.05	+ 250
Long 139 XYZ Jul 30 calls	0.07	+ 973
Total Vega:		+1,023

The vega is a positive 10.23 points ($1,023 since each point for these equity options is worth $100). The fact that the position has a positive vega means that it is exposed to variations in volatility. If volatility decreases, the position will lose money: $1,023 for each 1% decrease in volatility. However, if volatility increases, the position will benefit.

Vega is greatest for at-the-money options and approaches zero as the option is deeply in- or out-of-the-money. Again, this is common sense, since a deep in- or out- option will not be affected much by a change in volatility. In addition, for at-the-money options, longer-term options have a higher vega than short-term options. To verify this, think of it in the extreme. An at-the-money option with one day to expiration will not be overly affected by any change in volatility due to its pending expiration. However, a 3-month at-the-money option will certainly be sensitive to changes in volatility.

Vega does not directly correlate with either delta or gamma. One could have a position with no delta and no gamma (delta neutral and gamma neutral) and still have exposure to volatility. This does not mean that such a position would be undesirable, it merely means that if one had such a position, he would have removed most of the market risk from his position and would only be concerned with volatility risk.

In later sections, the use of volatility to establish positions and vega to monitor them will be discussed.

Theta

Theta measures the time decay of a position. All option traders know that time is the enemy of the option holder, and it is the friend of the option writer. Theta is the name given to the risk measurement of time in one's position. Theta is generally expressed as a negative number, and it is expressed as the amount by which the option value will change. Thus, if an option has a theta of -0.12, that means the option will *lose* 12 cents, or about an eighth of a point, *per day*. This is true for both puts and calls although the theta of a put and call with the same strike and expiration date are not equal to each other.

Very long-term options are not subject to much time decay in one day's time. Thus, the theta of a long-term option is nearly zero. On the other hand, short-term options, especially at-the-money ones, have the largest absolute theta, since they are subject to the ravages of time on a daily basis. The theta of options on a highly volatile stock will be higher than the theta of options on a low volatility stock. Obviously, the former options are more expensive (have more time value) and therefore have more time value to lose on a daily basis, thereby implying that they have a higher theta. Finally, the decay is not linear—an option will lose a greater percent of its daily value near the end of its life.

Figure 38-8 (see Table 38-7) depicts the relationships of thetas for various striking prices and for differing volatilities on options with three months of life remaining. Again, notice that for very volatile stocks, the out-of-the-money options have thetas as large as the at-the-moneys. This is saying that as each day passes, the probability of the stock reaching that out-of-the-money strike drops and causes the option to lose value.

FIGURE 38-8.
Theta comparison, with XYZ = 50, t = three months.

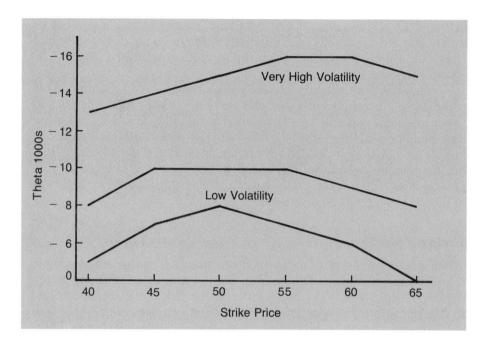

TABLE 38-7.
Theta comparison for differing volatilities (XYZ = 50, t = 3 months).

Strike	Low Volatility	Med Volatility	High Volatility
40	−0.005	−0.008	−0.013
45	−0.007	−0.010	−0.014
50	−0.008	−0.010	−0.015
55	−0.007	−0.010	−0.016
60	−0.006	−0.009	−0.016
65	−0.004	−0.008	−0.015

This does not change the fact that, for very short-term options, the theta is largest at-the-money.

Normally, the theta of an individual option is of little interest to the strategist. He generally would be more concerned with delta or gamma. However, as with the other risk measures, theta can be computed for an entire portfolio of options. This measure, the "position theta," can be quite important because it gives the strategist a good idea of how much gain or loss he can expect on a daily basis, due to time erosion. The following example demonstrates this point. Note that the underlying security itself has a theta of zero, since it cannot lose any value due to time decay.

Example: With XYZ at 49, the strategist has the following position in February, so that the April calls are nearer to expiration than the July calls. This position is similar to a large calendar spread position.

Position	Option Theta	Position Theta
Short 4,000 XYZ	0.00	0
Short 150 XYZ Apr 50 calls	−0.04	+600
Long 150 XYZ Apr 30 calls	−0.02	−300
Short 78 XYZ Jul 30 puts	−0.02	+156
	Total Theta:	+456

This position is expected to *make* $456 per day due to time decay. Note that *short options, whether puts or calls, have a positive position theta, while long options have a negative position theta.* A negative position theta means the position has risk due to time, while a positive position theta means time is working *for* the position.

Rho

Rho is the name given to the *price change of an option's value due to a change in interest rates.* Recall that one of the components that contributes to an option's price is interest rates. *As interest rates rise, call prices will rise, but put prices will fall.* Rho measures the amount by which these prices rise or fall.

This behavior of puts and calls with respect to interest rates may not be immediately obvious, but recall that the arbitrage that can be established with in-the-money calls (the "interest play," discussed in the chapter on Arbitrage) demonstrates that arbitrageurs are willing to pay more for an in-the-money call as interest rates rise because they will be earning more interest on the stock that they sell short against that in-the-money call. Thus, rising interest rates cause call prices to increase.

The opposite is true for puts—rising interest rates cause put prices to decline. Again, an arbitrage can be used to demonstrate the point. Recall that in a reversal arbitrage, the arbitrageur is selling the stock and the put while buying the call. We have just demonstrated that, as interest rates rise, he is willing to pay more for the call since he can earn extra interest on the short sale of his stock. This automatically means that he will be willing to sell the put for less.

Rho is expressed as a positive number for calls and a negative one for puts. *Rho is smallest for deeply out-of-the-money options and is largest for deeply-in-the-money options. It is larger for longer-term options and is nearly zero for very short-term options.* The following table of option prices may help to see these relationships:

Example: With XYZ at 49, the following options have the rho indicated (January is the short-term expiration):

Month/Strike	Call Rho	Put Rho
Jan 35	0.05	−0.01
Jan 50	0.03	−0.03
Jan 60	0.00	−0.05
Jul 35	0.18	−0.02
Jul 50	0.14	−0.15
Jul 60	0.07	−0.18

Note the in-the-money calls (35 strike) have larger rho than the out-of-the-money 60's, both in January and July. Similarly, the in-the-money puts (the 60's) have larger rho on an absolute basis than the out-of-the-money 35's. Again, this is true for both January and July.

Furthermore, note that the longer-term, July rhos are all larger (again as absolute numbers) than their shorter-term, January counterparts.

Rho can also be calculated for an entire portfolio to obtain a "position rho," similar to previous examples. Generally, one would not be overly concerned with his "position rho" unless his portfolio contained quite a few long-term options and/or deeply in-the-money ones. Thus, rho is more important as a consideration when one is trading LEAPS or warrants, both of which may be extremely long-term vehicles. Of the risk measures discussed so far, rho is the least used, since many traders tend to have relatively short-term options in their positions.

The Gamma of the Gamma

Occasionally, one may hear reference to the "six measures of risk." This is the sixth one and it is the most arcane. At any point, one knows the delta and gamma of an option. As the stock moves, the delta changes (by the amount of the gamma), but so does the gamma. Some traders are interested in knowing how much the *gamma* will change when the stock moves. Hence, they will compute the *gamma of the gamma, which is the amount by which the* gamma *will change when the stock price changes.*

This concept will be discussed at the end of this chapter. It is most important for strategists involved in positions on highly volatile stocks, for if the stock moves far enough, the gamma (and therefore the delta) may change dramatically. Thus, one might want to know how this risk measure affects his profitability.

Summary

Delta: Positive delta indicates that a position is currently bullish; if the underlying security goes up in price, the position should make money. A negative delta indicates a bearish slant.

Gamma: Positive gamma means that the delta will increase if the underlying security rises in price. Positive gamma generally implies that there is a preponderance of long options in the position, either puts or calls; negative gamma indicates written or naked options in the position.

Theta: Negative theta means that the position will lose money as time passes (typical of positions with long options); positive theta implies that time is working *for* the position (positions with written options).

Vega: Positive vega means that an increase of (perceived) volatility will benefit the position—usually true of positions with long options in them; negative vega means that a decrease of volatility would be beneficial.

STRATEGY CONSIDERATIONS—USING THE "GREEKS"

Before looking at how one operates a particular strategy using delta, gamma, etc., it might be beneficial to see how these factors relate to the individual strategies that have been described throughout this book. Table 38-8 is a *general* guide to how the various strategies are exposed to various market factors. It is not an all-purpose or *specific* table, because as the stock moves higher or lower, some of the risk measurement factors will certainly be affected.

    A few assumptions were made in constructing the table. First, it was assumed that the strategies where delta is noted as being zero are established in a neutral stance. The bull spread and bear spread strategies assumed that the stock was midway between the striking prices. Two other spread strategies—ratio call and ratio put—assumed the stock was at the striking price of the option that was *sold*. In all other cases, there is only one striking price involved, and it was assumed that the stock was at the strike.

TABLE 38-8.
General risk exposure of common strategies.

Strategy	Δ	Γ	θ	ν	ρ
Buy stock	+	0	0	0	0
Sell stock short	−	0	0	0	0
Call buy	+	+	−	+	+
Put buy	−	+	−	+	−
Straddle buy	0	+	−	+	+
Covered write	+	−	+	−	−
Naked call sale	−	−	+	−	−
Naked put sale	+	−	+	−	+
Ratio write (straddle sale)	0	−	+	−	−
Calendar spread	0	−	+	+	−
Bull spread	+	−	−	−	+
Bear spread	−	−	−	−	+
Ratio call spread	0	−	+	−	−
Ratio put spread	0	−	+	−	+

The table may help to clarify some of the concepts concerning the risk measurement factors. First, notice that stock or futures—or any underlying security—have only delta. None of the other factors pertains to the underlying security itself.

As might be expected, spread strategies involving both long and short options are less easily quantified than outright buys or sells. The calendar spread strategy is one in which the spreader does *not* want a lot of stock movement—he would prefer the underlying security to remain near the striking price, for that is the area of maximum profit potential. This is reflected by the fact that gamma is negative. Also, for calendar spreads, the passage of time is good, a fact which is reflected by the fact that theta is positive. Finally, since an increase in implied volatilities or interest rates would boost prices and widen the spread (creating a profit), vega is positive and rho is negative.

A bull spread has positive delta—reflecting the bullish nature of the spread, but it has negative gamma. The reason that gamma is negative is that the position comes less bullish as the underlying security rises, since the profit potential, and hence the bullishness of the position, is limited. For similar reasons, a bear spread has negative delta (reflecting bearishness) and negative gamma (reflecting limited bearishness). Both the bull spread and bear spread are the same with respect to the other risk measurements. Theta is negative, reflecting the fact that time decay can hurt the spread. Less obvious is the fact that these spreads are hurt by an increase in perceived volatility; a negative vega tells us this is true, however.

These risk measurement tools are important in that they can quite graphically depict the risk and reward characteristics of an option position or option portfolio. They are useful in establishing a new position because one can see how much exposure he is taking on. In addition, they are extremely useful for follow-up action since one can see how his position's characteristics have developed in the current marketplace at the present time. In the following sections, the use of the risk measurement tools as aids in establishing a position or in following up on a position will be discussed in detail.

Delta Neutral

One popular type of neutral position is to be "*delta neutral*"—that is, to have the equivalent stock position (ESP) or equivalent futures position (EFP) be zero. *A delta neutral position is one in which the sum of the projected price changes of the long options in the spread is essentially offset by the projected price changes of the short options in the same spread.*

Example: XYZ is trading at 50. The following three options are trading with the prices and deltas indicated. Furthermore, the "theoretical value" of each option is shown:

Option	Price	Delta	"Theoretical Value"
Jan 50 call	3	0.55	3.50
Jan 55 call	1½	0.35	1.48
Feb 50 put	3½	−0.40	3.44

Assuming that one can rely upon these "theoretical values" (a big assumption, by the way), it is obvious that the Jan 50 call is cheap with respect to the other options—they are close to their values, while the Jan 50 is 50 cents under. The neutral strategist would want to buy the Jan 50 call and hedge his purchase with one of the other two options presented. One choice would be to establish a spread wherein the Jan 50 calls are bought and a number of Jan 55's are sold. To determine how many are to be bought and sold, one merely has to divide the deltas of the two options:

Delta neutral spread ratio = 0.55/0.35 = 11-to-7.

Thus, a delta neutral ratio spread would consist of buying 7 Jan 50's and selling 11 Jan 55's. To verify that this spread is neutral with respect to the change in price of XYZ, notice that if XYZ moves up in price 1 point, the Jan 50 will increase in price by 0.55; so 7 of them will increase by 7 × 0.55, or 3.85 points total. Similarly, the Jan 55 will increase in price by 0.35, so 11 of them would increase in price by 11 × 0.35, or 3.85 points total. Hence, the long side of the spread would profit by 3.85 points, while the short side loses 3.85 points—a neutral situation.

The resulting position is a ratio spread. The profitability of the spread occurs between about 51 and 62 expiration as shown in Figure 38-9, but that is not the major point. The *real* attractiveness of the spread to the neutral trader is that if the underpriced nature of the Jan 50 call (vis-á-vis the Jan 55 call) should disappear, the spread should produce a profit, regardless of the short-term market movement of XYZ. The spread could then be closed if this should occur.

To illustrate this fact, suppose that XYZ actually falls to 49, but the Jan 50 call returns to "fair value"

Option	Price	Delta	"Theoretical Value"
Jan 50 call	3	0.52	3.00
Jan 55 call	1⅛	0.34	1.13
Feb 50 put	3⅞	−0.42	3.84

FIGURE 38-9.
XYZ ratio spread.

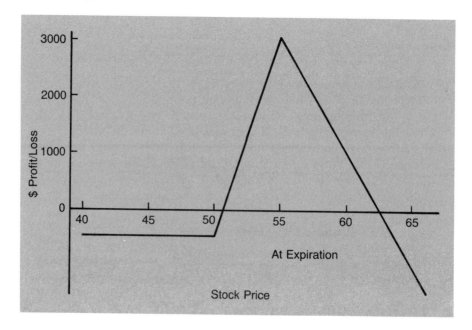

Notice that the "theoretical values" in this table are equal to the "theoretical values" from the previous table, less the amount of the delta. Since the XYZ Jan 50 call is no longer underpriced, the position would be removed, and the strategist would make nothing on his Jan 50's, but would make ⅜ on each of the 11 short Jan 55's, for a profit of $412.50 less commissions.

This example leans heavily on the assumption that one is able to accurately estimate the "theoretical value" and delta of the options. In real life, this chore can be quite difficult, since the estimate requires one to define the future volatility of the common stock. This is not easy. However, for the purposes of a spread, the *ratio* of the two deltas is used. Moreover, the example didn't require that one know the exact theoretical value of each option; rather, the only knowledge that was required was that one of the options was cheap with respect to the other options.

As an alternative to a ratio spread, another type of delta neutral position could be established from the previous data: buy the Jan 50 call (this is the basis of the position since it is supposedly the cheap option) and buy the Feb 50 put—the only other choice from the data given. This position is a long straddle of sorts. Recall that the delta of a put is negative—so again, the delta neutral ratio can be calculated by dividing the absolute value of two deltas:

$$\text{Delta neutral staddle ratio} = 0.55/|-0.40| = 11\text{-to-}8$$

Thus, a delta neutral straddle position would consist of buying 8 Jan 50 calls and buying 11 Feb 50 puts. The straddle has no market exposure, at least over the short term. Note that the delta neutral straddle has a significantly different profit picture from the delta neutral ratio spread, but they are both neutral and are both based on the fact that the Jan 50 call is cheap. The straddle makes money if the stock moves a lot, while the other makes money if the stock moves only a little. (See Figure 38-10.)

Can these two vastly different profit pictures be depicting strategies in which the same thing is to be accomplished (that is, to capture the underpriced nature of the XYZ Jan 50 call)? Yes, but in order to decide which strategy is "best," the strategist would have to take other factors into consideration: the historic volatility of the underlying security, for example, or how much actual time remains until January expiration, as well as his own psychological attitude towards selling uncovered calls. A more precise definition of the other risks of these two positions can be obtained by looking at their position gammas.

Delta Neutral is Not Entirely Neutral. In fact, delta neutral means that one is neutral *only with respect to small price changes in the underlying security.* A delta neutral position may have seriously un-neutral characteristics when some of the other risk measurements are considered. Con-

FIGURE 38-10.
XYZ straddle buy.

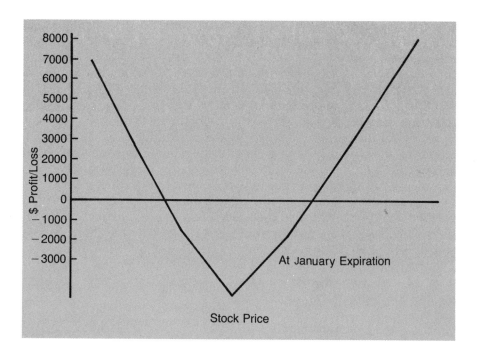

At January Expiration

Stock Price

sequently, one cannot blithely go around, establishing delta neutral positions and ignoring them, for they may have significant market risk as
certain factors change.

For example, it is obvious to the naked eye that the two positions described in the previous section—the ratio spread and the long straddle—
are not alike at all, but both are delta neutral. If one incorporates the usage
of some of the other risk measurements into his position, he will be able
to quantify the difference between "neutral" strategies. The sale of a straddle will be used to examine how these various factors work.

Positions with naked options in them have negative position gamma.
This means that as the underlying security moves, the position will acquire
traits opposite to that movement: if the security rises, the position becomes
short; if it falls, the position becomes long. This description generally fits
any position with naked options, such as a ratio spread, naked straddle,
or ratio write.

Example: XYZ is at 88. There are three months remaining until July
expiration, and the volatility of XYZ is 30%. Suppose 100 July 90 straddles
are sold for 10 points—the put and the call each selling for 5. Initially,

this position is nearly delta neutral as shown in Table 38-9. However, since both options are sold, each sale places negative gamma in the position.

TABLE 38-9.
Position delta and gamma of straddle sale. XYZ = 88.

Position	Option Delta	Position Delta	Option Gamma	Position Gamma
Sell 100 Jul 90 calls	0.505	− 5,050	0.03	− 300
Sell 100 Jul 90 puts	0.495	+ 4,950	0.03	− 300
Total shares		− 100		− 600

The usefulness of calculating gamma is shown by this example. The initial position is short only 100 shares of XYZ, a very small delta. In fact, a person who is a trader of small amounts of stock might actually be induced into believing that he could sell these 100 straddles, because that is equivalent to being short merely 100 shares of the stock.

Calculating the gamma quickly dispels those notions. The gamma is large: 600 shares of negative gamma. Hence, if the stock moves only two points lower, this trader's straddle position can be expected to behave as if it were now long 1,100 shares! (the original 100 shares short plus 1,200 that the gamma tells us we can expect to get long). The position might look like this after the stock drops two points:

XYZ: 86

Position	Option Delta	Position Delta
Sold 100 Jul 90 calls	0.44	− 4,400
Sold 100 Jul 90 puts	0.55	+ 5,500
		+ 1,100 shares

Hence, a two point drop in the stock means that the position is already acquiring a "long" look. Further drops will cause the position to become even "longer." This is certainly not a position—being short 100 straddles—for a small trader to be in, even though it might have erroneously appeared that way when one observed only the delta of the position. Paying attention to gamma more fully discloses the real risks.

In a similar manner, if the stock had risen two points to 90, the position would quickly have become delta short. In fact, one could expect it to be short 1,300 shares in that case: the original short 100 shares plus the 1,200 indicated by the negative gamma. A rise to 90, then, would make the position look like this:

XYZ: 90

Position	Option Delta	Position Delta
Sold 100 Jul 90 calls	0.56	− 5,600
Sold 100 Jul 90 puts	0.43	+ 4,300
		− 1,300 shares

These examples demonstrate how quickly a large position, such as being short 100 straddles, can acquire a large delta as the stock moves even a small distance. Extrapolating the moves is not completely correct because the gamma changes as the stock price changes, but it can give the trader some feel for how much his delta will change.

It is often useful to calculate this information in advance, at some point in the near future. Figure 38-11 depicts what the delta of this large short straddle position will be, two weeks after it was first sold. The points

FIGURE 38-11.
Projected delta, in 14 days.

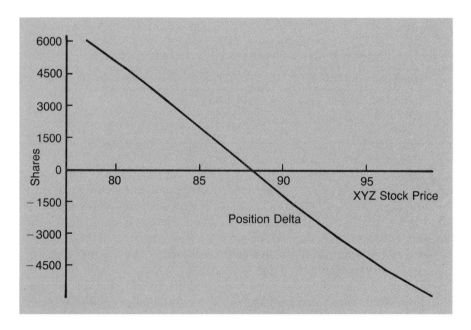

on the horizontal axis are stock prices. The quickness with which the neutrality of the position disappears is alarming. A small move up to 93— only one standard deviation—in two weeks makes the overall position short the equivalent of about 3,300 shares of XYZ. Figure 38-11 is really nothing more than the effect that gamma is having on the position, but it is presented in a form that may be more preferable for some traders.

What this means is that the position is "fighting" the market: as the market goes up, this position becomes shorter and shorter. That can be an unpleasant situation, both from the point of view of creating unrealized losses as well as psychologically. *The position delta and gamma can be used to estimate the amount of unrealized loss that will occur.* Just how much can this position be expected to lose if there is a quick move in the underlying stock? The answer is quickly obtained from the delta and gamma: the first point that XYZ moves, from 88 to 89, the position acts as if it is short 100 shares (the position delta), so it would lose $100. The *next* point that XYZ rises, from 89 to 90, the position will act as if it is short the original 100 shares (the position delta), *plus another* 600 shares (the position gamma). Hence, during that second point of movement by XYZ, the entire position will act as if it is short 700 shares, and therefore lose another $700. Therefore, an immediate 2-point jump in XYZ will cause an unrealized loss of $800 in the position. Summarizing:

Loss, first point of stock movement = position delta

Loss, second point of stock movement = position delta + gamma

Total loss for two points of stock movement

$$= 2 \times \text{position delta} + \text{position gamma}$$

Using the example data:

Loss, XYZ moves from 88 to 89: −$100 (the position delta)

Loss, XYZ moves from 89 to 90: −$100 (delta) −$600 (gamma)

: −$700

Total loss, XYZ moves from 88 to 90: −$100 × 2 − $600 = −$800

This can be verified by looking at the prices of the call and put after XYZ has jumped from 88 to 90. One could use a model to calculate expected prices if that happened. However, there is another way. Consider the following statements:

If the stock goes up by one point, the call will then have a price of:

$$p_1 = p_0 + \text{delta}$$

$$5.505 = 5.00 + 0.505 \text{ (if XYZ goes to 89 in the example)}$$

If the stock goes up two points, the call will have an increase of the above amount plus a similar increase for the next point of stock movement. The delta for that *second* point of stock movement is the original delta plus the gamma, since gamma tells one how much his delta is going to change.

$$p_2 = p_1 + \text{delta} + \text{gamma, or substituting from above}$$

$$p_2 = (p_0 + \text{delta}) + \text{delta} + \text{gamma}$$

$$= p_0 + 2 \times \text{delta} + \text{gamma}$$

$$6.04 = 5.00 + 2 \times 0.505 + 0.03 \text{ (in the example if XYZ} = 90)$$

By the same calculation, the put in the example will be priced at 4.04 if XYZ immediately jumps to 90:

$$4.04 = 5.00 - 2 \times 0.495 + 0.03$$

So, overall, the call will have increased by 1.04, but the put will only have decreased by 0.96. The unrealized loss would then be computed as $-\$10,400$ for the 100 calls, offset by a gain of $\$9,600$ on the sale of 100 puts, for a net unrealized loss of $\$800$. This verifies the result obtained above using position delta and position gamma. Again, this confirms the logical fact that a quick stock movement will cause unrealized losses in a short straddle position.

Continuing on, let us look at some of the other factors affecting the sale of this straddle. The straddle seller has time working in his favor. After the position is established, there will not be as much decay in the first two-week period as there will be when expiration draws near. The exact amount of time decay to expect can be calculated from the theta of the position:

XYZ: 88

Position	Option Theta	Position Theta
Sold 100 Jul 90 calls	-0.03	$+\$300$
Sold 100 Jul 90 puts	-0.03	$+\$300$
		$+\$600$

This is how the position looked with respect to time decay when it was first established (XYZ at 88 and three months remaining until expiration). The theta of the put and the call are essentially the same, and indicate that each option is losing about 3 cents of value each day. Note that the theta is expressed as a positive number, and since these options are sold, the *position theta* is a positive number. A positive position theta means time decay is working in your favor. One could expect to make $300 per day from the sale of 100 calls. He could expect to make another $300 per day from the sale of the 100 puts. Thus, his overall position is generating a theoretical profit from time decay of $600 per day.

The fact that the sale of a straddle generates profits from time decay is not earth-shattering. That is a well-known fact. However, the *amount* of that time decay is quantified by using theta. Furthermore, it serves to show that this position, which is *delta* neutral, is *not* neutral with respect to the passage of time.

Finally, let us examine the position with respect to changes in volatility. This is done by calculating the position vega.

XYZ: 88

Position	Option Vega	Position Vega
Sold 100 Jul 90 calls	0.18	− $1,800
Sold 100 Jul 90 puts	0.18	− $1,800
		− $3,600

Again, this information is displayed at the time the position was established: three months to expiration, and a volatility of 30% for XYZ. The vega is quite large. The fact that the call's vega is 0.18 means that the call price is expected to increase by 18 cents if the implied volatility of the option increases from 0.01 to 31%. Since the position is short 100 calls, an increase of 18 cents in the price of the call would translate into a loss of $1,800. The put has a similar vega, so the overall position would lose $3,600 if the options trade with an increase in volatility of just 0.01. Of course, the position would *make* $3,600 if the volatility decreased by 0.01 to 29%.

This volatility risk, then, is the greatest risk in this short straddle position. As before, it is obvious that an increase in volatility is not good for a position with naked options in it. The use of vega quantifies this risk and shows how important it is to attempt to sell overpriced options when establishing such positions. One should not adhere to any one strategy all the time. For example, one should not always be selling naked puts. If the implied volatilities of these puts are below historic norms, such a strategy is much more likely to encounter the risk represented by the position vega. There have been several times in the recent past—mostly during market crashes—when the implied volatilities of both index and equity options have leaped tremendously. Those times were not kind to sellers of options. However, in almost every case, the implied volatility of index options was quite low before the crash occurred. Thus, any trader who was examining his vega risk would not have been inclined to sell naked options when they were historically "cheap."

In summary then, this "neutral" position is, in reality, much more complex when one considers all the other factors.

Position summary

Risk Factor	Comment
Position delta = −100	Neutral; no immediate exposure to small market movements; lose $100 for one point move in underlying
Position gamma = −600	Fairly negative; position will react inversely to market movements, causing losses of $700 for second point of movement by underlying
Position theta = +$600	Favorable; the passage of time works in the position's favor
Position vega = −$3,600	Very negative; position is extremely subject to changes in implied volatility

This straddle sale only has one thing guaranteed to work for it initially: time decay (the risk factors will change as price, time, and volatility change). Stock price movements will not be helpful, but there will always be stock price movements, so one can expect to feel the negative effect of those price changes. Volatility is the big unknown. If it decreases, the straddle seller will profit handsomely. Realistically, however, it can only decrease by a limited amount. If it increases, very bad things will happen to the profitability of the position. Even worse, if the implied volatility is increasing, there is a fairly likely chance that the underlying stock will be jumping around quite a bit as well. That isn't good either. Thus, it is imperative that the straddle seller only engage in the strategy when there is a reasonable expectation that volatilities are high and can be expected to decrease. If there is significant danger of the opposite occurring, the strategy should be avoided.

If volatility remains relatively stable, one can anticipate what effects the passage of time will have on the position. The delta will not change much since the options are nearly at-the-money. However, the gamma will increase, indicating that nearer to expiration, short-term price movements will have more exaggerated effects on the unrealized profits of the position. The theta will grow even more, indicating that time will be an even better friend for the straddle writer. Shorter-term options tend to decay at a faster rate than do longer-term ones. Finally, the vega will decrease some as well, so that the effect of an increase in implied volatility alone will not be as damaging to the position when there is significantly less time remaining. So, the passage of time generally will improve most aspects of this naked straddle sale. However, that does not mitigate the current situation, nor does it imply that there will be no risk if a little time passes.

The type of analysis shown in the above examples gives a much more in-depth look than merely envisioning it as being delta short 100 shares or looking at how the position will do at expiration. In the above example, it is known that the straddle writer will profit if XYZ is between 80 and 100 in three months, at expiration. However, what might happen in the interim is another matter entirely. The delta, gamma, theta, and vega are useful for the purpose of defining how the position will behave or mis-behave at the current point in time.

Refer back to the table of strategies at the beginning of this section. Notice that ratio writing or straddle selling (they are equivalent strat-egies) have the characteristics that have been described in detail: delta is 0, and several other factors are negative. It has been shown how those negative factors translate into potential profits or losses. Observing other lines in the same table, note that covered writing and naked put selling (they are *also* equivalent, don't forget) have a description very similar to straddle selling: delta is positive, and the other factors are negative. This is a worse situation than selling naked straddles, for it entails all the same risks, but in addition will suffer losses on immediate down-ward moves by the underlying stock. The point to be made here is that if one felt that straddle selling is not a particularly attractive strategy after he had observed the above examples, he then should feel even *less* inclined to do covered writing, for it has all the same risk factors and isn't even delta neutral.

An example that was given back in the chapter on futures options trading will be expanded as promised at this time. To review, one may often find volatility skewing in futures options, but it was noted that one should not normally buy an at-the-money call (the cheapest one) and sell a large quantity of out-of-the-money calls just because that looks like the biggest theoretical advantage. The following example was given. It will now be expanded to include the concept of gamma.

Example: Heavy volatility skewing exists in the prices of January soybean options: the out-of-the-money calls are much more expensive than the at-the-money calls.

The following data is known:

January soybeans: 583

Option	Price	Implied Volatility	Delta	Gamma
575 call	19½	15%	0.55	.0100
675 call	2¼	23%	0.09	.0026

Using deltas, the following spread appears to be neutral.

Buy 1 Jan bean 575 call at 19½	19½ DB
Sell 6 Jan bean 675 calls at 2¼	13½ CR
Net position:	6 Debit

At the time the original example was presented, it was demonstrated through the use of the profit picture that the ratio was too steep and problems could result in a large rally.

Now that one has the concept of gamma at his disposal, he can quantify what those problems are.

The position gamma of this spread is quite negative:

$$\text{Position gamma} = .01 - 6 \times .0026 = -0.0056$$

That is, for every 10 points that January soybeans rally, the position will become short about ½ of one futures contract. The maximum profit point, 675, is 92 points above the current price of 583. While beans would not normally rally 92 points in only a few days, it does demonstrate that this position could become very short if beans quickly rallied to the point of maximum profit potential. Rest assured there would be no profit if that happened.

Even a small rally of 20 cents (points) in soybeans—less than the daily limit—would begin to make this tiny spread noticeably short. If one had established the spread in some quantity, say buying 100 and selling 600, he could become seriously short very fast.

A neutral spreader would not use such a large ratio in this spread. Rather, he would neutralize the gamma and then attempt to deal with the resulting delta. The following section deals with ways to accomplish that.

Creating Multi-Faceted Neutrality

So what is the strategist to do? He can attempt to construct positions that are neutral with respect to the other factors if he perceives them as a risk.

There is no reason why a position cannot be constructed as vega-neutral rather than delta neutral, if he wants to eliminate the risk of volatility increases or decreases. Or, maybe he wants to eliminate the risk of stock price movements, in which case he would attempt to be gamma neutral as well as delta neutral.

This seems like a simple concept until one first attempts to establish a position that is neutral with respect to more than one risk variable. For example, if one is attempting to create a spread that is neutral with respect to both gamma and delta, he could attempt it in the following way:

Example: XYZ is 60. A spreader wants to establish a spread that is neutral with respect to both gamma and delta, using the following prices:

Option	Delta	Gamma
Oct 60 call	0.60	0.050
Oct 70 call	0.25	0.025

The secret to determining a spread that is neutral with respect to both risk measures is to neutralize gamma first, for delta can always be neutralized by taking an offsetting position in the underlying security, whether it be stock or futures. First, determine a gamma-neutral spread by dividing the two gammas:

Gamma neutral ratio = 0.050/0.025 = 2-to-1

So, buying one Oct 60 and selling two Oct 70 calls would be a gamma neutral spread. Now, the position delta of that spread is computed:

Position	Delta	Position Delta
Long 1 Oct 60 call	0.60	+60 shares
Short 2 Oct 70 call	0.25	−50 shares
Net position delta:		+10 shares

Hence, this gamma neutral ratio is making the position delta long by 10 shares of stock for each 1-by-2 spread that is established. For example, if one bought 100 Oct 60 calls and sold 200 Oct 70 calls, his position delta would be long 1,000 shares.

This position delta is easily neutralized by selling short 1,000 shares of the stock. The resulting position is both gamma neutral and delta neutral:

Position	Option Delta	Position Delta	Option Gamma	Position Gamma
Short 1,000 XYZ	1.00	−1,000	0	0
Long 100 Oct 60 call	0.60	+6,000	0.050	+500
Short 200 Oct 70 calls	0.25	−5,000	0.025	−500
Net Position:		0		0

Hence, it is always a simple matter to create a position that is both gamma and delta neutral. In fact, it is just as simple to create a position that is neutral with respect to delta and *any* other risk measure, because all that is necessary is to create a neutral ratio of the other risk measure (gamma, vega, theta, etc.) and then eliminate the resulting position delta by using the underlying.

In theory, one could construct a position that was neutral with respect to all five risk measures (or six, if you really want to go overboard and include "gamma of the gamma" as well). Of course, there wouldn't be much profit potential in such a position, either. But such constructions are actually employed, or at least attempted, by traders such as market makers who try to make their profits from the difference between the bid and offer of an option quote, and not from assuming market risk.

Still, the concept of being neutral with respect to more than one risk factor is a valid one. In fact, if a strategist can determine what he is really attempting to accomplish, he can often negate other factors and construct a position designed to accomplish exactly what he wants. Suppose that one thought the implied volatility of a certain set of options was too high. He could just sell straddles and attempt to capture that volatility. However, he is then exposed to movements by the underlying stock. He would be better served to construct a position with negative vega to reflect his expectation on volatility, but then also have the position be delta neutral and gamma neutral, so that there would be little risk to the position of market movements. This can normally be done quite easily. An example will demonstrate how.

Example: XYZ is 48. There are three months to expiration, and the volatility of XYZ and its options is 35%. The following information is also known:

Option	Price	Delta	Gamma	Vega
Apr 50 call	2½	0.47	0.045	0.08
Apr 60 call	1	0.17	0.026	0.06

For whatever reasons—perhaps the historical volatility is much lower—the strategist decides that he wants to sell volatility. That is, he wants to have a negative position vega so that when the volatility decreases he will make money. This can probably be accomplished by buying some April 50 calls and selling more April 60 calls. However, he does not want any risk of price movement so some analysis must be done.

First, he should determine a *gamma* neutral spread. This is done in much the same manner as a delta neutral spread, except that gamma is used. Merely divide the two gammas to determine the neutral ratio to be used. In this case, assume that the Apr 50 call and the Apr 60 call are to be used:

Gamma neutral ratio: 0.045/0.026 = 1.73-to-1

Thus, a gamma neutral position would be created by buying 100 Apr 50's and selling 173 Apr 60's. Alternatively, buying 10 and selling 17 would be close to gamma neutral as well. The larger position will be used for the remainder of this example.

Now that this ratio has been chosen, what is the effect on delta and vega?

Position	Option Delta	Position Delta	Option Gamma	Position Gamma	Option Vega	Position Vega
Long 100 Apr 50	0.47	+4,700	0.045	+450	0.08	+ $800
Short 173 Apr 60	0.17	−2,941	0.026	−450	0.06	−1,038
Total:		+1,759		0		− $238

The position delta is long 1,759 shares of XYZ. This can easily be "cured" by shorting 1,700 or 1,800 shares of XYZ to neutralize the delta. Consequently, the complete position, including the short 1,700 shares, would be neutral with respect to both delta and gamma, and would have the desired negative vega.

The actual profit picture at expiration is shown in Figure 38-12. Bear in mind, however, that the strategist would normally not intend to hold a position like this until expiration. He would close it out if his expectations on volatility decline were fulfilled (or proved false).

One other point should be made: the fact that gamma and delta are neutral to begin with does not mean that they will remain neutral indefinitely as the stock moves (or even as volatility changes). However, there

FIGURE 38-12.
Spread with negative vega; gamma and delta neutral.

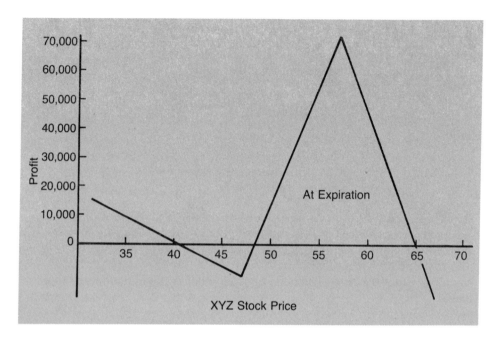

will be little or no effect of stock price movements on the position in the short run.

In summary, then, one can always create a position that is neutral with respect to both gamma and delta by first choosing a ratio that makes the gamma zero, and then using a position in the underlying security to neutralize the delta that is created by the chosen ratio. This type of position would always involve two options and some stock. The resulting position will *not* necessarily be neutral with respect to the other risk factors.

The Mathematical Approach

The strategist should be aware that the process of determining neutrality in several of the risk variables can be handled quite easily by a computer. All that is required is to solve a series of simultaneous equations.

In the above example, the resulting vega was negative: −$238. For each decline of 0.01 in volatility from the current level of 35%, one could expect to make $238. This result could have been reached by another method, as long as one were willing to spell out in advance the amount of vega risk he wants to accept. Then, he can also assume the gamma is zero and solve for the quantity of options to trade in the spread. The delta would be neutralized, as above, by using the common stock.

   Example: Prices are the same as in the above example. XYZ is 48. There are three months to expiration, and the volatility of XYZ and its options is 35%. The following information is also the same:

Option	Price	Delta	Gamma	Vega
Apr 50 call	2½	0.47	0.045	0.08
Apr 60 call	1	0.17	0.026	0.06

   A spreader expects volatility to decline and is willing to set up a position whereby he will profit by $250 for each 0.01 decrease in volatility. Moreover, he wants to be gamma and delta neutral. He knows that he can eventually neutralize any delta by using XYZ common stock as in the previous example. How many options should be spread to achieve the desired result?
   To answer the question, one must create two equations in two unknowns, x and y. The unknowns represent the quantities of options to be bought and sold, respectively. The constants in the equations are taken from the table above.
   The first equation represents gamma neutral:

$$0.045 \; x + 0.026 \; y = 0,$$

where

x is the number of Apr 50's in the spread and y is the number of Apr 60's. Note that the constants in the equation are the gammas of the two calls involved.

The second equation represents the desired vega risk of making 2.5 points, or $250 if the volatility decreases:

$$0.08 \; x + 0.06 \; y = -2.5,$$

where

x and y are the same quantities as in the first equation, and the constants in this equation are the gammas of the options. Furthermore, note that the vega risk is negative, since the spreader wants to profit if volatility decreases.

Solving the two equations in two unknowns by algebraic methods yields the following results:

Equations:

0.045 x + 0.026 y = 0

0.08 x + 0.06 y   = −2.5

Solutions:

x = 104.80

y = −181.45

This means that one would buy 105 Apr 50 calls, since x being positive means that the options would be bought. He would also sell 181 Apr 60 calls (y is negative, which implies that the calls would be sold). This is nearly the same ratio determined in the previous example. The quantities are slightly higher, since the vega here is −$250 instead of the −$238 achieved in the previous example.

Finally, one would again determine the amount of stock to buy or sell to neutralize the delta by computing the position delta:

Position delta = 105 × 0.47 − 181 × 0.17 = 18.58

Thus 1,858 shares of XYZ would be shorted to neutralize the position.

Note: all the equations cannot be set equal to zero, or the solution will be all zeros. This is easily handled by setting at least one equation equal to a small, non-zero quantity, such as 0.1. *As long as at least one of the risk factors is non-zero, one can determine the neutral ratio for all other factors merely by solving these simultaneous equations.* There are plenty of low-cost computer programs that can solve simultaneous equations such as these.

This concept can be carried to greater lengths in order to determine the best spread to create in order to achieve the desired results. One might even try to use three different options—using the third option to neutralize delta, so that he wouldn't have to neutralize with stock. The third equation would use deltas as constants and would be set to equal zero, representing delta neutral. Solving this would require solving three equations in three unknowns, a simple matter for a computer.

As long as at least one of the risk factors is non-zero, one can determine the neutral ratio for all other factors merely by solving these simultaneous equations. Even more importantly, the computer can scan many combinations of options that produce a position that is both gamma and delta neutral and has a specific position vega (−$238, for example). One would then choose the "best" spread of the available possibilities by logical methods including, if possible, choosing one with positive theta, so time is working in his favor.

To summarize, one can neutralize all variables, or he can specify the risk that he wants to accept in any of them. Merely write the equations and solve them. It is best to use a computer to do this, but the fact that it *can* be done adds an entirely new, broad dimension to option spreading and risk reducing strategies.

Evaluating a Position Using the Risk Measures

The previous sections have dealt with establishing a new position, and determining its neutrality or lack thereof. However, the most important use of these risk measures is to predict how a position will perform into the future. At a minimum, a serious strategist should use a computer to print out a projection of the profits and losses and position risk at future expected prices. Moreover, this type of analysis should be done at several future times in order to give the strategist an idea of how the passage of time and the resultant larger movements by the underlying security will affect the position.

First, one would choose an appropriate time period—say, 7 days hence—for the first analysis. Then he should use the statistical projection of stock prices (see the chapter on mathematical applications) to determine probable prices for the underlying security at that time. Obviously, this stock price projection needs to use volatility, and that is somewhat variable. But, for the purposes of such a projection, it is acceptable to use the current volatility. The results of as many as 9 stock prices might be displayed: every one half standard deviation from −2 through +2 (−2.0, −1.5, −1.0, −0.5, 0, 0.5, 1.0, 1.5, 2.0).

Example: XYZ is at 60 and has a volatility of 35%. A distribution of stock prices 7 days into the future would be determined using the equation:

$$\text{Future Price} = \text{Current Price} \times av\sqrt{t}$$

where

a corresponds to the constants in the following table (−2.0 . . . 2.0)

# Standard Deviations	Projected Stock Price
−2.0	54.46
−1.5	55.79
−1.0	57.16
−0.5	58.56
0	60
0.5	61.47
1.0	62.98
1.5	64.52
2.0	66.11

Again, refer to Chapter 30 on mathematical applications for a more in-depth discussion of this price determination equation.

Note that the formula used to project prices has time as one of its components. This means that as we look farther out in time, the range of possible stock prices will expand—a necessary and logical component of this analysis. For example, if the prices were being determined 14 days into the future, the range of prices would be from 52.31 to 68.82. That is, XYZ has the same probability of being at 54.46 in 7 days that it has of being at 52.31 in 14 days. At expiration, some 90 days hence, the range would be quite a bit wider still. *Do not make the mistake of trying to evaluate the position at the same prices for each time period (7 days, 14 days, 1 month, expiration, etc.).* Such an analysis would be wrong.

Once the appropriate stock prices have been determined, the following quantities would be calculated for each stock price: profit or loss, position delta, position gamma, position theta, and position vega (position rho is generally a less important risk measure for stock and futures short-term options). Armed with this information, the strategist can be prepared to face the future. An important item to note: a model will necessarily be used to make these projections. As was shown earlier, if there is a distortion in the current implied volatilities of the options involved in the position, *the strategist should use the current implieds as input to the model for future option price projections.* If he does not, the position may look overly attractive if expensive options are being sold or cheap ones are being bought. A truer profit picture is obtained by propagating the current implied volatility structure into the near future.

Using an example similar to the previous one—a ratio spread using short stock to make it delta neutral—the concepts will be described.

Initial Position: XYZ is at 60. The Jan 70 calls, which have three months until expiration, are expensive with respect to the Jan 60 calls. A strategist expects this discrepancy to disappear when the implied volatility of XYZ options decreases. He therefore established the following position, which is both gamma and delta neutral.

Position	Delta	Gamma	Theta	Vega
Buy 100 Jan 60 calls	0.57	0.0723	−0.020	0.109
Short 240 Jan 70 calls	0.20	0.0298	−0.019	0.080
Short 800 XYZ				

The risk measures for the entire position are:

Position delta: −38 shares (virtually delta neutral)

Position gamma: +7 shares (gamma neutral)

Position theta: +$263

Position vega: −$827

Thus, the position is both gamma and delta neutral. Moreover, it has the attractive feature of making $263 per day because of the positive theta. Finally, as was the intention of the spreader, it will make money if the volatility of XYZ declines: $827 for each 0.01 decrease in implied volatility. Two equations in two unknowns (gamma and vega) were solved to obtain the quantities to buy and sell. The resulting position delta was neutralized by selling 800 XYZ.

The following analyses will assume that the relative expensiveness of the April 70 calls persists. These are the calls that were sold in the position. If that overpricing should disappear, the spread would look more favorable, but there is no guarantee that they will cheapen—especially over a short time period such as one or two weeks.

How would the position look in 7 days at the stock prices determined above?

Stock Price	P&L	Delta	Gamma	Theta	Vega
54.46	19.05	− 7.40	1.62	−0.94	− 1.57
55.79	10.77	− 4.90	2.07	−1.18	− 1.96
57.16	6.06	− 1.97	2.13	−1.53	− 2.90
58.56	5.28	0.74	1.65	−2.00	− 4.62
60.00	7.71	2.38	0.56	−2.63	− 7.22
61.47	11.27	2.07	−1.01	−3.38	− 10.63
62.98	12.52	− 0.87	−2.85	−4.22	− 14.56
64.52	7.02	− 6.73	−4.67	−5.07	− 18.61
66.11	− 10.19	− 15.42	−6.21	−5.85	− 22.31

In a similar manner, the position would have the following characteristics after 14 days had passed:

Stock Price	P&L	Delta	Gamma	Theta	Vega
52.31	42.21	− 9.10	0.69	− 0.55	− 0.98
54.14	27.31	− 6.93	1.69	− 0.75	− 0.89
56.02	17.82	− 2.87	2.51	− 1.06	− 1.21
57.98	17.17	2.17	2.44	− 1.61	− 2.69
60.00	25.77	5.85	1.00	− 2.51	− 6.00
62.09	38.39	5.29	− 1.63	− 3.73	− 11.05
64.26	43.61	− 1.55	− 4.61	− 5.09	− 16.90
66.50	26.31	− 14.80	− 7.02	− 6.31	− 22.17
68.82	− 27.99	− 32.83	− 8.32	− 7.18	− 25.72

The same information will be presented graphically in Figure 38-13 so that those who prefer pictures instead of columns of numbers can follow the discussions easily.

First, the profitability of the spread can be examined. This profit picture assumes that the volatility of XYZ remains unchanged. Note that in 7 days, there is a small profit if the stock remains unchanged. This is to be expected, since theta was negative, and therefore time is working in favor of this spread. Likewise, in 14 days, there is an even bigger profit if XYZ remains relatively unchanged—again due to the negative theta. Overall, there is an *expected profit* (see Chapter 30) of $800 in 7 days, or $2,600 in 14 days from this position. This indicates that it is an attractive situation statistically, but, of course, it does not mean that one cannot lose money.

Continuing to look at the profit picture, the downside is favorable to the spread since the short stock in the position would contribute to ever larger profits in the case that XYZ tumbles dramatically (see Figure 38-13). The upside is where problems could develop. In seven days, the position breaks even at about 65 on the upside; in 14 days, it breaks even at about 67½.

The reader may be asking, "Why is there such a dramatic risk to the upside? I thought the position was delta neutral and gamma neutral." True, the position *was* originally neutral with respect to both those variables. That neutrality explains the flatness of the profit curves about the current stock price of 60. However, once the stock has moved 1½ standard deviations to the upside, the neutrality begins to disappear. To see this, let us look at Figures 38-14 and 38-15 that show both the position delta

FIGURE 38-13.
XYZ ratio spread, gamma and delta neutral.

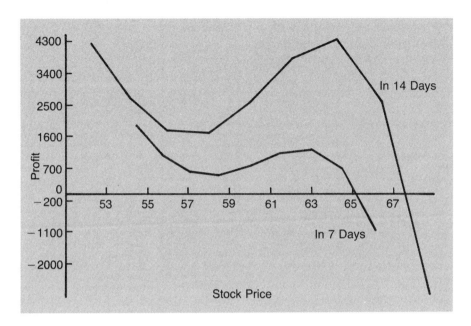

and position gamma 7 days and 14 days after the spread was established. Again, these are the same numbers listed in the previous tables.

First, look at the position delta in 7 days (Figure 38-14). Note that position remains relatively delta neutral with XYZ between 57 and 63— this is because the gamma was initially neutral. However, the position begins to get quite delta short if XYZ rises above 63 or falls below 57 in 7 days. What is happening to gamma while this is going on? Since we just observed that the delta eventually changes, that *has* to mean that the position is acquiring some gamma.

Figure 38-15 depicts the fact that gamma is not very stable, considering that it started at nearly zero. If XYZ falls, gamma increases a little, reflecting the fact that the position will get somewhat shorter as XYZ falls. But since there are only calls coupled with short stock in this position, there is no risk to the downside. Positive gamma, even a small positive gamma like this one, is beneficial to stock movement.

The upside is another matter entirely. The gamma begins to get seriously negative above a stock price of 63 in 7 days. Recall that negative gamma means that one's position is about to react poorly to price changes in the market—the position will soon be "fighting the market." As the stock goes even higher, the gamma becomes even more negative. These observations apply to stock price movements in either 7 days or 14 days—

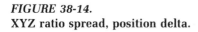

FIGURE 38-14.
XYZ ratio spread, position delta.

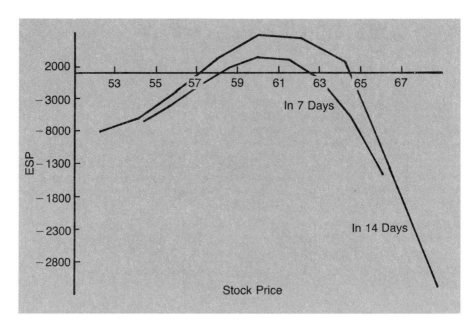

in fact, the effect on gamma does not seem to be particularly dependent
on time in this example, since the two lines on the Figure 38-15 are very
close to each other.

The above information depicts in detailed form the fact that this
position will not behave well if the stock rises too far in too short of a
time. However, stable stock prices will produce profits as will falling
prices. These are not earth-shattering conclusions since, by simple observation, one can see that there are extra short calls plus some short stock
in the position. However, the point of calculating this information in
advance is to be able to anticipate where to make adjustments and how
much to adjust.

Follow-Up Action. How should the strategist use this information? A
simplistic approach is to adjust the delta as it becomes non-neutral. This
won't do anything for gamma, however, and may therefore not necessarily
be the best approach. If one were to adjust only the delta, he would do it
in the following manner. The chart of delta (above) shows that the position
will be approximately delta short 800 shares if XYZ rises to 64½ in a
week. One simple plan would be to cover the 800 shares of XYZ that are
short if the stock rises to 64½. Covering the 800 shares would return the

FIGURE 38-15.
XYZ ratio spread, position gamma.

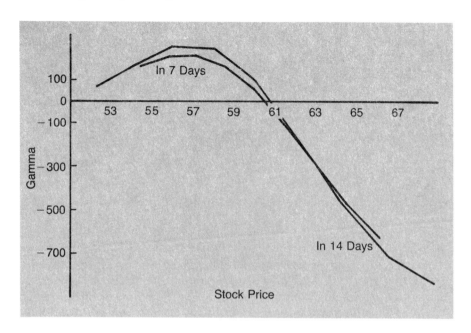

position to delta neutral at that time. Note that if the stock rises at a slower pace, the point at which the strategist would cover the 800 shares moves higher. For example, the delta in 14 days (again on Figure 38-14) shows that XYZ would have to be at about 65½ for the position to be delta short 800 shares. Hence, if it took two weeks for XYZ to begin rising, one could wait until 65½ before covering the 800 shares and returning the position to delta neutral.

In either case, the purchase of the 800 shares does not take care of the negative gamma that is creeping into the position as the stock rises. *The only way to counter negative gamma is to buy options, not stock.* To return a position to neutrality with respect to more than one risk variable requires one to approach the problem as he did when the position was established: neutralize the gamma first, and then use stock to adjust the delta. Note the difference between this approach and the one just described in the previous paragraph. Here, we are trying to adjust gamma first, and will get to delta later.

In order to add some positive gamma, one might want to buy back (cover) some of the Jan 70 calls that are currently short. Suppose that the decision is made to cover when XYZ reaches 65½ in 14 days. From the graph above, one can see that the position would be approximately gamma short 700 shares at the time. Suppose that the gamma of the Jan 70 call is 0.07. Then, one would have to cover 100 Jan 70 calls to add 700 shares of positive gamma to the position, returning it to gamma neutral. This purchase would, of course, make the position delta long, so some stock would have to be sold short as well in order to make the position delta neutral once again.

Thus, the procedure for follow-up action is somewhat similar to that for establishing the position: first neutralize the gamma and then eliminate the resulting delta by using the common stock. The resulting profit graphs will not be shown for this follow-up adjustment, since the process could go on and on. However, a few observations are pertinent. First, *the purchase of calls to reduce the negative gamma hurts the original thesis of the position*—to have negative vega and positive theta, if possible. Buying calls will add vega and subtract theta to the position, which is not desirable. However, it is more desirable than letting losses build up in the position as the stock continues to run to the upside. Second, *one might choose to remove the position if it is profitable*. This might happen if the volatility *did* decrease as expected. Then, when the stock rallies, producing negative gamma, one might actually have a profit, because his assumption concerning volatility had been right. If he does not see much further potential gains from decreasing volatility, he might use the point at which negative gamma starts to build up as the exit point from his position. Third, *one might choose to accept the acquired gamma risk*. Rather than jeopardize his initial thesis, one may just want to adjust the delta and let the gamma build up. This is no longer a neutral strategy, but one may have reasons for approaching the position this way. At least he has calculated the risk and is aware of it. If he chooses to accept it rather than eliminate it, that is his decision.

Finally, it is obvious that *the process is dynamic*. As factors change (stock price, volatility, time), the position itself changes and the strategist is presented with new choices. There is no absolutely correct adjustment. The process is more of an art than a science at times. Moreover, the strategist should continue to re-calculate these profit pictures and risk measures as the stock moves and time passes, or if there is a change in the securities involved in the position. There is one absolute truism and that is that *the serious strategist should be aware of the risk his position has with respect to at least the four basic measures of delta, gamma, theta, and vega*. To be ignorant of the risk is to be delinquent in the management of the position.

Trading Gamma From the Long Side

The strategist who is selling overpriced options and hedging that purchase with other options or stock will often have a position similar to the one described above. Large stock movements—at least in one direction—will typically be a problem for such positions. The opposite of this strategy would be to have a position that is *long* gamma. That is, the position does better if the stock moves quickly in one direction. While this seems pleasing to the psyche, these types of positions have their own brand of risk.

The simplest position with long gamma is a long straddle, or a backspread (reverse ratio spread). Another way to construct a position with long gamma would be to invert a calendar spread—to buy the near-term option and to sell a longer-term one. Since a near-term option has a higher gamma than a longer-term one with the same strike, such a position has long gamma. In fact, traders who expect violent action in a stock often construct such a position for the very reason that the public will come in behind them, bid up the short-term calls (increasing their implied volatility), and make the spread more profitable for the trader.

Unfortunately, all of these positions often involve being long just about everything else, including theta and vega as well. This means that time is working against the position, and that swings in implied volatility can be helpful or harmful as well. Can one construct a position that is long gamma, but is not so subject to the other variables? Of course he can, but what would it look like? The answer, as one might suspect, is not an ironclad one.

For the following examples, assume these prices exist:

XYZ: 60

Option	Price	Delta	Gamma	Theta	Vega
Mar 60 call	3.25	0.54	0.0510	0.033	0.089
June 60 call	5.50	0.57	0.0306	0.021	0.147

Example: Suppose that a strategist wants to create a position that is *gamma long, but is neutral with respect to both delta and vega.* He thinks the stock will move, but is not sure of the price direction, and does not want to have any risk with respect to quick changes in volatility. In order to quantify the statement that he "wants to be gamma long," let us assume that he wants to be gamma long 1,000 shares or 10 contracts.

It is known that delta can always be neutralized last, so let us concentrate on the other two variables first. The two equations below are used to determine the quantities to buy in order to make gamma long and vega neutral:

$$0.0510x + 0.0306y = 10 \text{ (gamma, expressed in \# of contracts)}$$
$$0.089x + 0.147y = 0 \text{ (vega)}$$

The solution to these equations is:

$$x = 308, y = -186$$

Thus, one would *buy* 308 Mar 60 calls and would *sell* 186 Jun 60 calls. This is the reverse calendar spread that was discussed just above: near-term calls are bought and longer-term calls are sold.

Finally, the delta must be neutralized. To do this, calculate the position delta using the quantities just determined:

$$\text{Position delta} = 0.54 \times 308 - 0.57 \times 186 = 60.30$$

So, the position is long 60 contracts, or 6,000 shares. It can be made delta neutral by selling short 6,000 shares of XYZ.

The overall position would look like this:

Position	Delta	Gamma	Vega
Short 6,000 XYZ	1.00	0	0
Long 308 Mar 60 calls	0.54	0.0510	0.089
Short 186 Jun 60 calls	0.57	0.0306	0.147

Its risk measurements are:

Position delta: long 30 shares (neutral)

Position vega: $7 (neutral)

Position gamma: long 1,001 shares

This position then satisfies the initial objectives of wanting to be gamma long 1,000 shares, but delta and vega neutral.

Finally, note that theta = −$625. The position will lose $625 per day from time decay.

The strategist must go further than this analysis, especially if one is dealing with positions that are not simple constructions. He should calculate a profit picture as well as look at how the risk measures behave as time passes and the stock price changes.

Figure 38-16 (see Tables 38-9, 38-10, and 38-11) show the profit potential in 7 days, in 14 days, and at March expiration. Figure 38-17 shows the position delta (ESP) at the 7- and 14-day time intervals. Before

FIGURE 38-16.
Trading long gamma, profit picture.

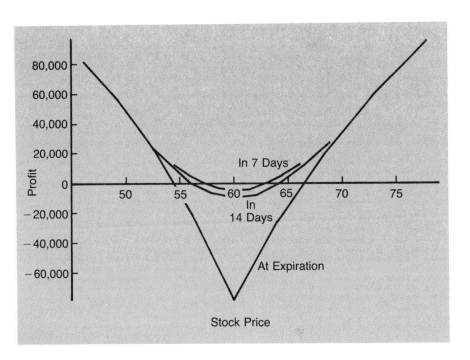

discussing these items, the data will be presented in tabular form at three different times: in 7 days, 14 days, and at March expiration.

The following data depict the position in 7 days:

TABLE 38-10.
Risk measures of long gamma position in 7 days.

Stock Price	P&L	Delta	Gamma	Theta	Vega
54.46	122.59	− 58.72	8.28	4.15	− 5.74
55.79	52.02	− 46.60	9.78	5.20	− 4.18
57.16	− 2.24	− 32.45	10.80	6.09	− 2.85
58.56	− 36.70	− 16.91	11.25	6.73	− 1.94
60.00	− 49.75	− 0.80	11.08	7.04	− 1.63
61.47	− 39.01	15.01	10.32	6.98	− 1.96
62.98	− 5.07	29.69	9.09	6.57	− 2.89
64.52	51.05	42.56	7.54	5.87	− 4.29
66.11	127.17	53.17	5.86	4.97	− 5.96

FIGURE 38-17.
Trading long gamma, position vega.

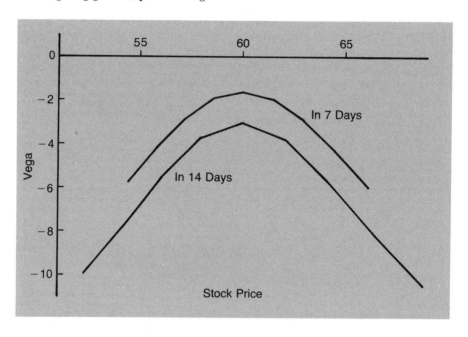

This table represents the results in 14 days:

TABLE 38-11.
Risk measures of long gamma position in 14 days.

Stock Price	P&L	Delta	Gamma	Theta	Vega
52.31	249.45	− 79.34	4.75	2.10	− 9.91
54.14	114.45	− 67.68	8.00	3.91	− 7.87
56.02	2.77	− 49.79	10.79	5.76	− 5.56
57.98	− 72.63	− 26.87	12.42	7.21	− 3.73
60.00	− 101.41	− 1.44	12.47	7.88	− 3.04
62.09	− 77.84	23.32	10.99	7.60	− 3.78
64.26	− 3.47	44.47	8.45	6.47	− 5.71
66.50	114.91	60.12	5.55	4.82	− 8.20
68.82	266.72	69.81	2.92	3.09	−10.48

Finally, the position as it looks at March expiration should be known as well:

TABLE 38-12.
Risk measures of long gamma position at March expiration.

Stock Price	P&L	Delta	Gamma	Theta	Vega
46.19	813.27	− 75.69	− 3.65	− 1.32	− 6.88
49.31	556.28	− 89.84	− 5.39	− 2.25	− 11.43
52.64	223.78	− 110.50	− 6.89	− 3.33	− 16.50
56.20	− 215.23	− 136.65	− 7.62	− 4.28	− 20.67
60.00	− 789.07	144.68	− 7.29	− 4.79	− 22.49
64.06	− 259.46	117.44	− 6.03	− 4.70	− 21.26
68.39	197.87	95.03	− 4.31	− 4.10	− 17.44
73.01	597.32	79.05	− 2.67	− 3.24	− 12.43
77.95	960.62	69.19	− 1.43	− 2.41	− 7.69

In each case, note that the stock prices are calculated in accordance with the statistical formula shown in the last section. The more time that passes, the farther it is possible for the stock to roam from the current price.

The profit picture (Figure 38-16) shows that this position looks much like a long straddle would—it makes large, symmetric profits if the stock goes either way up or way down. Moreover, the losses if the stock remains relatively unchanged can be large. These losses tend to mount right away, becoming significant even in 14 days. Hence, if one enters this type of position, he had better get the desired stock movement quickly, or be prepared to cut his losses and exit the position.

The most startling thing to note about the entire position is the devastating effect of time on the position. The profit picture shows that large losses will result if the stock movement that is expected does not materialize. These losses are completely due to time decay. Theta is negative in the initial position ($625 of losses per day), and remains negative—and surprisingly constant—until March expiration (when the long calls expire). Time also affects vega. Notice how the vega begins to get negative right away and keeps getting much more negative as time passes. Simply, it can be seen that as time passes, the position becomes *vulnerable to increases in implied volatility.*

This relationship between time and volatility might not readily be apparent to the strategist unless he takes the time to calculate these sorts of tables or figures. In fact, one may be somewhat confounded by this observation. What is happening is that as time passes, the options which are owned are less explosive if volatility increases, but the options which were sold have a lot of time remaining, and are therefore apt to increase violently if volatility spurts upward.

Figures 38-18 and 38-19 provide less enlightening information about delta and gamma. Since gamma was positive to start with, the delta increases dramatically as the stock rises, and decreases just as fast if the stock falls (Figure 38-19). This is standard behavior for positions with long gamma; a long straddle would look very similar. Notice that gamma remains positive throughout (Figure 38-18), although it falls to smaller levels if the stock moves towards the end of the pricing ranges used in the analyses. Again, this is standard action for a long straddle.

So, is this a good position? That is a difficult question to answer unless one knows what is going to happen to the underlying stock. Statistically, this type of position has a negative expected return and would generally produce losses over the long run. However, in situations where the near-term options are destined to get overheated—perhaps a takeover rumor or just a leak of material information about a company—many sophisticated traders establish this type of position to take advantage of the expected explosion in stock price.

Other Variations. Without going into as much detail, it is possible to compare the above position with similar ones. The purpose in doing so is to illustrate how a change in the strategist's initial requirements would

FIGURE 38-18.
Trading long gamma, position gamma.

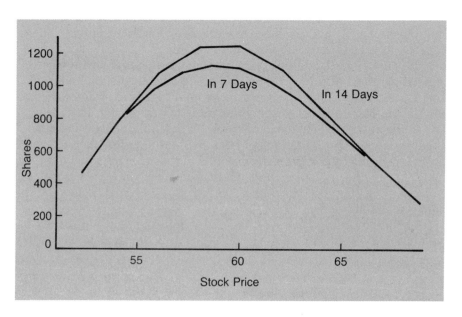

FIGURE 38-19.
Trading long gamma, position delta.

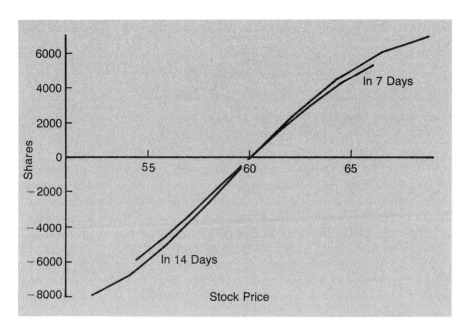

alter the established position. In the above position, the strategist wanted to be gamma long, but neutral with respect to delta and volatility. Suppose he not only expects price movement (meaning he wants positive gamma), but also expects an increase in volatility. If that were the case, he would want positive vega as well. Suppose that he quantifies that desire by deciding that he wants to make $1,000 for every 0.01 increase in volatility. The simultaneous equations would then be:

$$0.0501x + 0.0306y = 10 \text{ (gamma)}$$
$$0.089x + 0.147y = 10 \text{ (vega)}$$

The solution to these equations is:

$$x = 243, y = -80$$

Furthermore, 8,500 shares would have to be sold short in order to make the position delta neutral. The resulting position would then be:

Short 8,500 XYZ   Delta: neutral
Long 243 Mar 60 calls   Gamma: long 1,000 shares

Short 80 Jun 60 calls   Vega: long $1,000
                             Theta: long $630

Recall that the position discussed in the last section was vega neutral and was:

Short 6,000 XYZ   Delta: neutral
Long 308 Mar 60 calls   Gamma: long 1,000 shares
Short 186 Jun 60 calls   Vega: neutral
                             Theta: long $625

   Notice that in the new position there are now over three times as many long Mar 60 calls as there are short Jun 60 calls. This is a much larger ratio than in the vega neutral position, where about 1.6 calls were bought for each one sold. This even greater preponderance of near-term calls that are purchased means the newer position has an even larger exposure to time decay than did the previous one. That is, in order to acquire the positive vega, one is forced to take on even more risk with respect to time decay. For that reason, this is a less desirable position than the first one; it seems overly risky to want to be both long gamma and long volatility.
   This does not necessarily mean that one would never want to be long volatility. In fact, if one expected volatility to increase, he might want to establish a position that was delta neutral and gamma neutral, but had positive vega. Again, using the same prices as in the previous examples, the following position would satisfy these criteria:

Short 2,600 XYZ   Delta: neutral
Short 64 Mar 60 calls   Gamma: neutral
Long 106 Jun 60 calls   Vega: long $1,000
                             Theta: long $11

   This position has a more conventional form. It is a calendar spread, except that more long calls are purchased. Moreover, the theta of this position is only $11—it will only lose $11 per day to time decay. At first glance it might seem like the best of the three choices. Unfortunately, when one draws the profit graph (Figure 38-20) he finds that this position has significant downside risk—the short stock cannot compensate for the large quantity of Jun 60 calls. Still, the position *does* make money on the upside, and will also make money if volatility increases. If the near-term March calls were overpriced with respect to the June calls at the time the position was established, it would make it even more desirable.

FIGURE 38-20.
Trading long gamma, "conventional" calendar.

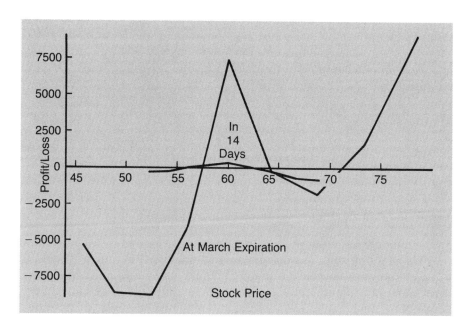

To summarize, defining the risks one wants to take or avoid specifies the construction of the eventual position. The strategist should examine the potential risks and rewards, especially the profit picture. If the potential risks are not desirable, the stategist should rethink his requirements and try again. Thus, in the above example, the strategist felt that he initially wanted to be long gamma, but it involved too much risk of time decay. A second attempt was made, introducing positive volatility into the situation, but that didn't seem to help much. Finally, a third analysis was generated involving *only* long volatility and not long gamma. The resulting position has little time risk, but has risk if the stock drops in price. It is probably the best of the three. The strategist arrives at this conclusion through a local process of analysis.

ADVANCED MATHEMATICAL CONCEPTS

The remainder of this chapter is a short adjunct to the chapter on mathematical applications. It is quite technical. Those who desire to understand the basic concepts behind the risk measures and perhaps to utilize them in more advanced ways will be interested in what follows.

Calculating "The Greeks"

It is known that the equation for delta is a direct byproduct of the Black-Scholes model calculation:

$$\Delta = N(d1)$$

Each of the risk measures can be derived mathematically by taking the partial derivative of the model. However, there is a shortcut approximation that works just as well. For example, the formula for gamma is as follows:

$$x = \ln\left(\frac{\rho}{s \times (1 + r)^t}\right)\Big/ v\sqrt{t} + \frac{v\sqrt{t}}{2}$$

$$\Gamma = \frac{e^{-\frac{x^2}{2}}}{\rho v \sqrt{2\pi t}}$$

There is a simpler, yet correct, way to arrive at the gamma. The delta is the partial derivative of the Black-Scholes model with respect to stock price—that is, it is the amount by which the option's price changes for a change in stock price. The gamma is the change in delta for the same change in stock price. Thus, one can approximate the gamma by the following steps:

1. calculate the delta with ρ = current stock price
2. set $\rho = \rho + 1$ and recalculate the delta
3. gamma = delta from step 1 − delta from step 2

The same procedure can be used for the other "greeks":

Vega: 1. Calculate the option price with a particular volatility.
        2. Calculate another option price with volatility increased by 1%.
        3. Vega = difference of the prices in steps 1 and 2.
Theta: 1. Calculate the option price with the current time to expiration.
        2. Calculate the option price with 1 day less time remaining to expiration.
        3. Theta: = difference of the price in steps 1 and 2.
Rho: 1. Calculate the option price with the current risk-free interest rate.
        2. Calculate the option price with the rate increased by 1%.
        3. Rho = difference of the price in steps 1 and 2.

The Gamma of the Gamma

This discussion of this concept was deferred from earlier sections because it is somewhat difficult to grasp. It is included now for those who may wish to use it at some time. Those readers who are not interested in such matters may skip to the next section.

Recall that this is the sixth risk measurement of an option position. *The gamma of the gamma is the amount by which the gamma will change when the stock price changes.*

Recall that in the earlier discussion of gamma, it was noted that gamma changes. This example is based on the same example used earlier.

Example: With XYZ at 49, assume the Jan 50 call has a delta of 0.50 and a gamma of 0.05. If XYZ moves up one point to 50, the delta of the call will increase by the amount of the gamma: it will increase from 0.50 to 0.55. Simplistically, if XYZ moves up another point to 51, the delta will increase by another 0.05 to 0.60.

Obviously, the delta cannot keep increasing by 0.05 each time XYZ gains another point in price, for it will eventually exceed 1.00 by that calculation, and it is known that the delta has a maximum of 1.00. Thus, it is obvious that the gamma changes.

In reality, the gamma decreases as the stock moves away from the strike. Thus, with XYZ at 51, the gamma might only be 0.04. Therefore, if XYZ moved up to 52, the call's delta would only increase by 0.04, to 0.64. Hence, the gamma of the gamma is -0.01, since the gamma decreased from .05 to .04 when the stock rose by one point.

As XYZ moves higher and higher, the gamma will get smaller and smaller. Eventually, with XYZ in the low 60's, the delta will be nearly 1.00 and the gamma nearly 0.00.

This change in the *gamma* as the stock moves is called the *gamma of the gamma*. It is probably referred to by other names, but since its use is limited to only the most sophisticated traders, there is no standard name. Generally, one would use this measure on his entire portfolio to gauge how quickly the portfolio would be responding to the "position gamma."

Example: With XYZ at $31\frac{3}{4}$ as in some of the previous examples, the following risk measures exist:

Position	Option Delta	Option Gamma	Option Gamma/Gamma	Position Gamma/Gamma
Short 4,500 XYZ	1.00	0.00	0.0000	0
Short 100 XYZ Apr 25 calls	0.89	0.01	-0.0015	-15

Long 50 XYZ Apr 30 calls	0.76	0.03	− 0.0006	− 3
Long 139 XYZ Jul 30 calls	0.74	0.02	− 0.0003	− 4
		Totals Gamma of Gamma:		− 22

Recall that, in the same example used to describe gamma, the position was delta long 686 shares and had a positive gamma of 328 shares. Furthermore, we now see that the gamma itself is going to *decrease* as the stock moves up (it is negative) or will increase as the stock moves down. In fact, it is expected to increase or decrease by 22 shares for each point XYZ moves.

So, if XYZ moves up by one point, the following should happen:

a) delta increases from 686 to 1,014, increasing by the amount of the gamma.

b) the gamma decreases from 328 to 306, indicating that a further upward move by XYZ will result in a smaller increase in delta.

One can build a general picture of how the gamma of the gamma changes over different situations—in- or out-of-the-money, or with more or less time remaining until expiration. The following table of two index calls, the Jan 350 with one month of life remaining, and the December 350 with eleven months of life remaining, shows the delta, gamma, and gamma of the gamma for various stock prices.

Index Price	*Jan 350 call* Delta	Gamma	Gamma/Gamma	*Dec 350 call* Delta	Gamma	Gamma/Gamma
310	.0006	.0001	.0000	.3203	.0083	.0000
320	.0087	.0020	.0004	.3971	.0082	.0000
330	.0618	.0100	.0013	.4787	.0080	− .0000
340	.2333	.0744	.0013	.5626	.0078	− .0001
350	.5241	.0309	− .0003	.6360	.0073	− .0001
360	.7957	.0215	− .0014	.6984	.0067	− .0001
370	.9420	.0086	− .0010	.7653	.0060	− .0001
380	.9892	.0021	− .0003	.8213	.0052	− .0001

Several conclusions can be drawn, not all of which are obvious at first glance. First of all, the gamma of the gamma for long-term options is very small. This should be expected, since the delta of a long-term option changes very slowly. The next fact can best be observed while looking at the shorter-term Jan 350 table. The gamma of the gamma is near zero for deeply out-of-the-money options. But, as the option comes closer to being in-the-money, the gamma of the gamma becomes a positive number, reaching its maximum, while the option is still out-of-the-money. By the time the option is *at* the money, the gamma of the gamma has turned negative. It then remains negative, reaching its most negative point when slightly in-the-money. From there on, as the option goes even deeper into-the-money, the gamma of the gamma remains negative but get closer and closer to zero, eventually reaching (minus) zero when the option is very far in-the-money.

Can one possibly reason this risk measurement out without making severe mathematical calculations? Well, possibly. Note that the delta of an option starts as a small number when the option is out-of-the-money. It then increases, slowly at first, then more quickly until it is just below 0.60 for an at-the-money option. From there on, it will continue to increase, but much more slowly as the option becomes in-the-money. This movement of the delta can be observed by looking at gamma: it is the change in the delta, so it starts slowly, increases as the stock nears the strike, and then begins to decrease as the option is in-the-money, always remaining a positive number, since delta can only change in the positive direction as the stock rises. Finally, the gamma of the gamma is the change in the gamma, so it in turn starts as a positive number as gamma grows larger, but then when gamma starts tapering off, this is reflected as a negative gamma of the gamma.

In general, the gamma of the gammma is used by sophisticated traders on large option positions where it is not obvious what is going to happen to the gamma as the stock changes in price. Traders often have some feel for their delta. They may even have some feel for how that delta is going to change as the stock moves (i.e., they have a feel for gamma). However, sophisticated traders know that even positions which start out with zero delta and zero gamma may eventually acquire some delta. The gamma of the gamma tells the trader how much and how soon that eventual delta will be acquired.

Measuring the Difference of Implied Volatilities

Recall that when the topic of implied volatility was discussed, it was shown that if one could identify situations in which the various options on the same underlying security had substantially different implied volatilities, then there might be an attractive neutral spread available. The strategist might ask how he is to determine if the discrepancies between the individual options are significantly large to warrant attention. Furthermore, is there a quick way (using a computer, or course) to determine this?

A logical way to approach this is to look at each individual implied volatility and compute the standard deviation of these numbers. This standard deviation can be converted to a percentage by dividing it by the overall implied volatility of the stock. This percentage, if it is large enough, alerts the strategist that there may be opportunities to spread the options of this underlying security against each other. An example should clarify this procedure:

Example: XYZ is trading at 50, and the following options exist with the indicated implied volatilities. We can calculate a standard deviation of these implieds, called implied deviation, via the formula:

Implied deviation = sqrt (sum of differences from mean)^2/(# options − 1)

XYZ: 50

Option	Implied Volatility	Difference from Average
Oct 45 call	25%	−9.44
Nov 45 call	25%	−9.44
Jan 45 call	23%	−7.44
Oct 50 call	32%	+1.56
Nov 50 call	30%	−0.44
Jan 50 call	28%	−2.44
Oct 55 call	40%	+9.56
Nov 55 call	37%	+6.56
Jan 55 call	34%	+3.56

Average: 30.44%

Sum of (difference from avg)^2 = 389.26

Implied deviation = sqrt (sum of diff)^2/(# options − 1)

= sqrt (389.26 / 8)

= 6.98

This figure represents the raw standard deviation of the implied volatilities. To convert it into a useful number for comparisons, one must divide it by the average implied volatility.

$$\text{Percent deviation} = \frac{\text{implied deviation}}{\text{average implied}}$$

= 6.98/30.44

= 23%

This "percent deviation" number is usually significant if it is larger than 15%. That is, if the various options have implied volatilities that are different enough from each other to produce a result of 15% or greater in the above calculation, then the strategist should take a look at establishing neutral spreads in that security or futures contract.

The above concept can be refined further by using a weighted average of the implieds (taking into consideration such factors as volume and distance from the striking price) rather than just using the raw average. That task is left to the reader.

Recall that a computer can perform a large number of Black-Scholes calculations in a short period of time. Thus, the computer can calculate each option's implied volatility and then perform the "percent deviation" calculation above even faster. The strategist who is interested in establishing this type of neutral spread would only have to scan down the list of percent deviations to find candidates for spreading. On a given day, the list is usually quite short—perhaps 20 stocks and 10 futures contracts will qualify.

SUMMARY

In today's highly competitive and volatile option markets, neutral traders must be extremely aware of their risks. That risk is not just risk at expiration, but also the current risk in the market. Furthermore, they should have an idea of how the risk will increase or decrease as the underlying stock or futures contract moves up and down in price. Moreover, the passage of time or the volatility that the options are being assigned in the marketplace—the implied volatility—are important considerations. Even changes in short-term interest rates can be of interest, especially if longer-term options (LEAPS) are involved.

Once the strategist understands these concepts, he can use them to select new positions, to adjust existing ones, and to formulate specific strategies to take advantage of them. He can select a specific criteria that he wants to exploit—selling high volatility, for example—and use the other measures to construct a position that has little risk with respect to any of the other variables. Furthermore, the market maker or specialist, who does not want to acquire any market risk if he can help it, will use these techniques to attempt to neutralize all of the current risk if possible.

Chapter 39

Taxes

In this chapter, the basic tax treatment of listed options will be outlined and several tax strategies will be presented. The reader should be aware of the fact that tax laws change, and therefore should consult tax counsel before actually implementing any tax-oriented strategy. The interpretation of certain tax strategies by the Internal Revenue Service is subject to reclarification or change, as well.

An option is a capital asset and any gains or losses are capital gains or losses. Differing tax consequences apply, depending on whether the option trade is a complete transaction by itself, or whether it becomes part of a stock transaction via exercise or assignment. Listed option transactions which are closed out in the options market or are allowed to expire worthless are capital transactions. Gains from option purchases could possibly be long-term gains if the holding period of the option exceeds the long-term capital gains holding period (currently one year).

Gains from the sale of options are short-term capital gains. In addition, the tax treatment of futures options and index options and other listed non-equity options may differ from that of equity options. We will review these points individually.

HISTORY

In the short life of listed option trading, there have been several major changes in the tax rules. When options were first listed in 1973, the tax laws treated the gains and losses from *writing* options as ordinary income. That is, the feeling was that only professionals or those people "in the business" actually wrote over-the-counter options, and thus their gains and losses represented their ordinary income, or means of making a living. This rule presented some interesting strategies involving spreads, because the long side of the spread could be treated as long-term gain (if held for more than 6 months) and the short side of the spread could be ordinary loss. Of course, the stock would have had to move in the desired direction in order to obtain this result.

In 1976, the tax laws changed. The major changes affecting option traders were that the long-term holding period was extended to one year and also that gains or losses from writing options were considered to be capital gains. The extension of the long-term period essentially removed all possibilities of listed option holders ever obtaining a long-term gain, because the listed option market's longest-term options only had 9 months of life.

All through this period there were a wide array of tax strategies that were available, legally, to allow investors to defer capital gains from one year to the next, thereby avoiding payment of taxes. Essentially, one would enter into a spread involving deep in-the-money options that expire in the next calendar year. Perhaps the spread would be established during October using January options. Then one would wait for the underlying stock to move. Once a move had taken place, the spread would have a profit on one side and a loss on the other. The loss would be realized by rolling the losing option into another deep in-the-money option. The realized loss could thus be claimed on that year's taxes. The remaining spread—now an unrealized profit—would be left in place until expiration, in the next calendar year. At that time, the spread would be removed and the gain would be realized. Thus, the gain was moved from one year to the next. Then, later in *that* year, the gain would again be rolled to the next calendar year, and so on.

These practices were effectively stopped by the new tax ruling issued in 1984. Two sweeping changes were made. First, the new rules stated that, in any spread position involving offsetting options—as the two deep in-the-money options in the above example—the losses can be taken only to the extent that they exceed the unrealized gain on the other side of the spread (the tax literature insists on calling these positions "straddles" after the old commodity term, but for options purposes they are really spreads or covered writes). As a by-product of this rule, the holding period of stock can be terminated or eliminated by writing options that are too deeply in-the-money. Second, the new rules required that all positions in non-equity options and all futures be marked to market at the end of the tax year, and that taxes be paid on realized and unrealized gains alike. The tax *rate* for non-equity options was lowered from that of equity options. Then in 1986, the long-term and short-term capital gains rates were made equal to the lowest ordinary rate. All of these points will be covered in detail.

BASIC TAX TREATMENT

Listed options which are exercised or assigned fall into a different category for tax purposes. The original premium of the option transaction is combined into the stock transaction. There is no tax liability on this stock position until the stock position itself is closed out. There are four different combinations of exercising or assigning puts or calls. Table 39-1 summarizes the method of applying the option premium to the stock cost or sale price.

Examples of how to treat these various transactions are given in the following sections. In addition to examples explaining the basic tax treatment, some supplementary strategies are included as well.

Call Buyer

If a call holder subsequently sells the call or allows it to expire worthless, he has a capital gain or loss. For equity options, the holding period of the option determines whether the gain or loss is long-term or short-term. As mentioned previously, a long-term gain would be possible if held for more than six months. For tax purposes, an option that expires worthless is considered to have been sold at zero dollars on the expiration date.

Example: An investor purchases an XYZ October 50 call for 5-points on July 1. He sells the call for 9 points on September 1. That is, he realizes a capital gain via a closing transaction. His taxable gain would be computed as follows, assuming that a $25 commission was paid on both the purchase and the sale.

TABLE 39-1.
Applying the option premium to the stock cost or sale price.

Action	Tax Treatment
Call buyer exercises	Add call premium to stock cost
Put buyer exercises	Subtract put premium from stock sale price
Call writer assigned	Add call premium to stock sale price
Put writer assigned	Subtract put premium from stock cost

Net proceeds of sale ($900 − $25)	$875
Net cost ($500 + $25)	− 525
Short-term gain:	$350

Alternatively, if the stock had fallen in price by October expiration and the October 50 call had expired worthless, the call buyer would have lost $525—his entire net cost. If he had held the call until it expired worthless, he would have a short-term capital loss of $525 to report among his taxable transactions.

Put Buyer

The holder of a put has much the same tax consequences as the holder of a call, provided that he is not also long the underlying stock. This initial discussion of tax consequences to the put holder will assume that he does *not* simultaneously own the underlying stock. If the put holder sells his put in the option market or allows it to expire worthless, the gain or loss is treated as capital gain, long-term for equity puts held more than six months. Historically, the purchase of a put was viewed as perhaps the only way an investor could attain a long-term gain in a declining market.

Example: An investor buys an XYZ April 40 put for 2 points with the stock at 43. Later, the stock drops in price and the put is sold for 5 points. The commissions were $25 on each option trade, so the tax consequences would be:

Net sale proceeds ($500 − $25)	$475
Net cost ($200 + $25)	− 225
Short-term capital gain:	$250

Alternatively, if he had sold the put at a loss, perhaps in a rising market, he would have a short-term capital loss. Furthermore, if he allowed the put to expire totally worthless, his short-term loss would be equal to the entire net cost of $225.

Call Writer

Written calls that are bought back in the listed option market or are allowed to expire worthless are short-term capital gains. A written call cannot produce a long-term gain, regardless of the holding period. This treatment of a written call holds true even if the investor simultaneously owned the underlying stock (that is, he had a covered write). As long as the call is bought back or allowed to expire worthless, the gain or loss on the call is treated separately from the underlying stock for tax purposes.

Example: A trader sells naked an XYZ July 30 call for 3 points and buys it back three months later at a price of 1. The commissions were $25 for each trade, so the tax gain would be:

Net sale proceeds ($300 − $25)	$275
Net cost ($100 + $25)	− 125
Short-term gain:	$150

If the investor had not bought the call back, but had been fortunate enough to be able to allow it to expire worthless, his gain for tax purposes would have been the entire $275, representing his net sale proceeds. The purchase cost is considered to be zero for an option that expires worthless.

Put Writer

The tax treatment of written puts is quite similar to that of written calls. If the put is bought back in the open market or is allowed to expire worthless, the transaction is a short-term capital item.

Example: An investor writes an XYZ July 40 put for 4 points, and later buys it back for 2 points after a rally by the underlying stock. The commissions were $25 on each option trade, so the tax situation would be:

Net put sale price $(400 − $25)	$375
Net put cost ($100 + $25)	− 125
Short-term gain:	$250

If the put were allowed to expire worthless, the investor would have a net gain of $375, and this gain would be short-term.

The 60/40 Rule

As mentioned earlier, *non-equity option positions and future positions must be marked to market at the end of the tax year and taxes paid on both the unrealized and realized gains and losses.* This same rule applies to futures positions. The tax rate on these gains and losses is lower than the equity options rate. *Regardless of the actual holding period of the*

positions, one treats 60% of his tax liability as long-term and 40% as
short-term. This ruling means that even gains made from extremely short-
term activity such as day-trading can qualify partially as long-term gains.

Since 1986, long-term and short-term capital gains rates have been
equal. If long-term rates should drop, then the rule would again be more
meaningful.

Example: A trader in non-equity options has made three trades during the tax year. It is now the end of the tax year and he must compute
his taxes. First, he bought S&P 500 calls for $1,500 and sold them 6 weeks
later for $3,500. Second, he bought an OEX January 160 call for 3¼ seven
months ago and still holds it. It currently is trading at 11½. Finally, he
sold 5 XMI Feb 250 puts for 1½ three days ago. They are currently trading
at 2. The net gain from these transactions should be computed without
regard to holding period.

Non-Equity Contract	Original Price	Current Price	Cost	Proceeds	Gain/ Loss	
S&P calls	—	—	$1,500	$3,500	+ $2,000	realized
OEX Jan 160	3¼	11½	$ 325	$1,150	+ 825	unrealized
XMI Feb 250	1½	2	$1,000	$ 750	− 250	unrealized
Total capital gains					+ $2,575	

The total tax liability is $2,575, regardless of holding period and regardless
of whether the item is realized or unrealized. Of this total liability, 60%
($1,545) is subject to long-term treatment and 40% ($1,030) is subject to
short-term treatment.

In practice, one computes these figures on a separate tax form and
merely enters the two final figures—$1,545 and $1,030—on the tax sched-
ule for capital gains and losses. Note that if one loses money in nonequity
options, he actually has a tax *disadvantage* in comparison to equity options, because he must take some of his loss as a long-term loss, while
the equity option trader can take all of his loss as short-term.

EXERCISE AND ASSIGNMENT

Except for a specified situation that we will discuss later, exercise and assignment do not have any *tax* effect for non-equity options because everything is marked to market at the end of the year. However, since equity options are subject to holding period considerations, the following discussion pertains to them.

Call Exercise

An equity call holder who has an in-the-money call might decide to exercise the call rather than sell it in the options market. If he does this, there are no tax consequences on the option trade itself. Rather, the cost of the stock is increased by the net cost of the original call option. Moreover, the holding period begins on the day the stock is purchased (the day after the call was exercised). The option's holding period has no bearing on the stock position that resulted from the exercise.

   Example: An XYZ October 50 call was bought for 5 points on July 1. The stock had risen by October expiration, and the call holder decided to exercise the call on October 20. The option commission was $25 and the stock commission was $85. The cost basis for the stock would be computed as follows:

Buy 100 XYZ at 50 via exercise	
($5,000 plus $85 commission)	$5,085
Original call cost ($500 plus $25)	525
Total tax basis of stock	$5,610
Holding period of stock begins on October 21.	

When this stock is eventually sold, it will be a gain or a loss, depending on the stock's sale price as compared to the tax basis of $5,610 for the stock. Furthermore, it will be a short-term transaction unless the stock is held until October 21 of the following year.

Call Assignment

If a written call is not closed out, but is instead assigned, the call's net sale proceeds are added to the sale proceeds of the underlying stock. The call's holding period is lost, and the stock position is considered to have been sold on the date of the assignment.

   Example: A naked writer sells an XYZ July 30 call for 3 points, and is later assigned rather than buying back the option when it was in-the-money near expiration. The stock commission is $75. His net sale proceeds for the stock would be computed as follows:

Net call sale proceeds ($300 − $25)	$ 275
Net stock proceeds from assignment of 100 shares at 30 ($3,000 − $75)	2,925
Net stock sale proceeds	$3,200

In the case where the investor writes a naked, or uncovered, call, he sells stock short upon assignment. He may, of course, cover the short sale by purchasing stock in the open market for delivery. Such a short sale of stock is governed by the applicable tax rules pertaining to short sales— that any gains or losses from the short sale of stock are short-term gains or losses.

Tax Treatment for the Covered Writer. If, on the other hand, the investor was assigned on a covered call—that is, he was operating the covered writing strategy—and he elects to deliver the stock that he owns against the assignment notice, he has a complete stock transaction. The net cost of the stock was determined by its purchase price at an earlier date and the net sale proceeds are, of course, determined by the assignment in accordance with the preceding example.

Determining the proceeds from the stock purchase and sale are easy, but determining the tax status of the transaction is not. In order to prevent stockholders from using deeply in-the-money calls to protect their stock while letting it become a long-term item, some complicated tax rules have been passed. They can be summarized as follows:

1. If the equity option was out-of-the-money when first written, it has no effect on the holding period of the stock.
2. If the equity option was too deeply in-the-money when first written *and the stock was not yet held long-term*, then the holding period of the stock is *eliminated*.
3. If the equity option was in-the-money, but not too deeply, then the holding period of the stock is suspended while the call is in place.

These rules are complicated and merit further explanation. The first rule merely says that one can write out-of-the-money calls without any problem. If the stock later rises and is called away, the sale proceeds for the stock include the option premium and the transaction is long-term or short-term depending on the holding period of the stock.

Example: On March 1, an investor buys 100 XYZ at 35. On July 15, the stock has risen to 43 and he sells an October 45 call for 3. At October expiration, he is called away. Assume $25 option commission and $75 stock commission each way.

Net call sale proceeds ($300 − $25)	$ 275	
Net stock proceeds from		
assignment ($4,500 − $75)	$4,425	
Net stock sale proceeds	$4,700	$4,700
Net stock cost ($3,500 + $75)		$3,575
Net long-term gain		+$1,125

Thus this covered writer has a net gain of $1,125 and it is a long-term gain because the stock was held for more than 6 months and the option, when written, was out-of-the-money.

Note that in a similar situation where the stock had been held for less than 6 months before being called away, the gain would be short-term.

Let us now look at the other two rules. They are related in that their differentiation relies on the definition of "too deeply in-the-money." They come into play only if the stock was *not* already held long-term when the call was written. If the written call is too deeply in-the-money, it can eliminate the holding period of short-term stock. Otherwise it can suspend it. If the call is in-the-money, but not *too* deeply in-the-money, it is referred to as a *qualified covered call.* There are several rules regarding the determination of whether an in-the-money call is qualified or not. Before actually getting to that definition, which is complicated, let us look at two examples to show the effect of qualified or not qualified.

Example: Qualified Covered Write: As in the previous example, on March 1, an investor buys 100 XYZ at 35. He again holds the stock for 3½ months, and, on July 15, the stock has risen to 43. This time he sells an in-the-money call, the October 40 call for 6. By October expiration, the stock has declined and the call expires worthless.

He would now have the following situation: a $575 short-term gain from the sale of the call, plus he is long 100 XYZ with a *holding period of only 3½ months.* Thus, the sale of the October call *suspended* his holding period, but did not *eliminate* it.

He could now hold the stock another 2½ months and then sell it as a long-term item.

If the stock in this example had stayed above 40 and been called away, the net result would have been that the option proceeds would have been added to the stock sale price as in previous examples, and the entire net gain would have been *short-term* due to the fact that the writing of the qualified covered call had suspended the holding period of the stock at 3½ months.

The above example was one of writing a call which was *not* too deeply in-the-money. If, however, one writes a call on stock that is not yet held long-term and that call is too deeply in-the-money, then the holding period of the stock is *eliminated.* That is, if the call is subsequently bought back or expires worthless, the stock must then be held *another* 6 months in order to qualify as a long-term investment. This rule can work to an investor's advantage. If one buys stock and it goes down and he is in jeopardy of having a long-term loss, but he really does not want to sell the stock, he can sell a call that is too deeply in-the-money (if one exists), and eliminate the holding period of the stock.

The above examples and discussion summarize the covered writing rules. Let us now look at what is a qualified covered call. The following rules are the literal interpretation. Most investors work from tables that are built from these rules. Such a table may be found in Appendix E. A covered call is qualified if:

1. the option has more than 30 days of life remaining when it is written, and

2. the strike of the written call is not lower than the following benchmarks:

    a. First determine the applicable stock price (ASP). That is normally the closing price of the stock on the previous day. However, if the stock opens more than 110% higher than its previous close, then the applicable stock price is that higher opening.

    b. If the ASP is less than $25, then the benchmark strike is 85% of ASP. So any call written with a strike lower than 85% of ASP would *not* be qualifed (for example, if the stock was at 12 and one wrote a call with a striking price of 10, it would *not* be qualified—it it too deeply in-the-money).

    c. If the ASP is between 25⅛ and 60, then the benchmark is the next lowest strike. Thus if the stock were at 39 and one wrote a call with a strike of 35, it *would* be qualified.

    d. If the ASP is greater than 60 and not higher than 150, *and the call has more than 90 days of life remaining,* the benchmark is two strikes below the ASP. There is a further condition here that the benchmark cannot be more than 10 points lower than the ASP. Thus, if a stock is trading at 90, one could write a call with a strike of 80 as long as the call had more than 90 days remaining until expiration, and still be qualified.

e. If the ASP is greater than 150 and the call has more than 90 days of life remaining, the benchmark is two strikes below the ASP. Thus, if there are 10-point striking price intervals, then one could write a call that was 20 points in-the-money and still be qualified. Of course, if there are 5-point intervals, then one could not write a call deeper than 10 points in-the-money and still be qualified.

These rules are complicated. That is why they are summarized in Appendix E. In addition, they are always subject to change, so if an investor is considering writing an in-the-money covered call against stock which is still short-term in nature, he should check with his tax advisor and/or broker to determine if the in-the-money call is qualified or not.

There is one further rule in connection with qualified calls. Recall that we stated that the above rules only apply if the stock is not yet held long-term when the call is written. If the stock is already long-term when the call is written, then it is considered long-term when called away, regardless of the position of the striking price when the call was written. However, if one sells an in-the-money call on stock already held long-term, and then subsequently buys that call back at a loss, *the loss on the call must be taken as a long-term loss* because the stock was long-term.

Overall, a rising market is the best, taxwise, for the covered call writer. If he writes out-of-the-money calls and the stock rises he could have short-term loss on the calls plus a long-term gain on the stock.

Example: On June 1, an investor bought 100 shares of XYZ at 32, paying $75 in commissions, and simultaneously wrote a July 35 call for 2 points. The July 35 expired worthless, and the investor then wrote an October 35 call for 3 points. In October, with XYZ at 39, the investor bought back the October 35 call for 6 points (it was in-the-money) and sold a January 40 call for 4 points. In January, on the expiration day, the stock was called away at 40. The investor would have a long-term capital gain on his stock because he had held it for more than 6 months. He would also have two short-term capital transactions from the July 35 and October 35 calls. Tables 39-2 and 39-3 show his net tax treatment from operating this covered writing strategy. The option commission on each trade was $25.

Things have indeed worked out quite well, both profitwise and taxwise, for this covered call writer. Not only has he made a net profit of $850 from his transactions on the stock and options over the period of one year, but he has received very favorable tax treatment. He can take a short-term loss of $175 from the combined July and October option transactions, and is able to take the $1,025 gain as a long-term gain.

TABLE 39-2.
Summary of trades.

June 1	Bought 100 XYZ at 32
	Sold 1 July 35 call at 2
July	July call expired worthless (XYZ at 32)
	Sold 1 October 35 call at 3
October	Bought back October 35 call for 6 points (XYZ at 39)
	Sold 1 January 40 call for 4 points
January	(of the following year)
	100 XYZ called away at 40

TABLE 39-3.
Tax treatment of trades.

Short-term capital items:		
July 35 call:	Net proceeds ($200 − $25)	$175
	Net cost (expired worthless)	0
	Short-term capital gain	$175
October 35 call:	Net proceeds ($300 − $25)	$275
	Net cost ($600 + $25)	− 625
	Short-term capital loss	($350)
Long-term capital item:		
100 shares XYZ:	Purchased June 1 of one year and sold at January expiration of the following year. Therefore, held for more than 6 months, qualifying for long-term treatment. Net sale proceeds of stock (assigned call):	
	January 40 call sale proceeds ($400 − $25)	$375
	Sold 100 XYZ at 40 strike ($4,000 − $75)	+ 3,925
		$4,300
	Net cost of stock (January 1 trade):	
	Bought 100 at 32 ($3,200 + $75)	− 3,275
	Long-term capital gain	$1,025

This example demonstrates an important tax consequence for the covered call writer: his optimum scenario taxwise is a rising market, for he may be able to achieve a long-term gain on the underlying stock if he holds it for at least 6 months, while simultaneously subtracting short-term losses from written calls that were closed out at higher prices. Unfortunately, in a declining market the opposite result could occur: short-term option gains coupled with the possibility of a long-term loss on the underlying stock. There are ways to avoid long-term stock losses, such as buying a put (discussed later in the chapter), or going short against the box before the stock becomes long-term. However, these maneuvers would interrupt the covered writing strategy, which may not be a wise tactic.

In summary, then, the covered call writer who finds himself with an in-the-money call written and expiration date drawing near, may have several alternatives open to him. If the stock is not yet held long-term, he might elect to buy back the written call and to write another call whose expiration date is beyond the date required for a long-term holding period on the stock. This is apparently what the hypothetical investor in the preceding example did with his October 35 call. Since that call was in-the-money, he could have elected to let the call be assigned and to take his profit on the position at that time. However, this would have produced a short-term gain, since the stock had not yet been held for 6 months, so he elected instead to terminate the October 35 call through a closing purchase transaction and to simultaneously write a call whose expiration date exceeded the 6-month period required to make the stock a long-term item. He thus wrote the January 40 call, expiring in the next year. Note that this investor not only decided to hold the stock for a long-term gain, but also decided to try for more potential profits—he rolled the call up to a higher striking price. This lets the holding period continue. An in-the-money write would have suspended it.

Delivering "New" Stock to Avoid a Large Long-Term Gain

Some covered call writers may not want to deliver the stock that they are using to cover the written call, if that call is assigned. For example, if a covered writer were writing against stock that had an extremely low cost basis, he might not be willing to take the tax consequences of selling that particular stock holding. Thus the writer of a call that is assigned may sometimes wish to buy stock in the open market to deliver against his assignment, rather than deliver the stock he previously owns. Recall that it is completely in accordance with the Options Clearing Corporation rules for a call writer to buy stock in the open market to deliver against an assignment. For tax purposes, the confirmation that the investor receives from his broker for the sale of the stock via assignment should clearly specify which particular shares of stock are being sold. This is usually accomplished by having the confirmation read "Versus Purchase" and listing the purchase date of the stock being sold. This is done to clearly identify that the "new" stock, and not the older long-term stock, is being delivered against the assignment.

Example: An investor owns 100 shares of XYZ and his cost basis—after multiple stock splits and stock dividends over the years—is $2 per share. With XYZ at 50, this investor decides to sell an XYZ July 50 call for 5 points to bring in some income to his portfolio. Subsequently, the call is assigned, but the investor does not want to deliver his XYZ, which he owns at a cost basis of $2 per share, because he would have to pay capital gains on a large profit. He may go into the open market and buy another 100 shares of XYZ at its current market price for delivery against the assignment notice. Suppose he does this on July 20—the day he receives the assignment notice on his XYZ July 50 call. The confirmation that he receives from his broker for the sale of 100 XYZ at 50—that is, the confirmation for the call assignment—should be marked "Versus Purchase July 20, 1985." This long-term holder of XYZ stock must, of course, pay for the additional XYZ bought in the open market for delivery against the assignment notice. Thus it is imperative that such an investor have a reserve of funds that he can fall back on if he feels that he must ever implement this sort of strategy to avoid the tax consequences of selling his low-cost-basis stock.

Put Exercise

If the put holder does not choose to liquidate the option in the listed market, but instead exercises the put—thereby selling stock at the striking price—the net cost of the put is subtracted from the net sale proceeds of the underlying stock.

Example: Assume an XYZ April 45 put was bought for 2 points. XYZ had declined in price below 45 by April expiration, and the put holder decides to exercise his in-the-money put rather than sell it in the option market. The commission on the stock sale is $85, so the net sale proceeds for the underlying stock would be:

Sale of 100 XYZ at 45 strike ($4,500 − $85)	$4,415
Net cost of put ($200 + 25)	− 225
Net sale proceeds of stock for tax purposes:	$4,190

If the stock sale represents a new position—that is, the investor has shorted the underlying stock—it will eventually be a short-term gain or loss, according to present tax rules governing short sales. If the put holder already owns the underlying stock and is using the put exercise as a means of selling that stock, his gain or loss on the stock transaction is computed, for tax purposes, by subtracting his original net stock cost from the sale proceeds as determined above.

Put Assignment

If a written put is assigned, stock is bought at the striking price. The net cost of this purchased stock is reduced by the amount of the original put premium received.

Example: If one initially sold an XYZ July 40 put for 4 points, and it was assigned, the net cost of the stock would be determined as follows, assuming a $75 commission charge on the stock purchase:

Cost of 100 XYZ assigned at 40 ($4,000 + $75)	$4,075
Net proceeds of put sale ($400 − $25)	− 375
Net cost basis of stock	$3,700

The holding period for stock purchased via a put assignment begins on the day of the put assignment. The period during which the investor was short the put has no bearing on the holding period of the stock. Obviously, the put transaction itself does not become a capital item—it becomes part of the stock transaction.

SPECIAL TAX PROBLEMS

The Wash Sale Rule

The call buyer should be aware of the *wash sale rule.* In general, the wash sale rule denies a tax deduction for a security sold at a loss if a substantially identical security, or an option to acquire that security, is purchased within 30 days before or 30 days after the original sale. This means that one cannot sell XYZ to take a tax loss and also purchase XYZ within the 61-day period that extends 30 days before and 30 days after the sale. Of course, an investor can legally make such a trade, he just cannot take the tax loss on the sale of the stock. A call option is certainly an option to acquire the security. *It would thus invoke the wash sale rule for an investor to sell XYZ stock to take a loss and also purchase any XYZ call within 30 days before or after the stock sale.*

Various series of call options are not generally considered to be substantially identical securities, however. If one sells an XYZ January 50 call to take a loss, he may then buy any other XYZ call option without jeopardizing his tax loss from the sale of the January 50. It is not clear whether he could repurchase another January 50 call—that is, an identical call—without jeopardizing the taxable loss on the original sale of the January 50.

It would also be acceptable for an investor to sell a call to take a loss and then immediately buy the underlying security. This would not invoke the wash sale rule.

Avoiding a Wash Sale. It is generally held that the sale of a put is not the acquisition of an option to buy stock, even though that is the effect of assignment of the written put. This fact may be useful in certain cases. If an investor holds a stock at a loss, he may want to sell that stock in order to take the loss on his taxes for the current year. The wash sale rule prevents him from repurchasing the same stock, or a call option on that stock, within 30 days after the sale. Thus the investor will be "out of" the stock for a month—that is, he will not be able to participate in any rally in the stock in the next 30 days. If this underlying stock has listed put options, the investor may be able to partially offset this negative effect. By selling an in-the-money put at the same time that the stock is sold, the investor will be able to take his stock loss on the current year's taxes and also will be able to participate in price movements on the underlying stock.

If the stock should rally, the put will decrease in price. However, if the stock rallies above the striking price of the put, the investor will not make as much from the put sale as he would have from the ownership of the stock. Still, he does realize some profits if the stock rallies.

Conversely, if the stock falls in price, the investor will lose on the put sale. This certainly represents a risk—although no more of a risk than owning the stock did. An additional disadvantage is that the investor who has sold a put will not receive the dividends, if any are paid by the underlying stock.

Once 30 days have passed, the investor can cover the put and re-purchase the underlying stock. The investor who utilizes this tactic should be careful to select a put sale in which early assignment is minimal. Therefore, he should sell a long-term, in-the-money put when utilizing this strategy (he needs the in-the-money put in order to participate heavily in the stock's movements). Note that if stock should be put to the investor before 30 days had passed, he would thus be forced to buy stock, and the wash sale rule would be invoked, preventing him from taking the tax loss on the stock at that time—he would have to postpone taking the loss until he makes a sale that does not invoke the wash sale rule.

Finally, this strategy must be employed in a margin account because the put sale will be uncovered. Obviously, the money from the sale of the stock itself can be used to collateralize the sale of the put. If the stock should drop in value, it is always possible that additional collateral will be required for the uncovered put.

The Short Sale Rule—Put Holder's Problem

A put purchase made by an investor who also owns the underlying stock
may have an effect on the holding period of the stock. If a stock holder
buys a put, he would normally do so to eliminate some of the downside
risk in case the stock falls in price. However, if a put option is purchased
to protect stock that is not yet held long enough to qualify for long-term
capital treatment, the entire holding period of the stock is wiped out.
Furthermore, the holding period for the stock will not begin again until
the put is disposed of. For example, if an investor has held XYZ for 5
months—not quite long enough to qualify as a long-term holding—and
then buys a put of XYZ, he will wipe out the entire accrued holding period
on the stock. Furthermore, when he finally disposes of the put, the holding
period for the stock must begin all over again—the previous 5-month
holding period is lost, as is the holding period during which the stock
and put were held together. This tax consequence of a put purchase is
derived from the general rules governing short sales, which state that the
acquisition of an option to sell property at a fixed price (that is, a put) is
treated as a short sale. This ruling has serious tax consequences for an
investor who has bought a put to protect stock that is still in a short-term
tax status.

"Married" Put and Stock. There are two cases in which the put purchase does *not* affect the holding period of the underlying stock. First, if
the stock has already been held long enough to qualify for long-term capital
treatment, the purchase of a put has no bearing on the holding period of
the underlying stock. Second, if the put and the stock that it is intended
to protect are bought at the same time, *and* the investor indicates that he
intends to exercise that particular put to sell those particular shares of
stock, the put and the stock are considered to be "married" and the normal
tax rulings for a stock holding would apply. The investor must actually
go through with the exercise of the put in order for the "married" status
to remain valid. If he instead should allow the put to expire worthless,
he could not take the tax loss on the put itself but would be forced to add
the put's cost to the net cost of the underlying stock. Finally, if the investor
neither exercises the put not allows it to expire worthless but sells both
the put and the stock in their respective markets, it would appear that
the short sale rules would come back into effect.

This definition of "married" put and stock, and its resultant ramifications, are quite detailed. What exactly are the consequences? The
"married" rule was originally intended to allow an investor to buy stock,
protect it, and still have a chance of realizing a long-term gain. This is
possible with options with more than 6 months of life remaining. The
reader must be aware of the fact that, if he initially "marries" stock and

a listed 3-month put, for example, there is no way that he can replace that put at its expiration with another put and still retain the "married" status. Once the original "married" put is disposed of—through sale, exercise, or expiration—no other put may be considered to be "married" to the stock.

Protecting a Long-Term Gain or Avoiding a Long-Term Loss. The investor may be able, at times, to use the short-sale aspect of put purchases to his advantage. The most obvious use is that he can protect a long-term gain with a put purchase. He might want to do this if he has decided to take the long-term gain, but would prefer to delay realizing it until the following tax year. A purchase of a put with a maturity date in the following year would accomplish that purpose.

Another usage of the put purchase, for tax purposes, might be to avoid a long-term loss on a stock position. If an investor owns a stock that has declined in price and also is about to become a long-term holding, he can buy a put on that stock to eliminate the holding period. This avoids having to take a long-term loss. Once the put is removed—either by its sale or by its expiring worthless—the stock holding period would begin all over again and it would be a short-term position. In addition, if the investor should decide to exercise the put that he purchased, the result would be a short-term loss. The sale basis of the stock upon exercise of the put would be equal to the striking price of the put less the amount of premium paid for the put, less all commission costs. Furthermore, note that this strategy does not lock in the loss on the underlying stock. If the stock rallies, the investor would be able to participate in that rally, although he would probably lose all of the premium that he paid for the put. Note that both of these long-term strategies can be accomplished via the sale of a deeply in-the-money call as well.

SUMMARY

This concludes the section of the tax chapter dealing with listed option trades and their direct consequences on option strategies. In addition to the basic tax treatment to option traders of liquidation, expiring worthless, or assignment or exercise, several other useful tax situations have been described. The call buyer should be aware of the wash sale rule. The put buyer must be aware of the short sale rules involving both put and stock ownership. The call writer should realize the beneficial effects of selling an in-the-money call to protect the underlying stock, while waiting for a realization of profit in the following tax year. The put writer may be able to avoid a wash sale by utilizing an in-the-money put write, yet still retaining profit potential from a rally by the underlying stock.

TAX PLANNING STRATEGIES FOR EQUITY OPTIONS

Deferring a Short-Term Call Gain

The call holder may be interested in either deferring a gain until the following year or possibly converting a short-term gain on the call into a long-term gain on the stock. It is much easier to do the former than the latter. A holder of a profitable call that is due to expire in the following year can take any of three possible actions that might let him retain his profit while deferring the gain until the following tax year. One way in which to do this would be to buy a put option. Obviously, he would want to buy an in-the-money put for this purpose. By so doing, he would be spending as little as possible in the way of time value premium for the put option and he would also be locking in his gain on the call. The gains and losses from the put and call combination would nearly equal each other from that time forward as the stock moves up or down, unless the stock rallies strongly, thereby exceeding the striking price of the put. This would be a happy event, however, since even larger gains would accrue. The combination could be liquidated in the following tax year, thus achieving a gain.

Example: On September 1, an investor bought an XYZ January 40 call for 3 points. The call is due to expire in the following year. XYZ has risen in price by December 1, and the call is selling for 6 points. The call holder might want to take his 3-point gain on the call, but would also like to defer that gain until the following year. He might be able to do this by buying an XYZ January 50 put for 5 points, for example. He would then hold this combination until after the first of the new year. At that time, he could liquidate the entire combination for at least 10 points, since the striking price of the put is 10 points greater than that of the call. In fact, if the stock should have climbed to or above 50 by the first of the year, or should have fallen to or below 40 by the first of the year, he would be able to liquidate the combination for more than 10 points. The increase in time value premium at either strike would also be a benefit. In any case, he would have a gain—his original cost was 8 points (3 for the call and 5 for the put). Thus he has effectively deferred taking the gain on the original call holding until the next tax year. The risk that the call holder incurs in this type of transaction is the increased commission charges of buying and selling the put as well as the possible loss of any time value premium in the put itself. The investor must decide for himself whether these risks—although they may be relatively small—outweigh the potential benefit from deferring his tax gain into the next year.

Another way in which the call holder might be able to defer his tax gain into the next year would be to sell another XYZ call against the one that he currently holds. That is, he would create a spread. To assure that he retains as much of his current gain as possible, he should sell an in-the-money call. In fact, he should sell an in-the-money call with a lower striking price than the call held long, if possible, to ensure that his gain remains intact even if the underlying stock should collapse substantially. Once the spread has been established, it could be held until the following tax year before being liquidated. The obvious risk in this means of deferring gain is that one could receive an assignment notice on the short call. This is not a remote possibility, necessarily, since an in-the-money call should be used as protection for the current gain. Such an assignment would result in large commission costs on the resultant purchase and sale of the underlying stock, and could substantially reduce one's gain. Thus, the risk in this strategy is greater than that in the previous one (buying a put), but it may be the only alternative available if puts are not traded on the underlying stock in question.

Example: An investor bought an XYZ February 50 call for 3 points in August. In December, the stock is at 65 and the call is at 15. The holder would like to "lock in" his 12-point call profit, but would prefer deferring the actual gain into the following tax year. He could sell an XYZ February 45 call for approximately 20 points to do this. If no assignment notice is received, he will be able to liquidate the spread at a cost of 5 points with the stock anywhere above 50 at February expiration. Thus in the end he would still have a 12-point gain—having received 20 points for the sale of the February 45 and having paid out 3 points for the February 50 plus 5 points to liquidate the spread to take his gain. If the stock should fall below 50 before February expiration, his gain would be even larger, since he would not have to pay out the entire 5 points to liquidate the spread.

The third way in which a call holder could lock in his gain and still defer the gain into the following tax year would be to sell the stock short while continuing to hold the call. This would obviously lock in the gain, since the short sale and the call purchase will offset each other in profit potential as the underlying stock moves up or down. In fact, if the stock should plunge downward, large profits could accrue. However, there is risk in using this strategy as well. The commission costs of the short sale will reduce the call holder's profit. Furthermore, if the underlying stock should go ex-dividend during the time that the stock is held short, the stategist will be liable for the dividend as well. In addition, more margin will be required for the short stock.

The three tactics discussed above showed how to defer a profitable call gain into the following tax year. The gain would still be short-term when realized. The only way in which a call holder could hope to convert his gain into a long-term gain would be to exercise the call and then hold the stock for more than 6 months. Recall that the holding period for stock acquired through exercise begins on the day of exercise—the option's holding period is lost. If the investor chooses this alternative, he of course is spending some of his gains for the commissions on the stock purchase as well as subjecting himself to an entire year's worth of market risk. There are ways to protect a stock holding while letting the holding period accrue—for example, writing out-of-the-money calls—but the investor who chooses this alternative should carefully weigh the risks involved against the possible benefits of eventually achieving a long-term gain. The investor should also note that he will have to advance considerably more money to hold the stock.

Deferring a Put Holder's Short-Term Gain

Without going into as much detail, there are similar ways in which a put holder who has a short-term gain in a put due to expire in the following tax year can attempt to defer the realization of that gain into the following tax year. One simple way in which he could protect his gain would be to buy a call option to protect his profitable put. He would want to buy an in-the-money call for this purpose. This resulting combination is similar in nature to the one described for the call buyer in the previous section.

A second way that he could attempt to protect his gain and still defer its realization into the following tax year would be to sell another XYZ put option against the one that he holds long. This would create a vertical spread. This put holder should attempt to sell an in-the-money put if possible. Of course, he would not want to sell a put that was so deeply in-the-money that there is risk of early assignment. The results of such a spread are analogous to the call spread described in detail in the last section.

Finally, the put holder could buy the underlying stock if he had enough available cash or collateral to finance the stock purchase. This would lock in the profit, as the stock and the put would offset each other in terms of gains or losses while the stock moved up or down. In fact, if the stock should experience a large rally—rising above the striking price of the put—even larger profits would become possible.

In each of the tactics described, the position would be removed in the following tax year, thereby realizing the gain that was deferred.

Difficulty of Deferring Gains from Writing

As a final point in this section on deferring gains from option transactions, it might be appropriate to describe the risks associated with the strategy of attempting to defer gains from uncovered option writing into the following tax year. Recall that in the previous sections, it was shown that a call or put holder who has an unrealized profit in an option that is due to expire in the following tax year could attempt to "lock in" the gain and defer it. The dollar risks to a holder attempting such a tax deferral were mainly commission costs and/or small amounts of time value premium paid for options. However, the option writer who has an unrealized profit may have a more difficult time finding a way to both "lock in" the gain and also defer its realization into the following tax year. It would seem, at first glance, that the call writer could merely take actions opposite to those that the call buyer takes: buying the underlying stock, buying another call option, or selling a put. Unfortunately, none of these actions "locks in" the call writer's profit—in fact, he could lose substantial investment dollars in his attempt to defer the gain into the following year.

Example: An investor has written an uncovered XYZ January 50 call for 5 points and the call has dropped in value to 1 point in early December. He might want to take the 4-point gain, but would prefer to defer realization of the gain until the following tax year. Since the call write is at a profit, the stock must have dropped and is probably selling around 45 in early December. Buying the underlying stock would not accomplish his purpose, because if the stock continued to decline through year-end, he could lose a substantial amount on the stock purchase and could only make 1 more point on the call write. Similarly, a call purchase would not work well either. A call with a lower striking price—for example, the XYZ January 45 or the January 40—could lose substantial value if the underlying stock continued to drop in price. An out-of-the-money call—the XYZ January 60—is also unacceptable, because if the underlying stock rallied to the high 50's, the writer would lose money both on his January 50 call write and on his January 60 call purchase at expiration. Writing a put option would not "lock in" the profit either. If the underlying stock continued to decline, the losses on the put write would certainly exceed the remaining profit potential of one point in the January 50 call. Alternatively, if the stock rose, the losses on the January 50 call could offset the limited profit potential provided by a put write. Thus there is no relatively safe way for an uncovered call writer to attempt to "lock in" an unrealized gain for the purpose of deferring it to the following tax year. The put writer seeking to defer his gains faces similar problems.

Unequal Tax Treatment on Spreads

There are two types of spreads in which the long side may receive different tax treatment than the short side. One is the normal equity option spread which is held for more than 6 months. The other is any spread between futures, futures options, or cash-based options and equity options.

With equity options, if one has a spread in place more than 6 months and if the movement of the underlying stock is favorable, one could conceivably have a long-term gain on the long side and a short-term loss on the short side of the spread.

Example: An investor establishes an XYZ bullish call spread in options that have 8 months of life: In January, he buys the August 70 call at 3 and sells the August 75 call at 1. In July, after he has held the spread for more than 6 months, XYZ has advanced to 90 and he decides to remove the spread. With XYZ at 90, the August 75 is trading at 16 and the August 70 is trading at 20½. The results are summarized for tax purposes (commissions are omitted from this example):

Option	Cost	Proceeds	Gain/Loss
XYZ August 70	$ 300	$2,050	$1,750 long term gain
XYZ August 75	$1,600	$ 100	−$1,500 short term loss

No taxes would be owed on this spread since one-half the long-term gain is less than the short-term loss. The investor with this spread could be in a favorable position since, even though he actually made money in the spread—buying it at a 2-point debit and selling it at a 4½ point debit— he can show a loss on his taxes due to the disparate treatment of the two sides of the spread.

The above spread requires that the stock move in a favorable direction in order for the tax advantage to materialize. If the stock were to move in the opposite direction, then one should liquidate the spread before the long side of the spread had reached a holding period of 6 months. This would prevent taking a long-term loss.

Another type of spread may be even more attractive in this respect. That is a spread in which non-equity options are spread against equity options. In this case, the trader would hope to make a profit on the non-equity or futures side, because part of that gain is automatically long-term gain. He would simultaneously want to take a loss on the equity option side, because that would be entirely short-term loss. The major problem with this scenario is that there are not many logical opportunities to spread equity options against non-equity options. Perhaps one might buy equity options instead of stocks upon occasion. Any strategist should be cautioned against establishing spreads merely for tax purposes—he might wind up losing money.

SUMMARY

Options can be used for many tax purposes. Short-term gains can be deferred into the next tax year, or can be partially protected with out-of-the-money options until they mature into long-term gains. Long-term losses can be avoided with the purchase of a put or sale of a deeply in-the-money call. Wash sales can be avoided without giving up the entire ownership potential of the stock. There are risks as well as rewards in any of the strategies. Commission costs and the dissipation of time value premium in purchased options will both work against the strategist.

A tax advisor should be consulted before actually implementing any tax strategy, whether that strategy employs options or not. Tax rules change from time to time. It is even possible that a certain strategy is not covered by a written rule, and only a tax advisor is qualified to give consultation on how such a strategy might be interpreted by the IRS.

Finally, the options strategist should be careful not to confuse tax strategies with his profit-oriented strategies. It is generally a good idea to separate profit strategies and tax strategies. That is, if one finds himself in a position that conveniently lends itself to tax applications—fine. However, one should not attempt to stay in a position too long or to close it out at an illogical time just to take advantage of a tax break. The tax consequences of options should never be considered to be more important than sound strategy management.

Postscript

Option strategies cannot be unilaterally classified as aggressive or conservative. There are certainly many aggressive applications—the simplest being the outright purchase of calls or puts. However, options can also have conservative applications, most notably in reducing some of the risks of common stock ownership. In addition, there are less polarized applications, particularly spreading techniques, which allow the investor to take a middle-of-the-road approach.

Consequently, *the investor himself—not options—becomes the dominant force in determining whether an option strategy is too risky*. It is imperative that the investor understands what he is trying to accomplish in his portfolio before actually implementing an option strategy. Not only should he be cognizant of the factors that go into determining the initial selection of the position, but he must also have in mind a plan of follow-up action. If he has thought out, in advance, what action he will take if the underlying entity rises or falls, he will be in a position to make a more rational decision when and if it does indeed make a move. The investor must also determine if the risk of the strategy is acceptable according to his financial means and objectives. If the risk is too high, the strategy is not suitable.

Every serious investor owes it to himself to acquire an understanding of listed option strategies. Since various options strategies are available for a multitude of purposes, *almost every money manager or dedicated investor will be able to use options in his strategies at one time or another.* For a stock-oriented investor to ignore the potential advantages of using options would be as serious a mistake as it would be for a large grain company to ignore the hedging properties available in the futures market, or as it would be for an income-oriented investor to concentrate only in utilities and Treasury bills while ignoring less well known, but equally compatible, alternatives, such as GNMA's.

Moreover, in today's markets, with options being available on futures, equities, and indices, the strategist in any one field should familiarize himself with the others, because any of them will provide profit opportunities at one time or another.

PART VI ——————————————————————

APPENDICES

Appendix A

Strategy Summary

Except for arbitrage strategies and tax strategies, the strategies we have described deal with risk of market movement. It is therefore often convenient to summarize option strategies by their risk and reward characteristics and by their market outlook—bullish, bearish, or neutral. Table A-1 lists all the risk strategies that were discussed and gives a general classification of their risks and rewards. If a strategist has a definite attitude about the market's outlook or about his own willingness to accept risks, he can scan Table A-1 and select the strategies that most closely resemble his thinking. The number in parentheses after the strategy name indicates the chapter in which the strategy was discussed.

Table A-1 gives a *broad* classification of the various risk and reward potentials of the strategies. For example, a bullish call calendar spread does not actually have unlimited profit potential unless its near-term call expires worthless. In fact, *all calendar spread or diagonal spread positions have limited profit potential at best until the near-term options expire.*

Also, the definition of limited risk can vary widely. Some strategies do have a risk that is truly limited to a relatively small percentage of the initial investment—the protected stock purchase, for example. *In other cases, the risk is limited but is also equal to the entire initial investment.* That is, one could lose 100% of his investment in a short time period— option purchases, and bull, bear, or calendar spreads are examples.

Thus, although Table A-1 gives a broad perspective on the outlook for various strategies, one must be aware of the differences in reward, risk, and market outlook when actually implementing one of the strategies.

TABLE A-1.
General strategy summary.

Strategy (Chapter)	Risk	Reward
Bullish strategies		
Call purchase (3)	Limited	Unlimited
Synthetic long stock (short put/long call) (21)	Unlimited[a]	Unlimited
Bull spread—puts or calls (7 and 22)	Limited	Limited
Protected stock purchase (long stock/long put) (17)	Limited	Unlimited
Bullish call calendar spread (9)	Limited	Unlimited
Covered call writing (2)	Unlimited[a]	Limited
Uncovered put write (19)	Unlimited[a]	Limited
Bearish Strategies		
Put purchase (16)	Limited	Unlimited[a]
Protected short sale (synthetic put) (4 and 16)	Limited	Unlimited[a]
Synthetic short sale (long put/short call) (21)	Unlimited	Unlimited[a]
Bear spread—put or call (and 22)	Limited	Limited
Covered put write (19)	Unlimited	Limited
Bearish put calendar spread (22)	Limited	Unlimited[a]
Naked call write (5)	Unlimited	Limited
Neutral strategies		
Straddle purchase (18)	Limited	Unlimited
Reverse hedge (simulated straddle buy) (4)	Limited	Unlimited
Fixed income + option purchase (25)	Limited	Unlimited
Diagonal sparead (14, 23, and 24)	Limited	Unlimited
Neutral calendar spread—puts or calls (9 and 22)	Limited	Limited
Butterfly spread (10 and 23)	Limited	Limited
Calendar straddle or combination (23)	Limited	Unlimited
Reverse spread (13)	Limited	Unlimited
Ratio write—put or call (6 and 19)	Unlimited	Limited
Straddle or combination write (20)	Unlimited	Limited
Ratio spread—put or call (11 and 24)	Unlimited	Limited
Ratio calendar spread—put or call (12 and 24)	Unlimited	Unlimited

[a]Wherever the risk or reward is limited only by the fact that a stock cannot fall below zero in price, the entry is marked. Obviously, although the potential may technically be limited, it could still be quite large if the underlying stock did fall a large distance.

Appendix *B*

Equivalent Positions

Some strategies can be constructed with either puts or calls to attain the same profit potential. These are called equivalent strategies and are given in Table B-1. They do not necessarily have the same potential returns, because the investment required may be quite different. However, equivalent positions have profit graphs with exactly the same shape.

Other equivalences can be determined by combining any two strategies in the left-hand column and setting that combination equivalent to the two corresponding strategies in the right-hand column.

TABLE B-1.
Equivalent strategies.

This Strategy . . .	is equivalent to . . . This Strategy
Call purchase	Long stock/long put
Put purchase	Short stock/long call (synthetic put)
Long stock	Long call/short put (synthetic stock)
Short stock	Long put/short call (synthetic short sale)
Naked call write	Short stock/short put
Naked put write	Covered call write (long stock/short call)
Bullish call spread (long call at lower strike/ short call at higher strike)	Bullish put spread (long put at lower strike/ short put at higher strike)
Bearish call spread (long call at higher strike/ short call at lower strike)	Bearish put spread (long put at higher strike/ short put at lower strike)
Ratio call write (long stock/short calls)	Straddle write (short put/short call)
. . . and is also equivalent to . . .	Ratio put write (short stock/short puts)
Straddle buy (long call/long put)	Reverse hedge (short stock/long calls) or buy stock/buy puts
Butterfly call spread (long 1 call at each outside strike/ short 2 calls at middle strike)	Butterfly put spread (long 1 put at each outer strike/ short 2 puts at middle strike)
All four of these "butterfly" strategies are equivalent	
Butterfly combination (bullish call spread at two lower strikes/bearish put spread at 2 higher strikes)	Protected straddle write (short straddle at middle strike/ long call at highest strike/ long put at lowest strike

Appendix *C*

Formulae

Chapter references are given in parentheses. The following notation is used throughout this appendix.

x = current stock price

s = striking price

c = call price

p = put price

r = interest rate

t = time (in years)

B = break-even point

U = upside break-even point

D = downside break-even point

P = maximum profit potential

R = maximum risk potential

Subscripts indicate multiple items. For example s_1, s_2, s_3 *would designate* three striking prices in a formula. The formulae are arranged alphabetically by title or by strategy.

Annualized Risk (Ch. 27)

$$\text{Annualized risk} = \sum_i \text{INV}_i \frac{360}{H_i}$$

where INV_i = percent of total assets invested in options
with holding periods, H_i

H_i = length of holding period in days

Bear Spread

$s_1 < s_2$

—Calls (Ch. 8)

$$P = c_1 - c_2$$

$$R = s_2 - s_1 - P$$

$$B = s_1 + P$$

—Puts (Ch. 22)

$$R = p_2 - p_1$$

$$P = s_2 - s_1 - R$$

$$B = s_1 + P = s_2 + p_1 - p_2$$

Black Model (Ch. 36):

Theoretical futures call price = $e^{-rt} \times \text{BSM}[r = 0\%]$

where $\text{BSM}[r = 0]$ is the Black-Scholes Model
using $r = 0\%$ as the short-term interest rate

Put price = Call price $- e^{-rt} \times (f - s)$

where f = futures price

---

x = current stock price	B = break-even point
s = striking price	U = upside break-even point
c = call price	D = downside break-even point
p = put price	P = maximum profit potential
r = interest rate	R = maximum risk potential
t = time (in years)	
f = futures price	

Subscripts indicate multiple items. For example s_1, s_2, s_3 would designate three striking prices in a formula. The formulae are arranged alphabetically by title or by strategy.

Formulae

Black-Scholes Model (Ch. 30)

$$\text{Theoretical call price} = xN(d_1) - se^{-rt}N(d_2)$$

$$\text{where } d_1 = \frac{\ln(x/s) + (r + \tfrac{1}{2}v^2)t}{v\sqrt{t}}$$

$$\text{and } d_2 = d_1 - v\sqrt{t}$$

$$\ln = \text{natural logarithm}$$
$$N() = \text{cumulative normal density function}$$
$$v = \text{annual volatility}$$

$$\text{Delta} = N(d_1)$$

Bull Spread

$$s_1 < s_2$$

—Calls (Ch. 7)

$$R = c_1 - c_2$$
$$P = s_2 - s_1 - R$$
$$B = s_2 - P = s_1 - c_2 + c_1$$

—Puts (Ch. 22)

$$P = p_2 - p_1$$
$$R = s_2 - s_1 - P$$
$$B = s_2 - P$$

Butterfly Spread

A butterfly spread combines a bull spread using strikes s_1 and s_2 with a bear spread using strikes s_2 and s_3.

$$s_1 < s_2 < s_3$$

$$s_3 - s_2 = s_2 - s_1$$

—if using all calls (Ch. 10)

$$R = c_1 + c_3 - 2c_2$$

—if using all puts (Ch. 23)

$$R = p_1 + p_2 - 2p_2$$

—if using put bull spread and call bear spread (Ch. 23)

$$P = c_2 + p_2 - c_3 - p_1$$

—if using call bull spread and put bear spread (Ch. 23)

$$R = p_2 + c_2 - p_1 - c_3 - s_3 + s_2$$

Then

$$P = s_3 - s_2 - R \quad \text{or} \quad R = s_3 - s_2 - P$$

$$D = s_1 + R$$

$$U = s_3 - R$$

Combination Buy (Ch. 18)

$$s_1 < s_2$$

Out-of-the-money: $R = c_2 + p_1$

In-the-money: $R = c_1 + p_2 - s_2 + s_1$

$$D = s_1 - P$$

$$U = s_2 + P$$

Combination Sale (Ch. 20)

$$s_1 < s_2$$

Out-of-the-money: $P = c_2 + p_1$

In the money: $P = c_1 + p_2 - s_2 + s_1$

$$D = s_1 - P$$

$$U = s_2 + P$$

---

x = current stock price	B = break-even point
s = striking price	U = upside break-even point
c = call price	D = downside break-even point
p = put price	P = maximum profit potential
r = interest rate	R = maximum risk potential
t = time (in years)	

Subscripts indicate multiple items. For example s_1, s_2, s_3 would designate three striking prices in a formula. The formulae are arranged alphabetically by title or by strategy.

Conversion and Reversal Profit (Ch. 29)

Conversion: $P = s + c - x - p +$ dividends $-$ carrying cost

Reversal: $P = x + p - c - s -$ dividends $+$ carrying cost

where

$$\text{carrying cost} = \begin{cases} \text{srt (simple interest)} \\ s[1 - (1 + r)^{-1}] \text{ (compound interest,} \\ \qquad\qquad\qquad\qquad \text{present worth)} \end{cases}$$

Covered Call Write (Ch. 2)

$P = s + c - x$

$B = x - c$

Covered Straddle Write (Ch. 20)

$P = s + c + p - x$

$B = s - \frac{1}{2}P = \frac{1}{2}(x + s - p - c)$

Cumulative Normal Density Function (Ch. 30)

Approximation by fifth-order polynomial

$a = 1 - z(1.330274y^5 - 1.821256y^4 + 1.781478y^3 - .3565638y^2$
$\quad + .3193815y)$

where $y = \dfrac{1}{1 + .2316419|\sigma|}$

$\quad z = .3989423e^{-\sigma^2/2}$

Then

$$N(s) = \begin{cases} a & \text{if } \sigma > 0 \\ 1 - a & \text{if } \sigma < 0 \end{cases}$$

Delta—see Black-Scholes Model

Delta Neutral Ratio:

—stock versus option (Ch. 6)

$$\text{Neutral ratio} = \frac{1}{\text{Delta of option}}$$

—spread (Chs. 11 and 24)

$$\text{Neutral ratio} = \frac{\text{Delta of long option}}{\text{Delta of short option}}$$

Equivalent Futures Position (Ch. 36)

$$\text{EFP} = \text{delta} \times \text{number of options}$$

Equivalent Stock Position (Ch. 30)

$$\text{ESP} = \text{unit of trading} \times \text{delta} \times \text{number of options}$$

where unit of trading is the number of shares of the underlying stock that can be bought or sold with the option (normally 100).

Future Stock Price (Ch. 30)

—lognormal distribution, assuming a movement of a fixed number of standard deviations

$$q = xe^{av_t}$$

Where
q = future stock price
v_t = volatility for the time period
a = number of standard deviations of movement
(normally $-3.0 \leq a \leq 3.0$)

Probability of Stock Movement (Ch. 30)

—lognormal distribution

$$P(\text{below } q) = N\left\{\frac{\ln(q/x)}{v_t}\right\}$$

$$P(\text{above } q) = 1 - P(\text{below } q)$$

---

x = current stock price B = break-even point
s = striking price U = upside break-even point
c = call price D = downside break-even point
p = put price P = maximum profit potential
r = interest rate R = maximum risk potential
t = time (in years)

Subscripts indicate multiple items. For example s_1, s_2, s_3 would designate three striking prices in a formula. The formulae are arranged alphabetically by title or by strategy.

where

q = stock price in question

$N()$ = cumulative normal density function

$\ln$ = natural logarithm

v_t = volatility for the time period

Put Pricing Model—Arbitrage Model (Ch. 30)

Theoretical put price = theoretical call price + s − x + dividends − carrying cost

where

$$\text{carrying cost} = \begin{cases} srt \text{ (simple interest)} \\ s\,[1 - (1 + r)^{-t}] \text{ (compound interest,} \\ \qquad\qquad\qquad\qquad \text{present worth)} \end{cases}$$

Ratio Call Write (Ch. 6)

General case: long m round lots of stock, short n calls

$$P = m(s - x) + nc$$

$$U = s + \frac{P}{n - m}$$

$$D = s - \frac{P}{m}$$

2:1 ratio (straddle sale)

$$P = s - x + 2c$$

$$U = s + p$$

$$D = s - p = x - 2c$$

Ratio Spread

—*Calls* (Ch. 11): buy n_1 calls at lower strike, s_1, and sell n_2 calls at higher strike, s_2

$$s_1 < s_2$$

$$n_1 < n_2$$

$$R = n_1 c_1 - n_2 c_2$$

$$P = (s_2 - s_1)n_1 - R$$

$$U = s_2 + \frac{P}{n_2 - n_1}$$

Break-even cost of long calls for follow-up action (Ch. 11)

$$\text{Break-even cost} = \frac{n_2(s_2 - s_1) - R}{n_2 - n_1}$$

—Puts (Ch. 24): buy n_2 puts at higher strike, s_2, and sell n_1 puts at lower strike, s_1

$$s_1 < s_2$$

$$n_2 < n_1$$

$$R = n_2p_2 - n_1p_1$$

$$P = n_2(s_2 - s_1) - R$$

$$D = s_1 - \frac{P}{n_1 - n_2}$$

Reversal—See Conversion and Reversal Profit
Reverse Hedge (Ch. 4)—simulated straddle purchase

General case: short m round lots of stock and long n calls

$$R = m(s - x) + nc$$

$$U = s + \frac{R}{n - m}$$

$$D = s - \frac{R}{m}$$

---

x = current stock price B = break-even point
s = striking price U = upside break-even point
c = call price D = downside break-even point
p = put price P = maximum profit potential
r = interest rate R = maximum risk potential
t = time (in years)

Subscripts indicate multiple items. For example s_1, s_2, s_3 would designate three striking prices in a formula. The formulae are arranged alphabetically by title or by strategy.

2:1 ratio (straddle buy):

$$R = s + 2c - x$$
$$U = s + R$$
$$D = s - R = x - 2c$$

Using puts (long 100 stock, long 2 puts) (Ch. 18)

$$R = x + 2p - s$$
$$U = s + R = x + 2p$$
$$D = s - R$$

Straddle Buy (Ch. 18)

$$R = p + c$$
$$U = s + R$$
$$D = -R$$

Straddle Sale (Ch. 20)

$$P = p + c$$
$$U = s + p$$
$$D = s - p$$

Synthetic Put Purchase—short stock and long call (Ch. 4)

$$R = s + c - x$$
$$B = s - c$$

Variable Ratio Write (Ch. 6)

—long 100 shares of stock, short one call at strike s_1, short one call at strike s_2

$s_1 < x < s_2$

$$P = c_1 + c_2 + s_1 - x$$
$$D = s_1 - P = x - c_1 - c_2$$
$$U = s_2 + P$$

Volatility—Standard Deviation (Ch. 30)

$$V_2 = \frac{\sum\limits_{i=1}^{n} (x_i - \bar{x})^2}{n - 1}$$

Where

x_i = daily stock closing price

$\bar{x}$ = mean *(average) of the* x_i's

n = number of observations

—if v is the annual volatility, then the volatility for a time period, t, is

$$v_t = v \sqrt{t}$$

Graphs

Chapter references are in parentheses.

A. Intrinsic Value—Call (Ch. 1)   B. Intrinsic Value—Put (Ch. 15)

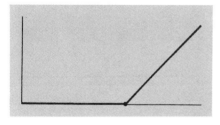
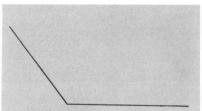

C. Call Option Pricing Curve (Ch. 1)

D. Put Option Pricing Curve (Ch. 15)

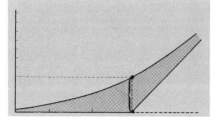
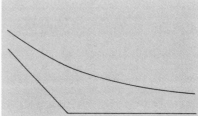

E. Time Value Premium Decay
(Ch. 1)

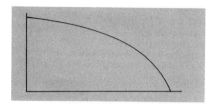

F. Lognormal Distribution
(Ch. 30)

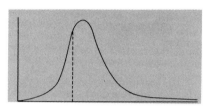

G. Call Purchase (Ch. 1)
(long stock/long put—Ch. 17)

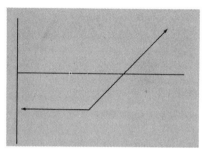

H. Put purchase (Ch. 16)
(short stock/long call—Ch. 4)

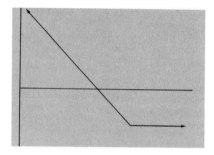

I. Covered Call Write (Ch. 2)
Naked Put Write (Ch. 19)

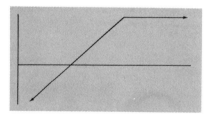

J. Naked Call Write (Ch. 5)
(short stock/short put—
Ch. 19)

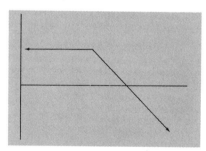

K. Bull Spread (Chs. 7 and 22)
(covered call write + long put
out-of-the-money—Ch. 17)

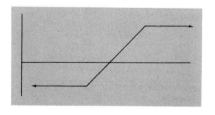

L. Bear Spread (Chs. 8 and 22)

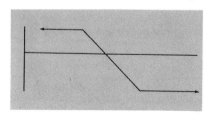

M. Calendar Spread (Chs. 9 and 22)

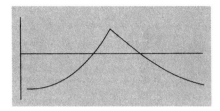

N. Butterfly Spread (Chs. 10 and 23)

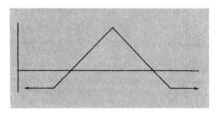

O. Naked Straddle Write (Ch. 20)
    Ratio Call Write (long 100 stock, short 2 calls—Ch. 6)
    Ratio Put Write (short 100 stock, short 2 puts—Ch. 19)

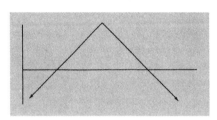

P. Straddle Purchase (Ch. 18)
    Reverse Hedge (short 100 stock, long 2 calls—Ch. 4)
    Put Hedge (long 100 stock, long 2 puts—Ch. 18)

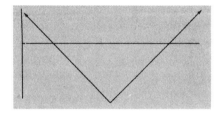

Q. Combination Sale (Ch. 20)
    Variable Ratio Write (long 100 stock—short 2 calls with different strikes—Ch. 6)

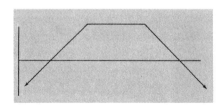

R. Combination Purchase (Ch. 18)
    (short 100 stock, long 2 calls with different strikes—Ch. 4)

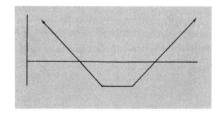

S. Ratio Call Spread (Ch. 11)

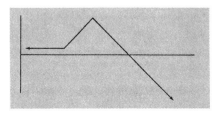

T. Ratio Put Spread (Ch. 24)

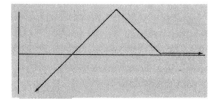

Appendix *E*

Qualified Covered Calls

For tax purposes, there is no effect on the holding period of the stock when one writes an out-of-the-money call. However, when one writes an in-the-money call, he eliminates the holding period on his common stock unless the stock is already held long-term. The only exception to this is that if the covered call is deemed to be qualified, then the holding period is merely suspended rather than eliminated. The following table shows the *lowest* striking price that may be written if the stock is in the price range shown.

TABLE E-1.
Qualified covered call options.

Applicable Stock Price(1)	Call is not "deep-in-the-money" if Stike price(2) is at least:		Applicable Stock Price(1)	Call is not "deep-in-the-money" if Strike price(2) is at least:	
	31–90 Day Call	*More than 90-Day Call*		*31–90 Day Call*	*More than 90-Day Call*
5⅛–5⅞	5	5	75⅛–80	75	70
6–10	None	None	80⅛–85	80	75
10⅛–11¾	10	10	85⅛–90	85	80
11⅞–15	None	None	90⅛–95	90	85
15⅛–17⅝	15	15	95⅛–100	95	90
17¾–20	None	None	100⅛–105	100	95
20⅛–23½	20	20	105⅛–110	100	100
23⅝–25	None	None	110⅛–120	110	110
25⅛–30	25	25	120⅛–130	120	120
30⅛–35	30	30	130⅛–140	130	130
35⅛–40	35	35	140⅛–150	140	140
40⅛–45	40	40	150⅛–160	150	140
45⅛–50	45	45	160⅛–170	160	150
50⅛–55	50	50	170⅛–180	170	160
55⅛–60	55	55	180⅛–190	180	170
60⅛–65	60	55	190⅛–200	190	180
65⅛–70	65	60	200⅛–210	200	190
70⅛–75	70	65	210⅛–220	210	200

(1) Applicable stock price is either the closing price of the stock on the day preceding the date the option was granted, or the opening price on the day the option is granted if such price is greater than 100% of the preceding day's closing price.

(2) Assumption is that strike prices are only at $5 intervals up to $100 and $10 intervals over $100. *Note:* If the stock splits, option strike prices will have smaller intervals for a period of time.

Glossary

American Exercise: a feature of an option that indicates it may be exercised at any time. Therefore, it is subject to early assignment.

Arbitrage: the process in which professional traders simultaneously buy and sell the same or equivalent securities for a riskless profit. *See also* Risk Arbitrage.

Assign: to designate an option writer for fulfillment of his obligation to sell stock (call option writer) or buy stock (put option writer). The writer receives an assignment notice from the Options Clearing Corporation. *See also* Early Exercise.

Assignment Notice: *see* Assign.

Automatic Exercise: a protection procedure whereby the Options Clearing Corporation attempts to protect the holder of an expiring in-the-money option by automatically exercising the option on behalf of the holder. For CAPS options: the automatic exercise of a CAPS option occurs when the index closes above the call cap price or below the put cap price.

Average Down: to buy more of a security at a lower price, thereby reducing the holder's average cost. (Average Up: to buy more at a higher price.)

Backspread: *see* Reverse Strategy.

Bearish: an adjective describing an opinion or outlook that expects a decline in price, either by the general market or by an underlying stock, or both. *See also* Bullish.

Bear Spread: an option strategy that makes its maximum profit when the underlying stock declines and has its maximum risk if the stock rises in price. The strategy can be implemented with either puts or calls. In either case, an option with a higher striking price is purchased and one with a lower striking price is sold, both options generally having the same expiration date. *See also* Bull Spread.

Beta: a measure of how a stock's movement correlates to the movement of the entire stock market. The Beta is not the same as volatility. *See also* Standard Deviation *and* Volatility.

Black Model: a model used to predict futures option prices; it is a modified version of the Black-Scholes model.

Board Broker: the exchange member in charge of keeping the book of public orders on exchanges utilizing the "market-maker" system, as opposed to the "specialist system," of executing orders. *See also* Market-Maker *and* Specialist.

Box Spread: a type of option arbitrage in which both a bull spread and a bear spread are established for a riskless profit. One spread is established using put options and the other is established using calls. The spreads may both be debit spreads (call bull spread vs. put bear spread), or both credit spreads (call bear spread vs. put bull spread).

Break-Even Point: the stock price (or prices) at which a particular strategy neither makes nor loses money. It generally pertains to the result at the expiration date of the options involved in the strategy. A "dynamic" break-even point is one that changes as time passes.

Broad-Based: Generally referring to an index, it indicates that the index is composed of a sufficient number of stocks or of stocks in a variety of industry groups. Broad-based indices are subject to more favorable treatment for naked option writers. *See also* narrow-based.

Bullish: describing an opinion or outlook in which one expects a rise in price, either by the general market or by an individual security. *See also* Bearish.

Bull Spread: an option strategy that achieves its maximum potential if the underlying security rises far enough, and has its maximum risk if the security falls far enough. An option with a lower striking price is bought and one with a higher striking price is sold, both generally having the same expiration date. Either puts or calls may be used for the strategy. *See also* Bear Spread.

Butterfly Spread: an option strategy that has both limited risk and limited profit potential, constructed by combining a bull spread and a bear spread. Three striking prices are involved, with the lower two being utilized in the bull spread and the higher two in the bear spread. The strategy can be established with either puts or calls; there are four different ways of combining options to construct the same basic position.

Calendar Spread: an option strategy in which a short-term option is sold and a longer-term option is bought, both having the same striking price. Either puts or calls may be used. A calendar combination is a strategy that consists of a call calendar spread and a put calendar spread at the same time. The striking price of the calls would be higher than the striking price of the puts. A calendar straddle would consist of selling a near-term straddle and buying a longer-term straddle, both with the same striking price.

Calendar Straddle or Combination: *see* Calendar spread.

Call: an option which gives the holder the right to buy the underlying security at a specified price for a certain, fixed period of time. See *also* Put.

Call Price: the price at which a bond or preferred stock may be called in by the issuing corporation; *see* redemption price.

Capitalization-Weighted Index: A stock index which is computed by adding the capitalizations (float times price) of each individual stock in the index, and then dividing by the divisor. The stocks with the largest market values have the heaviest weighting in the index. See *also* Float, Price-weighted index, Divisor.

Cap Price: the price at which a CAPS option reaches its maximum value. For calls, it is the higher strike; for puts, it is the lower strike; *see* Automatic exercise of CAPS.

Carrying Cost: the interest expense on a debit balance created by establishing a position.

Cash-Based: Referring to an option or future that is settled in cash when exercised or assigned. No physical entity, either stock or commodity, is received or delivered.

CBOE: the Chicago Board Options Exchange; the first national exchange to trade listed stock options.

Circuit Breaker: a limit applied to the trading of index futures contracts designed to keep the stock market from crashing.

Class: a term used to refer to all put and call contracts on the same underlying security.

Closing Transaction: a trade that reduced an investor's position. Closing buy transactions reduce short positions and closing sell transactions reduce long positions. *See also* Opening Transaction.

Collateral: the loan value of marginable securities; generally used to finance the writing of uncovered options.

Combination: any position involving both put and call options that is not a straddle. *See also* Straddle.

Commodities: *see* Futures Contract.

Contingent Order: an order to buy stock and sell a covered call option that is given as one order to the trading desk of a brokerage firm. Also called a "net order." This is a "not held" order. *See also* Market Not Held Order.

Conversion Arbitrage: a riskless transaction in which the arbitrageur buys the underlying security, buys a put, and sells a call. The options have the same terms. *See also* Reversal Arbitrage.

Conversion Ratio: *see* Convertible Security.

Converted Put: *see* Synthetic Put.

Convertible Security: a security that is convertible into another security. Generally, a convertible bond or convertible preferred stock is convertible into the underlying stock of the same corporation. The rate at which the shares of the bond or preferred stock are convertible into the common is called the conversion ratio.

Cover: to buy back as a closing transaction an option that was initially written.

Covered: a written option is considered to be covered if the writer also has an opposing market position on a share-for-share basis in the underlying security. That is, a short call is covered if the underlying stock is owned, and a short put is covered (for margin purposes) if the underlying stock is also short in the account. In addition, a short call is covered if the account is also long another call on the same security, with a striking price equal to or less than the striking price of the short call. A short put is covered if there is also a long put in the account with a striking price equal to or greater than the striking price of the short put.

Covered Call Write: a strategy in which one writes call options while simultaneously owning an equal number of shares of the underlying stock.

Covered Put Write: a strategy in which one sells put options and simultaneously is short an equal number of shares of the underlying security.

Covered Straddle Write: the term used to describe the strategy in which an investor owns the underlying security and also writes a straddle on that security. This is not really a covered position.

Credit: money received in an account. A credit transaction is one in which the net sale proceeds are larger than the net buy proceeds (cost), thereby bringing money into the account. See also Debit.

Cycle: the expiration dates applicable to various classes of options. There are three cycles: January/April/July/October, February/May/August/ November, and March/June/September/December.

Debit: an expense, or money paid out from an account. A debit transaction is one in which the net cost is greater than the net sale proceeds. See also Credit.

Deliver: to take securities from an individual or firm and transfer them to another individual or firm. A call writer who is assigned must deliver stock to the call holder who exercised. A put holder who exercises must deliver stock to the put writer who is assigned.

Delivery: The process of satisfying an equity call assignment or an equity put exercise. In either case, stock is delivered. For futures, the process of transferring the physical commodity from the seller of the futures contract to the buyer. Equivalent delivery refers to a situation in which delivery may be made in any of various, similar entities that are equivalent to each other (for example, Treasury bonds with differing coupon rates).

Delta: 1) the amount by which an option's price will change for a corresponding one point change in price by the underlying entity. Call options have positive deltas, while put options have negative deltas. Technically, the delta is an instantaneous measure of the option's price change, so that the delta will be altered for even fractional changes by the underlying entity. Consequently, the terms "up delta" and "down delta" may be applicable. They describe the option's change after a full 1-point change in price by the underlying security—either up or down. The "up delta" may be larger than the "down delta" for a call option, while the reverse is true for put options. 2) the percent probability of a call being in-the-money at expiration. See also Hedge Ratio.

Delta Spread: a ratio spread that is established as a neutral position by utilizing the deltas of the options involved. The neutral ratio is determined by dividing the delta of the purchased option by the delta of the written option. See also Ratio Spread and Delta.

Depository Trust Corporation (DTC): a corporation that will hold securities for member institutions. Generally used by option writers, the

DTC facilitates and guarantees delivery of underlying securities if assignment is made against securities held in DTC.

Diagonal Spread: any spread in which the purchased options have a longer maturity than do the written options as well as having different striking prices. Typical types of diagonal spreads are diagonal bull spreads, diagonal bear spreads, and diagonal butterfly spreads.

Discount: an option is trading at a discount if it is trading for less than its intrinsic value. A future is trading at a discount if it is trading at a price less than the cash price of its underlying index or commodity. See also Intrinsic Value and Parity.

Discount Arbitrage: a riskless arbitrage in which a discount option is purchased and an opposite position is taken in the underlying security. The arbitrageur may either buy a call at a discount and simultaneously sell the underlying security (basic call arbitrage) or may buy a put at a discount and simultaneously buy the underlying security (basic put arbitrage). See also Discount.

Discretion: see Limit Order and Market Not Held Order.

Dividend Arbitrage: in the riskless sense, an arbitrage in which a put is purchased and so is the underlying stock. The put is purchased when it has time value premium less than the impending dividend payment by the underlying stock. The transaction is closed after the stock goes ex-dividend. Also used to denote a form of risk arbitrage in which a similar procedure is followed except that the amount of the impending dividend is unknown and therefore risk is involved in the transaction. See also Ex-Dividend and Time Value Premium.

Divisor: a mathematical quantity used to compute an index. It is initially an arbitrary number that reduces the index value to a small, workable number. Thereafter the divisor is adjusted for stock splits (price-weighted index) or additional issues of stock (capitalization-weighted index).

Downside Protection: generally used in connection with covered call writing, this is the cushion against loss, in case of a price decline by the underlying security, that is afforded by the written call option. Alternatively, it may be expressed in terms of the distance the stock could fall before the total position becomes a loss (an amount equal to the option premium), or it can be expressed as percentage of the current stock price. See also Covered Call Write.

Dynamic: for option strategies, describing analyses made during the course of changing security prices and during the passage of time. This is as opposed to an analysis made at expiration of the options used in the strategy. A dynamic break-even point is one that changes as time passes. A dynamic follow-up action is one that will change as either the security price changes or the option price changes or time passes. *See also* Break-Even Point *and* Follow-up Action.

Early Exercise (assignment): the exercise or assignment of an option contract before its expiration date.

Equity Option: an option that has common stock as its underlying security. *See also* non-equity option.

Equity Requirement: a requirement that a minimum amount of equity must be present in a margin account. Normally, this requirement is $2,000, but some brokerage firms may impose higher equity requirements for uncovered option writing.

Equivalent Positions: positions that have similar profit potential, when measured in dollars, but are constructed with differing securities. Equivalent positions have the same profit graph. A covered call write is equivalent to an uncovered put write, for example. *See also* Profit Graph.

Escrow Receipt: a receipt issued by a bank in order to verify that a customer (who has written a call) in fact owns the stock and therefore the call is considered covered.

European Exercise: a feature of an option that stipulates that the option may only be exercised at its expiration. Therefore, there can be no early assignment with this type of option.

Ex-Dividend: the process whereby a stock's price is reduced when a dividend is paid. The ex-dividend date (ex-date) is the date on which the price reduction takes place. Investors who own stock on the ex-date will receive the dividend, and those who are short stock must pay out the dividend.

Exercise: to invoke the right granted under the terms of a listed options contract. The holder is the one who exercises. Call holders exercise to buy the underlying security, while put holders exercise to sell the underlying security.

Exercise Limit: the limit on the number of contracts which a holder can exercise in a fixed period of time. Set by the appropriate option exchange, it is designed to prevent an investor or group of investors from "cornering" the market in a stock.

Exercise Price: the price at which the option holder may buy or sell the underlying security, as defined in the terms of his option contract.

It is the price at which the call holder may exercise to buy the underlying security or the put holder may exercise to sell the underlying security. For listed options, the exercise price is the same as the Striking Price. *See also* Exercise.

Expected Return: a rather complex mathematical analysis involving statistical distribution of stock prices, it is the return which an investor might expect to make on an investment if he were to make exactly the same investment many times throughout history.

Expiration Date: the day on which an option contract becomes void. The expiration date for listed stock options is the Saturday after the third Friday of the expiration month. All holders of options must indicate their desire to exercise, if they wish to do so, by this date. *See also* Expiration Time.

Expiration Time: the time of day by which all exercise notices must be received on the expiration date. Technically, the expiration time is currently 5:00 PM on the expiration date, but public holders of option contracts must indicate their desire to exercise no later than 5:30 PM on the business day preceding the expiration date. The times are Eastern Time. *See also* Expiration Date.

Facilitation: the process of providing a market for a security. Normally, this refers to bids and offers made for large blocks of securities, such as those traded by institutions. Listed options may be used to offset part of the risk assumed by the trader who is facilitating the large block order. *See also* Hedge Ratio.

Fair Value: normally, a term used to describe the worth of an option or futures contract as determined by a mathematical model. Also sometimes used to indicate intrinsic value. *See also* Intrinsic Value *and* Model.

First Notice Day: the first day upon which the buyer of a futures contract can be called upon to take delivery. *See* notice period.

Float: the number of shares outstanding of a particular common stock.

Floor Broker: a trader on the exchange floor who executes the orders of public customers or other investors who do not have physical access to the trading area.

Follow-up Action: any trading in an option position after the position is established. Generally, to limit losses or to take profits.

Fundamental Analysis: a method of analyzing the prospects of a security by observing accepted accounting measures such as earnings, sales, assets, and so on. *See also* Technical Analysis.

Futures Contract: a standardized contract calling for the delivery of a specified quantity of a commodity at a specified date in the future.

Gamma: a measure of risk of an option that measures the amount by which the delta changes for a one point change in the stock price; alternatively, when referring to an entire option position, the amount of change of the delta of the entire position when the stock changes in price by one point.

Gamma of the gamma: a mathematical measure of risk that measures by how much the gamma will change for a one point move in the stock price. See Gamma.

Good Until Canceled (GTC): a designation applied to some types of orders, meaning that the order remains in effect until it is either filled or canceled. See also Limit, Stop, and Stop Limit.

Hedge Ratio: the mathematical quantity that is equal to the delta of an option. It is useful in facilitation in that a theoretically riskless hedge can be established by taking offsetting positions in the underlying stock and its call options. See also Facilitation and Delta.

Holder: the owner of a security.

Horizontal Spread: an option strategy in which the options have the same striking price, but different expiration dates.

Implied Volatility: a measure of the volatility of the underlying stock, it is determined by using prices currently existing in the market at the time, rather than using historical data on the price changes of the underlying stock. See also Volatility.

Incremental Return Concept: a strategy of covered call writing in which the investor is striving to earn an additional return from option writing against a stock position which he is targeted to sell—possibly at substantially higher prices.

Index: a compilation of the prices of several common entities into a single number. See price-weighted index, capitalization-weighted index.

Index Arbitrage: a form of arbitraging index futures against stock. If futures are trading at prices significantly higher than fair value, the arbitraguer sells futures and buys the exact stocks that make up the index being arbitraged; if futures are at a discount to fair value, the arbitrage entails buying futures and selling stocks.

Index Option: an option whose underlying entity is an index. Most index options are cash-based.

Institution: an organization, probably very large, engaged in investing in securities. Normally a bank, insurance company, or mutual fund.

Intermarket Spread: a futures spread in which futures contracts in one market are spread against futures contracts trading in another market. Examples: Currency spreads (Yen versus Deutschemark) or TED spread (T-Bills versus Eurodollars).

In-the-Money: a term describing any option that has intrinsic value. A call option is in-the-money if the underlying security is higher than the striking price of the call. A put option is in-the-money if the security is below the striking price. See also Out-of-the-Money and Intrinsic Value.

Intramarket Spread: a futures spread in which futures contracts are spread against other futures contracts in the same market; example, buy May soybeans, sell March soybeans.

Intrinsic Value: the value of an option if it were to expire immediately with the underlying stock at its current price; the amount by which an option is in-the-money. For call options, this is the difference between the stock price and the striking price, if that difference is a positive number, or zero otherwise. For put options it is the difference between the striking price and the stock price, if that difference is positive, and zero otherwise. See also In-the-Money, Time Value Premium, and Parity.

Last Trading Day: the third Friday of the expiration month. Options cease trading at 3:00 PM Eastern Time on the last trading day.

LEAPS: Long-term Equity AnticiPation Securities. These are long-term listed options, currently having maturities as long as two and one half years.

Leg: a risk-oriented method of establishing a two-sided position. Rather than entering into a simultaneous transaction to establish the position (a spread, for example), the trader first executes one side of the position, hoping to execute the other side at a later time and a better price. The risk materializes from the fact that a better price may never be available, and a worse price must eventually be accepted.

Letter of Guarantee: a letter from a bank to a brokerage firm which states that a customer (who has written a call option) does indeed own the underlying stock and the bank will guarantee delivery if the call is assigned. Thus the call can be considered covered. Not all brokerage firms accept letters of guarantee.

Leverage: in investments, the attainment of greater percentage profit and risk potential. A call holder has leverage with respect to a stock holder—the former will have greater percentage profits and losses than the latter, for the same movement in the underlying stock.

Limit: see Trading Limit.

Limit Order: an order to buy or sell securities at a specified price (the limit). A limit order may also be placed "with discretion"—a fixed, usually small, amount such as ⅛ or ¼ of a point. In this case, the floor broker executing the order may use his discretion to buy or sell at ⅛ or ¼ of a point beyond the limit if he feels it is necessary to fill the order.

Listed Option: a put or call option that is traded on a national option exchange. Listed options have fixed striking prices and expiration dates. *See also* Over-the-Counter Option.

Local: a trader on a futures exchange who buys and sells for his own account and may fill public orders.

Lognormal Distribution: a statistical distribution that is often applied to the movement of the stock prices. It is a convenient and logical distribution because it implies that stock prices can theoretically rise forever but cannot fall below zero—a fact which is, of course, true.

Margin: to buy a security by borrowing funds from a brokerage house. The margin requirement—the maximum percentage of the investment that can be loaned by the broker firm—is set by the Federal Reserve Board.

Market Basket: a portfolio of common stocks whose performance is intended to simulate the performance of a specific index. *See* Index.

Market-Maker: an exchange member whose function is to aid in the making of a market, by making bids and offers for his account in the absence of public buy or sell orders. Several market-makers are normally assigned to a particular security. The market-maker system encompasses the market-makers and the board brokers. *See also* Board Broker *and* Specialist.

Market Not Held Order: also a market order, but the investor is allowing the floor broker who is executing the order to use his own discretion as to the exact timing of the execution. If the floor broker expects a decline in price and he is holding a "market not held" buy order, he may wait to buy, figuring that a better price will soon be available. There is no guarantee that a "market not held" order will be filled.

Market Order: an order to buy or sell securities at the current market. The order will be filled as long as there is a market for the security.

Married Put and Stock: a put and stock are considered to be married if they are bought on the same day, and the position is designated at that time as a hedge.

Model: a mathematical formula designed to price an option as a function of certain variables—generally stock price, striking price, volatility, time to expiration, dividends to be paid, and the current risk-free interest rate. The Black-Scholes model is one of the more widely used models.

Naked Option: *see* Uncovered Option.

Narrow-Based: Generally referring to an index, it indicates that the index is composed of only a few stocks, generally in a specific industry group. Narrow-based indices are NOT subject to favorable treatment for naked option writers. *See also* broad-based.

"Net" Order: *see* Contingent Order.

Neutral: describing an opinion that is neither bearish or bullish. Neutral option strategies are generally designed to perform best if there is little or no net change in the price of the underlying stock. See *also* Bearish *and* Bullish.

Non-Equity Option: an option whose underlying entity is not common stock; typically refers to options on physical commodities, but may also be extended to include index options.

"Not Held": *see* Market Not Held Order.

Notice Period: the time during which the buyer of a futures contract can be called upon to accept delivery. Typically, the 3 to 6 weeks preceding the expiration of the contract.

Opening Transaction: a trade which adds to the net position of an investor. An opening buy transaction adds more long securities to the account. An opening sell transaction adds more short securities. See *also* Closing Transaction.

Open Interest: the net total of outstanding open contracts in a particular option series. An opening transaction increases the open interest, while any closing transaction reduces the open interest.

Option Pricing Curve: a graphical representation of the projected price of an option at a fixed point in time. It reflects the amount of time value premium in the option for various stock prices, as well. The curve is generated by using a mathematical model. The delta (or hedge ratio) is the slope of a tangent line to the curve at a fixed stock price. See *also* Delta, Hedge Ratio, *and* Model.

Options Clearing Corporation (OCC): the issuer of all listed option contracts that are trading on the national option exchanges.

Out-of-the-Money: describing an option that has no intrinsic value. A call option is out-of-the-money if the stock is below the striking price of the call, while a put option is out-of-the-money if the stock is higher than the striking price of the put. See *also* In-the-Money *and* Intrinsic Value.

Over-the-Counter Option (OTC): an option traded over-the-counter, as opposed to a listed stock option. The OTC option has a direct link between buyer and seller, has no secondary market, and has no standardization of striking prices and expiration dates. See *also* Listed Stock Option *and* Secondary Market.

Overvalued: describing a security trading at a higher price than it logically should. Normally associated with the results of option price predictions by mathematical models. If an option is trading in the market for a higher price than the model indicates, the option is said to be overvalued. See *also* Fair Value *and* Undervalued.

Pairs Trading: a hedging technique in which one buys a particular stock and sells short another stock. The two stocks are theoretically linked in their price history, and the hedge is established when the historical relationship is out of line in hopes that it will return to its former correlation.

Parity: describing an in-the-money option trading for its intrinsic value: that is, an option trading at parity with the underlying stock. Also used as a point of reference—an option is sometimes said to be trading at a half-point over parity or at a quarter-point under parity, for example. An option trading under parity is a discount option. *See also* Discount *and* Intrinsic Value.

PERCS: Preferred Equity Redemption Cumulative Stock. Issued by a corporation, this preferred stock pays a higher dividend than the common and has a price at which it can be called in for redemption by the issuing corporation. As such, it is really a covered call write, with the call premium being given to the holder in the form of increased dividends. *See* Call price, Redemption price, Covered call write.

Physical Option: an option whose underlying security is a physical commodity that is not stock or futures. The physical commodity itself—typically a currency or Treasury debt issue—underlies that option contract. *See also* equity option, index option.

Portfolio Insurance: a method of selling index futures or buying index put options to protect a portfolio of stocks.

Position: as a noun, a specific securities in an account or strategy. A covered call writing position might be long 1,000 XYZ and short 10 XYZ January 30 calls. As a verb, to facilitate; to buy or sell—generally a block of securities—thereby establishing a position. *See also* Facilitation *and* Strategy.

Position Limit: the maximum number of put or call contracts on the same side of the market that can be held in any one account or group of related accounts. Short puts and long calls are on the same side of the market. Short calls and long puts are on the same side of the market.

Premium: for options, the total price of an option contract. The sum of the intrinsic value and the time value premium. For futures, the difference between the futures price and the cash price of the underlying index or commodity.

Present Worth: a mathematical computation that determines how much money would have to be invested today, at a specified rate, in order to produce a designated amount at some time in the future. For example, at 10% for one year, the present worth of $110 is $100.

Price-Weighted Index: A stock index which is computed by adding the prices of each stock in the index, and then dividing by the divisor. See also Capitalization-weighted index, Divisor.

Profit Graph: a graphical representation of the potential outcomes of a strategy. Dollars of profit or loss are graphed on the vertical axis, and various stock prices are graphed on the horizontal axis. Results may be depicted at any point in time, although the graph usually depicts the results at expiration of the options involved in the strategy.

Profit Range: the range within which a particular position makes a profit. Generally used in reference to strategies that have two break-even points—an upside break-even and a downside break-even. The price range between the two break-even points would be the profit range. See also Break-Even Point.

Profit Table: a table of results of a particular strategy at some point in time. This is usually a tabular compilation of the data drawn on a profit graph. See also Profit Graph.

Program Trading: the act of buying or selling a particular portfolio of stocks and hedging with an offsetting position in index futures. The portfolio of stocks may be small or large, but it is not the makeup of any stock index. See Index arbitrage.

Protected Strategy: a position that has limited risk. A protected short sale (short stock, long call) has limited risk, as does a protected straddle write (short stradde, long out-of-the-money combination). See also Combination and Straddle.

Public Book (of orders): the orders to buy or sell, entered by the public, that are away from the current market. The board broker or specialist keeps the public book. Market-makers on the CBOE can see the highest bid and lowest offer at any time. The specialist's book is closed (only he knows at what price and in what quantity the nearest public orders are). See also Board Broker, Market-Maker, and Specialist.

Put: an option granting the holder the right to sell the underlying security at a certain price for a specified period of time. See also Call.

Put-Call Ratio: the ratio of put trading volume divided by call trading volume; sometimes calculated with open interest instead of trading volume. Can be calculated daily, weekly, monthly, etc. Moving averages are often used to smooth out short-term, daily figures.

Ratio Calendar Combination: a strategy consisting of a simultaneous position of a ratio calendar spread using calls and a similar position using puts, where the striking price of the calls is greater than the striking price of the puts.

Ratio Calendar Spread: selling more near-term options than longer-term ones purchased, all with the same strike; either puts or calls.

Ratio Spread: constructed with either puts or calls, the strategy consists of buying a certain amount of options and then selling a larger quantity of out-of-the-money options.

Ratio Strategy: a strategy in which one has an unequal number of long securities and short securities. Normally, it implies a preponderance of short options over either long options or long stock.

Ratio Write: buying stock and selling a preponderance of calls against the stock that is owned. (Occasionally constructed as shorting stock and selling puts.)

Redemption Price: for the price at which a PERCS may be called for redemption by the issuing corporation; the term is used to distinguish it from "call price," which may be confusing when discussing the imbedded call option that exists in PERCS. See Call price, PERCS.

Resistance: a term in technical analysis indicating a price area higher than the current stock price where an abundance of supply exists for the stock, and therefore the stock may have trouble rising through the price. See also Support.

Return (on investment): the percentage profit that one makes, or might make, on his investment.

Return If Exercised: the return that a covered call writer would make if the underlying stock were called away.

Return If Unchanged: the return that an investor would make on a particular position if the underlying stock were unchanged in price at the expiration of the options in the position.

Reversal Arbitrage: a riskless arbitrage that involves selling the stock short, writing a put, and buying a call. The options have the same terms. See also Conversion Arbitrage.

Reverse Hedge: a strategy in which one sells the underlying stock short and buys calls on more shares than he has sold short. This is also called a synthetic straddle and is an outmoded strategy for stocks that have listed puts trading. See also Straddle and Ratio Write.

Reverse Strategy: a general name that is given to strategies which are the opposite of better known strategies. For example, a ratio spread consists of buying calls at a lower strike and selling more calls at a higher strike. A reverse ratio spread also known as a backspread consists of selling the calls at the lower strike and buying more calls at the higher strike. The results are obviously directly opposite to each other. See also Reverse Hedge and Ratio Write.

Rho: the measure of how much an option changes in price for an incremental move (generally 1%) in short-term interest rates; more significant for longer-term or in-the-money options.

Risk Arbitrage: a form of arbitrage that has some risk associated with it. Commonly refers to potential takeover situations where the arbitrageur buys the stock of the company about to be taken over and sells the stock of the company that is effecting the takeover. See also Dividend Arbitrage.

Roll Down: close out options at one strike and simultaneously open other options at a lower strike.

Roll Forward: close out options at a near-term expiration date and open options at a longer-term expiration date.

Rolling: a follow-up action in which the strategist closes options currently in the position and opens other options with different terms, on the same underlying stock. See also Roll Down, Roll Forward, and Roll Up.

Roll Up: close out options at a lower strike and open options at a higher strike.

Rotation: a trading procedure on the open exchanges whereby bids and offers, but not necessarily trades, are made sequentially for each series of options on an underlying stock.

Secondary Market: any market in which securities can be readily bought and sold after their initial issuance. The national listed option exchanges provided, for the first time, a secondary market in stock options.

Serial Option: a futures option for which there is no corresponding futures contract expiring in the same month. The underlying futures contract is the next futures contract out in time. Example: there is no March gold futures contract, but there is an April gold futures contract, so March gold options—which are serial options—are options on April gold futures.

Series: all option contracts on the same underlying stock having the same striking price, expiration date, and unit of trading.

Specialist: an exchange member whose function it is to both make markets—buy and sell for his own account in the absence of public orders—and to keep the book of public orders. Most stock exchanges and some option exchanges utilize the specialist system of trading.

Spread Order: an order to simultaneously transact two or more option trades. Typically, one option would be bought while another would simultaneously be sold. Spread orders may be limit orders, not held orders, or orders with discretion. They cannot be stop orders, however. The spread order may be either a debit or credit.

Spread Strategy: any option position having both long options and short options of the same type on the same underlying security.

Standard Deviation: a measure of the volatility of a stock. It is a statistical quantity measuring the magnitude of the daily price changes of that stock.

Stop-Limit Order: similar to a stop order, the stop-limit order becomes a limit order, rather than a market order, when the security trades at the price specified on the stop. See also Stop Order.

Stop Order: an order, placed away from the current market, that becomes a market order if the security trades at the price specified on the stop order. Buy stop orders are placed above the market while sell stop orders are placed below.

Straddle: the purchase or sale of an equal number of puts and calls having the same terms.

Strangle: a combination involving a put and call at different strikes with the same expiration date.

Strategy: with respect to option investments, a preconceived, logical plan of position selection and follow-up action.

Striking Price: see Exercise Price.

Striking Price Interval: the distance between striking prices on a particular underlying security. Normally, the interval is 5 points for stocks selling up to $50 per share, 10 points for stocks between $50 and $200 per share, and 20 points thereafter. There may, however, be exceptions to this general guideline.

Subindex: see narrow-based index.

Suitable: describing a strategy or trading philosophy in which the investor is operating in accordance with his financial means and investment objectives.

Support: a term in technical analysis indicating a price area lower than the current price of the stock, where demand is thought to exist. Thus a stock would stop declining when it reached a support area. See also Resistance.

Synthetic Put: a security which some brokerage firms offer to their customers. The broker sells stock short and buys a call, while the customer receives the synthetic put. This is not a listed security, but a secondary market is available as long as there is a secondary market in the calls.

Synthetic Stock: an option strategy that is equivalent to the underlying stock. A long call and a short put is synthetic long stock. A long put and a short call is synthetic short stock.

Technical Analysis: the method of predicting future stock price movements based on observation of historical stock price movements.

Terms: the collective name denoting the expiration date, striking price, and underlying stock of an option contract.

Theoretical Value: the price of an option, or a spread, as computed by a mathematical model.

Theta: the measure of how much an option's price decays for each day of time that passes.

Time Spread: see Calendar Spread.

Time Value Premium: the amount by which an option's total premium exceeds its intrinsic value.

Total Return Concept: a covered call writing strategy in which one views the potential profit of the strategy as the sum of capital gains, dividends, and option premium income, rather than viewing each one of the three separately.

Tracking Error: the amount of difference between the performance of a specific portfolio of stocks and a broad-based index with which they are being compared. See market basket.

Trader: a speculative investor or professional who makes frequent purchases and sales.

Trading Limit: the exchange-imposed maximum daily price change that a futures contract or futures option contract can undergo.

Treasury Bill/Option Strategy: a method of investment in which one places approximately 90% of his funds in risk-free, interest-bearing assets such as Treasury bills, and buys options with the remainder of his assets.

Type: the designation to distinguish between a put or call option.

Uncovered Option: a written option is considered to be uncovered if the investor does not have a corresponding position in the underlying security. See also Covered.

Underlying Security: the security which one has the right to buy or sell via the terms of a listed option contract.

Undervalued: describing a security that is trading at a lower price than it logically should. Usually determined by the use of a mathematical model. See also Overvalued and Fair Value.

Variable Ratio Write: an option strategy in which the investor owns 100 shares of the underlying security and writes two call options against it, each option having a different striking price.

Vega: the measure of how much an option's price changes for an incremental change—usually 1%—in volatility.

Vertical Spread: any option spread strategy in which the options have different striking prices, but the same expiration dates.

Volatility: a measure of the amount by which an underlying security is expected to fluctuate in a given period of time. Generally measured by the annual standard deviation of the daily price changes in the security, volatility is not equal to the Beta of the stock.

Warrant: a long-term, non-standardized, security that is much like an option. Warrants on stocks allow one to buy (usually one share of) the common at a certain price until a certain date. Index warrants are generally warrants on the price of foreign indices. Warrants have also been listed on other things such as cross-currency spreads and the future price of a barrel of oil.

Write: to sell an option. The investor who sells is called the writer.

Index

A

Aggressive bull spreads, 157
American exercise, 503–5
American Stock Exchange Index, 498
Annualized risk, 411–12
Arbitrage:
  box arbitrage, 440–44, 646–47
  carrying costs, computing, 430, 431–32
  conversions/reversals, 428–42, 444, 645–46
    borrowing stock to sell short, 433–34
    risks in, 434–38
  definition of, 422
  discounting, 423–25, 644–45
  dividend arbitrage, 425–28
  effects of, 445–46
  equivalence arbitrage, variations on, 444–45
  facilitation (block positioning), 456
  futures options, 661–62
  index arbitrage, 549–59
  pairs trading, 455–56
  risk arbitrage, 427
    using options, 446–55
  See also Conversion arbitrage; Index arbitrage; Reversal arbitrage; Risk arbitrage
Assignment, 853
  call options, 17–21
    anticipating, 17–21
    honoring, 16
    taxes and, 810–16
  cash-based options, 502, 521–22
  circumstances signaling, 18
  covered call writing and, 80
  currency options, 679
  definition of, 7
  futures options, 679
  margin requirements and, 16
  put options, 232–35
    anticipating, 233–35
    position limits, 235
    taxes and, 818
  See also Early exercise
Automatic exercise, 18–19
  call CAPS, 608–9, 619

futures options, 665
put CAPS, 609–10
vertical CAPS spreads, 629

B

Backspreads, 212–16, 692–94
  diagonal, 221–22
  LEAPS and, 380–82
  See also Reverse ratio call spread (backspread)
Bearish calendar spreads, 319
Bear spreads:
  calls, 167–72
  puts, 309–12
  See also Bull spreads
Beta, volatility vs., 540–41
Bid-offer spread, 668
Black model, 649–50, 653, 682–83
  definition of, 854
Black-Scholes model, 457–67, 487, 647–50, 653, 682–83, 684
  characteristics of, 461–67
Board broker, 22
Box arbitrage, 440–44, 646–47
  with equity options, 646
Bullish calendar spreads, 177–79, 319
  follow-up action, 178–79
Bull spreads:
  calls, 100, 154–71
    degrees of aggressiveness, 157–58
    follow-up action, 160–62
    lowering break-even price, 162–64
    ranking, 158–60
    substituting for covered writing, 165–66
  puts, 312–13
  See also Bear spreads
Butterfly spreads, 181–90, 316–19
  CAP butterflies, 617–23
  collateral requirement, 182–84
  definition of, 181
  diagonal, 324–27
  follow-up action, 187–90

M

N

Q

R

SPECIAL OFFER

Trial subscriptions to either or both of these two services, written by Lawrence G. McMillan, author of two best selling books on options, are available to book owners. *The Option Strategist* is a twice-monthly newsletter that concentrates on strategies using equity, index, and futures. *The Daily Volume Alert* is a fax service (also available by e-mail) that uses equity Option volume to pinpoint stocks that are going to move.

The Option Strategist features:

- Specific recommendations for equity, index, and futures options, including follow-up action.
- FREE telephone HOTLINE
(toll call required outside of 973 area-code).
- Ideas to improve your trading and hedging; articles on timely topics.

The Daily Volume Alert fax service features:

- Specific entry and exit points for short-term trading of stocks and stock options.
- Occasional OEX recommendations, based on our proprietary indicator.
- Every business day, analysis of issues with unusual option activity.

YES! Sign me up for the following trial subscriptions:

❏ 3 months of *The Option Strategist* (6 issues) for $19 *(regularly $29)*
❏ 1 month of *Daily Volume Alert Service* for $60 *(regularly $95)*

Name _____

Address _____

City _____ State/Province ___ Zip/Postal _____

Charge to my: ❏ Master Card   ❏ Visa Card

Card Number _____

Expiration Date _____ Signature _____

Call 1-800-724-1817
or 908-850-7113
Website - http://www.optionstrategist.com

Or copy this form and mail to:
McMillan Analysis Corporation
P.O. Box 1323, Morristown NJ 07962-1323

OTHER RESOURCES AVAILABLE

Intensive Option Strategy Seminar Audio: A set of audio tapes, recorded at the most recent full day "Intensive Option Strategy" seminar. Includes a copy of all the view-graphs used in the seminar. Approximate running time: 4½ hours. See next item for description of topics covered. *Cost $250*

Intensive Option Strategy Seminar Video: A set of two video tapes consisting of excerpts from an "Intensive Option Strategy" seminar. Topics include: equity, index, and futures option strategies; volatility trading: pricing options; dynamic strategies; and short-term trading strategies. *Cost $500*

Put-Call Ratio Charts by email: Graphs of put-call ratios in 25 sectors and futures markets, plus OEX, total and all equity. Updated weekly on your email. *Cost $10 per month +$10 software setup fee*

Option Calculation Software: IBM PC-compatible program to calculate theoretical values and related statistics, such as implied volatility. Program is stand-alone (i.e., it does not connect to a data service), so price data can be entered manually. User manual included. *Cost $100.*

Also Available: a probability calculation program that computes the probability of a stock ever moving through a certain price during a specified time period. One of a kind! *Cost $30 +$1 shipping*

Implied Volatility Booklet: a booklet of charts that allow you to quickly compute implied volatility by plotting a point on the chart. Comes with complete instructions for usage. *Cost $30*

McMillan On Options: The new book (1996) on option trading. 600 pages on trading systems and tactics, replete with actual examples and stories. Emphasis on practical applications. Topics include "the versatility of options," "the predictive power of options," and neutral trading. *Cost $65. ($69.95 in stores)*

Back Issues Available: Back issues of *The Option Strategist* are available for $4.00 per copy. A complete list of topics is available upon request.

Call 1-800-724-1817
or 908-850-7113
Website - http://www.optionstrategist.com

CONTINUING EDUCATION ≡≡≡≡

3-DAY INTENSIVE OPTION SEMINAR

Join Lawrence G. McMillan author of the world's best-selling option book, *Options As A Strategic Investment*, at a 3 day seminar.

DAY 1: OPTION STRATEGY

DAY 2: CURRENT ANALYSIS

DAY 3: REAL-TIME TRADING!

Designed for the serious investor or trader interested in a better understanding of option trading methods and strategies. Learn how McMillan applies his strategies in real time in stock or futures markets.

TOPICS COVERED

DAY 1: McMillan's Intensive Option Strategy Seminar; Saturday, 8:30am to 3:30pm

1. **Definitions of Today's Terms:** derivative types; profit & pricing graphs; futures options.

2. **Trading Aids:** equivalent position; brokerage & margin; data services & software.

3. **Short-term trading strategies:** specific option or futures trading systems.

4. **Directional strategies:** option volume and price as indicators; put-call ratios; trading at expiration.

5. **Portfolio Protection:** buying index puts as insurance; buying equity puts; using collars.

6. **Volatility Trading:** factors affecting the price of an option, volatility skewing, implied volatility percentiles, strategies for buying cheap options, strategies for selling expensive options.

DAY 2: Preparation for Real-Time Trading; Sunday: 9am to 2pm
Experienced professionals, who trade extensively for their own accounts, will describe what they look for as they prepare to go into a trading day. Both stock and futures market will be analyzed. Current option and underlying data will be analyzed, using Friday's closing prices. How to prepare yourself mentally for a day of serious trading. Specific strategies will be laid out for Monday's trading.

Larry McMillan will divulge the specific computer analysis that he uses to make his trading decisions prior to beginning a trading day; set-ups for both directional trades and position trades (i.e., those of a longer-term Nature) will be analyzed using option volume, implied volatility skewing

Day 3: Real-Time Trading; Monday: Market hours

Real-time pricing feeds and computer analysis will be available at the seminar. Moreover, the phone system will be set up so that participants will be able to hear the conversations between Larry and the trading desks as he implemens his theories in actual practice, and what decisions and modifications they make as information is received during the trading day.

A limited number of reservations will be accepted. Payment is required at the time the reservation is made. The payment is fully refundable up until three days prior to the beginning of the seminar. If a minimum number of reservations is not received, *McMillan Analysis Corp.* reserves the right to cancel the seminar and refund all monies.

Call for a location near you.
CALL 800-724-1817 FOR RESERVATIONS
or 908-850-7113
Website - http://www.optionstrategist.com

PRICING --
COMPLETE SEMINAR: $2495
SATURDAY ONLY: $695
SUNDAY & MONDAY ONLY: $2095

Current subscribers to either *The Option Strategist* or *Daily Volume Alerts* are entitled to a discount. Call for details

THE COMPLETE SEMINAR PACKAGE
Includes the following:

- a 6-month subscription to *The Option Strategist* ($175value);
- a 3-month subscription to *Daily Volume Alerts* ($285 value);
- an Audio tape of the Saturday seminar ($275 value);

plus discounts for other McMillan products.

THE TRADING PORTION PACKAGE
(Those attending only Sunday and Monday) includes the following:

- a 3-month subscription to *The Option Strategist*;
- a one month subscription to *Daily Volume Alerts*;

plus discounts for other McMillan products.